Get the eBook FREE!

(PDF, ePub, Kindle, and liveBook all included)

We believe that once you buy a book from us, you should be able to read it in any format we have available. To get electronic versions of this book at no additional cost to you, purchase and then register this book at the Manning website.

Go to https://www.manning.com/freebook and follow the instructions to complete your pBook registration.

That's it!
Thanks from Manning!

Statistics Slam Dunk

Statistics Slam Dunk

STATISTICAL ANALYSIS WITH R ON REAL NBA DATA

GARY SUTTON

FOREWORD BY THOMAS W. MILLER

MANNING

SHELTER ISLAND

For online information and ordering of this and other Manning books, please visit www.manning.com. The publisher offers discounts on this book when ordered in quantity. For more information, please contact

Special Sales Department
Manning Publications Co.
20 Baldwin Road
PO Box 761
Shelter Island, NY 11964
Email: orders@manning.com

Manning Publications Co.
20 Baldwin Road
PO Box 761
Shelter Island, NY 11964

Development editor: Ian Hough
Technical editor: Rohit Goswami
Review editor: Aleksandar Dragosavljević
Production editor: Kathy Rossland
Copy editor: Julie McNamee
Proofreader: Melody Dolab
Technical proofreader: Eli Mayost
Typesetter: Gordan Salinovic
Cover designer: Marija Tudor

ISBN 9781633438682
Printed in the United States of America

To Liane, Chloe, and Carson

brief contents

contents

foreword

Data science begins with data. We gather data. We prepare data. And we use data in predictive models. The better the data, the better the models, whether they draw on traditional statistics or machine learning.

By creating new data and measures from original data and measures, by manipulating data, we enhance model performance and efficiency. This is the work of feature engineering.

Visualizations help us learn from data. They demonstrate relationships among variables. They suggest useful transformations. They point to modeling problems, outliers, and unusual patterns in data.

Put these together—data preparation, feature engineering, and visualization—and you have the essence of Gary Sutton's *Statistics Slam Dunk: Statistical analysis with R on real NBA data.* Drawing on many examples from professional basketball, Sutton provides a thorough introduction to exploratory data analysis for sports analytics and data science.

With its many packages and tools, R is the obvious choice for this book. We can expect Sutton's work to be well-received by R enthusiasts, especially those who wish to transition from base R to tidyverse functions. The mechanics of R programming are well-illustrated in *Statistics Slam Dunk.*

Many have been waiting for a sequel to Dean Oliver's *Basketball on Paper,* and Sutton's book represents a first step in that direction. Basketball involves continuous activity rather than plays with obvious beginning and ending times. Basketball presents the difficulty of extracting individual performance metrics from what are clearly team efforts. Addressing the special problems of basketball analytics begins with the data of basketball.

As we go from chapter to chapter in no prescribed order, we hear Sutton saying, "Here's data about players and teams in the National Basketball Association. Let's explore this data to see how basic concepts from probability and statistics (and economics) apply to the sport." Through well-worked examples, he teaches us about modeling best practices, classical inference, constrained optimization, methods for dealing with outliers, the Pareto principle and 80-20 rule, home versus road team referee biases, whether defense wins championships, the degree to which spending on player salaries translates into winning records (except for the New York Knicks), the Gini coefficient and Lorenz curve for representing income inequality, randomness, the Monte Hall problem, and the myth of the hot hand. It's a fun ride and one worth taking by sports fans and analysts alike.

Relevant measures and extensive data are the keys to analytics-guided competitive advantage in sports today. Dispassionate analysis serves managers and coaches when making decisions about team composition and in-game strategy, just as it serves those who benefit from accurate predictions of game outcomes. Going from data to decisions or from data to actions means programming with data. The truth is in the code—and Sutton provides extensive code to prove it.

— Dr. Thomas W. Miller
Faculty Director, Data Science Program, Northwestern University
Author of Sports Analytics and Data Science:
Winning the Game with Methods and Models

preface

Statistics Slam Dunk is the confluence of at least three factors.

First, I very much wanted to improve my own R programming skills. As the leader of an organization, I spend my time directing and project managing my staff's work, removing their blockers and other challenges, developing goals, creating and delivering executive-level presentations, hiring (and sometimes firing) staff, preparing and communicating performance evaluations, computing and allocating annual compensation adjustments and merit bonuses, and the like. In other words, there's no bandwidth left to write my own code and therefore sustain, much less improve, my programming skills.

Second, I wanted to satisfy some of my intellectual curiosity. I had read, for instance, about optimal stopping in *Algorithms to Live By: The Computer Science of Human Decisions*, by Brian Christian and Tom Griffiths; mass intelligence versus professionals and other experts in *The Wisdom of Crowds*, by James Surowiecki; power laws and the Lindy effect from Nassim Nicholas Taleb, most notably in *Fooled by Randomness*, *The Black Swan*, *Antifragile*, and *Skin in the Game*; and case studies touting the benefits of rest, such as afternoon naps and Fridays off, to produce performance and productivity gains. All along, I wondered how well these concepts translated to professional basketball (I played basketball competitively and noncompetitively for many years and, at the same time, had an intellectual curiosity about the game starting as a youngster). Furthermore, I had long-standing doubts about defense winning championships, games being won in the fourth quarter, and the NBA's salary cap creating intra-season and inter-season parity, and I wanted to discover what the data said. Finally, I wanted to determine if statistical analysis might justify tanking or might uncover referee, or official, biases.

Third, in spite of my desire (or need?) to upskill myself in R, I nonetheless believed I had expertise and experience worth imparting to others.

My original intent was to organize each chapter into two roughly equal halves: the first half would summarize my findings in layman terms, and the second half would more or less amount to a code review. There would be content for everyone! I finally realized, once I got around to writing my book proposal, that I was essentially writing two books . . . and one book was definitely going to be challenging enough. While I was targeting technical and nontechnical readers alike, my book maybe didn't have enough focus to attract anyone at all. Fundamentally, I knew I was writing a programming and statistics book; I subsequently restructured the manuscript accordingly and then updated my proposal.

Nevertheless, *Statistics Slam Dunk* remains unlike other "like" books. After all, my overarching goal from the beginning was to write a different sort of book that could not readily be compared to preceding manuals. Each chapter plays out, from beginning to end, like a real-world data science or statistics project.

Back in the day, I started out in SAS, but then saw that the future was in opensource technologies. I can't exactly remember why or how, but I chose R . . . and never looked back—nor should you.

acknowledgments

While my name is on the front cover, writing a book is, in fact, a team effort. I'd like to thank the following people for not just making this possible, but for making *Statistics Slam Dunk* better than it would otherwise be:

- First and foremost, my development editor, Ian Hough, who kept me on point, provided fantastic advice, and was always available when I needed additional guidance (which was often).
- Marjan Bace, Manning's publisher, and Andy Waldron, acquisitions editor, who believed in me and embraced my out-of-the-box idea for a book.
- Rohit Goswami, my technical editor, who provided keen insights and encouraged me to elaborate on many of the methods presented herein. He seemed especially pleased when, upon his suggestion, I swapped out the `gather()` and `spread()` functions in favor of `pivot_longer()` and `pivot_wider()`. Rohit is a software engineer at Quansight Labs and a Rannis-funded doctoral researcher at the Science Institute of the University of Iceland. He is an active reviewer for rOpenSci and maintains the "Software Carpentries" lesson on R. Much of his doctoral work focuses on R workflows and bindings to compiled C++ and Fortran with the `Rcpp` and `Cpp11` packages.
- Eli Mayost, technical proofreader, who checked my code and assured all of us that everything actually worked as designed.
- Aleks Dragosavljević, my review editor, who obtained reviewers and coordinated the peer review processes.

- Paul Wells and his team—especially Kathy Rossland, Julie McNamee, and Melody Dolab—for expertly running *Statistics Slam Dunk* through the Manning production process.
- The peer reviewers who dedicated many hours of their "free" time to read the manuscript and provide valuable feedback: Ayush Bihani, Bob Quintus, Chen Sun, Christian Sutton, David Cronkite, David Jacobs, Eli Mayost, George Carter, Giri Swaminathan, Jan Pieter Herweijer, John Williams, Juan Delgado, Kim Lokøy, Lachman Dhalliwal, Mark Graham, Maxim Volgin, Oliver Korten, Ravi Kiran Bamidi, Sander Zegveld, Simone Sguazza, Sleiman Salameh, Stefano Ongarello, and Ulrich Gauger.
- Dr. Thomas Miller for contributing the foreword and teaching me about constrained optimization (see chapter 4).
- The Manning Early Access Program (MEAP) participants who purchased the book while it was still raw, asked intelligent questions, and pointed out typos and other errors.

Additionally, acknowledgments are most definitely in order for the "silent heroes" who, without fame or monetary reward, create and share data sets. They are the true enablers for everything that follows.

Finally, I must thank my wife, Liane, who tolerated my mood swings (which were highly correlated with my nonlinear progress) and my general lack of availability throughout this journey.

about this book

Statistics Slam Dunk is rather different from other programming manuals. Other comparable books are usually organized by technique, or method; for instance, there might be a chapter on common data wrangling operations, another chapter on linear regression, another chapter on creating basic plots, and so on.

There's nothing wrong with that. However, there's no such thing in the real world as a data wrangling project, a linear regression project, or a data visualization project. *Statistics Slam Dunk* is instead project-based: any and every operation required to get from point zero to a predefined endpoint is executed in each chapter, from loading packages, to importing data, to wrangling data, to exploring it, visualizing it, testing it, and modeling it. *Statistics Slam Dunk* teaches you how to think about, set up, and run a data science or statistics project from beginning to end.

That's number one. Number two, *Statistics Slam Dunk* deals with NBA data sets throughout, attempting to discover something useful and relevant in every chapter that should be transferrable to your own world. My hope is that *Statistics Slam Dunk* is a more fun and effective way of learning R.

Who should read this book

It goes without saying that some prior exposure to R, or at least some previous experience with another statistical programming language, will help you get the most out of this book. In addition, some foundational knowledge of basic statistical concepts, a background in data visualization and best practices thereof, and even a basic understanding of the game of basketball and some familiarity with basic basketball statistics will be beneficial.

However, *Statistics Slam Dunk* presumes very little. R and RStudio, the integrated development environment (IDE) for R, are both free downloads. *Statistics Slam Dunk* presumes you can download software and then install it by clicking Next a few times. Otherwise, every operation is explained at a level of detail that is most appropriate for undergraduate and graduate students with little or no background in either R or statistics, junior-level or mid-level data scientists and data analysts with some prior R experience looking to upskill themselves, and other data scientists and data analysts transitioning from another programming language.

That being said, there's enough content in *Statistics Slam Dunk* for those already well-seasoned in R. If you're familiar with R, *Statistics Slam Dunk* will help you get further grounded in key statistical concepts, demonstrate how to create compelling graphical content outside the mainstream, and introduce packages and their functions that there's a good chance you haven't yet been exposed to.

Data-savvy basketball fans and those of you working in basketball will most definitely have an interest in the book's findings—but you'll have to sift through hundreds of lines of code and complementary text to get there. You need *not* be at all familiar with the game of basketball to get the most out of this book, any more than you need to be a horticulturist to use the iris data set (which comes bundled with R and is used, more often than any other data set, to demonstrate a plethora of techniques). Anything and everything you need to know about basketball and about the data sets are explained in thorough detail.

How this book is organized: A road map

Statistics Slam Dunk is organized into 20 chapters. Almost every chapter is a standalone project, or story, with a beginning, an end, and a plot in between. Take chapter 5, for example, where we examine and test the influence hustle has on wins and losses. Every operation is explained and demonstrated in detail, from loading packages, importing data, and exploring and wrangling the same, to developing models.

That being said, here is a chapter-by-chapter breakdown:

- Chapter 1 is essentially an introduction of sorts. By the end, you should be not only comfortable but also excited about making a learning investment in R. No code is included in this chapter.
- Chapter 2 demonstrates how to best go about interrogating a data set, computing basic statistics, and visualizing your results. You'll also learn how to load packages, import data, wrangle and summarize data, and create compelling graphical content using a mix of built-in and packaged functions.
- Chapter 3 is a build from the foundation established in the previous chapter. You'll learn how to visualize means and medians, create a flow chart called a Sankey diagram, set up and estimate an expected value analysis, and carry out an unsupervised learning problem called hierarchical clustering.

- Chapter 4 demonstrates how to set up and complete a constrained optimization problem. You'll also learn how to best visualize data distributions and add comments to your R code.

- Chapter 5 demonstrates how to identify outliers in your data, run and interpret statistical tests of normality, compute and visualize correlations between continuous variables, develop a multiple linear regression and interpret the results, and develop a decision tree and plot the same.

- Chapter 6 shows how to subset data sets, separate and join data sets, and rename and convert variables, among other data wrangling operations. Additionally, you'll learn how to apply many of the best practices in data visualization, including small touches that can make a big difference with your audience.

- Chapter 7 demonstrates how to run, interpret, and visualize t-tests, as well as run and interpret complementary effect size tests.

- Chapter 8 introduces the optimal stopping rule, oftentimes referred to as the 37% rule. Additionally, you'll learn how to create a derived variable from a substring; create a frequency table; add a theme to visualizations created in ggplot2, the premier graphics package used throughout the book; import and inset images into other ggplot2 content; and add multiple trend lines to the same data series in ggplot2 line charts.

- Chapter 9 includes a thorough discussion of permutations and combinations—how to distinguish one versus the other and how to compute the same. You'll also learn how to create awesome, if somewhat atypical, visual content, including facet plots, balloon plots, and mosaic plots; run and interpret statistical tests of significance on categorical data; and run and interpret complementary effect size tests on the same data.

- Chapter 10 shows how to compute correlation coefficients between pairs of continuous variables; perform correlation tests; create correlation plots, dot plots, and lollipop charts; modify labels through transformations and concatenations; and deal with missing values in your data.

- Chapter 11 demonstrates how to carry out another type of unsupervised learning problem, a K-means clustering. You'll learn how to compute and visualize competing optimal cluster counts, create the clusters, and plot the same. You'll also learn how to create a Cleveland dot plot, yet another type of visualization that might be atypical, but nonetheless tells a quick and compelling story.

- Chapter 12 introduces Gini coefficients and how to visualize inequality with Lorenz curves. You'll get additional exposure to significance tests and effect size tests.

- Chapter 13 again demonstrates how to compute and interpret Gini coefficients, but on top of a different data set from that used in the previous chapter. You'll also learn how to create alternative Lorenz curves, perform t-tests (again) and F-tests, and conduct other effect size tests not demonstrated in prior chapters. Also included are sections about creating for loops and writing your own functions.

- Chapter 14 might be the heaviest and most technical chapter in the book. You'll learn how to run correlation tests and interpret their results; develop an analysis of variance (ANOVA) model; develop a logistic regression; understand and differentiate probabilities, odds ratios, and log odds; create a receiver operating characteristic (ROC) curve; and create fairly unusual boxplots.

- Chapter 15 is mostly dedicated to a discussion of the 80-20 rule and alternative methods of creating Pareto charts. You'll also learn how to create violin plots and paired histograms.

- Chapter 16 is essentially a discussion of randomness when others might see causality. You'll learn about Laplace's rule of succession, how to simulate coin flips, and how to insert ggplot2 objects into other ggplot2 objects (a very cool feature).

- Chapter 17 opens with successive demonstrations of three competing automated exploratory data analysis packages. Advanced functional and aesthetic techniques that can be applied to ggplot2 bar charts are also introduced.

- Chapter 18 introduces several measures of statistical dispersion and discusses why or how they should best be used. You'll also learn how to compute churn and how to create a pyramid plot.

- Chapter 19 introduces several methods of data standardization or normalization and discusses why and how to apply them. You'll also learn how to color data frames and highlight observations and how to compare the contents of two data sets.

- Chapter 20 is a summary that reviews the techniques applied between chapters 2 and 19 and recaps the results these same techniques produced along the way. It's not a chapter-by-chapter rehash, but rather a consolidation of key findings from nine learning areas most often covered in this book, including cluster analysis, significance testing, effect size testing, modeling, operations research, probability, statistical dispersion, standardization, and summary statistics and visualization.

This was obviously a pretty high-level description of these chapters. *Statistics Slam Dunk* demonstrates a ton of data wrangling operations not mentioned in the preceding list—for instance, how to drop columns or rows; how to transpose your data from long to wide or vice versa; how to summarize data, and by groups if necessary; how to create segments from conditional logic; and how to manipulate date formats, to name just a few. *Statistics Slam Dunk* also contains approximately 300 visualizations and roughly 40 types of plots, most of which were developed in ggplot2 or with ggplot2 extensions. Often, the best and most effective way of getting your audience to understand results from other techniques or methods is by creating graphical content. Creating compelling visualizations can be hard. Employing best practices and applying finishing touches (adding titles and subtitles, adding captions, annotating your visualizations, reformatting labels, manipulating axes, etc.) can sometimes be even harder. Almost every *Statistics Slam Dunk* chapter teaches some subset of these techniques.

About the code

Code is intermingled with text throughout. More often than not, the code is explained first and the results are summarized or otherwise discussed afterward. Many functions, built-in and packaged, appear throughout the book; as such, explanatory text incrementally fades as functions and code repeat, on the assumption that you've read previous chapters. However, you'll periodically come across thorough reiterations when reminders are presumed to be in order. Source code in this book is formatted in a `fixed-width font like this` to separate it from ordinary text. In many cases, the original source code has been reformatted; we've added line breaks and reworked indentation to accommodate the available page space in the book.

You can get executable snippets of code from the liveBook (online) version of this book at https://livebook.manning.com/book/statistics-slam-dunk. Code and data sets are available at the following GitHub location: https://github.com/garysutton/statisticsplaybook. The complete code for the scripts in the book is also available for download from the Manning website at www.manning.com/books/statistics-slam-dunk.

liveBook discussion forum

Purchase of *Statistics Slam Dunk* includes free access to liveBook, Manning's online reading platform. Using liveBook's exclusive discussion features, you can attach comments to the book globally or to specific sections or paragraphs. It's a snap to make notes for yourself, ask and answer technical questions, and receive help from the author and other users. To access the forum, go to https://livebook.manning.com/book/statistics-slam-dunk/discussion. You can also learn more about Manning's forums and the rules of conduct at https://livebook.manning.com/discussion.

Manning's commitment to our readers is to provide a venue where a meaningful dialogue between individual readers and between readers and the author can take place. It is not a commitment to any specific amount of participation on the part of the author, whose contribution to the forum remains voluntary (and unpaid). We suggest you try asking the author some challenging questions lest his interest stray! The forum and the archives of previous discussions will be accessible from the publisher's website as long as the book is in print.

about the author

 **GARY SUTTON** has built and led high-performing business intelligence and analytics organizations across multiple verticals, where R was the preferred programming language for statistical analysis, predictive modeling, and other quantitative insights. Mr. Sutton earned his undergraduate degree from the University of Southern California, a master's from George Washington University, and a second master's, in data science, from Northwestern University. He is an avid reader, former Ironman triathlete, and former basketball player.

about the cover illustration

The figure on the cover of *Statistics Slam Dunk* is "Homme Koraik," or "Koryaks Man," taken from a collection by Jacques Grasset de Saint-Sauveur, published in 1788. Each illustration is finely drawn and colored by hand.

In those days, it was easy to identify where people lived and what their trade or station in life was just by their dress. Manning celebrates the inventiveness and initiative of the computer business with book covers based on the rich diversity of regional culture centuries ago, brought back to life by pictures from collections such as this one.

Getting started

Data is changing the way businesses and other organizations work. Back in the day, the challenge was *getting* data; now the challenge is making sense of it, sifting through the noise to find the signal, and providing actionable insights to decision-makers. Those of us who work with data, especially on the frontend—statisticians, data scientists, business analysts, and the like—have many programming languages from which to choose.

R is a go-to programming language with an ever-expanding upside for slicing and dicing large data sets, conducting statistical tests of significance, developing predictive models, producing unsupervised learning algorithms, and creating top-quality visual content. Beginners and professionals alike, up and down an organization and across multiple verticals, rely on the power of R to generate insights that drive purposeful action.

This book provides end-to-end and step-by-step instructions for discovering and generating a series of unique and fascinating insights with R. In fact, this book differs from other manuals you might already be familiar with in several meaningful ways. First, the book is organized by project rather than by technique, which means any and every operation required to start and finish a discrete project is contained within each chapter, from loading packages, to importing and wrangling data, to exploring, visualizing, testing, and modeling data. You'll learn how to think about, set up, and run a data science or statistics project from beginning to end.

Second, we work exclusively with data sets downloaded or scraped from the web that are available—sometimes for a small fee—to anyone; these data sets were created, of course, without any advance knowledge of how the content might be analyzed. In other words, our data sets are *not* plug and play. This is actually a good thing because it provides opportunities to introduce a plethora of data-wrangling techniques tied to specific data visualizations and statistical testing methods. Rather than learning these techniques in isolation, you'll instead learn how seemingly different operations can and must work together.

Third, speaking of data visualizations, you'll learn how to create professional-grade plots and other visual content—not just bar charts and time-series charts but also dendrograms, Sankey diagrams, pyramid plots, facet plots, Cleveland dot plots, and Lorenz curves, to name just a few visualizations that might be outside the mainstream but are nonetheless more compelling than what you're probably used to. Often, the most effective way to tell a story or to communicate your results is through pictures rather than words or numbers. You'll get detailed instructions for creating dozens of plot types and other visual content, some using base R functions, but most from ggplot2, R's premier graphics package.

Fourth, this book has a professional basketball theme throughout; that's because all the data sets are, in fact, NBA data sets. The techniques introduced in each chapter aren't just ends in themselves but also means by which unique and fascinating insights into the NBA are ultimately revealed—all of which are absolutely transferrable to your own professional or academic work. At the end of the day, this book provides a more fun and effective way of learning R and getting further grounded in statistical concepts. With that said, let's dive in; the following sections provide further background that will best position you to tackle the remainder of the book.

1.1   *Brief introductions to R and RStudio*

R is an open source and free programming language introduced in 1993 by statisticians for other statisticians. R consistently receives high marks for performing statistical computations (no surprise), producing compelling visualizations, handling massive data sets, and supporting a wide range of supervised and unsupervised learning methods.

In recent years, several integrated development environments (IDEs) have been created for R, where a source code editor, debugger, and other utilities are combined into a single GUI. By far, the most popular GUI is RStudio.

You don't *need* RStudio. But imagine going through life without modern conveniences such as running water, microwaves, and dishwashers; that's R without the benefits of RStudio. And like R, RStudio is a free download. All the code in this book was written in RStudio 1.4.1103 running on top of R 4.1.2 on a Mac laptop computer loaded with version 11.1 of the Big Sur operating system. R and RStudio run just as well on Windows and Linux desktops, by the way.

You should first download and install R (https://cran.r-project.org) and then do the same with RStudio (www.rstudio.com). You'll indirectly interact with R by downloading libraries, writing scripts, running code, and reviewing outputs directly in RStudio. The RStudio interface is divided into four panels or windows (see figure 1.1). The Script Editor is located in the upper-left quadrant; this is where you import data, install and load libraries (also known as packages), and otherwise write code. Immediately beneath the Script Editor is the Console.

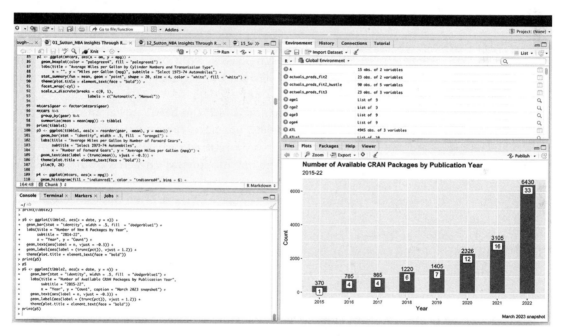

Figure 1.1 A snapshot of the RStudio interface. Code is written in the upper-left panel; programs run in the lower-left panel; the plot window is in the lower-right panel; and a running list of created objects is in the upper-right panel. Through preferences, you can set the background color, font, and font size.

The Console looks and operates like the basic R interface; this is where you review outputs from the Script Editor, including error messages and warnings when applicable. Immediately beside the Console, in the lower-right quadrant of the RStudio interface, is the Plot Window; this is where you view visualizations created in the Script Editor, manipulate their size if you so choose, and export them to Microsoft Word, PowerPoint, or other applications. And then there's the Environment Window, which keeps a running history of the objects—data frames, tibbles (a type of data frame specific to R), and visualizations—created inside the Script Editor.

RStudio also runs in the cloud (https://login.rstudio.cloud) and is accessible through almost any web browser. This might be a good option if your local machine is low on resources.

1.2   Why R?

The size of the digital universe is expanding along an exponential curve rather than a linear line; the most successful businesses and organizations are those that collect, store, and use data more than others; and, of course, we know that R is, and has been, the programming language of choice for statisticians, data scientists, and business analysts around the world for nearly 30 years now. But why should you invest your time polishing your R skills when there are several open source and commercial alternatives?

1.2.1   Visualizing data

This book contains some 300 or so plots. Often, the most effective way of analyzing data is to visualize it. R is absolutely best in class when it comes to transforming summarized data into professional-looking visual content. So let's first talk about pictures rather than numbers.

Several prepackaged data sets are bundled with the base R installation. This book does *not* otherwise use any of these objects, but here, the mtcars data set—an object just 32 rows long and 11 columns wide—is more than sufficient to help demonstrate the power of R's graphics capabilities. The mtcars data was extracted from a 1974 issue of *Motor Trend* magazine; the data set contains performance and other data on 32 makes and models of automobiles manufactured in the United States, Europe, and Japan.

The following visualizations point to mtcars as a data source (see figure 1.2); they were created with the ggplot2 package and then grouped into a single 2 × 2 matrix with the patchwork package. Both of these packages, especially ggplot2, are used extensively throughout the book. (More on packages in just a moment.)

Our visualizations include a correlation plot and facet plot along the top and a bar chart and histogram on the bottom, as described here:

- *Correlation plot*—A correlation plot displays the relationship between a pair of continuous, or numeric, variables. The relationship, or association, between two continuous variables can be positive, negative, or neutral. When positive, the variables move in the same direction; when negative, the two variables move in opposite directions; and when neutral, there is no meaningful relationship at all.

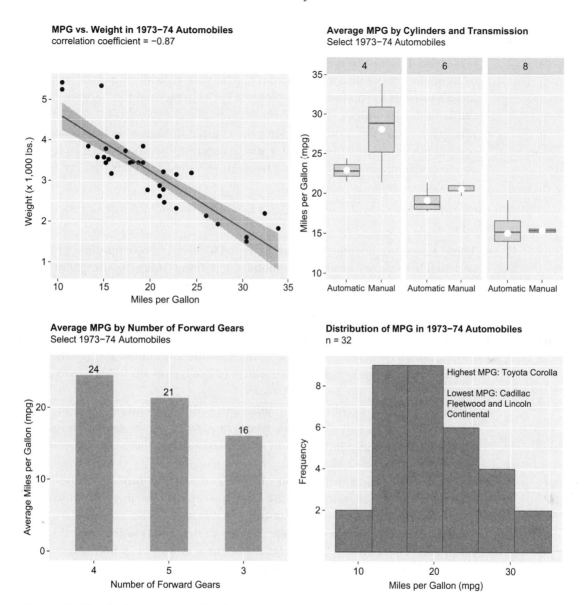

Figure 1.2   Visualizations of automobile data using the `ggplot2` package

- *Facet plot*—A facet plot is a group of subplots that share the same horizontal and vertical axes (x-axis and y-axis, respectively); thus, each subplot must otherwise be alike. The data is split, or segmented, by groups in the data that are frequently referred to as *factors*. A facet plot draws one subplot for each factor in the data and displays each in its own panel. We've drawn boxplots to display the distribution of miles per gallon segmented by the number of cylinders and the type of transmission.

- *Bar chart*—A bar chart, often called a bar graph, uses rectangular bars to display counts of discrete, or categorical, data. Each category, or factor, in the data is represented by its own bar, and the length of each bar corresponds to the value or frequency of the data it represents. The bars are typically displayed vertically, but it's possible to flip the orientation of a bar chart so that the bars are instead displayed horizontally.

- *Histogram*—Sometimes mistaken for a bar chart, a histogram is a graphical representation of the distribution of a single continuous variable. It displays the counts, or frequencies, of the data between specified intervals that are usually referred to as bins.

We can readily draw several interesting and meaningful conclusions from these four visualizations:

- There is a strong negative correlation, equal to –0.87, between miles per gallon and weight; that is, heavier automobiles get fewer miles to the gallon than lighter automobiles. The slope of the regression line indicates how strongly, or not so strongly, two variables, such as miles per gallon and weight, are correlated, which is computed on a scale from –1 to +1.

- Automobiles with fewer cylinders get more miles to the gallon than cars with more cylinders. Furthermore, especially regarding automobiles with either four or six cylinders, those with manual transmissions get more miles to the gallon than those with automatic transmissions.

- There is a significant difference in miles per gallon depending upon the number of forward gears an automobile has; for instance, automobiles with four forward gears get 8 miles to the gallon more than automobiles equipped with just three forward gears.

- The miles per gallon distribution of the 32 makes and models in the mtcars data set appears to be normal (think of a bell-shaped curve in which most of the data is concentrated around the mean, or average); however, there are more automobiles that get approximately 20 miles to the gallon or less than there are otherwise. The Toyota Corolla gets the highest miles per gallon, whereas the Cadillac Fleetwood and Lincoln Continental are tied for getting the lowest miles per gallon.

R's reputation in the data visualization space is due to the quantity of graphs, charts, plots, diagrams, and maps that can be created and the quality of their aesthetics; it isn't at all due to ease of use. R, and specifically the ggplot2 package, gives you the power and flexibility to customize any visual object and to apply best practices. But with customizations come complexities, such as the following:

- Concerning the facet plot, for instance, where paired boxplots were created and divided by the number of cylinders in an automobile's engine, an additional function—with six arguments—was called just to create white dots to represent the population means (ggplot2 otherwise prints a horizontal line inside a boxplot to designate the median). Another function was called so that ggplot2 returned x-axis labels that spelled out the transmission types rather than a 0 for automatic and a 1 for manual.

- The bar chart, a relatively straightforward visual object, nevertheless contains several customizations. Data labels aren't available out of the box; adding them required calling another function plus decision points on their font size and location. And because those data labels were added *atop* each bar, it then became necessary to extend the length of the y-axis, thereby requiring yet another line of code.

- When you create a histogram, ggplot2 does *not* automatically return a plot with an ideal number of bins; instead, that's your responsibility to figure out, and this usually requires some experimentation. In addition, the tick marks along the y-axis were hardcoded so that they included whole numbers only; by default, ggplot2 returns fractional numbers for half of the tick marks, which, of course, makes no sense for histograms.

This book provides step-by-step instructions on how to create these and some three dozen other types of ggplot2 visualizations that meet the highest standards for aesthetics and contain just enough bells and whistles to communicate clear and compelling messages.

1.2.2 *Installing and using packages to extend R's functional footprint*

Regardless of what sort of operation you want or need to perform, there's a great chance that other programmers preceded you. There's also a good chance that one of those programmers then wrote an R function, bundled it into a package, and made it readily available for you and others to download. R's library of packages continues to expand rapidly, thanks to programmers around the world who routinely make use of R's open source platform. In a nutshell, programmers bundle their source code, data, and documentation into packages and then upload their final products into a central repository for the rest of us to download and use.

As of this writing, there are 19,305 packages stored in the Comprehensive R Archive Network (CRAN). Approximately one-third of these were published in 2022; another one-third were published between 2019 and 2021; and the remaining one-third were published sometime between 2008 and 2018. The ggplot2 bar chart shown in figure 1.3 reveals the number of packages available in CRAN by publication year. (Note that the number of packages *available* is different from the number of packages *published* because many have since been deprecated.) The white-boxed labels affixed inside the bars represent the percentage of the total package count as of March 2023; so, for instance, of all the packages published in 2021, 3,105 remain in CRAN, which represents 16% of the total package count.

Clearly, new packages are being released at an increasing rate; in fact, the 2023 count of new packages is on pace to approach or even exceed 12,000. That's about 33 new packages on average every day. R-bloggers, a popular website with hundreds of

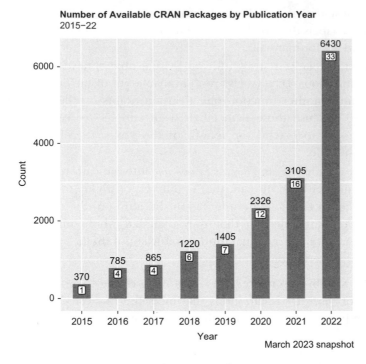

Figure 1.3   Package counts in CRAN displayed by publication year

tutorials, publishes a Top 40 list of new packages *every month*, just to help programmers sift through all the new content. These are the kinds of numbers that surely make heads spin in the commercial software world.

Packages are super easy to install: it takes just a single line of code or a couple of clicks inside the RStudio GUI to install one. This book will show you how to install a package, how to load a package into your script, and how to utilize some of the most powerful packages now available.

1.2.3   *Networking with other users*

R programmers are very active online, seeking support and getting it. The flurry of online activity helps you correct errors in your code, overcome other roadblocks, and be more productive. A series of searches on Stack Overflow, a website where statisticians, data scientists, and other programmers congregate for technical support, returned almost 450,000 hits for R versus just a fraction of that total, about 20%, for five leading commercial alternatives (JMP, MATLAB, Minitab, SAS, and SPSS) *combined*.

In the spirit of full disclosure, Python, another open source programming language, returned more hits than R—way more, in fact. But bear in mind that Python, while frequently used for data science and statistical computing, is really a general programming language, also used to develop application interfaces, web portals, and even video games; R, on the other hand, is strictly for number crunching and data analysis. So comparing R to Python is very much like comparing apples to oranges.

1.2.4   Interacting with big data

If you want or anticipate the need to interact with a typical big data technology stack (e.g., Hadoop for storage, Apache Kafka for ingestion, Apache Spark for processing), R is one of your best bets for the analytics layer. In fact, the top 10 results from a Google search on "best programming languages for big data" *all* list R as a top choice, while the commercial platforms previously referenced, minus MATLAB, weren't mentioned at all.

1.2.5   Landing a job

There's a healthy job market for R programmers. An Indeed search returned nearly 19,000 job opportunities for R programmers in the United States, more than SAS, Minitab, SPSS, and JMP *combined*. It's a snapshot in time within one country, but the point nevertheless remains. (Note that many of the SAS and SPSS job opportunities are *at* SAS or IBM.) A subset of these opportunities was posted by some of the world's leading technology companies, including Amazon, Apple, Google, and Meta (Facebook's parent company). The `ggplot2` bar chart shown in figure 1.4 visualizes the full results. Python job opportunities, of which there are plenty, aren't included for the reason mentioned previously.

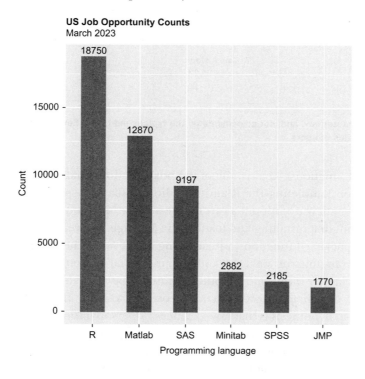

Figure 1.4   There's a healthy job market for R programmers.

1.3   How this book works

As previously mentioned, this book is organized so that each of the following chapters is a standalone project—minus the final chapter, which is a summary of the entire book. That means every operation required to execute a project from wing to wing is self-contained within each chapter. The following flow diagram, or process map, provides a visual snapshot of what you can expect going forward (see figure 1.5).

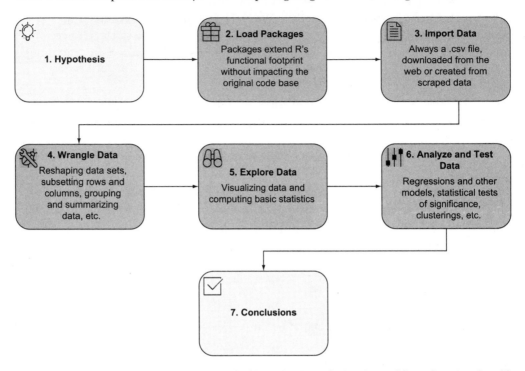

Figure 1.5   A typical chapter flow and, not coincidentally, the typical end-to-end flow of most real-world data science and statistics projects

We use only base R functions—that is, out-of-the-box functions that are immediately available to you after completing the R and RStudio installations—to load packages into our scripts. After all, you can't put a cart before a horse, and you can't call a packaged function without first installing and loading the package. Thereafter, we rely on a mix of built-in and packaged functions, with a strong lean toward the latter, especially for preparing and wrangling our data sets and creating visual content of the same.

We begin every chapter with some hypothesis. It might be a null hypothesis that we subsequently reject or fail to reject depending on test results. In chapter 7, for instance, our going-in hypothesis is that any variances in personal fouls and attempted free throws between home and visiting teams are due to chance. We then reject that hypothesis and assume officiating bias if our statistical tests of significance return a low probability of ever obtaining equal or more extreme results; otherwise, we fail to reject that same hypothesis. Or it might merely be an assumption that must then be confirmed or denied by applying other methods. Take chapter 15, for instance, where we assume nonlinearity between the number of NBA franchises and the number of games played and won, and then create Pareto charts, visual displays of unit and cumulative frequencies, to present the results. For another example, take chapter 19, where we make the assumption that standardizing points-per-game averages by season—that is, converting the raw data to a common and simple scale—would most certainly provide a very different historical perspective on the NBA's top scorers.

Then, we start writing our scripts. We begin every script by loading our required packages, usually by making one or more calls to the `library()` function. Packages must be installed before they are loaded, and they must be loaded before their functions are called. Thus, there's no hard requirement to preface any R script by loading any package; they can instead be loaded incrementally if that's your preference. But think of our hypothesis as the strategic plan and the packages as representing part of the tactical, or short-term, steps that help us achieve our larger goals. That we choose to load our packages up front reflects the fact that we've thoughtfully blueprinted the details on how to get from a starting line to a finish line.

Next, we import our data set, or data sets, by calling the `read_csv()` function from the `readr` package, which, like `ggplot2`, is part of the `tidyverse` universe of packages. That's because all of our data sets are .csv files downloaded from public websites or created from scraped data that was then copied into Microsoft Excel and saved with a .csv extension.

This book demonstrates how to perform almost any data-wrangling operation you'll ever need, usually by calling `dplyr` and `tidyr` functions, which are also part of the `tidyverse`. You'll learn how to transform, or reshape, data sets; subset your data by rows or columns; summarize data, by groups when necessary; create new variables; and join multiple data sets into one.

This book also demonstrates how to apply best exploratory data analysis (EDA) practices. EDA is an initial but thorough interrogation of a data set, usually by mixing computations of basic statistics with correlation plots, histograms, and other visual content. It's always a good practice to become intimately familiar with your data *after* you've wrangled it and *before* you test it or otherwise analyze it. We mostly call base R functions to compute basic statistical measures such as means and medians; however, we almost exclusively rely on `ggplot2` functions and even `ggplot2` extensions to create best-in-class visualizations.

We then test or at least further analyze our data. For instance, in chapter 5, we develop linear regression and decision tree models to isolate which hustle statistics—loose balls recovered, passes deflected, shots defended, and the like—have a statistically significant effect on wins and losses. In chapter 9, we run a chi-square test for independence, a type of statistical or hypothesis test run against two categorical variables, to determine whether permutations of prior days off between opposing home and road teams help decide who wins. Alternatively, let's consider chapter 3, where we develop a type of unsupervised learning algorithm called *hierarchical clustering* to establish whether teams should have very different career expectations of a top-five draft pick versus any other first-round selection. Or take chapter 16, where we evaluate the so-called hot hand phenomenon by "merely" applying some hard-core analysis techniques, minus any formal testing.

Finally, we present our conclusions that tie back to our hypothesis: yes (or no), officials are biased toward home teams; yes (or no), rest matters in wins and losses; yes (or no), defense does, in fact, win championships. Often, our conclusions are actionable, and therefore, they naturally mutate into a series of recommendations. If some hustle statistics matter more than others, then teams should coach to those metrics; if teams want to bolster their rosters through the amateur draft, and if it makes sense to tank, or purposely lose games, as a means of moving up the draft board to select the best available players, then that's exactly what teams should do; offenses should be designed around the probabilities of scoring within a 24-second shot clock.

Before jumping into the rest of the book, here are some caveats and other notes to consider. First, some chapters don't flow quite so sequentially with clear delineations between, let's say, data wrangling and EDA. Data-wrangling operations may be required throughout; it might be necessary to prep a data set as a prerequisite to exploring its contents, but other data wrangling might then be required to create visualizations. Regarding conclusions, they aren't always held in reserve and then revealed at the end of a chapter. In addition, chapter 3 is more or less a continuation of chapter 2, and chapter 11 is a continuation of chapter 10. These one-to-many breaks are meant to consign the length of these chapters to a reasonable number of pages. However, the same flow, or process, applies, and you'll learn just as much in chapter 2 as in chapter 3 or equally as much in chapter 10 as in chapter 11. We'll get started by exploring a data set of first-round draft picks and their subsequent career trajectories.

Summary

- R is a programming language developed by statisticians for statisticians; it's a programming language for, and only for, crunching numbers and analyzing data.
- RStudio is a GUI or IDE that controls an R session. Installing and loading packages, writing code, viewing and analyzing results, troubleshooting errors, and producing professional-quality reports are tasks made *much* easier with RStudio.
- Against many competing alternatives—open source and commercial—R remains a best-in-class solution with regard to performing statistical computations, creating elegant visual content, managing large and complex data sets, creating regression models and applying other supervised learning methods, and conducting segmentation analysis and other types of unsupervised learning. As an R programmer, you'll be bounded only by the limits of your imagination.
- R functionality is, and has been, on a skyrocketing trajectory. Packages extend R's functional footprint, and over half of the packages now available in CRAN were developed within the past three years. Next-generation programmers—studying at Northwestern, Berkeley, or some other college or university where the curriculum is naturally fixed on open source and free technologies—are likely to maintain R's current trajectory for the foreseeable future.

- There's no 1-800 number to call for technical support, but there are Stack Overflow, GitHub, and other similar websites where you can interact with other R programmers and get solutions, which beats requesting a level-1 analyst to merely open a support ticket any day of the week.
- R is one of the programming languages that make interacting with big data technologies user-friendly.
- There's a high demand for R programmers in today's marketplace. An ongoing symbiotic relationship between higher education and private industry has created a vicious circle of R-based curriculum and R jobs that is likely to self-perpetuate in the years to come.

Exploring data 2

This chapter and the next are a package deal—we'll explore a real data set in this chapter and then get practical implications from the same in chapter 3. An exploratory data analysis (EDA) is a process—or, really, a series of processes—by which a data set is interrogated by computing basic statistics and creating graphical representations of the same. We won't paint any broad strokes along the way; instead, we'll focus our analysis on a single variable, a performance metric called win shares, and discover how win shares is associated with the other variables in our data. Our going-in hypothesis in the next chapter will directly tie back to the findings from this chapter. Along the way, we'll demonstrate how to best use the power of R to thoroughly explore a data set—any data set.

But first, we must take care of the mandatory tasks of loading packages, importing our data set, and then tidying and wrangling it. If you're not spending *most* of your time dedicated to "intangible" tasks that can sometimes feel like grunt work—understanding that time allocations aren't necessarily correlated with lines of code—then you're most likely doing something wrong. Unfortunately, data isn't always collected and stored in anticipation of subsequent analytical needs; tidying and wrangling data help us avoid bad or misleading results. Nevertheless, we'll introduce several operations that will serve us well going forward, and in the process, you'll learn a great deal about win shares and other NBA data.

2.1 Loading packages

We begin by calling the `library()` function to load packages that allow us to then call functions not available in the base product. You're not using the best of R by relegating yourself to built-in functions. It may go without saying, but packages must be installed before loading them into a script and then calling their functions. This is just one reason why we reserve the very top of our scripts for loading packages we've previously installed. Just to be clear, when you install R, you're installing the base product only; any need thereafter to go above and beyond the features and functions of base R requires ongoing installs of packages, usually from the Comprehensive R Archive Network (CRAN), but every now and then from GitHub.

Packages are installed by calling the base R `install.packages()` function and passing the package name as an argument between a pair of single or double quotation marks, as shown:

```
install.packages("tidyverse")
```

To avoid the risk of confusing R, we use double quotation marks on the outside when quoting an entire line of code and use single quotation marks, if and when necessary, on the inside when quoting a portion of code.

While packages need to be installed just once, they must be loaded whenever and wherever you plan to use them. Packages extend the features and functions of R without modifying or otherwise affecting the original code base (which no one wants to touch today). Here's a rundown of the packages we plan to use in this chapter:

- The `dplyr` and `tidyr` packages contain *many* functions for manipulating and wrangling data. Both of these packages are part of the `tidyverse` universe of packages. This means you can call the `library()` function once and pass the `tidyverse` package, and R will automatically load `dplyr`, `tidyr`, and every other package that is part of the `tidyverse`.
- The `ggplot2` package includes the `ggplot()` function for creating elegant visual content that puts to shame most out-of-the-box plots. In addition, `ggplot2` contains several other functions for trimming your visualizations that, by and large, don't have base R equivalents. The `ggplot2` package is also part of the `tidyverse`.

- The readr package is used to quickly and easily read or import rectangular data from delimited files; readr is part of the tidyverse. Rectangular data is synonymous with structured data or tabular data; it simply means that the data is organized in rows and columns. A *delimited file* is a type of flat file by which the values are separated, or delimited, by a special character or sequence of characters; they are usually saved with an extension that indicates how the data is delimited. We'll be working exclusively with files previously saved with a .csv extension. A .csv, or *comma-separated values*, file is a Microsoft Excel file by which a comma is used as the delimiter.
- The reshape2 package includes functions that make it easy—it's just one line of code—to transform data between wide and long formats. Data is usually transformed to suit specific analysis methods and/or visualization techniques.
- The sqldf package is used to write SELECT statements and other Structured Query Language (SQL) queries. SQL is a programming language of its own that provides a mostly standardized way of interacting with stored data. Those migrating from another programming language might find some comfort in the fact that R supports SQL; however, we'll gradually wean you away from sqldf and toward dplyr.
- The patchwork package makes it very easy—again, it's just a single line of code—to bundle two or more visualizations into a single graphical object.

In the following chunk, the library() function is called four times to load four packages we've already installed. Note that it's *not* necessary to include the package name inside a pair of quotation marks when calling the library() function:

```
library(tidyverse)
library(reshape2)
library(sqldf)
library(patchwork)
```

To run one or more lines of code—which, by the way, should be entered in the Script Editor panel—highlight the code with your cursor and then click Run at the top of the Script Editor. If you're working on a Mac, you can instead hold down the Control key and press Return.

2.2   *Importing data*

The read_csv() function from the readr package is used to import a data set in the form of a flat file previously saved with a .csv extension. R reads .csv files very well, as long as the data is confined to a single worksheet (think of a Microsoft Excel file as a workbook that can contain one or more worksheets). R will throw an error otherwise. The read_csv() function requires just a single argument to be passed: the name of the file, preceded by its storage location, bounded by a pair of single or double quotation marks.

However, if you previously set a working directory and subsequently deployed your files in that location, you merely need to pass the name of the file, including the extension. You can set the working directory by calling the `setwd()` function and get the working directory you previously set by calling the `getwd()` function; both `setwd()` and `getwd()` are base R functions. When you then call the `read_csv()` function, R will automatically navigate through your folder structure, search your working directory, and import your file.

The following line of code imports a .csv file called draft since it's saved in our working directory and, through the assignment operator (`<-`), sets it equal to an object by the same name. The data set, downloaded from the http://data.world website, contains information on every NBA first-round draft pick between the 2000 and 2009 amateur drafts:

```
draft <- read_csv("draft.csv")
```

> **What is the NBA draft?**
> For those of you who might not be familiar with the NBA, the draft is an annual event, held during the offseason, where teams take turns selecting eligible players from the United States and abroad. Today, the draft is just two rounds. Barring trades between teams, each team is allowed one selection per round in an order determined by the prior year's finish, where the worst teams are allowed to select first.

A quick and easy way to confirm the success of a data import and, at the same time, return the dimension of your data set is to call the base R `dim()` function:

```
dim(draft)
## [1] 293  26
```

Our draft data set contains 293 rows and 26 columns. Anything and everything preceded by a pair of pound signs is a copy and paste of what R subsequently returns for us. Now that we have our data set, we'll wrangle it before exploring it, analyzing it, and drawing some meaningful conclusions from it.

2.3 *Wrangling data*

In the real world, most of the data sets you import will be less than perfect; it's therefore absolutely necessary to perform a series of operations to transform the data into a clean and tidy object that can then be properly and accurately analyzed. Many of the most common data wrangling operations include the following:

- Reshaping, or transposing, the layout of your data by gathering columns into rows or spreading rows into columns
- Subsetting your data by rows that meet some logical criteria
- Subsetting your data by columns to remove superfluous data
- Summarizing your data, usually through mathematical operations, and often grouped by some other variable in your data set

- Creating new variables, usually derived from one or more original variables in your data
- Converting variables from one class to another, for instance, from numeric to date or from character string to categorical
- Changing variable names
- Replacing attributes
- Combining or joining your data with one or more other data sets

We'll start by removing unnecessary columns or variables.

2.3.1   *Removing variables*

Our first data wrangling operation is to remove superfluous variables from the draft data set. For the most part, we're dropping career statistics that won't factor into our analysis. This is a purely discretionary operation, but it's always a best practice to retain only what you need and to discard everything else. When working with large data sets, dropping irrelevant or redundant data can absolutely improve computational efficiency.

In the following line of code, we make a call to the `select()` function from the `dplyr` package as well as the `c()` function from base R:

```
draft <- select(draft,-c(3,4,16:24))
```

The `select()` function is used to select or deselect variables by their name or index; the `c()` function is used to combine multiple arguments to form a vector. We're calling the `select()` function to subset the draft data set by removing the variables, denoted by their left-to-right position in our data set, passed to the `c()` function (notice the preceding minus [-] operator). There is usually more than one way to skin a cat in R, and this is one of those instances:

- The variable names could be substituted for the position numbers. This is actually a best practice and should be the preferred method, unless the number of variables to remove is prohibitive or there are extenuating circumstances. In fact, some of these variables include characters that would otherwise cause R to error out, so we elected to call out the position numbers this time rather than the variable names.
- The minus operator could be removed, and the variable names or positions to *include* could then be passed as arguments to the `c()` function.
- Base R functions could be used in lieu of `dplyr` code.

We'll apply all of these alternatives going forward, depending on the circumstances.

2.3.2   *Removing observations*

The next line of code removes observations (i.e., rows or records) 90 and 131 from draft for the very simple reason that these observations contain incomplete data that would otherwise interrupt ongoing operations. The records are mostly blank, thereby eliminating data imputation or other corrective action as options:

```
draft <- draft[-c(90, 131),]
```

Now that we've cut the dimension of draft by first dropping unnecessary variables and then removing mostly incomplete observations, we'll next view our data and perform more meaningful data wrangling operations.

2.3.3 Viewing data

The dplyr glimpse() function, where the name of our data set is passed as the lone argument, returns a transposed view of the data. In this view, the columns appear as rows, and the rows appear as columns, making it possible to see every column in the RStudio Console; this is especially useful when working with wide data sets.

The glimpse() function also returns the type, or class, for each variable and, at the very top, the dimension of the object:

```
glimpse(draft)
## Rows: 289
## Columns: 18
## $ Rk        <dbl> 1, 2, 3, 4, 5, 6, 7, 8, 9, 10, 11, 12, 13, 14, 1…
## $ Year      <fct> 2009, 2009, 2009, 2009, 2009, 2009, 2009, 2009, …
## $ Pk        <dbl> 1, 2, 3, 4, 5, 6, 7, 8, 9, 10, 11, 12, 13, 14, 1…
## $ Tm        <fct> LAC, MEM, OKC, SAC, MIN, MIN, GSW, NYK, TOR, MIL…
## $ Player    <chr> "Blake Griffin", "Hasheem Thabeet", "James Harde…
## $ Age       <dbl> 20.106, 22.135, 19.308, 19.284, 18.252, 20.144, …
## $ Pos       <chr> "F", "C", "G", "G-F", "G", "G", "G", "C-F", "G-F…
## $ Born      <fct> us, tz, us, us, es, us, us, us, us, us, us, us, …
## $ College   <chr> "Oklahoma", "UConn", "Arizona State", "Memphis",…
## $ From      <fct> 2011, 2010, 2010, 2010, 2012, 2010, 2010, 2010, …
## $ To        <fct> 2020, 2014, 2020, 2019, 2020, 2012, 2020, 2017, …
## $ G         <dbl> 622, 224, 826, 594, 555, 163, 699, 409, 813, 555…
## $ MP        <dbl> 34.8, 10.5, 34.3, 30.7, 30.9, 22.9, 34.3, 18.8, …
## $ WS        <dbl> 75.2, 4.8, 133.3, 28.4, 36.4, -1.1, 103.2, 16.4,…
## $ WS48      <dbl> 0.167, 0.099, 0.226, 0.075, 0.102, -0.015, 0.207…
## $ Born2     <fct> USA, World, USA, USA, World, USA, USA, USA, USA,…
## $ College2  <fct> 1, 1, 1, 1, 0, 1, 1, 1, 1, 0, 1, 1, 1, 1, 1, 1, …
## $ Pos2      <chr> "F", "C", "G", "G-F", "G", "G", "G", "C-F", "G-F…
```

The draft data set is now 291 rows long and 15 columns wide (versus its original 293 × 26 dimension), with a combination of numeric variables (int and dbl) and character strings (chr).

Alternatively (or additionally), R returns the first and last n rows of a data set when the base R head() and tail() functions, respectively, are called. This is especially useful if the transposed output from glimpse() is less than intuitive. By default, R displays the first six or last six observations in a data set for either or both of these functions. The following two lines of code return the first three and last three observations in the draft data set:

```
head(draft, 3)
      Rk Year    Pk Tm      Player        Age Pos   Born  College
## <dbl> <dbl> <dbl> <chr>  <chr>       <dbl> <chr> <chr> <chr>
## 1    1 2009     1 LAC    Blake Grif… 20.1  F     us    Oklaho…
## 2    2 2009     2 MEM    Hasheem Th… 22.1  C     tz    UConn
## 3    3 2009     3 OKC    James Hard… 19.3  G     us    Arizon…
      From    To     G    MP    WS   WS48
## <dbl> <dbl> <dbl> <dbl> <dbl> <dbl>
## 1 2011  2020    622  34.8  75.2 0.167
## 2 2010  2014    224  10.5   4.8 0.099
## 3 2010  2020    826  34.3 133.  0.226


tail(draft, 3)
        Rk Year    Pk Tm     Player       Age Pos   Born  College
## <dbl> <dbl> <dbl> <chr>   <chr>      <dbl> <chr> <chr> <chr>
## 1  291 2000    27 IND     Primo_ Bre… 20.3 C     si    0
## 2  292 2000    28 POR     Erick Bark… 22.1 G     us    St. Jo…
## 3  293 2000    29 LAL     Mark Madsen 24.2 F     us    Stanfo…
      From    To     G    MP    WS   WS48
## <dbl> <dbl> <dbl> <dbl> <dbl> <dbl>
## 291 2002  2010    342  18.1  10.8 0.084
## 292 2001  2002     27   9.9   0.2 0.027
## 293 2001  2009    453  11.8   8.2 0.074
```

Some of our variables that are now character strings or numeric should be converted to factor variables. We'll take care of that next.

2.3.4 *Converting variable types*

Some character strings and numeric variables are, in fact, categorical variables, or factors, even if they're not classed as such; that's because they can only take on a known or fixed set of values. Take the variable Year, just to provide one example. We've already established that our data set includes information on NBA first-round draft picks between 2000 and 2009; thus, Year can only equal some value between 2000 and 2009. Or, take the variable Tm, which is short for *Team*. There are only so many teams in the NBA; therefore, Tm has a fixed set of possibilities. If you plan to model or visualize data, converting variables to factors that are truly categorical is almost mandatory.

Now take a look at the next few lines of code. The $ operator in R is used to extract, or subset, a variable from a chosen data set. For example, in the first line of code here, we're extracting, or subsetting, the variable Year from the draft data set and converting it, and only it, to a factor variable:

```
draft$Year <- as.factor(draft$Year)
draft$Tm <- as.factor(draft$Tm)
draft$Born <- as.factor(draft$Born)
draft$From <- as.factor(draft$From)
draft$To <- as.factor(draft$To)
```

To directly confirm just one of these operations, and therefore the others indirectly, we next make a call to the base R class() function and pass the draft variable Year. We can see that Year is now, in fact, a factor variable. The glimpse() function can again be called as an alternative:

```
class(draft$Year)
## "factor"
```

Soon enough, we'll be visualizing and analyzing our data around the levels, or groups, in some of these variables that are now factors.

2.3.5   *Creating derived variables*

We've removed variables and converted other variables. Next, we'll create variables—three, in fact—and sequentially append them to the end of the draft data set. With respect to the first two variables, we'll call the dplyr mutate() function in tandem with the base R ifelse() function. This powerful combination makes it possible to perform logical tests against one or more original variables and add attributes to the new variables, depending on the test results. For the third variable, we'll duplicate an original variable and then replace the new variable's attributes by calling the dplyr recode() function.

Let's start with the variable Born; this is a two-byte variable that equals a player's country of birth where, for instance, us equals United States.

The first line of code in the following chunk creates a new, or derived, variable called Born2. If the value in the original variable Born equals us, then the same record in draft should equal USA; if the value in Born equals anything other than us, Born2 should instead equal World. The second line of code converts the variable Born2 to a factor variable because each record can take just one of two possible values and because some of our forthcoming analysis will, in fact, be grouped by these same levels:

```
mutate(draft, Born2 = ifelse(Born == "us", "USA", "World")) -> draft
draft$Born2 <- as.factor(draft$Born2)
```

> **NOTE** By the way, the = and == operators aren't the same; the first is an assignment or mathematical operator, whereas the second is a logical operator.

Now, let's work with the variable College, which equals the last college or university every NBA first-round pick in the draft data set attended, regardless of how long they might have been enrolled and regardless of whether or not they graduated. However, not every player attended a college or university; for those who didn't, College equals NA. An NA, or not available, in R is the equivalent of a missing value and therefore can't be ignored. In the next line of code, we call the base R is.na() function to replace every NA with 0.

In the second line of code, we again call the mutate() and ifelse() functions to create a new variable, College2, and to add values derived from the original variable College. If that variable equals 0, it should also equal 0 in College2; on the other hand, if College equals anything else, College2 should instead equal 1. The third line of code converts College2 to a factor variable:

```
draft$College[is.na(draft$College)] <- 0
mutate(draft, College2 = ifelse(College == 0, 0, 1)) -> draft
draft$College2 <- as.factor(draft$College2)
```

Finally, a quick check on the variable `Pos`, short for a player's position, reveals yet another tidying opportunity—provided we didn't previously glean the same when calling the `glimpse()` function. A call to the base R `levels()` function returns every unique attribute from `Pos`. Note that `levels()` only works with factor variables, so we therefore couple `levels()` with the `as.factor()` function to temporarily convert `Pos` from one class to another:

```
levels(as.factor(draft$Pos))
## [1] "C"  "C-F"  "F"  "F-C"  "F-G"  "G"  "G-F"
```

We readily see that, for instance, some players play center and forward (`C-F`), whereas others play forward and center (`F-C`). It's not clear if a player tagged as a C–F is predominantly a center and another player tagged as an F–C is predominantly a forward—or if this was simply the result of careless data entry. Regardless, these players play the same two positions because of their build and skill set.

In the first line of code that follows, we create a new variable called `Pos2` as an exact duplicate of `Pos`. In the next couple lines of code, we make a call to the `recode()` function to replace the `Pos2` attributes with new ones, as such (note that we apply quotation marks around the variable names because, at least for the time being, `Pos2` is still a character string):

- `C` is replaced by `Center`.
- `C-F` and `F-C` are replaced by `Big`.
- `F` is replaced by `Forward`.
- `G` is replaced by `Guard`.
- `F-G` and `G-F` are replaced by `Swingman`.

Then, we convert the variables `Pos` and `Pos2` to factors. Finally, we pass `Pos2` to the `levels()` function to confirm that our recoding worked as planned:

```
draft$Pos2 <- draft$Pos
draft$Pos2 <- recode(draft$Pos2,
                     "C" = "Center",
                     "C-F" = "Big",
                     "F" = "Forward",
                     "F-C" = "Big",
                     "F-G" = "Swingman",
                     "G" = "Guard",
                     "G-F" = "Swingman")
draft$Pos <- as.factor(draft$Pos)
draft$Pos2 <- as.factor(draft$Pos2)
levels(draft$Pos2)
## [1] "Big"      "Center"   "Forward"  "Guard"      "Swingman"
```

With all this wrangling and tidying out of the way—at least for the time being—it makes sense to baseline our working data set, which we'll do next.

2.4 Variable breakdown

After removing a subset of the original variables, converting other variables to factors, and then creating three new variables, the draft data set now contains the following 18 variables:

- Rk—A record counter only, with a maximum of 293. The draft data set, when imported, *had* 293 records, where Rk starts at 1 and then increments by one with each subsequent record. Two records were subsequently removed due to incomplete data, thereby reducing the length of draft to 291 records, but the values in Rk remained as is despite the deletions.

- Year—Represents the year a player was selected in the NBA draft, with a minimum of 2000 and a maximum of 2009. For what it's worth, the http:// data.world data set actually covers the 1989 to 2016 NBA drafts; however, 10 years of data is sufficient for our purposes here. Because our intent (see chapter 3) is to eventually track career trajectories, 2009 is a reasonable and even necessary stopping point. We'll sometimes summarize our data grouped by the variable Year.

- Pk—The draft data set containing first-round selections only. This is, therefore, the selection, or pick, number in the first round where, for instance, the number 7 indicates the seventh overall pick. We're particularly interested in win shares by the variable Pk; we expect to see differences between players picked high in the draft versus other players picked later in the first round.

- Tm—The abbreviated team name—for instance, NYK for New York Knicks or GSW for Golden State Warriors—that made the draft pick.

- Player—The name of the player selected, in firstname lastname format (e.g., Stephen Curry).

- Age—The age of each player at the time he was selected; for instance, Stephen Curry was 21.108 years old when the Warriors selected him seventh overall in 2009.

- Pos—The position, or positions, for each player, in abbreviated format.

- Born—The country where each player was born, in abbreviated format.

- College—The college or university that each player last attended before turning professional. Of course, many players, especially those born overseas, didn't attend college; where that is the case, the record now equals 0.

- From—The first professional season for each player where, for instance, 2010 equals the 2009–10 season. A typical NBA regular season starts in mid-October and concludes in mid-April of the following calendar year. Because the draft data set starts with the 2000 draft, the minimum value equals 2001.

- `To`—The last season for which the draft data set includes player statistics. The maximum value here is 2020.
- `G`—The total number of regular season games played by each player between the 2000-01 and 2019–20 seasons.
- `MP`—The average minutes played per regular season game by each player.
- `WS`—The number of win shares accrued by each player between the 2000–01 and 2019–20 seasons. Win shares is an advanced statistic used to quantify a player's contributions to his team's success. It combines each player's raw statistics with team and league-wide statistics to produce a number that represents each player's contributions to his team's win count. The sum of individual win shares on any team should approximately equal that team's regular season win total. Stephen Curry accrued 103.2 win shares between 2009 and 2020. In other words, approximately 103 of Golden State's regular season wins over that 10-year stretch tie back to Curry's offensive and defensive production. Most of the forthcoming EDA focuses on win shares, including its associations with other variables.
- `WS48`—The number of win shares accrued by each player for every 48 minutes played. NBA games are 48 minutes in duration, as long as they end in regulation and don't require overtime.
- `Born2`—Not in the original data set. This is a derived variable that equals USA if a player was born in the United States or World if the player was born outside the United States.
- `College2`—Not in the original data set. This is a derived variable that equals 0 if a player didn't attend a college or university or 1 if he did.
- `Pos2`—Not in the original data set. This is a derived variable that equals the full position name for each player so that, for instance, F-G and G-F both equal Swingman.

An NBA team might have as many as 15 players on its active roster, but only 5 players can play at a time. Teams usually play two guards, two forwards, and a center; what's more, there are point guards and shooting guards, and there are small forwards and power forwards, as described here:

- *Point guard*—Basketball's equivalent to a quarterback; he runs the offense and is usually the best passer and dribbler.
- *Shooting guard*—Often a team's best shooter and scorer.
- *Small forward*—Usually, a very versatile player; he can score from inside or outside and defend short or tall players.
- *Power forward*—Normally, a good defender and rebounder, but not necessarily much of a shooter or scorer.
- *Center*—A team's tallest player; he's usually counted on to defend the basket, block shots, and rebound.

The draft data set doesn't distinguish point guards from shooting guards or small forwards from power forwards; but it does single out those players who play multiple positions. A *swingman* is a player capable of playing shooting guard or small forward, and a *big* is a player who can play either power forward or center.

A call to the head() function returns the first six observations in the new and improved draft data set:

```
head(draft)
          Rk Year    Pk Tm     Player        Age  Pos   Born
##    <dbl> <fct> <dbl> <fct> <chr>        <dbl> <fct> <fct>
## 1     1 2009     1 LAC   Blake Griffin  20.1 F     us
## 2     2 2009     2 MEM   Hasheem Thabeet 22.1 C    tz
## 3     3 2009     3 OKC   James Harden   19.3 G     us
## 4     4 2009     4 SAC   Tyreke Evans   19.3 G-F   us
## 5     5 2009     5 MIN   Ricky Rubio    18.3 G     es
## 6     6 2009     6 MIN   Jonny Flynn    20.1 G     us
      College       From  To     G    MP    WS    WS48
##    <chr>         <fct> <fct> <dbl> <dbl> <dbl>  <dbl>
## 1 Oklahoma       2011  2020   622  34.8  75.2  0.167
## 2 UConn          2010  2014   224  10.5   4.8  0.099
## 3 Arizona State  2010  2020   826  34.3 133.   0.226
## 4 Memphis        2010  2019   594  30.7  28.4  0.075
## 5 0              2012  2020   555  30.9  36.4  0.102
## 6 Syracuse       2010  2012   163  22.9  -1.1 -0.015
      Born2 College2 Pos2
##    <fct> <fct>    <fct>
## 1 USA   1        Forward
## 2 World 1        Center
## 3 USA   1        Guard
## 4 USA   1        Swingman
## 5 World 0        Guard
## 6 USA   1        Guard
```

Now it's time to explore and analyze win shares and other variables from our data.

2.5 *Exploratory data analysis*

To reiterate, EDA is most often a mix of computing basic statistics and creating visual content. For our purposes, especially as a lead-in to chapter 3, the EDA effort that follows concentrates on a single variable—win shares—but nonetheless provides insights into how win shares is associated, or not associated, for that matter, with many of the remaining draft data set variables. As such, our investigation of the draft data set will be a combination univariate (one variable) and bivariate (multiple variable) exercise.

2.5.1 *Computing basic statistics*

The base R summary() function is called to kick-start the exploration and analysis of the draft data set, a process that will *mostly* focus on the variable win shares; that's because we're ultimately interested in understanding how much productivity teams can expect from their draft picks when win shares is pegged to other variables in our data set. The `summary()` function returns basic statistics for each variable in draft. For continuous, or numeric, variables such as `win shares`, the `summary()` function returns the minimum and maximum values, the first and third quartiles, and the median and mean; for categorical variables such as `Born2`, on the other hand, the `summary()` function returns the counts for each level. To elaborate, as far as continuous variables are concerned

- The *minimum* represents the lowest value.
- The *maximum* represents the highest value.
- The *mean* is the average.
- The *median* is the middle value when the data is sorted in ascending or descending order. When the data contains an even number of records, the median is the average between the two middle numbers.
- The *1st quartile* is the lower quartile; when data is arranged in ascending order, the lower quartile represents the 25% cutoff point.
- The *3rd quartile* is also known as the upper quartile; again, when the data is arranged in ascending order, the upper quartile represents the 75% cutoff point.

That all being said, we finally make our call to the `summary()` function:

```
summary(draft)
##       Rk              Year           Pk              Tm
## Min.   :  1.0    2006   : 30    Min.   : 1.00    BOS    : 13
## 1st Qu.: 73.5    2008   : 30    1st Qu.: 8.00    CHI    : 13
## Median :148.0    2009   : 30    Median :15.00    POR    : 13
## Mean   :147.3    2000   : 29    Mean   :15.12    MEM    : 12
## 3rd Qu.:220.5    2003   : 29    3rd Qu.:22.00    NJN    : 12
## Max.   :293.0    2004   : 29    Max.   :30.00    PHO    : 12
##                  (Other):114                     (Other):216
##    Player            Age           Pos            Born
## Length:291       Min.   :17.25   C  :42    us     :224
## Class :character 1st Qu.:19.33   C-F:10    es     :  6
## Mode  :character Median :21.01   F  :88    fr     :  6
##                  Mean   :20.71   F-C:24    br     :  4
##                  3rd Qu.:22.05   F-G:10    si     :  4
##                  Max.   :25.02   G  :95    de     :  3
##                                  G-F:22    (Other): 44
##    College           From           To
## Length:291       2005   : 31    2020   : 46
## Class :character 2009   : 31    2019   : 24
## Mode  :character 2002   : 30    2013   : 23
##                  2004   : 29    2017   : 23
##                  2006   : 29    2015   : 22
##                  2007   : 28    2018   : 18
##                  (Other):113    (Other):135
##       G              MP             WS              WS48
## Min.   :  6.0    Min.   : 4.30   Min.   : -1.60   Min.   :-0.32600
## 1st Qu.: 248.0   1st Qu.:15.60   1st Qu.:  4.05   1st Qu.: 0.05000
## Median : 549.0   Median :21.60   Median : 19.60   Median : 0.07900
## Mean   : 526.4   Mean   :21.53   Mean   : 29.35   Mean   : 0.07592
```

```
## 3rd Qu.: 789.5     3rd Qu.:27.70    3rd Qu.: 43.85    3rd Qu.: 0.10600
## Max.   :1326.0     Max.   :38.40    Max.   :236.10    Max.   : 0.24400
##    Born2        College2          Pos2
## USA  :224      0: 73      Center  :42
## World: 67      1:218      Big     :34
##                           Forward :88
##                           Swingman:32
##                           Guard   :95
```

The most interesting and meaningful takeaways include the following:

- There is a tremendous amount of variance in career win shares. At least one first-round pick between the 2000 and 2009 NBA drafts actually accrued a *negative* number of win shares over the course of their career. One player accrued more than 236 win shares.

- There are also significant variances in the other career statistics, namely regular season games played and average minutes played per regular season game.

- Going back to win shares, the mean, which is especially sensitive to outliers (or data points far removed from the population center), is significantly greater than the median, suggesting that the mean is skewed by a small number of superstars in the data set.

- First-round NBA draft picks between 2000 and 2009 were anywhere between 17.25 and 25.02 years old at the time they were selected.

- More than three-quarters of the players in draft, 224 of 291, to be exact, were born in the United States.

- Nearly the same number of players—218 to be specific—attended a college or university.

There are other basic statistics, however, that summary() doesn't return. The sd() function from base R, for instance, computes the standard deviation for continuous variables such as regular season games played (G), minutes played per regular season game (MP), and career win shares (WS). Once more, the $ operator tells R to compute and return results for just the one variable that's called out:

```
sd(draft$G)
## [1] 319.6035
sd(draft$MP)
## [1] 7.826054
sd(draft$WS)
## [1] 33.64374
```

The standard deviation is a measure of how dispersed the data is relative to the mean. Low standard deviations imply the data is clustered close to the mean; alternatively, high standard deviations suggest the data is more dispersed. *If* this data was Gaussian or normally distributed (think of a bell curve), approximately 68% of the players in the draft data set would be within ± one standard deviation of the mean, 95% would be within ± two standard deviations of the mean, and all but perhaps a couple of players would be within ± three standard deviations of the mean. Take minutes played per regular season game—approximately 68% of the players are likely to have averaged somewhere between 13.71 and 29.35 minutes, which is equal to the population mean ± the standard deviation. We can get to the variance for any continuous variable by squaring its standard deviation or by passing the variable name to the base R var() function.

2.5.2   *Returning data*

In the following chunk of code, we run a series of independent SELECT statements by calling the sqldf() function from the sqldf package. Our purpose here is to dig deeper into the data and fetch some specifics that summary() and other functions don't return:

```
sqldf("SELECT min(WS), Player, Tm, Pk, Year FROM draft")
##    min(WS)        Player  Tm Pk Year
## 1     -1.6 Mardy Collins NYK 29 2006
sqldf("SELECT max(WS), Player, Tm, Pk, Year FROM draft")
##    max(WS)        Player  Tm Pk Year
## 1    236.1 LeBron James CLE  1 2003
sqldf("SELECT min(G), Player, Tm, Pk, Year FROM draft")
##    min(G)           Player  Tm Pk Year
## 1       6 Pavel Podkolzin UTA 21 2004
sqldf("SELECT max(G), Player, Tm, Pk, Year FROM draft")
##    max(G)         Player  Tm Pk Year
## 1    1326 Jamal Crawford CLE  8 2000
sqldf("SELECT min(MP), Player, Tm, Pk, Year FROM draft")
##    min(MP)       Player  Tm Pk Year
## 1      4.3 Julius Hodge DEN 20 2005
sqldf("SELECT max(MP), Player, Tm, Pk, Year FROM draft")
##    max(MP)        Player  Tm Pk Year
## 1     38.4 LeBron James CLE  1 2003
sqldf("SELECT min(Age), Player, Tm, Pk, Year FROM draft")
##    min(Age)        Player  Tm Pk Year
## 1    17.249 Andrew Bynum LAL 10 2005
sqldf("SELECT max(Age), Player, Tm, Pk, Year FROM draft")
##    max(Age)           Player  Tm Pk Year
## 1    25.019 Mamadou N'Diaye DEN 26 2000
```

The SELECT and FROM clauses identify which variables to pull from which data source. As just one example, the first SELECT statement fetches from draft the record where the variable win shares equals the data set minimum, returning the number of win shares, the player's full name, the team that selected him, the pick number, and the year in which he was selected. SELECT statements—easy to write and usually quick to run—work best when you need just a data point or maybe a short list of records. If you need to instead create a data object that can subsequently be used as a source for further analysis, dplyr is a *way* better option. Going forward, we'll direct our attention squarely to win shares, starting with some frequency distribution analysis.

2.5.3 *Computing and visualizing frequency distributions*

Pulling data is constructive. But visualizing data is like pressing down on the gas pedal—pictures show relationships between variables, display outliers, and demonstrate trends that numbers alone don't reveal for us. In particular, frequency distributions are visual displays of continuous data counts. They are usually displayed as absolute frequencies, or representations of the raw data, but sometimes that same data is converted so that percentages or proportions are displayed instead. We'll visualize the raw data with histograms and boxplots and then demonstrate how to write `sqldf` and `dplyr` code to get additional insights.

HISTOGRAMS

No doubt the most common method of visualizing the frequency distribution of a continuous variable, like `win shares`, is with a histogram; so drawing a histogram is a logical starting point. A *histogram* is a graphical representation of the distribution of one continuous variable; it divides the data into what we call bins and then displays the frequency or count of observations within each bin.

Every visualization in this chapter was created with the `ggplot2` package; `ggplot2`, elegant yet powerful at the same time, is a big reason why R is a leader in the data visualization space. Building a `ggplot2` visualization is very much like creating a wedding cake—the `ggplot()` function establishes the foundation, and then other functions provide the frosting and decorations. Take note of the plus or addition operator (+) between successive calls to various `ggplot2` functions that add, change, or enhance a baseline build with the following:

- The `ggplot()` function initializes a `ggplot2` object. The first argument passed to `ggplot()` is a pointer to the data source, which, of course, is the draft data set. The second argument is a call to the `aes()` function, which defines the variables that should be plotted as well as which plot parameters, or axes, they should be mapped to.
- The `geom_histogram()` function—geom is short for geometric object—tells R to visualize the distribution of a single continuous variable by dividing the x-axis into a specified number of bins and counting the observations within each bin. The bins should be colored and filled with the same shade of royal blue.
- The `labs()` function adds a title, subtitle, and labels for the x- and y-axes.
- The `theme()` function applies a bold font to the title in place of the default plain font.
- The base R `print()` function prints the histogram, called `p1`; also, `p1` by itself will do the same.

Our histogram (see figure 2.1) provides a snapshot of the win shares data that makes it possible, in just a few seconds, to get a read on the distribution by simply eyeballing rows of data that would otherwise take much longer and potentially lead to false conclusions:

```
p1 <- ggplot(draft, aes(x = WS)) +
  geom_histogram(fill = "royalblue3", color = "royalblue3",
                 bins = 8) +
  labs(title = "Career Win Shares Distribution of
       NBA First-Round Selections",
       subtitle = "2000-09 NBA Drafts",
       x = "Career Win Shares",
       y = "Frequency") +
  theme(plot.title = element_text(face = "bold"))
print(p1)
```

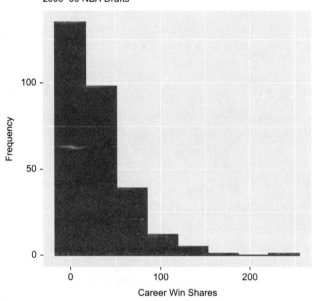

Career Win Shares Distribution of NBA First–Round Selections
2000–09 NBA Drafts

Figure 2.1   Career win shares has a right-skewed, or positive-skewed, distribution.

The variable win shares has a right-skewed, or positive-skewed, distribution—right-skewed because the distribution has a long right tail and positive-skewed because the long tail is in the positive direction of the x-axis. In lay terms, it simply means that many NBA first-round picks between the 2000 and 2009 drafts accrued very few career win shares while just a few players accrued lots of win shares.

Fills and colors

If you're reading this book as a physical copy, you've surely noticed by now that every plot is printed in grayscale. Nevertheless, we demonstrate how to enhance your visualizations—ggplot2 and otherwise—by adding custom fills and colors in almost every plot and referencing the same within the text. The following website is a ggplot2 reference guide for fills and colors that is quite handy: http://sape.inf.usi.ch/quick-reference/ggplot2/colour. In addition, anyone who purchased a new copy of this book has access to the e-book version (with full color); please do refer to that if you're interested in seeing visualizations in full color as coded.

The following pair of SELECT statements return the record counts in the draft data set where the number of career win shares is either greater than or equal to 75 or less than 75. We're therefore getting actual counts versus the approximate counts we got from our histogram. Including asterisks with the COUNT() function ensures that we get any observations with null values as part of the result set. More significantly, the WHERE clause identifies the conditions that must evaluate to true for any observation to be included in the results:

```
sqldf("SELECT COUNT (*) FROM draft WHERE WS >= 75")
##    COUNT (*)
## 1        27
sqldf("SELECT COUNT (*) FROM draft WHERE WS < 75")
##    COUNT (*)
## 1       264
```

Less than 10% of the first-round picks in the 2000 to 2009 NBA drafts then accrued at least 75 win shares in their respective careers. In fact, more than 50% of the players, 169 of 291, accrued fewer than 25 win shares:

```
sqldf("SELECT COUNT (*) FROM draft WHERE WS <= 25")
##    COUNT (*)
## 1       169
```

BOXPLOTS

Another way of visualizing the frequency distribution of a continuous variable is with boxplots. Our next visualization contains two pairs of boxplots inside a facet plot, where the distribution of win shares is first segmented by the derived variable Born2 and again by the derived variable College2.

No two ggplot2 visualizations are exactly alike, especially across geoms, or geometric objects; however, they all follow the same general syntax and structure. Following are a few notes regarding our facet plot, where the data is broken out and visualized in subplots that share the same x- and y-axes:

- The stat_summary() function adds a solid white dot to each boxplot to indicate the population means. The population medians are represented by horizontal lines, which ggplot2 adds automatically.
- The facet_wrap() function creates a panel—and therefore separate pairs of boxplots—for each level in the variable Born2; because Born2 has two levels, our facet plot therefore has two panels.
- The scale_x_discrete() function hardcodes the labels along the x-axis by converting 0 and 1, which are the levels in College2, to No College and College, respectively. Accurate or intuitive labeling goes a long way toward improving the readability and interpretability of your visual content.

Our second visualization (see figure 2.2) shows that win shares distributions vary depending on place of birth and whether or not players first attended a college or university:

```
p2 <- ggplot(draft, aes(x = College2, y = WS)) +
  geom_boxplot(color = "orange4", fill = "orange1") +
  labs(title = "Career Win Shares Distribution of
       NBA First-Round Selections",
       x = "",
       y = "Career Win Shares",
       subtitle = "2000-09 NBA Drafts") +
  stat_summary(fun = mean, geom = "point", shape = 20,
               size = 8, color = "white", fill = "white") +
  theme(plot.title = element_text(face = "bold")) +
  facet_wrap(~Born2) +
  scale_x_discrete(breaks = c(0, 1),
                   labels = c("No College", "College"))
print(p2)
```

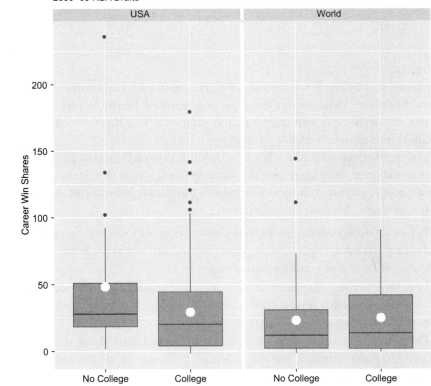

Figure 2.2   Distribution of win shares varies by place of birth and by whether a player first attended a college or university before turning professional.

Boxplots display the distribution of a continuous variable by isolating the following measures that align, but sometimes not exactly, with `summary()` function outputs:

- *Median*—The middle value, represented by a horizontal line.
- *First quartile*—The middle value between the smallest number (not necessarily the "minimum") and the median, otherwise known as the 25th percentile.
- *Third quartile*—The middle value between the median and the highest number (not necessarily the "maximum"), otherwise known as the 75th percentile.
- *Interquartile Range (IQR)*—The 25th to 75th percentiles; basically, the box. This can otherwise be derived by computing the difference between the first and third quartiles.
- *"Minimum"*—Equal to Q1 – (1.5 * IQR). This isn't necessarily the lowest value; there may, in fact, be one or more data points—outliers—beyond the so-called minimum.
- *"Maximum"*—Equal to Q3 + (1.5 * IQR). Likewise, this may not actually represent the highest value.

The mean isn't a usual measure for boxplots, which is presumably why `ggplot2` doesn't add it automatically. The whiskers are the lines extending below and above the IQR (boxplots are therefore often called box-and-whiskers plots). Dots, or circles, beyond the "minimum" and "maximum" are outliers.

This is otherwise a fascinating graphical representation of the data, rendering several truths:

- Players born in the United States *generally* accrued more career win shares than did players born outside the United States.
- Players born in the United States who bypassed college *generally* accrued more career win shares than did US-born players who did attend a college or university.
- Alternatively, players born in any country other than the United States who did *not* attend a college or university *generally* accrued fewer win shares over their respective careers than did other players born outside the United States who *did* attend college.
- The means are consistently higher than the medians, suggesting, of course, that average win shares, regardless of how the data is sliced and diced, are influenced by superstar production.

More boxplots display the distribution of win shares by year or draft class (see figure 2.3):

```
p3 <- ggplot(draft, aes(x = Year, y = WS)) +
  geom_boxplot(color = "dodgerblue4", fill = "dodgerblue" ) +
  labs(title = "Year-over-Year Win Shares Distribution of
      NBA First-Round Selections",
      x = "",
      y = "Win Shares",
```

```
        subtitle = "2000-09 NBA Drafts") +
    stat_summary(fun = mean, geom = "point", shape = 20,
                 size = 8, color = "white", fill = "white") +
    theme(plot.title = element_text(face = "bold"))
print(p3)
```

Year-over-Year Win Shares Distribution of NBA First–Round Selections
2000–09 NBA Drafts

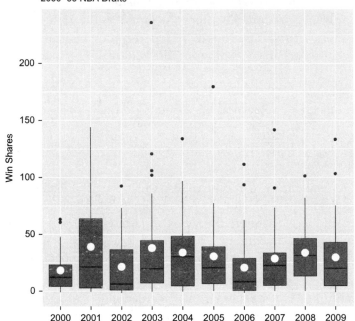

Figure 2.3   Not every
draft class between 2000
and 2009 was alike.

TABLES

Let's again take some deeper dives into our data. Rather than just writing a series of
SELECT statements again, we'll demonstrate how to expand your use of the dplyr package, which contains several functions for pulling and manipulating data. Once more,
sqldf is just fine if you merely need a few data points, but if you need a result set that
can subsequently be passed to ggplot2 or be used for other analysis, you'll want—and
need—to become comfortable with dplyr.

The first key to understanding the following few lines of code is knowing how the
pipe operator (%>%) works. In short, the pipe operator assigns each functional output
as an argument to the next function. Think of the pipe as the means by which the output from one function, or operation, is then transported to another function or operation. You can also think of the word "then" as the pseudocode substitute for the pipe:
"take the draft data set THEN compute a series of summary statistics."

The second key is knowing how the dplyr summarize() function works; summarize()
is somewhat similar to the base R summary() function, except that summarize() is much
more flexible and extendable, especially when it's paired with the dplyr group_by() function. Here, we're instructing summarize() to compute standard boxplot-type measures.

Results are then pushed (take note of the assignment operator) to a tibble called first_tibble. By far, the most important thing to know about tibbles, which are specific to R, is that they share many of the same properties as data frames, meaning they can be wrangled and used as data sources for visual content and other analysis. However, when printed, only the first 10 rows and whatever number of columns that fit onscreen are returned; you'll see and experience this repeatedly. In addition, some base R functions and other legacy code won't work with tibbles (or tibbles won't work with older code). When that's the case—and we'll see this much later on—simply convert the tibble to a data frame by passing it to the base R as.data.frame() function:

```
draft %>%
  summarize(MIN = min(WS),
            LQ = quantile(WS, .25),
            UQ = quantile(WS, .75),
            AVG = mean(WS),
            M = median(WS),
            MAX = max(WS)) -> first_tibble
print(first_tibble)
##    MIN   LQ   UQ     AVG    M    MAX
## 1 -1.6 4.05 43.85 29.34811 19.6 236.1
```

The following code chunk passes draft as an argument to the group_by() function, and then the group_by() function is subsequently passed as an argument to the summarize() function. Perhaps a better, more effective way of understanding these few lines of code is to think of the summarize() function as computing the mean of win shares by year rather than doing so holistically. The results are then thrown into a new object, or tibble, called second_tibble. These results align with our previous set of boxplots:

```
draft %>%
  group_by(Year) %>%
  summarize(avg = mean(WS)) -> second_tibble
print(second_tibble)
## # A tibble: 10 × 2
##    Year    avg
##    <fct> <dbl>
## 1  2000   18.3
## 2  2001   39.0
## 3  2002   21.4
## 4  2003   37.9
## 5  2004   34.0
## 6  2005   30.6
## 7  2006   20.6
## 8  2007   28.6
## 9  2008   33.7
## 10 2009   29.6
```

Here, the dplyr tally() function counts, or tallies, the number of players in the draft data set who accrued 75 or more win shares in their respective careers, and it breaks the results down by every factor, or level, in the variable Year. Clearly, means are influenced by the number of draft picks who then accrued a relatively high number of career win shares:

```
draft %>%
  group_by(Year) %>%
tally(WS >= 75) -> third_tibble
print(third_tibble)
## # A tibble: 10 × 2
##    Year       n
##    <fct> <int>
##  1 2000       0
##  2 2001       7
##  3 2002       1
##  4 2003       5
##  5 2004       2
##  6 2005       3
##  7 2006       2
##  8 2007       2
##  9 2008       2
## 10 2009       3
```

Now, alternating between dplyr code and sqldf code, the following SELECT statement returns the variables Player and Pk from draft where WS is greater than or equal to 75 *and* the variable Year equals 2001 (just to show who are/were the seven players from the 2001 draft who then accrued 75 or more win shares as professionals):

```
sqldf("SELECT Player, Pk FROM draft WHERE WS >= 75 AND Year == 2001")
##               Player Pk
## 1    Tyson Chandler  2
## 2         Pau Gasol  3
## 3     Shane Battier  6
## 4       Joe Johnson 10
## 5 Richard Jefferson 13
## 6     Zach Randolph 19
## 7       Tony Parker 28
```

The next SELECT statement returns those same variables where WS again is greater than or equal to 75 and where the variable Year this time equals 2003 (just to show who are/were the five players from the 2001 draft who then accrued 75 or more win shares). The results are returned sorted in descending order by win shares:

```
sqldf("SELECT Player, Pk, WS
       FROM draft WHERE WS >= 75 AND Year == 2003 ORDER BY WS DESC")
##             Player Pk    WS
## 1    LeBron James  1 236.1
## 2     Dwyane Wade  5 120.7
## 3      Chris Bosh  4 106.0
## 4 Carmelo Anthony  3 102.0
## 5      David West 18  85.9
```

In this next chunk of `dplyr` code, the draft data set is subset, or filtered, to include only those records where the variable `WS` is greater than or equal to `75`; between the `group_by()` and `summarize()` functions, the mean of `Pk` is then computed across each year in draft. The results are pushed to a 9×2 tibble called `fourth_tibble`. You might recall that no players selected in the 2000 draft then earned more than 75 career win shares; R doesn't return any results for that year's draft because it's impossible, of course, to compute anything from zero records. Otherwise, note how low the averages are when you consider there were either 29 or 30 first-round selections in each draft between 2000 and 2009:

```
draft %>%
  filter(WS >= 75) %>%
  group_by(Year) %>%
  summarize(avg = mean(Pk)) -> fourth_tibble
print(fourth_tibble)
## # A tibble: 9 x 2
##   Year    avg
##   <fct> <dbl>
## 1 2001   11.6
## 2 2002   9
## 3 2003   6.2
## 4 2004   5
## 5 2005   12.3
## 6 2006   13
## 7 2007   2.5
## 8 2008   4.5
## 9 2009   3.67
```

We can run relatively simple and straightforward computations with the `sqldf()` function. In the following, the mean for the variable `Pk` is computed where the variable `WS` is greater than or equal to `75`:

```
sqldf("SELECT AVG(Pk) FROM draft WHERE WS >= 75")
##    AVG(Pk)
## 1 8.111111
```

Next, the draft data set is again subset to include only those records where a player's career win share total equaled or exceeded 75 by calling the `dplyr` `filter()` function. Between the `dplyr` `group_by()` and `summarize()` functions, the median of `Pk` is computed by the variable `Year` and then thrown into a new object called `fifth_tibble`:

```
draft %>%
  filter(WS >= 75) %>%
  group_by(Year) %>%
  summarize(med = median(Pk)) -> fifth_tibble
print(fifth_tibble)
## # A tibble: 9 x 2
##   Year    med
##   <fct> <dbl>
## 1 2001   10
```

```
## 2 2002      9
## 3 2003      4
## 4 2004      5
## 5 2005      4
## 6 2006     13
## 7 2007      2.5
## 8 2008      4.5
## 9 2009      3
```

The following SELECT statement computes and returns the median of the variable Pk across the entire draft data set where, again, the variable WS is greater than or equal to 75. Notice how much lower the median, which is insensitive to outliers, is than the mean:

```
sqldf("SELECT MEDIAN(Pk) FROM draft WHERE WS >= 75")
##    MEDIAN(Pk)
## 1           4
```

As you might imagine by now, the mean and median for the variable Pk are even lower when the draft data set is subset to include only records where the variable WS is equal to or greater than 100, rather than 75. The following dplyr code returns the annual mean for Pk and casts the results into an object called sixth_tibble:

```
draft %>%
  filter(WS >= 100) %>%
  group_by(Year) %>%
  summarize(avg = mean(Pk)) -> sixth_tibble
print(sixth_tibble)
## # A tibble: 8 × 2
##   Year     avg
##   <fct> <dbl>
## 1 2001  11
## 2 2003   3.25
## 3 2004   1
## 4 2005   4
## 5 2006   2
## 6 2007   2
## 7 2008   4
## 8 2009   5
```

The next SELECT statement computes and returns the mean for the variable Pk across all of draft where the variable WS equals or exceeds 100:

```
sqldf("SELECT AVG(Pk) FROM draft WHERE WS >= 100")
##    AVG(Pk)
## 1 4.928571
```

Now, let's look at the same set of operations, except the median is substituted for the mean. The next chunk of dplyr code computes the median of Pk for each year in draft when the data set is previously subset where the variable WS is equal to or greater than 100:

```
draft %>%
  filter(WS >= 100) %>%
  group_by(Year) %>%
  summarize(med = median(Pk)) -> seventh_tibble
print(seventh_tibble)
## # A tibble: 8 x 2
##    Year    med
##    <fct>  <dbl>
## 1 2001      3
## 2 2003      3.5
## 3 2004      1
## 4 2005      4
## 5 2006      2
## 6 2007      2
## 7 2008      4
## 8 2009      5
```

The following SELECT statement then computes and returns the median of Pk where WS equals or exceeds 100:

```
sqldf("SELECT MEDIAN(Pk) FROM draft WHERE WS >= 100")
##    MEDIAN(Pk)
## 1          3
```

Let's pivot and pull some figures where WS is equal to or less than 25:

```
draft %>%
  filter(WS <= 25) %>%
  group_by(Year) %>%
  summarize(avg = mean(Pk),
            med = median(Pk)) -> eighth_tibble
print(eighth_tibble)
## # A tibble: 10 x 3
##     Year    avg    med
##     <fct>  <dbl>  <dbl>
## 1  2000   15.8   14.5
## 2  2001   14.9   16
## 3  2002   16.6   17
## 4  2003   15.6   16
## 5  2004   18.6   21
## 6  2005   17.8   18
## 7  2006   16.6   17.5
## 8  2007   16.2   16.5
## 9  2008   16.6   14
## 10 2009   17.5   16
```

On average, players who accrued fewer win shares were selected later in the first round than other players who earned significantly more win shares. The next SELECT statement computes and returns the mean and median of the variable Pk where WS is equal to or less than 25:

```
sqldf("SELECT AVG(Pk), MEDIAN(Pk) FROM draft WHERE WS <= 25")
##     AVG(Pk) MEDIAN(Pk)
## 1 16.55621         16
```

Let's go a step further and see what these same figures look like when draft is subset to just include players who earned fewer than five win shares in their respective careers. Once more, we use `dplyr` to get the annual results and `sqldf` to return the overall results:

```
draft %>%
  filter(WS <= 5) %>%
  group_by(Year) %>%
  summarize(avg = mean(Pk),
            med = median(Pk)) -> ninth_tibble
print(ninth_tibble)
## # A tibble: 10 × 3
##    Year    avg   med
##    <fct> <dbl> <dbl>
## 1  2000   17.4   15
## 2  2001   17.9   19
## 3  2002   15.3   18
## 4  2003   19.2   17
## 5  2004   17.1   16
## 6  2005   17.2 14.5
## 7  2006   18.5 18.5
## 8  2007   17.6   18
## 9  2008   23.8 28.5
## 10 2009   16.9 17.5
```

```
sqldf("SELECT AVG(Pk), MEDIAN(Pk) FROM draft WHERE WS <= 5")
##     AVG(Pk) MEDIAN(Pk)
## 1 17.65854       17.5
```

Many of the first-round selections in the 2000–2009 NBA drafts never amounted to much. For every LeBron James or Stephen Curry, there are dozens of other first-round picks who are mostly unknown today to most professional basketball fans. Almost 30% of the first-round picks between 2000 and 2009 earned fewer than five win shares in their respective professional careers. The next SELECT statement pulls a count of players in the draft data set where the variable WS is less than 5:

```
sqldf("SELECT COUNT (*) FROM draft WHERE WS < 5")
##    COUNT (*)
## 1        81
```

Our final SELECT statement pulls the number of players in draft who finished their NBA careers with a negative number of win shares:

```
sqldf("SELECT COUNT (*) FROM draft WHERE WS < 0")
##    COUNT (*)
## 1        20
```

Clearly, not every draft class was created equal. Here are the most significant take-aways from the latest set of boxplots as well as the returns from our chunks of `dplyr` and `sqldf` code:

- The 2001 class stands out: first-round selections from the 2001 NBA draft averaged more win shares over the course of their careers, 39, than any other class of first-round selections between 2000 and 2009. Only in 2001 does the top end of the IQR exceed 50 win shares.

- Furthermore, seven players from this same class accrued 75 or more win shares during their careers, the most of any class within the draft data set. Three of these players—Tyson Chandler, Pau Gasol, and Shane Battier—were among the top six picks that year; three other players—Joe Johnson, Richard Jefferson, and Zach Randolph—were selected between picks 10 and 19; and then there's Tony Parker, who was selected at 28 and then accrued 111.3 win shares, all while playing for the San Antonio Spurs.

- First-round selections from the 2003 NBA draft averaged almost as many win shares, 38, as did the first-round picks from the 2001 class. LeBron James, Dwyane Wade, Chris Bosh, Carmelo Anthony, and David West all accrued more than 75 win shares in their respective careers, and that's just through the 2019–20 season.

- Four of the five players just referenced—all but David West—were among the first five players selected in 2001.

- On the flip side, the 2000 class was probably the most disappointing; first-round selections from 2000 averaged barely 18 win shares in their respective careers, easily the lowest average of any class in the draft data set. Not surprisingly, no players drafted in 2000 earned up to 75 win shares in their respective careers. Only in 2000 does the top end of the IQR fall short of 25 win shares.

- Players who, so far, have accrued at least 75 win shares were selected eighth, on average; in fact, in the nine classes from draft that include at least one player who then accrued 75 or more win shares, in five of these classes, the average was 6 win shares or less. The median equals 4.

- When draft is subset on those players who have accrued a minimum of 100 win shares in their respective careers, the average pick, or selection number, equals 4, and the median is 3.

- Of the 291 first-round selections in the draft data set, 81 of them accrued fewer than 5 career win shares, and 20 of these players accrued a *negative* number of career win shares.

- There appears to be a relationship between win shares and where in the first round players were selected. Players who accrued a relatively high number of win shares were generally drafted before other players who earned a lesser number of win shares.

Let's now explore how `win shares` is correlated, or maybe not correlated, with the other continuous variables in our data set.

2.5.4 *Computing and visualizing correlations*

Correlation is a statistical measure that quantifies the linear relationship between a pair of continuous, or numeric, variables. That relationship can either be positive or negative. When positive, the variables increase together at constant rates; when negative, the variables change at constant rates, but one increases while the other decreases. The relationship might actually be neutral as well.

The relationship between two continuous variables is determined by computing the correlation coefficient between them. The result will always equal some number between –1 and +1. When the correlation coefficient equals or approximates –1, then the relationship is negative; when the correlation coefficient instead equals or approximates +1, the relationship is positive. As a rule of thumb, correlation coefficients less than –0.8 and greater than 0.8 are indications of a strong linear relationship; correlation coefficients between –0.6 and –0.8 and also between 0.6 and 0.8 are indications of a fairly strong linear relationship; and correlation coefficients at or near 0 are indications of no relationship at all. Just because a pair of continuous variables might be strongly correlated doesn't necessarily mean that one variable influences the other—correlation isn't the same as causation.

It's very easy in R to compute the correlation coefficient between two variables or between multiple pairs of variables at one time. There are also *many* options in R for visualizing the same. We'll demonstrate how to do the latter by creating a `ggplot2` heat map. A *heat map* is a diagram that associates different data values with different colors or shades.

With that in mind, our first step is to create a new object, `cor_draft`, by passing `draft` via the pipe operator (`%>%`) to the `dplyr` `select()` function to subset our original data set on its five continuous variables: `Age`, `G`, `MP`, `WS`, and `WS48`. After all, we only compute correlation coefficients between continuous variables; if we were to try otherwise, R would throw an error. Here's the first step:

```
draft %>%
    select(c(Age, G:WS)) -> cor_draft
```

The second step is to more or less convert `cor_draft` into a tabular format by passing it to the base R `cor()` function, which computes the correlation coefficient between every pair of variables. Our results are cast to a new object called `cor_matrix`. A subsequent call to the `print()` function is optional—as this isn't a required step to create a heat map—but it does, of course, return the results and shows us what a correlation matrix should look like. Here's the second step:

```
cor_matrix <- cor(cor_draft)
print(cor_matrix)
##               Age         G        MP        WS      WS48
```

```
## Age    1.0000000 -0.2189601 -0.2327846 -0.2509647 -0.1801535
## G     -0.2189601  1.0000000  0.7921621  0.8004797  0.6165429
## MP    -0.2327846  0.7921621  1.0000000  0.7758876  0.6597869
## WS    -0.2509647  0.8004797  0.7758876  1.0000000  0.6942061
## WS48  -0.1801535  0.6165429  0.6597869  0.6942061  1.0000000
```

For instance, the correlation coefficient between the variables MP and WS48 equals 0.66 (rounded). We actually see this twice because every pair of variables in a matrix intersects at two points, which isn't what we want in our heat map.

The third step requires a call to the melt() function from the reshape2 package. The melt() function racks and stacks every two-variable combination from cor_matrix between a pair of columns labeled Var1 and Var2 and also creates a third column called value where the cells are populated with the corresponding correlation coefficient. In consideration of space, rather than printing the entire result set, the head() and tail() functions are called to just return the first three and last three observations in our new object, cor_table. Here's the third step:

```
cor_table <- melt(cor_matrix)
head(cor_table, n = 3)
##    Var1 Var2       value
## 1   Age  Age  1.0000000
## 2     G  Age -0.2189601
## 3    MP  Age -0.2327846
tail(cor_table, n = 3)
##     Var1 Var2      value
## 23    MP WS48 0.6597869
## 24    WS WS48 0.6942061
## 25  WS48 WS48 1.0000000
```

The next chunk of code produces our heat map now that we have a perfectly formatted data source:

- As with any ggplot2 visualization, the object is initialized by calling the ggplot() function, where cor_table is passed as the data source for our heat map; the cor_table variables Var1 and Var2 are, respectively, our x- and y-axis variables; and the fill is based on the computed correlation coefficient.
- The geom_tile() function is the ggplot() function that draws the heat map.
- The scale_fill_gradient2() function establishes a two-color gradient scheme across correlation coefficients.
- Text geoms are called when labels or annotations are in order. By calling the geom_text() function, we're annotating our correlation matrix with the actual correlation coefficients between each pair of continuous variables in our data source. The base R round() function reduces our coefficients to only two digits right of the decimal point.

The purpose of a heat map, or correlation matrix, is to equate colors and their shades with different correlation coefficients (see figure 2.4). Positive correlations are represented by one color gradient, and negative correlations are represented by a different color gradient. Deeper shades represent stronger associations between variables, and vice versa. Following is our code, and right after that is our heat map created from the same:

```
p4 <- ggplot(data = draft_cor, aes(x = Var1,
                                   y = Var2, fill = value)) +
  geom_tile() +
  scale_fill_gradient2(midpoint = 0.5, mid = "grey84",
                       limits = c(-1, 1)) +
  labs(title = "Correlation Matrix",
    subtitle = "Correlation Coefficients between
    Win Shares and Other Continuous Variables",
    x = "",
    y = "",
    fill = "Correlation\nCoefficient",
    caption = "Source: draft data set") +
  theme(plot.title = element_text(face = "bold"),
    legend.title = element_text(face = "bold", color = "brown",
                                size = 10)) +
  geom_text(aes(x = Var1, y = Var2,
                label = round(value, 2)), color = "black",
    fontface = "bold", size = 5)
print(p4)
```

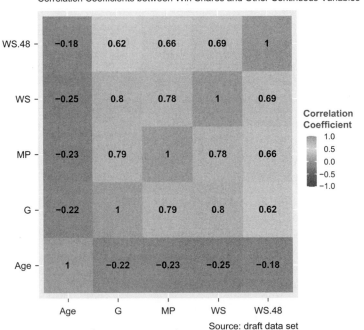

Figure 2.4   Matrix of correlation coefficients between all continuous variables in the draft data set

There are at least two conclusions that pop out:

- There are positive and strong, or at least fairly strong, correlations between win shares and regular season games played, minutes played per regular season game, and win shares for every 48 minutes of playing time. Mind you, correlation coefficients don't tell us which variable might be influencing another variable, if there is any causation at all.

- There is also a negative correlation between the variables Win Shares and Age, which is to say that players entering the NBA draft between 2000 and 2009 at younger ages then accrued, *generally*, more career win shares than players who turned professional at "older" ages. The correlation between these variables isn't strong, however. No doubt this is partially true because younger players likely have more years to play as professionals and therefore more opportunity to accrue more win shares. But it's also true—or at least likely—that better players turn professional at younger ages than lesser-skilled players.

Next, we'll visualize population means and medians with a series of bar charts so that we can determine how win shares compare across different levels in our factor variables.

2.5.5 *Computing and visualizing means and medians*

Finally, we're going to slice and dice our data set by computing and then visualizing the mean and median win shares broken down by the derived variables we created earlier. The following chunk of dplyr code again takes the group_by() and summarize() functions to summarize a subset of the data in the draft data set, thereby computing the mean and median win shares by the derived variable Born2. The results are pushed to a 2 × 3 tibble called tenth_tibble:

```
draft %>%
  group_by(Born2) %>%
  summarize(meanWS = mean(WS),
            medianWS = median(WS)) -> tenth_tibble
print(tenth_tibble)
## # A tibble: 2 × 3
##   Born2 meanWS medianWS
##   <fct> <dbl>    <dbl>
## 1 USA    31.1    21.5
## 2 World  23.5    12.8
```

These results are then visualized in a pair of ggplot2 bar charts, where the averages in career win shares are represented on the left, and the median win shares are represented on the right (see figure 2.5). In a typical bar chart, each level in a factor variable is represented by a separate bar, and the length of each bar (not necessarily the height because bar charts can also be oriented horizontally) corresponds to the value or frequency of the data it represents. In fact, bar charts are especially effective at visualizing categorical data, such as sales figures by region or net profits by fiscal year—or means and medians when Born2 equals USA or World. There are many variations of bar charts and even substitutes for bar charts, and we'll demonstrate many of these in subsequent chapters.

The y-axes are standardized between the two plots through similar calls to the ylim() function; otherwise, the y-axis scales would be different between the two visualizations, and the height of the bars would be identical, defeating the point of showing the differences between means and medians.

We've affixed the means and medians atop the bars by again calling the geom_text() function. But the values don't *exactly* match the results in tenth_tibble because we've also called the base R trunc() function, which rounds the means and medians *down* to their nearest whole number, just for aesthetic reasons. The label placements can be adjusted vertically and/or horizontally with the vjust and hjust arguments, respectively; be prepared to experiment with the vjust and hjust arguments until you're finally pleased with how it looks:

```
p5 <- ggplot(tenth_tibble, aes(x = Born2, y = meanWS)) +
  geom_bar(stat = "identity", width = .5, fill  = "darkorchid4") +
  labs(title = "Average Win Shares by Place of Birth",
       subtitle = "2000-09 NBA Drafts",
       x = "Where Born",
       y = "Average Career Win Shares") +
  geom_text(aes(label = trunc(meanWS), vjust = -0.3)) +
  ylim(0, 35) +
  theme(plot.title = element_text(face = "bold"))

p6 <- ggplot(tenth_tibble, aes(x = Born2, y = medianWS)) +
  geom_bar(stat = "identity", width = .5, fill  = "sienna1") +
  labs(title = "Median Win Shares by Place of Birth",
       subtitle = "2000-09 NBA Drafts",
       x = "Where Born",
       y = "Median Career Win Shares") +
  geom_text(aes(label = trunc(medianWS), vjust = -0.3)) +
  ylim(0, 35) +
  theme(plot.title = element_text(face = "bold"))
```

Our plots are temporarily held in memory rather than immediately printed. By calling the plot_layout() function from the patchwork package, our plots are bundled into a single graphical object in which the two bar charts are printed side by side (due to the fact that we passed the ncol, or number of columns, argument to equal 2):

```
p5 + p6 + plot_layout(ncol = 2)
```

There are two significant conclusions to draw from these two bar charts:

- Players born in the United States, on average, accrued more career win shares than players born elsewhere.
- The means are significantly greater than the medians. Means are sensitive to outliers, whereas medians are not; that the means are greater than the medians suggests they are influenced by superstar production where win shares per superstar are greater than 100.

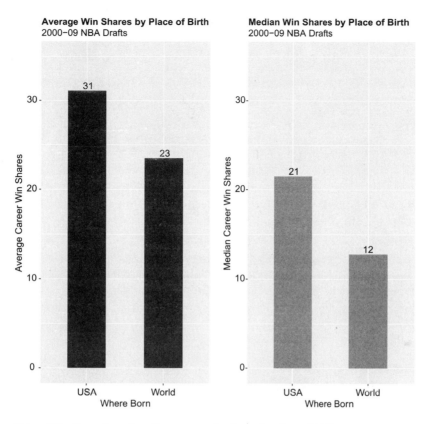

Figure 2.5   Average and median career win shares by place of birth

This same exercise is repeated here, except the variable Born2 is swapped out for the derived variable College2 (see figure 2.6):

```
draft %>%
  group_by(College2) %>%
  summarize(meanWS = mean(WS),
            medianWS = median(WS)) -> eleventh_tibble
print(eleventh_tibble)
## # A tibble: 2 × 3
##   College2 meanWS medianWS
##   <fct>     <dbl>    <dbl>
## 1 0          30.3     19.6
## 2 1          29.0     19.6

p7 <- ggplot(eleventh_tibble, aes(x = College2, y = meanWS)) +
  geom_bar(stat = "identity", width = .5, fill  = "darkorchid4") +
  labs(title = "Average Win Shares: College / No College",
       x = "College or No College",
       y = "Average Career Win Shares") +
  scale_x_discrete(breaks = c(0, 1),
                   labels = c("No College", "College")) +
  geom_text(aes(label = trunc(meanWS), vjust = -0.3)) +
```

```
  ylim(0, 35) +
  theme(plot.title = element_text(face = "bold"))

p8 <- ggplot(eleventh_tibble, aes(x = College2, y = medianWS)) +
  geom_bar(stat = "identity", width = .5, fill  = "sienna1") +
  labs(title = "Median Win Shares: College / No College",
       x = "College or No College",
       y = "Median Career Win Shares") +
  scale_x_discrete(breaks = c(0, 1),
                         labels = c("No College", "College")) +
  geom_text(aes(label = trunc(medianWS), vjust = -0.3)) +
  ylim(0, 35) +
  theme(plot.title = element_text(face = "bold"))
```

We then call the `plot_layout()` function a second time to pack our last two bar charts into a single graphical representation:

```
p7 + p8 + plot_layout(ncol = 2)
```

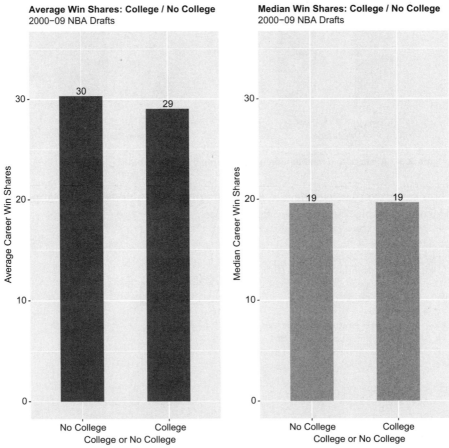

Figure 2.6   Average and median win shares between those players who first attended a college or university and those who did not

Between the two levels, or factors, in the variable `College2`, the means are essentially equal and the medians are essentially equal; however, the means are again significantly greater than the medians.

Our final chunk of `dplyr` code takes the draft data set and then passes `Born2`, `College2`, and the variable `Pos2` to the `summarize()` function to then compute the mean and median win shares for every combination of these three variables. We're doing this because we next intend to visualize mean and median win shares between every combination of `Born2`, `College2`, and `Pos2` in just a pair of complementary facet plots. The first three and last three observations of `twelfth_tibble`, where the results are cast, are returned by consecutive calls to the base R `head()` and `tail()` functions:

```
draft %>%
  group_by(Pos2, Born2, College2) %>%
  summarize(mean = mean(WS),
            median = median(WS)) -> twelfth_tibble
head(twelfth_tibble, n = 3)
## # A tibble: 3 x 5
## # Groups:   Pos2, Born2 [2]
##    Pos2  Born2 College2  mean median
##    <fct> <fct> <fct>    <dbl>  <dbl>
## 1 Big   USA   0         81.8   81.8
## 2 Big   USA   1         36.4   24.8
## 3 Big   World 0         39.9   22.1
tail(twelfth_tibble, n = 3)
## # A tibble: 3 x 5
## # Groups:   Pos2, Born2 [2]
##    Pos2      Born2 College2  mean median
##    <fct>     <fct> <fct>    <dbl>  <dbl>
## 1 Swingman  USA   1         39.6   30.4
## 2 Swingman  World 0         30.2   30.2
## 3 Swingman  World 1         18.2   18.2
```

Our final visualization is a pair of facet plots—once more, a facet plot is a type of visualization that displays two or more subsets of the data—with averages on the left and medians on the right, packed into one 2 × 2 object. Note that we've made a second call to the `theme()` function in order to orient our x-axis labels at 45 degrees in lieu of the `ggplot2` default, which, of course, orients the labels horizontally (see figure 2.7):

```
new_labels <- c("0" = "No College", "1" = "College")
p9 <- ggplot(twelfth_tibble, aes(x = Pos2, y = mean)) +
  geom_bar(stat = "identity", width = .5, fill = "slateblue4") +
  labs(title = "Average Win Shares by Place of Birth",
       x = "",
       y = "Win Shares",
       subtitle = "2000-09 NBA Drafts") +
  theme(plot.title = element_text(face = "bold")) +
  theme(axis.text.x = element_text(angle = 45, hjust = 1)) +
  facet_grid(Born2 ~ College2, labeller = labeller(College2 = new_labels))

new_labels <- c("0" = "No College", "1" = "College")
```

```
p10 <- ggplot(twelfth_tibble, aes(x = Pos2, y = median)) +
  geom_bar(stat = "identity", width = .5, fill  = "indianred3") +
  labs(title = "Median Win Shares by Place of Birth",
       x = "",
       y = "Win Shares",
       subtitle = "2000-09 NBA drafts") +
  theme(plot.title = element_text(face = "bold")) +
  theme(axis.text.x = element_text(angle = 45, hjust = 1)) +
  facet_grid(Born2 ~ College2, labeller = labeller(College2 = new_labels))
```

Again, rather than printing the two facet plots separately, they are instead bundled into one graphical object and then printed accordingly:

```
p9 + p10 + plot_layout(ncol = 2)
```

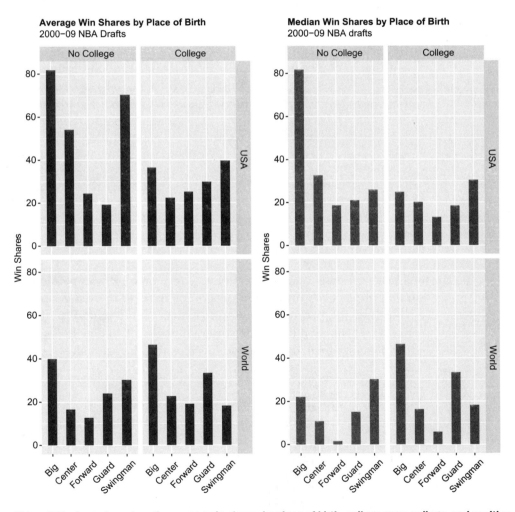

Figure 2.7   Average and median career win shares by place of birth, college or no college, and position

No doubt the most obvious and fascinating results from our pair of facet plots are in the upper-left panels. Bigs, Centers, and Swingmen born in the United States who did not attend a college or university before entering the NBA draft accrued significantly more win shares on average than other players at other positions regardless of where they were born and regardless of whether or not they first attended college.

The median win shares for these same players, however, aren't so distinct when compared to other players with different Born2 and College2 dispositions, again hinting at the effect just a few superstars can have.

This brings our exploration of the draft data set to a close. As you can see, a lot can be gleaned from a data set simply by applying standard or traditional exploration methods; it's not always necessary to test or model data, whatever the subject matter, in order to gain valuable insights. Before moving on, we'll save a copy of draft—after all the data wrangling—for chapter 3.

2.6 *Writing data*

One of our first operations was to call the read_csv() function to import a data set previously saved as a .csv file. Now, having finished our EDA, we want to generate an output file. To do that, we'll call the base R write.csv() function to create a new .csv file. This new file will be imported at the top of chapter 3. Rather than importing the original draft data set again—and then repeating the same data wrangling operations—a copy of draft, draft2, which equals the final configuration of the draft data set—will be imported instead. As long as you have a working directory set, write.csv() works very much like the read_csv() function; that is, you merely need to pass the name of the file:

```
draft -> draft2
write.csv(draft2, "draft2.csv")
```

One of the first operations in the following chapter will be to import draft2 for analysis above and beyond what was otherwise performed here—with implications that are profound and maybe even disconcerting.

Summary

- We learned how to install and load packages, read and write data, wrangle data, compute basic statistics, and create visual content—and we learned about win shares and other NBA data in the process.
- Most acquired data in the real world is messy, or at least not in a structure that works for subsequent analysis. Statisticians, data scientists, business analysts, and anyone working with data are therefore required to spend most of their time wrangling data rather than analyzing it.
- As far as wrangling data is concerned, we learned how to remove variables, remove observations, convert variables from one class to another, create new

variables, summarize data by groups, and even transform a data set from a wide format to a long one.

- We got our first glimpse of the ggplot2 package, which we used to create a histogram, paired boxplots, facet plots, a correlation heat map, and bar charts; we also called several ggplot() functions to customize our visual content and apply best practices.

- We demonstrated how to go about exploring a data set in full—but with purpose and with focus. Exploring data by computing it and visualizing it is a valuable exercise that leads to interesting and actionable insights and sets the table for deeper analysis.

- The methods applied here work on any data set, be they health records, sales figures, customer service statistics, or win shares.

- First-round NBA draft picks between 2000 and 2009 had very different professional careers. While a few players accrued many win shares over the course of their respective careers, most players accrued fewer than 25 career win shares.

- It would appear—at least based on the analysis conducted thus far—that players who accrued the most career win shares were picked very high in the first round, and lesser-skilled players were picked later in the first round. This will be further explored in great detail in chapter 3 through the application of more advanced analytical techniques.

Segmentation analysis 3

This chapter covers

- Loading packages with `c()` and `lapply()`
- Visualizing means and medians with bar charts
- Creating Sankey diagrams
- Computing expected values
- Performing a hierarchical clustering
- Creating and understanding dendrograms

In the previous chapter, we introduced several methods by which we can and should explore a data set as a prerequisite to conducting any statistical tests or performing specialized analysis. No doubt, the most significant finding from our analysis in chapter 2 is that, by and large, players who have the most productive professional careers were selected high in the first round of the NBA draft, whereas players who have modest careers, or even worse, were usually picked later in the first round—at least based on the 2000 to 2009 drafts. This finding creates an obvious incentive for teams to somehow get to the top of the draft board.

Tanking is the practice of purposely losing games in one season to secure a higher pick in the draft prior to the next season. The NBA draft, held annually during the offseason, is where teams take turns selecting the best eligible players from the United States and abroad. Like drafts in other US professional sports, the NBA draft is the exact opposite of a meritocracy; it's a worst-selects-first system that "awards" teams with the lowest number of wins with the opportunity to pick highest in the draft and therefore obtain rights to the best available players.

Given what we discovered in the previous chapter, our hypothesis in this chapter is that tanking is a rational and worthwhile strategy for losing teams that want to become winners. We intend to explore this hypothesis by segmenting our data and then demonstrating different and incrementally more technical analysis techniques against it. Segmentation analysis is the process by which data—usually customers, but it could also very well be NBA first-round draft picks—is divided based on one or more common characteristics.

Teams tank because it seems to work; superstars are an absolute requirement to win championships, and superstars are almost always top-five selections in the draft (though top-five selections are not always superstars). Therefore, teams must lose way more games than they win—intentionally, if that's what it takes—to draft a potential superstar. But let's see what the data says about this.

3.1   *More on tanking and the draft*

For those of you who are not overly familiar with the NBA, teams fixed on acquiring superstar talent to win championships generally follow one of two plans of action: through the draft or through veteran free agency. One of the unintended, yet perpetual, consequences of the NBA draft is that teams often tank when their rebuilding plans converge around it; that is, teams intentionally lose games by trading their best players and promoting benchwarmers in exchange for a long-term competitive edge made possible by the year-over-year accumulation of draft picks, especially *high* draft picks.

In 1985, right after the Houston Rockets tanked to the top of the draft and selected Hakeem Olajuwon, one of the league's all-time greats, the NBA inaugurated a lottery for its worst teams. (The Rockets subsequently won a pair of league titles.) The lottery disincentivized tanking—and preserved the integrity of play in the process—by randomizing the draft order and depriving teams of guaranteed outcomes based on wins and losses. Sort of.

The NBA draft remains a kakistocracy, where the worst teams from one season are rewarded before the next, because tanking gives teams no less than a reasonable chance of securing a top pick, and success provides virtually no chance. Take the Philadelphia 76ers: between 2013 and 2016, nearly 30 years after the first lottery, the 76ers tanked their way to the near top of the draft board, winning a *total* of 47 regular season games in the process, but then, minus the 2019–20 season shortened because of COVID-19, *averaging* 51 wins per season after selecting Joel Embiid and others. Every NBA team, by the way, plays an 82-game regular season schedule; so an average team would have 41 wins per season.

Championships are won with superstar talent, which is only available at or near the very top of the draft board. Aside from a previous trade, the only way to guarantee access to superstar talent is to tank.

The following analysis aims to establish beyond any reasonable doubt whether tanking is supported by the data. For this analysis, we'll use R's outstanding graphical capabilities, extend R's functional footprint to compute expected values, and even create an unsupervised learning algorithm.

3.2 Loading packages

The first order of business is to call the base R `library()` function to load packages that then make it possible to go above and beyond base R functionality; you aren't using the best of R without calling the latest or greatest packages and functions. As a reminder, packages must be loaded whenever and wherever they will be used; because we have a one-to-one relationship between scripts and chapters, some packages are loaded multiple times. Furthermore, packages must be loaded before calling any of their functions, which is why it's a good practice to load packages prior to writing or running other lines of code.

Two of our three packages, `tidyverse` and `patchwork`, were used in chapter 2. (Both of these packages, and especially `tidyverse`, will be used extensively going forward.) The one new package we're loading here is the `networkD3` package, which makes it possible to create Sankey diagrams, or flow diagrams, and other unique visualizations. The one Sankey diagram we'll create is one of just two visualizations in this chapter that are *not* created with the `ggplot2` graphics package, which is part of `tidyverse`. We then sequentially load these packages by making three calls to the `library()` function:

```
library(tidyverse)
library(networkD3)
library(patchwork)
```

There is, by the way, a method of loading multiple packages at the same time in lieu of sequentially calling the `library()` function. The first step is to create a vector containing the package names as arguments; next, we create a vector called packages—it can, in fact, be called anything you want—by calling the base R `c()` function and passing `tidyverse`, `networkD3`, and `patchwork` as arguments. Note that each package is bounded by quotation marks:

```
packages <- c("tidyverse", "networkD3", "patchwork")
```

The second and final step is to then call the base R `lapply()` function:

```
lapply(packages, library, character.only = TRUE)
```

Going forward, we'll continue to call the `library()` function, but the tandem of `c()` and `lapply()` is a good alternative if your script requires lots of packages. Now that we have our packages loaded, we're free to call any and all required functions to perform our analysis.

3.3   *Importing and viewing data*

Obviously, we need to import our data before we can do much else. We concluded chapter 2 by executing the following operations:

- A tibble called draft2 was created as a replica of the draft data set. The copy was made *after* draft was wrangled in which, for instance, many of the original variables were dropped, derived variables were created, and observations with missing data were deleted.
- A call was then made to the base R `write.csv()` function to create and save draft2 as a .csv file.

The readr `read_csv()` function is now called to import the draft2 data set. Because we're importing draft2 rather than draft, it won't be necessary to replicate the data wrangling operations performed in the previous chapter:

```
draft <- read_csv("draft2.csv")
```

The dplyr `glimpse()` function returns a transposed, yet truncated, version of draft2, where the column, or variable, names run vertically, and a subset of the data runs horizontally. A natural next step, albeit small, after importing a data set is to get its dimension as well as a sneak peek at its contents; `glimpse()` does this very well:

```
glimpse(draft2)
## Rows: 291
## Columns: 18
## $ Rk       <dbl> 1, 2, 3, 4, 5, 6, 7, 8, 9, 10, 11, 12, 13, 14,…
## $ Year     <dbl> 2009, 2009, 2009, 2009, 2009, 2009, 2009, 2009…
## $ Pk       <dbl> 1, 2, 3, 4, 5, 6, 7, 8, 9, 10, 11, 12, 13, 14,…
## $ Tm       <chr> "LAC", "MEM", "OKC", "SAC", "MIN", "MIN", "GSW…
## $ Player   <chr> "Blake Griffin", "Hasheem Thabeet", "James Har…
## $ Age      <dbl> 20.106, 22.135, 19.308, 19.284, 18.252, 20.144…
## $ Pos      <chr> "F", "C", "G", "G-F", "G", "G", "G", "C-F", "G…
## $ Born     <chr> "us", "tz", "us", "us", "es", "us", "us", "us"…
## $ College  <chr> "Oklahoma", "UConn", "Arizona State", "Memphis…
## $ From     <dbl> 2011, 2010, 2010, 2010, 2012, 2010, 2010, 2010…
## $ To       <dbl> 2020, 2014, 2020, 2019, 2020, 2012, 2020, 2017…
## $ G        <dbl> 622, 224, 826, 594, 555, 163, 699, 409, 813, 5…
## $ MP       <dbl> 34.8, 10.5, 34.3, 30.7, 30.9, 22.9, 34.3, 18.8…
## $ WS       <dbl> 75.2, 4.8, 133.3, 28.4, 36.4, -1.1, 103.2, 16.…
## $ WS48     <dbl> 0.167, 0.099, 0.226, 0.075, 0.102, -0.015, 0.2…
## $ Born2    <chr> "USA", "World", "USA", "USA", "World", "USA", …
## $ College2 <dbl> 1, 1, 1, 1, 0, 1, 1, 1, 1, 0, 1, 1, 1, 1, 1, 1…
## $ Pos2     <chr> "F", "C", "G", "G-F", "G", "G", "G", "C-F", "G…
```

The base R `dim()` function returns just the dimensions of an object; that is, the number of rows followed by the number of columns. It's a good alternative to `glimpse()`, especially if you want to pair `dim()` with the `head()` and `tail()` functions to get views of your data that haven't been transposed:

```
dim(draft2)
## [1] 291  18
```

We'll start by creating another derived variable that wasn't at all needed in chapter 2 but will, in fact, drive much of our analysis in this chapter. We'll go ahead and create that next.

3.4 *Creating another derived variable*

Now that we've gotten a peek at our data, we can proceed with prepping our data for why we're here: to perform segmentation analysis. In chapter 2, the dplyr mutate() function and the basic R ifelse() function were called in tandem to create variables that were then appended to the draft data set (and are therefore included in draft2). These same functions are called in a chunk of code (see the following discussion), where a new variable called Pk2 is created and populated with attributes that logically tie back to an original variable called Pk. To evaluate our data by segments, we first need to derive those segments because they don't natively exist.

The variable Pk is short for *pick*; it's a numeric variable that represents the pick, or first-round selection number. For example, James Harden was the third player chosen in the 2009 NBA draft; therefore, the variable Pk equals 3 where the variable Player equals James Harden. Because there are up to 30 first-round selections, Pk has a minimum of 1 and a maximum of 30. Following is a breakdown of our segmentations—our analysis will concentrate on these six Pk2 segments rather than the 30 Pk attributes:

- The derived variable Pk2 equals 1-5 when the original variable equals any number between 1 and 5. The %in% operator in R identifies whether an element, such as a number, is included in a vector or data frame. If affirmative, Pk2 is assigned the value 1-5; otherwise, the next line of code is read and executed, and so forth.
- Pk2 equals 6-10 if Pk equals any number between 6 and 10.
- Pk2 equals 11-15 if Pk equals any number between 11 and 15.
- Pk2 equals 16-20 if Pk equals any number between 16 and 20.
- Pk2 equals 21-25 if Pk equals any number between 21 and 25.
- Pk2 equals 26-30 if Pk equals any number between 26 and 30.
- If the original variable Pk equals anything other than a number between 1 and 30, the new variable Pk2 will equal NA.

Although Pk2 is a character string by default, it's really a categorical variable. All 291 players, or first-round selections, in the draft2 data set should be assigned to one of these six categories, or segments, depending on where exactly they were selected:

```
mutate(draft2, Pk2 = ifelse(Pk %in% 1:5, "1-5",
                     ifelse(Pk %in% 6:10, "6-10",
                     ifelse(Pk %in% 11:15, "11-15",
                     ifelse(Pk %in% 16:20, "16-20",
                     ifelse(Pk %in% 21:25, "21-25",
                     ifelse(Pk %in% 26:30, "26-30", "NA")))))) -> draft2
```

In fact, our next line of code converts `Pk2` to a factor variable by calling the base R `as.factor()` function. Again, this is a best practice for variables that can only assume a finite or fixed set of values:

```
draft2$Pk2 <- as.factor(draft2$Pk2)
```

Our subsequent analysis—we'll start by computing basic statistics and creating visual representations of the data—will be entirely focused on these and other segments.

3.5   *Visualizing means and medians*

You won't find more basic statistical measures than means and medians. These measures are helpful indicators of general differences between observed data and, therefore, represent a logical starting point for our segmentation analysis. The means and medians of the continuous variables in the draft2 data set will be visualized in a series of bar charts broken down by the six `Pk2` segments we just created:

- Total regular season games played
- Minutes played per regular season game
- Career win shares
- Win shares for every 48 minutes of playing time (NBA games that end in regulation are 48 minutes in duration)

We want to see where there are variances (if any) and where there are similarities (if any) in these performance and productivity measures between our six `Pk2` segments. We'll examine each of these variables one by one as we progress through the remainder of this section.

Based on our chapter 2 analysis of the 2000 to 2009 NBA drafts, we ultimately came to the conclusion—albeit preliminarily—that players who had the most productive professional careers, based on win shares, were generally picked higher in the first round than other players. We also discovered that the `win shares` variable is positively and highly correlated with regular season games played, minutes played per regular season game, and win shares for every 48 minutes of playing time. Thus, there could be a statistical justification for tanking if we see clear separation between the `1-5` segment and the other five segments—which is exactly what we intend to definitively determine.

3.5.1   *Regular season games played*

The total number of regular season games played is a fair measure of talent. Injuries aside, the NBA's best and most reliable players have longer careers and thus appear in more regular season games than lesser players who routinely get turned out in favor of younger and more promising players.

In the following chunk of `dplyr` code, we call the `summarize()` function to first compute the mean and median of regular season games played grouped by each factor, or segment, in variable `Pk2`. Then, using the preceding line of code, we instruct `summarize()` to compute the percentage of regular season games played for each segment of `Pk2` against the total number of games played by all 291 players in the draft2 data set. The result is a new 6 × 4 tibble called tibble1:

```
sumG <- sum(draft2$G)
draft2 %>%
  group_by(Pk2) %>%
  summarize(mean = mean(G),
            median = median(G),
            pct = sum(G)/sumG) -> tibble1
print(tibble1)
## # A tibble: 6 x 4
##    Pk2    mean median   pct
##    <fct> <dbl>  <dbl> <dbl>
## 1 1-5     716.   750. 0.234
## 2 11-15   444.   400  0.142
## 3 16-20   498.   550  0.163
## 4 21-25   453.   420  0.148
## 5 26-30   456.   478  0.125
## 6 6-10    579.   602. 0.189
```

These results are visualized with a pair of `ggplot2` bar charts between the mean and median:

- The `stat = "identity"` argument passed to the `geom_bar()` function tells R to compute the sum of the y-axis variable, grouped by the x-axis variable, and to display the results with a rectangular bar for each `Pk2` segment. Otherwise, `geom_bar()` would simply return counts of occurrences for each unique attribute in the x-axis variable. In addition, we're narrowing the width of the bars to 80% of the `ggplot2` default.

- The `scale_x_discrete()` function is called to hardcode the sequence of `Pk2` segments across the x-axis, from left to right. Otherwise, `ggplot2` would place the `Pk2` segment `6-10` last for the very simple reason that 6 is a digit that comes after 1 or 2.

- The `geom_text()` function is called to affix labels—truncated versions of the mean and median after passing those measures to the base R `trunc()` function, which reduces the raw results to the nearest whole number—atop the bars.

- The `geom_label()` function is called to add the tibble1 variable `pct`—truncated and multiplied by 100—inside the bars. Because the annotations in these and other plots have been truncated, some of the following results might seem "off," but actually, the totals and percentages have merely been rounded down to their nearest whole numbers.

- The `ylim()` function is called to extend the length of the y-axis so that it starts at 0 and ends at 800; this is often necessary for aesthetic reasons if and when the `geom_text()` or `geom_label()` functions is called to add labels *above* the bars.

```
g1 <- ggplot(tibble1, aes(x = Pk2, y = mean)) +
  geom_bar(stat = "identity", width = .8,
           fill = "coral", color = "coral4") +
  labs(title = "Average Career Games Played",
```

```
        subtitle = "First-Round Selections between
        2000 and 2009 NBA Drafts",
        x = "Segment",
        y = "Average Career Games Played",
        caption = "regular season games only") +
  scale_x_discrete(limits = c("1-5", "6-10", "11-15",
                              "16-20", "21-25", "26-30"),
                   labels = c("1-5", "6-10", "11-15",
                              "16-20", "21-25", "26-30")) +
  geom_text(aes(label = trunc(mean), vjust = -0.3)) +
  geom_label(aes(label = trunc(pct*100), vjust = 1.2)) +
  ylim(0, 800) +
  theme(plot.title = element_text(face = "bold"))

g2 <- ggplot(tibble1, aes(x = Pk2, y = median)) +
  geom_bar(stat = "identity", width = .8,
           fill = "coral3", color = "coral4") +
  labs(title = "Median Career Games Played",
        subtitle = "First-Round Selections between
        2000 and 2009 NBA Drafts",
        x = "Segment",
        y = "Median Career Games Played",
        caption = "regular season games only") +
  scale_x_discrete(limits = c("1-5", "6-10", "11-15",
                              "16-20", "21-25", "26-30"),
                   labels = c("1-5", "6-10", "11-15",
                              "16-20", "21-25", "26-30")) +
  geom_text(aes(label = trunc(median), vjust = -0.3)) +
  geom_label(aes(label = trunc(pct*100), vjust = 1.2)) +
  ylim(0, 800) +
  theme(plot.title = element_text(face = "bold"))
```

A subsequent call to the `plot_layout()` function from the `patchwork` package bundles these two visualizations, g1 and g2, into a single graphical object where the first visualization is positioned atop the second (see figure 3.1). If the `ncol` argument passed to `plot_layout()` instead equaled 2, these two visualizations would be printed side by side instead of g1 stacked on top of g2:

```
g1 + g2 + plot_layout(ncol = 1)
```

Visualizing data is much easier and quicker to interpret than reading rows of numbers. Following are the conclusions to draw from our first pair of bar charts:

- Players selected within the 1-5 segment played in more regular season games, based on means and medians, than any other group of first-round selections. In fact, though these players represent about 17% of the draft2 record count, they collectively played in more than 23% of the regular season games.
- Players selected within the 6-10 segment played in more regular season games than players selected later in the first round. They, too, represent approximately 17% of the draft2 record count but no less than 18% of the total regular season games played.

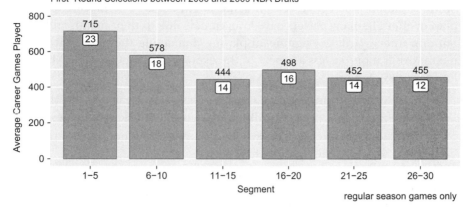

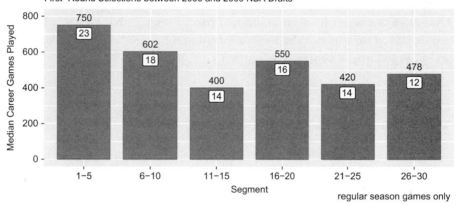

Figure 3.1 **Mean and median games played by the first-round segment affixed atop the bars. Percentages of the total games played are represented by the white-boxed labels inside the bars.**

- Therefore, about 34% of the first-round selections in draft2 account for more than 41% of the total regular season games played.
- In no other segment does the percentage of regular season games played exceed or even equal their respective percentage of draft2 record counts; in other words, segments 11-15, 16-20, 21-25, and 26-30 each contribute approximately 17% of the records to the draft2 data set, yet the percentage of total regular season games played across those four segments is consistently less than 17%. This absolutely supports our hypothesis—teams that tank and move up the draft board as a result are more likely to draft a player who will then play in more games than other players.

3.5.2 *Minutes played per game*

Minutes played per regular season game might actually be more telling than games played; after all, many players have long careers due to their health and dependability but don't necessarily get significant playing time along the way. That being said, our next move is more or less a repeat of the exercise we just completed but with the following series of changes:

- The variable minutes played per regular season game is inserted into similar `dplyr` and `ggplot2` code chunks in place of regular season games played.
- Our subsequent chunk of `dplyr` code produces a new object, tibble2, which is then passed to the `ggplot()` function.
- We then pass a different fill and color to the `geom_bar()` function.
- The plot title and y-axis label, just two of the arguments passed to the `labs()` function, are changed out due to the variable swap.
- The y-axis is rescaled accordingly, which is also due to the variable change.

Otherwise, we're creating an additional pair of `ggplot2` bar charts, where the means are displayed on top and the medians displayed on the bottom, broken down by our six `Pk2` segments, of course (see figure 3.2):

```
sumMP <- sum(draft2$MP)
draft2 %>%
  group_by(Pk2) %>%
  summarize(mean = mean(MP),
            median = median(MP),
            pct = sum(MP)/sumMP) -> tibble2

mp1 <- ggplot(tibble2, aes(x = Pk2, y = mean)) +
  geom_bar(stat = "identity", width = .8,
           fill = "deepskyblue", color = "deepskyblue4") +
  labs(title = "Average Minutes Played per Game",
       subtitle = "First-Round Selections between
       2000 and 2009 NBA Drafts",
       x = "Segment",
       y = "Average Minutes Played per Game",
       caption = "regular season games only") +
  scale_x_discrete(limits = c("1-5", "6-10", "11-15",
                              "16-20", "21-25", "26-30"),
                   labels = c("1-5", "6-10", "11-15",
                              "16-20", "21-25", "26-30")) +
  geom_text(aes(label = trunc(mean), vjust = -0.3)) +
  geom_label(aes(label = trunc(pct*100), vjust = 1.2)) +
  ylim(0, 30) +
  theme(plot.title = element_text(face = "bold"))

mp2 <- ggplot(tibble2, aes(x = Pk2, y = median)) +
  geom_bar(stat = "identity", width = .8,
           fill = "deepskyblue3", color = "deepskyblue4") +
```

```
    labs(title = "Median Minutes Played per Game",
         subtitle = "First-Round Selections between
         2000 and 2009 NBA Drafts",
         x = "Segment",
         y = "Median Minutes Played per Game",
         caption = "regular season games only") +
    scale_x_discrete(limits = c("1-5", "6-10", "11-15",
                                "16-20", "21-25", "26-30"),
                    labels = c("1-5", "6-10", "11-15",
                                "16-20", "21-25", "26-30")) +
    geom_text(aes(label = trunc(median), vjust = -0.3)) +
    geom_label(aes(label = trunc(pct*100), vjust = 1.2)) +
    ylim(0, 30) +
    theme(plot.title = element_text(face = "bold"))

mp1 + mp2 + plot_layout(ncol = 1)
```

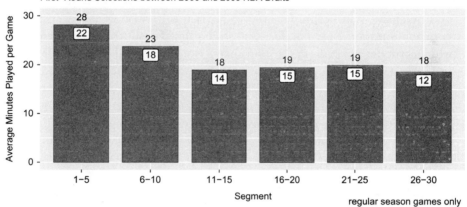

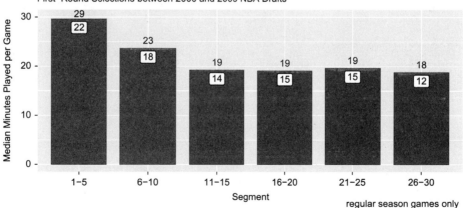

Figure 3.2   Mean and median minutes played per game by the first-round segment

These results are similar but, at the same time, more definite than our first set of results. They are summarized for you here:

- Players selected in the 1-5 segment played, on average, approximately 18% more minutes per game than players in the 6-10 segment and roughly 33% more minutes than players from the other four segments.
- There is clear and obvious separation between segments 1-5 and 6-10 and further separation between 6-10 and all other segments.
- There is almost no variance between segments 11-15, 16-20, 21-25, and 26-30.

All of this further supports our hypothesis that tanking makes sense—if that's what it takes for a team to select in the 1-5 segment, or even the 6-10 segment, versus anywhere else in the first round. Let's now take a look at win shares.

3.5.3 *Career win shares*

As discussed in chapter 2, win shares is basically a roll-up of every player's offensive and defensive statistics into a single metric. It otherwise equals each player's overall contribution to, or share of, his team's win total. To put things in perspective, players who accrued a minimum of 50 win shares over their careers were, for the most part, full-time starters for many years; players who accrued somewhere between 75 and 100 career win shares were frequent all-star selections; and players who accrued more than 100 career win shares are, without doubt, Hall of Fame material. On the flip side, players with 25 or fewer win shares were second-string, marginal, or sometimes worse.

Kareem Abdul-Jabbar, who was drafted by the Milwaukee Bucks but who then played most of his career with the Los Angeles Lakers, once accrued an all-time best 25.4 win shares over the course of just one season, and his 273.4 career win shares is still the all-time record. LeBron James, still playing, is not far behind.

The following chunk of code is similar to our previous `dplyr` and `ggplot2` code chunks, except that we're swapping in win shares. The corresponding changes to the `geom_bar()`, `labs()`, and `ylim()` functions apply:

```
sumWS <- sum(draft2$WS)
draft2 %>%
  group_by(Pk2) %>%
  summarize(mean = mean(WS),
            median = median(WS),
            pct = sum(WS)/sumWS) -> tibble3

ws1 <- ggplot(tibble3, aes(x = Pk2, y = mean)) +
  geom_bar(stat = "identity", width = .8,
           fill = "springgreen", color = "springgreen4") +
  labs(title = "Average Career Win Shares",
       subtitle = "First-Round Selections between
       2000 and 2009 NBA Drafts",
       x = "Segment",
       y = "Average Career Win Shares",
       caption = "regular season games only") +
  scale_x_discrete(limits = c("1-5", "6-10", "11-15",
```

```
                         "16-20", "21-25", "26-30"),
               labels = c("1-5", "6-10", "11-15",
                          "16-20", "21-25", "26-30")) +
    geom_text(aes(label = trunc(mean), vjust = -0.3)) +
    geom_label(aes(label = trunc(pct*100), vjust = 1.2)) +
    ylim(0, 60) +
    theme(plot.title = element_text(face = "bold"))

ws2 <- ggplot(tibble3, aes(x = Pk2, y = median)) +
  geom_bar(stat = "identity", width = .8,
           fill = "springgreen3", color = "springgreen4") +
  labs(title = "Median Career Win Shares",
       subtitle = "First-Round Selections between
       2000 and 2009 NBA Drafts",
       x = "Segment", y = "Median Career Win Shares",
       caption = "regular season games only") +
  scale_x_discrete(limits = c("1-5", "6-10", "11-15",
                              "16-20", "21-25", "26-30"),
                   labels = c("1-5", "6-10", "11-15",
                              "16-20", "21-25", "26-30")) +
    geom_text(aes(label = trunc(median), vjust = -0.3)) +
    geom_label(aes(label = trunc(pct*100), vjust = 1.2)) +
    ylim(0, 70) +
    theme(plot.title = element_text(face = "bold"))
```

For a third time, our end game is a pair of ggplot2 bar charts packed into one graphical representation of our results, with the computed means for every segment in the variable Pk2 visualized on the top and the computed medians per Pk2 segment on the bottom (see figure 3.3):

```
ws1 + ws2 + plot_layout(ncol = 1)
```

Wow, the separation between segments—1-5 versus 6-10, as well as 6-10 versus the remaining four segments—is even more pronounced than what we've previously seen. More specifically, consider the following:

- Players in the 1-5 segment, on average, accrued almost twice as many career win shares as players in the 6-10 segment and about three times as many win shares as players from any other segment.
- These same players—again, 17% of the draft2 population—account for 34% of all win shares, and players in the top-two segments, roughly 34% of the draft2 population, account for at least 53% of all win shares.
- While there are significant differences at the top end of the draft, there is little to no difference between the 11-15 through 26-30 segments.
- This is the best evidence we have so far that our going-in hypothesis is correct; on the most important metric, we have the greatest differentiation between the top segments and the remaining segments.

Finally, let's examine our second win shares variable, WS48. This variable represents win shares accrued for every 48 minutes of regular season playing time.

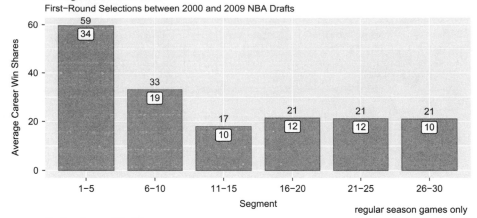

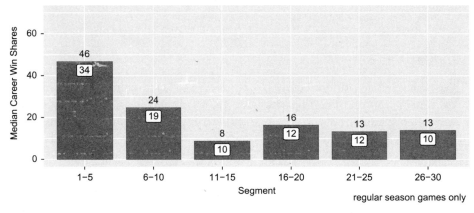

Figure 3.3   Mean and median career win shares by first-round segment

3.5.4   *Win shares every 48 minutes*

The following dplyr code computes means and medians for the variable WS48 for each Pk2 segment and the ggplot2 code to visualize the same:

```
sumWS48 <- sum(draft2$WS48)
draft2 %>%
  group_by(Pk2) %>%
  summarize(mean = mean(WS48),
            median = median(WS48),
            pct = sum(WS48)/sumWS48) -> tibble4

ws3 <- ggplot(tibble4, aes(x = Pk2, y = mean)) +
  geom_bar(stat = "identity", width = .8,
           fill = "gold", color = "gold4") +
  labs(title = "Average Win Shares per 48 Minutes",
       subtitle = "First-Round Selections between
       2000 and 2009 NBA Drafts",
       x = "Segment",
```

```
        y = "Average Win Shares per 48 Minutes",
        caption = "regular season games only") +
  scale_x_discrete(limits = c("1-5", "6-10", "11-15",
                               "16-20", "21-25", "26-30"),
                    labels = c("1-5", "6-10", "11-15",
                               "16-20", "21-25", "26-30")) +
  geom_text(aes(label = round(mean, 2), vjust = -0.3)) +
  geom_label(aes(label = trunc(pct*100), vjust = 1.2)) +
  ylim(0, 0.13) +
  theme(plot.title = element_text(face = "bold"))

ws4 <- ggplot(tibble4, aes(x = Pk2, y = median)) +
  geom_bar(stat = "identity", width = .8,
           fill = "gold3", color = "gold4") +
  labs(title = "Median Win Shares per 48 Minutes",
       subtitle = "First-Round Selections between
       2000 and 2009 NBA Drafts",
       x = "Segment", y = "Median Win Shares per 48 Minutes",
       caption = "regular season games only") +
  scale_x_discrete(limits = c("1-5", "6-10", "11-15",
                               "16-20", "21-25", "26-30"),
                    labels = c("1-5", "6-10", "11-15",
                               "16-20", "21-25", "26-30")) +
  geom_text(aes(label = round(median, 2), vjust = -0.3)) +
  geom_label(aes(label = trunc(pct*100), vjust = 1.2)) +
  ylim(0, 0.13) +
  theme(plot.title = element_text(face = "bold"))

ws3 + ws4 + plot_layout(ncol = 1)
```

A fourth and final pair of bar charts immediately follows—a different metric, of course, but the same layout and more or less the same results (see figure 3.4).

Because win shares for every 48 minutes of playing time is scaled significantly lower than our other measures, the variances between the top and bottom segments might appear less pronounced, but they are quite similar to our previous results. Our findings are summarized for you here:

- Players in the 1-5 segment accrued almost 20% more win shares for every 48 minutes of playing time than players in the 6-10 segment and nearly 40% more than players in the other segments.

- In other words, there's more than a 20% difference in win shares for every 48 minutes of playing time between the 6-10 segment and the remaining four segments.

- As with the other measures, there is clear and obvious separation between the 1-5 and 6-10 segments and further separation between the 6-10 segment and remaining segments.

- Performance and productivity are otherwise random across the 11-15 through 26-30 segments. Further evidence that our hypothesis is correct: tanking absolutely makes sense, especially for teams intent on rebuilding their rosters through the draft . . . if losing on purpose can elevate them enough to select a player in the 1-5 segment or, at worst, in the 6-10 segment.

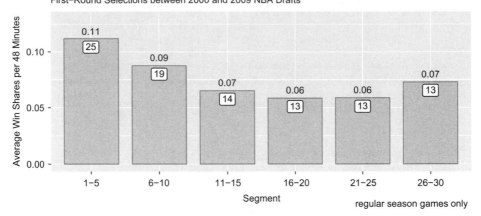

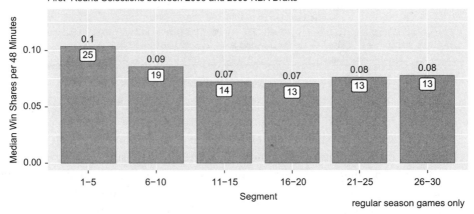

Figure 3.4   Mean and median win shares for every 48 minutes played by the first-round segment

Now that we've computed and visualized means and medians of the most significant draft2 variables—and in the process showed clear separation between the top of the draft and the rest of the first round—we should next document our most important takeaways thus far.

3.6   *Preliminary conclusions*

So what have we established so far? What are the implications? And what have we *not* established?

- Regardless of the measure, there is clear and obvious separation in performance and productivity between those players picked within the 1-5 segment versus those picked in the 6-10 segment, and there is further separation between the 6-10 segment and those players picked in the 11-15 segment.

- There are virtually no performance or productivity differences from the `11-15` segment through the rest of the first round, regardless of measure.

- Thus, there's a definite incentive for teams to somehow get to the top, or very close to the top, of the draft board. Teams are clearly best off selecting at or near the top of the draft if they want—or *need*—a potential superstar.

- But how to get there? Trading up is almost impossible because that, of course, would require another team to trade down. As long as the NBA rewards losing teams with high draft picks, teams will—*and should*—tank, which, of course, compromises the integrity of play.

- Finally, we need to avoid sweeping conclusions that are above and beyond what we're analyzing. Teams tanked in the 1970s too; they presumably did so because they wanted to increase their chances of selecting a potential superstar. But we can't rationalize that. We can only say that tanking makes sense based on an analysis of the 2000 to 2009 NBA drafts and the subsequent professional careers of those players who were selected in the first round in those drafts. Don't ever apply results to circumstances beyond the bounds of your testing and analysis.

With that being said, bear in mind that of the players in the draft2 data set with 100-plus career win shares, all but two were top-five picks when they entered the NBA draft; only Tony Parker, selected 28th overall by San Antonio in 2001, and Stephen Curry, drafted by Golden State in 2009 as the 7th overall selection, were drafted outside the top five and have more than 100 career win shares. NBA champions, more often than not, have a minimum of two top-five picks on their rosters (only two league champions since 2000 had but one top-five pick, and no championship-winning team since then had zero); yet, top-five picks are not necessarily guaranteed to win a championship. Of the 50 top-five picks in our data set, only 11 have since won a league championship.

3.7 *Sankey diagram*

Our next technique is a best attempt at consolidating our results into a single graphical object. A Sankey diagram is a type of flow diagram where the width of the connectors, or links, between a pair of nodes is proportional to quantity. Creating one is especially tedious—as you're about to discover—but the return is definitely worth the investment. Sankey diagrams not only look impressive but also provide revealing and actionable insights. You might not be all that familiar with Sankey diagrams, but you should be because there are plenty of use cases for them. For instance, consider the following:

- A human resources leader analyzes their company's end-to-end employment application process, starting with functional organizations and requisitions; then comprising the channels by which resumes and applications are ingested, including job boards, recruiting firms, and internal references; and, finally, a status breakdown of every candidate. They might then decide to advertise new opportunities on the two job boards that attracted the most or best candidates.

- A manager of a nonprofit tracks their organization's revenue from donations, grants, and membership fees; their capital and operational expenses; and the monetary value of their awards for educational, scientific, religious, and literary purposes. The manager might then decide to increase membership fees, seek additional grant money earmarked for scientific pursuits, or find more affordable office space.
- A marketing manager, without a machine learning background, diagrams yes/no responses to a direct marketing campaign by segmenting the customers using their education, job type, and marital status. The last pair of nodes— whether or not customers respond to the campaign—is the equivalent of a target, or response, variable in a machine learning model. The manager might then modify the marketing campaign by targeting customers with specific demographic attributes and ignoring other customers with other attributes.

Figure 3.5 shows a relatively simple Sankey diagram, just for illustrative purposes. We have a fictional NBA team attempting to sell the last remaining tickets to its next home game. The team sends a marketing email or text message to the men and women in its booster club. There are significantly more mobile phone numbers on file than email addresses; also, there are way more men in the booster club than women. Most of the men then purchase one or more tickets, whereas most of the women pass.

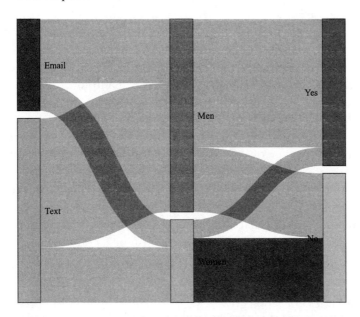

Figure 3.5   A sample Sankey diagram created for illustrative purposes only. The vertical rectangles are nodes, and the bands connecting a pair of nodes are links. The width of the links is a representation of quantity. In this example, more text messages are sent than emails, more men receive some type of digital communication than do women, and most men then respond affirmatively, whereas most women do not.

Our next code chunk produces a Sankey diagram where the node groupings, from left to right, originate from these derived variables:

- Born2—A binary variable created in chapter 2 that equals USA or World.
- College2—Another binary variable created in chapter 2 that equals 0 or 1 for No College and College, respectively.
- Age2—A new variable (discussed following this list) where the original variable Age is truncated to whole numbers. Every player in the draft2 data set was 17 to 25 years of age when they turned professional.
- Pos2—A variable created in chapter 2 where player positions were consolidated from the original variable Pos and also spelled out; this variable equals Big, Center, Forward, Guard, or Swingman.
- Pk2—A variable derived from the original variable Pk that equals 1-5, 6-10, 11-15, 16-20, 21-25, or 26-30.
- WS3—A new variable (discussed following this list) where the original variable WS (short for *win shares*) is truncated to whole numbers and then assigned to one of six categories or segments.

Our first order of business is to create the variables Age2 and then WS3. With respect to Age2, we pass the draft2 data set to the dplyr mutate() function and assign Age2 to equal a truncated version of the original variable Age. For WS3, we first call mutate() to create a variable called WS2, which is a truncated version of the original variable WS; then we pipe WS2 to the mutate() and case_when() functions (case_when() is the dplyr equivalent of the base R ifelse() function) to create WS3, which is WS2 split into six segments. For instance, if WS2 equals 47, then WS3 should equal 40-59. The net effect of creating Age2 and WS3 is to reduce the number of nodes and links in our Sankey diagram and therefore reduce the amount of code we need to write:

```
draft2 %>%
  mutate(Age2 = trunc(Age)) -> draft2

draft2 %>%
  mutate(draft2, WS2 = trunc(WS)) %>%
  mutate(WS3 = case_when(WS2 <= 19 ~ "<20",
                         WS2 >= 20 & WS2 <= 39 ~ "20-39",
                         WS2 >= 40 & WS2 <= 59 ~ "40-59",
                         WS2 >= 60 & WS2 <= 79 ~ "60-79",
                         WS2 >= 80 & WS2 <= 99 ~ "80-99",
                         WS2 >= 100 ~ "100+")) -> draft2
```

Our second order of business is to create the nodes. There should be a one-to-one relationship between variables and node groupings, which means our Sankey diagram will contain six node groupings. Additionally, there should be another one-to-one relationship between unique attributes across the six variables and the total number of nodes. For instance, Born2 and College2 are both binary variables, so those two node groupings should each contain two nodes. Our Sankey diagram will, in fact, contain 30 nodes. The next chunk of code creates a single-vector data frame, called nodes, by way of teaming the base R `data.frame()` and `c()` functions:

```
nodes <- data.frame(
"name" = c("USA", "World",
            "0", "1",
            "17", "18", "19", "20", "21", "22", "23", "24", "25",
            "Big",   "Center",  "Forward", "Guard",  "Swingman",
            "1-5",   "6-10",  "11-15", "16-20", "21-25", "26-30",
            "<20", "20-39", "40-59", "60-79", "80-99", "100+"))
```

Our third order of business is to create another data frame, called links. Each series of three numbers in the links data frame represents a link connecting two nodes, where the first number in the series is the node being connected from (source), the second number represents the node being connected to (target), and the third number represents the value, or quantity, of the flow between them (value):

```
links <- as.data.frame(matrix(c(
  0,2,21, 0,3,203,
  1,2,51, 1,3,16,
  2,4,1, 2,5,20, 2,6,19, 2,7,15, 2,8,12, 2,9,5, 2,10,0, 2,11,0, 2,12,0,
  3,4,0, 3,5,3, 3,6,32, 3,7,50, 3,8,58, 3,9,58, 3,10,14, 3,11,3, 3,12,1,
  4,13,0, 4,14,0, 4,15,1, 4,16,0, 4,17,0,
  5,13,2, 5,14,8, 5,15,6, 5,16,2, 5,17,5,
  6,13,11, 6,14,6, 6,15,15, 6,16,14, 6,17,5,
  7,13,7, 7,14,12, 7,15,19, 7,16,24, 7,17,3,
  8,13,9, 8,14,7, 8,15,19, 8,16,25, 8,17,10,
  9,13,5, 9,14,5, 9,15,23, 9,16,24, 9,17,6,
  10,13,0, 10,14,1, 10,15,4, 10,16,6, 10,17,3,
  11,13,0, 11,14,1, 11,15,2, 11,16,0, 11,17,0,
  12,13,0, 12,14,1, 12,15,0, 12,16,0, 12,17,0,
  13,18,7, 13,19,6, 13,20,8, 13,21,3, 13,22,2, 13,23,8,
  14,18,7, 14,19,6, 14,20,7, 14,21,7, 14,22,6, 14,23,9,
  15,18,16, 15,19,18, 15,20,13, 15,21,13, 15,22,13, 15,23,15,
  16,18,15, 16,19,13, 16,20,15, 16,21,22, 16,22,18, 16,23,12,
  17,18,5, 17,19,6, 17,20,7, 17,21,5, 17,22,3, 17,23,6,
  18,24,12, 18,25,9, 18,26,9, 18,27,6, 18,28,2, 18,29,12,
  19,24,19, 19,25,15, 19,26,5, 19,27,7, 19,28,3, 19,29,1,
  20,24,33, 20,25,9, 20,26,3, 20,27,3, 20,28,1, 20,29,0,
  21,24,27, 21,25,12, 21,26,8, 21,27,1, 21,28,2, 21,29,0,
  22,24,30, 22,25,10, 22,26,7, 22,27,2, 22,28,1, 22,29,0,
  23,24,26, 23,25,10, 23,26,2, 23,27,3, 23,28,0, 23,29,1),
  byrow = TRUE, ncol = 3))
names(links) = c("source", "target", "value")
```

Our fourth and final order of business is to render the Sankey diagram by calling the `sankeyNetwork()` function from the `networkD3` package (see figure 3.6). The arguments passed to the `sankeyNetwork()` function are mandatory and fixed:

```
sankeyNetwork(Links = links, Nodes = nodes,
              Source = "source", Target = "target",
              Value = "value", NodeID = "name",
              fontSize = 12, nodeWidth = 30)
```

A Sankey diagram is interactive in RStudio. When you navigate your cursor over one of the nodes, R will highlight the links to and from the node and produce a small pop-up that provides the node name and the flow quantity from it. When you navigate instead to a link, R will highlight it and provide a pop-up that identifies the connecting nodes and the flow quantity between them.

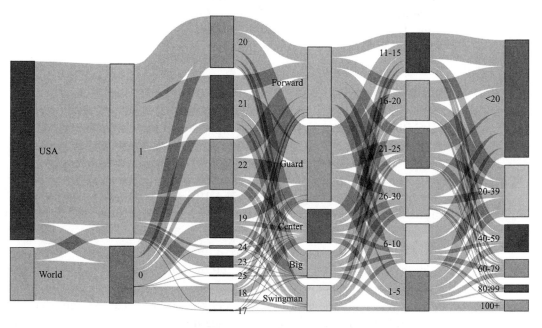

Figure 3.6   A Sankey diagram that displays the flow, or quantity, between adjacent sets of nodes. Going from left to right, most players selected in the first round of the 2000 to 2009 NBA drafts were born in the United States (USA) versus some other country (World). More players first attended a college or university (1) than those who did not (0). Most players were between 19 and 22 years of age when they entered the NBA draft. More players were selected as forwards and guards than other positions. Players are distributed across six equal "pick" segments, depending on where in the first round they were selected. All players then accrued some number of win shares; only a fraction of first-round picks then accrued many win shares, and most of them were picked in the 1-5 segment.

The following `dplyr` code returns the numbers, or values, that were previously supplied to the links data frame. The draft2 data set is piped five times to the `count()` function, which counts the number of draft2 observations between every combination of adjacent node groupings:

```
draft2 %>%
  count(Born2, College2)
draft2 %>%
  count(College2, Age2)
draft2 %>%
  count(Age2, Pos2)
draft2 %>%
  count(Pos2, Pk2)
```

```
draft2 %>%
  count(Pk2, WS3)
```

Due to space considerations, the results are not reproduced here, but they are, of course, reflected in the build-out of our Sankey diagram.

You might now appreciate why Sankey diagrams aren't all that prevalent. Just imagine if there were even more nodes. However, this one chart effectively visualizes the quantitative breakdowns of our derived variables as well as the relationships between them. The Sankey diagram works because the "process" depicted here is serial or linear. For instance, we can readily see the following:

- Approximately four times as many first-round picks between the 2000 and 2009 NBA drafts were born in the United States versus some other country.
- Most first-round picks born in the United States played in college before turning professional, whereas a majority of first-round picks born outside the United States didn't play in college.
- More first-round picks, regardless of where they were born and whether or not they first played in college, were aged 19 to 22 when they entered the NBA draft. Very few players were either younger than 19 or older than 22 when they turned professional.
- More first-round picks were forwards or guards than any other position.
- A large majority of the players with 100 or more win shares in their respective careers were selected at or near the very top of the draft.
- Most players with somewhere between 80 and 99 career win shares were selected between the 1-5 and 6-10 Pk2 segments.
- Players with fewer than 20 career win shares come from all Pk2 segments, but most of them were drafted somewhere between the 11-15 and 26-30 Pk2 segments.

Players selected in the 1-5 or 6-10 segments, especially 1-5, are more or less equally divided between the six segments of career win shares, but players drafted thereafter, starting with the 11-15 segment, were much more likely to accrue fewer than 20 win shares in their respective careers. When deciding to tank or not tank, teams should consider the results of our first segmentation analysis, but they should also bear in mind the demographics and other attributes of the best-available players.

3.8   *Expected value analysis*

Our analysis thus far clearly shows that NBA teams should have very different expectations of a top-five pick versus any other first-round selection. Let's carry that deduction forward by computing the expected value of a top-five pick, using results from the 2000 to 2009 NBA drafts, versus the expected value of any other first-round selection. *Expected value* is calculated by multiplying possible outcomes by their probability and then summing those results; it's a series of simple mathematical calculations that are computed when outcomes are uncertain, yet we nonetheless get a likely value based on a weighted average of every conceivable possibility. Expected value is an analysis technique most prevalent in finance and risk, but it's just as applicable in many other fields and endeavors. Following are some specifics about expected value:

- Expected value represents the average value, or payoff, that can be expected, usually from a specific decision or action, when more than one outcome is possible.
- Expected value is computed by multiplying each possible outcome by its probability of occurrence and then summing the products. Thus, Expected value = (Outcome$_1$ × Probability$_1$) + (Outcome$_2$ × Probability$_2$) + . . . + (Outcome$_N$ × Probability$_N$). The number of terms must equal the number of potential outcomes.
- Expected value is a common analysis technique when decisions must be made even as extenuating circumstances are uncertain and potentially risky. Whichever option returns the highest expected value should be considered the best choice.
- It may go without saying, but outcomes and probabilities must be known in advance, or, alternatively, they can be accurately estimated from historical data.

The draft2 data set is subset into two populations, based on where in the first round each player was drafted (1-5 or 6-30), and then subset again based on the number of win shares each player earned or has earned so far (some players are still active). For the sake of this exercise, the following designations are used:

- Players with 100 or more win shares are designated as *superstars.*
- Players with anywhere between 75 and 100 win shares are *stars.*
- Players with 50 to 75 career win shares are designated as *starters.*
- Players with 25 to 50 win shares are *reserves.*
- Players with fewer than 25 career win shares are designated as *marginal.*

Now, take a look at tables 3.1 and 3.2. Both are structured the same (meaning they have the same columns and rows), but table 3.1 is dedicated to the 1-5 segment, and table 3. 2 is dedicated to the 6-30 segment.

Table 3.1   Expected value for an NBA draft pick from the 1–5 segment

Segment (A)	Win Shares (B)	Probability (C)	Median (D)	Expected Value (E)
Superstar	> 100	0.24	127.00	30.48
Star	75–99.99	0.08	79.65	6.37
Starter	50–74.99	0.16	59.90	9.58
Reserve	25–49.99	0.20	39.95	7.99
Marginal	< 25	0.32	9.70	3.10
		1.00		**57.53**[a]

[a]The sum of the rows actually equals 57.52; 57.53 is the output from R.

Table 3.2   Expected value for an NBA draft pick from the `11–15` **through** `26–30` **segments**

Segment (A)	Win Shares (B)	Probability (C)	Median (D)	Expected Value (E)
Superstar	> 100	0.01	107.25	1.07
Star	75–99.99	0.04	83.00	3.32
Starter	50–74.99	0.11	60.60	6.67
Reserve	25–49.99	0.21	35.00	7.35
Marginal	< 25	0.63	5.00	3.15
		1.00		**21.21**[a]

[a]Once more, the printed sum is from the R output and not a sum of the rows; variances are due to rounding right of the decimal point.

Going from left to right, we have the following:

- The Segment (A) and Win Shares (B) columns together represent the player breakdown summarized in the previous list; that is, each of our two tables has, by necessity, five rows—one row for each segment of player designation.
- The Probability (C) column is really a conditional probability. For instance, teams have a 24% chance of selecting a future superstar when they own one of the first five picks (equal to 12 of 50 players with 100 win shares or more); teams drafting anywhere else in the first round instead have just a 1% probability of selecting a future superstar (equal to 2 of 50 players with 100 or more win shares). The five probability figures in each table therefore sum to 1.
- The Median (D) column represents the median number of career win shares for each Segment (A) and Win Shares (B) combination. For example, the median number of win shares for those players drafted within the `1–5` segment who then accrued 100 or more win shares equals 127. The median number of win shares was chosen here in lieu of the mean in order to mitigate the effect of outliers.
- The Expected Value (E) column represents the product of Probability (C) and Median (D). By then adding the result for each outcome, we get the Expected Value (E) of a `1–5` pick versus a `6–30` pick. A player selected in the `1–5` segment, based on the 2000 to 2009 NBA drafts, has an expected value of 57.53; in other words, an owner, a general manager, a fan—anyone—can expect a player drafted in spots 1, 2, 3, 4, or 5 to accrue about 58 win shares over the course of their career. Compare that to a player drafted sixth or below—these players can be expected to accrue just 21 win shares over their respective careers. This is the difference between a full-time starter for many years versus, at best, a career backup.

There are many ways in R to perform an expected value analysis, one not necessarily any better than the others. Here, the base R `c()` function is called to create a vector called `probs1`. Values for `probs1` are created with `dplyr` code; the draft2 data set is repeatedly piped to the `dplyr filter()` function that subsets draft2 where, for instance, the variable Pk is less than 6 and the variable WS is greater than 100. What remains of draft2 is counted with the dplyr tally() function and divided by 50, which equals the number of players in draft2 who were selected first to fifth in the NBA draft.

This series of operations is repeated four times, returning a vector that equals the probabilities supplied to table 3.1:

```
c(draft2 %>%
   filter(Pk < 6 & WS > 100) %>%
   tally() / 50,
draft2 %>%
   filter(Pk < 6 & WS > 75 & WS < 100) %>%
   tally() / 50,
draft2 %>%
   filter(Pk < 6 & WS > 50 & WS < 75) %>%
   tally() / 50,
draft2 %>%
   filter(Pk < 6 & WS > 25 & WS < 50) %>%
   tally() / 50,
draft2 %>%
   filter(Pk < 6 & WS < 25) %>%
   tally() / 50) -> probs1
print(probs1)
## $n
## [1] 0.24
##
## $n
## [1] 0.08
##
## $n
## [1] 0.16
##
## $n
## [1] 0.2
##
## $n
## [1] 0.32
```

The c() function is again called, this time to create a vector called vals1. Inside the c() function, we call the filter() function to subset the draft2 data set just as before; this time, however, the results are then piped to the dplyr summarize() function, which calculates the median win shares. The end result is a second vector that equals the medians in table 3.1:

```
c(draft2 %>%
   filter(Pk < 6 & WS > 100) %>%
   summarize(med = median(WS)),
draft2 %>%
   filter(Pk < 6 & WS > 75 & WS < 100) %>%
   summarize(med = median(WS)),
draft2 %>%
   filter(Pk < 6 & WS > 50 & WS < 75) %>%
   summarize(med = median(WS)),
```

```
draft2 %>%
  filter(Pk < 6 & WS > 25 & WS < 50) %>%
  summarize(med = median(WS)),
draft2 %>%
  filter(Pk < 6 & WS < 25) %>%
  summarize(med = median(WS))) -> vals1
print(vals1)
## $med
## [1] 127
##
## $med
## [1] 79.65
##
## $med
## [1] 59.9
##
## $med
## [1] 39.95
##
## $med
## [1] 9.7
```

The base R `sum()` function computes the expected value of a top-five pick by multiplying `probs1` and `vals1`, both of which are first converted to numeric variables by a pair of calls to the base R `as.numeric()` function:

```
sum(as.numeric(probs1) * as.numeric(vals1))
## [1] 57.53
```

The next chunk of code first produces a pair of vectors where

- `probs2` is more or less the same as `probs1`, except for the fact that the counts for each draft2 subset are divided by 241, which is the number of first-round picks in draft2 who were selected sixth or below.
- `vals2` is otherwise "equal" to `vals1`.

The final line of code includes a second call to the `sum()` function to compute the expected value of a first-round pick when selecting in the `6-30` segment:

```
c(draft2 %>%
  filter(Pk > 5 & WS > 100) %>%
  tally() / 241,
draft2 %>%
  filter(Pk > 5 & WS > 75 & WS < 100) %>%
  tally() / 241,
draft2 %>%
  filter(Pk > 5 & WS > 50 & WS < 75) %>%
  tally() / 241,
draft2 %>%
  filter(Pk > 5 & WS > 25 & WS < 50) %>%
  tally() / 241,
draft2 %>%
  filter(Pk > 5 & WS < 25) %>%
```

```
    tally() / 241) -> probs2
print(probs2)
## $n
## [1] 0.008298755
##
## $n
## [1] 0.0373444
##
## $n
## [1] 0.1120332
##
## $n
## [1] 0.2074689
##
## $n
## [1] 0.6348548
c(draft2 %>%
  filter(Pk > 5 & WS > 100) %>%
  summarize(med = median(WS)),
draft2 %>%
  filter(Pk > 5 & WS > 75 & WS < 100) %>%
  summarize(med = median(WS)),
draft2 %>%
  filter(Pk > 5 & WS > 50 & WS < 75) %>%
  summarize(med = median(WS)),
draft2 %>%
  filter(Pk > 5 & WS > 25 & WS < 50) %>%
  summarize(med = median(WS)),
draft2 %>%
  filter(Pk > 5 & WS < 25) %>%
  summarize(med = median(WS))) -> vals2
print(vals2)
## $med
## [1] 107.25
##
## $med
## [1] 83
##
## $med
## [1] 60.6
##
## $med
## [1] 35
##
## $med
## [1] 5
sum(as.numeric(probs2) * as.numeric(vals2))
## [1] 21.21452
```

Next, one last perspective that further supports our hypothesis: we'll generate what's called a hierarchical clustering algorithm and then create a plot called a dendrogram to visualize the results.

3.9 *Hierarchical clustering*

Hierarchical clustering is just one type of clustering algorithm (we'll demonstrate another clustering method in a subsequent chapter) that groups, or clusters, data points based on their similarities or dissimilarities. Hierarchical clustering is an unsupervised learning method that begins by assigning each observation, or data point, to its own cluster; the algorithm then churns and churns, reducing the number of clusters through each iteration, until we're left with just one cluster. (It's considered unsupervised because we're not attempting to predict the value of a response variable, but instead find structure within a data set.) We get the final results by plotting a dendrogram, which more or less resembles an upside-down tree, but which, more importantly, represents the hierarchy of clusters.

No doubt, the most common use case for clustering—hierarchical clustering included, of course—is in marketing. Marketing organizations typically segment their customers based on income, prior purchases, and demographic data, and then build tailored marketing campaigns that best fit each segment or cluster, thereby generating higher response rates than they would otherwise. Overall, hierarchical clustering is a powerful, yet moderately difficult, technique for discovering patterns and relationships within a data set where there is no shortage of use cases, not just in the marketing space but also in the biological and social sciences, for example. Hierarchical clustering doesn't require us to determine in advance an optimal number of clusters, unlike k-means, which will be demonstrated in chapter 11. In addition, the results are relatively easy to interpret. However, hierarchical clustering may bog down on large data sets, so be aware.

We're going to build our hierarchical clustering algorithm around just two of the draft2 variables: Pk and WS. So we start by calling the dplyr select() function to subset draft2 on those two variables and, in the process, create a new object called draft_clust:

```
draft2 %>%
  select(Pk, WS) -> draft_clust
```

Then, we pipe draft_clust to the group_by() and summarize() functions to compute the average, or mean, career win shares for every value, 1–30, in the variable Pk. Our results are then cast into a 30 × 2 tibble called draft_clust_final. Subsequent calls to the head() and tail() functions return the first three and last three observations, respectively:

```
draft_clust %>%
  group_by(Pk) %>%
  summarize(ws = mean(WS)) -> draft_clust_final

head(draft_clust_final, n = 3)
## # A tibble: 3 × 2
##      Pk     ws
##   <int>  <dbl>
## 1     1   69.6
```

```
## 2        2  51.5
## 3        3  66.9

tail(draft_clust_final, n = 3)
## # A tibble: 3 × 2
##      Pk     ws
##   <int>  <dbl>
## 1    28   25.6
## 2    29   8.12
## 3    30   19.7
```

This is where matters get a little more complicated. Our next step is to compute and print what's called a distance matrix by successively calling the base R `dist()` and `print()` functions. The `dist()` function takes two arguments: the data source and the preferred distance measure. The preferred distance measure, sometimes called the pairwise dissimilarity measure, requires some explanation.

With respect to hierarchical clustering algorithms, by far the most common method of computing the distance between two points is the Euclidean distance. Take a look at two of the first three observations in `draft_clust_final`: where the variable `Pk` equals `1`, the variable `ws` equals `69.6`; and where `Pk` equals `3`, `ws` equals `66.9`. Thus, the difference in average win shares between players selected first overall versus players selected third equals 2.7, or the difference between 69.6 and 66.9.

But that's *not* the Euclidean distance between these points. To compute the (approximate) Euclidean distance, the data points must be plotted as coordinates in a two-dimensional space, where each observation has an x-coordinate and a y-coordinate. The Euclidean distance between two points (x1, y1) and (x2, y2) is computed by doing the following:

- Squaring the differences between x2 and x1 and again between y2 and y1
- Adding the two differences together
- Computing the square root of the sum

Thus, the approximate Euclidean distance between two of the first three observations in `draft_clust_final` equals `3.36`, where x2 and x1 equal the `Pk` values `1` and `3`, respectively, and y2 and y1 equal the `ws` values `69.6` and `66.9`, respectively:

```
euclidean_distance <- sqrt((1 - 3)^2 + (69.6 - 66.9)^2)
euclidean_distance
## [1] 3.36006
```

This is a fairly short distance. Let's swap out the first `draft_clust_final` observation in favor of the second and compute the Euclidean distance between it and the third observation:

```
euclidean_distance <- sqrt((2 - 3)^2 + (51.5 - 66.9)^2)
euclidean_distance
## [1] 15.43243
```

This is still a short distance, but, obviously, the first and third draft_clust_final observations are more similar to one another than the second and third observations.

Now, we can call dist() and print(). Note that in consideration of space, only the first 30 rows of the distance matrix are displayed; the total output would otherwise take up approximately two additional pages:

```
distance_matrix <- dist(draft_clust_final, method = "euclidean")
print(distance_matrix)
##              1          2          3          4          5          6          7
## 2   18.177527
## 3    3.384213  15.452391
## 4   10.105568   8.732125   6.991881
## 5   19.661193   3.195309  16.640625   9.651943
## 6   44.660770  26.533241  41.757903  34.787539  25.149889
## 7   27.297562   9.844308  24.232416  17.242981   7.646202  17.778147
## 8   44.671852  26.654097  41.690911  34.701310  25.050287   2.016829  17.518564
## 9   30.536550  13.309485  27.404883  20.440949  10.974899  15.208817   3.473557
## 10  38.944218  21.299474  35.850043  28.870359  19.298953   7.623654  11.652794
## 11  53.777929  35.838472  50.744577  43.753584  34.121666   9.827085  26.513470
## 12  50.932042  33.125465  47.853944  40.870606  31.273478   8.038812  23.634932
## 13  53.366656  35.592450  50.274575  43.295756  33.712943  10.347193  26.069847
## 14  53.144528  35.471459  50.024394  43.057339  33.511168  10.729515  25.865228
## 15  54.209011  36.606125  51.069850  44.113472  34.596740  12.034953  26.954547
## 16  56.102438  38.542549  52.950627  46.002657  36.506658  13.917701  28.868753
## 17  50.217129  33.050000  47.003371  40.114866  30.785102  11.461605  23.232324
## 18  41.866784  25.698484  38.566577  31.851721  23.029983  13.470501  16.008026
## 19  49.573341  32.790877  46.311679  39.499008  30.360560  13.125399  22.947627
## 20  57.849197  40.688083  54.622780  47.750394  38.437639  17.357062  30.879768
## 21  46.428547  30.414840  43.107875  36.456309  27.731255  15.203631  20.716489
## 22  60.004701  42.994925  56.754827  49.918269  40.682202  19.898465  33.165892
## 23  54.745017  38.258599  51.446671  44.717227  35.743173  17.946100  28.429738
## 24  50.376903  34.572950  47.037943  40.458978  31.856316  18.005377  24.897311
## 25  54.678670  38.584458  51.351339  44.717674  35.955728  19.584752  28.814059
## 26  45.252607  30.967481  41.872426  35.664056  27.966782  21.079744  21.999730
## 27  59.204528  43.044182  55.876754  49.241564  40.446552  22.773144  33.248062
## 28  51.632161  36.670691  48.260112  41.911927  33.794343  22.003111  27.259208
## 29  67.587685  51.083493  64.278116  57.575848  48.603809  28.681148  41.242735
## 30  57.727872  42.344010  54.363814  47.929847  39.564406  24.629986  32.729058
```

Though we've truncated the results, the distance matrix nevertheless returns the Euclidean distance between every pair of observations in draft_clust_final. Thus, we can compare our previous computations with the returns from our call to the dist() function. The Euclidean distance between the first and third draft_clust_final observations is where (column) 1 and (row) 3 intersect. It equals 3.38, which is close enough to 3.36. Immediately to the right of that is the Euclidean distance between the second and third observations. It equals 15.45, which compares favorably to the 15.43 we previously computed.

We then call the base R hclust() function, which performs the hierarchical clustering. The algorithm starts by assigning each of the 30 draft_clust_final records to their own cluster; it then iterates 30 times, combining the most similar clusters each time based on the Euclidean distances, until every data point rolls up to the same cluster.

The `hclust()` function takes two arguments: our distance matrix, `distance_matrix`, is the first, and the preferred clustering method is the second. The *complete method* (aka *complete linkage method*) finds the maximum distance between points from different clusters to determine how close, or maybe not so close, a pair of clusters are to one another. R supports other methods, but this is by far the most common:

```
hc <- hclust(distance_matrix, method = "complete")
```

Now that we have our hierarchical clustering object, we can go about visualizing the results by calling the base R `plot()` function. We get a dendrogram, or a tree-like diagram, that displays the merging of clusters at different levels of similarity (see figure 3.7):

- The `as.dendrogram()` function, also from base R, is optional; however, we get a sharper visualization by adding it rather than just calling the `plot()` function.
- The `cex` argument is a number indicating how text and symbols should be scaled relative to the default; when set to `0.6`, we're telling R to print labels at 60% of their default size.
- The `hang` argument adjusts the height of the dendrogram leaves, or the endpoints of our upside-down tree; when set to `-1`, we're telling R to align or justify them along the width of the x-axis.
- The base R `rect.hclust()` function is also optional; it draws a *k* number of transparent boxes on top of the dendrogram to further delineate clusters, or segments. Considering our prior analysis centered on picks 1 through 5 versus every other first-round selection, it only makes sense to therefore set *k* equal to `2` and then await the results.
- The built-in `par()` function is used to set graphical parameters for base R plots. Here, we're merely instructing R to draw a dark sea-green background behind our dendrogram:

```
bg = par(bg = "darkseagreen1")
plot(as.dendrogram(hc, cex = 0.6, hang = -1),
     main = "Cluster Dendrogram:\nWin Shares by First-Round Selection",
     xlab = "First-Round Selection Number\n2000-2009 NBA Drafts",
     ylab = "Height (aka Euclidian Distance)")
rect.hclust(hc, k = 2)
```

It turns out, not surprisingly, that R draws one segment around first-round selections 1 through 5 and another segment around the remaining selection numbers. Otherwise, here's how to interpret our dendrogram:

- Each "leaf" at the very bottom of the dendrogram represents a separate observation from `draft_clust_final`.
- As we move up the dendrogram, observations that are similar to one another are fused to form a branch. Where our x-axis equals 1 and 3, for instance—or, put differently, where the `draft_clust_final` variable `Pk` equals `1` and `3`—those observations come together where the y-axis, or the Euclidean distance, equals 3.38.

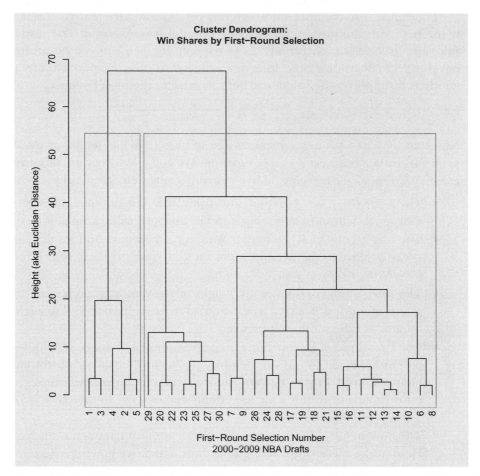

Figure 3.7   A dendrogram that displays hierarchical clusters based on win shares and pick number

- The closer observations are to one another, the more alike they are; conversely, the farther apart, the more dissimilar they are.
- The height of the branch connecting selection numbers 1 through 5 equals 19.66 because we chose a clustering method that computes the maximum distance separating any pair of "like" components. Take yet another look at our distance matrix—the maximum Euclidean distance across first-round picks 1 through 5 is between picks 1 and 5.
- Likewise, the height of the branch connecting picks 1 through 5 and the other selection numbers equals 67.59; again, that's because the greatest Euclidean distance separating any selection number between 1 and 5 and any other selection number is between picks 1 and 29, which equals 67.59 (take one last look at the distance matrix to confirm).
- These results are entirely consistent with our expected value analysis as well as our previous findings.

In this chapter, we told the same story through four separate and incrementally advanced statistical techniques. Only a few potential superstars are available in any NBA draft, and under the current set of league rules, the only way any team can control their own destiny and possibly draft one of these potential superstars is to tank. This is to otherwise say that the data and the methods we applied against it in whole support the hypothesis we presented in the very beginning. In the next chapter, we'll introduce a method by which teams can best build up their rosters, which is not through the draft by tanking, but through the free agent market.

Summary

- We showed that there's a better way to load many packages at once instead of making successive calls to the `library()` function.
- There are many ways in R to create segmentations from your original data. We called the `mutate()` and `ifelse()` functions in this and the previous chapter and, later on, called `mutate()` in tandem with the `case_when()` function.
- We demonstrated several methods by which to perform segmentation analysis, using mathematical operations and sophisticated visualization techniques.
- For instance, we further demonstrated how to visualize means and medians with `ggplot2` bar charts to display variances and similarities between our segmentations.
- Knowing how to create and to interpret Sankey diagrams is a key advanced analytics technique with many use cases. We showed how to create a fairly complex Sankey diagram that contained six node groupings and 30 nodes overall.
- Expected value is yet another technique with lots of use cases—investment opportunities and outcomes, indefinite weather patterns, gambling, and so on. We showed just one of the ways by which you can compute expected values in R.
- We demonstrated how to develop a hierarchical clustering and how to visualize and interpret the results.
- Regardless of method, it's clear that not all first-round picks are created equal. There is clear and obvious separation between players drafted at or near the very top of any NBA draft and almost every other available player.
- Acquiring superstar talent is an absolute necessity for teams wanting to build a championship-caliber roster.
- Therefore, teams must possess one of the first few picks to have a reasonable chance of selecting a potential superstar that can ultimately lead them to a championship.
- Even with the lottery, about the only chance of selecting a superstar is by having a losing record during the prior season; better yet, teams should tank to ensure their record is worse than other teams.

Constrained optimization

How often have you been asked to do more with less? In other words, what you're really being asked is to make the most of a situation compromised by trying circumstances. Constrained optimization is the operations research and quantitative solution to that end. In this chapter, we'll demonstrate how to organize and execute a typical constrained optimization problem. To accomplish this goal, we have a fictional NBA team fixed on acquiring veteran players from the free agent market. Their objective is *not* to acquire the five best players available, but the five best players that meet their specific requirements and needs. Our hypothesis, therefore, is that constrained optimization can successfully isolate the best group of free agents this team should acquire without breaching any of the constraints established in advance.

4.1   *What is constrained optimization?*

Constrained optimization is a method or technique that seeks to minimize or maximize some function while subject to constraints that curb freedom of movement. One such method might minimize costs or the depletion of resources; another might maximize profit margins. Constraints are effectively boundaries that can't be breached while crunching numbers to maximize or minimize some defined function. There are many use cases for constrained optimization:

- A chief financial officer, reviewing a long list of capital projects to fund against severe budgetary and resource constraints, needs to approve a subset of these projects to maximize the top line and load balance the projects across different departments.
- A triathlete needs the following on the bike: tools and spare parts in case of a flat tire or mechanical failure; water and a power drink to stay hydrated; salt tablets to cure cramps; and some combination of energy chews, energy gels, and Snickers bars to stay fueled. Between one saddle bag, two water bottle cages, and the rear pockets of the jersey, the triathlete must decide beforehand how to best use those spaces.
- For our purposes, a general manager of an NBA team is evaluating several players in the free agent market.

Our fictional NBA team intends to rebuild its roster, not through the draft, but rather by acquiring veteran players on the free agent market:

- The team is assessing 24 free agents of which they intend to sign *exactly* 5 players. That's their first requirement or constraint (these terms are used interchangeably in this chapter).
- They want one player for each position: one point guard, one shooting guard, one center, one power forward, and one small forward. That's their second requirement.
- Player salary demands are known and fixed. The team is willing to spend no more than $90 million (M) in annual salaries between the five players they acquire. That's their third requirement. It doesn't matter how the $90 M is distributed; all that matters is the total sum.
- The average age of whatever five players they acquire must be equal to or less than 30. That's their fourth and final requirement. Individual ages don't matter; all that matters is that the mean must be equal to or less than 30.

The flip side of the equation is the function that should be minimized or, in our case, maximized. The team's assessment included annual win share projections for each of the 24 free agents based on actual win shares from prior seasons, career trajectory, age, and other factors. Our fictional NBA team wants to maximize win shares while obeying *all* the constraints itemized here. Let's get started.

4.2   *Loading packages*

We have four packages to load: `tidyverse` and `patchwork`, which we've loaded and used in prior chapters, and two new packages, as described here:

- The `lpSolve` package contains several functions for solving linear programming problems, including those that require constrained optimization.
- The `scales` package—part of the `ggplot2` package, which, of course, is part of the `tidyverse` universe of packages—contains functions for, among other things, transforming `ggplot2` axis labels. Even though the `scales` package ties back to `tidyverse`, R might throw an error when you call `scales` functions if the `scales` package hasn't first been loaded separately and independently from the `tidyverse` package.

WARNING   Notice that the `S` in the `lpSolve` package is capitalized. R is a case-sensitive programming language. Even "innocuous" misapplications of lower-case and uppercase will generate error messages—some of which will be straightforward and others not so much—and prevent your code from running.

Before we make four successive calls to the `library()` function to load these four pack-ages, let's first introduce the concept of adding comments to your code chunks. Even though comments are comingled with your code, they aren't code at all; in fact, they are completely ignored when you execute your R script. Commenting is the practice of adding readable descriptions to help ease the potential pain later on when fixes or other changes are in order, especially when those changes are then assigned to another programmer.

Unlike many other programming languages, R makes allowances for single-line comments only; multi-line comments are only possible by "merging" two or more single-line comments. To add a comment to a chunk of code, simply preface it with the pound (#) sign:

```
# single line comment example: lpSolve is for constrained optimization
library(lpSolve)

# multi-line example: tidyverse includes dplyr and tidyr
# mult-line example continued: tidyverse also includes ggplot2
# mult-line example continued: tidyverse also includes readr
library(tidyverse)

# scales package is part of tidyverse, but it's best to load
# this as a standalone package
library(scales)

# we use the patchwork package to bundle multiple plots into one object
library(patchwork)
```

We'll import our data set next and further demonstrate the use of comments.

4.3   Importing data

The `readr read_csv()` function is called to import our data set, a Microsoft Excel file previously saved with a .csv extension. Through the assignment operator, we label our data set as free_agents.

The free_agents data set contained (when the data set was created) real-life soon-to-be free agents scraped from a website called Sportrac that were then joined with illustrative annual salary and win share projections based on historical data gathered from www.basketball-reference.com. An NBA player becomes a free agent once their contract expires; at that point, free agents are free to negotiate and sign a new contract with any team, including the team they most recently played for.

Note that we've added one comment, but this time, at the end of a line of code rather than in a separate line. R will execute the following code chunk until it sees the # sign; it will then ignore everything on the same line that comes after it:

```
free_agents <- read_csv("free_agents.csv") # saved in default directory
```

Next, we'll go about learning the basics of the data we just imported and then visualizing the same to acquire deeper insights.

4.4   Knowing the data

R provides several functions to get a quick, yet good, basic understanding of a data set. One is the base R `dim()` function, which returns the row and column counts:

```
dim(free_agents)
## [1] 24   7
```

The row count is provided first, followed by the column count.

Another is the `glimpse()` function from the `dplyr` package. The function also returns the dimension of a data set but with a truncated view of the data that has been rotated 90 degrees:

```
glimpse(free_agents)
## Rows: 24
## Columns: 7
## $ player        <chr> "Chris Paul", "Kawhi Leonard", "Blake Griff…
## $ current_team  <chr> "PHX", "LAC", "DET", "DAL", "DEN", "LAL", "…
## $ age           <dbl> 37, 31, 33, 29, 28, 28, 27, 36, 31, 29, 30,…
## $ position1     <chr> "PG", "SF", "PF", "SG", "SG", "PF", "SG", "…
## $ position2     <chr> "PG1", "SF1", "PF1", "SG1", "SG2", "PF2", "…
## $ annual_salary <dbl> 32000000, 37000000, 35000000, 11000000, 225…
## $ win_shares    <dbl> 6.9, 9.4, 5.2, 3.0, 3.7, 4.2, 3.8, 2.3, 4.7…
```

There is, by the way, a base R equivalent to `glimpse()`: the `str()` function. The `glimpse()` function is "cleaner" than `str()` and therefore the first choice between the two, but both functions return the same information in somewhat similar formats:

```
str(free_agents)
## 'data.frame':    24 obs. of  7 variables:
## $ player       : chr [1:24] "Chris Paul" "Kawhi Leonard" ...
## $ current_team : chr [1:24] "PHX" "LAC" "DET" "DAL" ...
## $ age          : num [1:24] 37 31 33 29 28 28 27 36 31 29 ...
## $ position1    : chr [1:24] "PG" "SF" "PF" "SG" ...
## $ position2    : chr [1:24] "PG1" "SF1" "PF1" "SG1" ...
## $ annual_salary: num [1:24] 32000000 37000000 35000000 11000000 ...
## $ win_shares   : num [1:24] 6.9 9.4 5.2 3 3.7 4.2 3.8 2.3 4.7 2.1 ...
```

The variables position1 and position2 should be factors rather than character strings (chr), so we then call the base R as.factor() function twice to convert both variables from one type or class to the other:

```
free_agents$position1 <- as.factor(free_agents$position1)
free_agents$position2 <- as.factor(free_agents$position2)
```

Let's run the base R levels() function to return the unique attributes of both variables. You must run the levels() function *after* converting variables to factors and not beforehand:

```
levels(free_agents$position1)
## [1] "C"   "PF" "PG" "SF" "SG"
levels(free_agents$position2)
## [1] "C1"  "C2"  "C3"  "C4"  "PF1" "PF2" "PF3" "PF4" "PF5" "PF6"
## [11] "PG1" "PG2" "PG3" "PG4" "PG5" "PG6" "SF1" "SF2" "SF3" "SF4"
## [21] "SF5" "SG1" "SG2" "SG3"
```

The variable position1 contains five levels, one for each position, which, of course, is what we would want or expect. Therefore, we've at least confirmed there are no typographical errors or other anomalies with position1. The variable position2, meanwhile, contains 24 levels, equaling the free_agents data set record count, which is a good thing.

Even the smallest of errors with either of these variables would compromise our constrained optimization problem, which is why it was worth our while to check the integrity of both variables.

If you don't care for glimpse() or str(), the head() and tail() functions are good alternatives; by default, head() returns the first six records, and tail() returns the last six. The following two lines of code return the first three and last three observations from free_agents:

```
head(free_agents, n = 3)
##   player        current_team  age position1 position2
##   <chr>         <chr>         <dbl> <fct>    <fct>
## 1 Chris Paul    PHX            37 PG        PG1
## 2 Kawhi Leonard LAC            31 SF        SF1
## 3 Blake Griffin DET            33 PF        PF1
##   annual_salary win_shares
##         <dbl>        <dbl>
```

```
## 1       32000000        6.9
## 2       37000000        9.4
## 3       35000000        5.2

tail(free_agents, n = 3)
##    player            current_team    age position1 position2
##    <chr>             <chr>          <dbl> <fct>     <fct>
## 1 Robert Covington  POR               31 PF        PF6
## 2 Serge Ibaka       LAC               33 C         C3
## 3 Aron Baynes       TOR               35 C         C4
##    annual_salary win_shares
##            <dbl>      <dbl>
## 1      13500000        3.1
## 2      12000000        2.9
## 3       7000000        2.5
```

Finally, the `summary()` function is a base R generic function that returns basic statistics for whatever data object is passed as an argument. It's mostly used to return the results of various model fitting functions (discussed in chapter 5); here, it returns basic statistics and other data for every variable in the free_agents data set. Once more, `summary()` returns boxplot-like measures for continuous variables and level counts for factor variables:

```
summary(free_agents)
##     player             current_team            age           position1
## Length:24          Length:24            Min.   :23.00    C :4
## Class :character   Class :character     1st Qu.:28.00    PF:6
## Mode  :character   Mode  :character     Median :30.50    PG:6
##                                         Mean   :30.42    SF:5
##                                         3rd Qu.:33.00    SG:3
##                                         Max.   :37.00
## C1      : 1    Min.   : 6500000   Min.   :1.700
## C2      : 1    1st Qu.:13500000   1st Qu.:2.975
## C3      : 1    Median :14750000   Median :3.800
## C4      : 1    Mean   :17312500   Mean   :3.992
## PF1     : 1    3rd Qu.:18750000   3rd Qu.:4.700
## PF2     : 1    Max.   :37000000   Max.   :9.400
## (Other):18
```

The `summary()` function returns some useful and interesting information, but even for short data sets such as free_agents, it's always best to also visualize the data to better understand it.

But first, one more housecleaning item is required: the `options()` function from base R, with the argument `scipen = 999`, tells R to not print any results in scientific notation (i.e., e+10), but instead to return them, without exception, in full digit numerals. We're essentially instructing R to return results in fixed notation unless those results are greater than scipen digits long. So any large scipen number will suffice, but 999 is the number most frequently used:

```
options(scipen = 999)
```

This setting can be reverted by again calling the `options()` function and adding the argument `scipen = 000`; this time, any small number will work, but 000 is preferred. The `options()` function is not universal, by the way—it applies only to the script to which it has been called.

4.5   *Visualizing the data*

Before we set up and run our constrained optimization problem, let's first get a better read on our data. We'll do just that by first creating a series of density plots covering the variables `annual_salary`, `win_shares`, and `age`; a sequence of boxplots over these same variables, but broken down by the variable `position1`; a single correlation plot between the variables `annual_salary` and `win_shares`; and, finally, a bar chart that displays the player counts by the variable `position1`.

4.5.1   *Density plots*

The first graphical representation of the free_agents data set is a set of density plots around the continuous variables salary (`annual_salary`), win shares (`win_shares`), and age (`age`). A density plot is essentially a smoothed version of a histogram, and like histograms, density plots display the distribution of continuous or numeric data. (Afterward, we'll create boxplots, a correlation plot, and a bar chart.)

The most significant advantage that density plots have over histograms is that density plots more accurately reflect the real distribution shape because there's no programmer option to fiddle with bin counts that can otherwise influence the appearance. But while the x-axis represents the range of values, just as it does for histograms, the y-axis represents a less-than-intuitive density function, or probability density function, rather than frequencies. However, at the end of the day, the probability density function actually correlates well with frequencies; in other words, the probability density function equals a low number when frequencies are low and, conversely, equals a high number (or at least a higher number) when frequencies are higher. Regardless, density plots are extremely useful for visualizing the underlying distribution of a continuous variable, identifying peaks or modes, and assessing skewness or symmetry.

Here's a walkthrough of our first `ggplot2` density plot out of three:

- The `ggplot()` function is always called first to initialize any `ggplot2` object.
- The `geom_density()` function computes the smoothed estimates and draws the plot. The `alpha` argument passed to the `geom_density()` makes the fill transparent so that the `ggplot2` grid lines remain visible throughout. For this effect to take, `alpha` should equal a number close to 0, such as .3.
- The `geom_vline()` function is called twice to draw a pair of vertical dashed lines, one that represents the population mean and the other that represents the population median. The thickness of the lines can be adjusted by modifying the `size` argument up or down; the default is 1, so any adjustments are therefore relative to the `ggplot2` default.

- The `scale_x_continuous()` function, in tandem with the `scales` package, adds commas to the x-axis tick marks, so that 10000000 is converted to a more readable 10,000,000.
- The `annotate()` function adds vertical text at the provided x- and y-coordinates:

```
p1 <- ggplot(free_agents, aes(x = annual_salary)) +
  geom_density(alpha = .3, fill = "salmon") +
  geom_vline(aes(xintercept = mean(annual_salary, na.rm = TRUE)),
          color = "red", linetype = "longdash", size = .8) +
  geom_vline(aes(xintercept = median(annual_salary, na.rm = TRUE)),
          color = "blue", linetype = "longdash", size = .8) +
  labs(title = "Annual Salary Distribution",
      subtitle = "Shortlisted Free Agents",
      x = "Annual Salary",
      y = "Density",
      caption = "Salary data is illustrative only") +
  scale_x_continuous(labels = comma) +
  theme(plot.title = element_text(face = "bold")) +
  annotate("text", x = 18000000,
          y = .000000025, label = "Mean", color = "black",
          size = 4, fontface = "bold", angle = 90) +
  annotate("text", x = 14000000,
          y = .000000025, label = "Median", color = "black",
          size = 4, fontface = "bold", angle = 90)
```

The second and third density plots—p2 and p3, respectively—are just like p1, minus a few modifications:

- The variable `annual_salary` has been swapped out in favor of the variables `win_shares` and `age`.
- Label changes have been incorporated.
- The `scale_x_continuous()` function and the `scales` package are no longer needed—after all, plots p2 and p3 don't have labels that require converting—and have therefore been removed:

```
p2 <- ggplot(free_agents, aes(x = win_shares)) +
  geom_density(alpha = .3, fill = "salmon") +
  geom_vline(aes(xintercept = mean(win_shares, na.rm = TRUE)),
          color = "red", linetype = "longdash", size = .8) +
  geom_vline(aes(xintercept = median(win_shares, na.rm = TRUE)),
          color = "blue", linetype = "longdash", size = .8) +
  labs(title = "Projected Annual Win Shares Distribution",
      subtitle = "Shortlisted Free Agents",
      x = "Win Shares", y = "Density",
      caption = "Win Shares data is illustrative only") +
  theme(plot.title = element_text(face = "bold")) +
  annotate("text", x = 4.1,
          y = .1, label = "Mean", color = "black",
          size = 4, fontface = "bold", angle = 90) +
  annotate("text", x = 3.7,
          y = .1, label = "Median", color = "black",
```

```
                  size = 4, fontface = "bold", angle = 90)

p3 <- ggplot(free_agents, aes(x = age)) +
  geom_density(alpha = .3, fill = "salmon") +
  geom_vline(aes(xintercept = mean(age, na.rm = TRUE)),
            color = "red", linetype = "longdash", size = .8) +
  geom_vline(aes(xintercept = median(age, na.rm = TRUE)),
            color = "blue", linetype = "longdash", size = .8) +
  labs(title = "Age Distribution", subtitle = "Shortlisted Free Agents",
      x = "Age", y = "Density",
      caption = "Player ages are real; source: Spotrac") +
  theme(plot.title = element_text(face = "bold")) +
  annotate("text", x = 30.2,
          y = .04, label = "Mean", color = "black",
          size = 4, fontface = "bold", angle = 90) +
  annotate("text", x = 30.7,
          y = .04, label = "Median", color = "black",
          size = 4, fontface = "bold", angle = 90)
```

The `plot_layout()` function from the `patchwork` package bundles the three density plots into one object (see figure 4.1), where plots `p1` and `p2` occupy the top row, and plot `p3`, assuming the same width as `p1` plus `p2`, is displayed on the bottom row:

```
p1 + p2 - p3 + plot_layout(ncol = 1)
```

Our first three visualizations tell us the following about the data:

- *Annual salaries*—These figures, which represent the year-over-year base salary expectations of our 24 free agents, are right skewed, or positively skewed. There are two ways of deducing this: (1) most values are obviously clustered around the left tail of the distribution while the right tail is longer, and (2) the mean is therefore greater than the median.

- *Win shares*—The same can be said for the annual win shares figures, which represent the projected number of accrued win shares per player per season. Given the means and medians of `annual_salaries` and `win_shares`, we can reasonably conclude that approximately $15 M in salary is the equivalent of about 3.5 to 4 win shares.

- *Age*—Unlike the variables `annual_salaries` and `win_shares`, the variable `age` is normally distributed; both the mean and the median equal approximately 30.5.

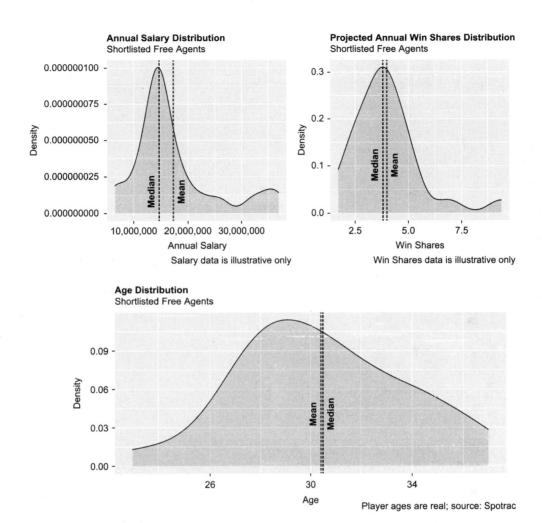

Figure 4.1 Density plots visualize the distribution of numeric data. Density plots are sometimes drawn in lieu of histograms or boxplots.

4.5.2 *Boxplots*

Our next series of visualizations again displays the distributions of these same variables, but this time through boxplots and also broken down by each level in variable position1. These boxplots are similar to the boxplots we created in previous chapters, but note that we're now using the scales package to transform our y-axis tick marks rather than those along the x-axis. Therefore, we call the scale_y_continuous() function instead of scale_x_continuous():

```
p4 <- ggplot(free_agents, aes(x = position1, y = annual_salary)) +
  geom_boxplot(color = "sienna4", fill = "sienna1" ) +
  labs(title = "Annual Salary Distribution by Position",
```

```
        subtitle = "Shortlisted Free Agents",
        x = "Position",
        y = "Annual Salary",
        caption = "Salary data is illustrative only") +
   scale_y_continuous(labels = comma) +
   stat_summary(fun = mean, geom = "point",
                shape = 20, size = 8, color = "white", fill = "white") +
   theme(plot.title = element_text(face = "bold"))

p5 <- ggplot(free_agents, aes(x = position1, y = win_shares)) +
   geom_boxplot(color = "steelblue4", fill = "steelblue1" ) +
   labs(title = "Annual Win Shares Distribution by Position",
        subtitle = "Shortlisted Free Agents",
        x = "Position",
        y = "Annual Win Shares",
        caption = "Win Share data is illustrative") +
   stat_summary(fun = mean, geom = "point",
                shape = 20, size = 8, color = "white", fill = "white") +
   theme(plot.title = element_text(face = "bold"))

p6 <- ggplot(free_agents, aes(x = position1, y = age)) +
   geom_boxplot(color = "gold4", fill = "gold1" ) +
   labs(title = "Age Distribution by Position",
        subtitle = "Shortlisted Free Agents",
        x = "Position",
        y = "Age",
        caption = "Player ages are real; source: Spotrac") +
   stat_summary(fun = mean, geom = "point",
                shape = 20, size = 8, color = "white", fill = "white") +
   theme(plot.title = element_text(face = "bold"))
```

We then make another call to the `plot_layout()` function, which pulls the three visualizations from memory and displays them as a single 3 × 1 graphical object (see figure 4.2):

```
p4 + p5 + p6 + plot_layout(ncol = 1)
```

Following are a few notes about our boxplots:

- It's no surprise that, given the variance in `annual_salary` and the low number of records in the free_agents data set, especially for each of the five levels in `position1`, the distributions are quite different from one position to the next.
- While there is less dispersion in the `win_shares` distributions, the position-by-position view appears to match the same for `annual_salary`.
- While we previously discovered that `age` is normally distributed, its distribution is nevertheless quite different when viewed by position. For instance, most centers and point guards are above the age of 30, whereas most small forwards and shooting guards are below the age of 30.

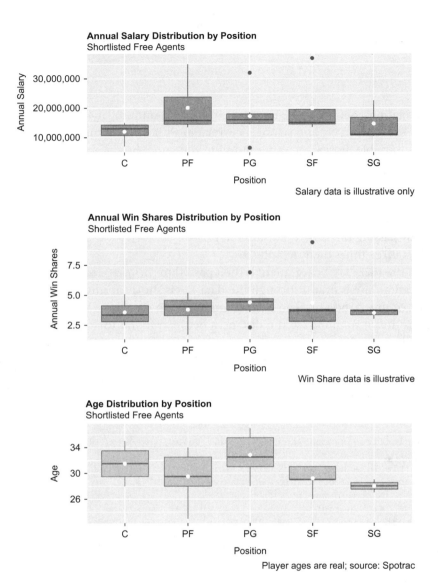

Figure 4.2   Another series of views into the distribution of numeric data

4.5.3   *Correlation plot*

In chapter 2, we demonstrated how to compute correlation coefficients between multiple continuous variables at once and then display the same in a heat map or correlation matrix. Here, we merely want to compute the correlation coefficient between just two variables and then add the result as a subtitle to a correlation plot, which visualizes the same by one variable running along the x-axis and the other variable running along the y-axis. That being said, we pass variables `annual_salary` and `win_shares` to the base R `cor()` function to compute the correlation coefficient between them:

```
cor(free_agents$annual_salary, free_agents$win_shares)
## [1] 0.7571507
```

The correlation coefficient, being equal to 0.76 (rounded), means that salaries and win shares are positively and strongly correlated with one another, which means that when one variable moves, the other moves in the same direction.

Our next chunk of code draws a `ggplot2` correlation plot, with `annual_salary` as the x-axis variable and `win_shares` as the y-axis variable (see figure 4.3). Whereas `geom_density()` is called to draw a `ggplot2` density plot and `geom_boxplot()` is called to draw a `ggplot2` boxplot, `geom_point()` tells R to draw a correlation plot, sometimes called a scatterplot. By passing the `size = 3` argument to `geom_point()`, we're instructing R to draw the points three times their default size.

When the `method = lm` argument is then passed to the `geom_smooth()` function, a linear regression line is drawn through the data (`lm` is short for linear model). A regression line, or line of best fit, is an annotation meant to visualize a trend in a data series; the line is drawn to minimize the distances between it and the data. The steeper the line, the stronger the correlation.

The `geom_smooth()` function automatically draws a 95% confidence interval around the regression line, unless instructed otherwise. The confidence interval can, in fact, be adjusted up or down or removed altogether. We've chosen to remove it by also passing the `se = FALSE` argument (se is short for standard error):

```
p7 <- ggplot(free_agents, aes(x = annual_salary, y = win_shares)) +
  geom_point(size = 3) +
  labs(title = "Annual Salaries vs. Win Shares",
       subtitle = "correlation coefficient = 0.76",
       x = "Annual Salaries",
       y = "Win Shares") +
  geom_smooth(method = lm, se = FALSE) +
  scale_x_continuous(label = scales::comma) +
  theme(plot.title = element_text(face = "bold"))
print(p7)
```

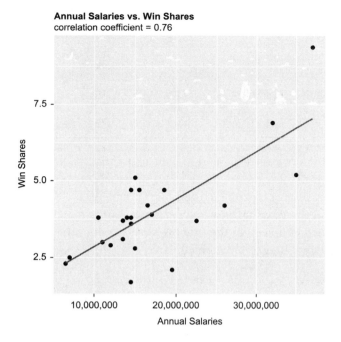

Figure 4.3   Salaries and win shares are positively and highly correlated with one another. The line is a regression line of best fit that minimizes the distances between it and the data.

4.5.4   *Bar chart*

In our next chunk of code, we pass the free_agents data set via the pipe operator to the dplyr group_by() and tally() functions. Together, group_by() and tally() count, or tally, the number of free_agents observations by each level, or factor, in variable position1. The results are then thrown into a tibble called tibble1:

```
free_agents %>%
  group_by(position1) %>%
  tally() -> tibble1
print(tibble1)
## # A tibble: 5 × 2
##   position1     n
##   <fct>      <int>
## 1 C              4
## 2 PF             6
## 3 PG             6
## 4 SF             5
## 5 SG             3
```

In this second chunk of code, we pass free_agents to the dplyr summarize() function to compute the means for annual_salary, win_shares, and age for each level in variable position1. The results are cast into a tibble called tibble2:

```
free_agents %>%
  group_by(position1) %>%
  summarize(meanSalary = mean(annual_salary),
```

```
            meanWinShares = mean(win_shares),
            meanAge = mean(age)) -> tibble2
print(tibble2)
## # A tibble: 5 × 4
##   position1 meanSalary meanWinShares meanAge
##   <fct>          <dbl>         <dbl>   <dbl>
## 1 C           12000000          3.58    31.5
## 2 PF          20083333.         3.8     29.5
## 3 PG          17250000          4.4     32.8
## 4 SF          19900000          4.36    29.2
## 5 SG          14666667.         3.5     28
```

In this third and final chunk of code, we make a call to the dplyr left_join() function to join the two tibbles we just created on their like variable position1. A left join is
an operation by which all the rows in one object are merged or matched with corresponding values in the second object. In the process, we also get every unique column
returned. The result is yet another tibble, tibble3:

```
left_join(tibble1, tibble2, by = "position1") -> tibble3
print(tibble3)
## A tibble: 5 × 5
## position1      n meanSalary meanWinShares meanAge
##   <fct>    <int>      <dbl>         <dbl>   <dbl>
## 1 C            4   12000000          3.58    31.5
## 2 PF           6   20083333.         3.8     29.5
## 3 PG           6   17250000          4.4     32.8
## 4 SF           5   19900000          4.36    29.2
## 5 SG           3   14666667.         3.5     28
```

We now have a data source for our next and final visualization, a ggplot2 bar chart:

- The geom_text() function is called to affix the counts for each level of position1
  atop the bars. The vjust argument moves or adjusts the location of ggplot2 plot
  elements such as labels, titles, and subtitles vertically; there is also an hjust argument, not called here, that adjusts similar plot elements horizontally. You'll
  likely want or need to experiment with different settings on a per-plot basis to
  get the best aesthetics.
- The geom_label() function is called three times to affix truncated values representing the means for annual_salaries, win_shares, and age *inside* the bars.
- The y-axis is extended, or otherwise fixed on minimum and maximum values,
  by calling the ylim() function to make all of this fit and not compromise the
  aesthetics.

These additional features enhance the aesthetics of our bar chart (see figure 4.4), converting it from a very ordinary graphical representation of the data to an object that
(hopefully) demands more of our attention. More importantly, these features provide
just enough information that wouldn't otherwise be included. We want to inform our
audience, not overwhelm them. Following is the code for our ggplot2 bar chart:

```
p8 <- ggplot(tibble3, aes(x = position1, y = n)) +
  geom_bar(stat = "identity", width = .8,
           fill = "darkorchid1", color = "darkorchid4") +
  labs(title = "Position Counts",
       subtitle = "Shortlisted Free Agents",
       x = "Position",
       y = "Counts",
       caption = "Salary mean ($M)\nWin Shares mean\nAge mean") +
  geom_text(aes(label = n, vjust = -0.3)) +
  geom_label(aes(label = trunc(meanSalary*.000001), vjust = 1.2)) +
  geom_label(aes(label = trunc(meanWinShares), vjust = 2.4)) +
  geom_label(aes(label = trunc(meanAge), vjust = 3.6)) +
  ylim(0, 8) +
  theme(plot.title = element_text(face = "bold"))
print(p8)
```

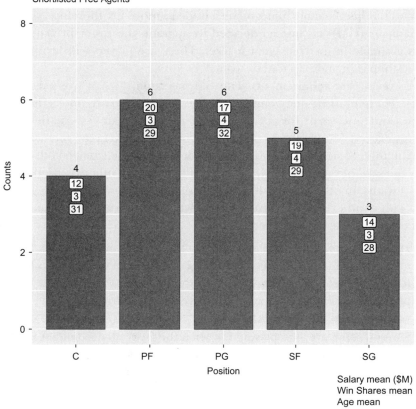

Figure 4.4 Counts of shortlisted free agents by position. Note the legend in the lower-right corner that explains the white-boxed labels inside the bars from top to bottom.

Our bar chart also includes a caption, positioned by default below the plot and to the right, that explains the three labels from top to bottom affixed to the inside of the bars. Aggregating the means across positions gives us a so-called mark on the wall: for $91 M (a slight constraint violation, but a violation nonetheless), our fictional NBA team can get 17 win shares from five players with an average age equal to 29.8.

The rest of this chapter is dedicated to organizing and executing a constrained optimization problem that, hopefully, gets us a better solution than our mark on the wall—without, of course, any constraint breaches. Regardless of where we ultimately land, constrained optimization takes out the guesswork and produces *the* optimal solution.

4.6   *Constrained optimization setup*

We're about to demonstrate how to design and develop a constrained optimization problem. The code is easily transferable to other use cases by merely swapping out the function to be maximized or minimized and changing out the constraints.

In the meantime, we have a fictional NBA team in need of a serious rebuilding effort. This team has recently failed in the draft, doesn't own a top pick for the next draft, and has been unable to negotiate a trade to move up; therefore, the team's general manager (GM) has instead decided to upgrade the roster by acquiring veteran players available in the free agent market. These are players with expiring contracts who can then sign and play for any team.

Let's revisit our requirements. The GM has room to sign five players (first constraint). There must be one point guard, one shooting guard, one center, one power forward, and one small forward (second constraint). Annual salaries, collectively, must not exceed $90 M (third constraint). Finally, the average age of these five players, at the time of signing, must be equal to or less than 30 (fourth constraint).

For the sake of this exercise, let's assume the team can otherwise sign whatever free agents it wants; in other words, there is no risk that any sought-after player will choose to sign with another team. The free_agents data set is therefore the team's short list of free agents, with the following variables:

- player—The full name of every player the team is evaluating, in firstname last-name format (e.g., Chris Paul); the free_agents data set is 24 rows long, so therefore we have 24 players in all. When the data was scraped from Spotrac, these players were, in fact, about to hit the free agent market.
- current_team—The abbreviated team name—for instance, PHX for Phoenix Suns—each player was playing for when the free_agents data set was created.
- age—The age of every player, in whole numbers, at the time free_agents was created.
- position1—The primary position played by each of the 24 players—C for center, PF for power forward, PG for point guard, SF for small forward, and SG for shooting guard.
- position2—The primary position combined with a one-digit integer starting at 1 and incrementing by one for each position as we move down the free_agents data set. For instance, Chris Paul happens to be the first point guard in our data set, so the variable position2 for Chris Paul equals PG1; Rajon Rondo is our second

point guard, so `position2` for Rondo equals `PG2`. Jonas Valančiūnas is our first center, so `position2` for Valančiūnas equals `C1`; the last of four centers is Aron Baynes, so `position2` for him equals `C4`. This variable will be required once we further set up and run our constrained optimization problem.

- `annual_salary`—The projected annual salary for each player. These figures are loosely based on prior salary information gathered from www.basketball-reference .com, but are otherwise illustrative.

- `win_shares`—The projected number of win shares to be accrued by each player per season. These figures tie back to actual win share totals from prior seasons grabbed from www.basketball-reference.com, but like variable `annual_salary`, these figures are illustrative. Our constrained optimization problem will *maximize win shares while obeying the hard constraints* previously mentioned.

Table 4.1 shows the team's short list of 24 players or free agents; the variables `current_team` and `position2` aren't included in this table. The players aren't listed in any particular order except for being grouped by position.

Table 4.1 List of available free agents

Player	Age	Position	Annual Salary	Win Shares
Chris Paul	37	PG	$32,000,000	6.9
Rajon Rondo	36	PG	$6,500,000	2.3
Ricky Rubio	31	PG	$18,500,000	4.7
Patrick Beverley	34	PG	$16,500,000	4.2
Marcus Smart	28	PG	$15,500,000	4.7
Cory Joseph	31	PG	$14,500,000	3.6
Josh Richardson	29	SG	$11,000,000	3.0
Gary Harris	28	SG	$22,500,000	3.7
Zach LaVine	27	SG	$10,500,000	3.8
Jonas Valančiūnas	30	C	$15,000,000	5.1
Jusuf Nurkić	28	C	$14,000,000	3.8
Serge Ibaka	33	C	$12,000,000	2.9
Aron Baynes	35	C	$7,000,000	2.5
Blake Griffin	33	PF	$35,000,000	5.2
Montrezl Harrell	28	PF	$26,000,000	4.2
Thaddeus Young	34	PF	$17,000,000	3.9
Marvin Bagley III	23	PF	$14,500,000	4.7
Taurean Prince	28	PF	$14,500,000	1.7

Table 4.1   List of available free agents *(continued)*

Player	Age	Position	Annual Salary	Win Shares
Robert Covington	31	PF	$13,500,000	3.1
Kawhi Leonard	31	SF	$37,000,000	9.4
Rodney Hood	29	SF	$19,500,000	2.1
Will Barton	31	SF	$14,500,000	3.8
Justise Winslow	26	SF	$15,000,000	2.8
TJ Warren	29	SF	$13,500,000	3.7

Though our problem scenario seems rather complex, you may be surprised at the simplicity of the solution that R and constrained optimization can provide. Let's turn to that solution between constructing the problem in section 4.7 and getting to the results in section 4.8.

4.7   *Constrained optimization construction*

Time to go about constructing our constrained optimization problem (note that these steps would be the same regardless of the use case). The first step in this process is to create a "copy" of the free_agents data set, called free_agents_sort, by calling the dplyr arrange() function, where the data is sorted by variable position2. The printed results are purposely limited to six observations, just for space considerations, by also calling the base R head() function:

```
head(free_agents_sort <- arrange(free_agents, position2))
##              player current_team age position1 position2 annual_salary
##     <chr>               <chr>       <dbl> <fct>     <fct>           <dbl>
## 1 Jonas Valanciunas      MEM   30        C        C1           15000000
## 2      Jusuf Nurkic      POR   28        C        C2           14000000
## 3       Serge Ibaka      LAC   33        C        C3           12000000
## 4       Aron Baynes      TOR   35        C        C4            7000000
## 5     Blake Griffin      DET   33       PF       PF1           35000000
## 6   Montrezl Harrell      LAL   28       PF       PF2           26000000
##    win_shares
##        <dbl>
## 1        5.1
## 2        3.8
## 3        2.9
## 4        2.5
## 5        5.2
## 6        4.2
```

Second, the free_agents_sort data set is subset to only include variables absolutely needed for our constrained optimization problem; the select() function from the dplyr package is called to reduce free_agents_sort to just the variables player, age, position2, annual_salary, and win_shares. The printed results are again limited by once more calling the head() function:

```
head(free_agents_sort <- select(free_agents_sort, player, age,
                                 position2, annual_salary, win_shares))
##               player age position2 annual_salary win_shares
##               <chr>       <dbl> <fct>         <dbl>      <dbl>
## 1 Jonas Valanciunas   30        C1      15000000        5.1
## 2      Jusuf Nurkic   28        C2      14000000        3.8
## 3       Serge Ibaka   33        C3      12000000        2.9
## 4       Aron Baynes   35        C4       7000000        2.5
## 5      Blake Griffin   33       PF1      35000000        5.2
## 6   Montrezl Harrell   28       PF2      26000000        4.2
```

Third, a constraint matrix is built, by which five vectors are created (note the $ operator separating the object and variable names), called centers, power_forwards, point_guards, small_forwards, and shooting_guards, and then appended to the free_agents_sort data set. We then use binary encoding to populate these vectors with ones and zeros, representing true and false, depending upon the corresponding value in position2.

To elaborate, each vector contains 24 elements, which, of course, matches the length of free_agents_sort. With respect to the vector centers, for instance, the top four values equal 1 because, after sorting our data, free agents that play the center position take up the top four records in free_agents_sort. The remaining values equal 0 because the other players in our data set play some position other than center. These results are subsequently printed in full:

```
free_agents_sort$centers = c(1,1,1,1,0,0,0,0,0,0,
                  0,0,0,0,0,0,0,0,0,0,0,0,0,0)
free_agents_sort$power_forwards = c(0,0,0,0,1,1,1,1,1,1,
                  0,0,0,0,0,0,0,0,0,0,0,0,0,0)
free_agents_sort$point_guards = c(0,0,0,0,0,0,0,0,0,0,0,
                  1,1,1,1,1,1,0,0,0,0,0,0,0,0)
free_agents_sort$small_forwards = c(0,0,0,0,0,0,0,0,0,0,0,
                  0,0,0,0,0,0,1,1,1,1,1,0,0,0)
free_agents_sort$shooting_guards = c(0,0,0,0,0,0,0,0,0,0,0,
                  0,0,0,0,0,0,0,0,0,0,0,1,1,1)
print(free_agents_sort)
##                  player age position2 annual_salary win_shares centers
## 1    Jonas Valanciunas   30        C1      15000000        5.1       1
## 2         Jusuf Nurkic   28        C2      14000000        3.8       1
## 3          Serge Ibaka   33        C3      12000000        2.9       1
## 4          Aron Baynes   35        C4       7000000        2.5       1
## 5        Blake Griffin   33       PF1      35000000        5.2       0
## 6     Montrezl Harrell   28       PF2      26000000        4.2       0
## 7       Thaddeus Young   34       PF3      17000000        3.9       0
## 8     Marvin Bagley III   23       PF4      14500000        4.7       0
## 9        Taurean Prince   28       PF5      14500000        1.7       0
## 10     Robert Covington   31       PF6      13500000        3.1       0
## 11           Chris Paul   37       PG1      32000000        6.9       0
## 12          Rajon Rondo   36       PG2       6500000        2.3       0
## 13          Ricky Rubio   31       PG3      18500000        4.7       0
```

```
## 14    Patrick Beverley    34       PG4       16500000          4.2          0
## 15      Marcus Smart      28       PG5       15500000          4.7          0
## 16       Cory Joseph      31       PG6       14500000          3.6          0
## 17    Kawhi Leonard       31       SF1       37000000          9.4          0
## 18       Rodney Hood      29       SF2       19500000          2.1          0
## 19       Will Barton      31       SF3       14500000          3.8          0
## 20    Justise Winslow     26       SF4       15000000          2.8          0
## 21        T.J. Warren     29       SF5       13500000          3.7          0
## 22    Josh Richardson     29       SG1       11000000          3.0          0
## 23       Gary Harris      28       SG2       22500000          3.7          0
## 24       Zach LaVine      27       SG3       10500000          3.8          0
##      power_forwards point_guards shooting_forwards shooting_guards
##           <dbl>         <dbl>           <dbl>             <dbl>
## 1           0             0               0                 0
## 2           0             0               0                 0
## 3           0             0               0                 0
## 4           0             0               0                 0
## 5           1             0               0                 0
## 6           1             0               0                 0
## 7           1             0               0                 0
## 8           1             0               0                 0
## 9           1             0               0                 0
## 10          1             0               0                 0
## 11          0             1               0                 0
## 12          0             1               0                 0
## 13          0             1               0                 0
## 14          0             1               0                 0
## 15          0             1               0                 0
## 16          0             1               0                 0
## 17          0             0               1                 0
## 18          0             0               1                 0
## 19          0             0               1                 0
## 20          0             0               1                 0
## 21          0             0               1                 0
## 22          0             0               0                 1
## 23          0             0               0                 1
## 24          0             0               0                 1
```

Fourth, we call the base R `rbind()` function (short for row-bind), which does more or less what the name suggests—it joins two or more vectors (or matrices or data sets), by rows, into a single object. Here, we call the `rbind()` function to combine several vectors into a new object called `constraint_matrix`, which has a dimension determined by variable `position2` as well as the hard constraints established at the beginning:

```
constraint_matrix <- as.matrix(rbind(free_agents_sort$centers,
                              free_agents_sort$centers,
                              free_agents_sort$power_forwards,
                              free_agents_sort$power_forwards,
                              free_agents_sort$point_guards,
                              free_agents_sort$point_guards,
                              free_agents_sort$small_forwards,
                              free_agents_sort$small_forwards,
                              free_agents_sort$shooting_guards,
```

```
                                   free_agents_sort$shooting_guards,
                                    t(rep(1, length = 24)),
                                   free_agents_sort$annual_salary,
                                   free_agents_sort$age))
```

Finally, we make a call to the base R `dimnames()` function to set the row and column names at once. We now have an object 13 rows long, in which each row represents a predetermined constraint, and 24 columns wide, in which each column ties back to the values from variable `position2`:

```
constraint_matrix <- as.matrix(rbind(free_agents_sort$centers,
                                     free_agents_sort$centers,
                                     free_agents_sort$power_forwards,
                                     free_agents_sort$power_forwards,
                                     free_agents_sort$point_guards,
                                     free_agents_sort$point_guards,
                                     free_agents_sort$small_forwards,
                                     free_agents_sort$small_forwards,
                                     free_agents_sort$shooting_guards,
                                     free_agents_sort$shooting_guards,
                                      t(rep(1, length = 24)),
                                     free_agents_sort$annual_salary,
                                     free_agents_sort$age))
dimnames(constraint_matrix) <-
  list(c("OneCenterMax",
         "OneCenterMin",
         "OnePowerForwardMax",
         "OnePowerForwardMin",
         "OnePointGuardMax",
         "OnePointGuardMin",
         "OneSmallForwardMax",
         "OneSmallForwardMin",
         "OneShootingGuardMax",
         "OneShootingGuardMin",
         "FivePlayerMax",
         "SalaryMax",
         "AgeMax"),
       free_agents_sort$position2)
print(constraint_matrix)
```

```
##                          C1        C2        C3        C4        PF1        PF2
## OneCenterMax              1         1         1         1         0         0
## OneCenterMin              1         1         1         1         0         0
## OnePowerForwardMax        0         0         0         0         1         1
## OnePowerForwardMin        0         0         0         0         1         1
## OnePointGuardMax          0         0         0         0         0         0
## OnePointGuardMin          0         0         0         0         0         0
## OneSmallForwardMax        0         0         0         0         0         0
## OneSmallForwardMin        0         0         0         0         0         0
## OneShootingGuardMax       0         0         0         0         0         0
## OneShootingGuardMin       0         0         0         0         0         0
## FivePlayerMax             1         1         1         1         1         1
## SalaryMax          15000000  14000000  12000000   7000000  35000000  26000000
## AgeMax                   30        28        33        35        33        28
##                         PF3       PF4       PF5       PF6       PG1        PG2
```

```
## OneCenterMax               0        0        0        0        0        0
## OneCenterMin               0        0        0        0        0        0
## OnePowerForwardMax         1        1        1        1        0        0
## OnePowerForwardMin         1        1        1        1        0        0
## OnePointGuardMax           0        0        0        0        1        1
## OnePointGuardMin           0        0        0        0        1        1
## OneSmallForwardMax         0        0        0        0        0        0
## OneSmallForwardMin         0        0        0        0        0        0
## OneShootingGuardMax        0        0        0        0        0        0
## OneShootingGuardMin        0        0        0        0        0        0
## FivePlayerMax              1        1        1        1        1        1
## SalaryMax           17000000 14500000 14500000 13500000 32000000  6500000
## AgeMax                    34       23       28       31       37       36
##                          PG3      PG4      PG5      PG6      SF1
## OneCenterMax               0        0        0        0        0
## OneCenterMin               0        0        0        0        0
## OnePowerForwardMax         0        0        0        0        0
## OnePowerForwardMin         0        0        0        0        0
## OnePointGuardMax           1        1        1        1        0
## OnePointGuardMin           1        1        1        1        0
## OneSmallForwardMax         0        0        0        0        1
## OneSmallForwardMin         0        0        0        0        1
## OneShootingGuardMax        0        0        0        0        0
## OneShootingGuardMin        0        0        0        0        0
## FivePlayerMax              1        1        1        1        1
## SalaryMax           18500000 16500000 15500000 14500000 37000000
## AgeMax                    31       34       28       31       31
##                          SF2      SF3      SF4      SF5      SG1
## OneCenterMax               0        0        0        0        0
## OneCenterMin               0        0        0        0        0
## OnePowerForwardMax         0        0        0        0        0
## OnePowerForwardMin         0        0        0        0        0
## OnePointGuardMax           0        0        0        0        0
## OnePointGuardMin           0        0        0        0        0
## OneSmallForwardMax         1        1        1        1        0
## OneSmallForwardMin         1        1        1        1        0
## OneShootingGuardMax        0        0        0        0        1
## OneShootingGuardMin        0        0        0        0        1
## FivePlayerMax              1        1        1        1        1
## SalaryMax           19500000 14500000 15000000 13500000 11000000
## AgeMax                    29       31       26       29       29
##                          SG2      SG3
## OneCenterMax               0        0
## OneCenterMin               0        0
## OnePowerForwardMax         0        0
## OnePowerForwardMin         0        0
## OnePointGuardMax           0        0
## OnePointGuardMin           0        0
## OneSmallForwardMax         0        0
## OneSmallForwardMin         0        0
## OneShootingGuardMax        1        1
## OneShootingGuardMin        1        1
## FivePlayerMax              1        1
## SalaryMax           22500000 10500000
## AgeMax                    28       27
```

All that remains is writing and running the constrained optimization algorithm, printing the results, and performing a series of simple checks.

4.8   *Results*

We can now solve our constrained optimization problem—that is, we can compute which five free agents this NBA team should acquire—by calling the lp() function from the lpSolve package. We're calling a *linear* programming function because our variables are continuous and all have a power of 1, meaning they are added and subtracted rather than multiplied or divided. Here's how it works:

- The const.mat argument references a matrix of numeric constraint coefficients where there must be one row for each constraint and one column for each variable, which, of course, is exactly how we constructed constraint_matrix.
- The objective argument equals the function that should be optimized, which is win shares.
- The direction argument is a character string indicating the optimization direction (this must equal either min or max).
- The const.rhs argument is a vector of numeric values that represents our constraints—a minimum of one player for each position on the floor, a maximum of one player for each position (that's 10 constraints), five players maximum, a maximum annual salary equal to $90 M, and a maximum age in years equal to 150.
- The const.dir argument is a vector of character strings indicating the direction of each constraint—no less and no more than one player per each of the five positions, five players total, annual salaries not to exceed $90 M, and the total age not to exceed 150 (thereby ensuring an average equal to or less than 30).
- The int.vec argument is a numeric vector specifying the number of integer variables.

The result is a new object called co_object. The print() function is *not* called at the end of the next code chunk; while it would return the objective function results—that is, how many win shares could be expected every year from the best free agents to acquire under the circumstances—it would not otherwise return anything else:

```
co_object <-
  lp(const.mat = constraint_matrix,
     objective = free_agents_sort$win_shares,
     direction = "max",
     const.rhs = c(1, 1, 1, 1, 1, 1, 1, 1, 1, 1, 5, 90000000, 150),
     const.dir = c("<=", ">=","<=", ">=", "<=", ">=",
                   "<=", ">=", "<=", ">=", "<=", "<=", "<="),
     int.vec = 1:24, all.bin = TRUE)
```

The following line of code returns the full results in the form of an object called df. The select() function is called to limit df to just include the variables in positions 1 through 5, these being player, age, position2, annual_salary, and win_shares:

```
print(df <- select(free_agents_sort[as.logical(co_object$solution),], 1:5))
##            player age position2 annual_salary win_shares
##    <chr>            <dbl> <fct>          <dbl>      <dbl>
## 3        Serge Ibaka  33        C3       12000000        2.9
## 8  Marvin Bagley III  23       PF4       14500000        4.7
## 15      Marcus Smart  28       PG5       15500000        4.7
## 17     Kawhi Leonard  31       SF1       37000000        9.4
## 24       Zach LaVine  27       SG3       10500000        3.8
```

We have five players, one player for each position on the floor.

A call to the base R sum() function computes the total of variable win_shares:

```
sum(df$win_shares)
## [1] 25.5
```

Another call to the sum() function computes the grand total of variable annual_salary. It turns out that this team will pay out approximately $3.5 M in salary for every win share:

```
sum(df$annual_salary)
## [1] 89500000
```

Finally, the base R mean() function is called to compute the average age of the five free agent acquisitions:

```
mean(df$age)
## [1] 28.4
```

Any other combination of players would either result in a lower win share total or would inevitably violate at least one of the hard constraints established up front. Thus, we've confirmed our hypothesis that constrained optimization can maximize a function while simultaneously obeying several constraints; our fictional NBA team is actually getting significantly more win shares at a slightly lower cost compared to the very rough estimates we computed after exploring the data.

So far, we've established how NBA teams can best take advantage of the draft or, as in the case here, the free agent market through constrained optimization to build up their rosters. Over the next several chapters, we'll apply several statistical techniques, most of which haven't yet been introduced, for in-game use. These same techniques are transferrable to other data and other real-world scenarios.

Summary

- We demonstrated how to add comments to your code. Comments improve the readability of your code and are especially useful during code reviews and post-production maintenance. R ignores and therefore doesn't execute lines in your script if they begin with the # sign.
- We introduced how to draw a ggplot2 density plot as a means of displaying the distribution of a single continuous variable as well as a ggplot2 correlation plot to visualize the correlation between two continuous variables.

- Sometimes, small touches to your visualizations can go a long way toward enhancing their aesthetics and improving their interpretability. The `scales` package makes it possible to transform your `ggplot2` labels without having to reformat your data. In fact, we'll apply other `scales` transformations in future chapters.

- Constrained optimization is a relatively straightforward operations research technique that quantitatively solves difficult and real-world problems by eliminating guesswork and producing the best possible solution. Calling the `lp()` function from the `lpSolve` package is just one way in R to go about this.

- Problems large or small, where less-than-ideal circumstances reduce available options, are best solved through constrained optimization methods.

- Constrained optimization problems are easily portable to other use cases; one algorithm applied to the NBA free agent market can subsequently be used elsewhere simply by substituting maximum or minimum functions and modifying the constraints.

- More often than not, you're probably seeking to minimize costs (acquisition costs, warehousing costs, supplier costs, salaries and benefits, etc.) or time (routes and deliveries, time to market, service level responses, delays and downtime, etc.).

- Most certainly, you're equally interested in maximizing some aspect of your business, perhaps in terms of profit margins, shelf space, or schedule adherence. Once more, anytime you're seeking to minimize or maximize a function where one or more constraints place restrictions on your options, you can and should apply constrained optimization to find your best option.

Regression models

This chapter covers

- Identifying and treating outliers
- Running and interpreting statistical tests of normality
- Computing and visualizing correlations between continuous variables
- Fitting and interpreting multiple linear regressions
- Fitting and interpreting regression trees

In this chapter, we'll demonstrate how to fit regression models, namely, multiple linear regressions and regression trees. Our dependent, or target, variable will be regular season wins, and our independent variables, or predictors, will be the full complement of hustle statistics that the NBA began recording during the 2016–17 season. These statistics include but aren't limited to blocked shots, deflections, and loose balls recovered. Hence, we'll be regressing wins against an order of hustle statistics.

Our hypothesis is that at least some of these hustle statistics have a meaningful influence on wins and losses, but which hustle statistics? And by how much? Following a thorough exploration of the data—during which we'll be laser-focused on identifying and treating outliers, testing for normal distributions, and computing correlation coefficients—we'll fit a multiple linear regression as a first test and then fit a regression tree as a second test.

A multiple linear regression is a model that estimates the relationship between a continuous target variable, such as regular season wins, and two or more predictor (and usually continuous) variables by producing an equation that draws a straight line through the data. (A simple linear regression is a model that does the same but with just one predictor variable.) The goal is to understand and quantify how two or more predictors collectively influence variances in the target variable.

A regression tree, on the other hand, often called a decision tree regression, generates a series of if-else rules to best fit the data. This type of model recursively partitions the data into subsets based on the values of the predictors and predicts the continuous value of the target variable for each subset. Results are displayed graphically and might best reflect our decision-making processes; thus, they are easier than linear regressions to interpret and then explain to others—but often less predictive. Which of the two might be best depends on the data.

Let's further set your expectations before loading our packages, importing our data, and otherwise moving forward with our analysis and testing:

- Linear modeling is based on the assumption that a linear relationship exists between the target variable and the predictors. Only when that assumption holds true is linear modeling a best test for explaining the past and predicting the future. Outliers in the data are sometimes the root cause when this assumption is violated. Linear models are especially sensitive to outliers; in fact, just a few outliers in a long data set can drastically change the slope of the regression line and thus cause a linear model to miss the overall pattern in the data and return inaccurate results. That all being said, in section 5.4, we'll identify and treat every outlier in our data.

- Every variable, especially the predictors, should be normally distributed. Treating outliers may be enough to transform a continuous variable from assuming a non-normal to a normal distribution, or it might not. In section 5.5, after we've identified outliers and treated them accordingly, we'll draw density plots and demonstrate how to run and interpret a common statistical test for normality. Predictors that fail our normality test will be excluded from model development.

- Predictors that are highly correlated with the target variable, positively or negatively, are more likely to have a statistically significant influence on target variable variances than other potential predictors. Thus, in section 5.6, we'll compute the correlation coefficients between wins and our remaining predictor variables to isolate those that have strong, or relatively strong, relationships with wins and to discard from model development those that don't.

- We'll fit our multiple linear regressions in section 5.7 and demonstrate how to interpret and apply the results. Along the way, we'll also provide instructions on how to apply best practices before and after fitting our models.

- In section 5.8, we'll fit and plot a regression tree and walk you through how to interpret the results and compare and contrast the same with our linear models.

Now we can go about loading our packages, importing our data, and starting our analysis.

5.1   *Loading packages*

With respect to our multiple linear regressions, we'll call the base R `lm()` function to fit our models and then a combination of packaged functions to return the results. Conversely, with respect to our regression tree, we'll call the `tree()` function from the `tree` package to fit the model and then call a pair of built-in functions to visualize the results.

Overall, we're introducing four packages that haven't been loaded or used previously, including the `tree` package and the following:

- From the `GGally` package, which is a `ggplot2` extension, the `ggpairs()` function will be called to return a correlation matrix that visualizes at once the associations between every continuous or numeric variable in our data set. There are many ways in R by which to visualize correlations; `GGally` actually goes above and beyond the heat map we created back in chapter 2.

- From the `car` package, the `vif()` function, which is short for variance inflation factor, will be called to check for multicollinearity among the independent variables, or predictors, in our linear regressions. Multicollinearity refers to two or more predictors that are strongly correlated with one another. When multicollinearity exists, at least one of the predictors should be removed, and a new or reduced model should be fit to ensure the highest levels of validity and reliability.

- From the `broom` package, a series of functions will be called to return our linear model results.

These packages, along with the `tidyverse` and `patchwork` packages, are loaded by making successive calls to the `library()` function:

```
library(tidyverse)
library(GGally)
library(car)
library(broom)
library(tree)
library(patchwork)
```

With our packages now loaded, we're ready to use their functions and then move on to the next step.

5.2   *Importing data*

We begin by creating an object or data set called hustle by calling the `readr` `read_csv()` function that imports a .csv file also called hustle. The hustle data set contains scraped data from the NBA's official website (www.nba.com):

```
hustle <- read_csv("hustle.csv")
```

The read_csv() function *automatically* imports the hustle data set at runtime because the file is stored in our default working directory. The preceding code would fail if hustle.csv were stored anywhere else.

There is more than one way to set or change your working directory. The best way—because other options can always change with subsequent software releases—is to call the base R setwd() function and add the full directory between a pair of single or double quotation marks:

```
setwd("/Users/garysutton/Library/Mobile Documents/com~apple~CloudDocs")
```

The following line of code *interactively* imports a .csv file by substituting the base R file.choose() function for the working directory. This is a good option if your .csv file is stored outside your working directory or if you've chosen to not define a working directory at all:

```
hustle <- read_csv(file.choose()
```

A dialog box opens at runtime prompting you to navigate your computer and then select the .csv file you want to import.

5.3 *Knowing the data*

Now that we've imported our data set, let's go about getting to know it. As in previous chapters, the glimpse() function from the dplyr package is called to return a transposed version of the hustle data set:

```
glimpse(hustle)
## Rows: 90
## Columns: 12
## $ team               <fct> Atlanta Hawks, Boston Celtics, Brooklyn…
## $ season             <fct> 2018-19, 2018-19, 2018-19, 2018-19, 201…
## $ team_season        <fct> ATL 19, BOS 19, BKN 19, CHA 19, CHI 19,…
## $ screen_assists     <dbl> 8.0, 8.6, 11.0, 11.1, 8.3, 9.8, 8.5, 9.…
## $ screen_assists_pts <dbl> 18.2, 20.0, 26.2, 25.7, 18.6, 22.4, 20.…
## $ deflections        <dbl> 14.5, 14.1, 12.1, 12.6, 12.6, 11.8, 11.…
## $ loose_balls        <dbl> 9.5, 8.3, 8.0, 8.1, 7.9, 7.6, 8.4, 8.6,…
## $ charges            <dbl> 0.5, 0.7, 0.3, 0.6, 0.4, 0.5, 0.8, 0.4,…
## $ contested_2pt      <dbl> 38.0, 35.9, 44.5, 39.2, 36.5, 34.6, 38.…
## $ contested_3pt      <dbl> 25.2, 26.4, 22.2, 25.3, 24.9, 23.9, 24.…
## $ contested_shots    <dbl> 63.2, 62.3, 66.7, 64.5, 61.3, 58.4, 62.…
## $ wins               <int> 29, 49, 42, 39, 22, 19, 33, 54, 41, 57,…
```

The hustle data set is 90 rows long and 14 columns wide. It contains the variables team, season, and team_season as character strings; several hustle statistics as numeric variables; and regular season wins.

We have one required and immediate action: converting those first three variables from character strings to factors. Therefore, we make three calls to the base R as.factor() function. Once again, it's a best practice to convert character strings to factors when the variables can otherwise assume just a fixed or finite set of values:

```
hustle$team <- as.factor(hustle$team)
hustle$season <- as.factor(hustle$season)
hustle$team_season <- as.factor(hustle$team_season)
```

We then call the summary() function from base R to return basic or descriptive statistics on every variable in the hustle data set:

```
summary(hustle)
##                      team           season       team_season  screen_assists
##   Atlanta Hawks       : 3   2016-17:30    ATL 17 : 1   Min.    : 6.800
##   Boston Celtics      : 3   2017-18:30    ATL 18 : 1   1st Qu.: 8.425
##   Brooklyn Nets       : 3   2018-19:30    ATL 19 : 1   Median : 9.350
##   Charlotte Hornets   : 3                 BKN 17 : 1   Mean    : 9.486
##   Chicago Bulls       : 3                 BKN 18 : 1   3rd Qu.:10.500
##   Cleveland Cavaliers : 3                 BKN 19 : 1   Max.    :13.100
##   (Other)             :72                 (Other):84
##   screen_assists_pts  deflections     off_loose_balls  def_loose_balls
##   Min.    :15.90      Min.    :11.40   Min.    :0.000   Min.    :0.000
##   1st Qu.:19.30       1st Qu.:13.32    1st Qu.:0.000    1st Qu.:0.000
##   Median :21.55       Median :14.45    Median :3.400    Median :4.500
##   Mean    :21.65      Mean    :14.38   Mean    :2.394   Mean    :3.181
##   3rd Qu.:23.90       3rd Qu.:15.30    3rd Qu.:3.700    3rd Qu.:4.900
##   Max.    :30.30      Max.    :18.70   Max.    :4.500   Max.    :5.500
##
##    loose_balls         charges        contested_2pt    contested_3pt
##   Min.    :6.20      Min.    :0.2000   Min.    :34.00   Min.    :18.10
##   1st Qu.:7.30       1st Qu.:0.4000    1st Qu.:37.73    1st Qu.:21.40
##   Median :8.00       Median :0.5000    Median :39.90    Median :22.95
##   Mean    :7.93      Mean    :0.5444   Mean    :40.19   Mean    :22.92
##   3rd Qu.:8.50       3rd Qu.:0.7000    3rd Qu.:42.23    3rd Qu.:24.65
##   Max.    :9.60      Max.    :1.1000   Max.    :49.10   Max.    :28.90
##
##   contested_shots       wins
##   Min.    :55.30     Min.    :17.00
##   1st Qu.:61.38      1st Qu.:32.25
##   Median :63.15      Median :42.00
##   Mean    :63.11     Mean    :41.00
##   3rd Qu.:64.67      3rd Qu.:49.00
##   Max.    :74.20     Max.    :67.00
##
```

Some of what we can deduce from our data follows:

- Our data set spans the last three NBA regular seasons, pre-COVID-19 (see the results on the season variable); the 2019–20 season was cut short, especially for those teams that failed to qualify for in-bubble play once the season resumed because of the pandemic. (Once the 2019–20 season resumed, all games were played at a neutral, controlled site in Orlando, Florida.)

- The variables `team` and `season` were concatenated to create an additional variable called `team_season` where, for instance, the 2016–17 Atlanta Hawks becomes ATL 17.
- The variables `off_loose_balls` and `def_loose_balls`, offensive and defensive loose balls recovered, respectively, have minimums of 0, thereby suggesting that for at least one season, the NBA tracked total loose balls recovered only. A loose ball recovered is just that—the offensive team has lost control but not necessarily possession of the ball, which is then recovered and controlled by the offense or defense.
- The statistics on the variable `charges` are modest, and the variances between them are negligible. When an offensive player in possession of the ball dribbles and drives toward the basket and there is contact between him and a defensive player, a personal foul is called (unless the contact was slight and didn't severely affect the play). In the NBA, as opposed to college basketball, contact on dribble drives to the basket usually results in a blocking foul or a foul against the defense. But every now and then, the offense is instead called for the foul; when this occurs, the defense is credited with a charge, or more specifically a drawn charge. Such a variable, where the frequency is rare and the variance is small, is unlikely to have much influence on a target variable.
- Other than `wins`, we see the most variance with the following variables:
  - `screen_assists_pts`—This variable equals the total points scored per game when one player makes a shot (i.e., field goal) immediately after a teammate sets a screen by placing his body between his teammate and a defensive player.
  - `contested_2pt`—This variable equals the average number of opponent two-point shot attempts that were closely defended.
  - `contested_shots`—This variable equals the average number of total shot attempts—two-pointers and three-pointers—that were closely defended. All shot (field goal) attempts are worth two or three points, depending on the distance from the basket.
- There is a moderate amount of variance with these variables:
  - `contested_3pt`—This variable equals the average number of opponent three-point shot attempts that were closely defended.
  - `screen_assists`—This variable equals the average number of screens set per game, regardless of what then happens on the floor.
  - `deflections`—This variable equals the average number of opponent passes broken up, or deflected, per game.

Based on the inconsistent tracking of *offensive* loose balls recovered versus *defensive* loose balls recovered, we make a call to the `select()` function from the `dplyr` package to remove the variables `off_loose_balls` and `def_loose_balls` from the hustle data set;

in this case, it's much easier to tell R what to delete—hence the minus operator preceding a subsequent call to the c() function—rather than what to retain:

```
hustle %>%
  select(-c(off_loose_balls, def_loose_balls)) -> hustle
```

We then call the base R dim() function to confirm the success of this operation by returning the new dimension of our data set:

```
dim(hustle)
## [1] 90 12
```

Our data set now contains 90 rows and just 12 columns, whereas before it had 14 columns.

5.4   *Identifying outliers*

As previously mentioned, linear regression models assume—actually, demand—that the source data be free of any outliers. Just a few outliers, which, for all we know, may be due to measurement errors, data entry mistakes, or rare events, can overwhelm the influence of the remaining data points, thereby injecting bias into any regression model. Therefore, data points that significantly deviate from the overall pattern or distribution of the remaining data will be identified and subsequently modified to effectively eliminate them as outliers. This might seem excessive to some of you, but when working with short data sets such as hustle, changing extreme values (known as *winsorization*) is a perfectly acceptable and legitimate alternative to removing observations and reducing the length of the data.

5.4.1   *Prototype*

There are many ways to go about identifying outliers. The visual approach might require the most work, but it's the most effective means of understanding the data. The easiest approach might be one of two statistical tests: Dixon's Q Test and Grubbs' Test, both of which require the outliers package. However, Dixon's Q only works with small data sets, where n, or the number of records, is less than 30; Grubbs' Test, on the other hand, has greater extensibility, but it only returns the one most significant outlier, even if other outliers are present.

Let's demonstrate the visual approach with the variable deflections. There are three visualization options for spotting outliers: scatterplot, histogram, and boxplot.

Creating a scatterplot with just an x-axis variable isn't the same as creating a correlation plot, which visualizes the relationship between a pair of x-axis and y-axis variables. That being said, rather than calling the ggplot() function from the ggplot2 package, we'll first create our scatterplot by calling the qplot() function, which is short for quick plot. Second, we'll pass the seq_along() function to qplot() to create a vector of evenly spaced numbers. The downside to scatterplots is that outliers won't always be so obvious.

The same can be said of histograms. They are usually a first option for displaying the distribution of a continuous variable, but in the end, tagging (or not tagging) values along the tails as outliers is often a subjective exercise. By contrast, boxplots are specifically designed to isolate values outside the whiskers and to qualify them as outliers.

For comparison purposes, the following chunk of code returns a scatterplot (`sp1`), histogram (`hist1`), and boxplot (`bp1`) around the variable `deflections` (see figure 5.1). However, with respect to the remaining variables in the hustle data set, only boxplots will be created:

```
sp1 <- qplot(seq_along(hustle$deflections), hustle$deflections) +
  labs(title = "Deflections",
       subtitle = "scatterplot",
       x = "",
       y = "Value") +
  theme(plot.title = element_text(face = "bold")) +
  annotate("text", x = 65, y = 18.5,
           label = "Outlier?", color = "red",
           size = 3, fontface = "bold") +
  annotate("text", x = 85, y = 18.3,
           label = "Outlier?", color = "red",
           size = 3, fontface = "bold")

hist1 <- ggplot(hustle, aes(x = deflections)) +
  geom_histogram(fill = "snow1", color = "dodgerblue4", bins = 8) +
  labs(title ="Deflections",
       subtitle = "histogram",
       x = "",
       y = "Frequency") +
  theme(plot.title = element_text(face = "bold")) +
  annotate("text", x = 18.75, y = 3,
           label = "  Outliers?", color = "red",
           size = 3, fontface = "bold")

bp1 <- ggplot(hustle, aes(x = "", y = deflections)) +
  labs(title = "Deflections",
       subtitle = "boxplot",
       x = "",
       y = "") +
  geom_boxplot(color = "dodgerblue4", fill = "snow1", width = 0.5) +
  stat_summary(fun = mean, geom = "point", shape = 20, size = 8,
               color = "dodgerblue4", fill = "dodgerblue4") +
  annotate("text", x = "", y = 18.6,
           label = "                        Outliers",
           color = "red", size = 3, fontface = "bold") +
  theme(plot.title = element_text(face = "bold"))
```

The spaces between the opening quotation marks and the `Outliers` annotations (e.g., "   `Outliers`") are purposeful; they were inserted to best position the text within the histogram and boxplot for aesthetic reasons. Otherwise, the `plot_layout()` function from the `patchwork` package prints our three visualizations as a single horizontal object:

```
sp1 + hist1 + bp1 + plot_layout(ncol = 3)
```

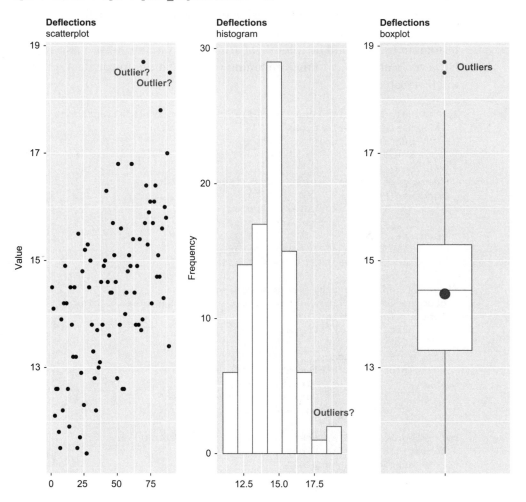

Figure 5.1 Left to right, a scatterplot, a histogram, and a boxplot around the variable `deflections` from the hustle data set. Identifying outliers can be subjective with respect to scatterplots and histograms, but not with boxplots.

The variable `deflections` does contain a pair of outliers. Our next step is to therefore winsorize the data by reducing the values of the two outliers just enough so that they instead equal the maximum. Recall that the maximum on a boxplot is the top end of the whisker (and that the minimum is the endpoint of the bottom whisker).

The following line of code modifies any values in the variable `deflections` greater than 17.8 to instead equal 17.8, the approximate endpoint of the top whisker from `bp1`:

```
hustle$deflections[hustle$deflections > 17.8] = 17.8
```

The maximum value for the variable `deflections` was originally 18.70 (check the `summary()` function returns). The `max()` function from base R returns the new maximum of 17.8, so there's no need to again call the `summary()` function when you just need a single statistic returned:

```
max(hustle$deflections)
## [1] 17.8
```

A second boxplot (see figure 5.2) displays the new distribution of the variable `deflections` post-winsorization:

```
bp2 <- ggplot(hustle, aes(x = "",
                          y = deflections)) +
  labs(title = "Deflections",
       subtitle = "post-winsorization boxplot",
       x = "", y = "") +
  geom_boxplot(color = "dodgerblue4", fill = "grey65", width = 0.5) +
  stat_summary(fun = mean, geom = "point", shape = 20, size = 8,
               color = "dodgerblue4", fill = "dodgerblue4") +
  theme(plot.title = element_text(face = "bold"))
print(bp2)
```

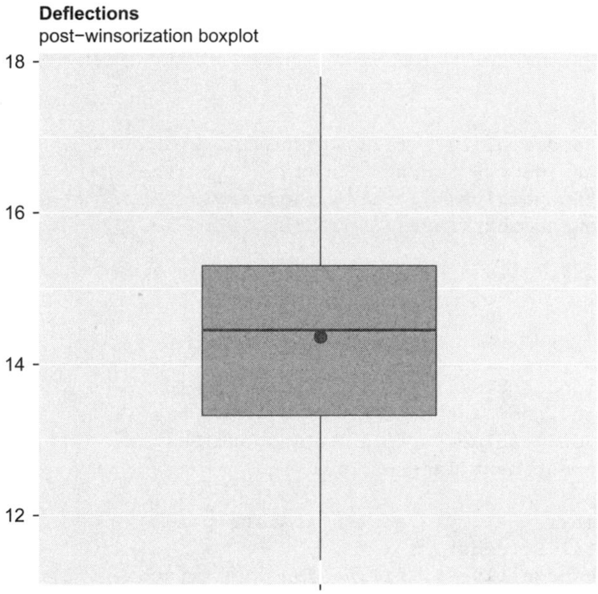

Figure 5.2 The new or revised distribution of the variable `deflections` post-winsorization. Note the absence of outliers, that is, any data points beyond the length of the whiskers.

The following summarizes what we've done so far:

- We selected a visual approach over a pair of statistical methods to spot outliers in the hustle data set.
- We then chose boxplots over scatterplots and histograms because identifying outliers in boxplots is less subjective than doing so with other visualization types. Furthermore, boxplots are better visuals than the alternatives when it comes to deciding how much to decrease or increase the values of outliers to effectively eliminate them as outliers.
- Rather than removing outliers from our data, we instead decided on winsorization due to the hustle data set being only 90 rows long.
- By calling the base R `max()` function and then creating a second boxplot, we twice confirmed that the outliers in the variable `deflections` are now gone.

This process will be repeated in the following section against the remaining variables in the hustle data set.

5.4.2   *Identifying other outliers*

In the long chunk of code that immediately follows, we'll create a boxplot for every remaining variable in the hustle data set. For those variables that contain one or more outliers, our boxplots include a second theme by which a red trim is added along the border. Otherwise, the syntax is exactly the same for each plot, which means you can review the code for our first boxplot and then skip to where the narrative resumes, if you like:

```
bp3 <- ggplot(hustle, aes(x = "", y = wins)) +
  labs(title = "Wins",
       x = "",
       y = "") +
  geom_boxplot(color = "dodgerblue4", fill = "snow1", width = 0.5) +
  stat_summary(fun = mean, geom = "point", shape = 20, size = 8,
               color = "dodgerblue4", fill = "dodgerblue4") +
  theme(plot.title = element_text(face = "bold"))

bp4 <- ggplot(hustle, aes(x = "", y = screen_assists)) +
  labs(title = "Screens",
       x = "",
       y = "") +
  geom_boxplot(color = "dodgerblue4", fill = "snow1", width = 0.5) +
  stat_summary(fun = mean, geom = "point", shape = 20, size = 8,
               color = "dodgerblue4", fill = "dodgerblue4") +
  theme(plot.title = element_text(face = "bold"))

bp5 <- ggplot(hustle, aes(x = "", y = screen_assists_pts)) +
  labs(title = "Points off Screens", x = "", y = "") +
  geom_boxplot(color = "dodgerblue4", fill = "snow1", width = 0.5) +
  stat_summary(fun = mean, geom = "point", shape = 20, size = 8,
               color = "dodgerblue4", fill = "dodgerblue4") +
  theme(plot.title = element_text(face = "bold"))
```

```
bp6 <- ggplot(hustle, aes(x = "", y = loose_balls)) +
  labs(title = "Loose Balls Recovered",
       x = "",
       y = "") +
  geom_boxplot(color = "dodgerblue4", fill = "snow1", width = 0.5) +
  stat_summary(fun = mean, geom = "point", shape = 20, size = 8,
               color = "dodgerblue4", fill = "dodgerblue4") +
  theme(plot.title = element_text(face = "bold"))

bp7 <- ggplot(hustle, aes(x = "", y = charges)) +
  labs(title = "Charges Drawn",
       x = "",
       y = "") +
  geom_boxplot(color = "dodgerblue4", fill = "snow1", width = 0.5) +
  stat_summary(fun = mean, geom = "point", shape = 20, size = 8,
               color = "dodgerblue4", fill = "dodgerblue4") +
  theme(plot.title = element_text(face = "bold"))

bp8 <- ggplot(hustle, aes(x = "", y = contested_2pt)) +
  labs(title = "Contested 2pt Shots",
       x = "",
       y = "") +
  geom_boxplot(color = "dodgerblue4", fill = "snow1", width = 0.5) +
  stat_summary(fun = mean, geom = "point", shape = 20, size = 8,
               color = "dodgerblue4", fill = "dodgerblue4") +
  theme(plot.title = element_text(face = "bold")) +
  theme(panel.background = element_rect(color = "red", size = 2))

bp9 <- ggplot(hustle, aes(x = "", y = contested_3pt)) +
  labs(title = "Contested 3pt Shots",
       x = "",
       y = "") +
  geom_boxplot(color = "dodgerblue4", fill = "snow1", width = 0.5) +
  stat_summary(fun = mean, geom = "point", shape = 20, size = 8,
               color = "dodgerblue4", fill = "dodgerblue4") +
  theme(plot.title = element_text(face = "bold"))

bp10 <- ggplot(hustle, aes(x = "", y = contested_shots)) +
  labs(title ="Contested Shots",
       x = "",
       y ="") +
  geom_boxplot(color = "dodgerblue4", fill = "snow1", width = 0.5) +
  stat_summary(fun = mean, geom = "point", shape = 20, size = 8,
               color = "dodgerblue4", fill = "dodgerblue4") +
  theme(plot.title = element_text(face = "bold")) +
  theme(panel.background = element_rect(color = "red", size = 2))
```

The first four of our eight boxplots (see figure 5.3) are packed into a single graphical object by again calling the plot_layout() function from the patchwork package. The remaining four plots are then packed into a separate object (see figure 5.4). It usually doesn't make sense—at least for aesthetic reasons if not also for practical purposes—to bundle more than four visualizations into one graphical representation:

```
bp3 + bp4 + bp5 + bp6 + plot_layout(ncol = 2)
bp7 + bp8 + bp9 + bp10 + plot_layout(ncol = 2)
```

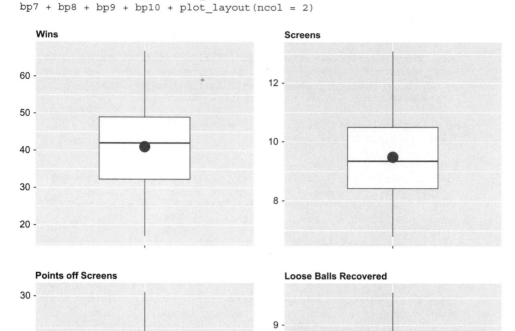

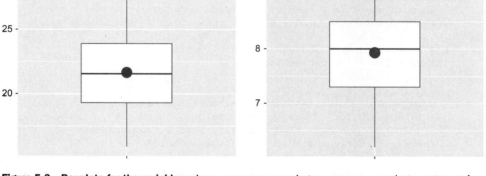

Figure 5.3 Boxplots for the variables `wins`, `screens_assists`, `screen_assists_pts`, **and** `loose_balls`. **There are no outliers present in any of these variables.**

Other than the variable `deflections`, just two other variables in the hustle data set contain outliers: `contested_2pt` and `contested_shots`. The variable `contested_2pt` has a single outlier beyond the maximum, and the variable `contested_shots` has a pair of outliers above the maximum and two more outliers below the minimum.

The next chunk of code decreases the values of those outliers above the maximum and increases the values of those outliers below the minimum:

```
hustle$contested_2pt[hustle$contested_2pt > 48.5] = 48.5
hustle$contested_shots[hustle$contested_shots > 69.3] = 69.3
hustle$contested_shots[hustle$contested_shots < 57.4] = 57.4
```

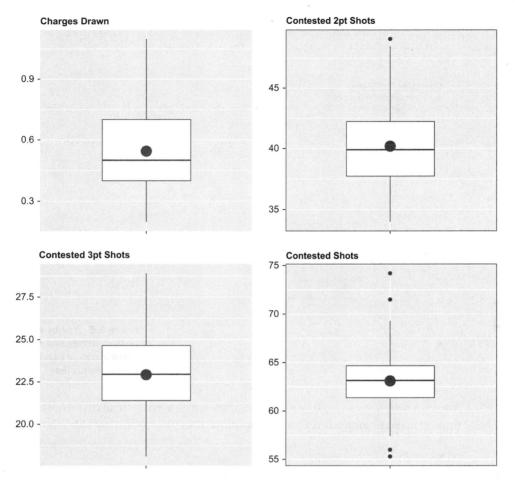

Figure 5.4 **Boxplots for the hustle data set variables** `charges`, `contested_2pt`, `contested_3pt`, **and** `contested_shots`. **Outliers are present in two of these four variables.**

A call to the `max()` function confirms that the maximum value for the variable `contested_2pt` has been reduced from 49.10 to 48.5:

```
max(hustle$contested_2pt)
## [1] 48.5
```

A second boxplot (see figure 5.5) is then drawn, showing that the variable `contested_2pt` is now free of any outliers:

```
bp11 <- ggplot(hustle, aes(x = "", y = contested_2pt)) +
  labs(title = "Contested 2pt Shots",
       subtitle = "post-winsorization boxplot",
       x = "",
       y = "") +
  geom_boxplot(color = "dodgerblue4", fill = "grey65", width = 0.5) +
```

```
stat_summary(fun = mean, geom = "point", shape = 20, size = 8,
             color = "dodgerblue4", fill = "dodgerblue4") +
theme(plot.title = element_text(face = "bold")) +
print(bp11)
```

Contested 2pt Shots
post-winsorization boxplot

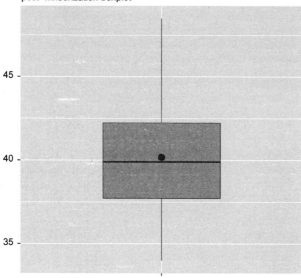

Figure 5.5 The new or revised distribution of the variable contested_2pt **post-winsorization**

Another call to the max() function immediately followed by a call to the base R min() function returns the new maximum and minimum values for the variable contested_shots:

```
max(hustle$contested_shots)
## [1] 69.3
min(hustle$contested_shots)
## [1] 57.4
```

The maximum value for contested_shots decreased from 74.20 to 69.30, and the minimum increased from 55.30 to 57.40.

Our next visualization displays the new distribution for the variable contested_shots, which now no longer contains any outliers, whereas before, it contained four of them (see figure 5.6):

```
bp12 <- ggplot(hustle, aes(x = "", y = contested_shots)) +
  labs(title = "Contested Shots",
       subtitle = "post-winsorization boxplot",
       x = "",
       y = "") +
  geom_boxplot(color = "dodgerblue4", fill = "grey65", width = 0.5) +
  stat_summary(fun = mean, geom = "point", shape = 20, size = 8,
               color = "dodgerblue4", fill = "dodgerblue4") +
  theme(plot.title = element_text(face = "bold"))
print(bp12)
```

Contested Shots
post–winsorization boxplot

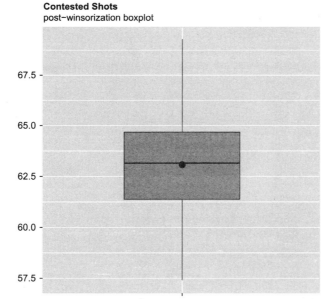

Figure 5.6 The new or revised distribution of the variable `contested_shots` **post-winsorization**

Linear regressions also expect the target variable and especially the predictor variables to be normally distributed to get best results (which is why non-normal variables are often transformed to make them normal). Although the hustle data set is now free of outliers, this by no means guarantees that our variables now assume normal or Gaussian distributions. Next, we'll visualize the distribution of every variable with a series of density plots and complement our ongoing visual approach with a statistical test against each variable to determine whether each is normally distributed.

5.5 Checking for normality

Now that outliers have been treated, we'll next create a series of density plots as a means of visualizing each variable's frequency distribution or shape. Additionally, the `shapiro.test()` function from base R will be called just before creating each density plot to run a Shapiro-Wilk test and determine whether each variable, regardless of how normal or not so normal their distributions may then appear, measures up. The Shapiro-Wilk test is just one of several normality tests, though no doubt the most common. Another fairly common normality test is the Kolmogorov-Smirnov test. R supports these and other similar tests.

The null hypothesis for a Shapiro-Wilk test is that the data is normally distributed. So if the p-value—defined as the probability that an observed difference could have otherwise occurred by chance—is less than or equal to 0.05, we'll reject the null hypothesis and conclude that the data is non-normal. Alternatively, when the p-value is greater than 0.05, we'll instead conclude that the data is normally distributed and that the null hypothesis shouldn't be rejected.

> ## Hypothesis testing and p-values
>
> Let's take a brief pause to raise a few additional points around hypothesis testing and p-values. Hypothesis testing, or statistical inference, is all about testing an assumption and drawing a conclusion from one or more data series. Hypothesis testing essentially evaluates how unusual or not so unusual the results are and whether they are too extreme or improbable to be the outcome of chance.
>
> Our starting assumption should *always* be what's known as the null hypothesis, designated as H_0, which suggests that nothing statistically significant or out of the ordinary exists in one variable or between two data series. We therefore require extraordinary evidence to reject the null hypothesis and to instead accept the alternative hypothesis, designated as H_1.
>
> That evidence is the p-value and specifically the generally accepted 5% threshold for significance. While 5% might be somewhat arbitrary, we can agree that it's a very low number, so we're setting a high bar to overturn or reject a null hypothesis.

As previously mentioned, linear modeling expects variables to be normally distributed, so any predictors that have Shapiro-Wilk test results where the p-value is less than or equal to 0.05 will be withheld from model development. There will be no data transformations or other corrective action applied.

5.5.1 *Prototype*

Once again, we'll use the variable `deflections` to prototype all this (see figure 5.7). But first, we make a call to the base R `options()` function to disable scientific notation; we prefer our results to be returned in full digit numerals rather than in scientific notation.

As a reminder, a density plot is a smoothed version of a histogram that doesn't allow us to contort the distribution shape by experimenting with different bin counts. We pass just a single hustle variable to the `ggplot()` function and then call the `geom_density()` function to draw a density plot. R subsequently returns a plot, not with frequency or counts as the y-axis variable, but rather a probability density function as the y-axis variable, where the probability is low when the frequency is low and the probability is high when the frequency is high. Otherwise, the x-axis represents the range of values in the data, just as it does for histograms:

```
options(scipen = 999)

shapiro.test(hustle$deflections)
##
##  Shapiro-Wilk normality test
##
## data:  hustle$deflections
## W = 0.98557, p-value = 0.4235
dp1 <- ggplot(hustle, aes(x = deflections)) +
  geom_density(alpha = .3, fill = "dodgerblue4") +
  labs(title = "Deflections",
```

```
                subtitle = "Shapiro-Wilk test of normality: p-value = 0.42",
                x = "",
                y = "Density") +
        theme(plot.title = element_text(face = "bold"))
print(dp1)
```

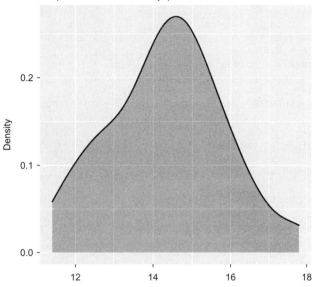

Deflections
Shapiro-Wilk test of normality: p−value = 0.42

Figure 5.7   Density plot for the variable deflections. **Because the Shapiro-Wilk normality test returned a p-value greater than 0.05, we can conclude that** deflections **assumes a normal distribution.**

The variable deflections *appears* to have a normal distribution and, based on the Shapiro-Wilk test results, where the p-value is significantly above the 0.05 threshold for significance, *is* normally distributed. This same process, if it can be called that, will be repeated in the following section against every remaining variable in the hustle data set.

5.5.2   *Checking other distributions for normality*

In our next code chunk, we once more take a variable-by-variable approach. We'll run a series of Shapiro-Wilk tests by calling the shapiro.test() function and also draw a sequence of density plots. The results are then divided into two panels (see figures 5.8 and 5.9). A red border will be drawn around any plot displaying a non-normal distribution, based on the Shapiro-Wilk test results. Once more, the code is more or less repeatable from one plot to the next:

```
shapiro.test(hustle$wins)
##
##   Shapiro-Wilk normality test
##
## data:  hustle$wins
## W = 0.98034, p-value = 0.1907
dp2 <- ggplot(hustle, aes(x = wins)) +
  geom_density(alpha = .3, fill = "dodgerblue4") +
```

```
    labs(title = "Wins",
         subtitle = "Shapiro-Wilk test of normality: p-value = 0.19",
         x = "",
         y = "Density") +
    theme(plot.title = element_text(face = "bold"))

shapiro.test(hustle$screen_assists)
##
##   Shapiro-Wilk normality test
##
## data:  hustle$screen_assists
## W = 0.98309, p-value = 0.2936
dp3 <- ggplot(hustle, aes(x = screen_assists)) +
  geom_density(alpha = .3, fill = "dodgerblue4") +
  labs(title = "Screens",
       subtitle = "Shapiro-Wilk test of normality: p-value = 0.29",
       x = "",
       y = "Density") +
  theme(plot.title = element_text(face = "bold"))

shapiro.test(hustle$screen_assists_pts)
##
##   Shapiro-Wilk normality test
##
## data:  hustle$screen_assists_pts
## W = 0.9737, p-value = 0.06464
dp4 <- ggplot(hustle, aes(x = screen_assists_pts)) +
  geom_density(alpha = .3, fill = "dodgerblue4") +
  labs(title = "Points off Screens",
       subtitle = "Shapiro-Wilk test of normality: p-value = 0.06",
       x = "",
       y = "Density") +
  theme(plot.title = element_text(face = "bold"))
shapiro.test(hustle$loose_balls)
##
##   Shapiro-Wilk normality test
##
## data:  hustle$loose_balls
## W = 0.98109, p-value = 0.2148
dp5 <- ggplot(hustle, aes(x = loose_balls)) +
  geom_density(alpha = .3, fill = "dodgerblue4") +
  labs(title = "Loose Balls Recovered",
       subtitle = "Shapiro-Wilk test of normality: p-value = 0.21",
       x = "",
       y = "Density") +
  theme(plot.title = element_text(face = "bold"))

shapiro.test(hustle$charges)
##
##   Shapiro-Wilk normality test
##
## data:  hustle$charges
## W = 0.95688, p-value = 0.004562
dp6 <- ggplot(hustle, aes(x = charges)) +
  geom_density(alpha = .3, fill = "dodgerblue4") +
```

```
    labs(title = "Charges Drawn",
         subtitle = "Shapiro-Wilk test of normality: p-value = 0.00",
         x = "",
         y = "Density") +
    theme(plot.title = element_text(face = "bold")) +
    theme(panel.background = element_rect(color = "red", size = 2))

shapiro.test(hustle$contested_2pt)
##
##  Shapiro-Wilk normality test
##
## data:  hustle$contested_2pt
## W = 0.97663, p-value = 0.1045
dp7 <- ggplot(hustle, aes(x = contested_2pt)) +
  geom_density(alpha = .3, fill = "dodgerblue4") +
  labs(title = "Contested 2pt Shots",
       subtitle = "Shapiro-Wilk test of normality: p-value = 0.10",
       x = "",
       y = "Density") +
  theme(plot.title = element_text(face = "bold"))

shapiro.test(hustle$contested_3pt)
##
##  Shapiro-Wilk normality test
##
## data:  hustle$contested_3pt
## W = 0.98301, p-value = 0.2899
dp8 <- ggplot(hustle, aes(x = contested_3pt)) +
  geom_density(alpha = .3, fill = "dodgerblue4") +
  labs(title = "Contested 3pt Shots",
       subtitle = "Shapiro-Wilk test of normality: p-value = 0.29",
       x = "",
       y = "Density") +
  theme(plot.title = element_text(face = "bold"))

shapiro.test(hustle$contested_shots)
##
##  Shapiro-Wilk normality test
##
## data:  hustle$contested_shots
## W = 0.98106, p-value = 0.2138
dp9 <- ggplot(hustle, aes(x = contested_shots)) +
  geom_density(alpha = .3, fill = "dodgerblue4") +
  labs(title = "Contested 2pt Shots",
       subtitle = "Shapiro-Wilk test of normality: p-value = 0.21",
       x = "",
       y = "Density") +
  theme(plot.title = element_text(face = "bold"))
```

Our density plots are then packed into a pair of 4 × 2 matrices:

```
dp2 + dp3 + dp4 + dp5 + plot_layout(ncol = 2)
dp6 + dp7 + dp8 + dp9 + plot_layout(ncol = 2)
```

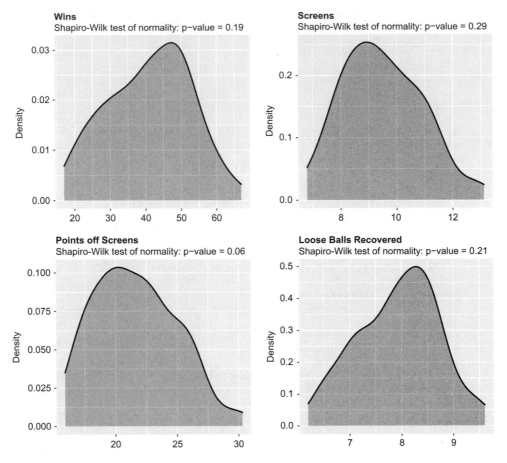

Figure 5.8   Density plots for the variables wins, screens_assists, screen_assists_pts, and loose_balls. All four of these variables are normally distributed due to Shapiro-Wilk tests that returned p-values above the 0.05 threshold for significance.

It turns out that only the variable charges has a non-normal distribution based on the Shapiro-Wilk tests, drawing a line in the sand where the p-value is equal to the predefined 5% threshold for significance. The variables screen_assists_pts and contested_2pt have Shapiro-Wilk p-values barely above 0.05, thereby indicating their respective distributions are almost non-normal. But again, we're applying a p-value of 0.05 as a hard cutoff; therefore, we'll withhold the variable charges from our linear modeling.

We nonetheless have several variables still in play. In the following section, we'll visualize and test the correlations between our remaining predictors and the variable wins to determine which of these might be best candidates for explaining and even predicting regular season wins.

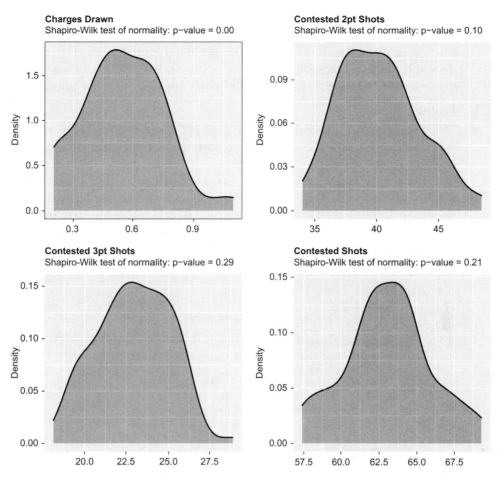

Figure 5.9   Density plots for the variables `charges`, `contested_2pt`, `contested_3pt`, **and** `contested_shots`. **Only Charges Drawn isn't normally distributed.**

5.6   *Visualizing and testing correlations*

To recap, we first identified outliers in our data and then subsequently capped those same data points so that they equal the maximum or minimum. Second, we tested our variables for normality to determine which of these to carry forward and which to withhold from any further analysis and testing.

Now, we'll compute the correlation coefficients between the variable `wins` and the remaining variables and then visualize the same with a correlation matrix. The correlation coefficient will always equal some value between −1 and +1. When a pair of variables has a correlation coefficient equal to or close to +1, we can conclude that a positive association exists between them; if their correlation coefficient instead equals −1 or close to that, we can alternately conclude that a negative association exists between them; and if their correlation coefficient is close to 0, then there is no meaningful association at all.

Our purpose here is to identify which variables might be best fits, or not fits at all, as predictors in our linear regression models. This is an especially relevant exercise when working with wide data sets as it makes much more sense to further examine the data and identify high-potential predictors as opposed to including every independent variable in a model regardless of whether any value is being added.

5.6.1   *Prototype*

The variable `deflections` will again be used for demonstration purposes. The base R `cor()` function is called to compute the correlation coefficient between the variables `deflections` and `wins`.

A `ggplot2` correlation plot is then created to visualize the relationship between these same two variables, where the x-axis variable is the potential predictor `deflections` and the y-axis variable is the future dependent, or target, variable `wins` (see figure 5.10). The correlation coefficient is added as a subtitle, and the `geom_smooth()` function is called to draw a regression line through the data. We get a correlation plot just like the one we drew in the previous chapter:

```
cor(hustle$deflections, hustle$wins)
## [1] 0.2400158
cor1 <- ggplot(hustle, aes(x = deflections, y = wins)) +
  geom_point(size = 3) +
  labs(title = "Deflections and Wins",
       subtitle = "correlation coefficient = 0.24",
       x = "Deflections per Game",
       y = "Regular Season Wins") +
  geom_smooth(method = lm, se = FALSE) +
  theme(plot.title = element_text(face = "bold"))
print(cor1)
```

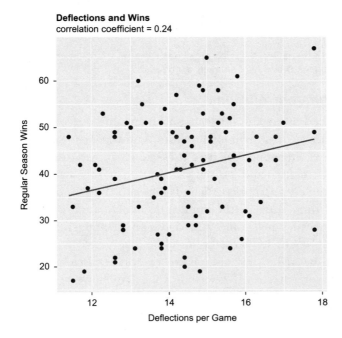

Figure 5.10
A correlation plot that
visualizes the relationship
between the variables
`deflections` **and** `wins`

With the correlation coefficient between deflections and wins equaling 0.24, there is a positive correlation between the two, but the association is otherwise unremarkable. Let's see how this stacks up against other correlation coefficients between additional predictors and the variable wins.

5.6.2 *Visualizing and testing other correlations*

As an alternative to plotting correlations serially, there is a big bang option that requires just two lines of code. In the first line of the next code chunk, we create a data set called hustle2, which is a copy of hustle minus the continuous variables deflections and charges and the factor variables team, season, and team_season. The discarded variables are in positions 1–3, 6, and 8.

Then we make a call to the ggpairs() function from the GGally package, thereby producing a matrix that uses a ggplot2 look and feel to visualize the correlations on the left, display the correlation coefficients on the right, and plot variable distributions in between. We then add or append a call to the theme() function in order to rotate our x-axis labels 90 degrees. (See figure 5.11.) Depending on your system, this could take several seconds to run:

```
hustle %>%
  select(-c(1:3, 6, 8)) -> hustle2
ggpairs(hustle2) +
  theme(axis.text.x = element_text(angle = 90, hjust = 1))
```

It turns out that none of the remaining hustle variables have a strong correlation one way or the other with wins; in fact, none have correlation coefficients with wins equal to or as meaningful as the correlation coefficient between deflections and wins.

A call to the base R cor() function returns a tabular view of these same results, which is a faster alternative to calling the ggpairs() function and rendering a correlation matrix:

```
cor(hustle2)
##                     screen_assists screen_assists_pts loose_balls
## screen_assists          1.00000000         0.98172006 -0.36232361
## screen_assists_pts      0.98172006         1.00000000 -0.31540865
## loose_balls            -0.36232361        -0.31540865  1.00000000
## contested_2pt           0.20713399         0.21707461 -0.24932814
## contested_3pt          -0.33454664        -0.31180170  0.45417789
## contested_shots         0.01946603         0.04464369  0.05003144
## wins                    0.12180282         0.16997124  0.12997385
##                     contested_2pt contested_3pt contested_shots
## screen_assists          0.2071340   -0.33454664      0.01946603
## screen_assists_pts      0.2170746   -0.31180170      0.04464369
## loose_balls            -0.2493281    0.45417789      0.05003144
## contested_2pt           1.0000000   -0.38772620      0.77579822
## contested_3pt          -0.3877262    1.00000000      0.25889619
## contested_shots         0.7757982    0.25889619      1.00000000
## wins                    0.1854940   -0.09666249      0.13024121
##                            wins
## screen_assists       0.12180282
## screen_assists_pts   0.16997124
## loose_balls          0.12997385
```

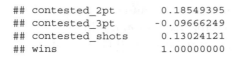

```
## contested_2pt        0.18549395
## contested_3pt       -0.09666249
## contested_shots      0.13024121
## wins                 1.00000000
```

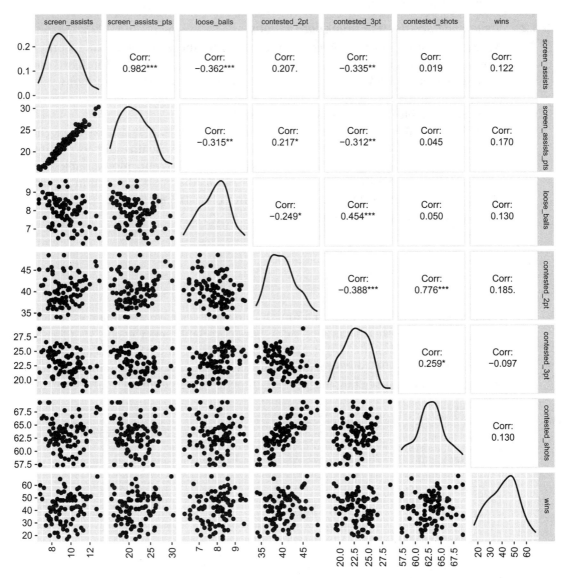

Figure 5.11   A correlation matrix that visualizes and computes the correlations between a subset of the hustle data set variables

That concludes all the linear regression prework. We've identified and then adjusted outlying values, tested for normality and then determined which subset of hustle variables to move forward with, and tested the correlations between potential predictors and the variable `wins`. Through this, we've determined that `deflections`, `contested_2pt`, and `screen_assists_pts` might have greater influence on wins than other predictors due to their correlation coefficients, with `wins` being the furthest from perfectly neutral.

5.7 Multiple linear regression

Whereas a simple linear regression tests a target variable against just one predictor variable (e.g., `wins` against `deflections`), a multiple linear regression tests a target variable against two or more predictors. A linear regression *must* contain a continuous target variable; the predictors are usually continuous, but they can also be categorical. In other words, linear models are intended to predict changes in a target variable that can assume any value within some range, such as test scores on a scale of 0–100 or regular season wins on a scale of 0–82. By contrast, a *logistic* regression (see chapter 14) contains a binary target variable, such as which students will or will not receive a passing grade or which NBA teams will or will not complete a regular season with a winning record.

Our immediate objectives are to demonstrate the following:

- How to randomly divide observations in a data set into a pair of mutually exclusive subsets, one of which will then be used for model fitting and the other for generating predictions
- How to fit a multiple linear regression
- How to return model results and interpret the same
- How to check for multicollinearity
- How to run model diagnostics and interpret the plots
- How to compare two competing linear models where the target variable is the same, but each model also contains a different mix of predictor variables
- How to predict

That all being said, let's get going with our regression testing.

5.7.1 Subsetting data into train and test

Our multiple regression exercise starts by subsetting 75% of the hustle observations into a data set called train and the remaining 25% into test; we'll fit our linear models against train and then predict on test. If instead we were to fit and predict on 100% of the records, we would run the risk of overfitting our models; that is, they would basically memorize the data and not necessarily respond well to new data.

The following chunk of `dplyr` code first extracts (i.e., filters) every fourth observation from the hustle data set and permanently casts the results into a new object called test; the row count for test, therefore, equals 23, or approximately 25% of the 90 observations in hustle. We then call the `anti_join()` function to create an object called train that contains the 67 hustle observations not already assigned to test:

```
hustle %>%
  filter(row_number() %% 4 == 1) -> test
train <- anti_join(hustle, test)
```

We then call the `dim()` function twice to return the dimensions of train and test, thereby confirming our train and test split worked as designed:

```
dim(train)
## [1] 67 12
dim(test)
## [1] 23 12
```

5.7.2   *Fitting the model*

The `lm()` function from base R is called to fit linear models. Our first model, fit1, regresses `wins` against the variables `screen_assists_pts`, `deflections`, `loose_balls`, `contested_2pt`, and `contested_shots`. These variables were selected as predictors based on the correlation coefficients we just computed.

The syntax is simple and straightforward enough. The target variable is separated from the predictors by a tilde, the predictors are separated by the addition operator, and there's a pointer to our data source:

```
fit1 <- lm(wins ~ screen_assists_pts + deflections + loose_balls +
    contested_2pt + contested_shots, data = train)
```

5.7.3   *Returning and interpreting the results*

We then call a series of functions from the `broom` package to incrementally return the results. A call to the `tidy()` function specifically returns a 6×5 tibble that, most importantly, contains the coefficient estimates and the p-values:

```
tidy(fit1)
## # A tibble: 6 × 5
##   term                 estimate std.error statistic p.value
##   <chr>                   <dbl>     <dbl>     <dbl>   <dbl>
## 1 (Intercept)            -62.9      38.6     -1.63   0.108
## 2 screen_assists_pts       1.04      0.441    2.35   0.0219
## 3 deflections              2.23      0.882    2.53   0.0138
## 4 loose_balls              5.38      2.19     2.45   0.0170
## 5 contested_2pt            0.525     0.763    0.688  0.494
## 6 contested_shots         -0.241     0.790   -0.305  0.761
```

Variables with p-values equal to or less than 0.05 have a statistically significant influence on variances in `wins`. We can otherwise combine the coefficient estimates returned from the `tidy()` function with actual values from the hustle data set to create a linear equation that takes the following form with respect to fit1:

$$y = B_0 + B_1 X_1 + B_2 X_2 + B_3 X_3 + B_4 X_4 + B_5 X_5$$

In this equation, note the following:

- y is the predicted value of the dependent variable `wins`.
- B_0 is the y-intercept, or constant term; it represents the value at which the fitted regression line crosses the y-axis.

- B_1X_1 is the regression coefficient of the first fit1 predictor, screen_assists_pts, where B_1 equals 1.04, and X_1 is the average number of points scored per game off of set screens.
- B_2X_2 is the regression coefficient of the second predictor, deflections, where B_2 equals 2.23, and X_2 is the average number of deflections per game.
- B_3X_3 is the regression coefficient of loose_balls, or 5.38 times the average number of loose balls recovered per game.
- B_4X_4 is the regression coefficient of contested_2pt, or 0.53 times the average number of two-point shot attempts contested per game.
- B_5X_5 is the regression coefficient of contested_shots, or -0.24 multiplied by the average number of total shot attempts contested per game.

Let's insert the relevant hustle statistics for the 2016–17 Miami Heat into our fit1 linear equation to demonstrate these results. The Heat averaged 22.3 points off screens, 14.2 deflections, 7.2 loose balls recovered, 45.5 two-point shot attempts contested, and 64.7 total shots contested per game during the 2016–17 regular season. Successive calls to the dplyr filter() and select() functions pull a subset of the MIA 17 record from the hustle data set:

```
hustle %>%
  filter(team_season == "MIA 17") %>%
  select(wins, screen_assists_pts, deflections, loose_balls,
         contested_2pt, contested_shots)
##    wins screen_assists_pts deflections loose_balls contested_2pt
## 1   41               22.3        14.2         7.2          45.5
##    contested_shots
## 2            64.7
```

Our linear regression would therefore "predict" (these figures were generated from train and not from test) Miami's win total as such:

```
wins = -62.91 + (1.04 * 22.3) + (2.23 * 14.2) + (5.38 * 7.2) +
  (0.52 * 45.5) - (0.24 * 64.7)
print(round(wins))
## [1] 39
```

Minus an error term, fit1 predicts 39 wins for the 2016–17 Heat (this was rounded to the nearest whole number by combining the print() function with the base R round() function), and the Heat actually won 41 games that season. That's not bad; however, subsequent evidence will reveal that fit1 is *way* more accurate when it comes to predicting regular season wins for .500 teams such as the 2016–17 Heat than for teams like the 2017–18 Houston Rockets, who won 65 games, or the 2018–19 New York Knicks, who won just 17 games. (Every NBA team plays an 82-game regular-season schedule.)

Let's now pretend the Heat actually recovered 8.2 loose balls per game rather than 7.2; in that case, fit1 would instead predict 44 wins (again, this has been rounded to the nearest whole number). We get to this by changing out 7.2 for 8.2 in our linear equation. More fundamentally, however, for every unit increase (or decrease) in the variable `loose_balls`, the predicted value for `wins` will increase (or decrease) by 5.38. By the same token, if the Heat had managed to deflect one more pass per game, fit1 would then predict 2.23 more wins (everything else being equal):

```
wins = -62.91 + (1.04 * 22.3) + (2.23 * 14.2) + (5.38 * 8.2) +
   (0.52 * 45.5) - (0.24 * 64.7)
print(round(wins))
## [1] 44
```

Not all fit1 predictors, however, have a statistically significant influence on wins. Only the variables `screen_assists_pts`, `deflections`, and `loose_balls` have p-values below the generally accepted and our predefined 0.05 threshold for significance, whereas the variables `contest_2pt` and `contested_shots` have p-values significantly above the 5% threshold. Therefore, our first multiple linear regression has revealed that only *some* hustle statistics have a significant influence on regular season win counts.

The `augment()` function from the `broom` package returns, among other things, actual values for wins as well as the fitted values for the same; the results are cast into a tibble called fit1_tbl. We then make a pair of calls to the `head()` function to return, at first, the top six values for the variable `wins`, and second, the top six values for the variable `.fitted`:

```
augment(fit1) -> fit1_tbl
head(fit1_tbl$wins)
## [1] 49 42 39 19 33 54
head(fit1_tbl$.fitted)
## [1] 37.84137 41.64023 40.52752 31.68228 33.81274 38.46419
```

Then, in the following chunk of `dplyr` code, we first call the `mutate()` function to create a new variable, `wins_dif`, which is the absolute difference (note the call to the base R `abs()` function) between the fit1_tbl variables `wins` and `.fitted`. We then call the `mean()` function from base R to compute the average difference between actual wins and fitted wins from fit1_tbl:

```
fit1_tbl %>%
   mutate(wins_dif = abs(wins - .fitted)) -> fit1_tbl
mean(fit1_tbl$wins_dif)
## [1] 8.274887
```

On average, our fit1 linear equation returned regular season win counts that are 8.27 wins above or below actual regular season win counts.

Finally, the `glance()` function from the `broom` package returns, most significantly, the R-squared (R^2) and adjusted R^2 statistics. R^2 is a statistical measure that represents the proportion of the variance in the target variable explained by the predictors. It therefore equals some number between 0 and 1, where a value of 1 indicates that the predictors explain all the variance, and a value of 0 indicates that the predictors fail to explain any of the variance.

Adjusted R^2 is a modified version of R^2 in that it takes into account the number of predictors. While R^2 will naturally increase as other predictors are added to a regression model, adjusted R^2 will actually decrease if those same predictors aren't contributing to the model's predictive power. The more complex the model, the more R^2 and adjusted R^2 will diverge:

```
glance(fit1)
## # A tibble: 1 × 12
##   r.squared adj.r.squared sigma statistic p.value    df logLik
##       <dbl>         <dbl> <dbl>     <dbl>   <dbl> <dbl>  <dbl>
## 1     0.202         0.137  10.9      3.09  0.0150     5  -252.
##       AIC   BIC deviance df.residual  nobs
##     <dbl> <dbl>    <dbl>       <int> <int>
## 1    518.  533.   7230.          61    67
```

Because R^2 equals 0.20, the fit1 predictors collectively explain approximately 20% of the variance in regular season wins, regardless of their respective p-values,

But the adjusted R^2 equals just 0.14, no doubt due to the fact that fit1 contains a pair of predictors, `contested_2pt` and `contested_shots`, that don't have statistically significant influences on wins due to their respective p-values being above the 5% threshold. In other words, our model contains noise. So based on this measure, it would actually be more accurate to say that fit1 best explains about 14%, rather than 20%, of the variance in wins.

5.7.4 *Checking for multicollinearity*

Let's now check for multicollinearity in fit1. Once more, multicollinearity is a situation in which two or more predictors are highly correlated; that is, the correlation coefficient between them is equal to or close to +1. The most significant consequence of multicollinearity is that it artificially inflates the explained variance. As we just mentioned, R^2 will automatically and incrementally increase in value with each additional predictor; at the same time, adjusted R^2 will decrease, but not so much if the additional predictors by themselves are statistically significant. But where and when there is multicollinearity, we're actually double counting; as a result, both the R^2 and adjusted R^2 measures will be artificially high.

We make a call to the `vif()` function from the `car` package to test for multicollinearity. Based on the correlation tests we ran earlier, it's doubtful fit1 contains a presence of multicollinearity, but it's nevertheless a best practice to test for it to ensure we're not overfitting:

```
vif(fit1)
## screen_assists_pts      deflections      loose_balls
##           1.155995         1.062677         1.314189
## contested_2pt   contested_shots
##      3.052934          2.637588
```

If the variance inflation factor for any of the fit1 predictors is above 5, we should discard those variables and then fit a reduced model, that is, a model with fewer predictors. But as we can see, the variance inflation factor for all fit1 predictors is less than 5.

5.7.5   *Running and interpreting model diagnostics*

The plot() function from base R returns the model diagnostics around linearity and normality (see figure 5.12). These are printed in a 2×2 matrix when plot() is preceded by the base R par() function. The plots confirm that fit1 satisfies prerequisites for linearity and normality, thereby validating the integrity of our first model, even if we might not be wholly satisfied with the results:

```
par(mfrow = c(2, 2))
plot(fit1)
```

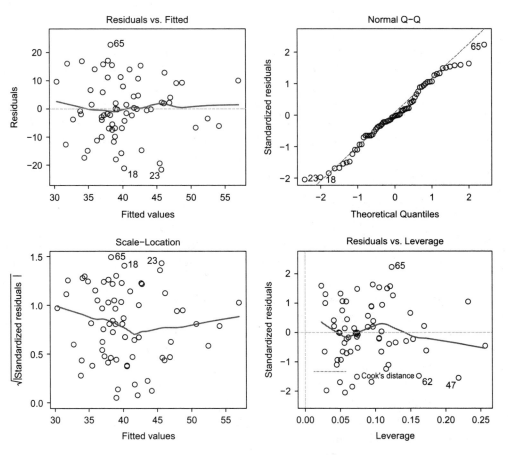

Figure 5.12   Model diagnostics for the first multiple linear regression model

Diagnostic plots help us assess the goodness of fit and validate going-in assumptions around linearity and normality. Let's go through these one by one.

The Residuals vs. Fitted plot in the upper-left quadrant displays the model residuals along the y-axis and the fitted values along the x-axis. A residual is a measure of the vertical distance from an actual value to the fitted regression line; the model residuals, or errors, should follow a normal distribution. The data points more or less hover around the horizontal line instead of following some obvious pattern, which is a good thing because it strongly suggests that the residuals do follow a normal distribution.

The Normal QQ plot in the upper-right quadrant is yet another check on whether the residuals follow a normal distribution. It compares the residuals, which are divided into quantiles, or four equal-sized proportions, against the quantiles of a theoretical normal distribution; the former is plotted along the y-axis, and the latter is plotted along the x-axis. Note that both data series have been converted to standardized scales. The residuals follow the diagonal line without any severe deviation, as they should. The alignment is hardly perfect, of course, and we do see some moderate deviation at both tails, but there's nothing here to trigger any serious concerns about normality and linearity or lack thereof.

The Scale-Location plot in the lower-left quadrant, also known as a spread-location plot or a square root of standardized residual plot, is used to assess what's called homoscedasticity. It also plots the square root of the standardized residuals along the y-axis and the fitted values along the x-axis. Homoscedasticity refers to a statistical assumption in regression analysis where the variance in the residuals—that is, the difference between the actual and fitted values—is constant across all levels of the predictors. In other words, it expects that the spread, or dispersion, of the residuals is more or less the same throughout the range of independent variables. The Scale-Location plot should and does resemble the Residuals vs. Fitted plot.

The Residuals vs. Leverage plot in the lower-right quadrant, more frequently called a Cook's Distance plot, is used to isolate any observations—outliers, basically—that have undue influence on the fitted regression line. It also plots the standardized residuals along the y-axis and what are called leverage values along the x-axis. Leverage values represent the influence of each observation. We're particularly concerned about any data points that fall below the dashed horizontal line annotated as Cook's Distance, and, of course, we have a few of those. But our actual concern should be focused on any data points below that line and in the lower-right corner, and we see only one observation that satisfies both criteria. Our results aren't perfect (they rarely are in the real world), but we don't have any cause for alarm or any reason to change course.

5.7.6 *Comparing models*

A logical next step would be to remove that one observation from train and then rerun our regression, but we're going to take a bigger next step instead. Because only a subset of the fit1 predictors has a statistically significant influence on wins, we'll now fit a second multiple regression where the predictors `screen_assist_pts`, `deflections`, and `loose_balls` remain in play, but the predictors `contested_2pt` and `contested_shots` are excluded. Therefore, our second regression, named fit2, is merely a reduced version of fit1. Subsequent calls to the tidy(), augment(), glance(), and other functions return the results, and figure 5.13 displays the diagnostics:

```
fit2 <- lm(wins ~ screen_assists_pts + deflections + loose_balls,
        data = train)

tidy(fit2)
## # A tibble: 4 × 5
##    term                estimate std.error statistic p.value
##    <chr>                  <dbl>     <dbl>     <dbl>   <dbl>
## 1 (Intercept)            -56.1      25.5     -2.20  0.0317
## 2 screen_assists_pts      1.12     0.422      2.65  0.0101
## 3 deflections             2.35     0.859      2.74  0.00805
## 4 loose_balls             4.81      1.98      2.42  0.0182
augment(fit2) -> fit_tbl2
print(fit_tbl2)
# A tibble: 67 × 10
##     wins screen_assists_pts deflections loose_balls .fitted  .resid
##    <int>              <dbl>       <dbl>       <dbl>   <dbl>   <dbl>
## 1    49                 20        14.1         8.3    39.3    9.66
## 2    42               26.2        12.1         8      40.1    1.85
## 3    39               25.7        12.6         8.1    41.2   -2.24
## 4    19               22.4        11.8         7.6    33.3  -14.3
## 5    33               20.1        11.5         8.4    33.8  -0.825
## 6    54               19.9        13.9         8.6    40.2   13.8
## 7    57               26.3        14.2         8.7    48.6    8.44
## 8    53               16.6        14.9         8.4    37.9   15.1
## 9    48               20.2        14.2         8.6    41.2    6.76
##10    37               20.1        11.9         8.5    35.2    1.75
##         hat .sigma   .cooksd  .std.resid
##       <dbl>  <dbl>     <dbl>       <dbl>
## 1   0.0224   10.8   0.00472       0.907
## 2   0.0726   10.8  0.000626       0.179
## 3   0.0568   10.8  0.000691      -0.214
## 4   0.0647   10.7    0.0324       -1.37
## 5   0.0749   10.9  0.000128      -0.0797
## 6   0.0316   10.7    0.0138        1.30
## 7   0.0792   10.8    0.0144       0.817
## 8   0.0550   10.7    0.0303        1.44
## 9   0.0298   10.8   0.00312       0.637
##10   0.0632   10.9  0.000478       0.168
## # … with 57 more rows

fit_tbl2 %>%
  mutate(wins_dif = abs(wins - .fitted)) -> fit_tbl2
mean(fit_tbl2$wins_dif)
## [1] 8.427093
glance(fit2)
## # A tibble: 1 × 12
##    r.squared adj.r.squared sigma statistic p.value    df logLik
##        <dbl>         <dbl> <dbl>     <dbl>   <dbl> <dbl>  <dbl>
## 1      0.194         0.156  10.8      5.06 0.00334     3  -252.
##        AIC    BIC deviance df.residual   nobs
##        dbl> <dbl>    <dbl>       <int> <int>
```

```
## 1     514.  525.    7302.          63    67

vif(fit2)
## screen_assists_pts       deflections        loose_balls
##          1.085184           1.031128           1.098619
par(mfrow = c(2,2))
plot(fit2)
```

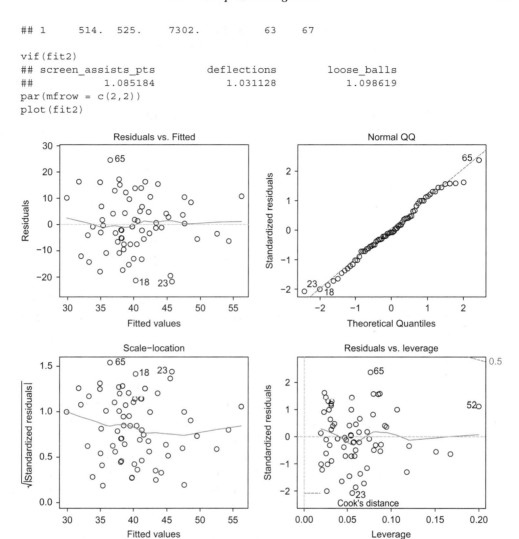

Figure 5.13 Model diagnostics for the second, or reduced, multiple linear regression model

Of the two fitted regressions, fit2 is a better model than fit1, at least for the following reasons:

- There's no noise in fit2—all fit2 predictors have p-values below the predefined 0.05 threshold for significance.
- Our second regression is merely a reduced version of our first model, yet fit2 better explains the variance in wins, albeit slightly, than fit1: the adjusted R^2 statistic for fit2 equals 0.16 versus 0.14 for fit1. That isn't to say fit2 explains the variance in wins *well*—but hold that thought.

- Our second model has a lower and therefore better Akaike Information Criterion (AIC) score than does our first model. AIC is one of the measures returned from the glance() function; alternatively, you can call the base R AIC() function to return the same. The best-fit model according to AIC is the one that explains most of the variance in a target variable using the smallest number of predictors; as such, it uses the independent variable count and the log-likelihood estimate—that is, the likelihood that a model could have generated observed y-values—as inputs. AIC is fairly meaningless by itself, but it's a key measure for comparing competing models. Furthermore, there's a rule of thumb that suggests that when one model has an AIC score two or more units lower than a competing model, the model with the lower AIC is a significantly better fit than the other model. Well, the AIC for fit1 equals 518, and the AIC for fit2 equals 514.
- The diagnostics are slightly better with fit2 than with fit1 primarily because the Residuals vs. Leverage plot doesn't contain any observations below the Cook's Distance line.

However, the average difference between actual and fitted wins is slightly greater in fit2 (8.43) versus fit1 (8.27), but this is hardly anything to haggle over given all the other results.

5.7.7   *Predicting*

Let's now see how fit2 performs on test. We therefore make a call to the base R predict() function to predict regular season wins, bounded by a 95% lower and upper confidence interval (CI). The CI is a range of values less than and greater than the predicted value for y that we can be 95% confident contains the actual value for y.

Three arguments are passed to the predict() function: the model and the data source are required while the CI, defaulted to 95%, is optional. The results are cast into an object called fit2_pred, where fit equals the predicted number of regular season wins, lwr represents the low end of our CI, and upr represents the high end of our CI:

```
fit2_pred <- predict(fit2, data.frame(test), interval = "confidence")
print(fit2_pred)
##          fit      lwr      upr
## 1   44.03632 37.33518 50.73746
## 2   32.32559 27.22836 37.42282
## 3   36.66966 31.99864 41.34067
## 4   33.97327 29.54744 38.39910
## 5   34.30091 28.39030 40.21152
## 6   43.32909 35.93216 50.72603
## 7   41.24102 35.64396 46.83807
## 8   44.46051 40.78216 48.13886
## 9   38.46246 34.58980 42.33511
## 10  41.12360 36.88138 45.36582
## 11  44.69284 40.73769 48.64799
## 12  37.34022 33.95924 40.72119
## 13  45.32616 39.41971 51.23261
## 14  50.02897 43.31042 56.74753
```

```
## 15 37.18162 33.31884 41.04439
## 16 42.25199 35.84835 48.65562
## 17 33.46908 27.89836 39.03979
## 18 34.15238 26.87326 41.43151
## 19 41.70479 36.39175 47.01783
## 20 34.30830 28.03565 40.58094
## 21 33.20151 27.19351 39.20951
## 22 43.30823 36.75603 49.86043
## 23 36.77234 29.78770 43.75698
```

We then call the `select()` function from the `dplyr` package to reduce the test data set to include only the variable `wins`:

```
test %>%
  select(wins) -> test
```

Next, we call the `cbind()` function from base R to join fit2_pred and test vertically and then the `mutate()` function from `dplyr` to create a new variable called `wins_dif`, which equals the absolute difference between the variables `wins` and `fit`. The results are thrown into a new object called fit_tbl_pred.

Finally, we compute the average of `wins_dif` using the `mean()` function from base R. The result equals 9.94, thereby suggesting that our second regression performs worse on test than it did against train:

```
cbind(fit2_pred, test) %>%
  mutate(wins_dif = abs(wins - fit)) -> fit_tbl_pred
mean(fit_tbl_pred$wins_dif)
## [1] 9.936173
```

A `ggplot2` histogram plots the frequency distribution of the fit_tbl_pred variable `wins_dif`, or the difference between actual and predicted wins (see figure 5.14):

```
p1 <- ggplot(fit_tbl_pred, aes(x = wins_dif)) +
  geom_histogram(fill = "snow1", color = "dodgerblue4", bins = 6) +
  labs(title = "Frequency of Differences between
       Actual and Predicted Wins",
       subtitle = "Wins ~ Points Off Screens + Deflections +
       Loose Balls Recovered",
       x = "Difference between Actual and Predicted Wins",
       y = "Frequency") +
  theme(plot.title = element_text(face = "bold"))
print(p1)
```

We get more accurate results when actual regular season wins equal 41 or thereabouts; conversely, we get less accurate results when teams won either very few or very many regular season games in an 82-game schedule.

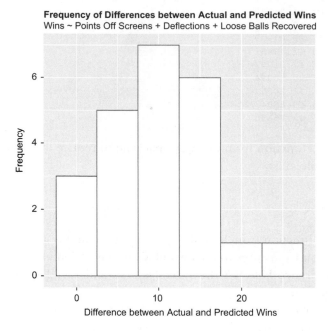

Figure 5.14 Frequency distribution displaying the absolute differences between predicted and actual regular season wins

The following short chunks of dplyr code return the fit_tbl_pred records where the variable wins_dif is greater than 15 and again where the same variable is less than 5:

```
fit_tbl_pred %>%
  filter(wins_dif > 15)
##         fit      lwr      upr wins  wins_dif
## 1  44.03632 37.33518 50.73746   29 15.03632
## 5  34.30091 28.39030 40.21152   60 25.69909
## 10 41.12360 36.88138 45.36582   24 17.12360
## 11 44.69284 40.73769 48.64799   65 20.30716
## 12 37.34022 33.95924 40.72119   22 15.34022
 fit_tbl_pred %>%
  filter(wins_dif < 5)
##         fit      lwr      upr wins   wins_dif
## 3  36.66966 31.99864 41.34067   41 4.3303443
## 13 45.32616 39.41971 51.23261   48 2.6738414
## 14 50.02897 43.31042 56.74753   52 1.9710281
## 16 42.25199 35.84835 48.65562   43 0.7480111
## 18 34.15238 26.87326 41.43151   37 2.8476181
## 22 43.30823 36.75603 49.86043   41 2.3082288
```

A second ggplot2 object, a line chart, compares actual wins with predicted wins, with the shaded areas immediately above and below the predicted values representing the upper and lower CIs (see figure 5.15).

But first, we call the dplyr arrange() function to sort fit_tbl_pred by the variable wins in ascending order and then append a new variable called row.num. This approach helps to make it more obvious that fit2 does a much better job of predicting wins for teams that finished at or near .500 versus teams that had an extreme number of regular season wins:

```
fit_tbl_pred %>%
  arrange(wins) -> fit_tbl_pred

fit_tbl_pred$row_num <- seq.int(nrow(fit_tbl_pred))

p2 <- ggplot(fit_tbl_pred, aes(x = row_num, y = wins, group = 1)) +
  geom_line(aes(y = wins), color = "navy", size = 1.5) +
  geom_line(aes(y = fit), color = "gold3", size = 1.5) +
  geom_ribbon(aes(ymin = lwr, ymax = upr), alpha = 0.2) +
  labs(title = "Actual Wins versus Predicted Wins",
       subtitle = "Results on test data set (23 observations)",
       x = "2016-17 through 2018-19\nSorted in Ascending Order
          by Actual Wins",
       y = "Wins",
       caption = "Actuals in dark\nPredictions in light") +
  theme(plot.title = element_text(face = "bold"))
print(p2)
```

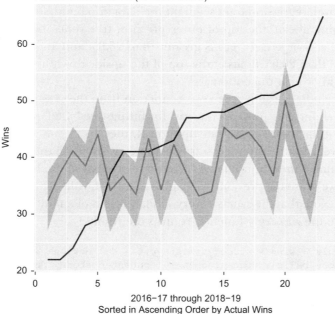

Figure 5.15   Another view between predicted and actual regular season wins

If our goal had been to fit a multiple linear regression to mostly account for the variance in wins from the 2016–17 to 2018–19 NBA regular seasons, then we would need a wider data set to include variables such as shots made and attempted, free throws made and attempted, turnover margin, and so on. Neither of our regressions, after all, adequately explain or predict regular season wins terribly well.

But our goal was more modest, or at least quite different from this. Our purpose instead was to identify which hustle statistics might have a statistically significant influence on wins and to quantify the effect of that influence. To that purpose, we've shown that points off screens, deflections, and loose balls recovered explain roughly 16% of the variance in regular season wins, which is far from insignificant. We've also discovered where and when it makes the most sense for players to give 100% efforts and where and when there isn't an equal return. Now, let's see what sort of insights a regression tree might reveal.

5.8   *Regression tree*

Regression trees, frequently referred to as decision tree regressions, are relatively easy to construct and just as easy to interpret and explain; their downside is that they are often less accurate than other supervised learning methods. For this reason, data scientists sometimes pivot toward bagging, random forest, and boosting models; each of these methods involves generating *many* trees, rather than just one, which are then combined to form a single prediction.

At a very basic level, regression trees segment the data into multiple regions of predictor space. Jumping ahead, the top of our regression tree splits the data into two regions: one where screen_assists_pts is greater than 26.05, and another where the same variable is less than 26.05. Splits at the top of the upside-down tree are more significant than splits at or near the bottom.

A regression tree is fit by calling the tree() function from the tree package. There are other R packages and functions, by the way, for fitting tree-based models and visualizing the results; in fact, with almost anything in R, there is usually more than one option or alternative, and one isn't necessarily better or worse than the others.

Our model contains the five predictors from our original multiple linear regression; additionally, we'll use the previous 75% split from the hustle data set called train as our data source. Note that the syntax is very similar to that of a multiple regression. A subsequent call to the summary() function returns the results:

```
fit3 <- tree(formula = wins ~ screen_assists_pts + deflections +
             loose_balls + contested_2pt + contested_shots, data = train)
summary(fit3)
##
## Regression tree:
## tree(formula = wins ~ screen_assists_pts + deflections + loose_balls +
##     contested_2pt + contested_shots, data = train)
## Number of terminal nodes:  10
## Residual mean deviance:  82.83 = 4722 / 57
## Distribution of residuals:
##     Min.  1st Qu.   Median    Mean  3rd Qu.     Max.
## -17.2500  -5.6670   0.2857  0.0000   6.3330  21.0000
```

Not every regression tree is necessarily constructed using every predictor in the model, but based on the fit3 results, our tree will contain one or more branches for each predictor variable. We know this, or can at least assume as much, because the model output would have otherwise called out the *subset* of predictors used in constructing the tree. We also know that our tree will contain 10 terminal nodes (i.e., leaves)—these are the endpoints at the bottom of the tree to which predicted regular season wins are affixed. Finally, the square root of the residual mean deviance, equal to 9.10, is the rough equivalent to the average difference between predicted and actual wins from our multiple regressions, which makes fit3 competitive to fit2, though less accurate.

To plot our regression tree, we call the `plot()` and `text()` functions from base R in succession (see figure 5.16); `plot()` draws the tree, and `text()` adds the variable names and conditions:

```
plot(fit3)
text(fit3)
```

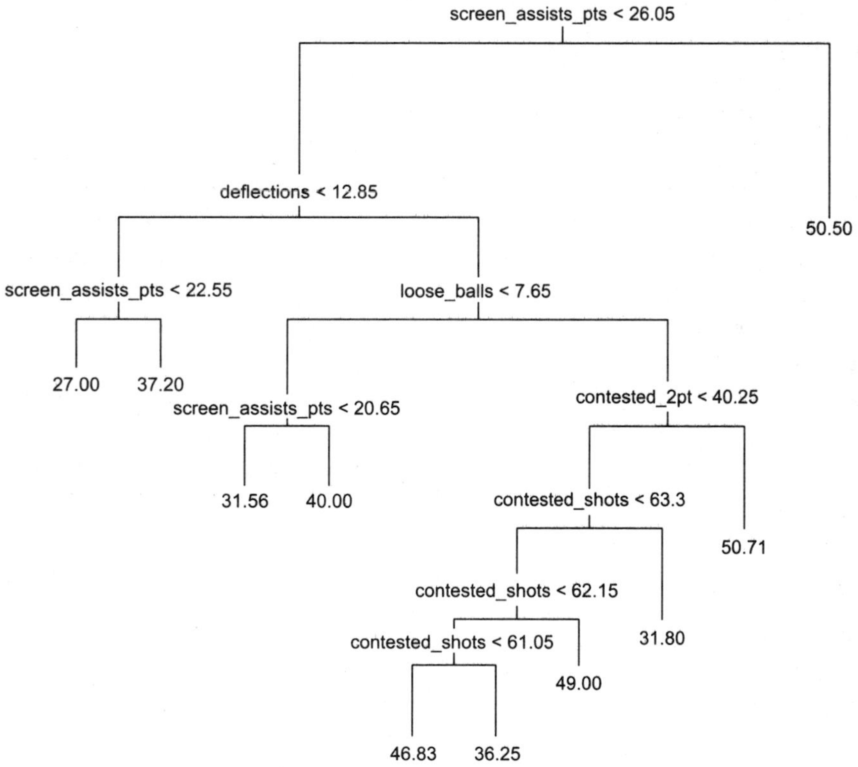

Figure 5.16   The visualized results of our regression tree

According to our regression tree

- Teams that average more than 26.05 points off screens per game can be expected to win 50 or 51 regular season games.
- Alternatively, teams that average fewer than 26.05 points off screens per game can be expected to win anywhere between 27 and 51 regular season games, depending on other variables and other splits.
- Teams that average fewer than 26.05 points off screens and fewer than 12.85 deflections per game can be expected to win somewhere between 27 and 37 regular season games.
- Teams that average fewer than 26.05 points off screens but more than 12.85 deflections per game can be expected to win somewhere between 31 and 51 regular season games.

There's a one-to-one correlation between if-else rules and splits in the tree. Our regression tree, therefore, produces results that tie back well to our multiple regressions and provide additional insights through a series of if-else rules that linear models can't return. The predictors `screen_assists_pts`, `deflections`, and `loose_balls` are more significant than `contested_2pt` and `contested_shots`, according to both model types tested here. And while neither model predicts wins with much certainty, our goal was to identify which of these hustle statistics has more of an influence on regular season wins than other like statistics.

At the end of the day, we've determined that setting screens on offense, which creates unfettered shot opportunities; deflecting passes on defense, which disrupts the opponent's offense; and grabbing loose balls while on offense or defense deserve a 100% effort, while other so-called hustle plays don't. Thus, we've confirmed our hypothesis that *some* hustle statistics do, in fact, have a statistically significant effect on wins and losses.

So our linear regression and our regression tree isolated the same three variables—the same three hustle statistics—as having the most significant influence on wins. They also provided different insights. According to our reduced linear model, points off screens, pass deflections, and loose balls recovered account for approximately 16% of the variance in regular season wins, based on a data set spanning three NBA seasons. Our regression tree, on the other hand, returned a series of predicted wins based on several if-else rules.

Going forward, we'll challenge some conventional wisdom and demonstrate, with data and statistical techniques, that these accepted conventions aren't necessarily true. In chapter 6, we'll explore the idea that games are won in the fourth quarter.

Summary

- Linear regressions done right first require a thorough analysis of the data. Outliers should be identified and treated, variables with non-normal distributions should be transformed or disregarded altogether, and preferences should be given to those potential predictors that have the strongest correlations with the target variable, especially when you're working with wide data sets.

- It's best to subset your data into two, developing your model against one and then predicting against the other, to avoid overfitting.

- Another way of avoiding overfitting is to check for multicollinearity and, if necessary, apply corrective action by then removing offending variables from your model.

- Linear regressions draw a straight line that minimizes the differences between the regression and the data. While linear models are quite common and likely more prevalent than other model types where the dependent (i.e., target) variable is continuous, it's important to understand that data isn't always linear.

- Our linear regressions didn't explain or predict wins with much accuracy, but we still successfully identified three hustle statistics—points off screens, pass deflections, and loose balls recovered—that collectively account for 16% of the variance in regular season wins over the three seasons tested. We therefore discovered where players should give 100% and where they can lay up, if necessary.

- Our regression tree isolated the same three variables as being more significant than the other hustle statistics in our data set; furthermore, it returned predicted regular season wins through a series of if-else rules.

- There are several use cases for linear regression, such as product sales based on a multichannel advertising strategy among online, radio, and television advertising; median price of a single-family home based on crime rates, average number of rooms per unit, and student-to-teacher ratios in local schools; marathon performance based on age, gender, and recent 10K and half-marathon paces; credit card default rates based on macroeconomic indicators; and CEO salaries based on years in position and year-over-year changes in stock prices. Linear regressions require a continuous target variable. In chapter 14, we'll fit a logistic regression, which instead requires a binary target variable.

- A tree-based model is a good alternative for these same use cases. Additionally, you can call the `tree()` function to also fit a classification tree; it has the same syntax as a regression tree, but your target variable must be binary rather than continuous.

More wrangling
and visualizing data

According to conventional wisdom, no doubt influenced by late-game bias where the final plays in a close game create the most indelible memories, NBA games are won in the fourth quarter. In other words, teams that win the fourth quarter and play best down the stretch, regardless of what might have happened over the first three quarters, will usually be victorious. This suggests that the last 12 minutes of an NBA game are more significant than the first 36 minutes (NBA games are 48 minutes in duration divided into four 12-minute quarters).

Our hypothesis is that this conventional wisdom is false. We'll examine almost every NBA regular season game over two contiguous seasons and then plot how winning teams fared in the fourth quarter versus the other three quarters. Along the way, we'll demonstrate a ton of data wrangling techniques that will serve you well in your professional or academic careers, such as changing layouts by reshaping whole data sets and sorting vectors, extracting records that meet logical criteria, selecting or deselecting columns by name, grouping and summarizing data, renaming existing variables and creating new ones, and joining data sets vertically and horizontally. And with our `ggplot2` bar charts, we'll demonstrate how to skillfully display results by highlighting some and de-emphasizing others.

6.1 *Loading packages*

We start by loading the three packages we'll need to wrangle, query, and visualize data in ways that are above and beyond the capabilities of base R. We make a series of calls to the `library()` function and pass our required packages as arguments. All of these packages should be familiar to you by now:

```
library(tidyverse)
library(sqldf)
library(patchwork)
```

Due to all the data wrangling ahead of us, when not relying on base R, we'll be calling `dplyr` and `tidyr` functions way more frequently than other packaged functions. Once more, `dplyr` and `tidyr` are part of the `tidyverse` package.

6.2 *Importing data*

We have two .csv files to import, both of which were downloaded from the website www.bigdataball.com. The first file, set to nba1819, contains box score data for every regular season and postseason game from the 2018–19 season; the second file, set to nba1920, contains similar box score data for every regular season and postseason game from the 2019–20 season.

We call the `read_csv()` function twice from the `readr` package, which is part of the `tidyverse`, to import these two files one at a time:

```
nba1819 <- read.csv("nba_boxscore_1819.csv")
nba1920 <- read.csv("nba_boxscore_1920.csv")
```

Box score data is mostly a combination of team-level and player-level basic statistics, such as the following:

- Total points scored
- Points scored per quarter
- Shots attempted and made
- Free throws attempted and made
- Offensive and defensive rebounds

- Assists
- Turnovers
- Starting lineups for both teams

Game-level attributes are also included; for example, the date of the game and where it was played, the names of the officials assigned to call the game, and opening and closing odds. We'll need only some of this data for our analysis.

The `dim()` function from base R returns the dimension—that is, the number of rows and columns—in the nba1819 and nba1920 data sets:

```
dim(nba1819)
## [1] 2624    57
dim(nba1920)
## [1] 2286    57
```

Both data sets have 57 columns, or variables. But nba1920 has fewer rows, or observations, than nba1819 because COVID-19 truncated the 2019–20 season; fewer games translates to fewer rows of data, of course.

6.3   Wrangling data

At the start, most of our data wrangling operations will be around subsetting data (including or excluding observations that meet or fail to meet some logical criteria, or reducing the width of whole data sets by removing variables that won't factor into our analysis) and combining, or joining, a pair of data sets into one object. Ultimately, we need data sources that can be cast into a series of complementary `ggplot2` visualizations that display quarter-by-quarter results in whole numbers and percentages. We're a long way from doing that with our two .csv files as is.

6.3.1   Subsetting data sets

We start by subsetting the nba1819 data set by calling the `filter()` function from the `dplyr` package so that nba1819 only includes observations where the variable DATASET equals NBA 2018-2019 Regular Season *and* the variable MIN (short for minutes) equals 240. This subsequently reduces the nba1819 data set to only regular season games that ended in regulation (240 is the product of 48 minutes times five players on the floor); or, put differently, we're excluding regular season games that went into overtime and all playoff games.

There is a base R equivalent to the `dplyr` `filter()` function, which is the `subset()` function—they operate similarly and return the same results. But if and when you're working with larger data sets, you might find that the `filter()` function provides a performance bump over `subset()`. Remember that R differentiates the = versus == operators; the former is an assignment operator, whereas the latter is an equal to operator. In addition, when filtering nba1819 where the variable DATASET equals NBA 2018-2019 Regular Season *and* (&) where the variable MIN equals 240, we're instructing R to subset our data where both conditions are met, not just one or the other.

We then call the `dim()` function to check the new dimension of nba1819:

```
nba1819 %>%
  filter(DATASET == "NBA 2018-2019 Regular Season" & MIN == 240) -> nba1819
dim(nba1819)
## [1] 2326    57
```

The nba1819 data set was 2,624 rows long when imported and now has a length of 2,326 rows.

With respect to the 2019–20 NBA season, where play was temporarily suspended due to the COVID-19 pandemic and then resumed (for most teams, not all) at a neutral site in Orlando, we subset the nba1920 data set to only include regular season games before the suspension of play that also ended in regulation. We therefore subset nba1920 so that the variable GAME_ID is equal to or less than 21900973 and the variable MIN equals 240:

```
nba1920 %>%
  filter(GAME_ID <= 21900973 & MIN == 240) -> nba1920
```

We then make another call to the `dim()` function, which, of course, returns the new dimension of the nba1920 data set. It now has a length of 1,820 rows, whereas it originally contained 2,286 observations:

```
dim(nba1920)
## [1] 1820    57
```

Let's now demonstrate some joining techniques.

6.3.2 Joining data sets

Base R and `dplyr` functions are available for combining two or more data sets into one object. While `dplyr` functions might perform best against larger data sets or when working with smaller machines, base R and `dplyr` functions otherwise operate alike and return equal results. Here, we'll call one base R function and then one `dplyr` function for the purposes of joining data sets, mixed with other data wrangling operations.

That being said, we first call the `rbind()` function from base R to row-bind the nba1819 and nba1920 data sets into a new object called nbadf1. This works because both data sets have the same width and the same variable names; any differences would cause R to throw an error. The variables do not need to be in the same order for this operation to be successful.

The `dim()` function is called immediately afterward to return the dimension of our new object:

```
nbadf1 <- rbind(nba1819, nba1920)
dim(nbadf1)
## [1] 4146    57
```

We see that nbadf1 contains 57 variables and 4,146 observations, comprising 2,326 observations from nba1819 and 1,820 from nba1920.

Then, we subset our new working data set by calling the select() function from the dplyr package to retain just the 16 variables positioned between DATASET and MIN; another call to the dim() function confirms that the width of nbadf1 has, in fact, been reduced from 57 columns to just 16. The semicolon in our code tells R to accept every variable from DATASET through MIN, which is a much better alternative than calling out all 16 variables:

```
nbadf1 %>%
  select(DATASET:MIN) -> nbadf1
dim(nbadf1)
## [1] 4146    16
```

Next, we split nbadf1 into equal halves by calling the dplyr filter() function twice: once where the variable VENUE equals R for road, and those observations are thrown into a data set called road, and then where VENUE instead equals H for home, and those observations are thrown into a data set called home. (Unless there are extenuating circumstances, NBA games—regular season and postseason—are *never* played at neutral sites. Regardless, teams are always designated as road or home.) Both calls are shown here:

```
nbadf1 %>%
  filter(VENUE == "R") -> road
dim(road)
## [1] 2073    16

nbadf1 %>%
  filter(VENUE == "H") -> home
dim(home)
## [1] 2073    16
```

The dim() function returns like dimensions for both objects, which is a good thing because there should be an equal number of road and home observations.

Our road and home data sets are about to be merged horizontally, but we first need to give them unique variable names. The rename() function from the dplyr package allows us to rename variables where the variable name on the left side of the assignment operator is the new variable name, and the variable name on the right side of the assignment operator is the old, or existing, variable name:

```
road %>%
  rename(dataset = DATASET, ID = GAME_ID, date = DATE,
         teamR = TEAM, venueR = VENUE, Q1R = Q1, Q2R = Q2,
         Q3R = Q3, Q4R = Q4, OT1R = OT1,
         OT2R = OT2, OT3R = OT3, OT4R = OT4,
         OT5R = OT5, FR = F, MINR = MIN) -> road
home %>%
  rename(dataset = DATASET, ID = GAME_ID, date = DATE,
```

```
teamH = TEAM, venueH = VENUE, Q1H = Q1, Q2H = Q2,
Q3H = Q3, Q4H = Q4, OT1H = OT1,
OT2H = OT2, OT3H = OT3, OT4H = OT4,
OT5H = OT5, FH = F, MINH = MIN) -> home
```

Most of the new variable names were appended with either the letter R or the letter H to distinguish road and home on otherwise like variables. The three exceptions to this are the variables now named `dataset`, `ID`, and `date`.

We then perform a left join on road and home by calling the `dplyr left_join()` function to merge the two data sets by matching rows; we specifically match road and home by the variables `dataset`, `ID`, and `date`.

We then immediately call the `dim()` function to again check the dimension of our working data set, called nbadf2; nbadf2 contains 2,073 rows (half of 4,146) and 29 variables (16 from the road data set and another 16 from the home data set, minus the common variables `dataset`, `ID`, and `date`):

```
left_join(road, home, by = c("dataset", "ID", "date")) -> nbadf2
dim(nbadf2)
## [1] 2073   29
```

Again, we call the `dplyr select()` function to remove unnecessary or duplicate variables (notice the minus sign that precedes the base R `c()` function); and again, we call the `dim()` function to return the row and column counts. As a reminder, the `c()` function is called when we need to create a vector or concatenate multiple objects into a single vector:

```
nbadf2 %>%
  select(-c(OT1R:OT5R, MINR, OT1H:OT5H, MINH)) -> nbadf2
dim(nbadf2)
## [1] 2073   17
```

We now have the data set nbadf2 containing 2,073 rows and 17 columns.

Next, we convert five of the remaining nbadf2 variables to factor variables by making successive calls to the base R `as.factor()` function. This is a good practice when your variables are categorical or ordinal and have a fixed set of possible values:

```
nbadf2$dataset <- as.factor(nbadf2$dataset)
nbadf2$teamR <- as.factor(nbadf2$teamR)
nbadf2$venueR <- as.factor(nbadf2$venueR)
nbadf2$teamH <- as.factor(nbadf2$teamH)
nbadf2$venueH <- as.factor(nbadf2$venueH)
```

Finally, we make a call to the `dplyr glimpse()` function to return a transposed snapshot of the nbadf2 data set:

```
glimpse(nbadf2)
## Rows: 2,073
## Columns: 17
```

```
## $ dataset <fct> NBA 2018-2019 Regular Season, NBA 2018-2019 Regular…
## $ ID      <int> 21800001, 21800002, 21800003, 21800004, 21800005, 2…
## $ date    <chr> "10/16/18", "10/16/18", "10/17/18", "10/17/18", "10…
## $ teamR   <fct> Philadelphia, Oklahoma City, Milwaukee, Brooklyn, M…
## $ venueR  <fct> R, R, R, R, R, R, R, R, R, R, R, R, R, R, R, R, R, …
## $ Q1R     <int> 21, 23, 36, 29, 16, 31, 24, 25, 35, 23, 30, 29, 24,…
## $ Q2R     <int> 21, 24, 31, 22, 23, 20, 25, 22, 36, 29, 38, 30, 22,…
## $ Q3R     <int> 24, 32, 26, 25, 19, 27, 35, 28, 30, 31, 25, 15, 27,…
## $ Q4R     <int> 21, 21, 20, 24, 25, 23, 23, 29, 30, 25, 30, 33, 27,…
## $ FR      <int> 87, 100, 113, 100, 83, 101, 107, 104, 131, 108, 123…
## $ teamH   <fct> Boston, Golden State, Charlotte, Detroit, Indiana, …
## $ venueH  <fct> H, H, H, H, H, H, H, H, H, H, H, H, H, H, H, H, H, …
## $ Q1H     <int> 21, 31, 23, 24, 27, 25, 23, 28, 29, 31, 34, 24, 37,…
## $ Q2H     <int> 26, 26, 31, 27, 29, 29, 49, 32, 25, 25, 21, 30, 19,…
## $ Q3H     <int> 30, 26, 29, 32, 20, 25, 34, 30, 30, 25, 32, 18, 27,…
## $ Q4H     <int> 28, 25, 29, 20, 35, 25, 20, 26, 28, 31, 30, 26, 38,…
## $ FH      <int> 105, 108, 112, 103, 111, 104, 126, 116, 112, 112, 1…
```

Here's a variable-by-variable breakdown of nbadf2:

- dataset—Equals NBA 2018-2019 Regular Season or NBA 2019-2020 Regular Season.
- ID—A unique identifier for each game that increments by one in chronological order.
- date—The date on which a game was played in *MM/DD/YY* format.
- teamR—The road, or visiting, team where, for instance, Golden State equals Golden State Warriors and Boston equals Boston Celtics.
- venueR—Always equals R, which is short for road.
- Q1R—Equals the number of points scored by the road team in the first quarter.
- Q2R—Equals the number of points scored by the road team in the second quarter.
- Q3R—Equals the number of points scored by the road team in the third quarter.
- Q4R—Equals the number of points scored by the road team in the fourth quarter.
- FR—Equals the total number of points scored by the road team for an entire game. Because we previously removed overtime games from our data set, FR *always* equals the sum of the previous four variables.
- teamH—The home team in the same format as the variable teamR.
- venueH—Always equals H.
- Q1H—Equals the number of points scored by the home team in the first quarter.
- Q2H—Equals the number of points scored by the home team in the second quarter.
- Q3H—Equals the number of points scored by the home team in the third quarter.
- Q4H—Equals the number of points scored by the home team in the fourth quarter.
- FH—Equals the total number of points scored by the home team for an entire game; also equals the sum of the previous four variables.

With our data sets successfully wrangled and joined, we're ready to start doing some analysis.

6.4   Analysis

Our analysis effort will be a three-pronged attack:

- First, we'll compute and visualize quarter-by-quarter results versus end-of-game results to determine if winning teams were more successful in the fourth quarter versus the first, second, and third quarters.

- Second, we'll subset our data set on the six most successful teams over the 2018–19 and 2019–20 NBA regular seasons and again on the six least successful teams and then compute and visualize their winning percentages when winning one quarter versus the other, broken down by playing on the road versus at home.

- Third, we'll reduce our data set to include only those games that were tied at half-time and then compare third- and fourth-quarter results versus end-of-game results.

We'll find that the preponderance of the evidence supports the idea that games are most often *not* won in the fourth quarter but rather most often in the third quarter, thereby confirming our hypothesis.

6.4.1   First quarter

Our first action is to create a new data set, nbadf3, by calling the `filter()` function to subset the nbadf2 data set where the variables Q1R and Q1H aren't equal; basically, we're subsetting nbadf2 by eliminating observations, or games, where the score was tied at the end of the first quarter. The NOT (`!`) operator evaluates `!TRUE` statements as `FALSE` and `!FALSE` statements as `TRUE`:

```
nbadf2 %>%
  filter(Q1R != Q1H) -> nbadf3
dim(nbadf3)
## [1] 1990    17
```

The nbadf3 data set has 1,990 rows.

In the following chunk of code, we call a pair of `dplyr` functions, `mutate()` and `case_when()`, to create a new nbadf3 variable called Q1vF that will be populated with one of four values based on conditional logic:

- When the home team scores more first-quarter points than the road team and then wins the game, Q1vF will equal HH.

- When the road team scores more first-quarter points than the home team and then wins the game, Q1vF will equal RR.

- When the home team scores more first-quarter points than the road team, but then the road team wins the game, Q1vF will equal HR.

- When the road team scores more first-quarter points than the home team, but then the home team wins the game, Q1vF will equal RH.

Our new variable is then converted to a factor:

```
nbadf3 %>% mutate(Q1vF = case_when(Q1H > Q1R & FH > FR ~ "HH",
                                   Q1R > Q1H & FR > FH ~ "RR",
                                   Q1H > Q1R & FR > FH ~ "HR",
                                   Q1R > Q1H & FH > FR ~ "RH")) -> nbadf3

nbadf3$Q1vF <- as.factor(nbadf3$Q1vF)
```

We then create a tibble that is more involved than other tibbles we've created in previous chapters:

- We start by calling the count() function from the dplyr package; it tallies the number of observations in nbadf3 for each of the four levels in the derived variable Q1vF and pipes the same to a pair of other dplyr functions, arrange() and desc(), to stack the results in a variable called n and to sort them in descending order.
- Our new object is then piped to a series of calls to the mutate() function to create three additional tbl1 variables. Our first call to mutate() creates a variable called pct_total, which is equal to n divided by the nbadf3 row count and then multiplied by 100.
- Our second call to mutate() creates a variable called cum_n, which equals the cumulative sum of n; cumsum() is a built-in function that returns a vector of cumulative sums derived from the raw data in another vector. For instance, if we have a vector containing the numerals 1, 2, and 3, cumsum() would return 1, 3, and 6.
- Our third and final call to mutate() creates a variable called cum_pct_total, which converts the values in cum_n to a percentage against the total record count in the nbadf3 data set.
- The variables pct_total and cum_pct_total are then formatted by calling the base R round() function so that only two digits to the right of the decimal point are returned.

The end result is a tibble with four rows and five columns:

```
count(nbadf3, Q1vF) %>% arrange(desc(n)) -> tbl1
tbl1 %>%
  mutate(pct_total = n/nrow(nbadf3)*100) %>%
  mutate(cum_n = cumsum(n)) %>%
  mutate(cum_pct_total = cumsum(pct_total)) -> tbl1
tbl1$pct_total <- round(tbl1$pct_total, digits = 2)
tbl1$cum_pct_total <- round(tbl1$cum_pct_total, digits = 2)
print(tbl1)
##   Q1vF   n pct_total cum_n cum_pct_total
## 1   HH 783     39.35   783         39.35
## 2   RR 550     27.64  1333         66.98
## 3   RH 365     18.34  1698         85.33
## 4   HR 292     14.67  1990        100.00
```

To check or reconcile our results, we then make a series of calls to the `sqldf()` function from the `sqldf` package. `SELECT` and `COUNT(*)` return the nbadf3 record counts that equal the variable n from tbl1:

```
sqldf("SELECT COUNT(*) FROM nbadf3 WHERE Q1H > Q1R AND FH > FR")
##   COUNT(*)
## 1      783
sqldf("SELECT COUNT(*) FROM nbadf3 WHERE Q1R > Q1H AND FR > FH")
##   COUNT(*)
## 1      550
sqldf("SELECT COUNT(*) FROM nbadf3 WHERE Q1R > Q1H AND FR < FH")
##   COUNT(*)
## 1      365
sqldf("SELECT COUNT(*) FROM nbadf3 WHERE Q1H > Q1R AND FH < FR")
##   COUNT(*)
## 1      292
```

By substituting the pipe operator in lieu of `FROM` and passing the `sqldf()` `WHERE` clause to the `count()` function, we can easily convert our `SELECT` statements to `dplyr` code. But note that `dplyr` uses `&`, whereas `sqldf()` uses `AND`, and `dplyr` returns counts for `TRUE` and `FALSE` observations, whereas `sqldf()` only returns the record count that actually satisfies the logic:

```
nbadf3 %>%
  count(Q1H > Q1R & FH > FR)
## # A tibble: 2 × 2
##   `Q1H > Q1R & FH > FR`     n
##   <lgl>                <int>
## 1 FALSE                 1207
## 2 TRUE                   783

nbadf3 %>%
  count(Q1R > Q1H & FR > FH)
## # A tibble: 2 × 2
##   `Q1R > Q1H & FR > FH`     n
##   <lgl>                <int>
## 1 FALSE                 1440
## 2 TRUE                   550

nbadf3 %>%
  count(Q1R > Q1H & FR < FH)
## # A tibble: 2 × 2
##   `Q1R > Q1H & FR < FH`     n
##   <lgl>                <int>
## 1 FALSE                 1625
## 2 TRUE                   365

nbadf3 %>%
  count(Q1H > Q1R & FH < FR)
## # A tibble: 2 × 2
##   `Q1H > Q1R & FH < FR`     n
##   <lgl>                <int>
## 1 FALSE                 1698
## 2 TRUE                   292
```

Thankfully, everything checks either way.

Let's now visualize our results with a pair of complementary `ggplot2` bar charts. The first of these, plot1a, displays the number of wins. Remember, these are regular season wins between the 2018–19 and 2019–20 seasons, minus games played in Orlando, games that went into overtime, and games that ended in a first-quarter tie between the four factors from our derived variable `Q1vF`.

Our second visualization, plot1b, returns more or less the same view, except winning percentages are substituted for wins. Thus, we have similar looks between plot1a and plot1b, with like results from different, yet complementary, measures.

A few additional points are warranted:

- In both plots, we call the base R `reorder()` function to sort the `Q1vF` factors in descending order by the tbl1 variables n (in the case of plot1a) and `pct_total` (in the case of plot1b). Note the minus operator that precedes the variable names; without this, the results would be sorted in ascending order.
- A custom color and fill scheme is added to emphasize results where the same team won the first quarter and won the game while simultaneously de-emphasizing the opposite results; we've chosen a bright color for the one and a light gray for the other.
- Labels affixed atop the bars tie back to the y-axis variables and are formatted with a bold font.
- Winning percentages might be off by a tenth of a percent due to rounding.

The code for both visualizations follows:

```
plot1a <- ggplot(tbl1, aes(x = reorder(Q1vF, -n), y = n)) +
  geom_bar(color = c("orange1", "orange1", "gray74", "gray74"),
           fill = c("orange1", "orange1", "gray74", "gray74"),
           stat = "identity") +
  labs(title = "Teams Winning the First Quarter",
       subtitle = "Win-Loss Record = 1,333-657",
       x = "Win Combinations",
       y = "Wins") +
  geom_text(aes(x = Q1vF, y = n, label = n, vjust = -0.3,
                fontface = "bold")) +
  theme(plot.title = element_text(face = "bold"))

plot1b <- ggplot(tbl1, aes(x = reorder(Q1vF, -pct_total), y = pct_total)) +
  geom_bar(color = c("orange1", "orange1", "gray74", "gray74"),
           fill = c("orange1", "orange1", "gray74", "gray74"),
           stat = "identity") +
  labs(title = "Teams Winning the First Quarter",
       subtitle = "Winning Percentage = 66.98%",
       x = "Win Combinations",
       y = "Winning Percentage") +
  geom_text(aes(x = Q1vF, y = pct_total, label = pct_total,
                vjust = -0.3, fontface = "bold")) +
  theme(plot.title = element_text(face = "bold"))
```

Our two visualizations are then paired side by side into a single object (see figure 6.1), which is made possible by calling the `plot_layout()` function from the `patchwork` package.

```
plot1a + plot1b + plot_layout(ncol = 2)
```

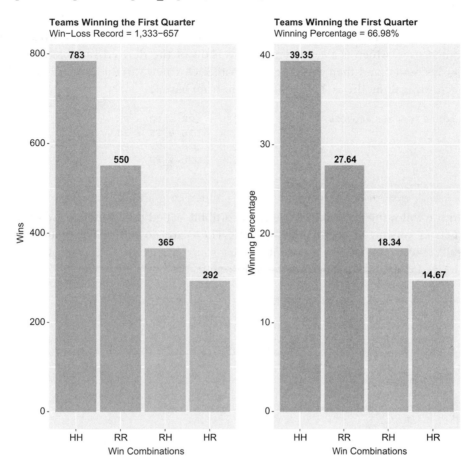

Figure 6.1   Teams that win the first quarter and then proceed to win the same game just over two-thirds of the time

Teams that won the first quarter subsequently won the game almost 67% of the time (equals 39.35% + 27.64% from plot1b). Home teams that won the first quarter had an overall winning percentage equal to almost 73% (equals 783 / 783 + 292 from plot1a); road teams, on the other hand, won about 60% of the time after winning the first quarter (equals 550 / 550 + 365 from plot1a).

6.4.2   Second quarter

Next, we repeat this exercise in full, except now our purpose is to compare second-quarter results to final scores. We call the `filter()` function to create a new object called nbadf4 that equals the nbadf2 data set, minus any observations where the road and home teams scored the same number of second-quarter points:

```
nbadf3 %>%
  filter(Q2R != Q2H) -> nbadf4
```

We then call the `mutate()` and `case_when()` functions to create a new nbadf4 variable called `Q2vF`, which is a second-quarter version of the derived variable `Q1vF` we previously created and then appended to nbadf3. Our new variable is then converted to a factor by calling the `as.factor()` function from base R:

```
nbadf4 %>% mutate(Q2vF = case_when(Q2H > Q2R & FH > FR ~ "HH",
                                   Q2R > Q2H & FR > FH ~ "RR",
                                   Q2H > Q2R & FR > FH ~ "HR",
                                   Q2R > Q2H & FH > FR ~ "RH")) -> nbadf4

nbadf4$Q2vF <- factor(nbadf4$Q2vF)
```

In the following code chunk, we create a tibble called tbl2, which is merely a second-quarter version of our first tibble, tbl1. There are no differences between tbl1 and tbl2, except that we've substituted data sources (nbadf3 in favor of nbadf4) and derived variables (`Q1vF` swapped out for `Q2vF`):

```
count(nbadf4, Q2vF) %>% arrange(desc(n)) -> tbl2
tbl2 %>%
  mutate(pct_total = n/nrow(nbadf4)*100) %>%
  mutate(cum_n = cumsum(n)) %>%
  mutate(cum_pct_total = cumsum(pct_total)) -> tbl2
tbl2$pct_total <- round(tbl2$pct_total, digits = 2)
tbl2$cum_pct_total <- round(tbl2$cum_pct_total, digits = 2)
print(tbl2)
##    Q2vF   n pct_total cum_n cum_pct_total
## 1    HH 711     37.84   711         37.84
## 2    RR 502     26.72  1213         64.56
## 3    RH 371     19.74  1584         84.30
## 4    HR 295     15.70  1879        100.00
```

Finally, we create a second pair of `ggplot2` bar charts and then bundle the two visualizations into a single graphical object (see figure 6.2):

```
plot2a <- ggplot(tbl2, aes(x = reorder(Q2vF, -n), y = n)) +
  geom_bar(color = c("skyblue3", "skyblue3", "gray74", "gray74"),
           fill = c("skyblue3", "skyblue3", "gray74", "gray74"),
           stat = "identity") +
  labs(title = "Teams Winning the Second Quarter",
       subtitle = "Win-Loss Record = 1,266-692",
       x = "Win Combinations",
       y = "Wins") +
  geom_text(aes(x = Q2vF, y = n, label = n,
                vjust = -0.3, fontface = "bold")) +
  theme(plot.title = element_text(face = "bold"))
```

```
plot2b <- ggplot(tbl2, aes(x = reorder(Q2vF, -pct_total), y = pct_total)) +
  geom_bar(color = c("skyblue3", "skyblue3", "gray74", "gray74"),
           fill = c("skyblue3", "skyblue3", "gray74", "gray74"),
           stat = "identity") +
  labs(title = "Teams Winning the Second Quarter",
       subtitle = "Winning Percentage = 64.66%",
       x = "Win Combinations",
       y = "Winning Percentage") +
  geom_text(aes(x = Q2vF, y = pct_total, label = pct_total,
                vjust = -0.3, fontface = "bold")) +
  theme(plot.title = element_text(face = "bold"))

plot2a + plot2b + plot_layout(ncol = 2)
```

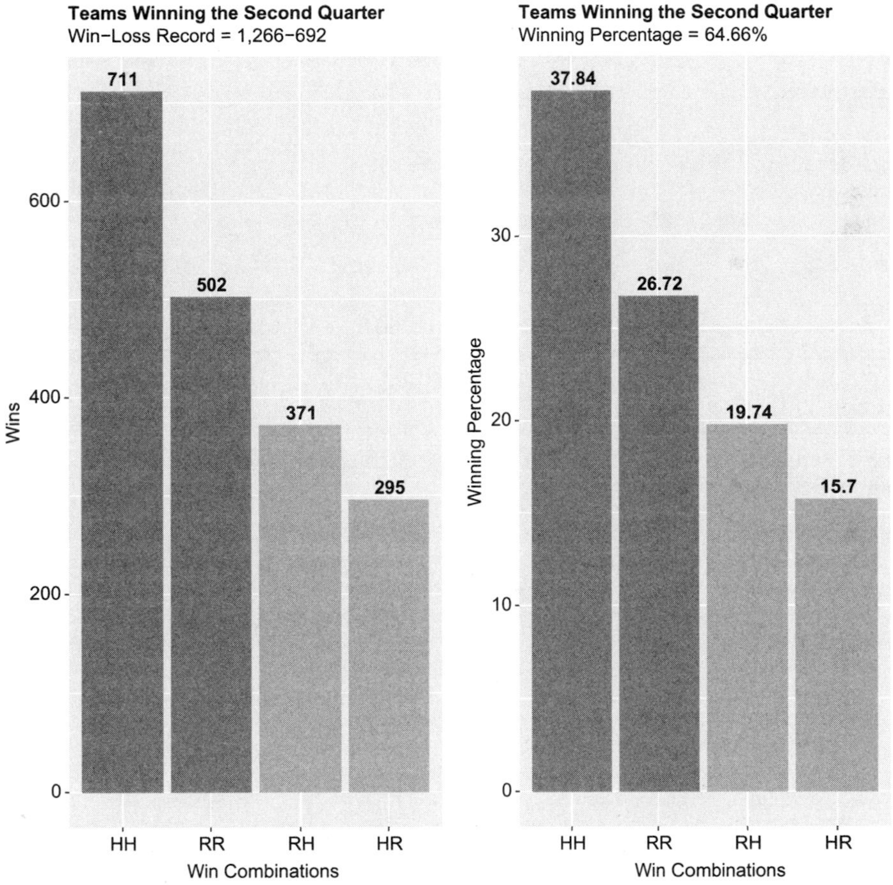

Figure 6.2 **Teams that win the second quarter then proceed to win the same game just under 65% of the time, a figure slightly below what we previously saw with respect to first-quarter results.**

Teams that won the second quarter subsequently won the same game almost 65% of the time, a figure more than two percentage points less than what we previously saw with respect to first-quarter results. Home teams that won the second quarter had an overall winning percentage of roughly 71%, versus 73% for home teams that won the first quarter; road teams won approximately 58% of the time after winning the second quarter, compared to a 60% winning percentage for road teams that won the first quarter.

6.4.3   *Third quarter*

Let's now look at the third-quarter results versus end-of-game results. This time, our code has been consolidated into one chunk, ending with another pair of `ggplot2` bar charts (see figure 6.3):

```
nbadf2 %>%
  filter(Q3R != Q3H) -> nbadf5

nbadf5 %>% mutate(Q3vF = case_when(Q3H > Q3R & FH > FR ~ "HH",
                                   Q3R > Q3H & FR > FH ~ "RR",
                                   Q3H > Q3R & FR > FH ~ "HR",
                                   Q3R > Q3H & FH > FR ~ "RH")) -> nbadf5

nbadf5$Q3vF <- factor(nbadf5$Q3vF)

count(nbadf5, Q3vF) %>% arrange(desc(n)) -> tbl3
tbl3 %>%
  mutate(pct_total = n/nrow(nbadf5)*100) %>%
  mutate(cum_n = cumsum(n)) %>%
  mutate(cum_pct_total = cumsum(pct_total)) -> tbl3
tbl3$pct_total <- round(tbl3$pct_total, digits = 2)
tbl3$cum_pct_total <- round(tbl3$cum_pct_total, digits = 2)
print(tbl3)
##    Q3vF   n pct_total cum_n cum_pct_total
## 1    HH 748     38.03   748         38.03
## 2    RR 574     29.18  1322         67.21
## 3    RH 378     19.22  1700         86.43
## 4    HR 267     13.57  1967        100.00

plot3a <- ggplot(tbl3, aes(x = reorder(Q3vF, -n), y = n)) +
  geom_bar(color = c("springgreen3", "springgreen3", "gray74", "gray74"),
           fill = c("springgreen3", "springgreen3", "gray74", "gray74"),
           stat = "identity") +
  labs(title = "Teams Winning the Third Quarter",
       subtitle = "Win-Loss Record = 1,322-645",
       x = "Win Combinations",
       y = "Wins") +
  geom_text(aes(x = Q3vF, y = n, label = n,
                vjust = -0.3, fontface = "bold")) +
  theme(plot.title = element_text(face = "bold"))

plot3b <- ggplot(tbl3, aes(x = reorder(Q3vF, -pct_total), y = pct_total)) +
  geom_bar(color = c("springgreen3", "springgreen3", "gray74", "gray74"),
           fill = c("springgreen3", "springgreen3", "gray74", "gray74"),
           stat = "identity") +
  labs(title = "Teams Winning the Second Quarter",
       subtitle = "Winning Percentage = 67.21%",
       x = "Win Combinations",
```

```
          y = "Winning Percentage") +
    geom_text(aes(x = Q3vF, y = pct_total, label = pct_total,
               vjust = -0.3, fontface = "bold")) +
    theme(plot.title = element_text(face = "bold"))

plot3a + plot3b + plot_layout(ncol = 2)
```

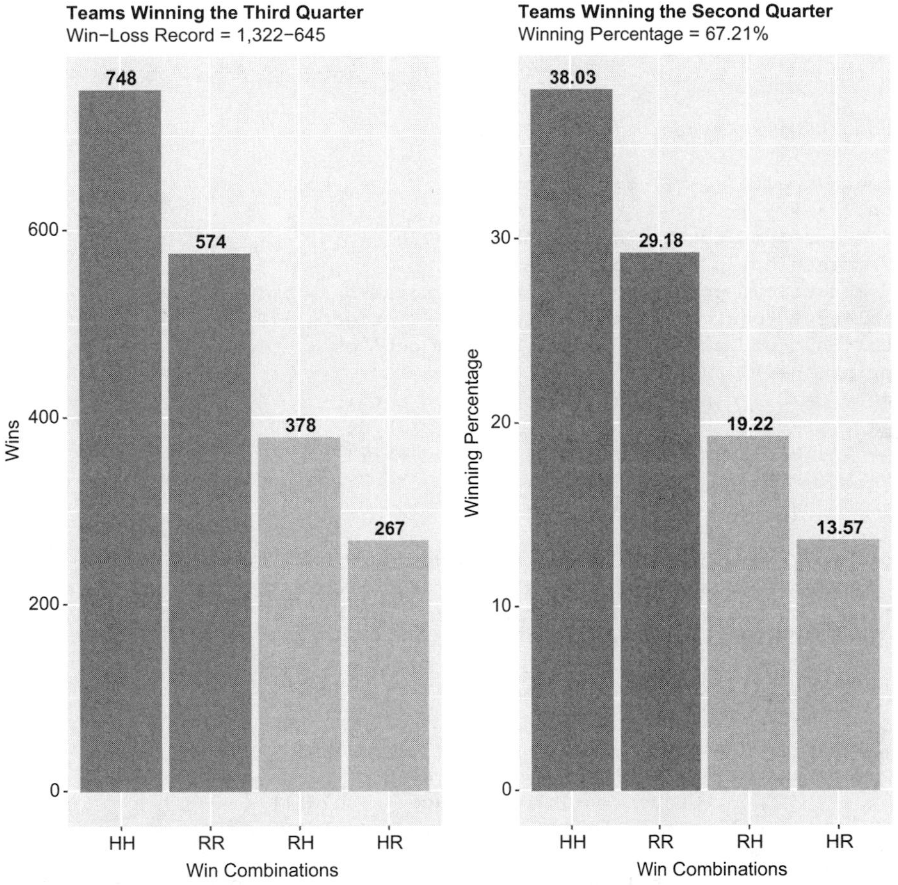

Figure 6.3 Teams that win the third quarter then proceed to win the same game more than 67% of the time, which is the highest winning percentage yet.

Home and road teams that won the third quarter then won more than 67% of those same games—the highest figure yet. Home team performance is mostly responsible for these results: 74% of the time, when the home team won the third quarter, it then went on to win the same game, compared to just a 60% winning percentage for road teams.

6.4.4 *Fourth quarter*

We then run our end-of-quarter versus end-of-game results one more time, this time focusing on the fourth quarter. Our code has again been consolidated into a single chunk, and our results are again visualized in a pair of `ggplot2` bar charts packed into a single graphical representation of the data (see figure 6.4):

```
nbadf2 %>%
  filter(Q4R != Q4H) -> nbadf6

nbadf6 %>% mutate(Q4vF = case_when(Q4H > Q4R & FH > FR ~ "HH",
                                   Q4R > Q4H & FR > FH ~ "RR",
                                   Q4H > Q4R & FR > FH ~ "HR",
                                   Q4R > Q4H & FH > FR ~ "RH")) -> nbadf6

nbadf6$Q4vF <- factor(nbadf6$Q4vF)

count(nbadf6, Q4vF) %>% arrange(desc(n)) -> tbl4
tbl4 %>%
  mutate(pct_total = n/nrow(nbadf6)*100) %>%
  mutate(cum_n = cumsum(n)) %>%
  mutate(cum_pct_total = cumsum(pct_total)) -> tbl4
tbl4$pct_total <- round(tbl4$pct_total, digits = 2)
tbl4$cum_pct_total <- round(tbl4$cum_pct_total, digits = 2)
print(tbl4)
##   Q4vF   n pct_total cum_n cum_pct_total
## 1   HH 767     39.05   767         39.05
## 2   RR 524     26.68  1291         65.73
## 3   RH 374     19.04  1665         84.78
## 4   HR 299     15.22  1964        100.00

plot4a <- ggplot(tbl4, aes(x = reorder(Q4vF, -n), y = n)) +
  geom_bar(color = c("darkorchid3", "darkorchid3", "gray74", "gray74"),
           fill = c("darkorchid3", "darkorchid3", "gray74", "gray74"),
           stat = "identity") +
  labs(title = "Teams Winning the Fourth Quarter",
       subtitle = "Win-Loss Record = 1,291-673",
       x = "Win Combinations",
       y = "Wins") +
  geom_text(aes(x = Q4vF, y = n, label = n,
                vjust = -0.3, fontface = "bold")) +
  theme(plot.title = element_text(face = "bold"))

plot4b <- ggplot(tbl4, aes(x = reorder(Q4vF, -pct_total), y = pct_total)) +
  geom_bar(color = c("darkorchid3", "darkorchid3", "gray74", "gray74"),
           fill = c("darkorchid3", "darkorchid3", "gray74", "gray74"),
           stat = "identity") +
  labs(title = "Teams Winning the Fourth Quarter",
       subtitle = "Winning Percentage = 65.73%",
       x = "Win Combinations",
       y = "Winning Percentage") +
  geom_text(aes(x = Q4vF, y = pct_total, label = pct_total,
                vjust = -0.3, fontface = "bold")) +
  theme(plot.title = element_text(face = "bold"))

plot4a + plot4b + plot_layout(ncol = 2)
```

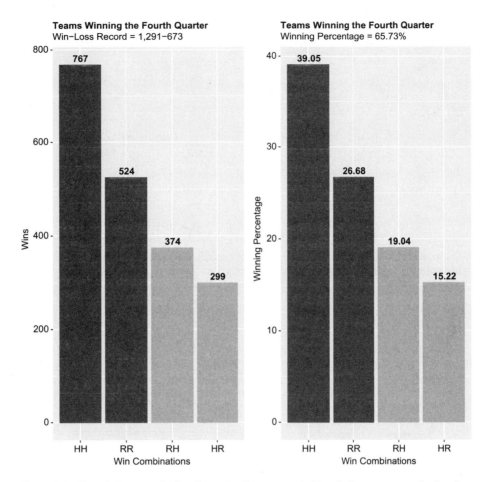

Figure 6.4   Teams that won the fourth quarter then proceeded to win the same game just under 66% of the time, which is the lowest winning percentage aside from our second-quarter results.

The winning team in the fourth quarter was also the game winner in nearly 66% of the applicable games in our data set. Home teams that won the fourth quarter also won about 72% of the time; road teams won approximately 58% of the games in which they scored the most points in the fourth quarter.

It's difficult, if not impossible, to say when games are won, especially if the choice is between one quarter versus another. Nevertheless, winning teams won the third quarter more than they won the fourth quarter, or any quarter for that matter, which, of course, is an affront to the conventional wisdom that games are won in the fourth quarter.

Our next analysis will focus on the best six and worst six teams over the 2018–19 and 2019–20 regular seasons.

6.4.5   *Comparing best and worst teams*

Let's now do a deeper yet more focused dive by repeating our analysis on a data set that includes just the six teams that won the most regular season games between the

2018–19 and 2019–20 regular seasons (not including neutral-site games following the COVID-19 suspension of play). These six teams are the Milwaukee Bucks (116 wins), Toronto Raptors (111), Denver Nuggets (100), Boston Celtics (97), Houston Rockets (97), and Los Angeles Clippers (97). We'll then do the same analysis on a data set that just includes the six worst teams.

BEST 6

To make this happen, we first create a data set called nbadf7, a subset of nbadf3, by calling the dplyr filter() function to include only those observations where one of the six aforementioned teams was the designated road team. Whereas the AND (&) operator takes two or more logical values and returns TRUE only if all values are, in fact, TRUE, the OR (|) operator returns TRUE if at least one of the values is TRUE.

Then, we subset nbadf7 on those observations where the variable Q1vF equals RR or RH. The results are saved in a new object called nbadf8:

```
nbadf3 %>%
  filter(teamR == "Milwaukee" | teamR == "Toronto" |
          teamR == "Boston" | teamR == "Denver" |
          teamR == "Houston" | teamR == "LA Clippers") -> nbadf7

nbadf7 %>%
  filter(Q1vF == "RR" | Q1vF == "RH") -> nbadf8
```

We then call the count() function to tally the number of observations in nbadf8 where Q1vF equals RR versus RH and then call the arrange() function to sort the results in descending order; the results are cast into a tibble called tbl5. We then call the mutate() function to create a variable called pct_total, which computes the percentage of n against the total record count; that variable is subsequently reduced to include just two digits right of the decimal point:

```
count(nbadf8, Q1vF) %>% arrange(desc(Q1vF)) -> tbl5
tbl5 %>%
  mutate(pct_total = n/nrow(nbadf8)*100) -> tbl5
tbl5$pct_total <- round(tbl5$pct_total, digits = 2)
print(tbl5)
##   Q1vF   n pct_total
## 1  RR 151     70.89
## 2  RH  62     29.11
```

This exercise is repeated three times, first by substituting the second quarter in place of the first quarter by swapping out the variable Q1vF for Q2vF:

```
nbadf4 %>%
  filter(teamR == "Milwaukee" | teamR == "Toronto" |
          teamR == "Boston" | teamR == "Denver" |
          teamR == "Houston" | teamR == "LA Clippers") -> nbadf9

nbadf9 %>%
  filter(Q2vF == "RR" | Q2vF == "RH") -> nbadf10
```

```
count(nbadf10, Q2vF) %>% arrange(desc(Q2vF)) -> tbl6
tbl6 %>%
  mutate(pct_total = n/nrow(nbadf10)*100) -> tbl6
tbl6$pct_total <- round(tbl6$pct_total, digits = 2)
print(tbl6)
##    Q2vF   n pct_total
## 1   RR 149     73.04
## 2   RH  55     26.96
```

Next, we replace the variable Q2vF with Q3vF:

```
nbadf5 %>%
  filter(teamR == "Milwaukee" | teamR == "Toronto" |
         teamR == "Boston" | teamR == "Denver" |
         teamR == "Houston" | teamR == "LA Clippers") -> nbadf11

nbadf11 %>%
  filter(Q3vF == "RR" | Q3vF == "RH") -> nbadf12

count(nbadf12, Q3vF) %>% arrange(desc(Q3vF)) -> tbl7
tbl7 %>%
  mutate(pct_total = n/nrow(nbadf12)*100) -> tbl7
tbl7$pct_total <- round(tbl7$pct_total, digits = 2)
print(tbl7)
##    Q3vF   n pct_total
## 1   RR 157     75.12
## 2   RH  52     24.88
```

Finally, we tally fourth-quarter results by inserting the variable Q4vF in lieu of Q3vF:

```
nbadf6 %>%
  filter(teamR == "Milwaukee" | teamR == "Toronto" |
         teamR == "Boston" | teamR == "Denver" |
         teamR == "Houston" | teamR == "LA Clippers") -> nbadf13

nbadf13 %>%
  filter(Q4vF == "RR" | Q4vF == "RH") -> nbadf14

count(nbadf14, Q4vF) %>% arrange(desc(Q4vF)) -> tbl8
tbl8 %>%
  mutate(pct_total = n/nrow(nbadf14)*100) -> tbl8
tbl8$pct_total <- round(tbl8$pct_total, digits = 2)
print(tbl8)
##    Q4vF   n pct_total
## 1   RR 142        71
## 2   RH  58        29
```

We next create a data set from scratch, which we'll name df1, by calling the data.frame() function from base R to store results where the variables Q1vF, Q2vF, Q3vF, and Q4vF equal RR. We then call the base R c() function to add a pair of vectors to our data frame. Our first vector is a character string called quarter (note the use of quotation marks around the attributes), and our second vector is a numeric variable called win_pct (note the lack of quotation marks). Creating a data set from scratch only makes sense when the row and column counts are kept to a minimum by design; otherwise, an investment in automation should be in order:

```
df1 <- data.frame(quarter = c("1Q", "2Q", "3Q", "4Q"),
                  win_pct = c(70.89, 72.81, 75.12, 71.01))
print(df1)
##   quarter win_pct
## 1      1Q   70.89
## 2      2Q   72.81
## 3      3Q   75.12
## 4      4Q   71.01
```

Our results are then visualized in a bar chart. We'll temporarily hold our plot in memory and then print it as one object alongside another ggplot2 bar chart:

```
plot5 <- ggplot(df1, aes(x = quarter, y = win_pct)) +
  geom_bar(color = c("gray74", "gray74", "skyblue", "gray74"),
           fill = c("gray74", "gray74", "skyblue", "gray74"),
           stat = "identity") +
  labs(title = "Top 6 Teams on the Road",
       subtitle = "Winning Percentages when Winning each Quarter",
       x = "Quarter",
       y = "Winning Percentage") +
  geom_text(aes(x = quarter, y = win_pct, label = win_pct,
                vjust = -0.3, fontface = "bold")) +
  theme(plot.title = element_text(face = "bold"))
```

Let's now see how these same teams performed at home:

```
nbadf3 %>%
  filter(teamH == "Milwaukee" | teamH == "Toronto" |
         teamH == "Boston" | teamH == "Denver" |
         teamH == "Houston" | teamH == "LA Clippers") -> nbadf15

nbadf15 %>%
  filter(Q1vF == "HR" | Q1vF == "HH") -> nbadf16

count(nbadf16, Q1vF) %>% arrange(Q1vF) -> tbl9
tbl9 %>%
  mutate(pct_total = n/nrow(nbadf16)*100) -> tbl9
tbl9$pct_total <- round(tbl9$pct_total, digits = 2)
print(tbl9)
##   Q1vF   n pct_total
## 1   HH 219     84.88
## 2   HR  39     15.12

nbadf4 %>%
  filter(teamH == "Milwaukee" | teamH == "Toronto" |
         teamH == "Boston" | teamH == "Denver" |
         teamH == "Houston" | teamH == "LA Clippers") -> nbadf17

nbadf17 %>%
  filter(Q2vF == "HR" | Q2vF == "HH") -> nbadf18

count(nbadf18, Q2vF) %>% arrange(Q2vF) -> tbl10
```

```
tbl10 %>%
  mutate(pct_total = n/nrow(nbadf18)*100) -> tbl10
tbl10$pct_total <- round(tbl10$pct_total, digits = 2)
print(tbl10)
##   Q2vF   n pct_total
## 1   HH 200     84.03
## 2   HR  38     15.97

nbadf5 %>%
  filter(teamH == "Milwaukee" | teamH == "Toronto" |
         teamH == "Boston" | teamH == "Denver" |
         teamH == "Houston" | teamH == "LA Clippers") -> nbadf19

nbadf19 %>%
  filter(Q3vF == "HR" | Q3vF == "HH") -> nbadf20

count(nbadf20, Q3vF) %>% arrange(Q3vF) -> tbl11
tbl11 %>%
  mutate(pct_total = n/nrow(nbadf20)*100) -> tbl11
tbl11$pct_total <- round(tbl11$pct_total, digits = 2)
print(tbl11)
##   Q3vF   n pct_total
## 1   HH 208     87.76
## 2   HR  29     12.24

nbadf6 %>%
  filter(teamH == "Milwaukee" | teamH == "Toronto" |
         teamH == "Boston" | teamH == "Denver" |
         teamH == "Houston" | teamH == "LA Clippers") -> nbadf21

nbadf21 %>%
  filter(Q4vF == "HR" | Q4vF == "HH") -> nbadf22

count(nbadf22, Q4vF) %>% arrange(Q4vF) -> tbl12
tbl12 %>%
  mutate(pct_total = n/nrow(nbadf22)*100) -> tbl12
tbl12$pct_total <- round(tbl12$pct_total, digits = 2)
print(tbl12)
##   Q4vF   n pct_total
## 1   HH 200     82.99
## 2   HR  41     17.01
df2 <- data.frame(quarter = c("1Q", "2Q", "3Q", "4Q"),
                  win_pct = c(84.88, 84.15, 87.76, 82.99))
print(df2)
##   quarter win_pct
## 1      1Q   84.88
## 2      2Q   84.15
## 3      3Q   87.76
## 4      4Q   82.99

plot6 <- ggplot(df2, aes(x = quarter, y = win_pct)) +
  geom_bar(color = c("gray74", "gray74", "brown3", "gray74"),
           fill = c("gray74", "gray74", "brown3", "gray74"),
           stat = "identity") +
  labs(title = "Top 6 Teams at Home",
       subtitle = "Winning Percentages when Winning each Quarter",
       x = "Quarter",
```

```
                  y = "Winning Percentage") +
      geom_text(aes(x = quarter, y = win_pct, label = win_pct,
                    vjust = -0.3, fontface = "bold")) +
      theme(plot.title = element_text(face = "bold"))
```

Once again, we make a call to the `plot_layout()` function to pack our last two bar charts, `plot5` and `plot6`, into a single object (see figure 6.5):

```
plot5 + plot6 + plot_layout(ncol = 2)
```

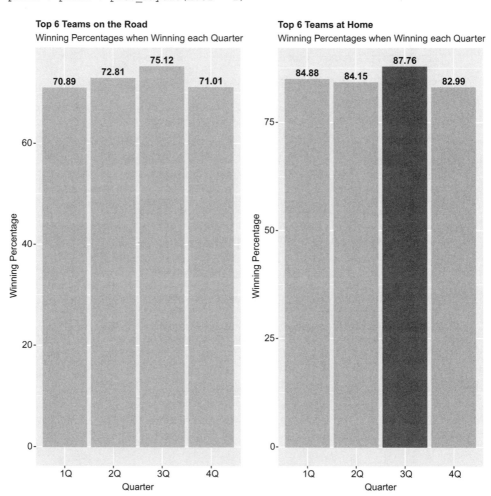

Figure 6.5   The NBA's best teams over the 2018–19 and 2019–20 regular seasons won the third quarter more frequently than other quarters in games they went on to win. This was true for both road and home games.

So the league's best teams most often won the third quarter, on the road and at home, when winning the same game. At the same time, these teams were *least* successful in the fourth quarter when road and home results are combined.

WORST 6

Now, what about the worst teams—do we see like or different results? We'll next reuse our code and apply it to the worst six teams over the 2018–19 and 2019–20 regular seasons. These teams are the Minnesota Timberwolves (55 wins), Phoenix Suns (53), Atlanta Hawks (49), Chicago Bulls (44), Cleveland Cavaliers (38), and New York Knicks (38). Results are summarized and visualized in another pair of `ggplot2` bar charts (see figure 6.6):

```
nbadf3 %>%
  filter(teamR == "Minnesota" | teamR == "Phoenix" |
         teamR == "Atlanta" | teamR == "Chicago" |
         teamR == "Cleveland" | teamR == "New York") -> nbadf23

nbadf23 %>%
  filter(Q1vF == "RR" | Q1vF == "RH") -> nbadf24

count(nbadf24, Q1vF) %>% arrange(desc(Q1vF)) -> tbl13
tbl13 %>%
  mutate(pct_total = n/nrow(nbadf24)*100) -> tbl13
tbl13$pct_total <- round(tbl13$pct_total, digits = 2)
print(tbl13)
##   Q1vF  n pct_total
## 1   RR 58     42.03
## 2   RH 80     57.97

nbadf4 %>%
  filter(teamR == "Minnesota" | teamR == "Phoenix" |
         teamR == "Atlanta" | teamR == "Chicago" |
         teamR == "Cleveland" | teamR == "New York") -> nbadf25

nbadf25 %>%
  filter(Q2vF == "RR" | Q2vF == "RH") -> nbadf26

count(nbadf26, Q2vF) %>% arrange(desc(Q2vF)) -> tbl14
tbl14 %>%
  mutate(pct_total = n/nrow(nbadf26)*100) -> tbl14
tbl14$pct_total <- round(tbl14$pct_total, digits = 2)
print(tbl14)
##   Q2vF  n pct_total
## 1   RR 43      34.4
## 2   RH 82      65.6

nbadf5 %>%
  filter(teamR == "Minnesota" | teamR == "Phoenix" |
         teamR == "Atlanta" | teamR == "Chicago" |
         teamR == "Cleveland" | teamR == "New York") -> nbadf27

nbadf27 %>%
  filter(Q3vF == "RR" | Q3vF == "RH") -> nbadf28

count(nbadf28, Q3vF) %>% arrange(desc(Q3vF)) -> tbl15
tbl15 %>%
  mutate(pct_total = n/nrow(nbadf28)*100) -> tbl15
tbl15$pct_total <- round(tbl15$pct_total, digits = 2)
print(tbl15)
##   Q3vF   n pct_total
```

```
## 1    RR   64       38.1
## 2    RH  104       61.9

nbadf6 %>%
  filter(teamR == "Minnesota" | teamR == "Phoenix" |
           teamR == "Atlanta" | teamR == "Chicago" |
           teamR == "Cleveland" | teamR == "New York") -> nbadf29

nbadf29 %>%
  filter(Q4vF == "RR" | Q4vF == "RH") -> nbadf30

count(nbadf30, Q4vF) %>% arrange(desc(Q4vF)) -> tbl16
tbl16 %>%
  mutate(pct_total = n/nrow(nbadf30)*100) -> tbl16
tbl16$pct_total <- round(tbl16$pct_total, digits = 2)
print(tbl16)
##    Q4vF  n pct_total
## 1    RR 54      37.76
## 2    RH 89      62.24
df3 <- data.frame(quarter = c("1Q", "2Q", "3Q", "4Q"),
                  win_pct = c(42.03, 33.33, 38.11, 37.76))
print(df3)
##    quarter win_pct
## 1       1Q   42.03
## 2       2Q   33.33
## 3       3Q   38.11
## 4       4Q   37.76

plot7 <- ggplot(df3, aes(x = quarter, y = win_pct)) +
  geom_bar(color = c("orange", "gray74", "gray74", "gray74"),
           fill = c("orange", "gray74", "gray74", "gray74"),
           stat = "identity") +
  labs(title = "Bottom 6 Teams on the Road",
       subtitle = "Winning Percentages when Winning each Quarter",
       x = "Quarter",
       y = "Winning Percentage") +
  geom_text(aes(x = quarter, y = win_pct, label = win_pct,
                vjust = -0.3, fontface = "bold")) +
  theme(plot.title = element_text(face = "bold"))

nbadf3 %>%
  filter(teamH == "Minnesota" | teamH == "Phoenix" |
           teamH == "Atlanta" | teamH == "Chicago" |
           teamH == "Cleveland" | teamH == "New York") -> nbadf31

nbadf31 %>%
  filter(Q1vF == "HR" | Q1vF == "HH") -> nbadf32

count(nbadf32, Q1vF) %>% arrange(Q1vF) -> tbl17
tbl17 %>%
  mutate(pct_total = n/nrow(nbadf32)*100) -> tbl17
tbl17$pct_total <- round(tbl17$pct_total, digits = 2)
print(tbl17)
##    Q1vF  n pct_total
## 1    HH 78      45.35
## 2    HR 94      54.65
```

```
nbadf4 %>%
  filter(teamH == "Minnesota" | teamH == "Phoenix" |
           teamH == "Atlanta" | teamH == "Chicago" |
           teamH == "Cleveland" | teamH == "New York") -> nbadf33

nbadf33 %>%
  filter(Q2vF == "HR" | Q2vF == "HH") -> nbadf34

count(nbadf34, Q2vF) %>% arrange(Q2vF) -> tbl18
tbl18 %>%
  mutate(pct_total = n/nrow(nbadf34)*100) -> tbl18
tbl18$pct_total <- round(tbl18$pct_total, digits = 2)
print(tbl18)
##   Q2vF  n pct_total
## 1   HH 86     51.81
## 2   HR 80     48.19


nbadf5 %>%
  filter(teamH == "Minnesota" | teamH == "Phoenix" |
           teamH == "Atlanta" | teamH == "Chicago" |
           teamH == "Cleveland" | teamH == "New York") -> nbadf35
nbadf35 %>%
  filter(Q3vF == "HR" | Q3vF == "HH") -> nbadf36

count(nbadf36, Q3vF) %>% arrange(Q3vF) -> tbl19
tbl19 %>%
  mutate(pct_total = n/nrow(nbadf36)*100) -> tbl19
tbl19$pct_total <- round(tbl19$pct_total, digits = 2)
print(tbl19)
##   Q3vF  n pct_total
## 1   HH 78     49.37
## 2   HR 80     50.63

nbadf6 %>%
  filter(teamH == "Minnesota" | teamH == "Phoenix" |
           teamH == "Atlanta" | teamH == "Chicago" |
           teamH == "Cleveland" | teamH == "New York") -> nbadf37

nbadf37 %>%
  filter(Q4vF == "HR" | Q4vF == "HH") -> nbadf38

count(nbadf38, Q4vF) %>% arrange(Q4vF) -> tbl20
tbl20 %>%
  mutate(pct_total = n/nrow(nbadf38)*100) -> tbl20
tbl20$pct_total <- round(tbl20$pct_total, digits = 2)
print(tbl20)
##   Q4vF  n pct_total
## 1   HH 97     52.72
## 2   HR 87     47.28

df4 <- data.frame(quarter = c("1Q", "2Q", "3Q", "4Q"),
                  win_pct = c(45.35, 52.02, 49.37, 52.72))
print(df4)
##   quarter win_pct
## 1      1Q   45.35
## 2      2Q   52.02
## 3      3Q   49.37
```

```
## 4      4Q    52.72

plot8 <- ggplot(df4, aes(x = quarter, y = win_pct)) +
  geom_bar(color = c("gray74", "gray74", "gray74", "orchid"),
           fill = c("gray74", "gray74", "gray74", "orchid"),
           stat = "identity") +
  labs(title = "Bottom 6 Teams at Home",
       subtitle = "Winning Percentages when Winning each Quarter",
       x = "Quarter",
       y = "Winning Percentage") +
  geom_text(aes(x = quarter, y = win_pct, label = win_pct,
              vjust = -0.3, fontface = "bold")) +
  theme(plot.title = element_text(face = "bold"))

plot7 + plot8 + plot_layout(ncol = 2)
```

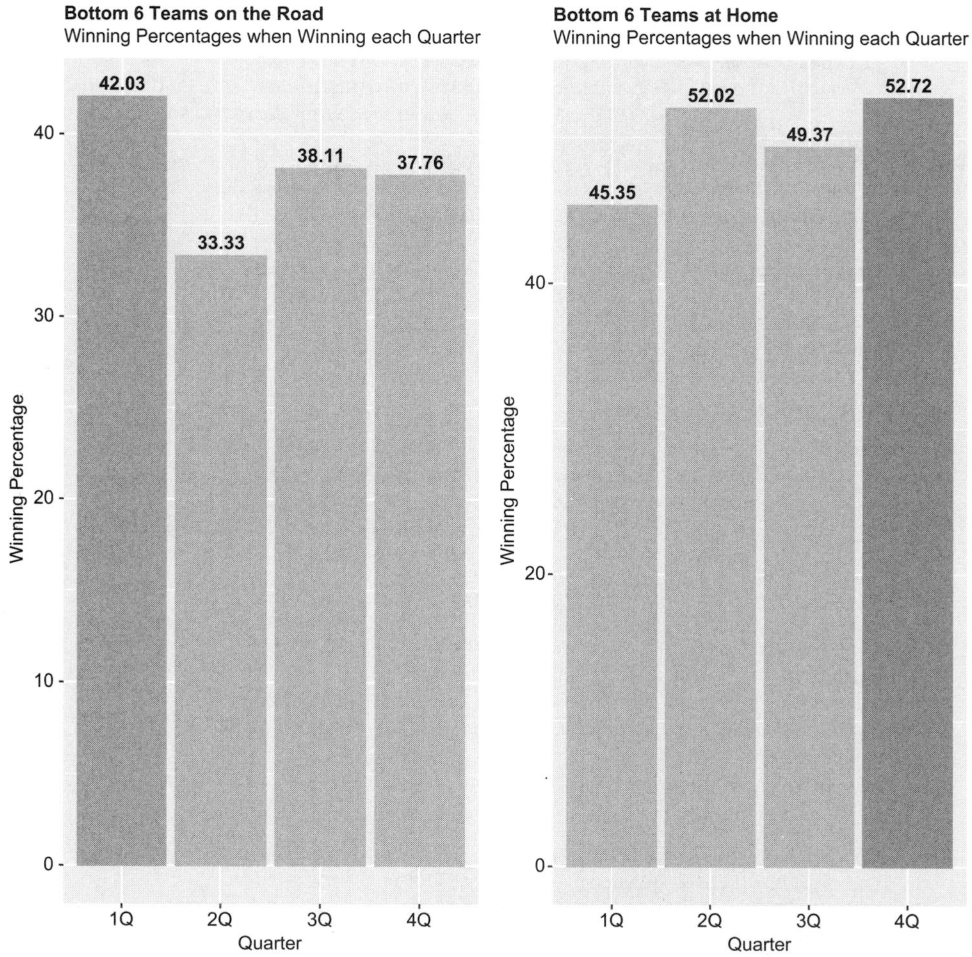

Figure 6.6   The NBA's worst teams over the 2018–19 and 2019–20 regular seasons. When they did manage to win, they most frequently won the first quarter when on the road and the fourth quarter when playing at home.

When playing on the road, the NBA's least successful teams most frequently won the first quarter when winning the same game. When playing at home instead, these same teams won the fourth quarter most frequently when also winning the game.

Most of the evidence so far suggests the *third* quarter matters most, in spite of these latest results; at a minimum, there is barely any evidence to otherwise suggest that fourth-quarter results are more significant than results over the first three quarters. Again, this finding further confirms our hypothesis. But let's take one more look.

6.4.6   *Second-half results*

In our final analysis, we'll investigate third- and fourth-quarter results against a data set that includes only those 2018–19 and 2019–20 regular season games that were tied at halftime. We're therefore pairing the last two quarters against one another and, in the process, disregarding the first two quarters; in other words, in this final analysis, we're examining the quarter thought to be decisive based on conventional wisdom (i.e., the fourth quarter) versus the one that, based on our analysis so far, *is* decisive (i.e., the third quarter).

We therefore call the `dplyr` `filter()` function to subset the nbadf2 data set on those observations where the road and home teams scored the same number of points between quarters 1 and 2. The results are cast into a new object called nbadf39:

```
nbadf2 %>%
  filter(Q1R + Q2R == Q1H + Q2H) -> nbadf39
```

We again call the `filter()` function, this time to subset nbadf39 on those observations where neither the third or fourth quarters ended with both the road and home teams scoring the same number of points. Therefore, the nbadf39 data set includes a winning team for every third and fourth quarter:

```
nbadf39 %>%
  filter(Q3R != Q3H & Q4R != Q4H) -> nbadf39
dim(nbadf39)
## [1] 61 17
```

By running the `dim()` function, we see that nbadf39 is just 61 rows long.

In the chunk of code that follows, we pipe the nbadf39 data set to a pair of `dplyr` functions: the `tally()` function counts the number of records in nbadf39 for every result combination called out in the `group_by()` function.

The arguments passed to the `group_by()` function map to every conceivable result combination between the third quarter, fourth quarter, and end of game. For instance, the first argument—where Q3H is greater than Q3R, Q4H is greater than Q4R, and FH is greater than FR—translates into the home team scoring more points than the road team in the third and fourth quarters and then winning the game. The last argument—where Q3R is less than Q3H, Q4R is greater than Q4H, and FR is greater than FH—translates into the home team outscoring the road team in the third quarter, the road team then outscoring the home team in the fourth quarter, and the road team winning the game.

This might go without saying, but mathematically impossible result combinations for games tied at the half aren't included. For example, it's impossible for the road team to win the third and fourth quarters and then *not* win the game, so there's no argument to the group_by() function to account for this scenario. The results are cast into a tibble called tbl21:

```
nbadf39 %>%
  group_by(Q3H > Q3R & Q4H > Q4R & FH > FR,
           Q3H > Q3R & Q4H < Q4R & FH > FR,
           Q3H < Q3R & Q4H > Q4R & FH > FR,
           Q3R > Q3H & Q4R > Q4H & FR > FH,
           Q3R > Q3H & Q4R < Q4H & FR > FH,
           Q3R < Q3H & Q4R > Q4H & FR > FH) %>%
tally() -> tbl21
print(tbl21)
## # A tibble: 6 × 7
## # Groups:   Q3H > Q3R & Q4H > Q4R & FH > FR,
## # Q3H > Q3R & Q4H < Q4R & FH > FR,
## # Q3H < Q3R & Q4H > Q4R & FH > FR,
## # Q3R > Q3H & Q4R > Q4H & FR > FH,
## # Q3R > Q3H & Q4R < Q4H & FR > FH [6]
## #  `Q3H > Q3R & Q4H > Q4R & FH > FR` `Q3H > Q3R & Q4H < Q4R & FH > FR`
##    <lgl>                             <lgl>
## 1 FALSE                             FALSE
## 2 FALSE                             FALSE
## 3 FALSE                             FALSE
## 4 FALSE                             FALSE
## 5 FALSE                             TRUE
## 6 TRUE                              FALSE
## #  `Q3H < Q3R & Q4H > Q4R & FH > FR` `Q3R > Q3H & Q4R > Q4H & FR > FH`
##    <lgl>                             <lgl>
## 1 FALSE                             FALSE
## 2 FALSE                             FALSE
## 3 FALSE                             TRUE
## 4 TRUE                              FALSE
## 5 FALSE                             FALSE
## 6 FALSE                             FALSE
## #  `Q3R > Q3H & Q4R < Q4H & FR > FH` `Q3R < Q3H & Q4R > Q4H & FR > FH`
##    <lgl>                             <lgl>
## 1 FALSE                             TRUE
## 2 TRUE                              FALSE
## 3 FALSE                             FALSE
## 4 FALSE                             FALSE
## 5 FALSE                             FALSE
## 6 FALSE                             FALSE
## #       n
##     <int>
## 1      6
## 2      8
## 3     13
```

```
## 4        8
## 5        8
## 6       18
```

These results aren't formatted in a way that's either quick or easy to decipher; therefore, we'll run a series of data wrangling operations to produce a tibble that translates well into a simple table that's much easier to interpret.

For starters, we call the base R `colnames()` function to set, or essentially rename, the tbl21 columns. Note that between the `colnames()` and `c()` functions, we're implementing a full replace of the tbl21 column names, so the length of the vector must equal the width of tbl21 to prevent R from throwing an error; thus, it's not necessary to include the original and changed column names in our code as we did previously by calling the `rename()` function.

The base R `head()` function, where `n = 1`, returns the new header information plus the first row of data in tbl21:

```
colnames(tbl21) <- c('HHH', 'HRH', 'RHH', 'RRR', 'RHR', 'HRR', 'count')
head(tbl21, n = 1)
## # A tibble: 1 × 7
## # Groups:   HHH, HRH, RHH, RRR, RHR [1]
##    HHH    HRH    RHH    RRR    RHR    HRR    count
##    <lgl>  <lgl>  <lgl>  <lgl>  <lgl>  <lgl>  <int>
## 1 FALSE FALSE FALSE FALSE FALSE  TRUE      6
```

> ### Avoid special characters and spaces
>
> Do *not* use special characters or spaces when changing or creating variable names because, depending on the function that's being called, R may throw an error. So, for instance, the column HHH—meaning the home team won the third quarter, fourth quarter, and game—should not instead be named anything resembling the following:
>
> H_H_H
>
> H H H
>
> H-H-H
>
> H@H@H

Most of our variables are logical data types, and our data wrangling operations will be made easier by converting logical variables to numeric. We do this by repeatedly calling the base R `as.numeric()` function:

```
tbl21$HHH <- as.numeric(tbl21$HHH)
tbl21$HRH <- as.numeric(tbl21$HRH)
tbl21$RHH <- as.numeric(tbl21$RHH)
tbl21$RRR <- as.numeric(tbl21$RRR)
tbl21$RHR <- as.numeric(tbl21$RHR)
tbl21$HRR <- as.numeric(tbl21$HRR)
```

Values that previously equaled FALSE now equal 0, and values that previously equaled TRUE now equal 1.

We then index the six values now equal to 1 by applying opening and closing square brackets so that they can be modified to equal the corresponding value from the count column instead. For instance, where variable HHH equals 1—row 6 and column 1—we change that so it equals 18 instead because tbl21 contains 18 records where the home team won the third quarter, fourth quarter, and game:

```
tbl21[6, 1] = 18
tbl21[5, 2] = 8
tbl21[4, 3] = 8
tbl21[3, 4] = 13
tbl21[2, 5] = 8
tbl21[1, 6] = 6
```

Because there is then no further need for the count column, we call the dplyr select() function to subset tbl21 on just those variables from HHH to HRR, thereby excluding the count column:

```
tbl21 %>%
  select(HHH:HRR) -> tbl21
```

We then call the tidyr pivot_longer() function, which reshapes a data object from wide to long by converting columns to rows. The pivot_longer() function essentially requires that we call out the existing columns to be collapsed and the new columns to then be created, where the following are true:

- cols equals the names of the columns to pivot.
- names_to equals the name of the new character column.
- values_to equals the name of the new values column.

The base R head() function returns the top six observations in tbl21. There are now six rows for each result combination (e.g., HHH, HRH, etc.) under the result column, of which only one contains the actual record count:

```
tbl21 %>%
  pivot_longer(cols = c("HHH", "HRH", "RHH", "RRR", "RHR", "HRR"),
               names_to = "result",
               values_to = "count") -> tbl21
head(tbl21)
## # A tibble: 6 × 2
##    result count
##    <chr>  <dbl>
## 1 HHH        0
## 2 HRH        0
## 3 RHH        0
## 4 RRR        0
## 5 RHR        0
## 6 HRR        6
```

By calling the `filter()` function one more time and subsetting tbl21 where the variable count is greater than 0, we finally have a 6 × 2 tibble that can easily be analyzed:

```
tbl21 %>%
  filter(count > 0)
print(tbl21)
## # A tibble: 6 × 2
##   result count
##   <chr>  <dbl>
## 1 HRR        6
## 2 RHR        8
## 3 RRR       13
## 4 RHH        8
## 5 HRH        8
## 6 HHH       18
```

Rather than visualizing these results, it actually might be more effective to throw them into a simple table (see table 6.1).

Table 6.1   Summary results for regular season games that were tied at halftime

Results combination	Explanation	Count
HHH	Home team won Q3 Home team won Q4 Home team won game	18
HRH	Home team won Q3 Road team won Q4 Home team won game	8
RHH	Road team won Q3 Home team won Q4 Home team won game	8
RRR	Road team won Q3 Road team won Q4 Road team won game	13
RHR	Road team won Q3 Home team won Q4 Road team won game	8
HRR	Home team won Q3 Road team won Q4 Road team won game	6

The results are unremarkable because there's nothing here to trigger any pivot from our previous conclusions. Not only are NBA games not usually won in the fourth quarter, but our analysis of the 2018–19 and 2019–20 regular seasons shows that the third quarter is most decisive:

- Of the 61 observations, or games, in tbl21, the home team won 34 times and the road team won 27 times. This is actually very close to the home/road split we see across an entire regular season.
- The home team won the third quarter 26 times and the fourth quarter 26 times in those games it also won.
- The road team won the third quarter 21 times and the fourth quarter 19 times in those games it then won.
- Therefore, for games tied at halftime, neither the third nor the fourth quarter is predominant over the other.

In the next chapter, we'll continue our in-game analyses by investigating a potential reason behind the NBA's home-court advantage.

Summary

- As with almost everything else in this book, there wasn't an available data set ideally structured to support the breadth of analysis performed here. Thankfully, any data set can be wrangled any number of ways in R, from creating variables to renaming, converting, or removing them; from subsetting data sets to reshaping them or joining them with other data sets; and from slicing and dicing data to visualizing the same.
- It's not at all uncommon for data-driven analysis to debunk conventional wisdom that was never based on data, but instead on what merely appeared to be logical. But when that's the case, you'll actually need *more* data, not just some, to shift people's mindsets.
- In the meantime, there is no evidence to support the conventional wisdom that the fourth quarter matters more than the first three quarters.
- If anything, the third quarter matters most; after all, winning teams, especially the league's best teams, won the third quarter more than they won any other quarter, at least over the 2018–19 regular season and most of the 2019–20 regular season.
- In an investigation into just those games that were tied at halftime, where the fourth quarter was then "competing" against the third quarter only, one quarter failed to stand out over the other. While this doesn't further support our previous findings that the third quarter actually matters more than the fourth quarter, or any quarter, it does in fact further discredit the going-in alternative hypothesis.

7

T-testing and
effect size testing

This chapter covers

- Running and interpreting statistical tests of significance with continuous data
- Visualizing statistical tests of significance
- Running and interpreting effect size testing with continuous data

Even if you're just a casual basketball fan, you nonetheless probably know that teams playing at home win way more often than they lose (this is true for other sports too). In chapter 9, we'll explore the actual win–loss percentages between home and visiting teams under different permutations of prior days off, but in the meantime, we want to determine if there is an officiating bias that might explain home-court advantage. We'll compare counts of foul calls and free throw attempts between home and visiting teams and then conduct statistical tests to determine if any variances in those counts are statistically significant and what their effect size may be. Which statistical tests to run mostly depends on the data. Because we'll be comparing two groups (and just two groups) where the outcomes are numeric, our plan is to therefore run t-tests to determine whether or not any variances are statistically significant and Cohen's d effect size tests to measure the size of those variances.

Our going-in, or null, hypothesis is that there are no statistically significant variances in personal foul calls or free throw attempts between road and home teams; we therefore start out by assuming that any differences are due to chance and not at all purposeful. We'll need overwhelming evidence from our t-tests to reject our null hypothesis and to then conclude that any variances we see in the data aren't due to chance. Cohen's d tests return quantitative and qualitative measures on the size of these same variances, independent and irrespective of the t-test results; we don't reject or fail to reject a null hypothesis based on what we get from an effect size test.

We'll cover much more on t-tests and effect size tests later, but here's a snapshot of how our journey will play out:

- We'll begin by loading packages, importing the same pair of data sets we imported in chapter 6, and then running a short series of data wrangling operations.
- With respect to the 2018–19 season, we'll run t-tests on personal foul calls and free throws (usually awarded to one team following a personal foul committed by the opposing team) on data split between the regular season and postseason. Then, we'll run effect size tests to complement our t-tests.
- With respect to the 2019–20 season, which was impacted by COVID-19, we'll again run a series of t-tests and effect size tests, but the data will be split on the regular season only this time. We'll first run our tests on a data set that contains regular season games played before COVID-19 temporarily suspended play and then again when the season resumed and all games were played at a neutral site in Orlando, Florida.

Let's start our journey by loading our packages.

7.1 Loading packages

As usual, we'll call a mix of base R and packaged functions to import data, wrangle data, conduct our significance tests, visualize results, and compute basic statistics. Our first order of business is to call the base R `library()` function to load the `tidyverse`, `ggpubr`, `sqldf`, `effsize`, and `patchwork` packages:

```
library(tidyverse)
library(ggpubr)
library(sqldf)
library(effsize)
library(patchwork)
```

The `ggpubr` package includes simple and straightforward functions for customizing `ggplot2` visualizations. The `effsize` package includes a function to perform effect size testing. Anything and everything in this chapter above and beyond base R ties back to one of these five packages.

7.2 Importing data

We now call the `readr read_csv()` function to import the same two .csv files we loaded in the previous chapter—nba_boxscore_1819.csv and nba_boxscore_1920.csv—both of which were downloaded from the website www.bigdataball.com and subsequently stored in our default working directory:

```
df1 <- read_csv("nba_boxscore_1819.csv")
df2 <- read_csv("nba_boxscore_1920.csv")
```

We set these to equal df1 and df2 data sets, respectively.

7.3 Wrangling data

Back in chapter 2, we saved a much-wrangled version of our original data set and then exported the content to a .csv file by calling the base R `write.csv()` function. That was done to avoid replicating the chapter 2 data wrangling operations in chapter 3. Even though we've imported the same pair of files that were first imported in the previous chapter, our purposes here are quite different from those in chapter 6, and therefore our data wrangling operations will be altogether different. In other words, there was no opportunity lost by *not* calling the `write.csv()` function in chapter 6.

That being said, we'll start with the 2018–19 box score data contained in df1. We call the `dplyr filter()` function to subset the df1 data set on those observations where the variable VENUE equals R and save the results in a new object called df3. Our new data set therefore contains road team data only:

```
df1 %>%
  filter(VENUE == "R") -> df3
```

Next, we call the `select()` function, also from the `dplyr` package, to reduce the df3 data set to only include those variables needed going forward:

```
df3 %>%
  select(DATASET, TEAM, VENUE, FT, FTA, PF) -> df3
```

Some of these will be familiar to you from the previous chapter, and some will be unfamiliar:

- DATASET—Now a character string, but essentially includes two levels to delineate regular season games versus playoff games.
- TEAM—Another character string; this equals the team name where, for instance, Milwaukee equals Milwaukee Bucks or Denver equals Denver Nuggets.
- VENUE—Always equals R as a designation for road teams (versus H for home teams).
- FT—Equals the number of free throws made by the road team in any particular game. Players are most often awarded free throws when fouled by an opposing player while in the act of attempting a field goal.

- FTA—Equals the number of free throws attempted by the road team.
- PF—Equals the number of personal fouls the road team committed during any particular game.

These same variables are then renamed to distinguish them later on from their home team equivalents (except for DATASET, which we merely convert to lowercase). The rename() function from dplyr is used to convert variable names on the right side of the assignment operator to names we have on the left:

```
df3 %>%
  rename(dataset = DATASET, teamR = TEAM, venueR = VENUE, ftR = FT,
         ftaR = FTA, pfR = PF) -> df3
```

Three of our df3 variables—dataset, teamR, and venueR—are then converted to factor variables by calling the base R as.factor() function three times. Once again, this is a best practice for variables that have a finite number of possible values:

```
df3$dataset <- as.factor(df3$dataset)
df3$teamR <- as.factor(df3$teamR)
df3$venueR <- as.factor(df3$venueR)
```

These same steps are repeated to create a data set called df4. This data set is just like df3 except for the fact that it contains home team box score data rather than road team data (and no DATASET variable):

```
df1 %>%
  filter(VENUE == "H") -> df4

df4 %>%
  select(TEAM, VENUE, FT, FTA, PF) -> df4

df4 %>%
  rename(teamH = TEAM, venueH = VENUE, ftH = FT, ftaH = FTA,
         pfH = PF) -> df4

df4$teamH <- as.factor(df4$teamH)
df4$venueH <- as.factor(df4$venueH)
```

We next instruct R to return the dimensions of df3 and df4 by calling the base R dim() function twice:

```
dim(df3)
## [1] 1312    6
dim(df4)
## [1] 1312    5
```

Both data sets contain 1,312 rows; df3 has six variables versus just five for df4 because we retained the variable dataset in the former and not in the latter.

Next, we merge the df3 and df4 data sets into a single object called fouls1819 (recall that we're working exclusively with 2018–19 data for the time being) by calling the base R cbind() function. The cbind() function makes it possible to join multiple data sets into one data set extended horizontally. We then call the dim() function one more time to check the row and column counts in fouls1819:

```
fouls1819 <- cbind(df3, df4)
dim(fouls1819)
## [1] 1312    11
```

Whereas df3 has 1,312 rows and 6 columns and df4 has 1,312 rows and 5 columns, our fouls1819 data set has 1,312 rows and 11 columns. We now have a data set containing 2018–19 regular season and postseason data that can be analyzed.

7.4 Analysis on 2018–19 data

Our analysis will be divided into two parts. First, we'll compute and test variances in foul calls and free throw attempts between home and visiting teams over the course of the 2018–19 regular season. Then, we'll compute and test the same for the 2018–19 playoffs.

7.4.1 2018–19 regular season analysis

We need to start by subsetting the fouls1819 data set so that it includes regular season games only. We therefore pass (or pipe) the fouls1819 data set to the filter() function, which reduces fouls1819 to a new data set called fouls1819reg, where the variable dataset equals NBA 2018-2019 Regular Season.

We then call the base R sum() and mean() functions to compute the variances on key measures between road and home teams using our new data set as the source. For the moment, we're merely interested in getting baseline data:

```
fouls1819 %>%
   filter(dataset == "NBA 2018-2019 Regular Season") -> fouls1819reg

sum(fouls1819reg$pfR) - sum(fouls1819reg$pfH)
## [1] 470
mean(fouls1819reg$pfR) - mean(fouls1819reg$pfH)
## [1] 0.3821138
mean(fouls1819reg$ftaR) - mean(fouls1819reg$ftaH)
## [1] -0.6504065
sum(fouls1819reg$ftR) / sum(fouls1819reg$ftaR)
## [1] 0.7655742
sum(fouls1819reg$ftH) / sum(fouls1819reg$ftaH)
## [1] 0.7670176
```

Following is a summary of these results:

- Road teams were called for 470 more personal fouls than home teams during the 2018–19 regular season; to be exact, road teams were called for a total of 25,947 personal fouls, versus 25,477 for home teams.

- Road teams were therefore whistled for approximately 0.38 more personal fouls per game than were home teams.
- As a result, home teams attempted approximately 0.65 more free throws per game than road teams.
- While home teams averaged more free throw attempts per game, home and road teams were equally efficient at making them; both home and road teams were successful on 77% of their free throw attempts.

These variances might *seem* immaterial, but the length of our data set must also be considered. Statistical tests of significance make allowance for both these factors—statistical significance is contingent upon group means, variances, and record counts. For instance, a "large" variance on short data could be statistically *insignificant*; conversely, a "small" variance on long data might be statistically *significant*. A t-test is one such statistical test, where two groups—and no more than two groups—are being compared and the data is continuous. Our null hypothesis, always, is that the means, regardless of measure, are essentially no different between road and home teams. Therefore, the p-value in either test must be equal to or less than the 0.05 threshold for significance to reject the null hypothesis that the means are statistically equal and instead accept the alternative hypothesis. While the 5% cutoff is rather arbitrary, it's undoubtedly a low number and therefore qualifies as a high bar by which to reject a null hypothesis.

There are *tons* of use cases for t-tests; for instance:

- A pharmaceutical company wants to test the efficacy of a new cholesterol-reducing drug versus one that's been on the market for several years. Afflicted patients are randomly selected and prescribed one drug or the other. A t-test will determine if one drug is better at treating high cholesterol levels than the other, or if any result differences are merely due to chance.
- A university wants to test and compare Business Analytics 101 exam scores between one group of randomly selected students who attended class in person versus another group of randomly selected students who attended online. A t-test will determine if one learning method is truly better than the other.
- A community bank that operates two branches conducts a survey where participating customers are asked to rate the service they received on a scale of 1 to 10. A t-test will determine if one branch provides superior customer service or if any variance is immaterial.

The data must otherwise be continuous (in chapter 9, we'll run a chi-square test for independence where the data is categorical), and no more than two groups should be compared. (In a subsequent chapter, we'll fit analysis of variance [ANOVA] models to compare more than two groups.)

T-TEST: PERSONAL FOULS

It's super easy to run a t-test in R; we simply call the out-of-the-box `t.test()` function and pass the two variables we're comparing as arguments. Our first t-test compares the means in personal fouls between road and home teams. Because R will return our t-test results in scientific notation by default, we first call the base R `options()` function to disable scientific notation in favor of their full numeric equivalents:

```
options(scipen = 999)

t.test(fouls1819reg$pfR, fouls1819reg$pfH)
##
##   Welch Two Sample t-test
##
## data:  fouls1819reg$pfR and fouls1819reg$pfH
## t = 2.2089, df = 2457.8, p-value = 0.02727
## alternative hypothesis: true difference in means is not equal to 0
## 95 percent confidence interval:
##   0.04290002 0.72132763
## sample estimates:
## mean of x mean of y
##   21.09512  20.71301
```

The p-value equals 0.03, which, of course, is below the accepted, or predefined, threshold for significance of 0.05. In other words, there is just a 3% probability of observing the same or more extreme difference if the null hypothesis were actually true. So we can reject the null hypothesis and conclude that the variance in personal foul counts between road and home teams over the 2018–19 NBA regular season isn't due to chance; in other words, the data points to a trend that may very well be causal.

T-TEST: FREE THROW ATTEMPTS

Let's now run a second t-test, this time comparing free throw attempts between road and home teams:

```
t.test(fouls1819reg$ftaR, fouls1819reg$ftaH)
##
##   Welch Two Sample t-test
##
## data:  fouls1819reg$ftaR and fouls1819reg$ftaH
## t = -2.1619, df = 2457.9, p-value = 0.03072
## alternative hypothesis: true difference in means is not equal to 0
## 95 percent confidence interval:
##   -1.24035782 -0.06045519
## sample estimates:
## mean of x mean of y
##   22.74715  23.39756
```

This variance is equally significant. Because the p-value again equals 0.03, we can again reject the null hypothesis and conclude with confidence that the variance in free throw attempts between road and home teams during the 2018–19 regular season is meaningful.

By the way, it's not accurate to state something like "road teams are always called for more fouls than home teams" or "the differences in free throw attempts between road and home teams are significant." It's always best to instead state specifically what was tested on what data and to not draw larger conclusions; what was true during the 2018–19 NBA regular season might not have been true in, let's say, the 1978–79 season.

VISUALIZING VARIANCES

The best way to visualize these variances is with paired boxplots. We go about doing this by first creating temporary data sets formatted for ggplot2 readability. For our first set of paired boxplots, we call the select() function from the dplyr package to create a data set called temp1, which includes just the variables pfR and pfH from the fouls1819reg data set.

We then call the pivot_longer() function from the tidyr package—tidyr is also part of the tidyverse universe of packages—to reshape temp1 by folding columns into rows; temp1 still has two columns, but now they are named team and fouls. The prior columns of pfR and pfH are now levels in the variable team, and their corresponding counts now occupy cells in the variable fouls.

Next, we make a call to the base R head() function, which prints the first six observations in temp1 to provide a visual of our results:

```
temp1 <- select(fouls1819reg, c(pfR, pfH))
temp1 %>%
  pivot_longer(cols = c(pfR, pfH),
               names_to = "team",
               values_to = "fouls") -> temp1
head(temp1)
## # A tibble: 6 x 2
##    team  fouls
##    <chr> <int>
## 1 pfR      20
## 2 pfH      20
## 3 pfR      21
## 4 pfH      29
## 5 pfR      25
## 6 pfH      19
```

Now, for our ggplot2 boxplots (see figure 7.1), we do the following:

- First, we call the base R c() function to create a vector, called tempt1.text, containing the values Home Team and Road Team. temp1.text is subsequently cast into the scale_x_discrete() function, so that Home Team and Road Team are our x-axis labels.
- Our boxplots are otherwise sourced from temp1, with team as our x-axis variable and fouls as our y-axis variable.
- The stat_summary() function adds a white dot to each boxplot to represent the mean, which is especially important because the t-tests are comparing the means of two groups, not the medians.

- The `stat_compare_means()` function from the `ggpubr` package essentially performs an independent t-test by comparing the means of the two variables we're visualizing and inserting the results, much like the `ggplot2` `geom_text()` or `annotate()` functions, where the specified x and y coordinates cross.

The full code chunk is as follows:

```
temp1.text <- c("Home Team", "Road Team")
p1 <- ggplot(temp1, aes(x = team, y = fouls, fill = team)) +
  geom_boxplot() +
  labs(title = "Personal Foul Calls: Home vs. Road Teams",
       subtitle = "2018-19 Regular Season",
       x = "",
       y = "Personal Fouls per Game") +
  stat_summary(fun = mean, geom = "point", shape = 20, size = 8,
               color = "white", fill = "white") +
  theme(legend.position = "none") +
  scale_x_discrete(labels = temp1.text) +
  theme(plot.title = element_text(face = "bold")) +
  stat_compare_means(method = "t.test",
                     label.x = 1.4, label.y = 34)
```

We now do the same with respect to free throw attempts in place of personal fouls. We first create a data source called temp2, which is structured just like temp1, and then call the `ggplot()` function to create a second pair of boxplots just like our first set:

```
temp2 <- select(fouls1819reg, c(5,10))
temp2 %>%
  pivot_longer(cols = c(ftaR, ftaH),
               names_to = "team",
               values_to = "ftattempts") -> temp2
head(temp2)
##    team ftattempts
## 1 ftaR         23
## 2 ftaH         14
## 3 ftaR         37
## 4 ftaH         18
## 5 ftaR         20
## 6 ftaH         22
```

```
temp2.text <- c("Home Team", "Road Team")
p2 <- ggplot(temp2, aes(x = team, y = ftattempts, fill = team)) +
  geom_boxplot() +
  labs(title = "Free Throw Attempts: Home vs. Road Teams",
       subtitle = "2018-19 Regular Season",
       x = "",
       y = "Free Throw Attempts per Game") +
  stat_summary(fun = mean, geom = "point", shape = 20, size = 8,
               color = "white", fill = "white") +
  theme(legend.position = "none") +
  scale_x_discrete(labels = temp2.text) +
  theme(plot.title = element_text(face = "bold")) +
  stat_compare_means(method = "t.test",
                     label.x = 1.4, label.y = 48)
```

We pack our two visualizations, p1 and p2, into a single graphical object by calling the plot_layout() function from the patchwork package:

```
p1 + p2 + plot_layout(ncol = 2)
```

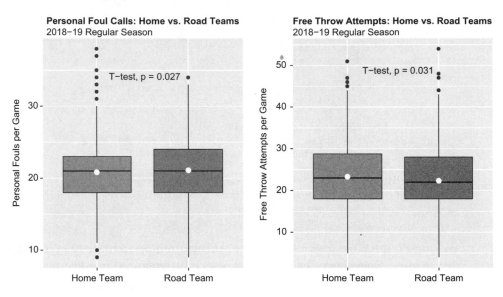

Figure 7.1   Paired boxplots for personal fouls per game between home and road teams on the left and free throw attempts per game between home and road teams on the right. The white dots represent the population means. Data is from the 2018–19 regular season. Both of these variances tested out as statistically significant.

Our paired boxplots clearly show the variances in population means (represented by the white dots inside the boxes) and additional differences in the length, or dispersion, of the interquartile ranges (represented by the boxes only) between home and road teams.

We might have otherwise been distracted by the outliers in both plots. For instance, at least five times during the 2018–19 regular season, teams were called for a minimum of 34 personal fouls, and at least twice, teams attempted more than 50 free throws.

We then call the sqldf() function from the sqldf package to return observations in the fouls1819reg data set where at least one team was called for 34 or more personal fouls:

```
sqldf("SELECT * from fouls1819reg WHERE pfH >= 34 OR pfR >= 34")
##                         dataset       teamR venueR ftR ftaR pfR
## 1  NBA 2018-2019 Regular Season  LA Clippers      R  33   43  26
## 2  NBA 2018-2019 Regular Season      Phoenix      R  13   24  34
## 3  NBA 2018-2019 Regular Season  LA Clippers      R  37   47  22
## 4  NBA 2018-2019 Regular Season Philadelphia      R  41   54  30
## 5  NBA 2018-2019 Regular Season      Phoenix      R  15   21  34
```

```
## 6  NBA 2018-2019 Regular Season       Brooklyn      R  26   34  23
## 7  NBA 2018-2019 Regular Season Oklahoma City       R  16   25  34
## 8  NBA 2018-2019 Regular Season        Chicago      R  35   48  30
## 9  NBA 2018-2019 Regular Season Oklahoma City       R  17   26  34
## 10 NBA 2018-2019 Regular Season       Brooklyn      R  33   54  23
##           teamH venueH ftH ftaH pfH
## 1  Oklahoma City      H  23   32  35
## 2   Philadelphia      H  31   42  27
## 3        Atlanta      H  17   19  38
## 4        Phoenix      H  30   36  34
## 5         Dallas      H  32   45  17
## 6      Cleveland      H  13   18  37
## 7         Denver      H  26   35  28
## 8        Atlanta      H  17   25  34
## 9    LA Clippers      H  31   46  26
## 10       Atlanta      H  26   32  37
```

It turns out that there were 10 games during the 2018–19 regular season where at least one of the competing teams was called for a minimum of 34 personal fouls—this was more often than not the home team.

Next, we call the sqldf() function again, this time to fetch all records in fouls1819reg where either the road team or home team attempted a minimum of 50 free throws. Two of our three times, the road team was actually the beneficiary:

```
sqldf("SELECT * from fouls1819reg WHERE ftaH > 50 OR ftaR > 50")
##                      dataset        teamR venueR ftR ftaR pfR
## 1 NBA 2018-2019 Regular Season      Detroit      R  28   41  32
## 2 NBA 2018-2019 Regular Season Philadelphia      R  41   54  30
## 3 NBA 2018-2019 Regular Season     Brooklyn      R  33   54  23
##        teamH venueH ftH ftaH pfH
## 1 Philadelphia      H  44   51  31
## 2      Phoenix      H  30   36  34
## 3      Atlanta      H  26   32  37
```

So there were actually three games in 2018–19 where a team attempted more than 50 free throws. Two of these three games tie back, not surprisingly, to the results from our first sqldf query; after all, personal fouls often lead to attempted free throws. But one game doesn't, which is why we're testing personal foul calls between road and home teams *and* free throw attempts between the same. Let's now examine the same measures using the same methods with respect to the 2018–19 playoffs.

7.4.2 *2019 postseason analysis*

Because not every NBA team qualifies for the postseason, and teams are then eliminated in each round, our analysis will be performed against a much shorter data set than before. Whereas the fouls1819reg data set contained 1,230 records, we'll now be working with a data set just 82 rows long. Therefore, to again get statistically significant results, our variances will presumably need to be more substantial than before.

We start by piping the fouls1819 data set to the `dplyr` `filter()` function to create a new object, fouls1819post, that just includes those 82 fouls1819 records where the variable `dataset` equals `NBA 2019 Playoffs`.

We then call the `sum()` and `mean()` functions to compute the same variances on the same measures we did previously; the only difference is that we've swapped out data sources. Once more, we're just trying to get an initial read on the data:

```
fouls1819 %>%
  filter(dataset == "NBA 2019 Playoffs") -> fouls1819post

sum(fouls1819post$pfR) - sum(fouls1819post$pfH)
## [1] 48
mean(fouls1819post$pfR) - mean(fouls1819post$pfH)
## [1] 0.5853659
mean(fouls1819post$ftaR) - mean(fouls1819post$ftaH)
## [1] -1.280488
sum(fouls1819post$ftR) / sum(fouls1819post$ftaR)
## [1] 0.7857143
sum(fouls1819post$ftH) / sum(fouls1819post$ftaH)
## [1] 0.7821068
```

Here's a summary of our results, including comparisons against the 2018–19 regular season:

- Road teams were called for 48 more personal fouls than home teams during the 2019 playoffs. To be more specific, road teams were called for a grand total of 1,843 fouls during the 2019 postseason, whereas home teams were called for 1,795 personal fouls.
- That averages out to a variance of 0.59, which is to say road teams on average were called for 0.59 more personal fouls per playoff game than were home teams. The difference during the regular season equaled 0.38.
- Consequently, home teams attempted 1.28 more free throws per playoff game than road teams; this variance is about twice that of regular season games.
- Road teams made almost 79% of their free throw attempts, while home teams were successful on about 78% of their attempted free throws. These figures are slightly higher than those during the regular season.

T-TEST: PERSONAL FOULS

Let's run a pair of t-tests to determine if these variances are statistically significant or not, starting with personal fouls called:

```
t.test(fouls1819post$pfR, fouls1819post$pfH)
##
##   Welch Two Sample t-test
##
## data:  fouls1819post$pfR and fouls1819post$pfH
## t = 1.0133, df = 161.46, p-value = 0.3124
## alternative hypothesis: true difference in means is not equal to 0
## 95 percent confidence interval:
```

```
##  -0.5553998  1.7261315
## sample estimates:
## mean of x mean of y
##  22.47561  21.89024
```

The p-value equals 0.31. Because it's greater than 0.05—much greater, in fact—we should fail to reject the null hypothesis and should therefore conclude that the variance in personal fouls called between road and home teams is not significant; the means are essentially equal. While the raw numbers are directionally consistent with the 2018–19 regular season, the results are neutral. It turns out that the drop in record count influenced the t-test results more than the increase in the variance did.

T-TEST: FREE THROW ATTEMPTS

Our next t-test will tell us whether or not the variance in attempted free throws between road and home teams during the 2019 playoffs is significant:

```
t.test(fouls1819post$ftaR, fouls1819post$ftaH)
##
##  Welch Two Sample t-test
##
## data:  fouls1819post$ftaR and fouls1819post$ftaH
## t = -1.1997, df = 159.16, p-value = 0.232
## alternative hypothesis: true difference in means is not equal to 0
## 95 percent confidence interval:
##  -3.3884143  0.8274387
## sample estimates:
## mean of x mean of y
##  24.07317  25.35366
```

Because the p-value is again greater than the 0.05 threshold for significance—0.23, to be exact—we must again conclude that the population means are essentially equal and therefore fail to reject the null hypothesis. While the results are again directionally consistent with our regular season results, we're nevertheless compelled to once more qualify the results as neutral.

VISUALIZING VARIANCES

We subsequently visualize and bundle our results just as we did before (see figure 7.2). The following chunk of code is very much like our previous chunks of code, except we've changed out data sources:

```
temp3 <- select(fouls1819post, c(6,11))
temp3 %>%
  pivot_longer(cols = c(pfR, pfH),
               names_to = "team",
               values_to = "fouls") -> temp3
head(temp3)
##    team fouls
## 1   pfR    19
## 2   pfH    19
## 3   pfR    27
```

```
## 4   pfH    24
## 5   pfR    22
## 6   pfH    22

temp3.text <- c("Home Team", "Road Team")
p3 <- ggplot(temp3, aes(x = team, y = fouls, fill = team)) +
  geom_boxplot() +
  labs(title = "Personal Foul Calls: Home vs. Road Teams",
       subtitle = "2019 Playoffs",
       x = "",
       y = "Personal Fouls per Game") +
  stat_summary(fun = mean, geom = "point", shape = 20, size = 8,
               color = "white", fill = "white") +
  theme(legend.position = "none") +
  scale_x_discrete(labels = temp1.text) +
  theme(plot.title = element_text(face = "bold")) +
  stat_compare_means(method = "t.test", label.x = 1.4, label.y = 34)
temp4 <- select(fouls1819post, c(5,10))
temp4 %>%
  pivot_longer(cols = c(ftaR, ftaH),
               names_to = "team",
               values_to = "ftattempts") -> temp4
head(temp4)
##    team ftattempts
## 1 ftaR         20
## 2 ftaH         14
## 3 ftaR         26
## 4 ftaH         42
## 5 ftaR         22
## 6 ftaH         20

temp4.text <- c("Home Team", "Road Team")
p4 <- ggplot(temp4, aes(x = team, y = ftattempts, fill = team)) +
  geom_boxplot() +
  labs(title = "Free Throw Attempts: Home vs. Road Teams",
       subtitle = "2019 Playoffs",
       x = "",
       y = "Free Throw Attempts per Game") +
  stat_summary(fun = mean, geom = "point", shape = 20, size = 8,
               color = "white", fill = "white") +
  theme(legend.position = "none") +
  scale_x_discrete(labels = temp2.text) +
  theme(plot.title = element_text(face = "bold")) +
  stat_compare_means(method = "t.test", label.x = 1.4, label.y = 48)

p3 + p4 + plot_layout(ncol = 2)
```

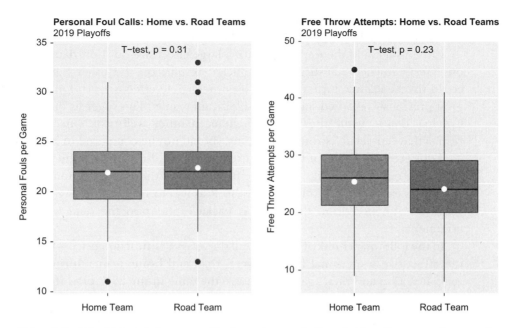

Figure 7.2   Paired boxplots for personal fouls per game and attempted free throws per game, road versus home teams. Differences in the populations means, represented by the white dots, are obvious. Though the results are directionally consistent with our first set of tests, these variances are statistically insignificant. Data is from 2019 playoff games.

The following summarizes our findings from the 2018–19 season:

- The variances in personal fouls called and free throw attempts during the regular season are statistically significant between road and home teams. Road teams are called for more personal fouls than home teams, while home teams attempt more free throws than road teams. These differences matter over the course of an entire regular season.
- The variances in these same two measures during postseason play are directionally consistent with our regular season results, but are neutral; they aren't statistically significant, mostly due to the low record count. It's for this very reason that we'll next perform a pair of effect size tests.

7.4.3   *Effect size testing*

While t-tests tell us if there is a statistically significant difference between the means of two populations (and whether we should reject or fail to reject a null hypothesis) based on a predefined threshold for significance, they don't tell us how large, or not so large, differences might be. That's where effect size testing comes in. One of the most common measurements of effect size is Cohen's d, which computes the difference between two means and divides it by the average standard deviation between the same two populations to return an effect size that is both quantified and classified. Results from effect size tests don't have any bearing on our null hypothesis; the results merely tell us how large or not so large the variances are. In large part, that's because a Cohen's d test doesn't consider record counts.

Cohen's d could theoretically return a large effect size on short data where a previous t-test returned statistically insignificant results; on the other hand, Cohen's d could theoretically return a small or even negligible effect size on long data where a t-test previously returned statistically significant results. This suggests that a t-test and a Cohen's d test, while they complement each other well, won't necessarily return results that "correlate" strongly and, thus, should not be compared in such a way.

Let's see how a pair of Cohen's d tests turn out, bearing in mind that our t-tests returned conflicting results where the figures were otherwise directionally consistent. It's just as easy to run a Cohen's d test in R as it is to run a t-test—we simply call the `cohen.d()` function from the `effsize` package and pass the data we're testing as arguments.

In the following chunk of code, we call the `cohen.d()` function twice—first to measure the effect size of personal fouls between road and home teams during the 2018–19 regular season and then again to measure the same in the 2019 playoffs:

```
cohen.d(fouls1819reg$pfR, fouls1819reg$pfH)
##
## Cohen's d
##
## d estimate: 0.08907251 (negligible)
## 95 percent confidence interval:
##       lower       upper
## 0.009960997 0.168184021

cohen.d(fouls1819post$pfR, fouls1819post$pfH)
##
## Cohen's d
##
## d estimate: 0.158254 (negligible)
## 95 percent confidence interval:
##       lower       upper
## -0.1506272  0.4671351
```

Both tests return the same results; whether or not there was a statistically significant difference in means, the Cohen's d tests tell us that the variances in personal fouls between road and home teams, regular season and postseason, are negligible. That's because the d estimate, which represents the number of standard deviations separating the means, is so trivial for both tests. In the first of our two tests, personal fouls called against road teams are 0.09 standard deviations greater than the same for home teams (0.09 being equal to the d estimate); in the second test, personal fouls against road teams are 0.16 standard deviations above the same for home teams. If and when a d estimate is negative, it merely means that the second group passed to the `cohen.d()` function has the higher of the two standard deviations. For the effect size to register as small, the d estimate would need to equal at least 0.20, plus or minus; by contrast, for the effect size to earn a large qualitative rating, the d estimate would need to equal at least 0.80, plus or minus.

Let's do the same with respect to attempted free throws:

```
cohen.d(fouls1819reg$ftaR, fouls1819reg$ftaH)
##
## Cohen's d
##
## d estimate: -0.08717524 (negligible)
## 95 percent confidence interval:
##       lower       upper
## -0.16628510 -0.00806538
cohen.d(fouls1819post$ftaR, fouls1819post$ftaH)
##
## Cohen's d
##
## d estimate: -0.1873661 (negligible)
## 95 percent confidence interval:
##      lower      upper
## -0.4964408  0.1217086
```

According to our second round of Cohen's d tests, the actual differences between attempted free throws—road teams versus home teams, regular season and postseason, prior statistical significance or not—are again negligible in both cases. Yet it's worth emphasizing at least one more time, but with a slightly different spin, that we should not throw a wet blanket on our t-tests that returned statistically significant results because our subsequent Cohen's d tests then returned negligible effect sizes. One considers the record counts, and the other doesn't. Differences in means between two samples or two populations should matter less when the record counts are small and should matter much more when we have more data.

7.5 Analysis on 2019–20 data

That does it for our analysis of the 2018–19 data set. But you might recall that we imported two seasons of data—so now it's time to explore the 2019–20 NBA season.

7.5.1 2019–20 regular season analysis (pre-COVID)

We'll use the same measures and statistical tests, but rather than testing postseason results, our 2019–20 analysis will be relegated to regular season games only, pre- and post-COVID. Before the pandemic, the 2019–20 NBA regular season proceeded just like any prior season. COVID suddenly suspended all play, and once the season resumed, every remaining game was played at a neutral site in Orlando with no fans present. So rather than again testing the regular season and then the postseason, we'll instead test the regular season pre-COVID and the regular season post-COVID. The steps we previously took to wrangle our 2018–19 data are replicated in the chunks of code that follow and are applied to the 2019–20 season.

We start by establishing a new data set, df5, which equals df2 where the variable VENUE equals R, for road, with a call to the `filter()` function:

```
df2 %>%
  filter(VENUE == "R") -> df5
```

We then make a call to the `select()` function to reduce the width of the df5 data set. Notice that we're retaining one additional variable, GAME_ID, that we previously discarded from the 2018–19 data:

```
df5 %>%
  select(DATASET, GAME_ID, TEAM, VENUE, FT, FTA, PF) -> df5
```

In preparation for further data wrangling operations, we call the `rename()` function to rename our df5 variables, sometimes appending a capital R at the end to later delineate the same measures between road and home teams:

```
df5 %>%
  rename(dataset = DATASET, gameID = GAME_ID, teamR = TEAM, venueR = VENUE,
         ftR = FT, ftaR = FTA, pfR = PF) -> df5
```

The variables dataset, teamR, and venueR are then converted to factor variables by making successive calls to the base R `as.factor()` function:

```
df5$dataset <- as.factor(df5$dataset)
df5$teamR <- as.factor(df5$teamR)
df5$venueR <- as.factor(df5$venueR)
```

Now we call these same functions to create a data set called df6, which is basically a home-team version of df5:

```
df2 %>%
  filter(VENUE == "H") -> df6

df6 %>%
  select(TEAM, VENUE, FT, FTA, PF) -> df6

df6 %>%
  rename(teamH = TEAM, venueH = VENUE, ftH = FT, ftaH = FTA,
         pfH = PF) -> df6
df6$teamH <- as.factor(df6$teamH)
df6$venueH <- as.factor(df6$venueH)
```

Next, we join the df5 and df6 data sets by calling the base R `cbind()` function:

```
fouls1920 <- cbind(df5, df6)
dim(df5)
## [1] 1143    7
dim(df6)
## [1] 1143    5
dim(fouls1920)
## [1] 1143   12
```

According to the returns from the `dim()` function, df5 contains 1,143 rows and 7 columns; the df6 data set contains 1,143 rows and 5 columns; and fouls1920, the aggregate of df5 and df6, contains 1,143 rows and 12 columns.

To subset the fouls1920 data set so that it only includes those games that were played pre-COVID, we call the `filter()` function to subset fouls1920 where the variable `gameID` is equal to or less than `21900973`. The result is a new object called fouls1920a.

We then compute the variances on our key measures by calling the base R `sum()` and `mean()` functions, using fouls1920a as our data source:

```
fouls1920 %>%
  filter(gameID <= 21900973) -> fouls1920a

sum(fouls1920a$pfR) - sum(fouls1920a$pfH)
## [1] 378
mean(fouls1920a$pfR) - mean(fouls1920a$pfH)
## [1] 0.3892894
mean(fouls1920a$ftaR) - mean(fouls1920a$ftaH)
## [1] -0.5983522
sum(fouls1920a$ftR) / sum(fouls1920a$ftaR)
## [1] 0.7707593
sum(fouls1920a$ftH) / sum(fouls1920a$ftaH)
## [1] 0.7712117
```

Our results are as follows:

- Road teams were called for 378 more personal fouls than home teams, equal to the difference between 20,171 fouls and 19,793 fouls.
- Road teams were, therefore, called for 0.39 more personal fouls per game than were home teams (the per-game average during the 2018–19 regular season equaled 0.38).
- Home teams attempted 0.60 more free throws per game than did road teams (the per-game average from the prior regular season was 0.65).
- Road and home teams were successful on 77% of their free throw attempts.

T-TEST: PERSONAL FOULS

Let's now run another t-test, this time to determine if the variance in personal foul calls between road and home teams during the 2019–20 regular season, pre-COVID, is statistically significant:

```
t.test(fouls1920a$pfR, fouls1920a$pfH)
##
##   Welch Two Sample t-test
##
## data:  fouls1920a$pfR and fouls1920a$pfH
## t = 1.9686, df = 1937.3, p-value = 0.04914
## alternative hypothesis: true difference in means is not equal to 0
## 95 percent confidence interval:
##   0.001474823 0.777103962
```

```
## sample estimates:
## mean of x mean of y
##   20.77343  20.38414
```

The results are barely significant if using a p-value of 0.05 as a line in the sand. That being said, we should nonetheless reject the null hypothesis that the population means are equal.

T-TEST: FREE THROW ATTEMPTS

Let's run yet another t-test, now comparing free throw attempts between road and home teams:

```
t.test(fouls1920a$ftaR, fouls1920a$ftaH)
##
##   Welch Two Sample t-test
##
## data:  fouls1920a$ftaR and fouls1920a$ftaH
## t = -1.8004, df = 1936.4, p-value = 0.07196
## alternative hypothesis: true difference in means is not equal to 0
## 95 percent confidence interval:
##   -1.25014956  0.05344513
## sample estimates:
## mean of x mean of y
##   22.59732  23.19567
```

This time, our results are barely insignificant; consequently, we must fail to reject the null hypothesis and accept that the population means is essentially equal—once more, because we're using 5% as a predefined cutoff. But otherwise, our results say that there is just a 7% probability of observing at least equal results if the null hypothesis is actually true. So while the variance is technically not significant, the p-value is low and obviously very close to our predefined threshold for significance.

VISUALIZING VARIANCES

We visualize and package the results just as we did with the 2018–19 data (see figure 7.3):

```
temp5 <- select(fouls1920a, c(7,12))
temp5 %>%
  pivot_longer(cols = c(pfR, pfH),
               names_to = "team",
               values_to = "fouls") -> temp5
head(temp5)
##    team fouls
## 1  pfR    34
## 2  pfH    24
## 3  pfR    24
## 4  pfH    25
## 5  pfR    20
## 6  pfH    18

temp5.text <- c("Home Team", "Road Team")
p5 <- ggplot(temp5, aes(x = team, y = fouls, fill = team)) +
```

```
geom_boxplot() +
labs(title = "Personal Foul Calls: Home vs. Road Teams",
     subtitle = "2019-20 Regular Season (pre-COVID)",
     x = "",
     y = "Personal Fouls per Game") +
stat_summary(fun = mean, geom = "point", shape = 20, size = 8,
             color = "white", fill = "white") +
theme(legend.position = "none") +
scale_x_discrete(labels = temp1.text) +
theme(plot.title = element_text(face = "bold")) +
stat_compare_means(method = "t.test", label.x = 1.4, label.y = 43)

temp6 <- select(fouls1920a, c(6,11))
temp6 %>%
  pivot_longer(cols = c(ftaR, ftaH),
               names_to = "team",
               values_to = "ftattempts") -> temp6
head(temp6)
##    team ftattempts
## 1 ftaR         20
## 2 ftaH         38
## 3 ftaR         21
## 4 ftaH         24
## 5 ftaR         22
## 6 ftaH         16

temp6.text <- c("Home Team", "Road Team")
p6 <- ggplot(temp6, aes(x = team, y = ftattempts, fill = team)) +
  geom_boxplot() +
  labs(title = "Free Throw Attempts: Home vs. Road Teams",
       subtitle = "2019-20 Regular Season (pre-COVID)",
       x = "",
       y = "Free Throw Attempts per Game") +
  stat_summary(fun = mean, geom = "point", shape = 20, size = 8,
               color = "white", fill = "white") +
  theme(legend.position = "none") +
  scale_x_discrete(labels = temp1.text) +
  theme(plot.title = element_text(face = "bold")) +
  stat_compare_means(method = "t.test", label.x = 1.4, label.y = 48)

p5 + p6 + plot_layout(ncol = 2)
```

There appears to be less of a difference in the length, or dispersion, of these two pairs of boxplots versus what we observed with the 2018–19 data, regular season and postseason. Nevertheless, we can clearly see that the population means aren't at all aligned.

In the next section, we'll compare and contrast these results by examining and testing the rest of the 2019–20 regular season.

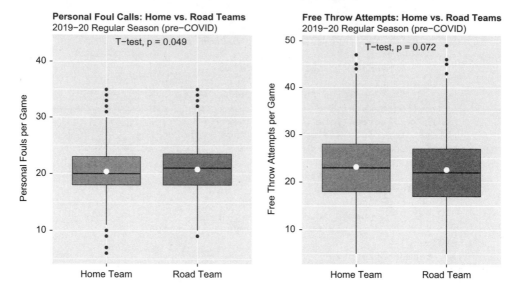

Figure 7.3   **This set of paired boxplots represents results from the 2019–20 regular season before COVID-19 temporarily suspended play.**

7.5.2 *2019–20 regular season analysis (post-COVID)*

Let's now examine the rest of the 2019–20 regular season, where every remaining game was played in Orlando without fans present. We need a data set, so we call the `filter()` function and subset fouls1920, where the variable `dataset` equals `NBA 2019 -2020 Regular Season` *and* the variable `gameID` is greater than `21901231`, to get a new object called fouls1920b. Then, we run the numbers:

```
fouls1920 %>%
  filter(dataset == "NBA 2019-2020 Regular Season" &
         gameID >= 21901231) -> fouls1920b

sum(fouls1920b$pfR) - sum(fouls1920b$pfH)
## [1] 54
mean(fouls1920b$pfR) - mean(fouls1920b$pfH)
## [1] 0.6067416
mean(fouls1920b$ftaR) - mean(fouls1920b$ftaH)
## [1] -0.2359551
sum(fouls1920b$ftR) / sum(fouls1920b$ftaR)
## [1] 0.7927369
sum(fouls1920b$ftH) / sum(fouls1920b$ftaH)
## [1] 0.7915753
```

We get the following results:

- Road teams—even though Orlando was technically a neutral site, teams were nevertheless designated as road and home, and the NBA decked the arena in the home team's logo and colors—were called for a grand total of 54 more personal fouls than were home teams. Over the course of an 89-game schedule, roughly equal to a typical postseason, the designated road team committed 2,064 personal fouls, and the designated home team committed 2,010 personal fouls. This equals a per-game variance equal to 0.61, which is a bit higher than we've otherwise observed.

- That variance didn't fully translate to free throw attempts, however. Home teams averaged only 0.24 more free throw attempts per game than road teams, which perhaps suggests that an inordinate number of personal foul calls were offensive or loose ball fouls, where free throws aren't awarded.

- Both road and home teams were successful on approximately 79% of their attempted free throws.

T-TESTS: PERSONAL FOULS AND FREE THROW ATTEMPTS

Let's see how these raw numbers translate into tests of statistical significance:

```
t.test(fouls1920b$pfR, fouls1920b$pfH)
##
##   Welch Two Sample t-test
##
## data:  fouls1920b$pfR and fouls1920b$pfH
## t = 0.93709, df = 173.63, p-value = 0.35
## alternative hypothesis: true difference in means is not equal to 0
## 95 percent confidence interval:
##   -0.6711954  1.8846785
## sample estimates:
## mean of x mean of y
##   23.19101  22.58427
```

```
t.test(fouls1920b$ftaR, fouls1920b$ftaH)
##
##   Welch Two Sample t-test
##
## data:  fouls1920b$ftaR and fouls1920b$ftaH
## t = -0.20855, df = 175.79, p-value = 0.835
## alternative hypothesis: true difference in means is not equal to 0
## 95 percent confidence interval:
##   -2.468889  1.996979
## sample estimates:
## mean of x mean of y
##   25.37079  25.60674
```

Number one, even though road teams were called for 0.61 more personal fouls per game than home teams, this didn't register on our first t-test. Whereas our data set is just 89 rows long, the computed p-value equals 0.35, way above the 0.05 threshold for significance, thereby compelling us to not reject the null hypothesis and to conclude that these means are essentially equal.

Number two, given the small difference in attempted free throws per game between road and home teams and the small record count in our data, it's no surprise that our second t-test returned a very high p-value (0.84). So, once again, the results are essentially neutral. Both results, however, are directionally consistent with our prior results.

Visualizing variances

As before, we visualize our results with paired boxplots that are combined into a single graphical representation (see figure 7.4):

```
temp7 <- select(fouls1920b, c(7,12))
temp7 %>%
  pivot_longer(cols = c(pfR, pfH),
               names_to = "team",
               values_to = "fouls") -> temp7
head(temp7)
##    team fouls
## 1  pfR    23
## 2  pfH    25
## 3  pfR    30
## 4  pfH    27
## 5  pfR    23
## 6  pfH    25

temp7.text <- c("Home Team", "Road Team")
p7 <- ggplot(temp7, aes(x = team, y = fouls, fill = team)) +
  geom_boxplot() +
  labs(title = "Personal Foul Calls: Home vs. Road Teams",
       subtitle = "2019-20 Regular Season (post-COVID)",
       x = "",
       y = "Personal Fouls per Game") +
  stat_summary(fun = mean, geom = "point", shape = 20, size = 8,
               color = "white", fill = "white") +
  theme(legend.position = "none") +
  scale_x_discrete(labels = temp1.text) +
  theme(plot.title = element_text(face = "bold")) +
  stat_compare_means(method = "t.test", label.x = 1.4, label.y = 38)

temp8 <- select(fouls1920b, c(6,11))
temp8 %>%
  pivot_longer(cols = c(ftaR, ftaH),
               names_to = "team",
               values_to = "ftattempts") -> temp8
head(temp8)
##    team ftattempts
## 1 ftaR         28
## 2 ftaH         18
## 3 ftaR         28
## 4 ftaH         37
## 5 ftaR         28
## 6 ftaH         23

temp8.text <- c("Home Team", "Road Team")
p8 <- ggplot(temp8, aes(x = team, y = ftattempts, fill = team)) +
  geom_boxplot() +
  labs(title = "Free Throw Attempts: Home vs. Road Teams",
       subtitle = "2019-20 Regular Season (post-COVID)",
```

```
        x = "",
        y = "Free Throw Attempts per Game") +
stat_summary(fun = mean, geom = "point", shape = 20, size = 8,
             color = "white", fill = "white") +
theme(legend.position = "none") +
scale_x_discrete(labels = temp1.text) +
theme(plot.title = element_text(face = "bold")) +
stat_compare_means(method = "t.test", label.x = 1.4, label.y = 43)
```

```
p7 + p8 + plot_layout(ncol = 2)
```

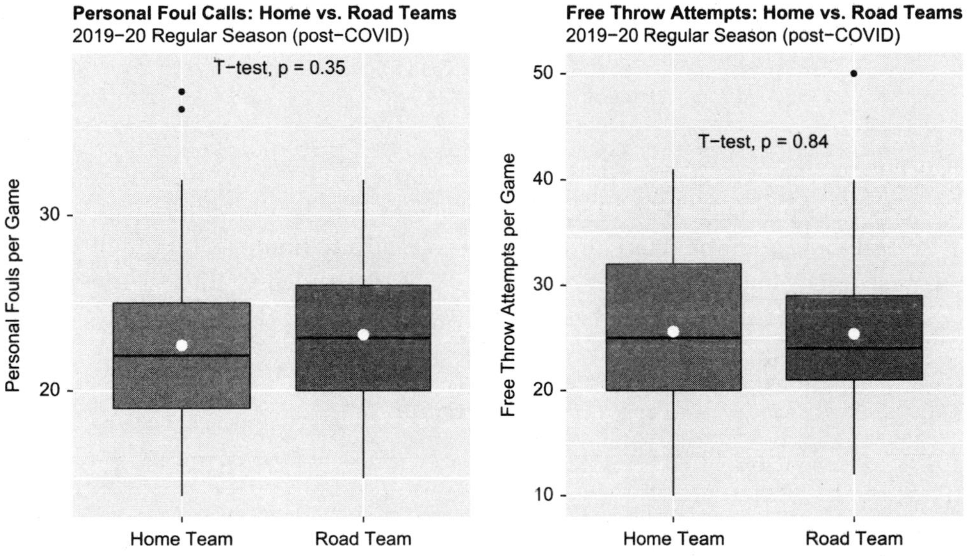

Figure 7.4   These two sets of paired boxplots display the most statistically insignificant results we've seen.

Our findings from the 2019–20 season are similar to those from 2018–19, as follows:

- Results pre- and post-COVID are directionally consistent in favor of home teams, regardless of measure.
- Variances are statistically significant pre-COVID and not statistically significant post-COVID; this is not so much because the variances changed but more because of the dissimilarity in record counts.

We'll otherwise conclude our 2019–20 regular season analysis by conducting another series of Cohen's d tests.

7.5.3   *More effect size testing*

Cohen's d tests on our 2019–20 data might be predictable, given the effect size test results from the 2018–19 regular season and 2019 playoffs and the computations on personal fouls and free throw attempts, pre- and post-COVID, over the 2019–20 regular season. We'll start with our pre-COVID data set:

```
cohen.d(fouls1920a$pfR, fouls1920a$pfH)
##
## Cohen's d
##
## d estimate: 0.08934564 (negligible)
## 95 percent confidence interval:
##       lower        upper
## 0.0002941679 0.1783971024

cohen.d(fouls1920a$ftaR, fouls1920a$ftaH)
##
## Cohen's d
##
## d estimate: -0.08934564 (negligible)
## 95 percent confidence interval:
##       lower        upper
## -0.170753099 0.007335309
```

Not surprisingly, according to our Cohen's d tests, the differences in personal foul calls and attempted free throws between road and home teams for all 2019–20 regular season games played before the COVID-19 pandemic hit are rated as negligible. Again, this is because the standard deviations are nearly identical.

Let's test the same with our post-COVID data set:

```
cohen.d(fouls1920b$pfR, fouls1920b$pfH)
##
## Cohen's d
##
## d estimate: 0.1404753 (negligible)
## 95 percent confidence interval:
##      lower       upper
## -0.1557346  0.4366853

cohen.d(fouls1920b$ftaR, fouls1920b$ftaH)
##
## Cohen's d
##
## d estimate: -0.03126236 (negligible)
## 95 percent confidence interval:
##      lower       upper
## -0.3271257  0.2646010
```

The quantitative results—that, is, the d estimates—are higher than our pre-COVID results, but not high enough to bump the qualitative ranking from negligible.

In the next chapter, we'll examine an aspect of the game controlled by the players, not by the officials: when to shoot the ball.

Summary

- Accurately comparing the means of two groups can have tremendous implications. The pharmaceutical company testing a pair of competing drugs might promote a more expensive alternative that really doesn't outperform a more affordable but otherwise like drug; a university might require every Business Analytics 101 student to attend class in person, thereby limiting enrollment, when the variances in exam scores compared to other students who only attended class online were actually not statistically significant; the branch manager of a bank could be demoted or even fired because the branch had lower customer service scores, despite minimal variances and mediocre participation.
- Our R code is absolutely transferrable to these and other t-test use cases.
- We ran t-tests to determine if variances were statistically significant and then Cohen's d tests to measure the size of these same variances. Once more, choose to run more than one test to get complete and thorough reads.
- All results—personal foul calls and attempted free throws from the 2018–19 regular season and postseason and from the 2019–20 regular season pre- and post-COVID—returned results that directionally favored home teams.
- Where we had relatively large record counts—namely, the 2018–19 regular season and the 2019–20 regular season before COVID—the road and home team variances in personal fouls called and attempted free throws, based on our t-tests, were statistically significant.
- Conversely, where we had lower record counts—the 2019 playoffs and the 2019–20 regular season games played in Orlando—variances in personal foul calls and attempted free throws between road and home teams weren't statistically significant, based on a 5% threshold.
- Our Cohen's d tests, which ignore record counts and instead use means and standard deviations, returned the same results every time: the differences in personal fouls and free throw attempts between road and home teams were always rated as negligible.
- We can therefore conclude that there was some officiating bias during the 2018–19 and 2019–20 seasons, but we can only speculate as to what might be causing this bias (crowd and other atmospheric influences?).
- Furthermore, we can only speculate how this bias affected outcomes. Our purpose was not to explain why or how home teams sometimes win games unfairly; rather, it was merely to explain, as it turned out, that home teams often get a slight, but statistically significant, edge in officiating.

Optimal stopping 8

There is a popular algorithm called the optimal stopping rule—which is frequently referred to as the 37% rule and sometimes called the look-then-leap rule—that solves the problem of when to take a specific course of action versus continuing to deliberate. Here's a common use case: Let's say you're a hiring manager interviewing candidates for an open role in your organization, and you're obligated to render a yea or nay decision immediately after interviewing each candidate because there are no second chances. According to the optimal stopping rule, you should automatically pass on the first 37% of the candidates in the applicant pool and then extend an offer to the first interviewed candidate who rates higher than every previous candidate.

Our purpose here is to explore how the optimal stopping rule might or might not apply to the NBA. Should teams not shoot during the first 37% of their allotted possession time? Should they then attempt a shot as soon as they have a scoring opportunity equal to or better than any previous chance? By rule, teams have 24 seconds to attempt a shot, and there are no resets; failure to take a shot results in a turnover whereby the opposing team takes possession. Teams use all or some of their allotted time passing and dribbling—the equivalent of interviewing candidates—expecting or hoping to create a high-percentage shot opportunity before their 24 seconds expire. Is there an optimal stopping point, measured in seconds, to passing and dribbling versus shooting? If so, is it consistent with the 37% rule? That's what we aim to find out.

We'll sequentially test the optimal stopping rule on three teams using 2019–20 regular season data, and then we'll test the same against the entire league. Along the way, we'll demonstrate a series of new visualization and data wrangling techniques.

8.1 Loading packages

We'll use base R functionality as well as a combination of familiar and not-so-familiar packages; packages not used previously and therefore introduced here include `stringr`, `janitor`, and `png`:

- The `stringr` package is actually part of the `tidyverse` universe of packages, so it's loaded by default when we load `tidyverse`; `stringr` makes it easy to manipulate character strings.
- The `janitor` package contains several functions for examining and cleaning dirty data.
- The `png` package contains functions for reading, writing, and displaying Portable Network Graphic (PNG) images.

We start by calling the base R `library()` function four times to sequentially load our required packages:

```
library(tidyverse)
library(janitor)
library(patchwork)
library(png)
```

We'll act on the last of these packages first.

8.2 Importing images

Images saved with a .png extension and stored in our default working directory are imported similarly to how we import .csv files—we simply call the `readPNG()` function from the `png` package and add the file path between a pair of single or double quotation marks. When inserted into any plot or chart, images accomplish more than merely enhancing their aesthetics; they also provide immediate clarity around scope or content. The presence of, let's say, the Milwaukee Bucks logo in a plot makes it instantly clear that we're visualizing Milwaukee Bucks results only.

In the following code chunk, we call the `readPNG()` function four times to sequentially import four NBA logos downloaded from the internet, saved as .png files, and then dragged and dropped into our default working directory. (There are dozens, probably hundreds, of websites from which these and other NBA images can be downloaded.) Because these are raster (or bitmap) images, the native argument is set to TRUE:

```
bucks <- readPNG("bucks.png", native = TRUE)

hawks <- readPNG("hawks.png", native = TRUE)

hornets <- readPNG("hornets.png", native = TRUE)

nba <- readPNG("nba.png", native = TRUE)
```

Once we get around to creating a series of `ggplot2` line charts, we'll inset these images as a way of augmenting our visual content. In the meantime, we'll move forward by importing and viewing our data set.

8.3   *Importing and viewing data*

We import our data by calling the `readr read_csv()` function and in the process establish an object called pbp (short for play-by-play). Our data was downloaded from the website www.bigdataball.com and subsequently saved in our default working directory with the filename pbp.csv.

Our data set contains almost every play from every regular season and postseason game from the 2019–20 NBA season. The types of plays included and not included in our data will be explored momentarily. For now, we merely want to understand, at a macro level, the size and scope of our data; the `glimpse()` function from the `dplyr` package returns the dimension of pbp and a transposed snapshot of the content—it's 543,149 rows long and 44 columns wide. If you're working on a personal computer and not a server, it may take several seconds to load the data:

```
pbp <- read_csv("pbp.csv")

glimpse(pbp)
## Rows: 543,149
## Columns: 44
## $ game_id      <chr> "0021900001", "0021900001", "0021900001", …
## $ data_set     <chr> "2019-2020 Regular Season", "2019-2020 Reg…
## $ date         <date> 2019-10-22, 2019-10-22, 2019-10-22, 2019-…
## $ a1           <chr> "Jrue Holiday", "Jrue Holiday", "Jrue Holi…
## $ a2           <chr> "Brandon Ingram", "Brandon Ingram", "Brand…
## $ a3           <chr> "Derrick Favors", "Derrick Favors", "Derri…
## $ a4           <chr> "JJ Redick", "JJ Redick", "JJ Redick", "JJ…
## $ a5           <chr> "Lonzo Ball", "Lonzo Ball", "Lonzo Ball", …
## $ h1           <chr> "OG Anunoby", "OG Anunoby", "OG Anunoby", …
## $ h2           <chr> "Pascal Siakam", "Pascal Siakam", "Pascal …
```

```
## $ h3              <chr> "Marc Gasol", "Marc Gasol", "Marc Gasol", …
## $ h4              <chr> "Kyle Lowry", "Kyle Lowry", "Kyle Lowry", …
## $ h5              <chr> "Fred VanVleet", "Fred VanVleet", "Fred Va…
## $ period          <dbl> 1, 1, 1, 1, 1, 1, 1, 1, 1, 1, 1, 1, 1, 1, …
## $ away_score      <dbl> 0, 0, 0, 0, 2, 2, 2, 2, 2, 2, 2, 2, 2, 2, …
## $ home_score      <dbl> 0, 0, 0, 0, 0, 0, 0, 0, 0, 0, 0, 0, 0, 0, …
## $ remaining_time  <time> 00:12:00, 00:12:00, 00:11:48, 00:11:47, 0…
## $ elapsed         <time> 00:00:00, 00:00:00, 00:00:12, 00:00:13, 0…
## $ play_length     <chr> "0:00:00", "0:00:00", "0:00:12", "0:00:01"…
## $ play_id         <dbl> 2, 4, 7, 8, 9, 10, 11, 12, 13, 14, 15, 16,…
## $ team            <chr> NA, "NOP", "NOP", "NOP", "NOP", "TOR", "NO…
## $ event_type      <chr> "start of period", "jump ball", "miss", "r…
## $ assist          <chr> NA, NA, NA, NA, NA, NA, NA, NA, NA, NA, NA…
## $ away            <chr> NA, "Derrick Favors", NA, NA, NA, NA, NA, …
## $ home            <chr> NA, "Marc Gasol", NA, NA, NA, NA, NA, …
## $ block           <chr> NA, NA, NA, NA, NA, NA, NA, NA, NA, NA, NA…
## $ entered         <chr> NA, NA, NA, NA, NA, NA, NA, NA, NA, NA, NA…
## $ left            <chr> NA, NA, NA, NA, NA, NA, NA, NA, NA, NA, NA…
## $ num             <dbl> NA, NA, NA, NA, NA, NA, NA, NA, NA, NA, NA…
## $ opponent        <chr> NA, NA, NA, NA, NA, NA, NA, NA, NA, NA, NA…
## $ outof           <dbl> NA, NA, NA, NA, NA, NA, NA, NA, NA, NA, NA…
## $ player          <chr> NA, "Marc Gasol", "Lonzo Ball", "Derrick F…
## $ points          <dbl> NA, NA, 0, NA, 2, 0, NA, 0, NA, 0, NA, 0, …
## $ possession      <chr> NA, "Lonzo Ball", NA, NA, NA, NA, NA, NA, …
## $ reason          <chr> NA, NA, NA, NA, NA, NA, NA, NA, NA, NA, NA…
## $ result          <chr> NA, NA, "missed", NA, "made", "missed", NA…
## $ steal           <chr> NA, NA, NA, NA, NA, NA, NA, NA, NA, NA, NA…
## $ type            <chr> "start of period", "jump ball", "unknown",…
## $ shot_distance   <dbl> NA, NA, 11, NA, 1, 3, NA, 8, NA, 25, NA, 1…
## $ original_x      <dbl> NA, NA, 2, NA, 0, 15, NA, 81, NA, 178, NA,…
## $ original_y      <dbl> NA, NA, 114, NA, -6, 28, NA, -1, NA, 176, …
## $ converted_x     <dbl> NA, NA, 24.8, NA, 25.0, 26.5, NA, 16.9, NA…
## $ converted_y     <dbl> NA, NA, 16.4, NA, 4.4, 86.2, NA, 4.9, NA, …
## $ description     <chr> NA, "Jump Ball Gasol vs. Favors: Tip to Ba…
```

Before we can properly analyze the data we've just loaded, we'll first have to explore it further and wrangle it.

8.4   *Exploring and wrangling data*

We start by converting the variable `data_set` from a character string to a factor by calling the built-in `as.factor()` function:

```
pbp$data_set <- as.factor(pbp$data_set)
```

By doing so, we can then call the base R `levels()` function, which returns the three factor levels associated with the variable `data_set`. Had we instead kept `data_set` as a character string, rather than converting it to a factor, and then called the `levels()` function, R would have returned NULL:

```
levels(pbp$data_set)
## [1] "2019-20 Playoffs"        "2019-20 Regular Season"
## [3] "2019-2020 Regular Season"
```

It appears that observations which tie back to regular season games are, for some reason, divided between two factor levels, 2019–20 Regular Season and 2019–2020 Regular Season, while playoff games are designated by the 2019–20 Playoffs factor level.

Our intent is to relegate our analysis to regular season games only instead of mixing regular season and postseason results; every NBA team plays a fixed regular season schedule, but only some teams then qualify for postseason play. Therefore, we pipe the pbp data set to the `dplyr` `filter()` function to subset pbp where the variable `data_set` does not equal 2019-20 Playoffs (the `!=` operator means not equal to).

We then call the `dim()` function from base R to check the new dimension of the pbp data set:

```
pbp %>%
  filter(data_set != "2019-20 Playoffs") -> pbp
dim(pbp)
## [1] 504445      44
```

By filtering out postseason plays and retaining every play from the 2019–20 regular season, pbp has thus been reduced to 504,445 rows.

The variable `play_length` is a bit more challenging. It's now a character string (which doesn't work for us) in an hours:minutes:seconds format (which also doesn't work for us). We want and need a numeric variable in seconds only. So we call the `mutate()` function from the `dplyr` package in tandem with the `str_sub()` function from the `stringr` package to create a new variable, `play_length2`, which will be in seconds only. The `str_sub()` function requires the following three inputs:

- The character string that requires manipulation, which is the original variable `play_length`.
- The first character from the variable `play_length` that should be extracted and ported to the derived variable `play_length2`. Because `play_length2` will be in seconds only, we're therefore interested in extracting and porting the last two characters from `play_length`, which, again, is in an hours:minutes:seconds format. Therefore, the second input is `-2`, which is the second-to-last character in `play_length`.
- The last character from `play_length` that should be extracted and ported to `play_length2`, which is the last character in the string. Therefore, the third input is `-1`.

Our new variable is then converted to a numeric class by calling the base R `as.numeric()` function:

```
pbp %>%
  mutate(play_length2 = str_sub(play_length, -2, -1)) -> pbp
pbp$play_length2 <- as.numeric(pbp$play_length2)
```

To compare and contrast the variables `play_length` and `play_length2`, we call the base R `head()` function twice to return the first six values in the pbp data set for each variable.

Usually, when we call the head() function, or even the tail() function, for that matter, we instruct R to return every variable in whatever number of top or bottom observations we need to view; here, by inserting the $ operator, we're instead telling R to just return play_length and then play_length2, ignoring the other pbp variables:

```
head(pbp$play_length)
## [1] "00:00:00" "00:00:00" "00:00:12" "00:00:01" "00:00:00" "00:00:18"
head(pbp$play_length2)
## [1]  0  0 12  1  0 18
```

So by calling the str_sub() function, we successfully created a new variable where, for instance, 00:00:12 is converted to 12 seconds, and 00:00:18 is converted to 18 seconds.

Let's now explore the variable event_type, which is also a character string. We convert it to a factor variable and then call the levels() function to return the factor levels:

```
pbp$event_type <- as.factor(pbp$event_type)
levels(pbp$event_type)
##  [1] "ejection"        "end of period"   "foul"          "free throw"
##  [5] "jump ball"       "miss"            "rebound"       "shot"
##  [9] "start of period" "sub"             "timeout"       "turnover"
## [13] "unknown"         "violation"
```

It turns out that the pbp data set contains 14 event types, including unknowns. We'll eventually work with just a small subset of the following 13 event types:

- ejection—A player has been permanently ejected from a game by one of the officials, usually after getting called for a second technical foul. Technical fouls are called subsequent to personal fouls that are especially violent or when players argue with the officials.
- end of period—Time has expired, thereby ending a period, or quarter.
- foul—A personal foul has been called.
- free throw—A free throw has been attempted, which could result in a make (a successful shot) or a miss. A free throw isn't the same as a shot or field goal. Neither the game clock nor the shot clock runs while a player is attempting a free throw.
- jump ball—This occurs after a pair of opposing players have equal possession of the ball. An official blows the whistle, thereby stopping play. The two players then jump for possession of the ball.
- miss—A field goal attempt is missed, or unsuccessful.
- rebound—An offensive or defensive rebound is made immediately following a missed shot.
- shot—A field goal attempt is made, or successful.
- start of period—A new period, or quarter, begins, including any overtime sessions, which take place following regulation when a game is tied.

- sub—One or both teams are substituting one or more players. Substitutions can only occur when the game clock is stopped.
- timeout—A break in play, usually requested by one of the teams. The game clock is stopped when a timeout is called and remains stopped until play resumes.
- turnover—The team in possession of the ball has committed some sort of sloppy play, resulting in the opposing team gaining possession.
- violation—One team, usually the team in possession of the ball, has committed some sort of violation such as traveling, double dribble, or three seconds in the key, which results in a change of possession.

In the following chunk of dplyr code, we call the group_by() and tally() functions to return the counts for each event type in the pbp data set in the form of a tibble called tbl1:

```
pbp %>%
  group_by(event_type) %>%
  tally() -> tbl1
print(tbl1)
## # A tibble: 15 × 2
##    event_type          n
##    <fct>           <int>
##  1 ejection           39
##  2 end of period    4315
##  3 foul            45295
##  4 free throw      49006
##  5 jump ball        1856
##  6 miss           101684
##  7 rebound        112803
##  8 shot            86633
##  9 start of period  4315
## 10 sub             51838
## 11 timeout         11911
## 12 turnover        30707
## 13 unknown          1306
## 14 violation        1947
## 15 <NA>              790
```

Following are a few observations and explanations:

- Ejections are rare. Players permanently foul out of a game once they've committed their sixth personal foul, but that is a disqualification and not an ejection.
- There is an equal number of events for end of period and start of period, which makes perfect sense.
- Personal fouls often immediately result in one or two free throw attempts, but sometimes don't result in attempted free throws at all. There is no way to readily derive the count for one measure from the count of another.

- There are approximately 15,000 more events where a player missed a shot attempt versus making a shot, meaning more shots are missed than made.
- Rebounds come after most missed shots and missed free throws, but not all.
- Passes between teammates might be the most obvious—certainly the most frequent—event type not accounted for in our data set.
- Note that our data set includes 790 observations in which no event type has been defined; our call to the `levels()` function failed to detect these. Otherwise, these numbers make perfect sense—just a few ejections, more missed than made field goal attempts, for instance—which, of course, suggests we're working with a reliable data set overall.

Our next operation is to convert the variable `team` to a factor. We can then call the `levels()` function once more to return the factor levels, but we'll call the base R `summary()` function instead, which returns the factor levels and the record counts for each. Thus, the `summary()` function returns factor levels and counts for the variable team, whereas we previously called the `levels()` function and then wrote a small chunk of `dplyr` code to return the same with respect to the variable `event_type`:

```
pbp$team <- as.factor(pbp$team)
summ ary(pbp$team)
##   ATL   BKN   BOS   CHA   CHI   CLE   DAL   DEN   DET   GSW   HOU   IND
## 15643 16578 16302 14012 14263 13986 16943 15999 14150 14337 16290 15477
##   LAC   LAL   MEM   MIA   MIL   MIN   NOP   NYK   OKC   ORL   PHI   PHX
## 16701 15996 17066 16013 17691 14847 16368 14940 15890 15877 16346 16333
##   POR   SAC   SAS   TOR   UTA   WAS  NA's
## 16601 15761 15812 15845 15931 16101 30346
```

The NBA is a 30-team league, yet the variable team contains 31 levels, due to 30,346 blanks that R returns as NAs.

Finally, we again call the `summary()` function to return a series of basic statistics for the variable points:

```
summary(pbp$points)
##   Min. 1st Qu.  Median    Mean 3rd Qu.    Max.    NA's
##      0       0       1       1       2       3  267122
```

Though our data set isn't necessarily perfect, the results are nonetheless consistent with our expectations:

- Points aren't possible through most event types, so we have the 267,122 NAs.
- Missed shots and missed free throws result in zero points.
- One point is awarded for a successful free throw.
- Two or three points are awarded for successful field goals, depending on how close or how far from the basket the shot was attempted.

Now that we've explored and wrangled our data, it's time to go about analyzing it.

8.5   *Analysis*

To reiterate, our purpose here is to establish how well the optimal stopping algorithm applies to the NBA. In other words, we want to determine if it makes sense for NBA teams to automatically abstain from shooting for some finite number of seconds and then take the first available shot that is equal to or better than any previous shot opportunity; if yes, we want to further determine if the 37% rule applies. As always, we must be careful not to make any sweeping conclusions. Because the analysis that follows uses just the data we've already imported and subsequently wrangled, our verdicts thus apply to the 2019–20 regular season only.

Our analysis is otherwise divided into two parts. We'll begin by isolating three teams that had very different points per game averages during the 2019–20 season, summarizing and visualizing their points scored and field goal percentages by 1-second increments, and then drawing some larger conclusions based on what R returns for us. Afterward, we'll do the same for the NBA as a whole by packing the league's 30 teams into a single data series. Let's start with the Milwaukee Bucks, who led the NBA in scoring during the 2019–20 regular season by averaging 118.7 points per game.

8.5.1   *Milwaukee Bucks*

Our first order of business is to create a Milwaukee Bucks data set from the pbp data set. We'll begin by calling the `dplyr filter()` function to reduce the length of pbp by only retaining observations that meet a specific series of criteria:

1 Where the variable `team` equals `MIL`, which is short for Milwaukee Bucks
2 Where our derived variable `play_length2` is equal to or greater than `5` *and* less than or equal to `24`
3 Where the variable `event_type` equals `shot` *or* `miss`

Some explanation is required here. Our interest here is in half-court possessions where teams can choose to deliberate by dribbling and passing or can instead take action by shooting. Attempted shots less than 5 seconds into a possession are usually fast-break opportunities against an out-of-position defense, easy returns near the basket immediately following an offensive rebound, or a desperate effort to beat an expiring game clock. In all three scenarios, shooting the ball is the only reasonable course of action. So times of possession less than 5 seconds in duration will be ignored by removing them altogether. Some cutoff is therefore an absolute must; 5 seconds is admittedly somewhat arbitrary, but it does represent the approximate duration of most fast breaks. Unfortunately, our data set doesn't contain an event type that indicates when teams in possession of the ball cross mid-court and establish their half-court sets.

Furthermore, the NBA employs a 24-second shot clock, which means teams must attempt a shot within 24 seconds of gaining possession or otherwise turn the ball over to the opposing team. The shot clock increases scoring by accelerating the pace of play and prevents teams from using stalling tactics to protect leads (and from boring the fans). For some reason—probably due to missing event types—the pbp data set includes a small number of observations where the variable play_length2 is greater than 24 seconds. Therefore, it only makes sense to remove these few records.

Finally, we're only interested in plays where a shot was made or missed. Because we're not interested in ejections, rebounds, violations, and other event types, it makes sense to also remove these records.

CREATING DATA SOURCES

The end result is a new object called MIL. One note about our dplyr code and specifically the logic we're passing to the filter() function: like other programming languages, R requires variable names to be explicitly called out whenever setting unique selection criteria. For instance, if we were to tell R that play_length2 must be equal to or greater than 5 seconds and less than or equal to 24 seconds, rather than telling R that play_length2 must be equal to or greater than 5 seconds and play_length2 should also be equal to or less than 24 seconds, R wouldn't have any idea which pbp variable should be equal to or less than 24; it would then throw an error.

We then call the dim() function to return the MIL row and columns counts:

```
pbp %>%
  filter(team == "MIL",
         play_length2 >= 5 & play_length2 <= 24,
         event_type == "shot" | event_type == "miss") -> MIL
dim(MIL)
## [1] 5436   45
```

MIL contains 5,436 rows and 45 columns. Our analysis requires only the variables event_type, points, and play_length2; therefore, we cut the width of MIL by calling the dplyr select() function, which subsets MIL by retaining these three variables only.

We then call the dim() function again, just to confirm that MIL now has a dimension of 5,436 rows and only three columns. It's always up to you when or how often you want to validate operations and display results of the same. We lean toward being safe rather than sorry:

```
MIL %>%
  select(event_type, points, play_length2) -> MIL
dim(MIL)
## [1] 5436    3
```

We then pipe the MIL data set to the dplyr group_by() and summarize() functions to compute the average number of points the Bucks scored by each value in the derived variable play_length2. Our result is a 20 × 2 tibble called MILx where play_length2 is one column (with a minimum of 5 and a maximum of 24 seconds) and avg is the other column, which represents the average, or mean, number of points scored:

```
MIL %>%
  group_by(play_length2) %>%
  summarize(avg = mean(points)) -> MILx
print(MILx)
## # A tibble: 20 × 2
##    play_length2   avg
```

```
##               <dbl> <dbl>
##  1               5  1.13
##  2               6  1.09
##  3               7  1.15
##  4               8  1.19
##  5               9  1.14
##  6              10  1.04
##  7              11  1.06
##  8              12  1.03
##  9              13  1.08
## 10              14  1.14
## 11              15  1.16
## 12              16  1.04
## 13              17  1.12
## 14              18  1.05
## 15              19  0.948
## 16              20  1.18
## 17              21  0.925
## 18              22  0.930
## 19              23  1.03
## 20              24  1.02
```

We'll keep these results in our back pocket for the time being.

Meanwhile, let's create a second data object that gets us the field goal percentages for every value in `play_length2`. We then pass MIL to the `tabyl()` function from the `janitor` package to create a frequency table, where the first argument is `play_length2` and the second argument is `event_type`. R returns a frequency table, or a data frame—called MILy—that tabulates the frequencies of every `event_type` factor for every `play_length2` value. Because we're only interested in the shot and miss event types, we then call the `select()` function to reduce MILy to include just those two variables, plus, of course, `play_length2`.

Finally, we make a call to the `mutate()` function from the `dplyr` package to create another variable, `fg_pct`, which is then appended to MILy. Our new variable computes the field goal (or shot) percentage by dividing the variable `shot` by the sum of variables `shot` and `miss`; the quotient is then multiplied by 100 to return a percentage. Our derived variable is then rounded to just two digits to the right of the decimal point:

```
MIL %>%
  tabyl(play_length2, event_type) -> MILy
MILy %>%
  select(play_length2, shot, miss) %>%
  mutate(fg_pct = shot / (shot + miss)*100) -> MILy
MILy$fg_pct <- round(MILy$fg_pct, digits = 2)
print(MILy)
##  play_length2 shot miss fg_pct
##             5  206  219  48.47
##             6  193  218  46.96
##             7  173  187  48.06
##             8  176  183  49.03
##             9  161  169  48.79
##            10  155  200  43.66
##            11  171  205  45.48
```

```
##               12   165   210   44.00
##               13   167   191   46.65
##               14   178   188   48.63
##               15   164   167   49.55
##               16   125   158   44.17
##               17   126   133   48.65
##               18   113   130   46.50
##               19    62    91   40.52
##               20    73    77   48.67
##               21    43    63   40.57
##               22    34    52   39.53
##               23    30    37   44.78
##               24    19    24   44.19
```

DISPLAYING RESULTS

We now have a pair of data sources, MILx and MILy, for two separate yet complementary ggplot2 line charts. The first of our two line charts, MILp1, pulls from the tibble MILx and displays the average number of points the Milwaukee Bucks scored during the 2019–20 regular season for every whole second of possession time, between 5 and 24 seconds, where a made or missed shot was the result:

- So play_length2 is our x-axis variable, and avg, which we created using a combination of the dplyr group_by() and summarize() functions, is our y-axis variable.

- The geom_line() function draws the line, and the geom_point() function adds a layer of points to the line.

- The geom_smooth() function, called three times, draws a trio of regression lines over the data, which allow us to readily see how the average number of points scored trended as the length of play increased. Regression lines are drawn to minimize the distances between it and the applicable data points. The blue line illustrates the trend covering the entire data series, whereas the gold and purple lines, respectively, display the trends before and after 12 seconds, or the 37% mark (12 seconds equals 5 plus 7 seconds; 7 divided by 19 seconds equals 37%). By passing the se = FALSE argument, we're instructing R to not draw shaded confidence intervals above and below our regression lines.

- The theme_classic() function replaces the ggplot2 default background with one that is solid white. The theme_classic() function must be called before the theme() function to preserve the bold font for the title; otherwise, the theme_classic() function, which renders the header in plain font, would overwrite the theme() function preferences.

- The inset_element() function, which is actually part of the patchwork package, insets a .png file called bucks. The left, bottom, right, and top arguments collectively determine where the image should be placed and how large or small it should be. Because those arguments equal numbers close to 1, our image will be placed in the upper-right corner of the plot. You'll likely want to experiment with these settings.

All of this is thrown together in the following code chunk:

```
MILp1 <- ggplot(MILx, aes(x = play_length2, y = avg, group = 1)) +
  geom_line(aes(y = avg), color = "darkgreen", size = 2) +
  geom_point(color = "wheat2", size = 3) +
  labs(title = "Points Scored per Second Increment",
       subtitle = "2019-20 Milwaukee Bucks",
       caption = "regular season only",
       x = "Number of Seconds into Possession",
       y = "Average Number of Points Scored") +
  geom_smooth(method = lm, color = "blue", se = FALSE) +
  geom_smooth(method = lm, color = "gold",
              data = MILx[MILx$play_length2 < 13,], se = FALSE) +
  geom_smooth(method = lm, color = "purple",
              data = MILx[MILx$play_length2 > 11,], se = FALSE) +
  theme_classic() +
  theme(plot.title = element_text(face = "bold")) +
  inset_element(bucks, left = 0.80, bottom = 0.80,
                right = 0.95, top = 0.95)
```

Our second line chart, MILp2, pulls from MILy, the frequency table we previously created by calling the `tabyl()` function from the `janitor` package. The variable `play_length2` is again our x-axis variable, and `fg_pct` is our y-axis variable. Otherwise, the syntax for our second line chart is just like our first one, thereby returning a graphical object with the forms, features, and functions equivalent to MILp1:

```
MILp2 <- ggplot(MILy, aes(x = play_length2, y = fg_pct, group = 1)) +
  geom_line(aes(y = fg_pct), color = "darkgreen", size = 2) +
  geom_point(color = "wheat2", size = 3) +
  labs(title = "Field Goal Percentage per Second Increment",
       subtitle = "2019-20 Milwaukee Bucks",
       caption = "regular season only",
       x = "Number of Seconds into Possession",
       y = "Field Goal Percentage") +
  geom_smooth(method = lm, color = "blue", se = FALSE) +
  geom_smooth(method = lm, color = "gold",
              data = MILy[MILy$play_length2 < 13,], se = FALSE) +
  geom_smooth(method = lm, color = "purple",
              data = MILy[MILy$play_length2 > 11,], se = FALSE) +
  theme_classic() +
  theme(plot.title = element_text(face = "bold")) +
  inset_element(bucks, left = 0.80, bottom = 0.80,
                right = 0.95, top = 0.95)
```

We then call the `plot_layout()` function from the `patchwork` package to bundle our two line charts into a single object where the plots are placed side by side (see figure 8.1). Our attention is immediately drawn to the fact that points scored and field goal percentage both drop precipitously as time of possession increases, although the relationship isn't exactly linear:

```
MILp1 + MILp2 + plot_layout(ncol = 2)
```

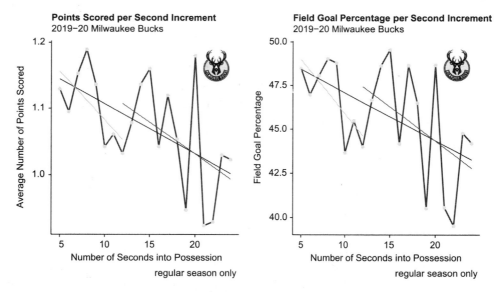

Figure 8.1   Average number of points scored (on the left) and field goal percentage (on the right) for the Milwaukee Bucks during the 2019–20 regular season computed at each second of a half-court possession, with trendlines

CONCLUSIONS

Before summarizing our first set of results, let's discuss optimal stopping a bit more: first, the intended purpose of the optimal stopping rule is to prescribe a *specific* amount of intended deliberation before acting, that is, how many candidates a hiring manager should interview for an open role before extending an offer, or how long an NBA team should dribble and pass before attempting a shot.

Second, when applied properly, optimal stopping returns a maximum gain and prevents valueless effort. The maximum gain might not equate to a "great" return in any absolute sense, but it does produce the highest chance of a *best* return against several alternatives. Defying the optimal stopping rule doesn't increase chances for a best outcome: a hiring manager won't increase chances of landing the best applicant by breaching the optimal stopping point; an NBA team won't, at least theoretically, make more shots by ignoring the optimal stopping point and pursuing the false hope of a better scoring opportunity.

Third, regardless of the situation, the point at which a hiring manager or an NBA team—or anyone—should leap rather than continuing to look is the 37% mark. There are two ways of computing what that mark is or where it is. If, for instance, *n* equals 20—there are 20 candidates in an applicant pool or 20 seconds remaining on the shot clock—the optimal stopping point is the product of 20 and 37%, which equals 7 (when rounded down to the nearest whole number). Alternatively, we get the same result when *n* is divided by *e*, the mathematical constant approximately equal to 2.72.

So if a hiring manager has an applicant pool of 20 candidates, the manager should automatically pass on the first seven candidates, continue interviewing, and then stop immediately after interviewing the first candidate that compares well to the first seven. By the same token, an NBA team should refrain from shooting until the 24-second shot clock is half expired equal to 12, or 5 plus 7, seconds and then attempt a shot once it has a scoring opportunity as good or better than any previous opportunity.

That being said, from these two plots, we can draw a combination of obvious and maybe not-so-obvious conclusions, as there's a lot to unpack here:

- Trendlines are visual representations of direction where the slope further illustrates the rate of change. Though the downward trends are hardly linear, our two y-axis variables, average points scored and field goal percentage, are nevertheless positively and strongly correlated with one another—meaning they move in the same direction at the same time.

- With respect to the average number of points scored for every second of possession time, the Bucks were most successful when our x-axis variable equaled 8 seconds or 20 seconds; the Bucks averaged 1.19 points when x equaled 8 and 1.18 points when x equaled 20.

- That's significant because it means the Bucks were never as successful at scoring points after the 37% mark as they were before then. In other words, Milwaukee's optimal stopping point was actually before the 37% mark and not after that.

- However, those results don't translate to field goal percentage. The Bucks shot 49.03% from the floor when x equaled 8 and 49.55% when x equaled 15. Of course, this means Milwaukee was better off not shooting before the 37% mark, based on this measure, at least.

- At any rate, the Bucks were generally better off scoring points and shooting from the floor when there was more time remaining on the shot clock. We say "generally" because, once more, the trends aren't exactly linear; most of the data points are, in fact, well below or well above our regression lines. This suggests that what we're really seeing is a regression to the mean phenomenon, where opposite results offset one another, rather than the letter of the optimal stopping rule.

- To carry this last point a step further, take a closer look at either or both plots where x equals 19 to 21 seconds—these three consecutive data points are significantly and alternately below or above the regression lines. Milwaukee's success at scoring points and shooting the basketball when just 4 seconds remain on the shot clock (x therefore equals 20) is as much an offset to their relative lack of success when x equals 19, and their further lack of success when x equals 21 is yet another offset in the opposite direction.

- Regression to the mean, sometimes called regression *toward* the mean, is a phenomenon by which extreme outcomes are succeeded by more moderate outcomes or equally extreme outcomes in the opposite direction that average each other out. What we're seeing is natural variation due to chance, or, at a minimum, results that are the natural byproduct of just a few data points. After all, our data contains significantly fewer records when there are no more than 5 seconds remaining on the shot clock than otherwise. We'll see the same phenomenon as we next evaluate results for two more teams; however, we'll instead observe smoothed-over results when we analyze the entire NBA in a single data series.

Next, we'll see how well these results hold up, or don't hold up, with a pair of lesser-scoring teams.

8.5.2 Atlanta Hawks

We'll first repeat this exercise by substituting the Atlanta Hawks for the Bucks. The Hawks scored 111.8 points per game during the 2019–20 regular season, which was the league average.

CREATING DATA SOURCES

We subset the pbp data set where the variable `team` equals `ATL` (short for Atlanta Hawks), the derived variable `play_length2` is equal to or greater than 5 and less than or equal to 24, and the variable `event_type` equals `shot` or `miss`. We then call the `dim()` function to return the dimension of our new data set:

```
pbp %>%
  filter(team == "ATL",
         play_length2 >= 5 & play_length2 <= 24,
         event_type == "shot" | event_type == "miss") -> ATL
dim(ATL)
## [1] 4945   45
```

The ATL data set is 4,945 rows long, which is considerably shorter than the MIL data set. The following chunk of `dplyr` code returns the miss and shot counts for the Hawks and Bucks for comparison purposes.

```
ATL %>%
  group_by(event_type) %>%
  tally()
## # A tibble: 2 × 2
##   event_type      n
##   <fct>       <int>
## 1 miss         2807
## 2 shot         2138

MIL %>%
  group_by(event_type) %>%
  tally()
## # A tibble: 2 × 2
##   event_type      n
##   <fct>       <int>
## 1 miss         2902
```

```
## 2 shot        2534
```

The Hawks attempted 441 fewer field goals than the Bucks and made 396 fewer shots. That's why the ATL row count is less than the MIL row count—and why the Hawks scored seven fewer points per game, on average, than the Milwaukee Bucks.

We then call the `select()` function to reduce the width of ATL by just retaining the variables `event_type`, `points`, and `play_length2`:

```
ATL %>%
  select(event_type, points, play_length2) -> ATL
dim(ATL)
## [1] 4945     3
```

A rerun of the `dim()` function confirms that our ATL data set now includes just those three variables.

Next, we create a tibble called ATLx, the Atlanta equivalent to MILx, by calling the dplyr `group_by()` and `summarize()` functions to compute the average number of points the Hawks scored for every second in the variable `play_length2`:

```
ATL %>%
  group_by(play_length2) %>%
  summarize(avg = mean(points)) -> ATLx
print(ATLx)
## # A tibble: 20 × 2
##    play_length2   avg
##           <dbl> <dbl>
##  1            5  1.04
##  2            6  1.03
##  3            7  1.17
##  4            8  0.897
##  5            9  1.02
##  6           10  1.11
##  7           11  1.04
##  8           12  0.912
##  9           13  1.08
## 10           14  0.976
## 11           15  0.984
## 12           16  0.938
## 13           17  0.878
## 14           18  1.06
## 15           19  0.994
## 16           20  0.831
## 17           21  1.04
## 18           22  1.04
## 19           23  0.678
## 20           24  1.06
```

We then create a frequency table called ATLy, the Atlanta equivalent to MILy, by passing ATL to the `tabyl()` function and adding `play_length2` and `event_type` as additional arguments. Because we only need the variable `play_length2` and the shot and miss factors from the variable `event_type`, which are now also variables, we then call the `select()` function to reduce ATLy to include just `play_length2`, `shot`, and `miss`.

Next, we call the `mutate()` function to create a variable called `fg_pct`; our new variable computes the field goal percentage by dividing the variable `shot` by the sum of the variables `shot` and `miss`, which is then multiplied by 100 to return a percentage. Our derived variable is then rounded to two digits to the right of the decimal point:

```
ATL %>%
  tabyl(play_length2, event_type) -> ATLy
ATLy <- select(ATLy, play_length2, shot, miss)
ATLy %>%
  mutate(fg_pct = shot / (shot + miss)*100) -> ATLy
ATLy$fg_pct <- round(ATLy$fg_pct, digits = 2)
print(ATLy)
##  play_length2 shot miss fg_pct
##             5  147  180  44.95
##             6  139  170  44.98
##             7  150  155  49.18
##             8  124  195  38.87
##             9  131  170  43.52
##            10  155  171  47.55
##            11  163  206  44.17
##            12  136  204  40.00
##            13  164  188  46.59
##            14  141  191  42.47
##            15  128  181  41.42
##            16  116  160  42.03
##            17   92  153  37.55
##            18   93  113  45.15
##            19   75  102  42.37
##            20   53   89  37.32
##            21   53   62  46.09
##            22   39   44  46.99
##            23   16   43  27.12
##            24   23   30  43.40
```

DISPLAYING RESULTS

We'll pull the tibble ATLx into one chunk of `ggplot2` code to source one line chart and the frequency table ATLy into another chunk of `ggplot2` code to source a second line chart. These line charts (see figure 8.2) are just like the first pair we created, except that we've swapped out data sources and images:

```
ATLp1 <- ggplot(ATLx, aes(x = play_length2, y = avg, group = 1)) +
  geom_line(aes(y = avg), color = "red", size = 2) +
  geom_point(color = "black", size = 3) +
  labs(title = "Points Scored per Second Increment",
       subtitle = "2019-20 Atlanta Hawks",
       caption = "regular season only",
       x = "Number of Seconds into Possession",
       y = "Average Number of Points Scored") +
  geom_smooth(method = lm, color = "blue", se = FALSE) +
```

```
    geom_smooth(method = lm, color = "gold",
                data = ATLx[ATLx$play_length2 < 13,], se = FALSE) +
    geom_smooth(method = lm, color = "purple",
                data = ATLx[ATLx$play_length2 > 11,], se = FALSE) +
    theme_classic() +
    theme(plot.title = element_text(face = "bold")) +
    inset_element(hawks, left = 0.78, bottom = 0.78,
                  right = 0.95, top = 0.95)

ATLp2 <- ggplot(ATLy, aes(x = play_length2, y = fg_pct, group = 1)) +
    geom_line(aes(y = fg_pct), color = "red", size = 2) +
    geom_point(color = "black", size = 3) +
    labs(title = "Field Goal Percentage per Second Increment",
         subtitle = "2019-20 Atlanta Hawks",
         caption = "regular season only",
         x = "Number of Seconds into Possession",
         y = "Field Goal Percentage") +
    geom_smooth(method = lm, color = "blue", se = FALSE) +
    geom_smooth(method = lm, color = "gold",
                data = ATLy[ATLy$play_length2 < 13,], se = FALSE) +
    geom_smooth(method = lm, color = "purple",
                data = ATLy[ATLy$play_length2 > 11,], se = FALSE) +
    theme_classic() +
    theme(plot.title = element_text(face = "bold")) +
    inset_element(hawks, left = 0.62, bottom = 0.78,
                  right = 0.79, top = 0.95)
```

After temporarily holding ATLp1 and ATLp2 in memory, we bundle them together by again calling the `plot_layout()` function from the `patchwork` package and print the two as a single object:

```
ATLp1 + ATLp2 + plot_layout(ncol = 2)
```

CONCLUSIONS

Our results are both the same and not quite the same as before:

- With respect to points scored and field goal percentage, the 2019–20 Hawks were most successful just 7 seconds into their time of possession, when they averaged 1.17 points and made 49.18% of their field goal attempts.
- This means that at no point after the 37% mark did the Hawks average as many points or shoot an equal or better field goal percentage than they did when their time of possession equaled 7 seconds. So once more, we're not seeing the optimal stopping, or 37%, rule in effect.
- Like the Bucks, the Atlanta Hawks were generally more successful on offense, regardless of which measure we're considering, when more time remained on the shot clock.
- Also like the Bucks, we see ongoing regressions to the mean as the x-axis variable increases and the observation counts decrease.

Let's take a look at just one more team.

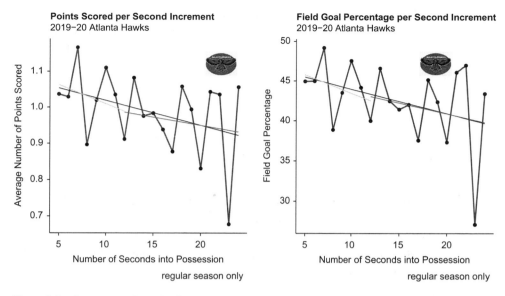

Figure 8.2   Average number of points scored (on the left) and field goal percentage (on the right) for the Atlanta Hawks during the 2019–20 regular season computed at each second of a half-court possession, with trendlines

8.5.3   *Charlotte Hornets*

We'll again repeat this exercise, this time by inserting the Charlotte Hornets for the Bucks or Hawks. The Hornets averaged just 102.9 points per game during the 2019–20 regular season, which was lowest in the league.

CREATING DATA SOURCES

We pass the pbp data set to the `filter()` function to subset it where the variable `team` equals `CHA`, the variable `play_length2` is again equal to or greater than `5` and less than or equal to `24`, and the variable `event_type` equals `shot` or `miss`. We then cast the results to equal a tibble called CHA. Next, we pass CHA to the `select()` function to reduce its width by just retaining the variables `event_type`, `points`, and `play_length2`. Finally, we call the `dim()` function to return the final dimension of the CHA data set:

```
pbp %>%
  filter(team == "CHA",
         play_length2 >= 5 & play_length2 <= 24,
         event_type == "shot" | event_type == "miss") -> CHA

CHA %>%
  select(event_type, points, play_length2) -> CHA
dim(CHA)
## [1] 4539    3
```

The CHA data set contains 4,539 observations between the `miss` and `made` event types. We then pipe CHA to the `group_by()` and `tally()` functions to return the miss and made counts so we can compare and contrast the Hornets with the Bucks and Hawks:

```
CHA %>%
  group_by(event_type) %>%
  tally()
## # A tibble: 2 × 2
##   event_type      n
##   <fct>       <int>
## 1 miss         2624
## 2 shot         1915
```

The 2019–20 Charlotte Hornets attempted 897 fewer shots than the Bucks and 406 fewer shots than the Hawks; they made 619 fewer shots than the Bucks and made 223 fewer shots than the Hawks.

We then create a tibble called CHAx and a frequency table called CHAy, just as we've done twice before:

```
CHA %>%
  group_by(play_length2) %>%
  summarise(avg = mean(points)) -> CHAx
print(CHAx)
## # A tibble: 20 × 2
##    play_length2   avg
##           <dbl> <dbl>
## 1             5  1.05
## 2             6  1.14
## 3             7  1.03
## 4             8  0.986
## 5             9  0.981
## 6            10  0.913
## 7            11  0.992
## 8            12  1.04
## 9            13  0.907
## 10           14  0.956
## 11           15  0.900
## 12           16  1.06
## 13           17  0.950
## 14           18  1.19
## 15           19  1.10
## 16           20  0.839
## 17           21  1.02
## 18           22  0.843
## 19           23  0.906
## 20           24  0.931

CHA %>%
  tabyl(play_length2, event_type) -> CHAy
CHAy %>%
  select(play_length2, shot, miss) -> CHAy
CHAy %>%
```

```
  mutate(fg_pct = shot / (shot + miss)*100) -> CHAy
CHAy$fg_pct <- round(CHAy$fg_pct, digits = 2)
print(CHAy)
##   play_length2 shot miss fg_pct
##              5  124  152  44.93
##              6  124  132  48.44
##              7  109  139  43.95
##              8   88  127  40.93
##              9   87  121  41.83
##             10   97  145  40.08
##             11  108  144  42.86
##             12  123  159  43.62
##             13  118  183  39.20
##             14  129  187  40.82
##             15  111  178  38.41
##             16  125  158  44.17
##             17  101  141  41.74
##             18  114  115  49.78
##             19   89  103  46.35
##             20   71  122  36.79
##             21   70   89  44.03
##             22   43   84  33.86
##             23   47   80  37.01
##             24   37   65  36.27
```

DISPLAYING RESULTS

We then create a third pair of line charts to visualize Charlotte's points-per-game average and field goal percentage per second of possession time (see figure 8.3):

```
CHAp1 <- ggplot(CHAx, aes(x = play_length2, y = avg, group = 1)) +
  geom_line(aes(y = avg), color = "cyan3", size = 2) +
  geom_point(color = "black", size = 3) +
  labs(title = "Points Scored per Second Increment",
       subtitle = "2019-20 Charlotte Hornets",
       caption = "regular season only",
       x = "Number of Seconds into Possession",
       y = "Average Number of Points Scored") +
  geom_smooth(method = lm, color = "blue", se = FALSE) +
  geom_smooth(method = lm, color = "gold",
              data = CHAx[CHAx$play_length2 < 13,], se = FALSE) +
  geom_smooth(method = lm, color = "purple",
              data = CHAx[CHAx$play_length2 > 11,], se = FALSE) +
  theme_classic() +
  theme(plot.title = element_text(face = "bold")) +
  inset_element(hornets, left = 0.73, bottom = 0.73,
                right = 0.95, top = 0.95)

CHAp2 <- ggplot(CHAy, aes(x = play_length2, y = fg_pct, group = 1)) +
  geom_line(aes(y = fg_pct), color = "cyan3", size = 2) +
  geom_point(color = "black", size = 3) +
  labs(title = "Field Goal Percentage per Second Increment",
       subtitle = "2019-20 Charlotte Hornets",
       caption = "regular season only",
       x = "Number of Seconds into Possession",
```

```
          y = "Field Goal Percentage") +
geom_smooth(method = lm, color = "blue", se = FALSE) +
geom_smooth(method = lm, color = "gold",
            data = CHAy[CHAy$play_length2 < 13,], se = FALSE) +
geom_smooth(method = lm, color = "purple",
            data = CHAy[CHAy$play_length2 > 11,], se = FALSE) +
theme_classic() +
theme(plot.title = element_text(face = "bold")) +
inset_element(hornets, left = 0.73, bottom = 0.73,
              right = 0.95, top = 0.95)
CHAp1 + CHAp2 + plot_layout(ncol = 2)
```

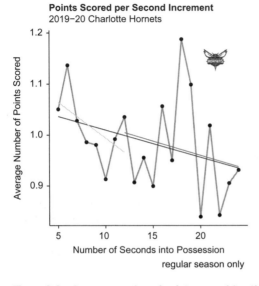
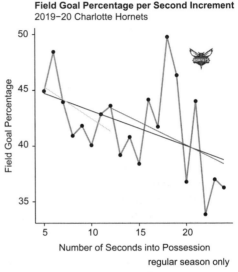

Figure 8.3   Average number of points scored (on the left) and field goal percentage (on the right) for the Charlotte Hornets during the 2019–20 regular season computed at each second of a half-court possession, with trendlines

CONCLUSIONS

For Charlotte, we have a mix of like and unlike results compared to the previous teams:

- Interestingly, with respect to both average points and field goal percentage, the Charlotte Hornets were best off applying the optimal stopping rule.
- Where time of possession equals 6 seconds, the Hornets averaged 1.14 points and made 48.44% of their shot attempts, which is when the Hornets were most successful on offense before the 37% mark.
- But where time of possession instead equals 18 seconds, the Hornets averaged 1.19 points and were successful on 49.78% of their attempted shots, which actually compares well to Milwaukee's best figures.
- Otherwise, we see like trends as well as ongoing regressions to the mean—just as we did with the Bucks and Hawks.

Finally, let's examine the whole NBA—Bucks, Hawks, and Hornets included—in one final pair of `ggplot2` line charts.

8.5.4 *NBA*

No doubt, you're now familiar with the code, but note that the first argument passed to the `filter()` function is optional; as it turns out, there are no observations in the pbp data set where the variable `team` is blank *and* the variable `event_type` equals `shot` or `miss`. The end result, as you might expect by now, is yet another pair of complementary `ggplot2` line charts (see figure 8.4):

```
pbp %>%
  filter(team != "",
         play_length2 >= 5 & play_length2 <= 24,
         event_type == "shot" | event_type == "miss") -> NBA

NBA %>%
  select(event_type, points, play_length2) -> NBA
dim(NBA)
## [1] 155130      3

NBA %>%
  group_by(play_length2) %>%
  summarise(avg = mean(points)) -> NBAx
print(NBAx)
## # A tibble: 20 × 2
##    play_length2    avg
##           <dbl>  <dbl>
##  1            5   1.13
##  2            6   1.10
##  3            7   1.07
##  4            8   1.08
##  5            9   1.06
##  6           10   1.06
##  7           11   1.06
##  8           12   1.05
##  9           13   1.01
## 10           14   1.04
## 11           15   1.04
## 12           16   1.04
## 13           17   1.01
## 14           18   1.04
## 15           19   1.00
## 16           20  0.992
## 17           21  0.942
## 18           22  0.937
## 19           23  0.928
## 20           24  0.927

NBA %>%
  tabyl(play_length2, event_type) -> NBAy
NBAy %>%
  select(play_length2, shot, miss) -> NBAy
NBAy %>%
  mutate(fg_pct = shot / (shot + miss)*100) -> NBAy
NBAy$fg_pct <- round(NBAy$fg_pct, digits = 2)
```

```
print(NBAy)
##  play_length2 shot miss fg_pct
##             5 4522 4774  48.64
##             6 4421 4919  47.33
##             7 4169 4891  46.02
##             8 4182 4902  46.04
##             9 4280 5088  45.69
##            10 4439 5308  45.54
##            11 4693 5599  45.60
##            12 4772 5768  45.28
##            13 4710 5976  44.08
##            14 4649 5673  45.04
##            15 4345 5336  44.88
##            16 3951 4768  45.31
##            17 3399 4356  43.83
##            18 3152 3851  45.01
##            19 2649 3434  43.55
##            20 2224 2972  42.80
##            21 1809 2591  41.11
##            22 1451 2132  40.50
##            23 1099 1683  39.50
##            24  867 1326  39.53
```

```
NBAp1 <- ggplot(NBAx, aes(x = play_length2, y = avg, group = 1)) +
  geom_line(aes(y = avg), color = "red", size = 2) +
  geom_point(color = "blue", size = 3) +
  labs(title = "Points Scored per Second Increment",
       subtitle = "2019-20 NBA Regular Season (all teams)",
       x = "Number of Seconds into Possession",
       y = "Average Number of Points Scored") +
  geom_smooth(method = lm, color = "blue", se = FALSE) +
  geom_smooth(method = lm, color = "gold",
              data = NBAx[NBAx$play_length2 < 13,], se = FALSE) +
  geom_smooth(method = lm, color = "purple",
              data = NBAx[NBAx$play_length2 > 11,], se = FALSE) +
  theme_classic() +
  theme(plot.title = element_text(face = "bold")) +
  inset_element(nba, left = 0.65, bottom = 0.65, right = 0.95, top = 0.95)

NBAp2 <- ggplot(NBAy, aes(x = play_length2, y = fg_pct, group = 1)) +
  geom_line(aes(y = fg_pct), color = "red", size = 2) +
  geom_point(color = "blue", size = 3) +
  labs(title = "Field Goal Percentage per Second Increment",
       subtitle = "2019-20 NBA Regular Season (all teams)",
       x = "Number of Seconds into Possession",
       y = "Field Goal Percentage") +
  geom_smooth(method = lm, color = "blue", se = FALSE) +
  geom_smooth(method = lm, color = "gold",
              data = NBAy[NBAy$play_length2 < 13,], se = FALSE) +
  geom_smooth(method = lm, color = "purple",
              data = NBAy[NBAy$play_length2 > 11,], se = FALSE) +
  theme_classic() +
  theme(plot.title = element_text(face = "bold")) +
  inset_element(nba, left = 0.65, bottom = 0.65, right = 0.95, top = 0.95)

NBAp1 + NBAp2 + plot_layout(ncol = 2)
```

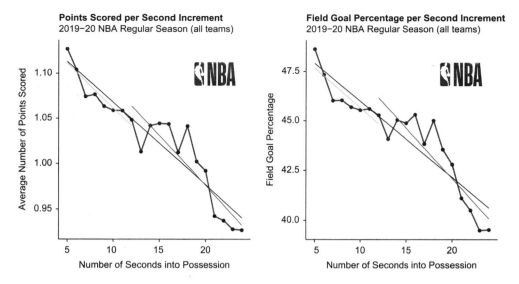

Figure 8.4 **Average number of points scored (on the left) and field goal percentage (on the right) for all 30 NBA teams during the 2019–20 regular season computed at each second of a half-court possession, with trendlines**

We see some really fascinating results here, but not necessarily unexpected results due to the size of the data:

- For starters, we don't see the second-over-second variation that we do when visualizing results for just one team at a time. That's because the results have been more or less smoothed out as a result of plotting the whole NBA in a single data series rather than just 1 of 30 teams.
- Instead, we see three regression lines with roughly equal but steep slopes and, of course, relatively minimal distances between any of them and the data.
- These regression lines suggest that neither the optimal stopping rule nor regressions to the mean are in effect.
- Most significantly, teams are *way* better off shooting earlier than later.

As far as the optimal stopping rule is concerned, our results, at least to the *letter* of the rule, are mixed at best; in fact, where some might see optimal stopping, we instead see regressions to the mean. But the *spirit* of the optimal stopping rule does apply to the NBA. Remember that optimal stopping, in part, is aimed at preventing wasteful effort—pull the trigger on a qualified candidate and stop interviewing; take a good shot and stop passing and dribbling. Our team-level and league-level analysis strongly suggests that teams are most successful scoring points and shooting higher field goal percentages when there is more time remaining on the shot clock, at least based on 2019–20 regular season data.

In this chapter and the one prior, we explored different facets of NBA games controlled by the officials or by the players and coaches, but in the next chapter, we'll examine how the league schedule can significantly influence wins and losses when one team is playing on more rest than its opponent.

Summary

- We all have opportunities in our personal and professional lives to apply the optimal stopping rule. For example, if you're in the market for a new home and absolutely want or need to submit an offer within 60 days, you should spend the first 22 days (37% of 60) noncommittally attending open houses; you should then submit an offer on the first house that favorably compares to the best house you previously inspected. Similarly, if you're speed dating, you should spend the first 37% of the evening more or less warming up, and then make a match with the first person who is just as appealing as everyone you've already met. Finally, if you're a lawyer researching the best legal precedent among 25 qualifying cases, you should automatically dismiss the first nine cases and then proceed with the first case that best compares to that initial batch.

- However, keep the following in mind: optimal stopping is fixed on providing the highest *probability* of a best outcome, without any guarantees, while proactively eliminating wasteful efforts. And it only works when you don't have second chances.

- Optimal stopping isn't necessarily a best fit for the NBA, at least based on our analysis of the 2019–20 regular season data. What might be construed as optimal stopping are more likely regressions to the mean, where positive and negative results are continuously offsetting one another. However, NBA teams during the 2019–20 regular season were generally better off—much better off, in fact—shooting earlier in their half-court sets rather than later.

- It's usually not worth it for a team to pass up good or even decent shot opportunities and to use what's left, or mostly left, on the 24-second shot clock. The mostly old-school idea that teams are more frequently than not better off passing and dribbling until a best shot opportunity comes to fruition is absolutely false. In other words, while the letter of the optimal stopping rule might not be generally applicable, the spirit of optimal stopping absolutely applies.

- In the meantime, we otherwise demonstrated how to create a frequency table and how to create a character string derived from another character string.

- We also showed how you can overwrite default `ggplot2` settings by adding a theme, how to inset images that improve the quality of your visual content, and how to add multiple trendlines to the same line chart.

Chi-square testing
and more effect size testing

This chapter covers

- Running and interpreting statistical tests of significance on categorical data
- Running and interpreting effect size tests on categorical data
- Computing permutations and differentiating permutations from combinations
- Creating facet plots, balloon plots, and mosaic plots

Rest was once thought to be the antithesis of work and activity. Today, it's considered a critical enabler for achieving the highest levels of productivity and performance. Our purpose here is to explore—first by visualizing and then by statistical testing—the effect that rest, defined herein as the number of days off prior to a regular season game, has on wins and losses in the NBA.

Back in chapter 7, we ran t-tests because we were working with numeric dependent variables. In this chapter, we'll instead be working with a categorical dependent variable, so we'll run a chi-square test for independence. But like t-tests, our going-in, or null, hypothesis is that there is no meaningful relationship between variables. Again, like t-tests, we'll reject our null hypothesis if our chi-square test returns a p-value less than 0.05, or we'll fail to reject our null hypothesis if we instead get a p-value greater than 0.05. Afterward, we'll demonstrate two ways by which you can run a Cramer's V test, which is an effect size test that complements a chi-square test, just as a Cohen's d effect size test complements a t-test. Once more, which tests to run should tie back to your data.

The NBA regular season schedule is essentially a constrained optimization problem. Every team plays 82 games, split evenly between home and away. Each team must play 16 games against other teams from their division, 36 games against other teams from the same conference, and 30 games against teams from the opposing conference. The best teams are showcased on Christmas and other days to maximize TV viewership; venues are available on some days but not others; and there are blackout dates. All the while, the league aims to minimize air travel and travel-related expenses.

Consequently, teams play dissimilar and irregular schedules—a pair of opposing teams might have an equal or an unequal number of days off before their scheduled matchup. Our null hypothesis is that rest has no bearing on wins and losses; therefore, our alternative hypothesis is that rest does, in fact, affect who wins and loses.

After we're done loading our packages, importing our data set, and wrangling the same, our subsequent steps are as follows:

- We'll lead off with a brief examination of combinations and permutations and discuss how to differentiate one versus the other; additionally, we'll demonstrate how to compute permutations with R code.
- We'll baseline our data and visualize the same with a facet plot.
- We'll next run our statistical tests, starting with a chi-square test for independence and finishing with a pair of Cramer's V effect size tests.
- A chi-square test is a tad more encompassing than other tests of statistical significance, such as a correlation test or a t-test. We have to first create a contingency table—a table or matrix, sometimes referred to as a crosstab, that displays the frequency distribution involving two or more variables—and then we pass the contingency table to our chi-square test. There are many ways to visualize a contingency table, but we'll demonstrate just two of these.

Let's get started.

9.1 Loading packages

The function to run our statistical test of significance and return the results comes out-of-the-box; however, wrangling data, querying data, and creating our visualizations require functions that aren't available in base R. We therefore make a series of calls to the `library()` function to load packages that allow us to go above and beyond the base install.

You're by now intimately familiar with the `tidyverse` and `sqldf` packages. We'll load these two packages plus five others that haven't previously been loaded or used:

```
library(tidyverse)
library(sqldf)
library(gtools)
library(gplots)
library(vcd)
library(questionr)
library(rcompanion)
```

The first of these is `gtools`, which contains several utility functions, including some for counting and printing permutations and combinations. Permutations are essentially combinations where we care about the order. For instance, the numbers 24, 16, and 31 are equivalent to 16, 31, and 24 if the order is immaterial; if so, these numbers qualify as a combination. But if 24, 16, and 31 is the "combination" to open your locker at the gym, it's really a permutation because 16, 31, 24 won't work. We'll cover much more on permutations and combinations in a bit. For now, understand that computing the maximum number of possible permutations isn't the same as computing the maximum number of combinations; we'll need to first differentiate which is which before plotting and analyzing our data.

The second and third of these packages are `gplots` and `vcd`. While our facet plot will be created with `ggplot2` functions, we'll also use the `balloonplot()` function from the `gplots` package to create a balloon chart and the `mosaic()` function from the `vcd` package to create a mosaic plot. Balloon plots and mosaic plots are just two ways of visualizing a contingency table.

The fourth and fifth packages are `questionr` and `rcompanion`, and we'll demonstrate two ways, one from each of these packages, to run a Cramer's V effect size test. We'll import our data set next.

9.2   Importing data

We now import our data, a .csv file downloaded from Kaggle, by calling the `readr` `read_csv()` function (recall that `readr` is part of the `tidyverse`). Our file was previously saved with the filename 2012_18_officialBoxScore and stored in our default working directory; our data set is called NBAboxscores, and it contains tabulated results of every regular season NBA game between the 2012–13 and 2017–18 seasons.

We then call the base R `dim()` function to return the dimension of the NBAboxscores data set:

```
NBAboxscores <- read_csv("2012_18_officialBoxScore.csv")

dim(NBAboxscores)
## [1] 44284    119
```

Our data has a row count equal to 44,284 and a column count equal to 119. In the following section, we'll run a series of operations to reduce the NBAboxscores data set, length-wise and width-wise, into an object we can better work with.

9.3   *Wrangling data*

For starters, we absolutely don't need the last name (offLNm) and first name (offFNm) of the officials or referees assigned to each game. So we call the dplyr select() function to remove those two variables from NBAboxscores. Here, we demonstrate another application of the select() function; rather than calling out the variable names or variable positions to deselect, we instead tell R to remove all variables in the NBAboxscores data set that start with off. We then call the dim() function again, only to confirm that our data set has, in fact, been reduced from 119 columns to 117 columns:

```
NBAboxscores %>%
  select(-starts_with("off")) -> NBAboxscores
dim(NBAboxscores)
## [1] 44284    117
```

However, by simply removing those two variables from our data set, we now have duplicate rows. The last and first names of the officials were the only variables distinguishing one record from the next because we have a vertical rather than horizontal data set in which single game records are divided between multiple observations. Therefore, we next call the base R unique() function to remove every duplicate record in our data set.

We then call the dim() function for a third time to check on the reduced dimension of the NBAboxscores data set. Don't be alarmed if this operation takes more than a few seconds to complete:

```
NBAboxscores <- unique(NBAboxscores)
dim(NBAboxscores)
## [1] 14758    117
```

Because most NBA games are called by three officials, we should expect the row count in NBAboxscores to have been cut by approximately two-thirds, resulting in our data set being reduced from 44,284 rows to 14,758 rows.

Although everything seems to be in good order, we'll nevertheless pause momentarily to run an integrity check against our data set. The count() function from the dplyr package makes it possible to quickly and easily pull counts of unique values or conditions. The frequency by which the variable teamPTS (representing the total points scored in a game by one of the participating teams) is greater than the variable opptPTS (representing the number of points scored by the opposing team) should equal the frequency by which the exact opposite condition is true:

```
NBAboxscores %>%
  count(teamPTS > opptPTS)
##    teamPTS > opptPTS       n
## 1            FALSE 7379
## 2             TRUE 7379
```

This checks out, but just to be sure, we'll run a second integrity check by reversing the condition:

```
NBAboxscores %>%
  count(teamPTS < opptPTS)
##    teamPTS < opptPTS     n
## 1             FALSE 7379
## 2              TRUE 7379
```

Because R returned the results we were hoping for and expecting, we can now move forward with confidence to further wrangle the NBAboxscores data set. Next, we call the `dplyr` `filter()` function to subset NBAboxscores where the variable `teamPTS` is greater than the variable `opptPTS`.

Another call to the `dim()` function confirms that we've effectively cut the NBAboxscores row count by exactly 50%—our data set now contains 7,379 records and, at least for now, 117 columns:

```
NBAboxscores %>%
  filter(teamPTS > opptPTS) -> NBAboxscores
dim(NBAboxscores)
## [1] 7379  117
```

Let's save NBAboxscores and create a copy called mydata. Yet another call to the `dim()` function confirms that mydata has the exact same dimension as NBAboxscores:

```
mydata <- NBAboxscores
dim(mydata)
## [1] 7379  117
```

We then make another call to the `select()` function to subset mydata on just six variables. The base R `head()` and `tail()` functions print, respectively, the first six and last six observations in the mydata data set:

```
mydata %>%
  select(teamLoc, teamRslt, teamDayOff, opptLoc, opptRslt,
         opptDayOff) -> mydata
head(mydata)
##    teamLoc teamRslt teamDayOff opptLoc opptRslt opptDayOff
##    <chr>   <chr>         <dbl> <chr>   <chr>         <dbl>
## 1  Home    Win               0 Away    Loss              0
## 2  Home    Win               0 Away    Loss              0
## 3  Away    Win               0 Home    Loss              0
## 4  Home    Win               0 Away    Loss              0
## 5  Away    Win               0 Home    Loss              0
## 6  Away    Win               0 Home    Loss              0
tail(mydata)
##       teamLoc teamRslt teamDayOff opptLoc opptRslt opptDayOff
##       <chr>   <chr>         <dbl> <chr>   <chr>         <dbl>
## 7374  Home    Win               2 Away    Loss              2
## 7375  Home    Win               2 Away    Loss              1
```

```
## 7376    Home       Win        1    Away       Loss       2
## 7377    Away       Win        1    Home       Loss       2
## 7378    Home       Win        2    Away       Loss       1
## 7379    Home       Win        2    Away       Loss       1
```

Here's a breakdown of our "surviving" variables:

- teamLoc—Equals either Home or Away, but will always equal the opposite of the variable opptLoc
- teamRslt—Equals Win for all observations
- teamDayOff—Equals the number of off days for the winning team prior to a game, and has a minimum of 0 and a maximum of 11
- opptLoc—Equals either Home or Away, but will always equal the opposite of teamLoc
- opptRslt—Equals Loss for all observations
- opptDayOff—Equals the number of off days for the losing team prior to a game, and has a minimum of 0 and a maximum of 11

The minimum and maximum values for the variables teamDayOff and opptDayOff were pulled by calling the base R min() and max() functions:

```
min(mydata$teamDayOff)
## [1] 0
max(mydata$teamDayOff)
## [1] 11
min(mydata$opptDayOff)
## [1] 0
max(mydata$opptDayOff)
## [1] 11
```

To make this a manageable exercise and avoid having an unreasonable number of days-off permutations between home and visiting teams, most of which would have very few observations anyway, we call the filter() function twice to subset mydata by retaining only those observations where the variable teamDayOff is less than or equal to 4 and then again where the variable opptDayOff is less than or equal to 4.

We then call the dim() function yet again and discover that we now have 7,191 rows and six columns in our working data set. So we merely stripped 188 rows from mydata, or less than 3% of the total record count:

```
mydata %>%
  filter(teamDayOff <= 4,
         opptDayOff <= 4) -> mydata
dim(mydata)
## [1] 7191    6
```

Next, we call the map_df() function from the purrr package, which is part of the tidyverse universe of packages, to return the class for each of our six variables. (We automatically loaded the purrr packaged when we loaded the tidyverse.) They are all character strings or integers, but they all should be factors instead, so we convert them accordingly by calling the base R as.factor() function:

```
map_df(mydata, class)
## # A tibble: 1 × 6
##   teamLoc   teamRslt  teamDayOff opptLoc   opptRslt  opptDayOff
##   <chr>     <chr>     <chr>      <chr>     <chr>     <chr>
## 1 character character integer    character character integer
```

```
mydata$teamLoc <- as.factor(mydata$teamLoc)
mydata$teamRslt <- as.factor(mydata$teamRslt)
mydata$teamDayOff <- as.factor(mydata$teamDayOff)
mydata$opptLoc <- as.factor(mydata$opptLoc)
mydata$opptRslt <- as.factor(mydata$opptRslt)
mydata$opptDayOff <- as.factor(mydata$opptDayOff)
```

We then pipe the mydata data set to the dplyr group_by() and tally() functions to compute the number of home and away wins:

```
mydata %>%
  group_by(teamLoc, teamRslt) %>%
tally()
## # A tibble: 2 × 3
## # Groups:   teamLoc [2]
##   teamLoc teamRslt     n
##   <fct>   <fct>    <int>
## 1 Away    Win       2967
## 2 Home    Win       4224
```

It turns out that the home team won 4,224 games, and the away team won 2,967 games. So the home team won 58.7% of the regular season games between the 2012–13 and 2017–18 seasons—that's our benchmark.

Before we get into our analysis, let's have that conversation about permutations and combinations that we promised in the beginning.

9.4 Computing permutations

The first thing to understand about permutations is that they are *not* synonymous with combinations. The starting lineup for the Golden State Warriors might consist of Otto Porter Jr., Andrew Wiggins, Draymond Green, Klay Thompson, and Stephen Curry. That's a combination, not a permutation, because it doesn't matter in what order these players are announced before tip-off; either way, Golden State's starting lineup remains unchanged.

On the other hand, if we're concerned with division standings at the end of the 2021–22 season, that's a permutation, not a combination, because the order is everything—the place at which each team finished absolutely matters.

So the first thing to understand is that if or when the order doesn't matter, it's a combination, but if or when the order does matter, it's a permutation. The second thing to understand about permutations is the concept of *with replacement* versus *without replacement.* A pair of plays called by a head coach for their team's next two possessions is a permutation *with replacement* because the same player could be the primary option for zero, one, or both plays. The NBA lottery is a permutation *without replacement* because the same team can't be selected more than once.

What's the point of all this? In just a moment, we're going to compute and visualize the number of wins between home and away teams based on permutations of prior days off. In fact, these are permutations with replacement due to the following:

- The order matters. For any given game, the home team might have two prior days off and the away team just one prior day off; that's very different, of course, from the home team having just one day off and the away team having two days. Therefore, these are permutations and not combinations.

- The home and away teams may absolutely have the same number of prior days off; in fact, this is quite common. For instance, a pair of opposing home and road teams may both have two prior days off. This means we can use the same number (2, in this example) twice in our permutations rather than just once. Therefore, these are permutations with replacement.

For our purposes here, there are five prior days off to select from (0–4), and each permutation will contain two of them. It's easy to compute the number of permutations we need to account for; the formula is n^r, where n represents the number of potential selections (5) and r represents the number of selections per permutation (2).

We can perform this or any other mathematical operation in R. We square 5 and set the output to equal an object called permutationsCount. The `paste0()` function from base R is a sort of enhanced version of the `print()` function; here, it concatenates a character string with permutationsCount and prints the full result as a character string. The `^` operator takes the first numeral and raises it to the exponent of the second numeral:

```
n = 5
r = 2
permutationsCount = n^r
paste0("The permuation count equals: ", permutationsCount)
## [1] "The permuation count equals: 25"
```

We can also call on the `permutations()` function from the gtools package to compute the permutations count where n equals the number of prior days off to select from, r equals the number of days off per permutation, and `repeats.allowed` is set to TRUE because replacement is allowed. We front the `permutations()` function with the base R `nrow()` function to return the permutations count:

```
nrow(permutations(n = 5, r = 2, repeats.allowed = TRUE))
## [1] 25
```

We then call the `permutations()` function again, this time without the `nrow()` function, to print our 25 permutations. We conveniently subtract our results by one so that R returns prior days off between 0 and 4 rather than between 1 and 5:

```
permutations(n = 5, r = 2, repeats.allowed = TRUE) - 1
##        [,1] [,2]
##  [1,]    0    0
##  [2,]    0    1
##  [3,]    0    2
##  [4,]    0    3
##  [5,]    0    4
##  [6,]    1    0
##  [7,]    1    1
##  [8,]    1    2
##  [9,]    1    3
## [10,]    1    4
## [11,]    2    0
## [12,]    2    1
## [13,]    2    2
## [14,]    2    3
## [15,]    2    4
## [16,]    3    0
## [17,]    3    1
## [18,]    3    2
## [19,]    3    3
## [20,]    3    4
## [21,]    4    0
## [22,]    4    1
## [23,]    4    2
## [24,]    4    3
## [25,]    4    4
```

Given that *n* and *r* are both small numbers, we certainly could have performed this operation by hand, but that's not how statisticians, data scientists, and data analysts are supposed to roll. Besides, we can't always count on *n* and *r* being small numbers; therefore, it's imperative to understand what distinguishes a permutation from a combination and to further understand the differences between with replacement and without replacement—the formulas are very different depending on the problem type.

We can now proceed to computing and visualizing our results.

9.5 *Visualizing results*

Our plan is to display counts of home team and road team wins by every possible permutation in a single facet plot. We'll create a data source, plot our results, and summarize the key takeaways.

9.5.1 *Creating a data source*

We start by resuming—and completing—our data wrangling operations with another call to the `group_by()` and `tally()` functions; this time, however, our objective is to compute the home and away win totals for each of our 25 permutations. Because there are home wins and away wins for every permutation, our results are cast into a tibble, called finaldf, that is 50 rows long rather than 25. Because R prints only the first 10 rows of our tibble by default, we add the argument `n = 50` to the `print()` function so that R instead prints finaldf in its entirety:

```
mydata %>%
  group_by(teamLoc, teamDayOff, opptLoc, opptDayOff) %>%
tally() -> finaldf
print(finaldf, n = 50)
## # A tibble: 50 × 5
## # Groups:   teamLoc, teamDayOff, opptLoc [10]
##     teamLoc teamDayOff opptLoc opptDayOff       n
##     <fct>   <fct>      <fct>   <fct>        <int>
##  1 Away     0          Home    0               35
##  2 Away     0          Home    1               31
##  3 Away     0          Home    2               33
##  4 Away     0          Home    3                8
##  5 Away     0          Home    4                1
##  6 Away     1          Home    0               26
##  7 Away     1          Home    1              334
##  8 Away     1          Home    2              477
##  9 Away     1          Home    3              148
## 10 Away     1          Home    4               33
## 11 Away     2          Home    0               12
## 12 Away     2          Home    1              201
## 13 Away     2          Home    2              969
## 14 Away     2          Home    3              195
## 15 Away     2          Home    4               47
## 16 Away     3          Home    0                4
## 17 Away     3          Home    1               46
## 18 Away     3          Home    2              191
## 19 Away     3          Home    3               82
## 20 Away     3          Home    4               17
## 21 Away     4          Home    0                2
## 22 Away     4          Home    1               11
## 23 Away     4          Home    2               35
## 24 Away     4          Home    3               17
## 25 Away     4          Home    4               12
## 26 Home     0          Away    0               66
## 27 Home     0          Away    1               35
## 28 Home     0          Away    2               20
## 29 Home     0          Away    3                8
```

```
## 30 Home    0          Away    4              1
## 31 Home    1          Away    0             47
## 32 Home    1          Away    1            431
## 33 Home    1          Away    2            242
## 34 Home    1          Away    3             70
## 35 Home    1          Away    4              4
## 36 Home    2          Away    0             54
## 37 Home    2          Away    1            795
## 38 Home    2          Away    2           1335
## 39 Home    2          Away    3            275
## 40 Home    2          Away    4             49
## 41 Home    3          Away    0             10
## 42 Home    3          Away    1            216
## 43 Home    3          Away    2            280
## 44 Home    3          Away    3            110
## 45 Home    3          Away    4             13
## 46 Home    4          Away    0              4
## 47 Home    4          Away    1             56
## 48 Home    4          Away    2             69
## 49 Home    4          Away    3             21
## 50 Home    4          Away    4             13
```

The win totals are represented in the far-right column labeled n. Take a look, for instance, at the first row. When the away and home teams both had no prior days off, the away team won 35 times. Now take a look at row 26; again, when the away and home teams had no prior days off, the home team won 66 times.

We then call the base R sum() function against finaldf to return the sum of n—it equals 7,191, which, of course, is identical to the mydata row count once we subset mydata so that the variables teamDayOff and opptDayOff were both equal to or less than 4:

```
sum(finaldf$n)
## [1] 7191
```

We now have a data source for our facet plot.

9.5.2 *Visualizing the results*

Our ggplot2 facet plot visualizes the number of home team and away team wins for every possible days-off permutation in finaldf. (Once more, a facet plot is a type of visualization made up of several subplots that have the same axes where each subplot represents a mutually exclusive subset of the data.) Because there are five days off possibilities (0–4) and two teams (Home and Away), the number of days off permutations equals 5^2, or 25. Therefore, our facet plot has 25 panels. Affixed atop each panel is the prior days-off permutation, where the top number applies to the home team and the bottom number applies to the away team. The specific instructions for creating our facet plot are as follows:

- We set n as the x-axis variable and teamLoc as the y-axis variable; therefore, our results will be visualized horizontally rather than vertically.

- The `geom_bar()` function is called to visualize the results with a bar chart per panel; the `stat = identify` argument tells R to draw the length of the bars to match the variable `n`.

- The `facet_wrap()` function instructs R to match `teamDayOff`/`opptDayOff` permutations with the 25 panels. R will automatically arrange the 25 panels in a 5 × 5 grid, but the layout can be customized by adding the `ncol` argument to the `facet_wrap()` function and then specifying the number of columns, which, of course, would then increase or decrease the row count to stay fixed on 25 panels. In addition, x-axis scales are fixed by default to be harmonized across all the panels. But this, too, can be customized by using the `scales` package in tandem with the `facet_wrap()` function and setting it to `free`; R will then scale each panel, or x-axis, independently based on the per-permutation results. We experimented with both of these options, and suffice to say, the defaults are there for a reason.

- The `xlim()` function is added to extend the length of the x-axes. We do this so that our labels affixed to the "top" of our horizontal bars fit inside all the panels, especially where the record counts are highest.

- These labels are made possible by the addition of the `geom_text()` function; the `vjust` and `hjust` arguments adjust the placement of the labels vertically and horizontally.

We create our facet plot (see figure 9.1)—any `ggplot2` object, really—by first calling the `ggplot()` function; then we incrementally add bells and whistles by alternately calling the plus (+) operator and other `ggplot2` functions. Note that R might not merely bypass `ggplot()` functions that aren't preceded by the + operator; instead, R could very well throw an error or return NULL. It all depends on the function that's not preceded by the + operator. The following calls the object:

```
ggplot(data = finaldf, aes(x = n, y = teamLoc, fill = teamLoc)) +
  geom_bar(stat = "identity") +
  facet_wrap(teamDayOff~opptDayOff) +
  labs(title =
        "Home and Away Win Totals Broken Down by Days Off Permutations",
      subtitle = "2012-13 to 2017-18 Regular Seasons",
      caption = "Top Numbers: Home team prior days off
      Bottom Numbers: Away team prior days off",
      x = "Win Totals",
      y = "") +
  xlim(0,1500) +
  geom_text(aes(label = n, vjust = 0.1, hjust = -0.1)) +
  theme(plot.title = element_text(face = "bold")) +
  theme(legend.position = "none")
```

Home and Away Win Totals Broken Down by Days Off Permutations
2012–13 to 2017–18 Regular Seasons

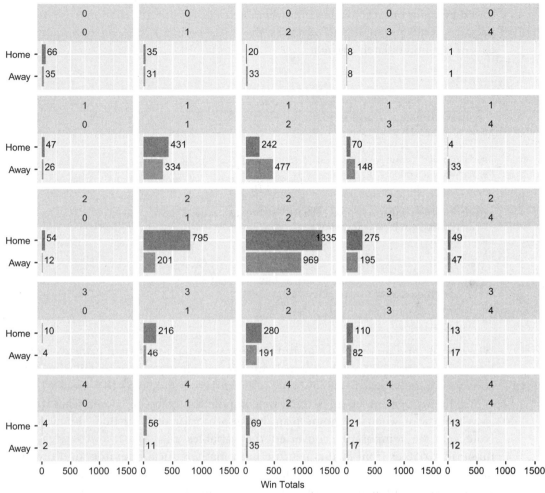

Top Numbers: Home team prior days off
Bottom Numbers: Away team prior days off

Figure 9.1   A facet plot divided into 25 panels that visualizes with a series of bar charts the breakdown in home and away wins by permutations of prior days off

9.5.3   Conclusions

It's fascinating to see these results because rest appears to have a tremendous influence on wins and losses. As just one example, consider where the home team had two days off and the away team had just one—the home team won 795 of the 996 games, or almost 80%. But when the away team had two days off and the home team just one day off, the away team won about two-thirds of the games. Recall that our reference point is 58.7%—this is the home team winning percentage regardless of prior days off between home and away teams.

In the chunk of `dplyr` code shown next, we compute the number of wins for home and away teams when both teams had an equal number of prior days off. That's followed by a pair of SELECT statements where we call the `sqldf()` function from the `sqldf` package, just for comparison purposes; the `sqldf` code is otherwise equivalent to the `dplyr` code immediately above it:

```
finaldf %>%
  filter(teamDayOff == opptDayOff) %>%
  group_by(teamLoc) %>%
  summarize(wins = sum(n))
## # A tibble: 2 × 2
##    teamLoc  wins
##    <fct>    <int>
## 1 Away      1432
## 2 Home      1955

sqldf("select SUM(n) FROM finaldf WHERE teamLoc ='Home' and
      teamDayOff = opptDayOff")
##    SUM(n)
## 1   1955

sqldf("select SUM(n) FROM finaldf WHERE teamLoc ='Away'
      and teamDayOff = opptDayOff")
##    SUM(n)
## 1   1432
```

When home and away teams squared off with an equal number of prior days off, the home team won 57.7% of the games, which is very close to their overall winning percentage in regular season games between the 2012–13 and 2017–18 seasons.

In the next chunk of `dplyr` code, we compute the counts of home team wins and away team wins when the home team had more prior days off than the away team. Note that we temporarily converted the variables `teamDayOff` and `opptDayOff` to numeric variables from factors because most mathematical operators don't work on factors. Again, we follow up by calling the `sqldf()` function twice and writing another pair of SELECT statements that provide the same output as our `dplyr` code:

```
finaldf %>%
  filter(as.numeric(teamDayOff) > as.numeric(opptDayOff)) %>%
  group_by(teamLoc) %>%
  summarize(wins = sum(n))
## # A tibble: 2 × 2
##    teamLoc  wins
##    <fct>    <int>
## 1 Away       545
## 2 Home      1552

sqldf("select SUM(n) FROM finaldf WHERE teamLoc ='Home'
      and teamDayOff > opptDayOff")
##    SUM(n)
## 1   1552
```

```
sqldf("select SUM(n) FROM finaldf WHERE teamLoc ='Away'
      and teamDayOff > opptDayOff")
##   SUM(n)
## 1    545
```

The home team won 74% of games in which it had at least one additional prior day off than the away team.

In the next and final chunk of `dplyr` code, we compute the counts of home team wins and away team wins when the away team had more prior days off than the home team. Following that, we again call the `sqldf()` function to return the same output:

```
finaldf %>%
  filter(as.numeric(teamDayOff) < as.numeric(opptDayOff)) %>%
  group_by(teamLoc) %>%
  summarize(wins = sum(n))
## # A tibble: 2 x 2
##   teamLoc  wins
##   <fct>   <int>
## 1 Away      990
## 2 Home      717

sqldf("select SUM(n) FROM finaldf WHERE teamLoc ='Home'
      and teamDayOff < opptDayOff")
##   SUM(n)
## 1    717

sqldf("select SUM(n) FROM finaldf WHERE teamLoc ='Away'
      and teamDayOff < opptDayOff")
##   SUM(n)
## 1    990
```

The away team won 58% of the games in which it had at least one more prior day off than the home team. These results seem significant, but let's perform a statistical test to confirm (or discover otherwise).

9.6 Statistical test of significance

Let's now conduct what is called a chi-squared test for independence to determine whether or not these differences are statistically significant. Whereas a t-test computes the statistical significance or lack thereof, when the dependent variable is numeric, a chi-square test is used when the dependent variable is categorical. Like a t-test, our null hypothesis is that there is no meaningful relationship between two variables and that the value of one variable doesn't help to predict the value of the other variable. We'll therefore need a p-value equal to or less than our predefined 0.05 threshold for significance to reject the null hypothesis and alternately conclude that rest matters in wins and losses.

Here are three hypothetical yet real-world examples of a chi-square test:

- We want to determine if there is a relationship between voter sentiment toward a bill to increase public school funding and marital status. The null hypothesis, or H_0, is that sentiment and marital status are independent of one another; the alternative hypothesis, or H_1, is that sentiment and marital status aren't independent. This sort of data would usually be collected by a survey. Chi-square tests for independence are frequently used by researchers studying survey responses.

- We have an interest in testing the potential relationship between gender and political beliefs. The null hypothesis is that no relationship exists between gender and whether one associates as liberal or conservative; the alternative hypothesis is that gender and politics are related.

- We want to measure customer counts in a restaurant by day of week. The null hypothesis is that the restaurant serves the same, or roughly the same, number of customers regardless of the day of the week; the alternative hypothesis is that customer counts vary, perhaps significantly so, by day of week.

All things considered, we're comparing the p-value from a chi-square test to a pre-defined 5% threshold for statistical significance—just like we did with our t-tests earlier. If the p-value is less than 5%, we'll reject a null hypothesis that any differences are more or less due to chance; if greater than 5%, we'll fail to reject that same null hypothesis—again, just like we did with our t-tests. We're running a chi-square test for independence rather than a t-test because we're now working with categorical data, whereas back in chapter 6, we instead worked with numeric data. This is why we'll run a Cramer's V effect size test afterward rather than a Cohen's d effect size test.

9.6.1   *Creating a contingency table and a balloon plot*

The outputs we computed in the previous section are thrown into a 3×2 contingency table called chisq_table. A contingency table is a way of summarizing categorical data by showing one distribution horizontally (or by rows) and another distribution vertically (or by columns); shortly, we'll pass our contingency table to a chi-square test. We initialize the contingency table by calling the base R matrix() function; therefore, our contingency table, at least for the time being, is really a matrix rather than a table. The three rows are labeled More Rest, Same Rest, and Less Rest (after all, each team has more, less, or the same rest as the opposing team) while the two columns are labeled Home Wins and Home Losses (all games end with one of these two outcomes, but clearly there are alternatives in the labeling):

```
chisq_table <- matrix(c(1552, 545, 1955, 1432, 717, 990),
                      ncol = 2, byrow = TRUE)
rownames(chisq_table) <- c("More Rest", "Same Rest", "Less Rest")
colnames(chisq_table) <- c("Home Wins", "Home Losses")
print(chisq_table)
##           Home Wins Home Losses
## More Rest      1552         545
## Same Rest      1955        1432
## Less Rest       717         990
```

One way of visualizing a contingency table is through a balloon chart (see figure 9.2), and one way of creating a balloon chart in R is to call the `balloonplot()` function from the `gplots` package in combination with the `t()` function from base R. The `t()` function transposes a matrix or data frame by switching the rows and columns. It's not absolutely required, but the `balloonplot()` function by itself automatically transposes our contingency table. The `t()` function therefore merely reverts the contingency table to its original dimension.

The `balloonplot()` function requires a table as a data source, so we first convert chisq_table from a matrix to a table by passing chisq_table as a matrix to the base R `as.table()` function and then create our visualization:

```
chisq_table <- as.table(as.matrix(chisq_table))
balloonplot(t(chisq_table), main = "Home Wins and Home Losses",
           xlab = "", ylab = "",
           label = TRUE, show.margins = TRUE)
```

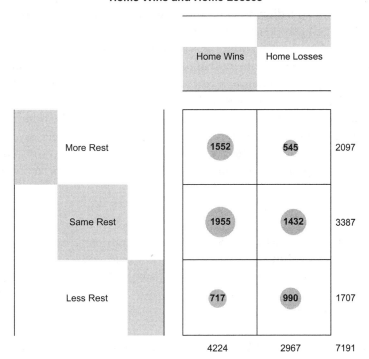

Figure 9.2 A balloon chart is just one way to visualize a contingency table in R.

Our balloon chart isn't necessarily the most elegant visualization we've created so far, but it does the job. It's basically a graphical contingency table or matrix where the dot sizes reflect the record counts. We can readily see that home teams are even more successful when they have more rest than their visiting opponents and less successful when their opponents instead have more rest.

When `label` equals TRUE, R adds the record counts inside the dots; when `show.margins` equals TRUE, R sums every row and column and prints the totals just outside the table.

9.6.2   *Running a chi-square test*

We then run our chi-squared test for independence by calling the base R `chisq.test()` function and passing our contingency table—now really a table—as the only parameter. This is just as simple and straightforward as running a t-test:

```
options(scipen = 999)

test <- chisq.test(chisq_table)
test
##
##   Pearson's Chi-squared test
##
## data:  chisq_table
## X-squared = 400.5, df = 2, p-value < 0.00000000000000022
```

Our results are returned in full digit numerals because we fronted our code by disabling scientific notation via the `options()` function from base R and passing the `scipen = 999` argument. Because the p-value is less than the 0.05 threshold for significance (much less, in fact), we can therefore reject the null hypothesis and conclude that a statistically significant relationship does exist between rest and wins and losses. Our null hypothesis—here and always—is that the variables are independent of one another and that the value of one variable therefore doesn't and can't predict the value of the other variable. We can and should reject the null hypothesis and instead accept the alternative hypothesis only when the evidence tells us there is almost zero chance our results could be random. This is why we generally require a p-value at or below 5% to reject any null hypothesis.

9.6.3   *Creating a mosaic plot*

A mosaic plot is another graphical representation of a contingency table (see figure 9.3). However, the `mosaic()` function from the `vcd` package goes a step further—in addition to drawing a picture that represents the relationship between categorical variables, the `mosaic()` function adds the results of our chi-squared test for independence by independently computing the p-value and returning the result in the lower-right corner.

We call the `mosaic()` function and add our contingency table as the first argument. When `shade` equals TRUE, R adds colors to the plot where the actual outcomes are at variance with the expected outcomes; when `legend` also equals TRUE, R adds a legend, in the form of Pearson residuals, to the right of the plot. Pearson residuals represent the standardized distances between actual and expected outcomes:

```
mosaic(chisq_table, shade = TRUE, legend = TRUE,
       main = "Home Wins and Home Losses")
```

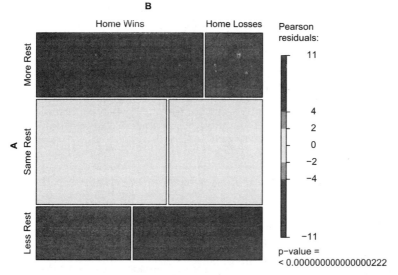

Figure 9.3   A mosaic plot is yet another way to visualize a contingency table in R. It's not at all necessary to create a balloon chart and a mosaic plot—one or the other is recommended—and you should pick the plot that works best for you.

The size, or length, of the rectangles represent proportional values. When compared to equal amounts of rest, home teams win even more frequently when they have at least one additional prior day off than visiting teams, and they win less frequently when the opposite is true.

9.7 *Effect size testing*

A Cramer's V test is to categorical data what a Cohen's d test is to continuous data; so whereas a Cohen's d test complements a t-test, a Cramer's V test complements a chi-square test for independence. Our purpose here is to demonstrate two ways of computing a Cramer's V effect size test where we pass our contingency table, chisq_table, to a pair of similar functions that return similar results.

From our chi-square test, we learned that a statistically significant relationship exists between rest and wins and losses; however, a chi-square test doesn't provide any insight as to *how* significant that relationship might be. A Cramer's V test, regardless of what function is called from which package, will return some number between 0 and 1, where 0 indicates absolutely no association between two variables, and 1 indicates a strong association between two variables.

We first call the `cramer.v()` function from the `questionr` package:

```
cramer.v(chisq_table)
## [1] 0.2359978
```

Then, we call the `cramerV()` function from the `rcompanion` package:

```
cramerV(chisq_table)
## Cramer V
##    0.236
```

So we get the same results from both operations; based on the results equaling 0.24, we can conclude that the effect size is small. Back in chapter 6, we emphasized that an effect size test like Cohen's d complements and doesn't replace a test of statistical significance, such as a t-test, and that we shouldn't correlate the results between the two. It's the same here between our chi-square test for independence and our subsequent Cramer's V effect size tests.

In the following chapter, we'll explore what sort of relationship there might be between team payrolls, regular season wins, postseason appearances, and league championships.

Summary

- Rest is quite obviously a significant factor in wins and losses. Our chi-square test for independence confirmed what we previously computed and visualized—wins and losses between home and away teams flip as prior days off flip. In R, you can write and run a significance test with just one or two lines of built-in code.
- The same is true with effect size tests on categorical data; just one line of code is all that's needed to run a Cramer's V test in R, regardless of what function from which package you choose.
- It's critical to understand the differences between permutations and combinations and between with replacement and without replacement. There are radically different formulas depending on the problem type; it just so happens that permutations with replacement are probably the easiest.
- While the brainpower must come from you, R can perform the grunt work and the heavy lifting. Computing permutations is hardly an everyday task, yet R includes more than one package and more than one function for accomplishing this task. Moreover, it took just one line of code to compute the permutations count and just one additional line of code to print all the permutations.
- Transforming a bar chart into a `ggplot2` facet plot requires just one additional line of code. Our balloon plot and mosaic plot might not be the most sophisticated plots we've created thus far, but they are nevertheless just as compelling as they were easy to produce.
- Due to the importance and benefits of rest, the NBA should consider days off, if at all possible, when generating the regular season schedule. Additionally, the Las Vegas sportsbooks should incorporate prior days off into their algorithms if they aren't already doing so.

Doing more with ggplot2

10

This chapter covers

- Creating correlation plots, dot plots, and lollipop charts
- Modifying `ggplot2` labels through transformations and concatenations
- Enhancing `ggplot2` visualizations with legends, annotations, and shapes
- Changing `ggplot2` colors by groups
- Revealing Simpson's Paradox

Our purpose in this chapter is to quantify and visualize the relationship in the NBA between team payrolls and team accomplishments. Along the way, we'll demonstrate ways to go above and beyond with the `ggplot2` graphics package—by experimenting with unconventional types of plots; by transforming and augmenting axis labels; by adding legends, annotations, and shapes; and by segmenting groups by color. When we visualize data instead of relegating it to rows and columns in a table, we accelerate our capacity to learn from it and our ability to act on it. We readily see correlations between variables, trends over time, unusual patterns, frequencies, distributions, and outliers that are near impossible to spot in a spreadsheet or some other like output. Sometimes small touches can have major effects on your visual content.

That being said, we need to consider a couple of notes before moving forward. First, team payrolls are equal to the sum of player salaries, which doesn't, therefore, include endorsement money and other income sources that typically supplement player salaries. We're only counting the monies that teams pay out to their employees. Second, team accomplishments will be measured three ways going forward: by regular season wins, postseason appearances, and league championships. Our journey will cover several paths:

- Quantifying and visualizing the year-over-year correlation between team payrolls and regular season wins (see section 10.4.1)
- Rank ordering team payrolls from one season to the next and classifying their end-of-season results across three-level factor variables (see section 10.4.2)
- Comparing average team payrolls against different season-ending results through a series of lollipop charts (see section 10.4.3)

But first, let's take care of some housecleaning tasks.

10.1 *Loading packages*

To accomplish these goals, we'll need to go above and beyond base R; thus, we call the `library()` function three times to load three packages we've used before. As a reminder, the `scales` package, which we introduced earlier in chapter 4, includes functions for converting `ggplot2` label formats:

```
library(tidyverse)
library(scales)
library(patchwork)
```

Next, we'll import our data sets.

10.2 *Importing and viewing data*

We'll be working with two data sets in this chapter. The first of these, called cap, is merely 18 rows long and three columns wide. It contains the real NBA salary cap for every season between 2000 and 2017, downloaded from www.basketball-reference .com, as well as the salary cap for the same in 2021 dollars, adjusted for inflation using a tool from www.usinflationcalculator.com.

Our second data set, called salaries, contains the real and inflation-adjusted payrolls for every NBA team between 2000 and 2017; the real salaries were obtained from a Boston Celtics fan site called Celtics Hub (www.celticshub.com; site was under maintenance at time of printing), and the adjusted salaries were computed with the help of www.usinflationcalculator.com. Additionally, the salaries data set contains regular season win totals and postseason results for every team and season combination, scraped from www.basketball-reference.com.

Both of these data sets are .csv files previously stored in our default working directory. We therefore make two calls to the readr read_csv() function to import both:

```
cap <- read_csv("salary_cap.csv")

salaries <- read_csv("salaries.csv")
```

Following are a couple of short notes with respect to the salaries data set:

- The NBA had 29 teams between the 1999–2000 and 2003–04 seasons and 30 teams every year thereafter; consequently, our salaries data set contains several Not Available (NA) values. We'll demonstrate how to deal with NAs so that missing values don't get in the way of our analysis.
- We use current team names throughout, despite the fact that some teams previously played their home games in another city or maybe even another state. So, for instance, the Nets are referred to as the Brooklyn Nets only, even though they previously played in New Jersey and were then known as the New Jersey Nets; the Thunder, previously known as the Supersonics when they played in Seattle, are referred to as the Oklahoma City Thunder only. Teams sometimes move and therefore change names, but they are nevertheless the same franchise, usually with the same ownership group.

A call to the dplyr glimpse() function returns the salaries row and column counts plus a transposed view of the data. However, we first make a call to the options() function so that glimpse(), and, of course, almost every operation thereafter, returns results in their original or raw format instead of in scientific notation. You should expect scientific notation to automatically take effect, unless disabled in advance, when working with numbers containing lots of digits. Even the most marginal players in the NBA are millionaires many times over; so all of our salary or payroll data contains *many* zeroes. Our preference is to return payroll data in full digit numerals and then, as necessary, override the results with smart and readable transformations:

```
options(scipen = 999)
```

> **Scientific notation and tibbles**
>
> We mentioned in a previous chapter that tibbles don't always work with base R functions. It turns out that disabling scientific notation works on tibbles some of the time, but other times it doesn't. However, there's a very easy workaround that we'll demonstrate in section 10.3.

In consideration of space, we pass salaries to the dplyr select() function to reduce our data so that glimpse() then returns just the variable Team and a subset of the 2017 data:

```
salaries %>%
  select(Team, s2017, sa2017, w2017, pc2017) %>%
  glimpse()
## Rows: 30
## Columns: 5
## $ Team   <chr> "Atlanta Hawks", "Boston Celtics", "Brooklyn Nets", …
## $ s2017  <dbl> 95471579, 87272327, 72926799, 99780303, 94291373, 13…
## $ sa2017 <dbl> 102154590, 93381390, 78031675, 106764924, 100891769,…
## $ w2017  <dbl> 43, 53, 20, 36, 41, 51, 33, 40, 37, 67, 55, 42, 51, …
## $ pc2017 <dbl> 10, 10, 0, 0, 10, 10, 0, 0, 0, 11, 10, 10, 10, 0, 10…
```

A subsequent call to the dim() function gets us the full dimension of the salaries data set:

```
dim(salaries)
## [1] 30 73
```

The salaries data set is almost two and a half times as wide as it is long. Here is what you need to immediately know about the data:

- Columns s2017 through s2000 represent annual team payrolls in real dollars where, for instance, s2017 equals the 2016–17 season.
- Columns sa2017 through sa2000 represent annual team payrolls in dollars adjusted for inflation.
- Columns w2017 through w2000 represent annual regular season win totals (all NBA teams play an 82-game schedule, minus unplanned disruptions due to strikes and pandemics).
- Columns pc2017 through pc2000 represent annual end-of-season results where 0 indicates a team failed to make the playoffs, 10 means it qualified for postseason play but then lost somewhere along the way, and 11 means it won the league championship.

Now for some time-series analysis on player salaries and the salary cap. The cap is the limit teams are allowed to spend on player salaries; the league adjusts the cap almost every year, at least to account for inflation.

10.3 *Salaries and salary cap analysis*

Our first of many visualizations in this chapter is a ggplot2 line chart that displays the NBA salary cap between 2000 and 2017 in both real dollars (USD) and inflation-adjusted dollars (2021 USD). The first data set we imported, cap, is our data source (see figure 10.1):

- We therefore call the geom_line() function twice to draw two lines, one solid and the other dashed. R defaults all lines to solid unless otherwise instructed; there are several alternatives besides dashed.
- To convert our y-axis labels from, let's say, 90000000 to a much more readable $90,000,000, we call the scale_y_continuous() function twice—first, to add commas to these large (some might say outrageous) salary figures, and, second, to

preface these same figures with US dollar signs. Both of these operations are performed in tandem with the `scales` package. While the `scales` package is part of the `tidyverse` by way of the `ggplot2` package, it's not uncommon for R to throw an error when calling `scales` functions without loading it separately and independently from the `tidyverse` or `ggplot2`.

- Because we're not adding a legend, we also call the `annotate()` function twice to add a pair of labels where the designated x and y coordinates meet; our labels take the place of a legend by designating which lines represent which data series.

Once more, we initialize a `ggplot2` object by first calling the `ggplot()` function. We then specify the plot type we want R to draw and accessorize the same by subsequently calling other `ggplot2` functions:

```
p1 <- ggplot(cap, aes(x = year, y = real, group = 1)) +
  geom_line(aes(y = real), color = "steelblue", size = 1.5,
            linetype = "dashed") +
  geom_line(aes(y = adjusted), color = "black", size = 1.5) +
  labs(title = "NBA Salary Cap in USD and 2021 USD",
       subtitle = "2000-2017",
       x = "Season",
       y = "Dollars") +
  theme(plot.title = element_text(face = "bold")) +
  scale_y_continuous(labels = comma) +
  scale_y_continuous(labels = dollar) +
  annotate("text", x = 2005, y = 68000000, label = "2021 USD",
           fontface = "bold", color = c("black")) +
  annotate("text", x = 2008, y = 50000000, label = "USD",
           fontface = "bold", color = c("steelblue"))
print(p1)
```

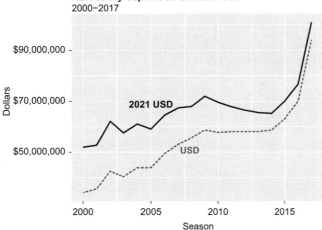

Figure 10.1 The NBA salary cap in USD and 2021 USD between 2000 and 2017. For instance, the salary cap in 2010 was just under $60 M. Converting that figure to 2021 dollars, the cap becomes approximately $70 M, which is why the two lines eventually converge. Whether we view the cap in real dollars or when adjusted for inflation, player salaries have more or less skyrocketed since 2000.

According to our first plot, the NBA salary cap was approaching $100 M back in 2017. The salary cap represents the most teams are allowed to spend on player salaries for the year (though there are allowable exceptions). Most teams carry about 15 players on their active roster at any time, which suggests an average player could be banking as much as $7 M annually in salary.

Working with ggplot2 line types and line widths

By default, `ggplot2` line charts are drawn with solid lines; in other words, if you want a solid line, `ggplot2` will take care of it for you automatically. But `ggplot2` supports other line types as well: dashed, dotted, dotdash, longdash, and twodash. You just need to pass the `linetype` argument to the `geom_line()` function and indicate within a pair of single or double quotation marks which type of line you want or need `ggplot2` to draw in lieu of the default.

In addition, you can fiddle with the width of any line, regardless of type. When, for instance, the size argument passed to `geom_line()` equals `1.5`, you're telling `ggplot2` to draw the line 50% wider than the default. When the size argument is set to, let's say, `0.8`, you're telling `ggplot2` to draw the line at 80% of its default.

Our second visualization is another `ggplot2` line chart that requires some leading data wrangling. We start by creating a new data set from salaries called mean_salaries_real. The `summarize()` function computes the average team payroll in real dollars, and the `dplyr` `across()` function applies the computation to a contiguous subset of the salaries variables. The `na.rm` argument is set to `TRUE` so that the mean calculation effectively ignores the NA values in the salaries data set; R would error out otherwise.

In addition, take note that we've converted mean_salaries_real from a tibble to a classic data frame at the time of print by calling the base R `as.data.frame()` function. That's because R would otherwise have returned results in scientific notation; the workaround is to simply convert the object from a tibble to a data frame:

```
salaries %>%
  summarize(across(s2017:s2000, mean, na.rm = TRUE)) -> mean_salaries_real
print(as.data.frame(mean_salaries_real))
##       s2017     s2016     s2015     s2014     s2013     s2012
## 1 95461491 79261793 73862841 71669986 70503755 67299568
##       s2011     s2010     s2009     s2008     s2007     s2006
## 1 67529008 70437138 71950425 68796241 64645788 63248999
##       s2005     s2004     s2003     s2002     s2001     s2000
## 1 59122201 57676465 57580407 53744919 51853886 45314984
```

Our new data set has a dimension of one row and 18 columns. Next, we call the `pivot_longer()` function from the `tidyr` package to transpose mean_salaries_real into a longer and leaner data set containing 18 rows and two columns called year and real. The previous columns s2017 through s2000 are converted to values in the column year, and the salaries are converted to values in the column real. We get a new object called new_mean_salaries_real:

```
mean_salaries_real %>%
  pivot_longer(col = c(s2017:s2000),
                 names_to = "year",
                 values_to = "real") -> new_mean_salaries_real
print(new_mean_salaries_real)
## # A tibble: 18 × 2
##    year        real
##    <chr>      <dbl>
##  1 s2017 95461491.
##  2 s2016 79261793.
##  3 s2015 73862841.
##  4 s2014 71669986.
##  5 s2013 70503755.
##  6 s2012 67299568.
##  7 s2011 67529008.
##  8 s2010 70437138.
##  9 s2009 71950425.
## 10 s2008 68796241.
## 11 s2007 64645788.
## 12 s2006 63248999.
## 13 s2005 59122201.
## 14 s2004 57676465.
## 15 s2003 57580407.
## 16 s2002 53744919.
## 17 s2001 51853886.
## 18 s2000 45314984
```

These two steps are then repeated:

- First, the adjusted salaries variables are substituting for real salaries, and the average adjusted team payroll between 2000 and 2017 is computed.
- Then, the pivot_longer() function is called to transpose the data from a wide to a long format. This produces an 18×2 data set called new_mean_salaries_adjusted where the cells in year_temp are populated with the former columns sa2017 through sa2000, and the values in those columns are now values in the adjusted column.

Our code chunk and the results follow:

```
salaries %>%
  summarize(across(sa2017:sa2000, mean,
                   na.rm = TRUE)) -> mean_salaries_adjusted

mean_salaries_adjusted %>%
  pivot_longer(col = c(sa2017:sa2000),
                 names_to = "year_temp",
                 values_to = "adjusted") -> new_mean_salaries_adjusted
print(new_mean_salaries_adjusted)
## # A tibble: 18 × 2
##    year_temp    adjusted
##    <chr>           <dbl>
##  1 sa2017     102143796.
##  2 sa2016      87187972.
##  3 sa2015      81987754.
##  4 sa2014      79553685.
```

```
## 5  sa2013      79669243.
## 6  sa2012      77394503.
## 7  sa2011      79008939.
## 8  sa2010      85228938.
## 9  sa2009      88499022.
## 10 sa2008      83931414.
## 11 sa2007      82100151
## 12 sa2006      82223699.
## 13 sa2005      79814972.
## 14 sa2004      80170286.
## 15 sa2003      82339982.
## 16 sa2002      78467582.
## 17 sa2001      77262290.
## 18 sa2000      69331926.
```

We then create a new object, or data set, called salaries_temp, by combining new_mean_salaries_real and new_mean_salaries_adjusted with a call to the base R cbind(), or column bind, function:

```
salaries_temp <- cbind(new_mean_salaries_real, new_mean_salaries_adjusted)
print(salaries_temp)
##      year      real year_temp   adjusted
## 1   s2017 95461491    sa2017  102143796
## 2   s2016 79261793    sa2016   87187972
## 3   s2015 73862841    sa2015   81987754
## 4   s2014 71669986    sa2014   79553685
## 5   s2013 70503755    sa2013   79669243
## 6   s2012 67299568    sa2012   77394503
## 7   s2011 67529008    sa2011   79008939
## 8   s2010 70437138    sa2010   85228938
## 9   s2009 71950425    sa2009   88499022
## 10  s2008 68796241    sa2008   83931414
## 11  s2007 64645788    sa2007   82100151
## 12  s2006 63248999    sa2006   82223699
## 13  s2005 59122201    sa2005   79814972
## 14  s2004 57676465    sa2004   80170286
## 15  s2003 57580407    sa2003   82339982
## 16  s2002 53744919    sa2002   78467582
## 17  s2001 51853886    sa2001   77262290
## 18  s2000 45314984    sa2000   69331926
```

Because we don't need the variables year *and* year_temp, we remove year_temp by passing the salaries_temp data set to the dplyr select() function and essentially deselecting it:

```
salaries_temp %>%
  select(-c(year_temp)) -> salaries_temp
```

We then convert the variable year to a factor by calling the base R as.factor() function. At the same time, we pass the values 2017 through 2000 to as.factor() as a full replacement for s2017 through s2000:

```
salaries_temp$year <- as.factor(2017:2000)
print(salaries_temp)
##    year      real   adjusted
## 1  2017 95461491 102143796
## 2  2016 79261793  87187972
## 3  2015 73862841  81987754
## 4  2014 71669986  79553685
## 5  2013 70503755  79669243
## 6  2012 67299568  77394503
## 7  2011 67529008  79008939
## 8  2010 70437138  85228938
## 9  2009 71950425  88499022
## 10 2008 68796241  83931414
## 11 2007 64645788  82100151
## 12 2006 63248999  82223699
## 13 2005 59122201  79814972
## 14 2004 57676465  80170286
## 15 2003 57580407  82339982
## 16 2002 53744919  78467582
## 17 2001 51853886  77262290
## 18 2000 45314984  69331926
```

Finally, we can now create our second `ggplot2` line chart (see figure 10.2). Here, we're showing the progression of the average payroll per team in real and adjusted dollars from 2000 through 2017; otherwise, our second line chart has the exact same fit, form, and function as our first visualization, p1, except for the fact that we've rotated the x-axis labels 45 degrees by making a second call to the `theme()` function:

```
p2 <- ggplot(salaries_temp, aes(x = year, y = real, group = 1)) +
  geom_line(aes(y = real), color = "steelblue",
            size = 1.5, linetype = "dashed") +
  geom_line(aes(y = adjusted), color = "black", size = 1.5) +
  labs(title = "Average Payroll per NBA Team in USD and 2021 USD",
       subtitle = "2000-2017",
       x = "Season",
       y = "Dollars") +
  theme(plot.title = element_text(face = "bold")) +
  scale_y_continuous(labels = comma) +
  scale_y_continuous(labels = dollar) +
  annotate("text", x = "2003", y = 85000000,
           label = "2021 USD", fontface = "bold", color = c("black")) +
  annotate("text", x = "2007", y = 61000000,
           label = "USD", fontface = "bold", color = c("steelblue")) +
  theme(axis.text.x = element_text(angle = 45, hjust = 1))
print(p2)
```

When adjusted for inflation, the average team payroll was actually very stable from 2001 through 2014. It has grown at an increasing rate since then. Now that we've provided some context, we'll next get into the heavy lifting.

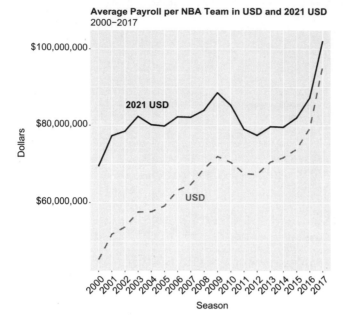

Figure 10.2   Average team payrolls from 2000 through 2017 in real and adjusted dollars

10.4   *Analysis*

The more successful teams in the NBA—that is, teams that win more regular season games, qualify for postseason play, and win championships—spend more money on player salaries than teams that win fewer regular season games and fail to make the postseason. For some additional context, especially for those of you not familiar with a typical NBA season, consider the following:

- The NBA's 30 teams are divided into two 15-team conferences; the top eight teams from each conference at the end of the regular season qualify for the postseason.
- The NBA regular season usually starts in mid-October and ends the following year in mid-April. It's equally correct to reference an NBA season that starts, let's say, in October 2021 and ends in April 2022 as the 2021–22 season, the 2022 season, or the 2022 year. All mean the same and are equally correct, so we'll use these interchangeably.
- Playoffs start immediately following the conclusion of the regular season, usually ending in early June. Postseason and playoffs are synonymous, so we'll use these additional terms interchangeably.

Although there are exceptions to almost every rule, we'll see if it can be proven that higher-paid NBA teams are more successful than lesser-paid teams, at least between 2000 and 2017. We'll do this primarily by summarizing and visualizing our data: correlation plots that display the positive and significant year-over-year relationship between team payrolls and regular season wins; dot plots that rank order team payrolls and classify their season-ending disposition into one of three discrete bins, or categories; and lollipop charts that display year-over-year average team payrolls broken down by these same categories.

10.4.1 *Plotting and computing correlations between team payrolls and regular season wins*

Our journey begins by computing and plotting the year-over-year correlation between team payrolls and regular season wins and performing a correlation test across our data.

COMPUTING CORRELATIONS AND PERFORMING A CORRELATION TEST

In R, you can compute the correlation coefficient between numeric variables in many ways. The most common and straightforward method of computing the correlation coefficient between two numeric variables at a time is to call the base R `cor()` function. In the following code, we call the `cor()` function to compute the correlation coefficient between salaries and wins from the 2000 season. By adding the `use = "complete.obs"` argument, we're telling R to ignore NAs in the salaries data set and return the correlation anyway; R would otherwise return NA rather than the correlation coefficient:

```
cor(salaries$s2000, salaries$w2000, use = "complete.obs")
## [1] 0.5721255
```

By default, R returns the *Pearson* correlation coefficient, which evaluates the linear relationship between two numeric or continuous variables. If you want or need R to instead return the *Spearman* correlation coefficient, which is based on ranked values for each variable rather than the raw data, simply add the `method = "spearman"` argument to the `cor()` function:

```
cor(salaries$s2000, salaries$w2000, method = 'spearman',
    use = "complete.obs")
## [1] 0.4988909
```

Because we're working with interval data (i.e., data measured along a numeric scale where the distances between adjacent values are always the same) and not ordinal data (i.e., categorical data that has a natural ordering or hierarchy among its categories), we'll compute Pearson correlations throughout. If and when you find it appropriate to compute Spearman correlation coefficients, note that like Pearson correlation coefficients, they will always equal some number between –1 and +1 and should therefore be interpreted just the same.

Of course, we're interested in the correlation between team payrolls and wins for all 18 seasons in our data set, not just for the 2000 season. So while this method is simple and straightforward enough, it's not the most scalable solution. Another method is to subset the salaries data set on just the relevant variables and then compute the correlation coefficient for every conceivable pair of variables with just a single line of code.

First, we call the dplyr select() function to subset the salaries data set on just the 18 variables between s2017 and s2000 and the 18 additional variables between w2017 and w2000. We then call the base R dim() function to return the dimension:

```
salaries %>%
  select(s2017:s2000, w2017:w2000) -> salaries_cor
dim(salaries_cor)
## [1] 30 36
```

Our new data set, salaries_cor, has the same row count as salaries, but has effectively been reduced width-wise to 36 columns.

We can now compute the correlation coefficient for every pair of variables in salaries_cor by again the calling the cor() function; however, rather than passing two variables as arguments, this time, we'll pass the entire data set.

To limit the result set, we first call the options() function where the "max.print" argument equals 100; we don't want to give R the option of returning the correlation coefficient between every pair of 36 variables. Additionally, we bound the cor() function with the base R round() function so that R returns correlations with only two digits right of the decimal point instead of the default, which is seven digits. Still, we're printing just a subset of the full result set:

```
options("max.print" = 100)

round(cor(salaries_cor, use = "complete.obs"), digits = 2)
##        s2017 s2016 s2015 s2014 s2013 s2012 s2011 s2010 s2009 s2008
## s2017  1.00  0.42  0.41  0.09 -0.09  0.20  0.01  0.20  0.34  0.11
## s2016  0.42  1.00  0.49  0.16 -0.14 -0.20 -0.48 -0.07 -0.04 -0.07
##        s2007 s2006 s2005 s2004 s2003 s2002 s2001 s2000 w2017 w2016
## s2017  0.08  0.04  0.16  0.00  0.10 -0.16 -0.06 -0.02  0.40  0.59
## s2016 -0.21 -0.32 -0.35 -0.38 -0.46 -0.44 -0.22 -0.34  0.48  0.56
##        w2015 w2014 w2013 w2012 w2011 w2010 w2009 w2008 w2007 w2006
## s2017  0.48  0.23 -0.10 -0.10 -0.05  0.21  0.06 -0.07  0.11  0.11
## s2016  0.53  0.43  0.30 -0.03 -0.15 -0.13 -0.16 -0.17  0.16  0.33
##        w2005 w2004 w2003 w2002 w2001 w2000
## s2017 -0.09 -0.11 -0.21 -0.10 -0.21 -0.25
## s2016  0.29 -0.05 -0.38 -0.33 -0.54 -0.57
```

This works when every variable is of type numeric, which is why we subset the salaries data set first; R would otherwise throw an error if that weren't the case. But it's too much data. We don't care, for instance, about the correlation between 2017 and 2016 payrolls; likewise, we also don't care about 2017 payrolls and 2014 wins. This makes it difficult to find correlations that are meaningful (like the correlation coefficient between s2017 and w2017, e.g., which equals 0.40).

Let's try another way. In our next code chunk, the following occurs:

- We first call the dplyr select() function to subset the salaries_cor data set on just those variables between s2017 and s2000.
- Next, we call the pivot_longer() function from the tidyr package to reshape salaries_cor from a wide layout to a thin layout, where the two remaining columns assume the variable names of year1 and salary. The results are cast to a tibble called salaries_sals.

Finally, we run a series of familiar base R commands against salaries_sals to examine the results:

```
salaries_cor %>%
  select(s2017:s2000) %>%
  pivot_longer(col = c(s2017:s2000),
               names_to = "year1",
               values_to = "salary") -> salaries_sals
dim(salaries_sals)
## [1] 540    2

head(salaries_sals, n = 3)
## # A tibble: 3 × 2
##    year1  salary
##    <chr>   <dbl>
## 1 s2017 95471579
## 2 s2016 72902950
## 3 s2015 58470278

tail(salaries_sals, n = 3)
## # A tibble: 3 × 2
##    year1  salary
##    <chr>   <int>
##    year1  salary
##    <chr>   <dbl>
## 1 s2002 54776087
## 2 s2001 59085969
## 3 s2000 53194441
```

Next, we repeat this exercise in full where the following are true:

- The salaries_cor data set is subset on the variables w2017 through w2000 in lieu of s2017 through s2000.
- The data set is then reshaped from wide to long with variables called year2 and wins.

The results are cast to a tibble called salaries_wins, and then we call the dim(), head(), and tail() functions from base R to examine the results of our work:

```
salaries_cor %>%
  select(w2017:w2000) %>%
  pivot_longer(col = c(w2017:w2000),
               names_to = "year2",
               values_to = "wins") -> salaries_wins
dim(salaries_wins)
## [1] 540    2

head(salaries_wins, n = 3)
## # A tibble: 3 × 2
##    year2  wins
##    <chr> <dbl>
## 1 w2017    43
## 2 w2016    48
## 3 w2015    60

tail(salaries_wins, n = 3)
## # A tibble: 3 × 2
##    year2  wins
##    <chr> <dbl>
## 1 w2002    37
## 2 w2001    19
## 3 w2000    29
```

We then call the cbind() function from base R to combine salaries_sals and salaries_wins into a new data set called salaries_cor2:

```
salaries_cor2 <- cbind(salaries_sals, salaries_wins)
dim(salaries_cor2)
## [1] 540    4

head(salaries_cor2, n = 3)
##    year1    salary year2 wins
## 1 s2017 95471579 w2017   43
## 2 s2016 72902950 w2016   48
## 3 s2015 58470278 w2015   60

tail(salaries_cor2, n = 3)
##      year1    salary year2 wins
## 538 s2002 54776087 w2002   37
## 539 s2001 59085969 w2001   19
## 540 s2000 53194441 w2000   29
```

The salaries_cor2 data set is 540 rows long and four columns wide with the following characteristics:

- Every payroll for every team is now consolidated into one column.
- Every regular season win total for every team is consolidated into one column.
- The variables year1 or year2 can be used as group identifiers.

This means we can write a chunk of dplyr code where we call the group_by() and summarize() functions to compute the correlation coefficient between the variables salary and wins for each factor, or unique identifier, in the variable year1 (or year2 if we wish). The results are cast into a tibble called tbl1:

```
salaries_cor2 %>%
  group_by(year1) %>%
  summarize(cor = round(cor(salary, wins, use = "complete.obs"),
    digits = 2)) -> tbl1
print(tbl1)
## # A tibble: 18 x 2
##     year1    cor
##     <chr> <dbl>
##  1 s2000   0.57
##  2 s2001   0.37
##  3 s2002   0.13
##  4 s2003   0.31
##  5 s2004   0.21
##  6 s2005   0.15
##  7 s2006   0.02
##  8 s2007   0.1
##  9 s2008   0.16
## 10 s2009   0.43
## 11 s2010   0.48
## 12 s2011   0.54
## 13 s2012   0.39
## 14 s2013   0.25
## 15 s2014   0.26
## 16 s2015   0.3
## 17 s2016   0.54
## 18 s2017   0.39
```

After all that, we now have our 18 correlation coefficients packed into a single data object that we will pull from to plot and analyze.

In the meantime, let's run a correlation test between payrolls and wins. We call the base R cor.test() function to determine if there is any meaningful or statistically significant relationship between the variables payrolls and wins. Our null hypothesis is no, but if our test returns a p-value, or a significance level, equal to or less than our predefined threshold of 0.05, we'll instead conclude that there is, in fact, a meaningful relationship between these two variables:

```
cor.test(salaries_cor2$salary, salaries_cor2$wins)
##
##  Pearson's product-moment correlation
##
## data:  salaries_cor2$salary and salaries_cor2$wins
## t = 4.9844, df = 533, p-value = 0.0000008417
## alternative hypothesis: true correlation is not equal to 0
## 95 percent confidence interval:
##   0.1285648 0.2906084
## sample estimates:
##       cor
## 0.2110361
```

The p-value is way below the 0.05 threshold for significance; therefore, we can reject the null hypothesis and instead accept the alternative hypothesis that the association between team payrolls and regular season wins between the 2000 and 2017 NBA seasons is statistically significant. It's important to also make the distinction between association and causation; our correlation test results, especially when considered in isolation of other results and inferences, are evidence of the former and not necessarily the latter.

VISUALIZING YEAR-OVER-YEAR CORRELATIONS

With that, let's now visualize the correlation between the variables s2000 and w2000, or between real salaries and regular season wins, from the 2000 season. We first call the select() function to subset the salaries data set on the variables Team, s2000, w2000, and pc2000, thereby creating a new data set called salaries2000. We then call the base R na.omit() function to ignore any and all values from salaries2000 that equal NA.

Here are the additional parameters:

- Our x-axis is Team Payrolls (s2000). We twice comingle the scale_x_continuous() function with the scales package to reformat the x-axis labels so that they include commas and US dollar signs.
- Our y-axis is Wins (w2000).
- The data points are increased three times their default size by adding the size = 3 argument to the geom_point() function.
- All NBA teams are thrown into one of three groups, depending on how their respective 2000 seasons ended. Put differently, the three levels in the variable pc2000—0, 10, and 11—are more or less converted to equal No playoffs, Made playoffs, and Won title, respectively.
- We call the geom_smooth() function twice to draw three trendlines without confidence intervals. Our first call to geom_smooth() draws trendlines for two of our three factors; the second call to geom_smooth() draws a third trendline across the entire data series, disregarding factors.
- A legend is added and affixed to the bottom on the plot.
- Our x-axis labels are rotated 45 degrees for fit.

Here's the code for our first plot:

```
salaries2000 <- select(salaries, Team, s2000, w2000, pc2000)
salaries2000 <- na.omit(salaries2000)

cor1 <- ggplot(salaries2000, aes(x = s2000, y = w2000,
                                 color = factor(pc2000))) +
  geom_point(size = 3) +
  labs(title = " Team Payrolls vs. Wins (1999-2000)",
       subtitle = "correlation coefficient = 0.57",
       x = "Team Payrolls",
       y = "Wins") +
  scale_x_continuous(labels = comma) +
  scale_x_continuous(labels = dollar) +
```

```
geom_smooth(method = lm, se = FALSE) +
geom_smooth(method = lm, color = "green4",
            data = salaries2000[salaries2000$s2000 > 20000000,],
            se = FALSE) +
theme(plot.title = element_text(face = "bold")) +
scale_color_manual(name = "",
                   labels = c("No playoffs",
                              "Made playoffs",
                              "Won title"),
                   values = c("0" = "navy",
                              "10" = "gold3",
                              "11" = "red")) +
theme(legend.position = "bottom") +
theme(axis.text.x = element_text(angle = 45, hjust = 1))
```

Let's now create a similar plot for 2001 by swapping out 2000 variables for 2001 but otherwise maintaining our previous syntax:

```
salaries2001 <- select(salaries, Team, s2001, w2001, pc2001)
salaries2001 <- na.omit(salaries2001)

cor2 <- ggplot(salaries2001, aes(x = s2001, y = w2001,
                                 color = factor(pc2001))) +
  geom_point(size = 3) +
  labs(title = " Team Payrolls vs. Wins (2000-01)",
       subtitle = "correlation coefficient = 0.37",
       x = "Team Payrolls", y = "Wins") +
  scale_x_continuous(labels = comma) +
  scale_x_continuous(labels = dollar) +
  geom_smooth(method = lm, se = FALSE) +
  geom_smooth(method = lm, color = "green4",
              data = salaries2001[salaries2001$s2001 > 20000000,],
              se = FALSE) +
  theme(plot.title = element_text(face = "bold")) +
  scale_color_manual(name = "",
                     labels = c("No playoffs",
                                "Made playoffs",
                                "Won title"),
                     values = c("0" = "navy",
                                "10" = "gold3",
                                "11" = "red")) +
  theme(legend.position = "bottom") +
  theme(axis.text.x = element_text(angle = 45, hjust = 1))
```

We then call the plot_layout() function from the patchwork package to return our two correlation plots as a single graphical object (see figure 10.3):

```
cor1 + cor2 + plot_layout(ncol = 2)
```

The remaining correlation plots, covering the 2002 to 2017 seasons, are displayed in the appendix to this book. All told, other than the statistical significance between payrolls and wins, we can draw the following conclusions, bearing in mind that correlation

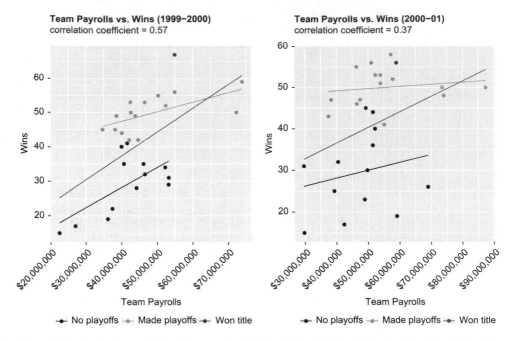

Figure 10.3   A pair of correlation plots, one for 2000 and the other for 2001, visualize the relationship between team payrolls and regular season wins.

coefficients will always equal some number between −1 and +1 and that results close to those extremes indicate a strong negative or positive relationship:

- Year over year, or season over season, there is a positive correlation between team payrolls and regular season wins. In other words, as payrolls increase, regular season wins increase.
- There appears to be no year-over-year consistency in the correlation coefficients and, in fact, a substantial amount of variance in our results. For instance, the correlation coefficient between team payrolls and regular season wins was as low as 0.02 in 2006 and as high as 0.57 in 2000.
- Additionally, we even see a lack of continuity in correlation coefficients between consecutive seasons. Take 2008 and 2009, for example, where the correlation coefficient between team payrolls and regular season wins jumped from 0.16 to 0.43.
- The few teams year over year with the highest payrolls almost always make the playoffs, while teams with the absolute lowest payrolls almost always fail to qualify for postseason play.
- Championship-winning teams are usually near the top in both regular season wins and payroll.

In addition, let's introduce and very briefly discuss the statistical phenomenon known as Simpson's Paradox. Simpson's Paradox is in play when the association between two variables, when cut into multiple subpopulations, is at odds with the association between the same pair of variables when otherwise examining the entire data series. Results from the 2012–13 season might be the best example (see the appendix). Overall, there is a positive correlation between payrolls and regular season wins. However, the relationships between these same variables are flat when the data is subset on our season-ending factors. We get this sort of insight by cutting the data and assigning different colors to different factors; there's absolutely no way we would see this if we had instead kept the data whole and not applied a color scheme.

PLOTTING CORRELATIONS OVER TIME

Our next visualization displays the year-over-year correlation coefficient between team payrolls and regular season wins using the tibble we created earlier as a data source. But first, we call the dplyr mutate() function and the built-in replace() and sprintf() functions to effectively overwrite all the values in the tbl1 variable year1 so that, for instance, s2014 is replaced by 14:

- We've previously called the mutate() function to create new, or derived, variables; here, it's called to help change out the values in an existing variable.
- The replace() function takes three arguments: the name of the vector we're modifying (year1), the elements we're replacing (all 18), and the replacement values (00 through 17).
- The sprintf() function formats character strings; here, we're instructing R to format the replacement values with two digits left of the decimal point and zero digits to the right. R would otherwise return 00 through 09 as 0, 1, 2, 3, and so on.

We then call the as.factor() function to convert year1 from a character string to a factor variable:

```
tbl1 %>%
  mutate(year1 = replace(year1, 1:18, sprintf("%02.0f", 00:17))) -> tbl1
tbl1$year1 <- as.factor(tbl1$year1)
print(tbl1)
## # A tibble: 18 × 2
##    year1   cor
##    <fct> <dbl>
##  1 00     0.57
##  2 01     0.37
##  3 02     0.13
##  4 03     0.31
##  5 04     0.21
##  6 05     0.15
##  7 06     0.02
##  8 07     0.1
##  9 08     0.16
## 10 09     0.43
## 11 10     0.48
## 12 11     0.54
## 13 12     0.39
## 14 13     0.25
## 15 14     0.26
## 16 15     0.3
```

```
## 17 16    0.54
## 18 17    0.39
```

We can now proceed with creating our visualization, a `ggplot2` line chart containing multiple trendlines, as follows:

- The tibble tbl1 is our data source, where the variable `year1` occupies the x-axis and the variable `cor` occupies the y-axis.
- Our first call to the `geom_smooth()` function draws one trendline over the entire data series. The argument `se = FALSE` tells R to *not* draw confidence intervals around the trendline.
- Our next and final two calls to the `geom_smooth()` function draw other trendlines covering mutually exclusive subsets of the data to accentuate a sharp change in trends starting in 2006.
- Finally, we call the `geom_segment()` and `annotate()` functions in succession four times to draw two vertical arrows and two horizontal arrows, and then we add complementary text. Arrows are drawn *from* the supplied x and y coordinates *to* the supplied xend and yend coordinates. Take note that the forward tip of an arrow is the endpoint. Arrows can be vertical, horizontal, or diagonal as well as up or down. The x and xend coordinates equal the positions of the x-axis tick marks, whereas the y and yend coordinates equal the correlation coefficient. The size of an arrow's head can be manipulated by playing or experimenting with the `unit()` function.
- By calling the `annotate()` function, we're adding text where the given x and y coordinates are the collective centerpoint. When adding shape and text layers to a `ggplot2` object, be prepared to perform a lot of experimentation before locking down your code.

Our `ggplot` code chunk is shown here:

```
p3 <- ggplot(tbl1, aes(x = year1, y = cor, group = 1)) +
  geom_line(aes(y = cor), color = "orange2", size = 2.5) +
  labs(title ="YoY Correlation between Payrolls and Wins",
       subtitle = "2000-17",
       x = "Season",
       y = "Correlation Coefficient") +
  geom_smooth(method = lm, color = "blue", se = FALSE) +
  geom_smooth(method = lm, color = "purple", se = FALSE,
          data = tbl1[as.numeric(tbl1$year1) < 08,]) +
  geom_smooth(method = lm, color = "red", se = FALSE,
          data = tbl1[as.numeric(tbl1$year1) > 06,]) +
  theme(plot.title = element_text(face = "bold")) +
  geom_segment(aes(x = 10,
                   y = 0.5,
                   xend = 11,
                   yend = 0.5),
               arrow = arrow(length = unit(0.3, "cm"))) +
  annotate("text", x = 8.7, y = 0.5,
           label = "YoY Correlations", size = 3) +
```

```
geom_segment(aes(x = 4,
                 y = 0.34,
                 xend = 3,
                 yend = 0.34),
             arrow = arrow(length = unit(0.3, "cm"))) +
annotate("text", x = 6.3, y = 0.34,
         label = "Trend between\n2000 and 2006", size = 3) +
geom_segment(aes(x = 11.5,
                 y = 0.24,
                 xend = 11.5,
                 yend = 0.29),
             arrow = arrow(length = unit(0.3, "cm"))) +
annotate("text", x = 11.5, y = 0.22,
         label = "Trend between\n2006 and 2017", size = 3) +
geom_segment(aes(x = 17.5,
                 y = 0.31,
                 xend = 17.5,
                 yend = 0.36),
             arrow = arrow(length = unit(0.3, "cm"))) +
annotate("text", x = 17.5, y = 0.27,
         label = "Trend\nbetween\n2000 and\n2017", size = 3)
print(p3)
```

The output is next (see figure 10.4). There is a slight upward trend in the correlation coefficient between 2000 and 2017. More significantly, however, two trends have been in effect: first, between 2000 and 2006, we see a sharp *downward* trend, and second,

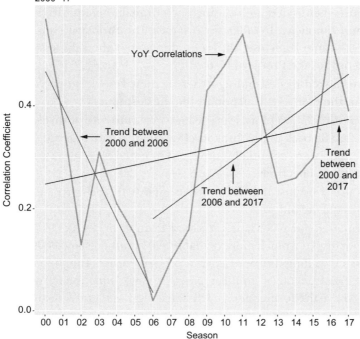

Figure 10.4 The year-over-year correlation coefficient between team payrolls and regular season wins, with three trendlines layered on top of the data. Correlation coefficients trended downward before the 2006 season and then trended sharply upward from 2006 forward.

from 2006 to 2017, we see an equally sharp *upward* trend. So while the correlation coefficient fluctuated year over year, sometimes substantially, our most important takeaway here is that the association between payrolls and wins is stronger post-2006 than it was pre-2006.

Let's pivot by exploring possible connections between team payrolls and where or how teams completed their seasons, regardless of how many games they won during the regular season.

10.4.2 *Payrolls versus end-of-season results*

Our journey continues with an examination of team payrolls plotted against one of three season-ending classifications for each team:

- Qualifies for postseason play but fails to win a title
- Qualifies for postseason play and wins the league championship
- Doesn't win enough regular season games and therefore doesn't make the playoffs

We'll visualize our results with a series of dot plots, one for each NBA season, where our data source for each is a temporary subset of the salaries data set. Following are a few additional notes about our dot plots:

- We're plotting real team payrolls or salaries, and not adjusted salaries; therefore, the x-axis variable in our first dot plot, for instance, is `s2000` rather than `sa2000`, where the former contains real 2000 salaries and the latter contains adjusted 2000 salaries.
- As previously mentioned, we're using current team names throughout for consistency and simplicity. In 2000, for instance, the Brooklyn Nets were the New Jersey Nets—same franchise, different name—but the salaries data set makes reference only to the Brooklyn Nets.
- Teams are ranked in descending order by their respective payrolls, hence the addition of the `reorder()` function inside the aesthetic.
- As with our correlation plots, every team is cast into one of three bins, or classifications, that tie back to the three-level variables `pc2000` to `pc2017` where the factors `0`, `10`, and `11` are essentially converted to equal `No playoffs`, `Made playoffs`, and `Won title`, respectively.
- Our dots are sized just the way our data points in the correlation plots were: three times the default size.
- We've formatted our x-axis labels (rotated again at 45 degrees for fit) so that, for instance, we display a much more readable $20 M rather than 20000000. We make this happen by calling the ggplot2 `scale_x_continuous()` function in conjunction with the `label_dollar()` and `cut_short_scale()` functions from the `scales` package, where the former adds a US dollar sign as a prefix to the x-axis labels, and the latter converts the same labels to millions and adds an M as a suffix.
- A legend is affixed to the bottom of each dot plot.

- Finally, before calling the `ggplot()` function and creating our dot plots, we preface that code by subsetting the salaries data set on just the variables required for the succeeding plot and then, when necessary, omitting any and all rows with NAs by calling the base R `na.omit()` function. We don't want to permanently delete all rows in salaries that might have a few NAs, so we instead create a temporary subset and then apply the `na.omit()` function. This is necessary because of franchise adds, moves, and changes between 2000 and 2004.

That being said, our first dot plot is created with the following chunk of code:

```
salaries2000 <- select(salaries, Team, s2000, pc2000)
salaries2000 <- na.omit(salaries2000)

dot1 <- ggplot(salaries2000) +
  geom_point(aes(x = s2000, y = reorder(Team, s2000),
                color = factor(pc2000)), size = 3) +
  labs(title= "NBA Team Payrolls (USD)",
       subtitle = "1999-2000",
       x = "Team Payroll",
       y = "") +
  scale_x_continuous(labels = label_dollar(scale_cut = cut_short_scale())) +
  theme(plot.title = element_text(face = "bold")) +
  scale_color_manual(name = "",
                     labels = c("No playoffs",
                                "Made playoffs",
                                "Won title"),
                     values = c("0" = "navy",
                                "10" = "gold3",
                                "11" = "red")) +
  theme(legend.position = "bottom") +
  theme(axis.text.x = element_text(angle = 45, hjust = 1))
```

We create our second dot plot—this one for the 2000–01 season—by changing out variables and creating a new, but temporary, subset of the salaries data set called salaries2001. Everything else remains consistent with our first dot plot:

```
salaries2001 <- select(salaries, Team, s2001, pc2001)
salaries2001 <- na.omit(salaries2001)

dot2 <- ggplot(salaries2001) +
  geom_point(aes(x = s2001, y = reorder(Team, s2001),
                color = factor(pc2001)), size = 3) +
  labs(title= "NBA Team Payrolls (USD)",
       subtitle = "2000-01",
       x = "Team Payroll",
       y = "") +
  scale_x_continuous(labels = label_dollar(scale_cut = cut_short_scale())) +
  theme(plot.title = element_text(face = "bold")) +
  scale_color_manual(name = "",
                     labels = c("No playoffs",
                                "Made playoffs",
                                "Won title"),
```

```
        values = c("0" = "navy",
                   "10" = "gold3",
                   "11" = "red")) +
   theme(legend.position = "bottom") +
   theme(axis.text.x = element_text(angle = 45, hjust = 1))
```

We bring our pair of dot plots together by again calling the `plot_layout()` function from the `patchwork` package and printing both visualizations as one graphical object (see figure 10.5):

```
dot1 + dot2 + plot_layout(ncol = 2)
```

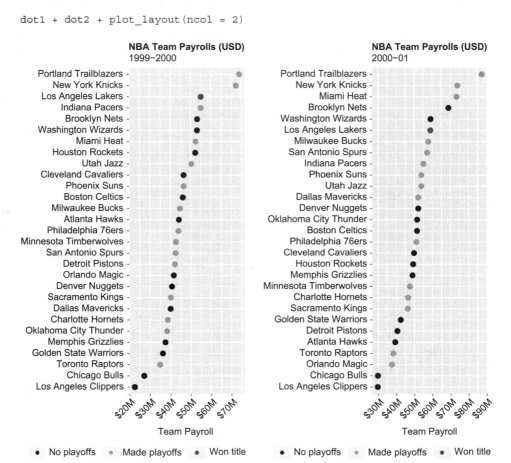

Figure 10.5   NBA team payrolls for the 1999–2000 and 2000–01 seasons ranked in descending order where the shades of the dots tie back to season-ending results

Dot plots for the remaining NBA seasons in our data set are in the appendix. Here's what these plots most significantly reveal from our data:

- League champions infrequently have the NBA's highest payroll. In fact, over the 18 seasons in our data set, just twice—in 2010 and again in 2016—did the league champion have the highest payroll.

- However, these same teams frequently have payrolls higher than 50% or more of the remaining teams and often have one of the NBA's highest payrolls.
- Teams with the highest payrolls usually make the playoffs; in fact, these teams usually have payrolls significantly, not just modestly, higher than all other teams.
- Teams with the lowest payrolls—teams with payrolls appreciably lower than the payrolls from all other teams—usually don't make the playoffs.
- That higher payrolls are mostly associated with successful teams and lower payrolls are mostly associated with less successful teams is more obvious and more prevalent in recent years than in the early 2000s.

Next, we'll compute the mean payroll year over year, comparing and contrasting teams that qualified for postseason play versus other teams that didn't versus the league champion. We'll visualize the results with a series of lollipop charts.

10.4.3 Payroll comparisons

Let's again pivot and take a year-over-year look at average team payrolls, sliced three ways just as before, where every team does one of the following:

- Qualifies for the playoffs but then fails to win a championship
- Wins the league championship
- Fails to even qualify for postseason play

We'll visualize these results for every NBA season between 2000 and 2017 with lollipop charts, a contemporary alternative to bar charts. The use cases for bar charts that were pitched back in chapter 2 apply just as well to lollipop charts.

First, however, we create a tibble to source each lollipop chart by executing the following commands:

- Tell R to ignore NA values where they exist in any per-season subset of the salaries data set.
- Compute the average salary for that season by each of our three season-ending classifications by calling the dplyr `group_by()` and `summarize()` functions and casting the results into a variable called mean.
- Call the `mutate()` function to create a new variable called mean2, where the values are essentially transformed versions of what is otherwise contained in the variable mean. The `paste()` function from base R is called to concatenate three terms—a US dollar sign, the corresponding value from the variable mean rounded to the nearest millionth, and a capital M—without any spaces separating each term. Consequently, a value such as 41611202 in mean is transformed to $42M in mean2.
- Convert the factors 0, 10, and 11 from the variables pc2000, pc2001, and so forth, to equal No playoffs, Made playoffs, and Won title, respectively.

Our lollipop charts have the following characteristics:

- Our three season-ending classifications run along the x-axis.
- The average team payroll is on the y-axis.

- The `geom_segment()` function draws three lollipops, one for each factor in our x-axis variable, with stems starting where y equals 0 and ending where y equals the mean payroll.

- The `geom_point()` function draws circles atop each stem based on our size, color, and fill specifications.

- Our y-axis labels—which are pulled from the variable `mean` rather than `mean2`—are transformed by calls to the ggplot2 `scale_y_continuous()` function and the scales `label_dollar()` and `cut_short_scale()` functions.

- The `geom_text()` function adds text inside the top of the lollipops that ties back to the variable `mean2`.

Our data wrangling and data visualization code for our first lollipop chart follows:

```
salaries2000 <- na.omit(salaries2000)

salaries2000 %>%
  group_by(pc2000) %>%
  summarize(mean = mean(s2000)) %>%
  mutate(mean2 = paste("$", round(mean/1000000),
                       "M", sep = "")) -> tbl2
  tbl2$pc2000 <- c("No playoffs", "Made playoffs", "Won title")

lol1 <- ggplot(tbl2, aes(x = pc2000, y = mean)) +
  geom_segment(aes(x = pc2000, xend = pc2000,
                   y = 0, yend = mean)) +
  geom_point(size = 15, color = c("navy", "gold3", "red"),
             fill = c("navy", "gold3", "red")) +
    labs(title = "Team Payroll Comparisons (USD)",
         subtitle = "1999-2000",
         x = "",
         y = "Averqge Team Payroll") +
  scale_y_continuous(labels =
                       label_dollar(scale_cut = cut_short_scale())) +
  scale_x_discrete(limits = c("No playoffs", "Made playoffs",
                              "Won title")) +
  geom_text(aes(label = mean2), color = "white",
            fontface = "bold", size = 3) +
  theme(plot.title = element_text(face = "bold")) +
  theme(axis.text.x = element_text(angle = 45, hjust = 1))
```

Following is the data wrangling and data visualization code chunk for our second lollipop chart, where we've merely swapped out 2000 variables for their 2001 equivalents:

```
salaries2001 <- na.omit(salaries2001)

salaries2001 %>%
  group_by(pc2001) %>%
  summarize(mean = mean(s2001)) %>%
  mutate(mean2 = paste("$", round(mean/1000000),
                       "M", sep = "")) -> tbl2
  tbl2$pc2001 <- c("No playoffs", "Made playoffs", "Won title")

lol2 <- ggplot(tbl2, aes(x = pc2001, y = mean)) +
```

```
geom_segment(aes(x = pc2001, xend = pc2001, y = 0, yend = mean)) +
geom_point(size = 15, color = c("navy", "gold3", "red"),
           fill = c("navy", "gold3", "red")) +
  labs(title = "Team Payroll Comparisons (USD)",
       subtitle = "2000-01",
       x = "",
       y = "Averqge Team Payroll") +
scale_y_continuous(labels =
                    label_dollar(scale_cut = cut_short_scale())) +
scale_x_discrete(limits = c("No playoffs", "Made playoffs",
                            "Won title")) +
geom_text(aes(label = mean2), color = "white",
          fontface = "bold", size = 3) +
theme(plot.title = element_text(face = "bold")) +
theme(axis.text.x = element_text(angle = 45, hjust = 1))
```

Once again, we consolidate our two charts by calling the `plot_layout()` function from the `patchwork` package and printing both visualizations as a single object (see figure 10.6):

```
lol1 + lol2 + plot_layout(ncol = 2)
```

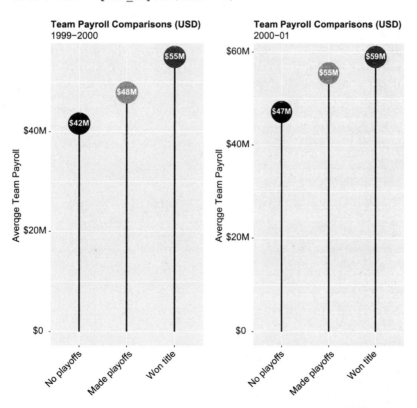

Figure 10.6   NBA team payroll comparisons for the 1999–2000 and 2000–01 seasons broken down by three season-ending classifications. The No playoffs and Made playoffs figures represent the average payroll for all teams rolling up to those respective classifications, where, of course, the Won title figure is the actual payroll for the one team that won the league title.

Here's what our series of lollipop charts tells us about the data (the remainder of these, like our correlation plots and dot plots, are in the appendix):

- More frequently than not, championship-winning teams have payrolls equal to or greater than the average payroll for all other teams that qualified for postseason play. Just as frequently, teams that make the playoffs but don't win a title have payrolls equal to or greater than the average payroll for those teams that fail to make the playoffs.
- *Both* conditions are true in 11 of the 18 seasons in our data set, including 9 of the last 11 seasons.
- In *every* year between 2000 and 2017, the average payroll for teams that made the playoffs but failed to win a title is equal to or (usually) greater than the average payroll for teams that failed to make the postseason.

Let's now redirect some of the data wrangling operations we ran earlier toward adjusted salaries as a way of summarizing and visualizing in one snapshot the average salary spends between our three season-ending classifications and across the breadth of the salaries data set. First, we call the dplyr select() function to subset the salaries data set on the variables between sa2017 and sa2000. Then, we call the tidyr pivot_longer() function to transform our results from a wide to a long format. The results are cast to a tibble called salaries_mean, which we can view by examining the returns from the dim(), head(), and tail() functions:

```
salaries %>%
  select(sa2017:sa2000) %>%
  pivot_longer(col = c(sa2017:sa2000),
               names_to = "year1",
               values_to = "salary") -> salaries_mean
dim(salaries_mean)
## [1] 540    2

head(salaries_mean, n = 3)
## # A tibble: 3 x 2
##    year1    salary
##    <chr>     <dbl>
## 1 sa2017 102154590
## 2 sa2016  80193245
## 3 sa2015  64902009

tail(salaries_mean, n = 3)
## # A tibble: 3 x 2
##    year1    salary
##    <chr>     <dbl>
## 1 sa2002 79973087
## 2 sa2001 88038094
## 3 sa2000 81387495
```

We repeat these very same operations, except this time we swap out the adjusted salary variables in favor of the variables pc2017 through pc2000, thereby creating yet another tibble, salaries_flag:

```
salaries %>%
  select(pc2017:pc2000) %>%
  pivot_longer(col = c(pc2017:pc2000),
               names_to = "year2",
               values_to = "flag") -> salaries_flag
dim(salaries_flag)
## [1] 540    2

head(salaries_flag, n = 3)
## # A tibble: 3 × 2
##    year2    flag
##    <chr>   <dbl>
## 1 pc2017      10
## 2 pc2016      10
## 3 pc2015      10

tail(salaries_flag, n = 3)
## # A tibble: 3 × 2
##    year2    flag
##    <chr>   <dbl>
## 1 pc2002       0
## 2 pc2001       0
## 3 pc2000       0
```

We then call the base R cbind() function to combine salaries_mean and salaries_flag into a single data set called salaries2:

```
salaries2 <- cbind(salaries_mean, salaries_flag)
dim(salaries2)
## [1] 540    4

head(salaries2, n = 3)
##    year1     salary  year2 flag
## 1 sa2017 102154590 pc2017   10
## 2 sa2016  80193245 pc2016   10
## 3 sa2015  64902009 pc2015   10

tail(salaries2, n = 3)
##      year1   salary  year2 flag
## 538 sa2002 79973087 pc2002    0
## 539 sa2001 88038094 pc2001    0
## 540 sa2000 81387495 pc2000    0
```

Finally, we tell R to ignore NAs in salaries2 by calling the base R na.omit() function and then write a chunk of dplyr code. We call the group_by() and summarize() functions to compute the average adjusted salary between 2000 and 2017 by each factor in the salaries2 variable called flag, which matches our three end-of-season classifications. We then call the mutate() function to create a variable called mean2, which is a transformed yet cleaner version of the variable `mean`. Our results are cast to a tibble called tbl3:

```
salaries2 <- na.omit(salaries2)

salaries2 %>%
  group_by(flag) %>%
  summarize(mean = mean(salary, na.rm = TRUE)) %>%
  mutate(mean2 = paste("$", round(mean/1000000),"M", sep = "")) -> tbl3
print(tbl3)
## # A tibble: 3 x 3
##    flag      mean mean2
##   <int>     <dbl> <chr>
## 1     0 78363267. $78M
## 2    10 85059950. $85M
## 3    11 88149764. $88M
```

We next create one more lollipop chart, this time displaying the average team payrolls adjusted for inflation between the 2000 and 2017 seasons broken down by our three season-ending classifications (see figure 10.7). The one aesthetic difference between this lollipop chart and the others we previously created is that here we've added a light blue border around the plot by calling the `theme()` function a second time:

```
tbl3$flag <- c("No playoffs", "Made playoffs", "Won title")
p4 <- ggplot(tbl3, aes(x = flag, y = mean)) +
  geom_segment(aes(x = flag, xend = flag,
                   y = 0, yend = mean)) +
  geom_point(size = 15, color = c("navy", "gold3", "red"),
             fill = c("navy", "gold3", "red")) +
  labs(title = "Adjusted Team Payroll Comparisons (2021 USD)",
       subtitle = "2000-2017 Seasons",
       x = "",
       y = "Averqge Team Payroll\nAdjusted for Inflation") +
  scale_y_continuous(labels =
                       label_dollar(scale_cut = cut_short_scale())) +
  scale_x_discrete(limits = c("No playoffs", "Made playoffs",
                              "Won title")) +
  geom_text(aes(label = mean2), color = "white",
            fontface = "bold", size = 3) +
  theme(plot.title = element_text(face = "bold")) +
  theme(panel.border = element_rect(fill = "transparent",
                                    color = "lightskyblue", size = 2))
print(p4)
```

Teams that win titles, on average, spend more on player salaries than teams that make the playoffs but don't win a championship; and playoff-qualifying teams spend, on average, more on player salaries than teams that fail to qualify for postseason play. Moreover, the difference in average salaries between teams that won a championship versus other teams that make the playoffs is minimal (only $3 M), whereas the subsequent difference separating postseason teams and those teams that don't make the postseason is more substantial ($8 M).

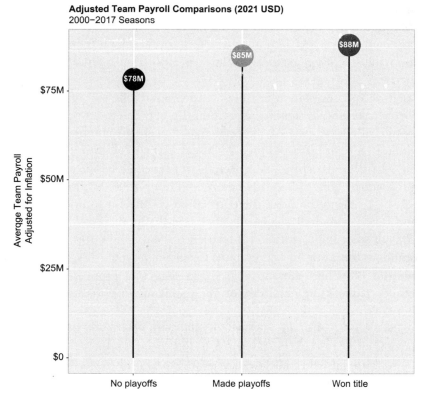

Figure 10.7 Payroll comparisons where the amounts have been adjusted for inflation

We'll work with the same data set in chapter 11, first by quantifying and visualizing per-team payrolls for every regular season win, and second by building an unsupervised learning algorithm that segments the NBA's 30 teams into like clusters based on a combination of salary spends and their regular season win totals.

Summary

- We demonstrated the full power of R in this chapter. For instance, we called on base R functions such as `cor()` and `cor.test()` to deliver some of our most significant and nifty results.
- We then went beyond base R to create compelling but not-so-common visualizations such as dot plots and lollipop charts. We even called on other packaged functions to transform our `ggplot2` labels to make our visualizations that much more aesthetically pleasing. Dare to go beyond conventional visualizations, and never hesitate to add or modify aesthetics, such as transforming x- and y-axis labels to more readable formats, when and where it adds value for your readers.

- Know your options when it comes to NAs in your data. Here, we performed several operations by ignoring NAs. In chapters 2 and 3, we removed records that contained several NAs, but, in other cases, you may want to impute data.

- Don't rely on just one test when two or more would tell a more compelling story.

- Based on our correlation test between team payrolls and regular season wins, there is a statistically significant relationship between the two. While correlation doesn't, of course, necessarily mean causation, when bumped up against other evidence, it's hard to avoid the conclusion that payrolls influence wins.

- The year-over-year correlation coefficient between payrolls and regular season wins trended quite differently before and after 2006. While hardly consistent from one year to the next, the correlation coefficient trended downward and then upward, thereby suggesting that payrolls more recently matter more in terms of wins and losses than they used to. Make the effort to insert multiple trendlines into your time-series plots to tell a complete story.

- Our dot plots and lollipop charts also suggest a more definite association between payrolls and qualifying or not qualifying for postseason play, especially after 2006.

- Teams with the absolute highest payrolls, with very few exceptions, reach the playoffs.

- Teams with the absolute lowest payrolls, with even fewer exceptions, fail to make the playoffs.

- Championship-winning teams almost always have one of the league's highest payrolls, especially recently.

- Along the way, we demonstrated several techniques that can bump up your ggplot2 visualizations a notch or two—transforming axis labels without having to change your data source, adding legends, inserting annotations and shapes, and color-coding data points by factor levels. These sorts of touches can avert questions about the data and instead allow people to focus on analyzing it.

- Finally, we introduced Simpson's Paradox and demonstrated how to reveal it. Simpson's Paradox, while maybe excessive and not terribly prevalent, is nevertheless a critical statistical phenomenon to be familiar with. Conclusions drawn on an entire data series may actually be the exact opposite of the truth for every subpopulation of the same.

K-means clustering

This chapter covers

- Developing a K-means clustering algorithm
- Computing and visualizing optimal cluster counts
- Understanding standard deviations and computing z-scores
- Creating Cleveland dot plots

Our primary purpose in this chapter is to demonstrate how to develop a K-means clustering algorithm. K-means clustering is a popular unsupervised learning method and multivariate analysis technique that enables purposeful and made-to-order strategies around smart clusters, or groups, cut from the data. Unsupervised learning is a learning method where the goal is to find patterns, structures, or relationships in data using only input variables and therefore no target, or output, data. By contrast, supervised learning methods use both input and output variables, usually to make predictions. In the former, you have no idea what you might be looking for; in the latter, you've already figured that out. Multivariate analysis refers to statistical techniques and methods used to analyze and understand relationships among two or more variables simultaneously.

The most obvious application for K-means clustering—maybe even the most proven—is customer segmentation. K-means is used to segment customers based on, for example, prior purchases; demographic variables such as age, gender, and home address; and other attributes. Companies with this sort of insight can then develop different marketing strategies for different clusters of customers, which in turn can drive sales and bump customer satisfaction scores.

The most significant differentiator in K-means clustering from hierarchical clustering is that K-means requires a predetermined number of clusters, denoted as *K*, to run. It's perfectly acceptable to experiment with different cluster counts or even run the algorithm on a fixed number of clusters. However, there are methods to determine an optimal number of clusters based on differentiation in the data. We'll demonstrate two of those methods, and then we'll run the K-means algorithm and analyze the results. We'll even experiment with incrementally different values for *K* and evaluate the sequential changes in the results.

Before that, we'll get you grounded by introducing a discussion on standard deviations and z-scores (K-means clusters are visualized in a two-dimensional plane where the raw data has been standardized) and then by plotting a pair of unlike numeric variables that have been converted to like scales.

Whereas in chapter 10 we examined the relationship between team payrolls and regular season wins, postseason appearances, and league championships at an aggregate level, in this chapter, we'll be concentrating on payrolls and wins down to the team level. First, we'll load the same set of packages we loaded near the beginning of the prior chapter, plus one new package for our K-means clustering.

11.1 Loading packages

Our one new package is `factoextra`, which is a popular package for extracting and plotting the results of multivariate data analyses, including K-means clustering. We'll call one function from `factoextra` to compute and visualize optimal cluster counts and then a second function to plot our clusters. Otherwise, our first order of business is to make four successive calls to the `library()` function to load `factoextra` plus three other packages you're already familiar with:

```
library(tidyverse)
library(scales)
library(patchwork)
library(factoextra)
```

Next, we'll import and take a glance at our data.

11.2 Importing data

In the previous chapter, we worked briefly with a data set called cap and then quite extensively with another data set called salaries. In this chapter, we'll work exclusively with salaries. Our second order of business is to therefore call the `readr` `read_csv()` function to (again) import the salaries data set:

```
salaries <- read_csv("salaries.csv")
```

Here are a few reminders about the salaries data set:

- The data set contains 30 rows—one row for every NBA team. Some teams relocated between the 2000 and 2017 seasons (which is the time horizon of our data) and changed their name as a result. The Supersonics moved from Seattle to Oklahoma City and are now the Oklahoma City Thunder; the Nets moved from New Jersey to Brooklyn and are now known as the Brooklyn Nets rather than the New Jersey Nets. But the data is nevertheless consigned to one observation per team; the salaries data set contains current team names only.

- There are 73 columns. Other than the variable Team, salaries is more or less divided into four 18-column sections, where each column represents an NBA season between 2000 and 2017: real salaries (numeric), inflation-adjusted salaries (numeric), regular season wins (numeric), and season-ending disposition (categorical). In this chapter, we'll concern ourselves only with adjusted salaries (these are player salaries that, when summed for every factor in the variable Team and grouped by season, equal a team's payroll) and regular season wins.

- Because the Charlotte Hornets and New Orleans Pelicans, unlike the other NBA teams, played in just 16 and 15 seasons, respectively, between 2000 and 2017, we're obligated to wrangle the salaries data set and make other adjustments that would otherwise be unnecessary. You'll see these momentarily.

In the following code, we pipe the salaries data set to a pair of dplyr functions—first to the select() function to subset salaries on the variables Team, sa2017 (equal to 2017 adjusted salaries), and w2017 (equal to 2017 regular season wins); and second, to the glimpse() function, which returns a transposed view of our salaries subset:

```
salaries %>%
  select(Team, sa2017, w2017) %>%
  glimpse
## Rows: 30
## Columns: 3
## $ Team   <chr> "Atlanta Hawks", "Boston Celtics", "Brooklyn Nets", "Ch…
## $ sa2017 <dbl> 102154590, 93381390, 78031675, 106764924, 100891769, 13…
## $ w2017  <dbl> 43, 53, 20, 36, 41, 51, 33, 40, 37, 67, 55, 42, 51, 26,…
```

Before we wrangle and analyze our data, it's important to get grounded in standard deviations and z-scores first.

11.3 A primer on standard deviations and z-scores

Understanding the basics of standard deviations and z-scores will serve us well in this chapter and beyond. Back in chapter 2, we mentioned that when data is normally distributed, approximately 68% of it would be within one standard deviation from the mean, plus or minus; 95% would be within two standard deviations from the mean; and all but a few outliers would be within three standard deviations from the mean. In chapter 7, we conducted Cohen's d effect size tests, which measure the difference in

two means from a pooled standard deviation. So we've at least had some prior exposure to standard deviations, but let's go a little deeper.

Standard deviation is a statistical measure that quantifies the amount of variability,
or dispersion, in a numeric vector. A low standard deviation indicates that the data is
closely gathered around the mean; a high standard deviation, on the other hand, indicates that the data, or much of it, is spread out. A z-score is a statistical measure that
represents the number of standard deviations a single data point is from the mean of
its distribution.

Let's create a small data frame to demonstrate. We first make two calls to the base
R `c()` function to create a pair of numeric vectors, `var1` and `var2`, that each contain
five values. Then, we pass `var1` and `var2` to the base R `data.frame()` function to create a
data frame called df—simple and straightforward:

```
var1 <- c(2, 4, 6, 8, 10)
var2 <- c(1, 2, 3, 10, 14)
df <- data.frame(var1, var2)
print(df)
##   var1 var2
## 1    2    1
## 2    4    2
## 3    6    3
## 4    8   10
## 5   10   14
```

But computing the standard deviation by hand or by using a spreadsheet application
such as Microsoft Excel or Google Sheets actually requires six steps. Let's use `var1` as
an example:

1 Find the mean by adding the values in `var1` and dividing the sum by the number of observations. This equals 6.
2 Find each value's deviation from the mean by subtracting the mean from each
   value. For the first value in `var1`, the deviation equals $2 - 6$, or -4.
3 Square each deviation from the mean by itself so that, for instance, -4
   becomes 16.
4 Find the sum of squares by adding the squared deviations. This equals 40.
5 Find the variance, which equals the sum of squares divided by $n - 1$, where n
   equals the number of observations. This equals $40 \div 4$, or 10.
6 Take the square root of the variance to get the standard deviation. This
   equals 3.16.

Fortunately, we can instead just pass `var1` and `var2` to the base R `sd()` function to get
the standard deviations:

```
sd(df$var1)
## [1] 3.162278
sd(df$var2)
## [1] 5.700877
```

Both vectors have the same means, but the standard deviation for var2 is almost double the standard deviation for var1. In other words, the mean can be indicative of a sample or population if and when the standard deviation is low, but when the standard deviation is high, the mean can actually be misleading.

Let's now compute the z-score for each value in both var1 and var2. To get the z-score for any data point, we subtract the mean from the value and divide the difference by the standard deviation. In R, we simply pass df to the dplyr mutate() function to create a pair of new variables, zvar1 and zvar2, and append them to our data frame:

```
df %>%
  mutate(zvar1 = (var1 - mean(var1)) / sd(var1),
         zvar2 = (var2 - mean(var2)) / sd(var2)) -> df
print(df)
##   var1 var2      zvar1       zvar2
## 1    2    1 -1.2649111 -0.8770580
## 2    4    2 -0.6324555 -0.7016464
## 3    6    3  0.0000000 -0.5262348
## 4    8   10  0.6324555  0.7016464
## 5   10   14  1.2649111  1.4032928
```

The middle value in var1, for example, equals the var1 mean, so it therefore has a z-score equal to 0; the middle value in var2 has a z-score equal to –0.53, which means it's approximately half a standard deviation below the var2 mean.

Standard deviations and z-scores provide context that we can't always get from the raw data. The Boston Celtics spent just over $1.5 billion (B) in player salaries between the 2000 and 2017 seasons. That's a tremendous amount of money—or is it? When we then compute the z-score, we get 0.21; in other words, Boston's total spent on player salaries between 2000 and 2017 was just 0.21 standard deviations above the league mean—that is, barely average.

Standard deviations are also key for performing unbiased multivariate analysis. When evaluating the association between a pair of numeric variables that are on very different scales—such as team payrolls and regular season wins—it's absolutely essential to put both variables on the same scale before completing your analysis to avoid getting results that are weighted toward one variable at the expense of the other. We do that by standardizing the data and computing z-scores. That is just what we'll be doing in the first half of our analysis and again when we compute our K-means clusters.

11.4 Analysis

We established in chapter 10 that a positive correlation exists between team payrolls and regular season wins, at least between the 2000 and 2017 NBA seasons; in fact, the correlation incrementally increased—not linearly, but it nevertheless increased overall—from 2006 through 2017. Furthermore, we ran a correlation test that returned a p-value below the 5% threshold, thereby indicating that the association between team payrolls and regular season wins is, in fact, statistically significant.

Our purpose here is to further interrogate the salaries data set and twice visualize, down to the team level, the relationship between payrolls and wins. We'll first demonstrate how to create what is called a `ggplot2` Cleveland dot plot, where payrolls and wins are displayed by dots on the same standardized scale. Then, we'll show you how to create a `ggplot2` horizontal bar chart, sorted by payroll amounts per regular season win, where the data is in its raw format.

As you might suspect by now, our data must first be wrangled some to support our ongoing analysis. We'll take care of those needs next.

11.4.1 *Wrangling data*

As previously mentioned, the NBA was a 29-team league between 2000 and 2004 and then a 30-team league every season thereafter; minor adjustments are therefore required to offset missing or Not Available (NA) values in our data and to ensure we return fair and accurate results. Furthermore, the raw data by itself is insufficient for the analysis we have in mind, so we have no choice but to transform and augment salaries in ways that weren't needed in the prior chapter.

The Charlotte Hornets and New Orleans Pelicans are the two teams in the salaries data set with missing data because neither team was around every year between 2000 and 2004. As such, we're about to create three mostly similar data sets subset from salaries: one fixed for the Hornets, another fixed for the Pelicans, and a third fixed for the remaining 28 teams. At the end, we'll combine these into one data set for plotting and analysis.

We'll start with the Hornets, who were active during 16 of the 18 NBA seasons in our data set. We therefore call the `dplyr filter()` function to subset the salaries data set where the variable `Team` equals Charlotte Hornets, thereby creating a new object called cha.

However, before moving forward with that and other data wrangling operations, let's disable scientific notation by passing the `scipen = 999` argument to the base R `options()` function:

```
options(scipen = 999)
```

Later on, we'll actually re-enable scientific notation:

```
salaries %>%
  filter(Team == "Charlotte Hornets") -> cha
```

We then call the `dplyr select()` function to reduce the cha data set so that it only includes the 33 columns, or variables, we absolutely need going forward—these being `Team`, the 16 adjusted salary variables, and the 16 regular season wins variables. We're purposely excluding the 2003 and 2004 seasons and the NAs in our data:

```
cha %>%
  select(Team, sa2017:sa2005, sa2002:sa2000, w2017:w2005,
         w2002:w2000) -> cha
```

Next, we call the `mutate()` function to create four derived variables:

- The first variable, `sumSalaries`, equals the sum of the adjusted salary variables in positions 2 through 17.
- The second variable, `sumWins`, equals the sum of the regular season wins variables in positions 18 through 33.
- The third variable, `efficiency`, equals the sum of variables 2 through 17 divided by the sum of variables 18 through 33. We're therefore summing the adjusted salary for 16 seasons and dividing it by the number of regular season wins the Hornets had over those same 16 seasons.
- The fourth and final variable, `meanWins`, equals the sum of variables 18 through 33 divided by 16 seasons, rounded to the nearest whole number. It's therefore computing and returning the average number of Charlotte Hornets wins per regular season.

Following are a few notes about the following chunk of code:

- The `rowSums()` function is a built-in R function that sums numeric variables by row in a data set (the cha data set contains just one row of data). There is also a base R `colSums()` function that does the same for columns.
- Square brackets are used for indexing a vector, matrix, array, list, or data frame; they are sometimes referred to as extraction operators when they are specifically used to extract a subset of elements from the same.
- The dots (`.`) are used as substitutes for cha, so they represent pointers to the cha data set:

```
cha %>%
  mutate(sumSalaries = rowSums(.[2:17]),
         sumWins = rowSums(.[18:33]),
         efficiency = rowSums(.[2:17]) / rowSums(.[18:33]),
         meanWins = round(rowSums(.[18:33]) / 16)) -> cha
```

Finally, we pipe the cha data set to the `dplyr` `select()` function and create a new object, cha_final, which contains only the variable `Team` plus the four derived variables we just created:

```
cha %>%
  select(Team, sumSalaries, sumWins, efficiency, meanWins) -> cha_final
print(cha_final)
##                Team sumSalaries sumWins efficiency meanWins
## 1 Charlotte Hornets  1124300389     549    2047906       34
```

We then repeat this exercise two times, once for the New Orleans Pelicans and again for the remainder of the NBA, creating two new data sets, nop_final and league_final, in the process.

The league_final data set should include records for every NBA team *except* the Charlotte Hornets and New Orleans Pelicans. We therefore call the logical operator not equal to (!=) to pull every record in the salaries data set where the variable Team doesn't equal Charlotte Hornets or New Orleans Pelicans:

```
salaries %>%
  filter(Team == "New Orleans Pelicans") -> nop

nop %>%
  select(Team, sa2017:sa2003, w2017:w2003) -> nop

nop %>%
  mutate(sumSalaries = rowSums(.[2:16]),
         sumWins = rowSums(.[17:31]),
         efficiency = rowSums(.[2:16]) / rowSums(.[17:31]),
         meanWins = round(rowSums(.[17:31]) / 15)) -> nop

nop %>%
  select(Team, sumSalaries, sumWins, efficiency, meanWins) -> nop_final
print(nop_final)
##                   Team sumSalaries sumWins efficiency meanWins
## 1 New Orleans Pelicans  1150489652     562    2047135       37

salaries %>%
  filter(Team != "Charlotte Hornets" &
         Team != "New Orleans Pelicans") -> league

league %>%
  select(Team, sa2017:sa2000, w2017:w2000) -> league

league %>%
  mutate(sumSalaries = rowSums(.[2:19]),
         sumWins = rowSums(.[20:37]),
         efficiency = rowSums(.[2:19]) / rowSums(.[20:37]),
         meanWins = round(rowSums(.[20:37]) / 18)) -> league

league %>%
  select(Team, sumSalaries, sumWins, efficiency, meanWins) -> league_final
print(league_final)
##                    Team sumSalaries sumWins efficiency meanWins
## 1        Atlanta Hawks  1331370577     672    1981206       37
## 2       Boston Celtics  1502338683     782    1921149       43
## 3        Brooklyn Nets  1572394745     635    2476212       35
## 4        Chicago Bulls  1350128086     696    1939839       39
## 5  Cleveland Cavaliers  1513579016     715    2116894       40
## 6    Dallas Mavericks  1793863099     911    1969114       51
## 7       Denver Nuggets  1359921484     741    1835252       41
## 8      Detroit Pistons  1374565213     750    1832754       42
## 9 Golden State Warriors 1401640477     709    1976926       39
## 10     Houston Rockets  1464712564     810    1808287       45
## 11      Indiana Pacers  1464126069     781    1874681       43
## 12 Los Angeles Clippers 1307071048     681    1919341       38
## 13   Los Angeles Lakers  1682631996     821    2049491       46
## 14    Memphis Grizzlies  1436199380     681    2108957       38
## 15          Miami Heat  1575463391     815    1933084       45
## 16      Milwaukee Bucks  1423272015     657    2166320       36
```

```
## 17 Minnesota Timberwolves  1424852176   616  2313072   34
## 18         New York Knicks  2034231301   626  3249571   35
## 19   Oklahoma City Thunder  1360935249   790  1722703   44
## 20           Orlando Magic  1494331249   694  2153215   39
## 21      Philadelphia 76ers  1471662937   638  2306682   35
## 22            Phoenix Suns  1420327702   777  1827964   43
## 23   Portland Trailblazers  1815095481   773  2348118   43
## 24        Sacramento Kings  1398565630   677  2065828   38
## 25      San Antonio Spurs   1458067975  1040  1401988   58
## 26         Toronto Raptors  1418504110   695  2041013   39
## 27              Utah Jazz   1333886430   786  1697057   44
## 28     Washington Wizards   1443384399   615  2346967   34
```

We then call the built-in `rbind()` function to combine the cha_final, nop_final, and league_final data sets by rows into a single object called final. The `head()` function returns the first six observations:

```
final <- rbind(cha_final, nop_final, league_final)
head(final)
##                    Team sumSalaries sumWins efficiency meanWins
## 1     Charlotte Hornets  1124300389     549    2047906       34
## 2 New Orleans Pelicans  1150489652     562    2047135       37
## 3         Atlanta Hawks  1331370577     672    1981206       37
## 4        Boston Celtics  1502338683     782    1921149       43
## 5         Brooklyn Nets  1572394745     635    2476212       35
## 6         Chicago Bulls  1350128086     696    1939839       39
```

Now that we have our data consolidated into a single object, we'll call the `mutate()` function twice to create a pair of additional derived variables that both require computations within numeric vectors. The variable zSalaries equals the z-score, sometimes called a standard score, for the variable sumSalaries. Once more, the z-score represents the number of standard deviations a data point is above or below the distribution mean; it's computed by subtracting the distribution mean from the raw data and dividing the difference by the standard deviation. If the variable sumSalaries were normally distributed, we could expect approximately 20 NBA teams, or two-thirds of the league, to be within one standard deviation of the mean and maybe all but one or two teams to be within two standard deviations of the mean. The variable zWins equals the z-score for the variable sumWins.

Subsequent calls to the `head()` and `tail()` functions return the first three and last three observations:

```
final %>%
  mutate(zSalaries = (sumSalaries - mean(sumSalaries)) / sd(sumSalaries),
         zWins = (sumWins - mean(sumWins)) / sd(sumWins)) -> final

head(final, n = 3)
## # A tibble: 3 × 7
##   Team                sumSalaries sumWins efficiency meanWins
##   <chr>                     <dbl>   <dbl>      <dbl>    <dbl>
## 1 Charlotte Hornets    1124300389     549   2047906.       34
```

```
## 2 New Orleans Pelicans  1150489652    562   2047135.      37
## 3 Atlanta Hawks          1331370577    672   1981206.      37
##    zSalaries  zWins
##        <dbl>  <dbl>
## 1      -1.86  -1.71
## 2      -1.71  -1.58
## 3     -0.723 -0.501

tail(final, n = 3)
## # A tibble: 3 × 7
##   Team                sumSalaries sumWins efficiency meanWins
##   <chr>                     <dbl>   <dbl>      <dbl>    <dbl>
## 1 Toronto Raptors      1418504110     695   2041013.       39
## 2 Utah Jazz            1333886430     786   1697057.       44
## 3 Washington Wizards   1443384399     615   2346967.       34
##    zSalaries  zWins
##        <dbl>  <dbl>
## 1     -0.246 -0.276
## 2     -0.710  0.616
## 3     -0.110 -1.06
```

Take the Utah Jazz, as just one example. (By the way, the Utah Jazz once played their home games in New Orleans; when they moved to Salt Lake City, they decided to keep their name as the Jazz, which is what most NBA teams do when relocating.) Utah spent just over $1.3 B in player salaries between 2000 and 2017. They won 786 regular season games over those 18 seasons, an average of 44 wins per season. Therefore, they spent about $1.7 M in player salaries for every regular season win. Their total spend in salaries was 0.71 standard deviations below the league mean, and their regular season wins were 0.62 standard deviations above the mean.

11.4.2 *Evaluating payrolls and wins*

We plan to evaluate team payrolls and regular season wins between the 2000 and 2017 NBA seasons by creating a Cleveland dot plot and then a horizontal bar chart. Our analysis will set us up well for what comes next: K-means clustering.

CLEVELAND DOT PLOT

Our first visualization, a ggplot2 Cleveland dot plot, displays the difference between our standardized variables for all 30 NBA teams; in other words, it shows how close or how distant investments are to returns (see figure 11.1). One of the goals of this book is to introduce visualizations, mostly through the ggplot2 graphics package, that might be outside the mainstream, discuss when they should best be presented, and demonstrate how to create them. A Cleveland dot plot, designed by prominent statistician and data visualization expert William S. Cleveland, is the next visualization in line, as described here:

- The NBA's 30 teams are sorted in alphabetical order along the x-axis. The labels are angled at 45 degrees and aligned horizontally just beneath the plot.
- Our y-axis measure is standard deviations, or z-scores.

- The geom_segment() function draws 30 lines perpendicular to the x-axis, each of which connects a pair of points, or dots, created by two calls to the geom_point() function, starting where y equals zSalaries and ending where y equals zWins.
- The points representing the variable zSalaries are drawn in a dark hue, whereas the points representing the variable zWins are drawn in a light hue. All points are increased in size by a factor of three times the ggplot2 default.
- The \n in the caption acts as a carriage return. By default, captions are placed in the lower-right area and are right-justified.

Following is the code chunk for our Cleveland dot plot:

```
p1 <- ggplot(final) +
  geom_segment(aes(x = Team, xend = Team,
                   y = zSalaries, yend = zWins), color = "grey50") +
  geom_point(aes(x = Team, y = zSalaries), color = "springgreen3",
             size = 3) +
  geom_point(aes(x = Team, y = zWins), color = "darkred", size = 3) +
  labs(title = "Inflation-Adjusted Payrolls vs. Regular Season Wins",
       subtitle = "2000-17",
       x = "",
       y = "Standard Deviations",
       caption = "green/light = salaries\nred/dark = wins") +
  theme(plot.title = element_text(face = "bold")) +
  theme(axis.text.x = element_text(angle = 45, hjust = 1))
print(p1)
```

Clearly, we could not have drawn a Cleveland dot plot without first standardizing very different measures. The length of the stems indicates how well or not so well player salaries align with wins; this is the first clue toward correctly interpreting our plot.

The second clue is then understanding the *direction* in which each stem was drawn; as a reminder, the stems are drawn *from* zSalaries *to* zWins. Therefore, when the stems are ascendant, it means returns in the form of regular season wins exceed a team's investment in player salaries. When the stems are instead descendant, it means, of course, just the opposite.

As it turns out, 17 teams earned returns on their respective investments, but 13 did not. These totals are computed easily enough by piping the final data set to the dplyr tally() function twice, once to return the number of NBA teams where zWins is greater than zSalaries and again where zWins is less than zSalaries:

```
final %>%
  tally(zWins > zSalaries)
##    n
## 1 17
final %>%
  tally(zWins < zSalaries)
##    n
## 1 13
```

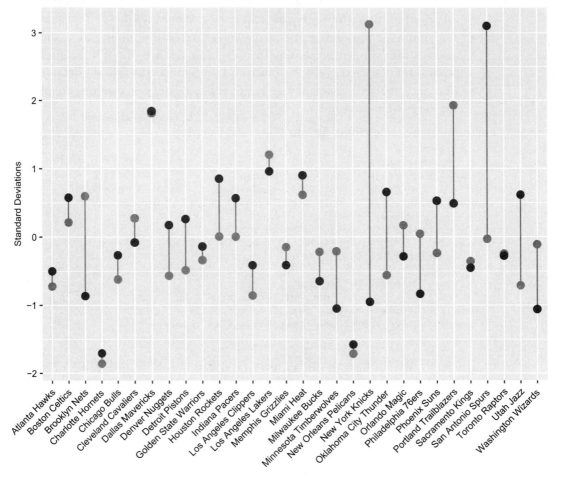

Figure 11.1   A comparison of inflation-adjusted payrolls and regular season wins after both variables have been standardized

When the `dplyr` `filter()` function is called to subset the final data set on the 17 observations where `zWins` is greater than `zSalaries` and the `dplyr` `summarize()` function is called to then compute the mean and median differences between `zWins` and `zSalaries`, we see that the average difference equals 0.68 standard deviations, and the median difference equals 0.44 standard deviations:

```
final %>%
  filter(zWins > zSalaries) %>%
  summarize(mean = mean(zWins - zSalaries),
```

```
          median = median(zWins - zSalaries))
##        mean    median
## 1 0.6776743 0.4434517
```

The mean is greater than the median because of teams such as the Houston Rockets, Utah Jazz, and especially the San Antonio Spurs; San Antonio's investment in player salaries between 2000 and 2017 roughly equaled the league average, but their total regular season win count was more than three standard deviations above the average.

When we flip the variables zWins and zSalaries, we see that the mean and median are almost one half of one standard deviation apart, with the mean being greater than the median:

```
final %>%
  filter(zSalaries > zWins) %>%
  summarize(mean = mean(zSalaries - zWins),
            median = median(zSalaries - zWins))
##        mean    median
## 1 0.8861895 0.4552426
```

This is true because of the Brooklyn Nets to some extent and the New York Knicks to a very large extent. The Knicks are the diametric opposite of the Spurs—their year-over-year payroll was more than three standard deviations above the NBA average, and their total number of regular season wins was about one standard deviation below the mean.

Otherwise, just by reviewing our plot, we can see investments and returns are very well aligned—where the absolute difference between the variables zWins and zSalaries is less than 0.5 standard deviations—for approximately half the NBA. Minus the obvious outliers (the Spurs and the Knicks), our conclusions from chapter 10 would no doubt have been even more definite.

HORIZONTAL BAR CHART

In our second look, total salaries divided by wins is visualized in a ggplot2 horizontal bar chart where efficiency, equal to dollars spent on player salaries for every regular season win between 2000 and 2017, drops from top to bottom (see figure 11.2):

- The reorder() and coord_flip() functions more or less work in tandem here. If our intent was to instead create a vertical bar chart, our results would be sorted, left to right, as the variable efficiency decreased, but by flipping our plot to a horizontal layout, we get lower (and better) efficiency numbers on top and higher (and worse) efficiency numbers on the bottom. Note that the x- and y-axes are part of the plot; as such, they also flip.

- The scale_y_continuous() function plus the label_dollar() and cut_short_ scale() functions from the scales package transform our y-axis labels from seven-digit numerals to $1M, $2M, and $3M.

- The geom_text() function affixes values from the variable meanWins as labels beside the bars; these can be adjusted vertically or horizontally with the vjust and hjust arguments, respectively. In addition, we've added a caption as another argument to the labs() function to note that these figures represent the average count of regular season wins for each team.

Now, here's the code:

```
p2 <- ggplot(final, aes(x = reorder(Team, -efficiency), y = efficiency)) +
  geom_bar(stat = "identity", width = .5, fill = "darkorange1") +
  coord_flip() +
  labs(title = "NBA Team Efficiency: Salary Spend per Win (2000-17)",
       subtitle = "2021 USD",
       x = "",
       y = "Salary Spend per Regular Season Win",
       caption = "Average number of regular season wins
       affixed atop bars") +
  scale_y_continuous(labels =
                        label_dollar(scale_cut = cut_short_scale())) +
  geom_text(aes(label = meanWins, fontface = "bold",
                vjust = 0.3, hjust = -0.4)) +
  theme(plot.title = element_text(face = "bold"))
print(p2)
```

From our sorted bar chart, we can glean the following:

- The San Antonio Spurs averaged significantly more regular season wins per year than every other team and paid out less than \$1.5 M in player salaries for every win. By the way, the Spurs won four league titles between 2003 and 2014.
- The New York Knicks, on the other hand, paid more than twice what the Spurs paid in player salaries for every regular season win and averaged only 35 wins per season in the process. The Knicks haven't won an NBA title since 1973.
- Once more, minus these two rather obvious outliers in our data, our chapter 10 conclusions around payrolls and wins would certainly be even more convincing.
- In between the Spurs and Knicks, we don't see too much variance in efficiency or average wins per season.
- However, teams in the top half of our plot, for the most part, averaged more regular season wins than the teams in the bottom half. Only 4 of the 15 teams in the top half averaged fewer than 40 wins per season, and only 3 teams in the bottom half averaged at least 40 wins per season.

No question, payrolls influence wins, but when you see results like these, you also have to figure that other factors, such as competent management (or incompetent management) and maybe luck (good or bad), are also relevant.

Next, we'll divide the NBA's 30 teams into like and unlike clusters based on team payrolls and regular season wins.

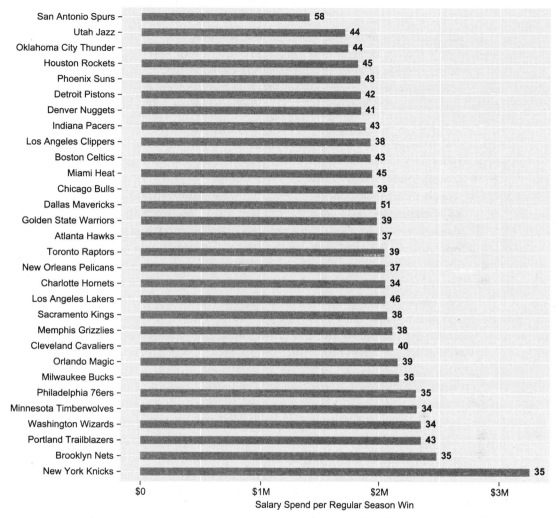

NBA Team Efficiency: Salary Spend per Win (2000–17)
2021 USD

Team	Average number of wins
San Antonio Spurs	58
Utah Jazz	44
Oklahoma City Thunder	44
Houston Rockets	45
Phoenix Suns	43
Detroit Pistons	42
Denver Nuggets	41
Indiana Pacers	43
Los Angeles Clippers	38
Boston Celtics	43
Miami Heat	45
Chicago Bulls	39
Dallas Mavericks	51
Golden State Warriors	39
Atlanta Hawks	37
Toronto Raptors	39
New Orleans Pelicans	37
Charlotte Hornets	34
Los Angeles Lakers	46
Sacramento Kings	38
Memphis Grizzlies	38
Cleveland Cavaliers	40
Orlando Magic	39
Milwaukee Bucks	36
Philadelphia 76ers	35
Minnesota Timberwolves	34
Washington Wizards	34
Portland Trailblazers	43
Brooklyn Nets	35
New York Knicks	35

Salary Spend per Regular Season Win

Average number of regular season wins affixed atop bars

Figure 11.2 Spend on player salaries for every regular season win between 2000 and 2017, sorted from top to bottom between most efficient to least efficient

11.5 K-means clustering

K-means clustering is a popular unsupervised learning algorithm used for data segmentation. Here are the basics:

- The goal is to partition an entire data set into distinct and therefore nonoverlapping clusters, where every data point is assigned to a cluster with the nearest mean, or centroid. The number of clusters is equal to K. It thus aims to minimize intra-cluster variance and maximize inter-cluster variance.

- The K-means algorithm operates iteratively by randomly initializing K centroids and then alternating between two steps—(1) assigning or reassigning each data point to the nearest centroid and (2) recalculating the centroids as the mean of all the data points assigned and then reassigned to them—until convergence. Convergence occurs when the centroids become fixed or a predefined maximum number of iterations is reached. There's no hard requirement to set a maximum number of iterations, but it's a good practice nonetheless.

- Like hierarchical clustering, the distance between data points and centroids is typically computed by applying the Euclidean distance metric, which measures the straight-line distance between a pair of data points in a two-dimensional space (see chapter 3 for details).

- Unlike hierarchical clustering, the number of clusters, or K, must be determined in advance. Choosing K isn't always straightforward. If you're in charge of a marketing team at a department store, for instance, and you only have enough resources to develop and maintain two advertising campaigns, there's only one choice for K. Likewise, if you're running a debt collection agency and decide up front that anything more than three strategies for three delinquent customer segmentations is untenable, then K can't exceed three. But if K can be almost any reasonable and logical number, there are several ways to go about calculating how many clusters *might* be optimal. We'll demonstrate two of those methods. On the whole, too few clusters might oversimplify the data and not add much value, but too many clusters may lead to overfitting.

- The K-means algorithm is fast, simple, and scalable—and with plenty of use cases. A police department could associate categories of criminal offenses (violent crime, property crime, white-collar crime, organized crime, and consensual or victimless crime) with geospatial points, identify any patterns, and deploy police accordingly; a department store could profile its customers using demographic attributes and purchasing history to develop tailored marketing strategies; a debt collection agency could segment its customers around their outstanding balance and credit history to implement made-to-order collections strategies; or a clerk at the National Archives could use K-means for document classification using tags, topics, and content.

- But it's generally understood that K-means returns best results when the variables in play are normally distributed. NBA payrolls and regular season wins aren't normally distributed, however, so we'll test that and show that later.

Our results will be plotted in a single visualization with team payrolls as our x-axis variable and regular season wins as our y-axis variable. The K-means algorithm automatically converts raw numbers into z-scores. You'll see that the results tie back extremely well to our Cleveland dot plot, except for the fact that all 30 NBA teams have been assigned to one cluster or another. But first, we have some further data wrangling to take care of.

11.5.1 *More data wrangling*

Back to the Charlotte Hornets. We start by piping the cha data set we created earlier to the dplyr mutate() function twice to create a pair of derived variables. The first of these is called salarytotal, which is merely the sum of Charlotte's adjusted salaries between 2000 and 2002 and between 2005 and 2017 from columns 2 through 17. The second derived variable is called wintotal, which is the sum of Charlotte's regular season win totals in columns 18 through 33. The results are cast to a new object called cha_kmeans:

```
cha %>%
  mutate(salarytotal = rowSums(.[2:17]),
         wintotal = rowSums(.[18:33])) -> cha_kmeans
```

To even up the Charlotte Hornets with NBA teams that played every season between 2000 and 2017, we bump the derived variables salarytotal and wintotal by 11% (the Hornets "missed" two seasons, or approximately 11% of the 18 NBA seasons contained in the salaries data set). This is by no means an exact science, but it will lead to more reasonable and even more accurate results than doing nothing; take a second look at our Cleveland dot plot, where we left the Hornets and the Pelicans as they were. Because wintotal should not contain any fractional or decimal part, we call the base R round() function to round the wintotal result to the nearest whole number:

```
cha_kmeans$salarytotal <- cha_kmeans$salarytotal * 1.11
cha_kmeans$wintotal <- round(cha_kmeans$wintotal * 1.11)
```

We then reduce the dimension of cha_kmeans by calling the select() function to only include the three variables we absolutely need to enable our forthcoming K-means clustering algorithm—Team, salarytotal, and wintotal:

```
cha_kmeans %>%
  select(Team, salarytotal, wintotal) -> cha_kmeans
```

We then repeat this exact same exercise two times, first for the New Orleans Pelicans and then for the remaining NBA teams. Because the Pelicans "missed" three seasons, we increase their salarytotal and wintotal sums by 17%. As a result, we have two new data objects, nop_kmeans and league_kmeans:

```
nop %>%
  mutate(salarytotal = rowSums(.[2:16]),
         wintotal = rowSums(.[17:31])) -> nop_kmeans

nop_kmeans$salarytotal <- nop_kmeans$salarytotal * 1.17
nop_kmeans$wintotal <- round(nop_kmeans$wintotal) * 1.17

nop_kmeans %>%
  select(Team, salarytotal, wintotal) -> nop_kmeans
```

```
league %>%
  mutate(salarytotal = rowSums(.[2:19]),
         wintotal = rowSums(.[20:37])) -> league_kmeans

league_kmeans %>%
  select(Team, salarytotal, wintotal) -> league_kmeans
```

In the chunk of code that follows, we first call the base R rbind() function to merge the cha_kmeans, nop_kmeans, and league_kmeans data sets into a single object called final_kmeans. Then, we call the select() function to subset final_kmeans on the variables salarytotal and wintotal, thereby removing the variable Team. Immediately thereafter, we call the base R trunc() function to essentially convert the variable wintotal from a float to an integer. Finally, we call the print() function to return the entire final_kmeans data set:

```
final_kmeans <- rbind(cha_kmeans, nop_kmeans, league_kmeans)

final_kmeans %>%
  select(salarytotal, wintotal) %>%
  trunc(final_kmeans$wintotal) -> final_kmeans
print(final_kmeans)
##    salarytotal wintotal
## 1   1247973431      609
## 2   1346072892      657
## 3   1331370577      672
## 4   1502338683      782
## 5   1572394745      635
## 6   1350128086      696
## 7   1513579016      715
## 8   1793863099      911
## 9   1359921484      741
## 10  1374565213      750
## 11  1401640477      709
## 12  1464712564      810
## 13  1464126069      781
## 14  1307071048      681
## 15  1682631996      821
## 16  1436199380      681
## 17  1575463391      815
## 18  1423272015      657
## 19  1424852176      616
## 20  2034231301      626
## 21  1360935249      790
## 22  1494331249      694
## 23  1471662937      638
## 24  1420327702      777
## 25  1815095481      773
## 26  1398565630      677
## 27  1458067975     1040
## 28  1418504110      695
## 29  1333886430      786
## 30  1443384399      615
```

Our final data wrangling operation is a call to the base R rownames() function to over-write the numeric row names in the final_kmeans data set with three-letter abbreviations representing all 30 NBA teams. Our data is sorted with Charlotte (CHA) and New Orleans (NOP) at the top and then alphabetically by the remaining 28 teams. Our results will, of course, be much easier to interpret if they contain team abbreviations rather than numerals:

```
rownames(final_kmeans) <- c("CHA", "NOP", "ATL", "BOS", "BKN", "CHI",
                            "CLE", "DAL", "DEN", "DET", "GSW", "HOU",
                            "IND", "LAC", "LAL", "MEM", "MIA", "MIL",
                            "MIN", "NYK", "OKC", "ORL", "PHI", "PHO",
                            "POR", "SAC", "SAS", "TOR", "UTA", "WAS")
```

Now, let's move on to our analysis.

11.5.2 K-means clustering

A K-means algorithm, as opposed to the hierarchical clustering algorithm we created back in chapter 3, first requires that we specify the number of clusters to generate. It's not uncommon to randomly specify a cluster count, designated by *K,* or experiment with different cluster counts; however, we'll demonstrate a pair of methods to gener-ate optimal cluster counts and then make a decision on *K* subsequent to completing both methods.

CALCULATING OPTIMAL CLUSTER COUNTS

The first method is frequently referred to as the elbow method or, more technically, the within sum of squares method. We draw a type of line chart called a scree plot, which displays the number of clusters along the x-axis and the within-cluster sum of squares (aka the within-cluster variance) along the y-axis. It computes and recomputes the sum of squares of the distances separating every data point and their assigned clus-ters, minimizing the sum with each iteration by increasing the number of clusters. The variance usually decreases at a decreasing rate until diminishing returns set in, which is where additional increases in *K* fail to further decrease the within-cluster vari-ance. That's typically where the plot bends—the elbow point—and we should accept that as an optimal number of clusters.

However, the elbow method is more subjective than objective; unfortunately, scree plots don't always display a definitive elbow point. In fact, the elbow point and where we see diminishing returns for *K* might not be the same. That's where the second method, known as the average silhouette method, comes in. It starts by computing a silhouette coefficient, or some number between −1 and +1, for every data point, based on the dissimilarity between a data point and other data points within the same cluster as well as the average dissimilarity between a data point and every data point in the nearest cluster. The silhouette coefficient is computed by taking the difference between those dissimilarities and dividing it by the maximum between the two. The clustering configuration stops when most data points have high, or at least positive, silhouette coefficients; conversely, low silhouette coefficients suggest too-low or too-high cluster counts, thereby triggering additional iterations. We get a plot that displays the number of clusters along the x-axis and the silhouette coefficients along the y-axis. It also reveals a precise optimal value for *K*.

In the next code chunk, we twice call on the `fviz_nbclust()` function from the `factoextra` package to compute and visualize optimal cluster counts, first using the within-cluster sum of squares method and then the silhouette method. The `fviz_nbclust()` function takes the following three arguments: the data source, the clustering algorithm (it doesn't necessarily have to be K-means), and the method, which are all pretty simple. In fact, the `fviz_nbclust()` function automatically inserts labels for both plots and defaults the y-axis tick marks for the second plot based on our preference for full digit numerals versus scientific notation. Because the sum of squares values are very large numbers, we first re-enable scientific notation by passing the `scipen = 000` argument to the `options()` function and then make our successive calls to `fviz_nbclust()`:

```
options(scipen = 000)
p3 <- fviz_nbclust(final_kmeans, kmeans, method = "wss")
p4 <- fviz_nbclust(final_kmeans, kmeans, method = "silhouette")
```

The `patchwork` package works just as well with these plots as it does with `ggplot2` visualizations. Therefore, we call the `plot_layout()` function to group these two plots into a single graphical object, displaying plot `p3` on top of `p4` (see figure 11.3):

```
p3 + p4 + plot_layout(ncol = 1)
```

While the silhouette method (bottom of figure 11.3) returns a definite, or unambiguous, optimal cluster count, the within-cluster sum of squares method (scree plot at top of figure 11.3) returns an optimal number of clusters that is open to interpretation. On one hand, the sharpest drop in the sum of squares is between one and two clusters, thereby suggesting two clusters would be optimal; on the other hand, the plot bends, and the slope approaches 0 between five and six clusters, alternatively suggesting—more convincingly—that six clusters would instead be best.

RUNNING THE ALGORITHM

We're going to split the difference and proceed with four clusters, also taking into account the fact that small cluster counts sometimes run the risk of oversimplifying the data. We then call the `kmeans()` function, which is part of base R, to construct our four clusters and group the NBA's 30 teams based on the final_kmeans variables `salarytotal` and `wintotal`. The `kmeans()` function requires just two arguments: the data set (final_kmeans) and the number of desired clusters (4), otherwise known as *K*.

We'll additionally pass two optional arguments to the `kmeans()` function: `iter.max` and `nstart`. The `iter.max` argument represents the number of times the algorithm should run before returning any results. Bear in mind that the `kmeans()` function churns through several iterative steps, if allowed, and returns a configuration where

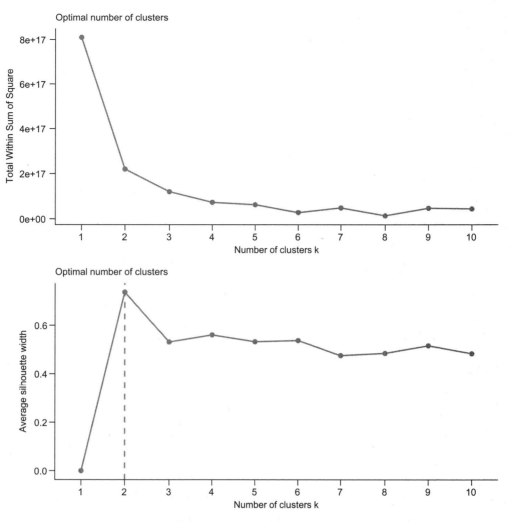

Figure 11.3   Two solutions on optimal cluster counts visualized, where the plot on the top is a scree plot that represents the within-cluster sum of squares method, and the plot on the bottom represents the silhouette method

the total sum of squares between the data and its respective centroid—that is, the center position of a cluster—is minimized. The optimal configuration may very well be obtained after just one run, or it may not—relegating the algorithm to one run may leave more optimal configurations on the table. Therefore, it's best to enable more than one iteration, which is the default; here, we're telling R to iterate through the algorithm 25 times.

The nstart argument represents the number of random data sets used to initialize the algorithm. We've specified four clusters and set the nstart argument to equal 25. Consequently, R will extract four sets of data, one per cluster, 25 times every time the algorithm is set to run. The print() function returns the results:

```
k <- kmeans(final_kmeans, 4, iter.max = 25, nstart = 25)
print(k)
## K-means clustering with 4 clusters of sizes 15, 1, 3, 11
##
## Cluster means:
##   salarytotal wintotal
## 1  1366605768 700.8667
## 2  2034231301 626.0000
## 3  1763863525 835.0000
## 4  1490569128 746.0000
##
## Clustering vector:
## CHA NOP ATL BOS BKN CHI CLE DAL DEN DET GSW HOU IND LAC LAL MEM MIA MIL
##   1   1   1   4   4   1   4   3   1   1   1   4   4   1   3   4   4   1
## MIN NYK OKC ORL PHI PHO POR SAC SAS TOR UTA WAS
##   1   2   1   4   4   1   3   1   4   1   1   4
##
## Within cluster sum of squares by cluster:
## [1] 3.519544e+16 0.000000e+00 1.012325e+16 2.254863e+16
## (between_SS / total_SS =  91.6 %)
##
## Available components:
##
## [1] "cluster"      "centers"      "totss"        "withinss"
## [5] "tot.withinss" "betweenss"    "size"         "iter"
## [9] "ifault"
```

This gives us the following information:

- The number of teams assigned to each cluster (1, 15, 11, 3).
- The `salarytotal` and `wintotal` means for each cluster, which also represent the centroids for every cluster. The returned data is sorted in ascending order by the variable `wintotal`.
- The cluster assignments for every team, where each cluster is identified by a number between 1 and 4. Every NBA team has been assigned to a cluster.

We then visualize these results with a `ggplot2` look and feel by calling the `fviz_cluster()` function from the `factoextra` package (see figure 11.4). A legend is automatically added to the right of the plot unless otherwise specified (we've decided to not include a legend). We also have the option of adding our own title and subtitle, x-axis and y-axis labels, and changing the font to bold:

```
p5 <- fviz_cluster(k, data = final_kmeans,
            main = "K-means Cluster of Payrolls and Wins (2000-17)",
            subtitle = "k = 4",
            xlab = "Team Payrolls",
            ylab = "Regular Season Wins",
            font.main = "bold") +
      theme(legend.position = "none")
print(p5)
```

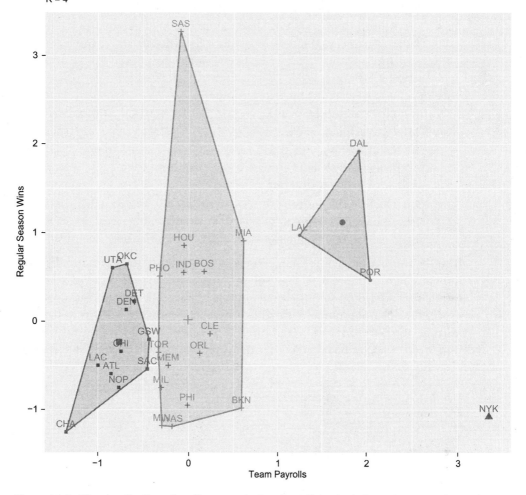

K−means Cluster of Payrolls and Wins (2000−17)
K = 4

Figure 11.4 The visualization of our K-means cluster where _K_ equals 4. The clusters are based on a combination of team payrolls and regular season wins, where each variable has been standardized.

The labels along the x- and y-axes represent the number of standard deviations from the distribution means (you can cross-check these with our Cleveland dot plot). Here's what we can glean from our K-means algorithm and the visualization of the same:

- The San Antonio Spurs (SAS), which, in our estimation, were the NBA's most efficient team between 2000 and 2017, had a regular season win count more than three standard deviations above the league average and a total payroll that was actually below average. Yet they're clustered with the Nets and not with the Lakers or Mavericks.

- The New York Knicks (NYK) are in a "cluster" all by themselves because their regular season win count was more than one standard deviation below the league average while their payroll was more than three standard deviations above it. You might think the Nets should be aligned with the Knicks, not San Antonio.

- The Boston Celtics (BOS), Miami Heat (MIA), Los Angeles Lakers (LAL), and Dallas Mavericks (DAL) were more or less equally above the league averages in wins and payrolls. These four teams won a combined 10 NBA championships between 2000 and 2013.

- Teams that averaged the fewest number of regular season wins between the 2000 and 2017 seasons—the Charlotte Hornets (CHA), Minnesota Timberwolves (MIN), Washington Wizards (WAS), Philadelphia 76ers (PHI), Brooklyn Nets (BKN), and Milwaukee Bucks (MIL)—by and large had payrolls, plus or minus, very close to the league average while, of course, their regular season win counts were at or even beyond one standard deviation below the league mean.

- Our clusters run more vertically than they do horizontally; that is, it more or less appears that a line in the sand, so to speak, has been drawn where the variable `Team Payrolls` equals one standard deviation above the mean.

Bear in mind that neither `salarytotal` nor `wintotal` are normally distributed. The K-means algorithm works *best*—it still otherwise works—when the plotted variables are evenly distributed around their means. A Shapiro-Wilk test returns a p-value that tells us whether or not a numeric variable is normally distributed. Our null hypothesis is a normal distribution; we would therefore reject that hypothesis if Shapiro-Wilk returned a p-value below 5%. That being said, we pass the variables `salarytotal` and `wintotal` to the base R `shapiro.test()` function:

```
shapiro.test(final_kmeans$salarytotal)
##  Shapiro-Wilk normality test
##
## data:  final_kmeans$salarytotal
## W = 0.82724, p-value = 0.0002144

shapiro.test(final_kmeans$wintotal)
##  Shapiro-Wilk normality test
##
## data:  final_kmeans$wintotal
## W = 0.89706, p-value = 0.007124
```

Both tests returned p-values below the 5% threshold for significance; so we would reject the null hypothesis twice and conclude that both variables aren't normally distributed. This might help explain the anomalies in the results.

EXPERIMENTING WITH OTHER VALUES FOR K

Rather than finishing with just a single K-means algorithm where *K* equals 4, let's next iterate our code and test where *K* equals 2 through 7. Our results—just the results, no code—are displayed over the next few pages (see figures 11.5a through 11.5c).

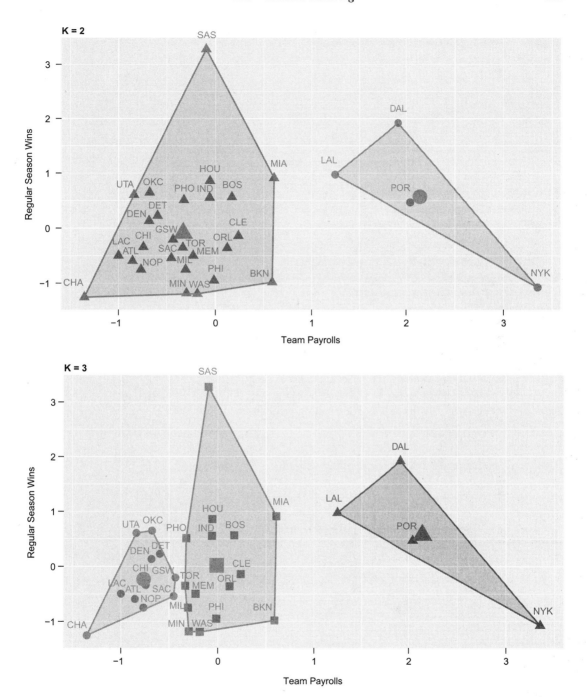

Figure 11.5a   K-means clusters where the number of clusters, otherwise known as K, starts at 2 and completes at 7

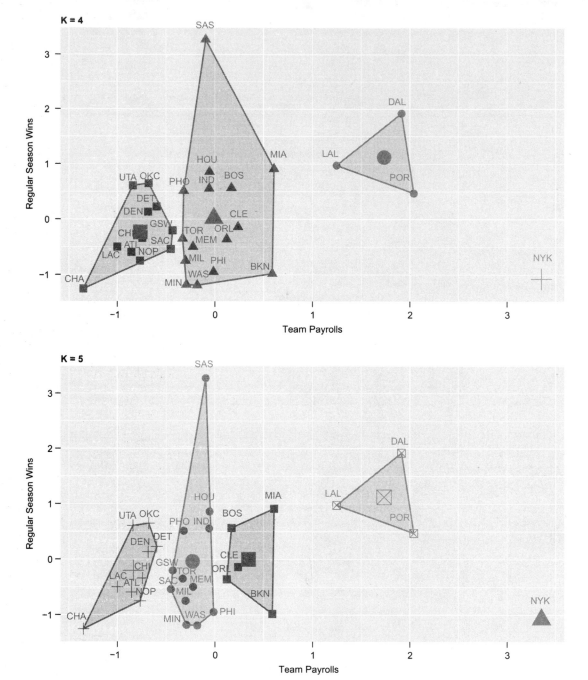

Figure 11.5b   K-means clusters where the number of clusters, otherwise known as K, starts at 2 and completes at 7

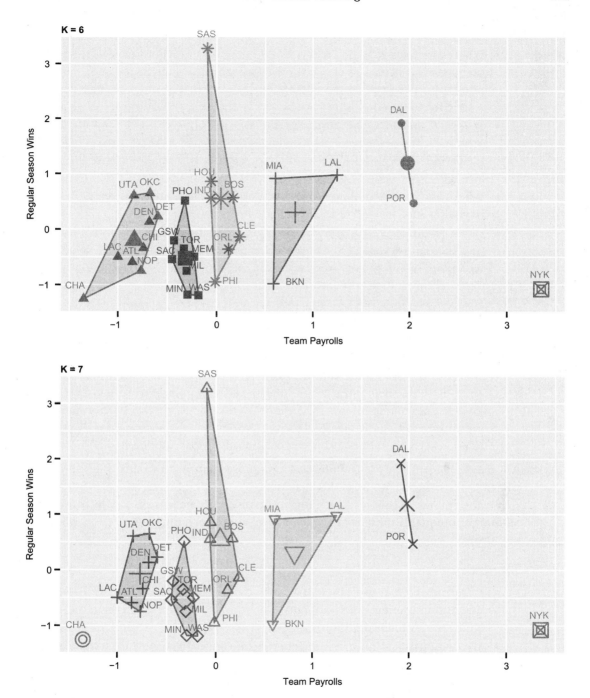

Figure 11.5c   K-means clusters where the number of clusters, otherwise known as K, starts at 2 and completes at 7

In the results, note the following:

- Where *K* equals 2, K-means throws every data point where payroll is less than one standard deviation above the NBA mean into one cluster and every data point where payroll is more than one standard deviation greater than the league mean into the other cluster.
- Where *K* equals 3, the largest of the two previous clusters is split into two groups. In the new cluster, every data point has a `salarytotal` z-score below the mean and a `wintotal` z-score less than one standard deviation above the league average.
- Where *K* equals 4, the algorithm has merely thrown the New York Knicks into its own group.
- Where *K* equals 5, the previous two clusters plotted where payroll is less than one standard deviation above the mean are divided into three clusters. Every data point within those three clusters has a `wintotal` z-score less than one standard deviation above the mean.
- Where *K* equals 6, the Los Angeles Lakers (LAL) are separated from the Dallas Mavericks (DAL) and Portland Trailblazers (POR) and cast into a cluster with a pair of teams that have payrolls less than one standard deviation above the mean.
- Where *K* equals 7, the Charlotte Hornets, with a payroll greater than one standard deviation below the league mean and a regular season win count also greater than one standard deviation below the mean, are thrown into their own group. Overall, the K-means algorithm, when instructed to iteratively add one new cluster, did so by splitting the data mostly by payroll rather than by wins.

A K-means algorithm can absolutely include more than just two attributes; however, you can only visualize two variables at a time.

In the following chapter, we'll further explore player salaries by measuring the amount of inequality there is at the team level and associating those results with wins and losses.

Summary

- Regardless of your use case and what kind of data you're working with—customers, criminal offenses, documents, whatever—you, too, can create a K-means algorithm by following these exact steps.
- We demonstrated how to first generate an optimal count of clusters, based on differentiation in the data, by introducing a pair of methods called within-cluster sum of squares and average silhouette. The former is the most popular of the two methods, but the latter doesn't leave any room for interpretation. Both are equally acceptable.

- The upside to K-means is that it's fast, easy, and can scale to large data sets; the downside is that it works best when the variables in play are normally distributed around their respective means—and that's not the case with the pair of variables we worked with here.

- Our breakdown of standard deviations and z-scores was meant to prepare you for the subsequent analysis to come. Once more, standard deviation is a quantitative measure of variability, or dispersion, in a numeric vector; a z-score is a measure that equals the number of standard deviations that any data point within a numeric vector is above or below the mean of its distribution.

- We've previously stated that R is a best-in-class programming language for data visualization (among other things). One of the reasons for that is the breadth of plots that can be created, especially with the `ggplot2` graphics package. We've demonstrated in prior chapters how to develop plots outside the mainstream, such as Sankey diagrams and lollipop charts. Here, we showed how to create a Cleveland dot plot that not only has a slick look and feel but also lots of easy-to-interpret information.

- As for our results, payrolls and wins are aligned fairly well to very well across almost half the teams in the league.

- We discovered further evidence to support our conclusions from chapter 10 that payrolls have a significant influence on regular season wins.

- The clusters produced from our K-means algorithm are interesting and surprising. The "best" teams with the smartest front offices—the Lakers, Mavericks, Spurs, Rockets, Celtics, Heat, and Jazz—are scattered across three of our four clusters. You can also consider the Spurs and Nets in the same cluster or Utah mixed with the Hornets.

- However, the New York Knicks are in their own cluster (at least when K equals 4), which makes perfect sense.

12

Computing and plotting inequality

This chapter covers

- Computing and understanding Gini coefficients
- Creating and interpreting Lorenz curves
- Performing significance testing
- Conducting effect size testing

Social scientists, economists, philosophers, and others have claimed for many years that income inequality exacerbates crime and other social ills. This is why, they say, taxation, income redistribution, and other state-level corrective actions aren't zero-sum, but critical for the common good. An equal society is a prosperous society, and an unequal society is a declining society.

How might this idea translate to the NBA? The NBA is a remarkably unequal "society" in that most of the money paid out in salaries is distributed to just a few players. In fact, you'll discover soon enough that salary inequality across the league is most recently much higher than it used to be. But at the same time, salary inequality varies significantly from one team or "community" to the next.

Might it be true that teams with relatively *equal* salary distributions are more prosperous than other teams? That is, do such teams win more regular season games and more league championships than teams with relatively *unequal* salary distributions? In any event, that's our going-in hypothesis.

Here's what you can expect to get out of this chapter:

- You'll learn anything and everything you need to know about the Gini coefficient, which is a statistical measure of inequality. We'll discuss what the Gini coefficient is exactly, how to compute it manually, how to do the same in R, and how to interpret results.
- You'll learn how to create a Lorenz curve, which is a graphical representation of inequality, and how to estimate the Gini coefficient from the same.
- You'll get refreshers on t-testing and Cohen's d effect size testing.
- You'll learn some data wrangling operations that we haven't yet had an opportunity to introduce—until now.

Because so much in this chapter hinges on the Gini coefficient and Lorenz curves, let's start with a primer on both topics before we load our packages, import our data, and perform our analysis.

12.1 Gini coefficients and Lorenz curves

The Gini coefficient is a statistical measure of income inequality across a population, usually applied at the nation-state level, where 0 represents perfect equality (i.e., everyone earns the same income or has the same amount of wealth) and 1 represents perfect inequality (just one person possesses all the income or wealth, and everyone else is left with nothing). Generally speaking, the following are true:

- Low inequality translates to a Gini coefficient of less than 0.3.
- Moderate inequality translates to a Gini coefficient between 0.3 and 0.4.
- Significant inequality translates to a Gini coefficient between 0.4 and 0.6.
- High inequality translates to a Gini coefficient greater than 0.6.

The Gini coefficient was developed by the Italian statistician Corrado Gini in 1912, and while Gini's worldview has long since fallen out of favor (Gini was a eugenicist), his coefficient to measure income inequality is regularly computed and published by the World Bank, the United Nations, and many other organizations to this day. This is why we've selected the Gini coefficient as our measure of inequality over a short list of alternatives, such as the standard deviation (see the previous chapter).

Regarding the Gini coefficient, it's critical to point out the following:

- The Gini coefficient is a *relative* measure, not an *absolute* measure, which conceals distributions and other details; for example, two countries might have equal Gini coefficients but radically different standards of living. From a statistical perspective, that means one country might have a negative-skewed income distribution with a long left tail, while the other country might have a positive-skewed income distribution with a long right tail.

- The Gini coefficient probably loses some of its accuracy where products and services are partially or wholly subsidized by the government; it's not easy, after all, to convert socialist or mixed economy benefits such as medicine, housing, and education into personal income or wealth.

A Lorenz curve is a graphical representation of cumulative income or wealth distribution within a population that was developed, interestingly enough, in 1905 by an American doctoral student named Max Lorenz, seven years before Gini developed the Gini coefficient. Drawing a Lorenz curve involves plotting a pair of numeric variables: the cumulative share of income or wealth along either axis and the cumulative share of the population along the opposite axis. (We'll plot cumulative salary distribution as our x-axis variable and cumulative share of NBA players as our y-axis variable.) A diagonal line is drawn to represent a state of perfect equality where, for instance, half the income is earned by half the population, and a Lorenz curve is drawn beneath the diagonal line to show, let's say, that half the income or wealth is actually owned by just 25% of the population. When perfect inequality exists, a Lorenz curve will take on a shape resembling a backward C.

We can estimate or even compute the Gini coefficient from a Lorenz curve; the Gini coefficient is the ratio of the area between the Lorenz curve and the line of perfect equality to the total area beneath the perfect equality line. So the greater the area between a Lorenz curve and the line of perfect equality, the greater the inequality.

Now that we have Gini coefficients and Lorenz curves out of the way, at least for the time being, we'll load our packages, import our data, and then start with our analysis.

12.2 *Loading packages*

We'll go above and beyond built-in R functions to wrangle, pull, and test data and otherwise compute and visualize our results. This time, we'll call the `library()` function six times to load packages that extend R's functional footprint:

```
library(tidyverse)
library(sqldf)
library(ineq)
library(gglorenz)
library(scales)
library(effsize)
```

Four of these packages—`tidyverse`, `sqldf`, `scales`, and `effsize`—we've loaded before; two others, `ineq` and `gglorenz`, are used here for the first time. The `ineq` package contains the `ineq()` function, which takes a vector of numerals and computes the Gini coefficient; the `gglorenz` package is a `ggplot2` extension that draws Lorenz curves.

As a friendly reminder, packages must be installed prior to importing them, and packages must be imported before calling their functions. For example, if the `ineq` package had not already been installed, we would have first called the `install.packages()`

function and passed the `ineq` package between a pair of single or double quotation marks as an argument:

```
install.packages("ineq")
```

We'll import our first data set next.

12.3   *Importing and viewing data*

Our first data set is in the form of a .csv file, previously downloaded from https://data.world. We therefore make a call to the `read_csv()` function from the `readr` package to import our data that's since been stored in our default working directory. In the process, we create an object called gini:

```
gini <- read_csv("salaries_1985to2018.csv")
```

Our data set contains annual salaries for every NBA player between 1985 and 2018.

We then call the `glimpse()` function from the `dplyr` package to perform a quick assessment of our data:

```
glimpse(gini)
## Rows: 14,163
## Columns: 7
## $ league       <chr> "NBA", "NBA", "NBA", "NBA", "NBA", "NBA", "NB…
## $ player_id    <chr> "abdelal01", "abdelal01", "abdelal01", "abdel…
## $ salary       <dbl> 395000, 494000, 500000, 805000, 650000, 15300…
## $ season       <chr> "1990-91", "1991-92", "1992-93", "1993-94", "…
## $ season_end   <dbl> 1991, 1992, 1993, 1994, 1995, 1985, 1986, 198…
## $ season_start <dbl> 1990, 1991, 1992, 1993, 1994, 1984, 1985, 198…
## $ team         <chr> "Portland Trail Blazers", "Portland Trail Bla…
```

The gini data set is 14,163 rows long and seven columns wide; it contains a combination of numeric variables (`int`) and character strings (`chr`). Some back-of-the-envelope math—taking into account the number of NBA seasons contained in our data set, the number of teams, and the number of players a team usually carries on its active roster—suggests that 14,163 records is rather high. It might be due to so many players rotating in and out of the league on short-term or temporary contracts, or it could be the result of something entirely different.

Because players frequently change teams *during* a season—they can be traded to another team or signed by another team after being waived, the equivalent of being fired or laid off—it's only fitting to check and tag duplicate records between the variables `player_id` (a unique identifier) and `season_end` (the calendar year in which an NBA regular season concluded). This is a good example of the importance of understanding the ecosystem in which your data resides; a blind analysis that lacks context in terms of the potential movement or interaction of variables is liable to spoil the integrity of your analysis.

It would be nice if there were some quick and easy way of detecting or confirming the presence of duplicate records, but unfortunately, the data dictionary that attended our data makes no mention of intra-season player movements or if salaries are double-counted in such instances, meaning we'll have to fend for ourselves. But this is how it often works in the real world.

In the following chunk of `dplyr` code, we first pass the gini data set to the `group_by()` function, where the variables `player_id` and `season_end` are additional arguments, and then we call the `mutate()` function to create a logical variable called `duplicate`. The `duplicate` variable will equal TRUE if and when gini contains more than one record where `player_id` *and* `season_end` are identical, or `duplicate` will equal FALSE if otherwise. Our results are cast to a tibble called gini2, which we'll use only temporarily:

```
gini %>%
  group_by(player_id, season_end) %>%
  mutate(duplicate = n() > 1) -> gini2
```

Then, we pass gini2 to the `group_by()` and `tally()` functions to return row counts where the variable `duplicate` equals TRUE or FALSE to get a count of (potentially) duplicate records in our data:

```
gini2 %>%
  group_by(duplicate) %>%
  tally()
## # A tibble: 2 × 2
##    duplicate      n
##    <lgl>      <int>
## 1 FALSE      13367
## 2 TRUE         796
```

Our data set does contain duplicates—lots of them, or so it would seem if we stopped here.

Next, we call the `sqldf()` function from the `sqldf` package and the `head()` function from base R to return the first six observations from gini2 where the variable `duplicate` equals TRUE. This gives us a read on a few of our duplicate records as well as a starter set by which to do some additional research:

```
head(sqldf("SELECT * FROM gini2 WHERE duplicate = TRUE"))
##    league player_id  salary  season season_end season_start
## 1     NBA  acyqu01 1914544 2016-17       2017         2016
## 2     NBA  acyqu01 1050961 2016-17       2017         2016
## 3     NBA afflaar01 1500000 2017-18       2018         2017
## 4     NBA afflaar01 1471382 2017-18       2018         2017
## 5     NBA aguirma01 1471000 1993-94       1994         1993
## 6     NBA aguirma01  150000 1993-94       1994         1993
##                     team  duplicate
## 1       Brooklyn Nets          TRUE
## 2     Dallas Mavericks          TRUE
## 3     Sacramento Kings          TRUE
```

```
## 4      Orlando Magic              TRUE
## 5      Detroit Pistons            TRUE
## 6      Los Angeles Clippers       TRUE
```

Upon further investigation, it turns out our duplicates aren't really duplicates after all. Quincy Acy is a typical case in point (see `player_id acyqu01` from our `sqldf` output). Acy was a marginal and forgettable player, but he did earn more than $8 M in salary over a seven-year professional career. According to his www.basketball-reference.com profile, Acy started the 2016–17 season as a member of the Dallas Mavericks. About a month into the season, in which he appeared in only six games, Acy was waived and, two months later, signed by the Brooklyn Nets. Most importantly for us, the Mavericks paid Acy more than $1 M, *and* the Nets paid him an additional $1.9 M; thus, Acy earned more than $2.9 M during the 2016–17 season. Other checks on other "duplicates" reveal the same pattern; there are, indeed, duplicates on the variables `player_id` and `season_end`, but the salaries are unique. That last part is what's key for us: the salaries are unique, or mutually exclusive, for each `player_id`, `season`, *and* `team` combination. Now that we have that settled, we know what needs to be done and what doesn't need to be done from a data wrangling perspective.

12.4 *Wrangling data*

Going forward, we only need three of the eight variables in gini—these being `salary`, `season_end`, and `team`. There's no use keeping unnecessary data around, so we'll reduce the gini data set by calling the `select()` function from the `dplyr` package to include just these three variables:

```
gini %>%
  select(salary, season_end, team) -> gini
```

Next, we convert the variables `season_end` and `team` to factors by calling the base R `as.factor()` function twice:

```
gini$season_end <- as.factor(gini$season_end)
gini$team <- as.factor(gini$team)
```

Then, we run the base R `summary()` function to return descriptive statistics for each of the three remaining variables in gini; the `maxsum` argument tells R to return up to but no more than 40 levels for factors. The variable `season_end` contains 34 levels, one for each season or year, and the variable `team`, because our data recognizes iterations in team names, contains 39 levels.

For variables that are numeric, such as `salary`, the `summary()` function returns the mean, median, minimum and maximum values, and the first and third quartiles; for variables that are factors, such as `season_end` and `team`, `summary()` instead returns the observation counts for each group:

```
summary(gini, maxsum = 40)
##     salary          season_end                                     team
## Min.    :    2706  1985:210                                      :   4
## 1st Qu.:  630000   1986:296   Atlanta Hawks                      :494
## Median :  1500000  1987:  40  Boston Celtics                     :502
## Mean    : 3164870  1988:303   Brooklyn Nets                      :103
## 3rd Qu.: 3884239   1989:321   Charlotte Bobcats                  :156
## Max.    :34682550  1990:  64  Charlotte Hornets                  :253
##                    1991:353   Chicago Bulls                      :496
##                    1992:387   Cleveland Cavaliers                :491
##                    1993:404   Dallas Mavericks                   :519
##                    1994:394   Denver Nuggets                     :490
##                    1995:418   Detroit Pistons                    :481
##                    1996:388   Golden State Warriors              :491
##                    1997:413   Houston Rockets                    :509
##                    1998:444   Indiana Pacers                     :484
##                    1999:432   Kansas City Kings                  :  11
##                    2000:526   Los Angeles Clippers               :503
##                    2001:464   Los Angeles Lakers                 :475
##                    2002:459   Memphis Grizzlies                  :298
##                    2003:459   Miami Heat                         :453
##                    2004:458   Milwaukee Bucks                    :491
##                    2005:478   Minnesota Timberwolves             :436
##                    2006:494   New Jersey Nets                    :413
##                    2007:511   New Orleans Hornets                :143
##                    2008:486   New Orleans Pelicans               :  95
##                    2009:471   New Orleans/Oklahoma City Hornets  :  31
##                    2010:472   New York Knicks                    :499
##                    2011:467   Oklahoma City Thunder              :163
##                    2012:468   Orlando Magic                      :463
##                    2013:496   Philadelphia 76ers                 :519
##                    2014:410   Phoenix Suns                       :509
##                    2015:543   Portland Trail Blazers             :487
##                    2016:527   Sacramento Kings                   :482
##                    2017:556   San Antonio Spurs                  :488
##                    2018:551   Seattle SuperSonics                :308
##                               Toronto Raptors                    :375
##                               Utah Jazz                          :456
##                               Vancouver Grizzlies                :  93
##                               Washington Bullets                 :153
##                               Washington Wizards                 :346
```

The summary() function output has revealed a couple of problems—one fairly minor but the other not so much. First, we have four observations in gini where the variable team is blank. This might have been an oversight when the data set was created, maybe these are players who had guaranteed contracts but didn't play for any team due to injury, or it's something else altogether. The following SELECT statement returns these four records from the gini data set:

```
sqldf("SELECT * FROM gini WHERE team == ''")
##   salary season_end team
## 1  65000       1985
```

```
## 2 600000          1985
## 3 450000          1985
## 4 120000          1985
```

It's interesting that all are from the 1984–85 season.

The second problem is that the record counts are low—very low in some cases—where the variable season_end is less than, or before, 1991. This is likely because salaries weren't always so public back in the day. The following pair of SELECT statements returns every record for two random teams, one from 1987 and the other from 1990, where, it turns out, the record counts are especially low:

```
sqldf("SELECT * FROM gini WHERE team == 'Boston Celtics' AND
      season_end == 1987")
##    salary season_end           team
## 1 1800000       1987 Boston Celtics
## 2  200000       1987 Boston Celtics
## 3  425000       1987 Boston Celtics


sqldf("SELECT * FROM gini WHERE team == 'Los Angeles Lakers' AND
      season_end == 1990")
##    salary season_end               team
## 1 1500000       1990 Los Angeles Lakers
## 2 3100000       1990 Los Angeles Lakers
## 3 1100000       1990 Los Angeles Lakers
## 4 1500000       1990 Los Angeles Lakers
```

It's possible to pull the same data and, of course, return the same results with dplyr code by substituting the WHERE clause in favor of the filter() function. That's up to you. Just be aware that dplyr and sqldf don't usually share the same syntax; for instance, sqldf uses AND, whereas dplyr uses &:

```
gini %>%
  filter(team == "Boston Celtics" & season_end == 1987)
##    salary season_end           team
## 1 1800000       1987 Boston Celtics
## 2  200000       1987 Boston Celtics
## 3  425000       1987 Boston Celtics


gini %>%
  filter(team == "Los Angeles Lakers" & season_end == 1990)
##    salary season_end               team
## 1 1500000       1990 Los Angeles Lakers
## 2 3100000       1990 Los Angeles Lakers
## 3 1100000       1990 Los Angeles Lakers
## 4 1500000       1990 Los Angeles Lakers
```

The gini data set contains just three records for the 1987 Boston Celtics and just four records for the 1990 Los Angeles Lakers.

Due to these discoveries, we then subset the gini data set by removing all rows where the factor variable season_end equals 1985, 1986, 1987, 1988, 1989, or 1990 to remove NBA seasons with incomplete data. We then have a new working data set called gini3.

To make this happen, we call the base R c() function to create a vector containing the season_end levels 1985 through 1990. Next, because we're filtering by vector, we use the %in% operator, which instructs R to sift through the variable season_end and remove— rather than retain because our code is fronted by the logical negation operator denoted by !—those records where the level equals one of the values inside our vector:

```
gini[!(gini$season_end %in% c(1985, 1986, 1987, 1988,
                              1989, 1990)),] -> gini3
```

We then call the dim() function to return the dimension of the gini3 data set:

```
dim(gini3)
## [1] 12929     3
```

As a result, our working data set has been reduced to 12,929 records from an original row count of 14,163, which is a difference of 1,234 records.

Following are two quick points on our data:

- A typical NBA regular season starts in mid-October and ends in mid-April, thereby starting in one calendar year and ending in another. So, for instance, because the 2018 season actually started in October 2017, it's sometimes called the 2017–18 season. We previously removed the variables season and season_start from the gini data set because neither one, or even the two together, add more value than the variable season_end by itself.
- Unlike the salaries data set, which we worked with in the prior two chapters, the gini data set recognizes franchise moves and subsequent changes in team names that occurred between the 1985 and 2018 seasons. This is why the variable team contains significantly more than 30 levels.

In the following chunk of code, we further reduce the gini3 data set by retaining no more than the top 14 player salaries for each team and season_end combination. Our results would otherwise be unfairly or inaccurately skewed by including the league's lowest salary players, who are usually playing on short-term or temporary contracts. We make this happen by following these steps:

1 We start by passing the gini3 data set via the pipe operator to the dplyr arrange() function, which sorts gini by each of its three variables.
2 We then call the dplyr group_by() and mutate() functions and the base R rank() function to create a new variable called rank, where the variable salary is sorted in descending order, 1 through n, by every team and season_end combination. The minus, or negative, sign inside the rank() function sorts, or ranks, the variable salary in descending order. The ties.method argument specifies how ties should be handled; when equal to first, R assigns tied elements consecutive, and thus different, ranks.

3 Finally, we call the dplyr `filter()` function to include only those records where the variable rank is less than or equal to 14. The results are thrown into a tibble called gini4:

```
gini3 %>%
  arrange(season_end, team, salary) %>%
  group_by(season_end, team) %>%
  mutate(rank = rank(-salary, ties.method = "first")) %>%
  filter(rank <= 14) -> gini4
```

This leaves us with a working data set in which the record count for every season_end and team combination equals a maximum of 14. But let's perform a series of integrity checks to validate that.

In the next code chunk, we twice call the `sqldf()` function from the sqldf package to write SELECT statements that pull data from the gini3 data set and the gini4 tibble where the variable season_end equals 2012 and the variable team equals Denver Nuggets for both. Notice that we use double quotation marks on the outside and single quotation marks on the inside; this style makes it easier for R to read and interpret the code:

```
sqldf("SELECT * FROM gini3 WHERE season_end = 2012 AND
       team = 'Denver Nuggets'")
##       salary season_end         team
## 1    7562500       2012 Denver Nuggets
## 2    4234000       2012 Denver Nuggets
## 3    3059000       2012 Denver Nuggets
## 4     289382       2012 Denver Nuggets
## 5    1254720       2012 Denver Nuggets
## 6    2180443       2012 Denver Nuggets
## 7    4190182       2012 Denver Nuggets
## 8    1073286       2012 Denver Nuggets
## 9    6226200       2012 Denver Nuggets
## 10  13000000       2012 Denver Nuggets
## 11   2203792       2012 Denver Nuggets
## 12   1654440       2012 Denver Nuggets
## 13   7807728       2012 Denver Nuggets
## 14   3343896       2012 Denver Nuggets
## 15    473604       2012 Denver Nuggets

sqldf("SELECT * FROM gini4 WHERE season_end = 2012 AND
       team = 'Denver Nuggets'")
##       salary season_end         team rank
## 1     473604       2012 Denver Nuggets   14
## 2    1073286       2012 Denver Nuggets   13
## 3    1254720       2012 Denver Nuggets   12
## 4    1654440       2012 Denver Nuggets   11
## 5    2180443       2012 Denver Nuggets   10
## 6    2203792       2012 Denver Nuggets    9
## 7    3059000       2012 Denver Nuggets    8
## 8    3343896       2012 Denver Nuggets    7
## 9    4190182       2012 Denver Nuggets    6
## 10   4234000       2012 Denver Nuggets    5
```

```
## 11  6226200     2012 Denver Nuggets    4
## 12  7562500     2012 Denver Nuggets    3
## 13  7807728     2012 Denver Nuggets    2
## 14 13000000     2012 Denver Nuggets    1
```

The first SELECT statement returns every record and every variable from gini3 where season_end equals 2012 and team equals Denver Nuggets; 15 records are returned, one for each player who was on Denver's payroll that season.

The second SELECT statement returns every record and every variable from gini4 where season_end also equals 2012 and team also equals Denver Nuggets; 14 records are then returned where the variable salary is sorted in ascending order and the variable rank is sorted in descending order. This is exactly what we were expecting.

Let's try this again, this time by swapping out the 2012 Denver Nuggets for the 2018 Chicago Bulls:

```
sqldf("SELECT * FROM gini3 WHERE season_end = 2018 AND
      team = 'Chicago Bulls'")
##      salary season_end          team
## 1   1471382       2018 Chicago Bulls
## 2  10595505       2018 Chicago Bulls
## 3    200000       2018 Chicago Bulls
## 4   4046760       2018 Chicago Bulls
## 5    100353       2018 Chicago Bulls
## 6   7843500       2018 Chicago Bulls
## 7   1713840       2018 Chicago Bulls
## 8   4615385       2018 Chicago Bulls
## 9   2163006       2018 Chicago Bulls
## 10  3202217       2018 Chicago Bulls
## 11 13788500       2018 Chicago Bulls
## 12  3821640       2018 Chicago Bulls
## 13  1312611       2018 Chicago Bulls
## 14  2203440       2018 Chicago Bulls
## 15  3853931       2018 Chicago Bulls
## 16  1516320       2018 Chicago Bulls
## 17  1471382       2018 Chicago Bulls
## 18  3000000       2018 Chicago Bulls
## 19    50000       2018 Chicago Bulls
## 20  2186400       2018 Chicago Bulls
## 21  3505233       2018 Chicago Bulls
## 22 15550000       2018 Chicago Bulls
## 23  1312611       2018 Chicago Bulls

sqldf("SELECT * FROM gini4 WHERE season_end = 2018 AND
      team = 'Chicago Bulls'")
##     salary season_end          team rank
## 1  2163006       2018 Chicago Bulls   14
## 2  2186400       2018 Chicago Bulls   13
## 3  2203440       2018 Chicago Bulls   12
## 4  3000000       2018 Chicago Bulls   11
## 5  3202217       2018 Chicago Bulls   10
## 6  3505233       2018 Chicago Bulls    9
## 7  3821640       2018 Chicago Bulls    8
```

```
## 8    3853931    2018 Chicago Bulls    7
## 9    4046760    2018 Chicago Bulls    6
## 10   4615385    2018 Chicago Bulls    5
## 11   7843500    2018 Chicago Bulls    4
## 12  10595505    2018 Chicago Bulls    3
## 13  13788500    2018 Chicago Bulls    2
## 14  15550000    2018 Chicago Bulls    1
```

The first SELECT statement returns 23 records, and the second returns the top 14 player salaries sorted from lowest to highest. That's perfect.

Finally, let's run two more SELECT statements that compute the gini4 row counts where the variable team equals Denver Nuggets and then when the variable team equals Chicago Bulls. Row counts should equal a maximum of 392, which is the product of 28 seasons multiplied by a maximum of 14 player salaries per season (some teams in some seasons had fewer than 14 players on their respective payrolls):

```
sqldf("SELECT COUNT (*) FROM gini4 WHERE team = 'Denver Nuggets'")
##    COUNT(*)
## 1      388
```

```
sqldf("SELECT COUNT (*) FROM gini4 WHERE team = 'Chicago Bulls'")
##    COUNT(*)
## 1      387
```

Because the row counts equal 388 for the Nuggets and 387 for the Bulls, these two checks further validate the integrity of our data.

It's always a worthwhile investment of time and effort to validate operations that aren't necessarily performed every day. Let's now start our analysis by computing Gini coefficients.

12.5 *Gini coefficients*

Once more, the Gini coefficient is a measure of inequality, so higher coefficients therefore mean greater dispersion. Let's demonstrate Gini coefficients with a series of very simple examples.

For starters, suppose we have a group of 10 individuals who each earn an income of \$50 per month. We create a vector with 10 like elements by calling the rep() and c() functions and telling R to repeat 50 ten times. Then, we pass our vector to the ineq() function from the ineq package to compute the Gini coefficient:

```
a <- rep(c(50), each = 10)
print(a)
##  [1] 50 50 50 50 50 50 50 50 50 50

ineq(a)
## [1] 0
```

Because everyone earns the exact same income, there's perfect equality, and therefore, the Gini coefficient equals 0.

In our second example, we have five individuals earning $50 per month and another five individuals earning twice that; thus, two-thirds of the total income is earned by just half the individuals:

```
b <- rep(c(50, 100), each = 5)
print(b)
##  [1]   50  50  50  50  50 100 100 100 100 100

ineq(b)
## [1] 0.1666667
```

As a result, we have a Gini coefficient equal to 0.17.

In our third example, half the individuals earn $150 per month, and the other half earn $300 per month:

```
c <- rep(c(150, 300), each = 5)
print(c)
##  [1] 150 150 150 150 150 300 300 300 300 300

ineq(c)
## [1] 0.1666667
```

Compared to our prior example, monthly incomes are higher across the board; nevertheless, the Gini coefficient also equals 0.17 because exactly two-thirds of the total income is again earned by just half the individuals. As previously mentioned, we can have right- and left-skewed distributions but equal Gini coefficients.

In our fourth example, we have a perfectly normal monthly income distribution where both the mean and the median equal 80 and the standard deviation is minimal:

```
d <- rep(c(60, 70, 80, 90, 100), each = 2)
print(d)
##  [1]   60  60  70  70  80  80  90  90 100 100

ineq(d)
## [1] 0.1
```

Nearly half of the total monthly income is earned by just four individuals; as a result, we have a Gini coefficient equal to 0.10.

In our fifth example, we again have a perfectly normal income distribution; this time, the mean and median equal 100, and the standard deviation is twice what it was before:

```
e <- rep(c(50, 75, 100, 125, 150), each = 2)
print(e)
##  [1]   50  50  75  75 100 100 125 125 150 150

ineq(e)
## [1] 0.2
```

As a result, 55% of the monthly income is earned by just 4 of the 10 individuals, and our Gini coefficient doubles to 0.20.

In our sixth and final example, nine individuals earn just $10 every month while a 10th individual earns $100:

```
f <- rep(c(10, 100), times = c(9, 1))
print(f)
##  [1]  10  10  10  10  10  10  10  10  10 100

ineq(f)
## [1] 0.4263158
```

This last individual is therefore earning just more than twice the income of everyone else combined, so we have a much higher Gini coefficient, 0.43, as a result.

Now, in the following chunk of code, we pass the most recent version of our working data set, gini4, to the dplyr group_by() and summarize() functions and the ineq() function to compute the Gini coefficient by each remaining factor in the variable season_end. The results are cast into a tibble called gini_summary. By calling the base R round() function, we're limiting the results to include just two digits right of the decimal point:

```
gini4 %>%
  group_by(season_end) %>%
  summarize(gc = round(ineq(salary), digits = 2)) -> gini_summary
print(gini_summary)
## # A tibble: 28 × 2
##    season_end    gc
##    <fct>      <dbl>
##  1 1991        0.41
##  2 1992        0.41
##  3 1993        0.41
##  4 1994        0.39
##  5 1995        0.42
##  6 1996        0.45
##  7 1997        0.52
##  8 1998        0.51
##  9 1999        0.49
## 10 2000        0.5
## # … with 18 more rows
```

These results are then visualized in a ggplot2 line, or time series, chart (see figure 12.1). Following are some pointers around the key ggplot2 functions that are called:

- The geom_line() function draws a single line that is 1.5 times the default ggplot2 width.
- The geom_point() function adds points along the line that are three times the default size.
- The geom_smooth() function draws a thin regression line across the entire data series without any confident band because we're adding the se = FALSE argument to geom_smooth() to overwrite the default functionality.

- The second call to the `theme()` function orients the x-axis labels at 45 degrees and aligns them horizontally just beneath the plot.
- Descriptive statistics are annotated in the lower-right corner of the plot by making successive calls to the `annotate()` function.

That being said, here's our code chunk:

```
ggplot(gini_summary, aes(x = season_end, y = gc, group = 1)) +
  geom_line(aes(y = gc), color = "coral3", size = 1.5) +
  geom_point(size = 3, color = "coral3") +
  geom_smooth(method = lm, se = FALSE) +
  labs(title = "Gini Coefficient of NBA Player Salaries by Season",
       subtitle = "1991-2018",
       x = "Season",
       y = "Gini Coeffiicient",
       caption = "includes a maximum top 14 salaries for each team") +
  annotate("text", x = "2014", y = .38, label = "min = 0.39",
           fontface = "bold") +
  annotate("text", x = "2014", y = .40, label = "max = 0.52",
           fontface = 'bold') +
  annotate("text", x = "2014", y = .39, label = "mean = 0.47",
           fontface = 'bold') +
  annotate("text", x = "2014", y = .37,
           label = "standard deviation = 0.03", fontface = 'bold') +
  theme(plot.title = element_text(face = "bold")) +
  theme(axis.text.x = element_text(angle = 45, hjust = 1))
```

These results are really fascinating:

- Between 1991 and 1995, the Gini coefficient equaled 0.41 or 0.42 every year except in 1994, when it then equaled a gini_summary minimum of 0.39.
- The Gini coefficient then spiked in 1995, again in 1996, and especially in 1997, where it equaled a gini_summary maximum of 0.52, despite static populations.
- The coefficient then dropped modestly in 1998 and again in 1999.
- A new norm was established by 1999 and maintained through 2018, where the Gini coefficient "bounced" between 0.47, the 1991–2018 mean, and 0.50.
- This all suggests that, while NBA salary distributions were *moderately* unequal back in the day, they are without doubt *significantly* unequal now.

Inequality is visualized with a Lorenz curve, as we discussed earlier in the chapter. Next, we'll demonstrate how to build a Lorenz curve with a `ggplot2` extension, show how a Gini coefficient can be estimated or even computed, and then discuss how to properly interpret the results.

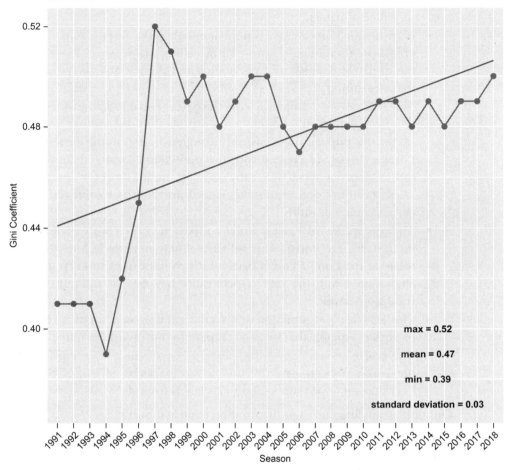

includes a maximum top 14 salaries for each team

Figure 12.1   The year-over-year, or season-over-season, Gini coefficient of salary distribution across the NBA

12.6   *Lorenz curves*

Once more, the Lorenz curve is a graphical representation of income or wealth distribution, where the percentage of income or salary distribution is usually the x-axis variable, and the percentage of individuals earning that income or drawing that salary is then the y-axis variable (though it would be perfectly fine to flip the variables).

It's possible to create a Lorenz curve using built-in R functions; however, we'll instead use the ggplot2 package in conjunction with a ggplot2 extension called gglorenz. Our first Lorenz curve visualizes salary distribution for the 1993–94 season, where the Gini coefficient equaled 0.39, the minimum in our data set (see figure 12.2):

- We start by calling the dplyr filter() function to subset the gini4 data set where the variable season_end equals 1994. In the process, we create a new data set called gini1994.

- Because our Lorenz curve is fundamentally no different from any other ggplot2 object, we then initialize our plot by calling the ggplot() function and passing the gini1994 data set as a parameter and the variable salary as the only aesthetic mapping.

- The stat_lorenz() function from the gglorenz package draws the Lorenz curve. When set to TRUE, the population is arranged in descending order; when set to FALSE, the population is instead arranged in ascending order. Because most Lorenz curves are created with the population arranged in ascending order, rather than vice versa, we set the desc argument, short for descending, to equal FALSE. Furthermore, we instruct R to draw the line a solid red and to make it twice the default width.

- The ggplot2 coord_fixed() function fixes the ratios of the x- and y-axes so that their scales are equal. This isn't absolutely necessary, but it's highly recommended for Lorenz curves because it's so important to keep the x- and y-axes aligned and with the same aspect ratio. It would be difficult to interpret the results otherwise.

- The geom_abline() function draws a dashed diagonal line that represents a state of perfect equality that we can compare to our inequality curve.

- The scale_x_continuous() and scale_y_continuous() functions, combined with the scales package—part of the ggplot2 package, which, of course, is part of tidyverse—convert our x- and y-axis labels from decimals to percentages.

Our data wrangling and data visualization code is shown here:

```
gini1994 <- filter(gini4, season_end == 1994)

ggplot(gini1994, aes(salary)) +
  stat_lorenz(desc = FALSE, color = "red", lwd = 2) +
  coord_fixed() +
  geom_abline(linetype = "dashed", lwd = 1.5) +
  labs(title = "Lorenz Curve\n1993-94 Season",
       subtitle = "Gini coefficient = 0.39",
       x = "Salary Distribution",
       y = "Percentage of NBA Players",
       caption = "includes a maximum top 14 salaries for each team") +
  scale_x_continuous(labels = percent) +
  scale_y_continuous(labels = percent) +
  theme(plot.title = element_text(face = "bold"))
```

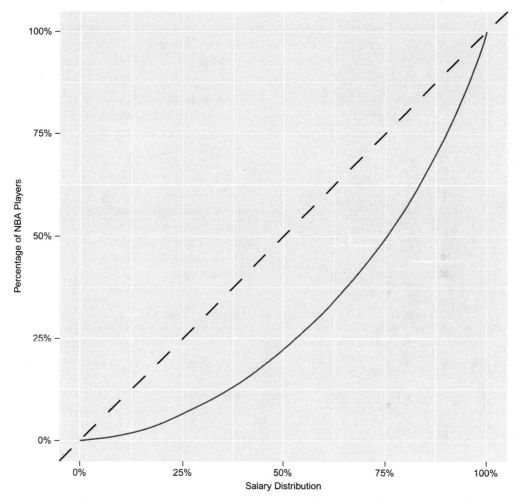

Figure 12.2   Lorenz curve for the 1993–94 NBA season when the Gini coefficient equaled 0.39

Here's how to interpret our Lorenz curve:

- The x-axis represents the percentage of US dollars paid out in player salaries.
- The y-axis represents the percentage of NBA players.

- The dashed line represents a state of perfect equality where, for instance, 50% of all dollars paid out in salaries are distributed to exactly 50% of the players in the league.
- The Lorenz curve represents the measure of salary inequality; the larger the area between it and the dashed line, the more inequality there is, and vice versa. In 1994, 75% of all dollars paid out in salaries were earned by just 50% of the players.
- The Gini coefficient can be derived by computing the area between the Lorenz curve and the line of perfect equality and dividing that by the total area beneath the line of perfect equality (you'll see much more on this in chapter 13).

Let's draw a second Lorenz curve, if only for comparison purposes (see figure 12.3). This can best be done by subsetting the gini4 data set where the variable season_end equals 1997, when the Gini coefficient equaled a maximum of 0.52. You'll see how much additional area there is between the Lorenz curve and the line of perfect equality versus our previous plot. More of a gap between the Lorenz curve and the line of perfect equality means more inequality:

```
gini1997 <- filter(gini4, season_end == 1997)

ggplot(gini1997, aes(salary)) +
  stat_lorenz(desc = FALSE, color = "red", lwd = 2) +
  coord_fixed() +
  geom_abline(linetype = "dashed", lwd = 1.5) +
  labs(title = "Lorenz Curve\n1996-97 Season",
       subtitle = "Gini coefficient = 0.52",
       x = "Salary Distribution",
       y = "Percentage of NBA Players",
       caption = "includes a maximum top 14 salaries for each team") +
  scale_x_continuous(labels = percent) +
  scale_y_continuous(labels = percent) +
  theme(plot.title = element_text(face = "bold"))
```

Whereas 75% of salaries were paid out to 50% of the players in 1994, 75% of salaries were distributed to just 38% of the players in 1997; that's the difference between Gini coefficients equal to 0.39 versus 0.52.

Now that you have a good understanding of Gini coefficients and Lorenz curves, let's apply what we've just learned by exploring how salary inequality might be associated with winning and losing.

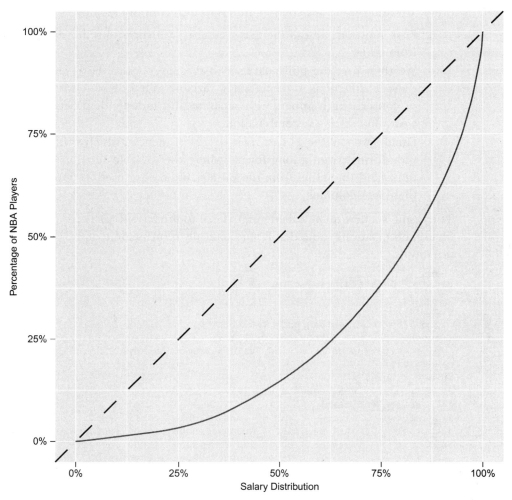

Figure 12.3   Lorenz curve for the 1996–97 NBA season when the Gini coefficient equaled 0.53

12.7 Salary inequality and championships

We'll begin by comparing and contrasting championship-winning teams versus all other teams. Recall that our going-in hypothesis is that teams with more equal salary distributions are generally more successful than other teams with less equal salary distributions.

We'll need to wrangle our data first, however.

12.7.1 Wrangling data

The following chunk of code reshapes the gini4 data set so that each player salary for every `team` and `season_end` combination is its own column:

1. First, however, we call the dplyr `select()` function to remove the variable `rank` from gini4.
2. We then pass the gini4 data set to the dplyr `group_by()`, `mutate()`, and `row_number()` functions to create a new variable called `id`, which is merely a column of consecutive numbers with separate and independent sequences for every `team` and `season_end` combination.
3. Finally, we call the tidyr `pivot_wider()` function, which transposes gini4 to a wide format from a long format where the variable `id` is broken out into columns and the values from the variable `salary` are used to populate the cells in these new columns.

The result is a new tibble called gini5. A call to the base R `head()` function returns the first six observations (note that R automatically returns some of the values in scientific notation):

```
gini4 <- select(gini4, -c(rank))

gini4 %>%
  group_by(team, season_end) %>%
  mutate(id = row_number(salary)) %>%
  pivot_wider(names_from = id, values_from = salary) -> gini5
head(gini5)
## # A tibble: 6 × 16
## # Groups:   team, season_end [6]
##   season_end team         `1`    `2`    `3`    `4`    `5`    `6`
##   <fct>      <fct>      <dbl>  <dbl>  <dbl>  <dbl>  <dbl>  <dbl>
## 1 1991       Atlant… 125000 200000 510000 510000 590000 650000
## 2 1991       Boston…  80000 222000 315000 375000 400000 525000
## 3 1991       Charlo…  75000 200000 322000 355000 485000 675000
## 4 1991       Chicag… 150000 385000 425000 450000 600000 750000
## 5 1991       Clevel… 100000 120000 200000 350000 525000 525000
## 6 1991       Dallas…  30000 115000 150000 250000 600000 730000
##      `7`    `8`    `9`   `10`   `11`
##    <dbl>  <dbl>  <dbl>  <dbl>  <dbl>
## 1 685000 775000 8   e5 8.95e5 1.55e6
## 2 547000 550000 7.5 e5 8.5 e5 1.21e6
## 3 805000 900000 1   e6 1.2 e6 1.25e6
## 4 765000 915000 1   e6 1   e6 1.1 e6
## 5 548000 630000 9.25e5 1.26e6 1.32e6
## 6 765000 880000 9.85e5 1   e6 1.5 e6
```

Note that columns 1 through 14 are now merely column names and not ranks; in fact, salaries are now sorted horizontally in ascending order from left to right. This is okay—we previously ranked salaries just to subset our data on the top 14 salaries for every `team` and `season_end` combination. How salaries are otherwise arranged no longer matters.

Then, we call the base R `names()` function to rename most of the gini5 column names; `season_end` and `team` will be left as is, but the remaining columns that originated as values in the former variable `rank` will be renamed so that 1, for instance, is converted to `s1` (s being short for salaries), 2 is converted to `s2`, and so forth.

Once more, note that R returns the larger values in scientific notation when we again call the `head()` function to get the first six observations, which is perfectly fine for our purposes here:

```
names(gini5) = c("season_end", "team", "s1", "s2", "s3", "s4", "s5",
                 "s6", "s7", "s8", "s9", "s10", "s11", "s12", "s13", "s14")
```

```
head(gini5)
## # A tibble: 6 × 16
## # Groups:   team, season_end [6]
##    <fct>        <fct>         <dbl>  <dbl>  <dbl>  <dbl>
## 1 1991         Atlanta Hawks 125000 200000 510000 510000
## 2 1991         Boston Celtics 80000 222000 315000 375000
## 3 1991         Charlotte Hor…  75000 200000 322000 355000
## 4 1991         Chicago Bulls 150000 385000 425000 450000
## 5 1991         Cleveland Cav… 100000 120000 200000 350000
## 6 1991         Dallas Maveri…  30000 115000 150000 250000
##     <dbl>  <dbl>  <dbl>  <dbl>  <dbl>
## 1 90000  650000 685000 775000 8    e5
## 2 400000 525000 547000 550000 7.5  e5
## 3 485000 675000 805000 900000 1    e6
## 4 600000 750000 765000 915000 1    e6
## 5 525000 525000 548000 630000 9.25e5
## 6 600000 730000 765000 880000 9.85e5
##     <dbl>  <dbl>  <dbl>   <dbl>   <dbl>
## 1 8.95e5 1.55e6 2.06e6 2406000      NA
## 2 8.5 e5 1.21e6 1.4 e6 1500000 2500000
## 3 1.2 e6 1.25e6 1.5 e6 1650000      NA
## 4 1   e6 1   e6 1.1 e6 2.5 e6       NA
## 5 1.26e6 1.32e6 1.4 e6 2640000 3785000
## 6 1   e6 1.5 e6 1.52e6 1519000 1650000
```

Then, we call the `mutate()` function from the `dplyr` package to create a new variable called `gini_index`, which equals the computed Gini coefficient for every `team` and `season_end` combination in the gini5 data set, rounded to two digits right of the decimal point. The Gini coefficient is again computed by calling the `ineq()` function from the `ineq` package, which takes the variables `s1` through `s14` as arguments. By setting the `na.rm` argument to `TRUE`, we're instructing the `ineq()` function to skip Not Available (NA) values in our data; if we had instead set it to `FALSE`, the `ineq()` function would return NA for every `team` and `season_end` combination with fewer than 14 salaries. (Remember, we set 14 players/salaries as the maximum per team per season, not the minimum.)

The result is a new data set called gini6. The `head()` function prints the first six observations:

```
gini5 %>%
  mutate(gini_index = round(ineq(c(s1, s2, s3, s4, s5, s6, s7, s8,
                                   s9, s10, s11, s12, s13, s14,
                                   na.rm = TRUE)), digits = 2)) -> gini6
head(gini6)
## # A tibble: 6 × 17
## # Groups:   team, season_end [6]
##   season_end team                   s1     s2     s3     s4
##   <fct>      <fct>               <dbl>  <dbl>  <dbl>  <dbl>
## 1 1991       Atlanta Hawks      125000 200000 510000 510000
## 2 1991       Boston Celtics      80000 222000 315000 375000
## 3 1991       Charlotte Hornets   75000 200000 322000 355000
## 4 1991       Chicago Bulls      150000 385000 425000 450000
## 5 1991       Cleveland Cavaliers 100000 120000 200000 350000
## 6 1991       Dallas Mavericks    30000 115000 150000 250000
##       s5     s6     s7     s8      s9    s10
##    <dbl>  <dbl>  <dbl>  <dbl>   <dbl>  <dbl>
## 1 590000 650000 685000 775000  800000 895000
## 2 400000 525000 547000 550000  750000 850000
## 3 485000 675000 805000 900000 1000000 1200000
## 4 600000 750000 765000 915000 1000000 1000000
## 5 525000 525000 548000 630000  925000 1260000
## 6 600000 730000 765000 880000  985000 1000000
##        s11     s12     s13     s14 gini_index
##      <dbl>   <dbl>   <dbl>   <dbl>      <dbl>
## 1 1550000 2.06e6 2406000      NA       0.42
## 2 1212000 1.4 e6 1500000 2500000       0.45
## 3 1250000 1.5 e6 1650000      NA       0.39
## 4 1100000 2.5 e6      NA      NA       0.38
## 5 1320000 1.4 e6 2640000 3785000       0.52
## 6 1500000 1.52e6 1519000 1650000       0.41
```

Next, we call the `read_csv()` function again to import a second data set, called records:

```
records <- read_csv("records.csv")
```

A subsequent call to the `dplyr` `glimpse()` function returns the records row and column counts as well as a small sample of the data:

```
glimpse(records)
## Rows: 816
## Columns: 6
## $ season_end <dbl> 1991, 1991, 1991, 1991, 1991, 1991, 1991, 199…
## $ team       <chr> "Atlanta Hawks", "Boston Celtics", "Charlotte…
## $ wins       <dbl> 43, 56, 26, 61, 33, 28, 20, 50, 44, 52, 41, 3…
## $ losses     <dbl> 39, 26, 56, 21, 49, 54, 62, 32, 38, 30, 41, 5…
## $ pct        <dbl> 0.52, 0.68, 0.32, 0.74, 0.40, 0.34, 0.24, 0.6…
## $ champ      <dbl> 0, 0, 0, 1, 0, 0, 0, 0, 0, 0, 0, 0, 0, 0, 0, …
```

The records data set includes variables called `season_end` and `team` that align perfectly with the same variables from gini6. It also contains the following variables:

- `wins`—Equals the number of regular season wins. As a reminder, teams play an 82-game regular season schedule. But in 1999 and again in 2012, the seasons were cut short due to lockouts over disagreements between the owners and players over money. As a result, the 1999 season was cut to just 50 games, and the 2012 season was reduced to 66 games.
- `losses`—Equals the number of regular season losses.
- `pct`—Short for winning percentage, a derived variable equal to wins divided by the sum of wins and losses.
- `champ`—A binary variable equal to 0 or 1, where 0 indicates a team didn't win a championship and 1 indicates otherwise.

We then convert the variables `season_end`, `team`, and `champ` to factor variables:

```
records$season_end <- as.factor(records$season_end)
records$team <- as.factor(records$team)
records$champ <- as.factor(records$champ)
```

Next, we perform a left join on the gini6 and records data sets by calling the `left_join()` function from the `dplyr` package. The two data sets are joined on the variables `season_end` and `team`; otherwise, `left_join()` returns a new data set, gini_records, that contains every row and every column from gini6 and records:

```
gini_records <- left_join(gini6, records, by = c("season_end", "team"))
```

Our new data set has a dimension of 816 rows and 21 columns—816 rows because that's the row count from gini6 and records, and 21 columns because that's the number of mutually exclusive variables between gini6 and records, plus the two shared variables `season_end` and `team`:

```
dim(gini_records)
## [1] 816  21
```

The `head()` function returns the first three observations from gini_records:

```
head(gini_records, n = 3)
## # A tibble: 3 x 21
## # Groups:   team, season_end [3]
##   season_end team                 s1     s2     s3     s4     s5
##   <fct>      <fct>             <dbl>  <dbl>  <dbl>  <dbl>  <dbl>
## 1 1991       Atlanta Hawks    125000 200000 510000 510000 590000
## 2 1991       Boston Celtics    80000 222000 315000 375000 400000
## 3 1991       Charlotte Hornets 75000 200000 322000 355000 485000
##       s6     s7      s8      s9     s10     s11     s12
##    <dbl>  <dbl>   <dbl>   <dbl>   <dbl>   <dbl>   <dbl>
## 1 650000 685000  775000  800000  895000 1550000 2065000
## 2 525000 547000  550000  750000  850000 1212000 1400000
```

```
## 3 675000 805000  900000 1000000 1200000 1250000 1500000
##       s13     s14 gini_index  wins losses   pct champ
##     <dbl>   <dbl>      <dbl> <dbl>  <dbl> <dbl> <fct>
## 1 2406000      NA       0.42    43     39  0.52 0
## 2 1500000 2500000       0.45    56     26  0.68 0
## 3 1650000      NA       0.39    26     56  0.32 0
```

Now that the gini6 and records data sets have been joined into a single object, we can perform operations that would not otherwise be possible and then execute on our analysis goals.

12.7.2 T-test

Because we're first evaluating championship-winning teams versus all other teams, we'll compute the average Gini coefficient grouped by the gini_records binary variable champ and then perform a t-test to determine if any variance is statistically significant. The variable champ equals 0 for those teams that failed to win a league championship or 1 for the one team per season where a team did win a title. Two reminders are in order:

- Our expectation is that teams with more equal salary distributions are more successful than teams with less equal salary distributions. In other words, we should expect championship-winning teams to have, on average, a lower Gini coefficient than the average team that didn't win a championship.

- From a purely statistical perspective, our null hypothesis is that any variance, one way or the other, is due to chance. We'll therefore need our t-test to return a p-value below the 5% threshold for significance to reject the null hypothesis and accept the alternative hypothesis that differences in salary distributions are meaningful.

We start with a chunk of dplyr code by which the gini_records data set is passed to the group_by() and summarize() functions; again, we're computing the average of the variable gini_index by the binary variable champ. Our results are cast into a tibble called gini_summary2:

```
gini_records %>%
  group_by(champ) %>%
  summarize(mean = round(mean(gini_index), digits = 2)) -> gini_summary2
print(gini_summary2)
## # A tibble: 2 × 2
##   champ mean
##   <fct> <dbl>
## 1 0      0.48
## 2 1      0.53
```

So the 28 championship-winning teams in our data set—one per season between 1991 and 2018—have an average Gini coefficient equal to 0.53, while teams that didn't win a league championship had an average Gini coefficient equal to 0.48. In other words, championship-winning teams between 1991 and 2018 had more unequal salary distributions than other teams.

Is this variance statistically significant? Let's perform our t-test to find out. A t-test is a statistical test that compares the means from two, and only two, data series. It considers the difference in means, group variances, and record counts to determine if the variance is essentially equal to zero or different from zero. If the former, we'll fail to reject our null or going-in hypothesis that the means are equal; if the latter, we'll reject the null hypothesis and instead accept the alternative hypothesis that the means are different.

With that in mind, we establish two new data sets, giniX, which is gini_records filtered on the variable champ equaling 0, and giniY, which is gini_records filtered on the variable champ instead equaling 1. The t-test is performed against the gini_records variable gini_index by calling the t.test() function from base R:

```
gini_records %>%
  filter(champ == 0) -> giniX
gini_records %>%
  filter(champ == 1) -> giniY

t.test(giniX$gini_index, giniY$gini_index)
##
##  Welch Two Sample t-test
##
## data:  giniX$gini_index and giniY$gini_index
## t = -2.9526, df = 28.54, p-value = 0.006245
## alternative hypothesis: true difference in means is not equal to 0
## 95 percent confidence interval:
##  -0.08297073 -0.01503507
## sample estimates:
## mean of x mean of y
## 0.4795685 0.5285714
```

The p-value, defined as the probability that a statistical measure will be greater than or equal to the observed results, of the t-test essentially equals 0. Because it's below the predefined and generally accepted 5% threshold for significance, we reject the null hypothesis that the means are statistically equal. This means the variance is statistically significant: that championship-winning teams have more *unequal* salary distributions than all other teams is a statistically significant differentiator. This is likely due to championship-winning teams having superstar and high-priced talent on their respective rosters, which, because of the salary cap, leaves less money available for other players.

We'll visualize these results with paired ggplot2 boxplots. Consider just a few notes about our code first:

- We first call the rbind() function from base R to join the giniX and giniY data sets by rows, thereby creating a new object called giniXY in the process.
- Our data source is therefore the giniXY data set.

- Our x-axis variable is the binary variable `champ`, and our y-axis variable is `gini_index`.
- The `ggplot()` function automatically draws horizontal lines to represent the medians. The `stat_summary()` function adds light dots to represent the means.
- The `scale_x_discrete()` function adds the labels `League Champions` and `All Other Teams` in lieu of the `1` and `0`, respectively, from the binary variable `champ`.

Shape options with ggplot2

We digressed in a previous chapter by briefly mentioning the different types of lines that you can draw with the `ggplot2` graphics package, so it's about time we did the same with respect to shapes. Because there are many options, shapes are referenced by numbers:

Circles: 1, 10, 13, 16, 19, 20, 21

Triangles: 2, 6, 17, 24, 25

Diamonds: 5, 9, 18, 23

Squares: 0, 7, 12, 14, 15, 22

Other: 3, 4, 8, 11

All of these can be manipulated by adding or changing colors, fills, and sizes. As always, you'll want to experiment with different combinations of shapes, colors, fills, and sizes.

Here's our data wrangling and data visualization code; the fruits of this, our paired box plots, follow (see figure 12.4):

```
giniXY <- rbind(giniX, giniY)
ggplot(giniXY, aes(x = champ, y = gini_index)) +
  geom_boxplot() +
  labs(title = "Comparison of Gini Coefficients based on
       Season-End Disposition ",
       subtitle = "1991-2018",
       x = "",
       y = "Gini Coefficients") +
  geom_boxplot(color = "skyblue4", fill = "skyblue1") +
  stat_summary(fun = mean, geom = "point", shape = 20, size = 8,
               color = "white", fill = "white") +
  theme(plot.title = element_text(face = "bold")) +
  scale_x_discrete(breaks = c("1", "0"),
                   labels = c("League Champions", "All Other Teams"))
```

We already know, of course, that the mean Gini coefficient is greater for championship-winning teams than it is for all other teams. The boxplots show that the medians, too, are quite different and that the distribution for league champions is less dispersed than it is for the remaining teams. Recall that the boxplots decompose the distribution of a

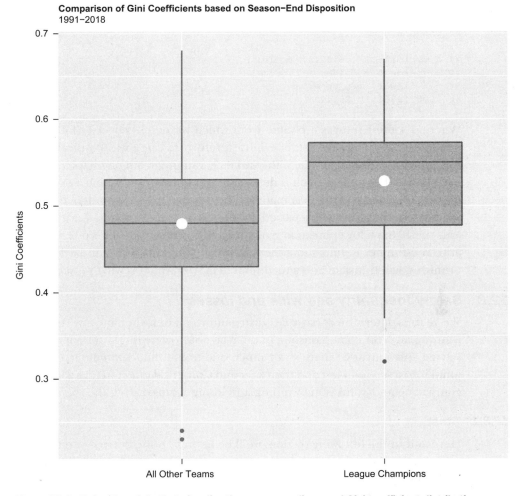

Comparison of Gini Coefficients based on Season-End Disposition
1991–2018

Figure 12.4 Paired boxplots that visualize the means, medians, and Gini coefficient distributions between championship-winning teams and all other teams. The variances are statistically significant.

data series between the Interquartile Range (IQR), which represents the middle 50% of the data; the whiskers that extend below and above the IQR that represent, respectively, the lower 25% and upper 25% of the data; and outliers, represented by solid dots beyond the whiskers.

Next, we'll complement our t-test with a Cohen's d effect size test.

12.7.3 Effect size testing

Let's now perform a Cohen's d test, which is a type of effect size test based on population means and standard deviations. Unlike a t-test, a Cohen's d test isn't influenced by record counts. The syntax resembles that of a t-test, or even a correlation test, for that matter; we merely substitute the `t.test()` function or the `cor.test()` function with the `cohen.d()` function from the `effsize` package, as follows:

```
cohen.d(giniX$gini_index, giniY$gini_index)
##
## Cohen's d
##
## d estimate: -0.6331437 (medium)
## 95 percent confidence interval:
##      lower      upper
## -1.0118781 -0.2544094
```

Whereas a t-test returns a p-value from which we either reject or fail to reject a null hypothesis, a Cohen's d test, by contrast, returns a categorical indicator representing the effect size, or magnitude of the variance, ranging from negligible to large, that ties back to the d estimate, which is defined as the number of standard deviations separating the two means. The d estimate will be positive or negative depending on how we sequenced the arguments passed to the cohen.d() function. Because the variable gini_index has a lower mean in giniX than in giniY, our Cohen's d test returned a negative d estimate. Results somewhere between 0.40 and 0.70 standard deviations, plus or minus, will translate into a medium effect size, which is what we see here.

12.8   *Salary inequality and wins and losses*

We've thus determined that salary distributions matter when it comes to winning or not winning an NBA championship, but maybe not how we might have imagined when we started this journey. There's not much additional data wrangling required, so we'll jump into a second t-test and then a second Cohen's d effect size test; this time, we'll be comparing and contrasting winning and losing teams during the regular season.

12.8.1   *T-test*

Here and in the following section, we'll be keying on the derived variable pct, which is equal to regular season winning percentage. We start by passing the gini_records data set to the dplyr group_by() and summarize() functions; the summarize() function computes the Gini coefficient, rounded to two digits right of the decimal point, and the group_by() function divides the results between teams that had winning percentages equal to or greater than 0.50 versus less than 0.50. Because we've included a logical operator inside the argument to the group_by() function, our results will therefore be split between TRUE and FALSE:

```
gini_records %>%
  group_by(pct >= 0.50) %>%
  summarize(mean = round(mean(gini_index), digits = 2)) -> gini_summary3
print(gini_summary3)
## # A tibble: 2 × 2
##   `pct >= 0.5`  mean
##   <lgl>        <dbl>
## 1 FALSE         0.46
## 2 TRUE          0.5
```

Winning teams, on average, have higher Gini coefficients, and therefore more unequal salary distributions, than teams with losing records, at least between the 1991 and 2018 seasons. These results are probably statistically significant, but let's see for sure.

We therefore create two more data sets, giniA, which is gini_records subset where the variable pct is equal to or greater than 0.50, and giniB, which is gini_records subset where the variable pct is less than 0.50. Our t-test compares the gini_index means between the giniA and giniB data sets:

```
gini_records %>%
  filter(pct >= 0.50) -> giniA
gini_records %>%
  filter(pct < 0.50) -> giniB

t.test(giniA$gini_index, giniB$gini_index)
##
##  Welch Two Sample t-test
##
## data:  giniA$gini_index and giniB$gini_index
## t = 8.8145, df = 767.61, p-value < 0.00000000000000022
## alternative hypothesis: true difference in means is not equal to 0
## 95 percent confidence interval:
##   0.03594185 0.05653782
## sample estimates:
## mean of x mean of y
## 0.5013666 0.4551268
```

The p-value, not surprisingly, is again essentially 0; therefore, we again reject the null hypothesis and instead accept the alternative hypothesis that the variance in means is statistically significant.

In the following chunk of code, we call the base R rbind() function to join giniA and giniB into a new data set called giniAB. Then, we call the dplyr mutate() function to create a new variable called win_pct to divide teams into one of two populations, depending on their regular season winning percentage. The ggplot2 code that follows has a syntax similar to our first set of boxplots (see figure 12.5):

```
giniAB <- rbind(giniA, giniB)
mutate(giniAB, win_pct = ifelse(pct >= 0.50, "y", "n")) -> giniAB
ggplot(giniAB, aes(x = win_pct, y = gini_index)) +
  geom_boxplot() +
  labs(title = "Comparison of Gini Coefficients based on
       Regular Season Winning Percentage",
       subtitle = "1991-2018",
       x = "",
       y = "Gini Coefficients") +
  geom_boxplot(color = "skyblue4", fill = "skyblue1") +
  stat_summary(fun = mean, geom = "point", shape = 20, size = 8,
               color = "white", fill = "white") +
  theme(plot.title = element_text(face = "bold")) +
  scale_x_discrete(breaks = c("y", "n"),
                   labels = c("Winning Teams", "Losing Teams"))
```

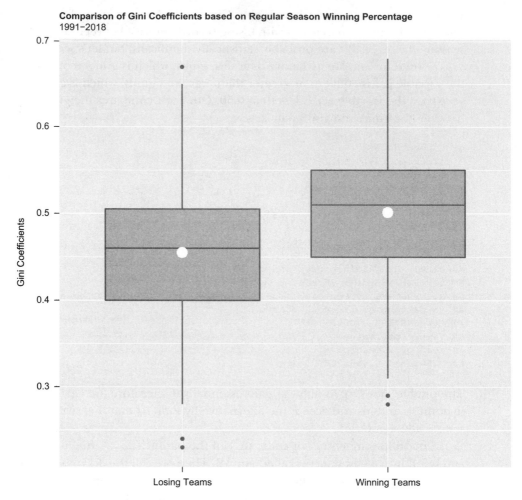

Figure 12.5   Paired boxplots that visualize the means, medians, and Gini coefficient distributions between winning and losing teams. Once more, the variances are statistically significant.

While our test results are rather straightforward, they nevertheless become more compelling when visualized. We could almost (if it weren't for the relevance of record counts) set aside our t-test and instead put our complete trust in these paired boxplots, which clearly show significant enough differences in means, medians, and distributions. Let's run a second Cohen's d test to get a read on the effect size.

12.8.2 *Effect size testing*

We call the `cohen.d()` function and pass the same pair of arguments we originally passed for our t-test:

```
cohen.d(giniA$gini_index, giniB$gini_index)
##
## Cohen's d
##
## d estimate: 0.6210674 (medium)
## 95 percent confidence interval:
##     lower     upper
## 0.4792167 0.7629181
```

Because the d estimate equals 0.62, our Cohen's d test returns a medium effect size. Our d estimate is positive this time because the first argument passed to the `cohen.d()` function has a larger mean than the second argument passed; that is, the average Gini coefficient for salary distribution is higher for teams that won at least half of their regular season games than it is for teams that won fewer than half their games. Thus, our analysis so far has returned results we weren't necessarily expecting, as summarized here:

- Championship-winning teams between the 1991 and 2018 NBA seasons had, on average, more unequal salary distributions, at least based on Gini coefficients, than teams that didn't win a championship.
- These variances are statistically significant, and according to our Cohen's d effect size test, which measures the practical significance rather than the statistical significance, the differences in means are graded as medium (which is less than large, but greater than negligible or small).
- Teams that won at least half of their regular season games between 1991 and 2018 had, on average, more unequal salary distributions than other teams that finished their regular seasons with losing records.
- These variances, too, are statistically significant, and our subsequent Cohen's d test returned more or less the same result as our first effect size test.

We'll take these last results a step further by categorizing every NBA team in our data set into one of five bins, or bands, and computing the average Gini coefficient for each.

12.9   *Gini coefficient bands versus winning percentage*

Finally, we'll create a `ggplot2` bar chart that plots Gini coefficients against regular season winning percentages. We're about to see how well unequal salary distributions and higher regular season winning percentages are correlated with one another. This will first require some additional data wrangling, however.

We'll start by passing the gini_records data set to the `dplyr mutate()` and `case_when()` functions to create a categorical variable called gini_band derived from the numeric variable gini_index. When the variable gini_index, for instance, is equal to or greater than `0.60`, gini_band will equal `>0.60`; when gini_index is greater than or equal to `0.50` and less than `0.60`, gini_band will equal `>0.50`; and so forth. We want to see how Gini coefficients trend as regular season winning percentages increase from one band to the next.

Our new variable is then converted to a factor variable. The `head()` function returns the first three observations:

```
gini_records %>%
  mutate(gini_band =
           case_when(gini_index >= .60 ~ ">0.60",
                     gini_index >= .50 & gini_index < .60 ~ ">0.50",
                     gini_index >= .40 & gini_index < .50 ~ ">0.40",
                     gini_index >= .30 & gini_index < .40 ~ ">0.30",
                     gini_index < .30 ~ ">0.20")) -> gini_records

gini_records$gini_band <- as.factor(gini_records$gini_band)

head(gini_records, n = 3)
## # A tibble: 3 × 22
## # Groups:   team, season_end [3]
##   season_end team                      s1     s2     s3     s4     s5
##   <fct>      <fct>                  <dbl>  <dbl>  <dbl>  <dbl>  <dbl>
## 1 1991       Atlanta Hawks         125000 200000 510000 510000 590000
## 2 1991       Boston Celtics         80000 222000 315000 375000 400000
## 3 1991       Charlotte Hornets      75000 200000 322000 355000 485000
##       s6     s7     s8     s9    s10    s11    s12
##    <dbl>  <dbl>  <dbl>  <dbl>  <dbl>  <dbl>  <dbl>
## 1 650000 685000 775000  8  e5 8.95e5 1.55e6 2.06e6
## 2 525000 547000 550000 7.5e5 8.5 e5 1.21e6 1.4 e6
## 3 675000 805000 900000  1  e6 1.2 e6 1.25e6 1.5 e6
##      s13    s14 gini_index  wins losses   pct champ gini_band
##    <dbl>  <dbl>      <dbl> <dbl>  <dbl> <dbl> <fct> <fct>
## 1 2.41e6 NA          0.42    43     39  0.52 0     >0.40
## 2 1.5 e6 2.5e6       0.45    56     26  0.68 0     >0.40
## 3 1.65e6 NA          0.39    26     56  0.32 0     >0.30
```

Then, we pass gini_records to the `dplyr` `group_by()` and `summarize()` functions, by which the `summarize()` function computes the mean of the variable pct, rounded two digits to the right of the decimal point, and the `group_by()` function separates the results for each factor in the variable gini_band. The results are cast to a tibble called gini_summary3:

```
gini_records %>%
  group_by(gini_band) %>%
  summarize(mean_pct = round(mean(pct), digits = 2)) -> gini_summary3
print(gini_summary3)
## # A tibble: 5 × 2
##   gini_band mean_pct
##   <fct>        <dbl>
## 1 >0.20         0.37
## 2 >0.30         0.43
## 3 >0.40         0.58
## 4 >0.50         0.54
## 5 >0.60         0.57
```

Here's our `ggplot2` bar chart that takes gini_summary3 as a data source and plots the variable `gini_band` along the x-axis and the variable `mean_pct` along the y-axis (see figure 12.6):

```
ggplot(gini_summary3, aes(x = gini_band, y = mean_pct)) +
  geom_bar(stat = "identity", width = .6, fill = "sienna1") +
  labs(title = "Gini Coefficients and Winning Percentages",
       subtitle = "1991-2018",
       x = "Gini Coefficient Bands",
       y = "Average Regular Season Winning Percentage") +
  ylim(0, 0.65) +
  geom_text(aes(x = gini_band, y = mean_pct, label = mean_pct,
                vjust = -0.3, fontface = "bold")) +
  theme(plot.title = element_text(face = "bold"))
```

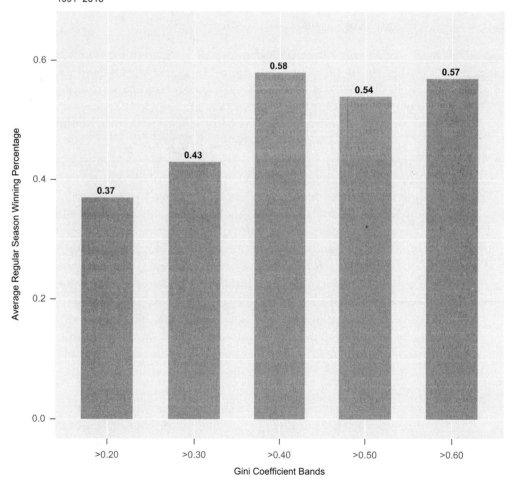

Figure 12.6   A bar chart that shows higher Gini coefficients—that is, more unequal salary distributions—to be very well aligned with higher regular season winning percentages

There is a significant increase in regular season winning percentages as salary distributions become more unequal. Teams with Gini coefficients equal to or greater than 0.40 win, on average, at least 54% of their regular season games. By contrast, teams with Gini coefficients less than 0.40 win, on average, 43% or less of their regular season games. This is the difference between possibly winning a league championship and not even qualifying for postseason play.

Salary inequality, then, at least in the NBA between 1991 and 2018, actually *creates* prosperity. That's because superstars—who are fairly paid (based on performance) millions more per year than other players—are the motor that powers the NBA. We learned in chapter 3 that teams can't even entertain the idea of winning a championship without one or, probably, two legitimate superstars on their roster.

In the next chapter, we'll explore inequality around win share distributions and how that may or may not be associated with winning and losing.

Summary

- Maybe the most important point worth understanding about t-tests is that their results are dependent upon the difference in means *and* the record counts. Small variances on small data sets won't register as statistically significant, but small variances on larger data sets might very well return different results. By the same token, large variances will absolutely return statistically significant results on large data sets and might or might not return the same on smaller data sets.

- Effect size tests, by contrast, don't consider record counts. You can therefore get like returns on a pair of effect size tests when the variances are equal, but the record counts are not. As such, effect size tests should complement t-tests or other "like" statistical tests and should never be a substitute. You reject or fail to reject a null hypothesis based on the results of a statistical test such as a t-test or a chi-square test for independence; you would never do likewise based on the results of an effect size test. In addition, you should never draw like conclusions from like variances where the record counts are very different.

- Make the investment in exploring your data. Not only does a thorough data exploration exercise return valuable insights, but often it will help guide your subsequent data wrangling and data analysis operations. Would our results have been any different had we heedlessly removed supposedly duplicate records in our data set?

- Make additional investments in the course of your data wrangling activities to periodically check and verify the integrity of your operations, especially when those operations are atypical and relatively complex. Repetition, if it's fair to call it that, should always take a back seat to periodic and even frequent integrity checks.

- With respect to our results, championship-winning teams have, on average, more unequal salary distributions than other teams, and winning teams have, on average, more unequal salary distributions than losing teams. Our t-tests proved that these variances are, in fact, statistically significant. Our Cohen's d tests further verified that these same variances are above negligible in magnitude.

- We know from prior chapters that winning teams, and especially championship-winning teams, usually have one or more superstars on their rosters who, of course, command the highest salaries. This leaves less money for other player salaries and undoubtedly helps explain our results.

- The league-wide Gini coefficient in player salaries has been and remains up significantly—by eight or so percentage points—since 1997 than before 1997. Some of this is surely due to league expansion over the years and the increase in roster sizes. But the remainder may very well be due to increased awareness around the efficacy of larger investments in superstar talent.

More with Gini coefficients and Lorenz curves

13

This chapter covers

- Working (again) with Gini coefficients
- Creating alternative Lorenz curves
- Running significance tests (t-tests and F-tests)
- Running other effect size tests (aside from Cohen's d)
- Writing `for` loops
- Writing user-defined functions

It's true that we're going to again compute Gini coefficients, plot inequality by drawing Lorenz curves, perform more significance testing, and conduct additional effect size tests to complement our t-tests—but there's a lot of new material packed into this chapter too:

- We'll demonstrate how to intelligently plot multiple Lorenz curves with the least amount of code. You'll learn how to plot two Lorenz curves in the same plot to compare two Gini coefficients in one object rather than two.

- Furthermore, we'll demonstrate how to create a simple `for` loop as an alternative to writing repeatable lines of code and then demonstrate how to apply what we've learned by drawing four Lorenz curves with one short chunk of code.

- Because we're demonstrating how to create a `for` loop, we'll show how you can create your own function just in case R doesn't already have a function for what you need. We'll first demonstrate how to create a pair of simple functions and then provide further instruction on creating a function that can estimate a Gini coefficient.

- In previous chapters, including chapter 12, we've conducted Cohen's d effect size tests to quantitatively and qualitatively measure the statistical relationship between two variables on a numeric scale. There are actually other effect size tests, above and beyond Cohen's d, that do the same thing. We'll demonstrate how to run those tests and then discuss which tests are best under which circumstances.

- Finally, we'll demonstrate how to run an F-test, which is yet another statistical test used to compare the variances between two or more groups. An F-test actually evaluates whether the ratio of two variances is statistically significant or just the result of chance. We'll briefly discuss how and when an F-test best fits into your analysis.

Along the way, we'll compute Gini coefficients on the distribution of win shares, the player-level advanced statistic that was at the heart of our analysis in chapters 2 and 3. While Gini coefficients have mostly been used to measure inequality in income or wealth, they can actually be used to measure any sort of inequality, as we demonstrated in the prior chapter. Our purpose in this chapter is to determine whether Gini coefficients on win share distributions are linked to winning or losing and if any variances are statistically significant. Our null hypothesis is that Gini coefficients, regardless of whether they are low or high or somewhere in between, have no effect on winning. However, if player salaries are truly aligned with productivity, we shouldn't be surprised to see results similar to those from chapter 12, but let's find out one way or the other. We'll start by loading our required packages.

13.1 Loading packages

The same set of packages we loaded and used in the previous chapter—`tidyverse`, `sqldf`, `ineq`, `gglorenz`, `scales`, and `effsize`—is again required, along with two other packages, `effectsize` and `car`:

- In prior chapters, including chapter 12, we performed one type of effect size test, Cohen's d, by way of the `effsize` package. In this chapter, we'll again compute Cohen's d estimates through the `effsize` package, and then we'll perform other effect size testing through the `effectsize` package.

- In chapter 5, we called the `vif()` function from the `car` package to check for multicollinearity in our multiple linear regressions; here, we'll load the `car` package and then call its `recode()` function to recode, or rename, elements in a character vector.

Our eight packages are loaded by sequentially calling the base R `library()` function:

```
library(tidyverse)
library(sqldf)
library(ineq)
library(gglorenz)
library(scales)
library(effsize)
library(effectsize)
library(car)
```

We'll next import our data set and then take a quick glance at what we'll be working with going forward.

13.2   *Importing and viewing data*

Our data set is a .csv file downloaded from Kaggle and then stored in our default working directory; it contains player statistics, including win shares, from every NBA season between 1950 and 2017. We therefore make a call to the readr `read_csv()` function to import our data and in the process establish an object called ws_gini:

```
ws_gini <- read_csv("seasons_stats.csv")
```

The base R `dim()` function returns the dimension, or row and column counts, of the ws_gini data set:

```
dim(ws_gini)
## [1] 24624    53
```

Our data set is 24,624 observations long and 53 columns wide where each player/year/team combination occupies a unique record in the ws_gini data set. It's always a best practice to reduce the dimension of your data by eliminating unnecessary or unwanted variables and records, if for no other reason than to allow your queries and other lines of code to run faster and for you to maintain focus where it's needed most. Thus, we'll start our data wrangling operations by reducing the width and then the length of our data.

13.3   *Wrangling data*

We begin by calling the dplyr `select()` function to subset ws_gini on just three variables: Year (e.g., 2012, which represents the 2011–12 season), Tm (e.g., CLE for Cleveland Cavaliers or DAL for Dallas Mavericks), and WS (short for win shares):

```
ws_gini %>%
  select(Year, Tm, WS) -> ws_gini
```

Then, we call the `dplyr filter()` function to subset ws_gini where the variable `Year` is equal to or greater than `1991`. Our data set will hereafter contain the 1991 through 2017 NBA seasons, which closely aligns with our data from chapter 12:

```
ws_gini %>%
  filter(Year >= 1991) -> ws_gini
```

Next, we call the `filter()` function again to further reduce the ws_gini data set by only including those records where the variable `Tm` doesn't equal `TOT`; we therefore add the logical operator not equal to `(!=)` to exclude those records going forward. It turns out that players who played for more than one team in a single NBA season are represented multiple times in the data downloaded from Kaggle. For instance, Spencer Hawes, now retired, played for both the Charlotte Hornets and Milwaukee Bucks in 2017; there are thus three Spencer Hawes observations in ws_gini for 2017, one where the variable `Tm` equals `CHO` (for Charlotte), one where `Tm` equals `MIL` (for Milwaukee), and a third where `Tm` equals `TOT`, which is an aggregate of `CHO` and `MIL`:

```
ws_gini %>%
  filter(Tm != "TOT") -> ws_gini
```

Another call to the `dim()` function gets the reduced dimension of the ws_gini data set:

```
dim(ws_gini)
## [1] 13356      3
```

This is now just 13,356 rows long and, of course, three columns wide.

We then convert the variables `Year` and `Tm` to factor variables by twice calling the base R `as.factor()` function:

```
ws_gini$Year <- as.factor(ws_gini$Year)
ws_gini$Tm <- as.factor(ws_gini$Tm)
```

Successive calls to the base R `head()` and `tail()` functions return the first six and last six observations, respectively, in ws_gini—just so you can see what a few records actually look like:

```
head(ws_gini)
##    Year   Tm     WS
##    <fct> <fct> <dbl>
## 1 1991   POR   0.5
## 2 1991   DEN  -1.0
## 3 1991   ORL   2.5
## 4 1991   DEN   6.3
## 5 1991   DET   5.5
## 6 1991   POR   6.2

tail(ws_gini)
##          Year   Tm     WS
```

```
##         <fct> <fct> <dbl>
## 13351 2017   IND    4.6
## 13352 2017   CHO    5.6
## 13353 2017   BOS    1.0
## 13354 2017   ORL    0.0
## 13355 2017   CHI    0.5
## 13356 2017   LAL    1.1
```

Then, we call the summary() function from base R, which returns descriptive statistics for the three variables remaining in ws_gini. By adding the maxsum argument, we're instructing R to return as many as, but no more than, 40 levels for factors. The variable Year contains 26 levels, and the variable Tm contains 38 levels (our data includes different levels, or factors, for multiple iterations in team names even when the franchises remained the same).

As a reminder, for variables that are numeric, such as WS, the summary() function returns the mean, median, minimum and maximum values, and the first and third quartiles. For variables that are factors, such as Year and Tm, summary() instead returns the observation counts for each group:

```
summary(ws_gini, maxsum = 40)
##      Year          Tm            WS
##  1991:415    ATL:464    Min.    :-2.100
##  1992:425    BOS:465    1st Qu.: 0.200
##  1993:421    BRK: 93    Median : 1.300
##  1994:444    CHA:183    Mean    : 2.422
##  1995:430    CHH:207    3rd Qu.: 3.700
##  1996:489    CHI:445    Max.    :20.400
##  1997:511    CHO: 53
##  1998:494    CLE:473
##  1999:474    DAL:477
##  2000:468    DEN:474
##  2001:490    DET:428
##  2002:470    GSW:480
##  2003:456    HOU:471
##  2004:517    IND:422
##  2005:526    LAC:457
##  2006:512    LAL:425
##  2007:487    MEM:288
##  2008:527    MIA:458
##  2009:515    MIL:452
##  2010:512    MIN:440
##  2011:542    NJN:394
##  2012:515    NOH:161
##  2013:523    NOK: 34
##  2014:548    NOP: 89
##  2015:575    NYK:452
##  2016:528    OKC:163
##  2017:542    ORL:455
##              PHI:481
##              PHO:459
##              POR:439
##              SAC:449
```

```
##              SAS:456
##              SEA:280
##              TOR:402
##              UTA:416
##              VAN: 98
##              WAS:351
##              WSB:122
```

The upcoming chunk of code should be familiar if you've already read chapter 12. The intent is to further reduce the length of our data set by subsetting ws_gini on a maximum of the top 14 win shares for each Year and Tm combination. The NBA includes many players who come and go on short-term contracts; by subsetting the ws_gini data set, we're fairly and accurately excluding the NBA equivalent of temporary contract help and focusing exclusively on full-time and permanent employees:

- We begin by passing our data to the dplyr arrange() function, which sorts ws_gini by each of the three ws_gini variables.
- We then call the dplyr group_by() and mutate() functions and the base R rank() function to create a new variable called rank, where the variable WS is sorted in descending order, 1 through *n*, by every Year and Tm combination in our data. The minus, or negative, sign inside the rank() function instructs R to sort, or rank, the variable WS in descending order. The ties.method argument specifies how ties should be handled; when equal to first, R assigns tied elements to consecutive, and thus different, ranks.
- Finally, we call the dplyr filter() function to include only those records where the variable rank is less than or equal to 14.

The results are thrown into a tibble called ws_gini2:

```
ws_gini %>%
  arrange(Year, Tm, WS) %>%
  group_by(Year, Tm) %>%
  mutate(rank = rank(-WS, ties.method = "first")) %>%
  filter(rank <= 14) -> ws_gini2
```

We then call the base R head() function, this time to return the top 14 records in the ws_gini2 data set, to display the outcomes of these last few operations:

```
head(ws_gini2, n = 14)
## # A tibble: 14 × 4
## # Groups:   Year, Tm [1]
##    Year  Tm        WS  rank
##    <fct> <fct> <dbl> <int>
## 1 1991  ATL    -0.5    14
## 2 1991  ATL    -0.1    13
## 3 1991  ATL     0      11
## 4 1991  ATL     0      12
## 5 1991  ATL     1.1    10
## 6 1991  ATL     1.8     9
```

```
##  7 1991  ATL     1.9      8
##  8 1991  ATL     2.5      7
##  9 1991  ATL     4        6
## 10 1991  ATL     4.4      5
## 11 1991  ATL     5.4      4
## 12 1991  ATL     5.6      3
## 13 1991  ATL     6.3      2
## 14 1991  ATL    11.4      1
```

Here are a couple of observations (note, by the way, that ATL is short for Atlanta Hawks):

- The variable ws is clearly sorted in ascending order, and just as clearly, we see that the variable rank is sorted in descending order. This makes it possible to subset each Year and Tm combination on no more than the top 14 win shares.
- The Atlanta Hawks had two players who "earned" 0.0 win shares during the 1991 season. By design, they are assigned different but contiguous ranks; otherwise, we would run the risk of subsetting at least some of our Year and Tm combinations on more than 14 records.

While this looks perfect, let's nevertheless perform a series of integrity checks similar to those we performed in the prior chapter. We start by twice calling the sqldf() function from the sqldf package to (1) to return every record from ws_gini where the variable Year equals 2012 and the variable Tm equals GSW, short for Golden State Warriors; and (2) return every record from ws_gini2 where the variable Year also equals 2012 and the variable Tm also equals GSW:

```
sqldf("SELECT * FROM ws_gini WHERE Year = 2012 AND Tm = 'GSW'")
##    Year  Tm   WS
## 1  2012 GSW   0.0
## 2  2012 GSW   0.0
## 3  2012 GSW   1.3
## 4  2012 GSW   0.1
## 5  2012 GSW   2.2
## 6  2012 GSW   1.5
## 7  2012 GSW   0.2
## 8  2012 GSW   0.7
## 9  2012 GSW   0.5
## 10 2012 GSW   5.0
## 11 2012 GSW   1.5
## 12 2012 GSW   0.1
## 13 2012 GSW   2.8
## 14 2012 GSW   3.5
## 15 2012 GSW   0.1
## 16 2012 GSW   1.7
## 17 2012 GSW  -0.2
## 18 2012 GSW   0.9
## 19 2012 GSW   0.6
## 20 2012 GSW   3.4

sqldf("select * FROM ws_gini2 WHERE Year = 2012 AND Tm = 'GSW'")
##    Year  Tm  WS rank
## 1  2012 GSW 0.2   14
```

```
## 2   2012 GSW 0.5   13
## 3   2012 GSW 0.6   12
## 4   2012 GSW 0.7   11
## 5   2012 GSW 0.9   10
## 6   2012 GSW 1.3    9
## 7   2012 GSW 1.5    7
## 8   2012 GSW 1.5    8
## 9   2012 GSW 1.7    6
## 10  2012 GSW 2.2    5
## 11  2012 GSW 2.8    4
## 12  2012 GSW 3.4    3
## 13  2012 GSW 3.5    2
## 14  2012 GSW 5.0    1
```

Our first SELECT statement returned 20 records, sorted in no particular order, and our second SELECT statement returned 14 records, where the variable WS is sorted in ascending order and the variable rank is sorted in descending order. This checks out.

Next, we do the same by swapping out the Golden State Warriors in favor of the Boston Celtics (BOS) and by writing two short chunks of dplyr code rather than sqldf code. We pass the ws_gini and then the ws_gini2 data sets to the filter() function to subset the results where the variable Year equals 2017 and the variable Tm equals BOS:

```
ws_gini %>%
  filter(Year == 2017 & Tm == "BOS")
##     Year  Tm   WS
## 1   2017 BOS   3.1
## 2   2017 BOS   1.5
## 3   2017 BOS   6.7
## 4   2017 BOS   0.6
## 5   2017 BOS   6.3
## 6   2017 BOS   0.1
## 7   2017 BOS   2.1
## 8   2017 BOS   5.0
## 9   2017 BOS   0.1
## 10  2017 BOS   4.1
## 11  2017 BOS   1.4
## 12  2017 BOS   3.2
## 13  2017 BOS  12.6
## 14  2017 BOS   0.3
## 15  2017 BOS   1.0

ws_gini2 %>%
  filter(Year == 2017 & Tm == "BOS")
## # A tibble: 14 × 4
## # Groups:   Year, Tm [1]
##     Year  Tm       WS  rank
##     <fct> <fct> <dbl> <int>
## 1 2017   BOS     0.1    14
## 2 2017   BOS     0.3    13
## 3 2017   BOS     0.6    12
## 4 2017   BOS     1      11
## 5 2017   BOS     1.4    10
## 6 2017   BOS     1.5     9
```

```
##  7 2017  BOS    2.1     8
##  8 2017  BOS    3.1     7
##  9 2017  BOS    3.2     6
## 10 2017  BOS    4.1     5
## 11 2017  BOS    5       4
## 12 2017  BOS    6.3     3
## 13 2017  BOS    6.7     2
## 14 2017  BOS   12.6     1
```

Our first chunk of `dplyr` code returned 15 unsorted records, and our second code chunk returned just 14 records by filtering out one of two players who earned 0.1 win shares during the 2017 season. This checks out.

Finally, let's run two more SELECT statements that compute the ws_gini2 row counts where the variable Tm equals GSW and then when Tm equals BOS. Row counts should equal a maximum of 378, which is the product of 27 seasons times a maximum of 14 players/win shares per season (some teams in some seasons had fewer than 14 players on their respective rosters):

```
sqldf("select COUNT(*) FROM ws_gini2 WHERE Tm = 'GSW'")
##    COUNT(*)
## 1      377

sqldf("select COUNT(*) FROM ws_gini2 WHERE Tm = 'BOS'")
##    COUNT(*)
## 1      378
```

The row counts equal 377 and 378, respectively. This also checks out.

Now that we know our data is in a good spot, we can next begin our analysis by computing Gini coefficients.

13.4 *Gini coefficients*

Once more, the Gini coefficient is a frequently reported measure of inequality, usually income inequality across some population, where a coefficient equal to 0 represents a state of perfect equality and a coefficient equal to 1 represents a state of perfect inequality. In chapter 12, we computed Gini coefficients to measure salary inequality; here, we'll compute Gini coefficients to measure win share inequality.

In the next chunk of code, we pass ws_gini2 to the `dplyr` group_by() and summarize() functions to compute the league-wide Gini coefficient for win shares for each level in the variable Year. The ineq() function from the ineq package is otherwise doing our heavy lifting, returning the annual Gini coefficient, rounded to two digits right of the decimal point, through a new variable called gc. Our results are cast to a tibble called ws_gini_summary:

```
ws_gini2 %>%
  group_by(Year) %>%
  summarize(gc = round(ineq(WS), digits = 2)) -> ws_gini_summary
print(ws_gini_summary)
```

```
## # A tibble: 27 × 2
##    Year      gc
##    <fct> <dbl>
##  1 1991   0.56
##  2 1992   0.56
##  3 1993   0.54
##  4 1994   0.54
##  5 1995   0.53
##  6 1996   0.54
##  7 1997   0.55
##  8 1998   0.53
##  9 1999   0.55
## 10 2000   0.53
## # … with 17 more rows
```

Our results are then plotted in a `ggplot2` line chart (see figure 13.1). We've switched up some of the aesthetics from previous line charts:

- The `geom_line()` function draws a black line one-half the `ggplot2` default width.
- The `geom_point()` function adds points along the line that are five times the default size. Our plot therefore assumes the look and feel of a connected scatterplot.
- The `geom_text()` function adds labels above the points that tie back to the ws_gini_summary variable `gc`. The `nudge_x` and `nudge_y` arguments are used to position the labels relative to the points—the smaller the number, the closer the labels. If negative, R places the numbers below the points rather than above. The `check_overlap` argument is an instruction to R to avoid, as much as possible, overlapping the labels.
- The first and second calls to the `theme()` function center the title and subtitle, thereby overwriting the `ggplot2` default, which is to left-justify both. By setting the `hjust` argument, short for horizontal adjustment, equal to `0.5`, we're shifting the title and subtitle halfway across the width of the plot. Alternatively, we could right-justify the title and subtitle by instead setting the `hjust` argument equal to `1`.
- The third call to the `theme()` function orients the x-axis labels at 45 degrees and aligns them horizontally just beneath the plot.
- The `annotate()` function is called twice to add a pair of transparent rectangular shapes, where the `xmin`, `xmax`, `ymin`, and `ymax` arguments establish the horizontal and vertical boundaries. This is a nice touch that immediately suggests the plot has two different stories to tell.

Finally, here's the chunk of code for our first plot:

```
ggplot(ws_gini_summary, aes(x = Year, y = gc, group = 1)) +
  geom_line(aes(y = gc), color = "black", size = .5) +
  geom_point(size = 5, color = "seagreen3") +
  geom_text(aes(label = gc),
            nudge_x = 0.01, nudge_y = 0.01,
```

```
              check_overlap = TRUE, size = 2.5) +
    labs(title = "Gini Coefficient for Win Shares",
         subtitle = "1991-2017",
         x = "Season",
         y = "Gini Coeffiicient",
         caption = "includes a maximum top 14 win shares for each team") +
    ylim(0.42, 0.60) +
    theme(plot.title = element_text(hjust = 0.5, face = "bold")) +
    theme(plot.subtitle = element_text(hjust = 0.5)) +
    theme(axis.text.x = element_text(angle = 45, hjust = 1)) +
    annotate("rect", xmin = "1991", xmax = "2009",
             ymin = 0.42, ymax = 0.60, alpha = 0.1, fill = "orange") +
    annotate("rect", xmin = "2010", xmax = "2017",
             ymin = 0.42, ymax = 0.60, alpha = 0.1, fill = "blue")
```

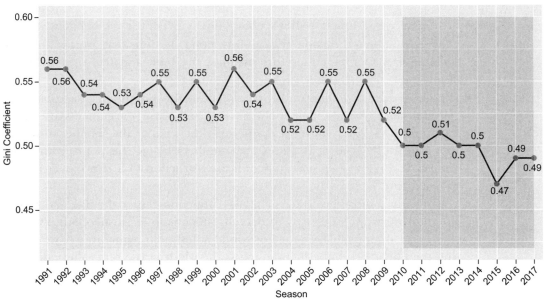

Figure 13.1   The year-over-year, or season-over-season, Gini coefficient for win shares distribution across the NBA

Our immediate takeaways are the following:

- These are high Gini coefficients: between 1991 and 2017, the Gini coefficient peaked twice at 0.56 and never dropped below 0.47. Once more, a Gini coefficient equal to or greater than 0.40 indicates significant inequality, regardless of what's being measured.
- We added a pair of shaded rectangles to the plot to highlight a contrast in results. Between 1991 and 2009, the Gini coefficient was never below 0.52, but

between 2010 and 2017, the Gini coefficient peaked at 0.51 once and was otherwise never above 0.50. Again, this is a fairly simple-enough technique that readily makes it clear that we have two distinct sets of results.

■ The league-wide Gini coefficient for win shares therefore trended *downward* between 1991 and 2017; by contrast, the Gini coefficient for salaries, which we explored in chapter 12, spiked *upward* in the mid-1990s and stabilized from there through 2018. Consequently, the Gini coefficients between salaries and win shares were unaligned in the 1990s and then identical, or nearly identical, every year between 2010 and 2017; put differently, they gradually converged over time.

In the next sections, we'll demonstrate different methods for visualizing the inequality of player productivity with Lorenz curves.

13.5   *Lorenz curves*

For starters, R will throw an error if we try to create a Lorenz curve from a vector that contains negative elements, so we need to query our data and then apply corrective action. We learned in chapters 2 and 3 that it's possible for players to "accrue" negative win shares, even over the course of a career. In the following code, we make a call to the `sqldf()` function to return a record count from ws_gini2 where the variable `WS` is less than 0:

```
sqldf("SELECT COUNT(*) FROM ws_gini2 WHERE WS < 0")
##   COUNT(*)
## 1      227
```

Sure enough, we have 227 records where the variable `WS` equals some number less than 0. There are at least two obvious fixes. One is to call the `filter()` function and remove these 227 records from our data set; the other is to adjust negative win shares to equal 0 instead. We'll take the latter approach.

In the following line of code, we apply square brackets, also known as extraction operators, to index the `WS` vector in the ws_gini2 data set where the value is less than 0 and then modify those elements so that they equal 0 instead. Then, we call the base R `min()` function to return the minimum value in the variable `WS`; as expected, it now equals 0:

```
ws_gini2$WS[ws_gini2$WS < 0] = 0.0
min(ws_gini2$WS)
## [1] 0
```

Our first Lorenz curve is created with our next code chunk (see figure 13.2):

■ We begin by calling the `filter()` function from the `dplyr` package to subset the ws_gini2 data set where the variable `Year` equals `1991`. The end result is a new data set called gini91.

- Even though our Lorenz curve is essentially an extension of `ggplot2`, requiring not only the `ggplot()` function but also the `gglorenz stat_lorenz()` function, the syntax is otherwise entirely consistent with any other `ggplot2` object. Therefore, our plot is initialized by calling the `ggplot()` function, passing gini91 as our data source, and then passing the variable `WS` as the lone aesthetic mapping.

- The `stat_lorenz()` function from the `gglorenz` package draws the Lorenz curve. When set to `TRUE`, the population is arranged in descending order; when set to `FALSE`, the population is instead arranged in ascending order. Because most Lorenz curves are created with the population arranged in ascending order, rather than vice versa, we set the `desc` argument, short for descending, equal to `FALSE`. Furthermore, we instruct R to draw the line a solid red and to make it twice the default width.

- The `ggplot2 coord_fixed()` function fixes the ratios of the x- and y-axes so that their scales are equal.

- The `geom_abline()` function draws a dashed diagonal line that represents a state of perfect equality.

- The `scale_x_continuous()` and `scale_y_continuous()` functions, combined with the `scales` package, converts our x- and y-axis labels, respectively, from decimals to percentages.

Following is our `dplyr` and `ggplot2` code:

```
ws_gini2 %>%
  filter(Year == 1991) -> gini91

ggplot(gini91, aes(WS)) +
  stat_lorenz(desc = FALSE, color = "red", lwd = 2) +
  coord_fixed() +
  geom_abline(linetype = "dashed", lwd = 1.5) +
  labs(title = "Lorenz Curve\n1990-91 Season",
       subtitle = "Gini coefficient = 0.56",
       x = "Win Share Distribution",
       y = "Percentage of NBA Players",
       caption = "includes a maximum top 14 salaries for each team") +
  scale_x_continuous(labels = percent) +
  scale_y_continuous(labels = percent) +
  theme(plot.title = element_text(face = "bold"))
```

Approximately 25% of the win shares during the 1990–91 NBA season were generated by about 1% of the players; approximately 50% of all win shares were generated by about 12% of the players; and approximately 75% of the win shares were generated by about 37% of the players. This is exactly how we created our chapter 12 Lorenz curves. But let's say we want to compare and visualize Gini coefficients between two seasons in a single graphical representation and, at the same time, create a plot that's more aesthetically pleasing than our previous Lorenz curves.

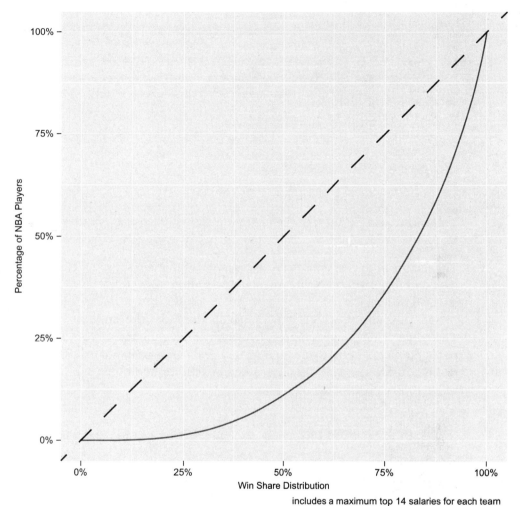

Figure 13.2   League-wide Lorenz curve for win share distribution for the 1990–91 NBA season when the Gini coefficient equaled 0.56

Our first step is to call the dplyr filter() function to subset the ws_gini2 data set where the variable Year equals 1991 or 2017, where the Gini coefficients equal 0.56 and 0.49, respectively. The pipe (|) is a logical operator meaning "or." We cast the results to a new object called gini9117:

```
ws_gini2 %>%
  filter(Year == 1991 | Year == 2017) -> gini9117
```

We then call the base R `head()` and `tail()` functions to return the first three and last three records in gini9117:

```
head(gini9117, n = 3)
## # A tibble: 3 × 4
## # Groups:   Year, Tm [1]
##   Year  Tm       WS  rank
##   <fct> <fct> <dbl> <int>
## 1 1991  ATL       0    14
## 2 1991  ATL       0    13
## 3 1991  ATL       0    11

tail(gini9117, n = 3)
## # A tibble: 3 × 4
## # Groups:   Year, Tm [1]
##   Year  Tm       WS  rank
##   <fct> <fct> <dbl> <int>
## 1 2017  WAS     8.5     3
## 2 2017  WAS     8.8     2
## 3 2017  WAS     9.4     1
```

The factors in the variable `Tm` are arranged in alphabetical order. That being said, our data set begins with the 1991 Atlanta Hawks and ends with the 2017 Washington Wizards. So this checks out.

Our next chunk of code draws a new and improved Lorenz curve (see figure 13.3). The syntax is the same as before, but with two exceptions—(1) we added an aesthetic parameter, `fill`, equal to the variable `Year`, and (2) we replaced the single Lorenz curve, or line, inside the `stat_lorenz()` function with an additional `geom` equal to `polygon`, which draws a pair of filled area curves:

```
ggplot(gini9117, aes(WS, fill = Year)) +
  stat_lorenz(geom = "polygon", desc = FALSE) +
  coord_fixed() +
  geom_abline(linetype = "dashed") +
  labs(title = "Lorenz Curve\n1990-91 versus 2016-17 Seasons",
       subtitle = "Gini coefficients = 0.56 and 0.49",
       x = "Win Share Distribution",
       y = "Percentage of NBA Players",
       caption = "includes a maximum top 14 salaries for each team") +
  scale_x_continuous(labels = percent) +
  scale_y_continuous(labels = percent) +
  theme(plot.title = element_text(face = "bold"))
```

The smaller curve represents the Gini coefficient in win share distribution for 2017, whereas the larger curve represents the Gini coefficient in win share distribution for 1991. Don't be fooled by the shades—we're still measuring the distance between each of the Lorenz curves and the dashed diagonal line. This is both a more effective and more efficient way of visually comparing two Gini coefficients versus creating a pair of side-by-side plots.

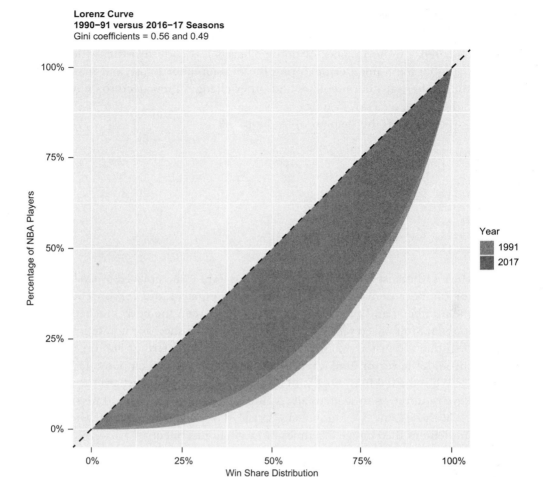

Lorenz Curve
1990–91 versus 2016–17 Seasons
Gini coefficients = 0.56 and 0.49

Figure 13.3   League-wide Lorenz curves for win share distributions in 1991 and 2017 consolidated into a single graphical object

We'll demonstrate one more way to create a Lorenz curve—actually, a series of Lorenz curves—in the next section.

13.6   *For loops*

So far, we've demonstrated two methods for creating ggplot2 Lorenz curves. But let's say we want or need to create a separate Lorenz curve for each of the 27 NBA seasons in our data set. One way to do that is to create one Lorenz curve, copy and paste the code 26 times, and then change maybe a couple of parameters on each iteration. This is tedious, yes, but not difficult. Another method is to write a for loop.

13.6.1 *Simple demonstration*

A `for` loop is an efficient and common alternative when the same task must be repeated a finite number of times. There's less code to write, which minimizes the potential for human error during the development phase and maximizes maintainability afterward because fixes and other changes then need to be applied just once, rather than, let's say, 27 times.

Following is the simplest of `for` loops:

```
for (i in 1:5)  {
  print(i * 2)
}
## [1]  2
## [1]  4
## [1]  6
## [1]  8
## [1] 10
```

Here's what just happened: An index, `i`, is iteratively replaced by each value in the vector 1:5. Because the first value in our vector equals 1, our `for` loop first replaces `i` with the number 1 and then executes the code between the curly brackets. Frequently, `for` loops are initialized with `i` as the counter, which is short for iteration, but `for` loops can be initialized just as well with any letter or character string. The `for` loop then iterates through the vector until it reaches the final value, at which point it stops and exits.

We returned five values with one small chunk of code where the alternative would have required us to sequentially multiply five numbers by two. If we should have multiplied those same five numbers by 3 instead of 2, we would have then been required to implement the change five times rather than just once.

13.6.2 *Applying what we've learned*

Now, for our Lorenz curves, we're going to first wrangle our data to best demonstrate the use of `for` loops to create multiple plots. We start by calling the `dplyr ungroup()` function to decouple, or ungroup, the two variables, `Year` and `Tm`, that were previously combined by calling the `group_by()` function. We want to subset our data on the variables `Year` and `WS` only, but because `Year` and `Tm` are currently grouped, R will otherwise force us to also retain the variable `Tm`:

```
ws_gini2 %>%
  ungroup(Tm, Year) -> ws_gini2
```

Next, we call the `dplyr filter()` function to reduce the length of ws_gini2 by only including those records where the variable `Year` equals 1991, 1992, 1993, or 1994. We can just as effectively demonstrate the worth of `for` loops with 4 years of data as we can with 27. We then cast the results to a new tibble called ws9194. The `head()` and `tail()` functions return the first six and last six observations:

```
ws_gini2 %>%
  filter(Year == 1991 | Year == 1992 | Year == 1993 |
          Year == 1994) -> ws9194

head(ws9194)
## # A tibble: 6 x 4
##    Year  Tm      WS  rank
##    <fct> <fct> <dbl> <int>
## 1 1991  ATL     0     14
## 2 1991  ATL     0     13
## 3 1991  ATL     0     11
## 4 1991  ATL     0     12
## 5 1991  ATL     1.1    10
## 6 1991  ATL     1.8     9

tail(ws9194)
## # A tibble: 6 x 4
##    Year  Tm      WS  rank
##    <fct> <fct> <dbl> <int>
## 1 1994  WSB    1.3     6
## 2 1994  WSB    1.9     5
## 3 1994  WSB    3.1     4
## 4 1994  WSB    3.8     3
## 5 1994  WSB    3.9     2
## 6 1994  WSB    5.6     1
```

Then, we transpose ws9194 from a long format to a wide format by calling the `pivot_wider()` function from the `tidyr` package. By doing so, the variable `Year` is broken out into four columns, `1991` through `1994`, populated with elements from the variable `WS`. The `head()` function then returns the top six records:

```
ws9194 %>%
  pivot_wider(names_from = Year, values_from = WS) -> ws9194
head(ws9194)
## # A tibble: 6 x 6
##    Tm     rank `1991` `1992` `1993` `1994`
##    <fct> <int> <dbl> <dbl> <dbl> <dbl>
## 1 ATL      14    0     0     0     0
## 2 ATL      13    0     0.1   0.1    0
## 3 ATL      11    0     1.1   0.2   1.3
## 4 ATL      12    0     0.2   0.2   0.2
## 5 ATL      10    1.1   1.1   0.3   1.4
## 6 ATL       9    1.8   2.1   1.1   2.2
```

We don't need the variables `Tm` and `rank` to create our Lorenz curves, so we next call the `dplyr` `select()` function to subset ws9194 on every variable but `Tm` and `rank` (notice the minus sign that precedes our call to the `c()` function):

```
ws9194 %>%
  select(-c(Tm, rank)) -> ws9194
```

Then, we convert ws9194 from a tibble to a data frame by calling the base R as.data.frame() function. Back when we created our first tibble, we mentioned that tibbles share many of the same properties as data frames, but there are at least three important differences as well. The first is that tibbles return only the first 10 rows and whatever number of columns fit on screen when the print() function is called (which we've seen). This is usually convenient when working with large data sets but sometimes frustrating otherwise. The second is that tibbles sometimes require "work-arounds" when subsetting the data (which we've also seen).

The third is much more significant—tibbles don't always work with older code. It turns out that our forthcoming Lorenz curves, created in part with base R code, can't read ws9194 as a tibble but can when ws9194 is a data frame instead. So we call the as.data.frame() function to convert ws9194 from a tibble to a data frame. Then, we call the base R class() function, which returns the class of ws9194 and confirms that it's now a data frame:

```
ws9194 <- as.data.frame(ws9194)
class(ws9194)
## [1] "data.frame"
```

Finally, we call the names() function from base R to rename the four remaining columns in ws9194 to a, b, c, and d:

```
names(ws9194) <- c("a", "b", "c", "d")
head(ws9194)
##     a   b   c   d
## 1 0.0 0.0 0.0 0.0
## 2 0.0 0.1 0.1 0.0
## 3 0.0 1.1 0.2 1.3
## 4 0.0 0.2 0.2 0.2
## 5 1.1 1.1 0.3 1.4
## 6 1.8 2.1 1.1 2.2
```

Now we can go about writing a for loop, and with that, creating four Lorenz curves, one for each of the four years in the ws9194 data set. First, we call the base R par() function to arrange our four Lorenz curves in a single 2 × 2 matrix. The mfrow argument tells R to arrange the plots with 1991 and 1992 on the top and 1993 and 1994 along the bottom; if we had instead called the mfcol argument, R would arrange 1991 and 1992 on the left and 1993 and 1994 on the right.

Within the remaining chunk of code, the following occurs:

- We first create a loop vector, called loop.vector, that will eventually iterate four times, or otherwise loop through each of the four columns, or vectors, in the ws9194 data set.
- The loop object is then initialized as i.

- The code inside the opening and closing brackets is then executed four times, once per column or vector that then generates four corresponding plots.
- The data is stored as x and then used to source our Lorenz curves, created with the combination of the base R plot() function and the Lc() function from the ineq package (see figure 13.4).
- The paste0() function is a built-in R function that concatenates elements without the need for separators. The title for each of our Lorenz curves is essentially a title on top and subtitle on the bottom, where the Lorenz curve is printed along the top and the applicable year is printed along the bottom; the \n in R acts like a carriage return when applied within a character string. The year is returned by appending, or concatenating, 199 and i (or 1, 2, 3, 4 with each successive loop).

The result is four Lorenz curves consolidated into a single graphical object:

```
par(mfrow = c(2, 2))

loop.vector <- 1:4

for (i in loop.vector) {
x <- ws9194[,i]

plot(Lc(x), col = "red", lwd = 2,
     main = paste0("Lorenz Curve\n", "199", i),
     xlab = "Win Share Distribution",
     ylab = "Percentage of NBA Players")
}
```

If we didn't know otherwise, we would likely estimate the Gini coefficients to equal approximately 0.50. (According to our time-series plot where we displayed the year-over-year league-wide Gini coefficients in win shares, the actual coefficients equal 0.56 in 1991 and 1992 and 0.54 in 1993 and 1994.) But more importantly, we've demonstrated how you can write a for loop and, in this case, create four plots with less than one-fourth the code that would otherwise be required.

In the next section, we'll imagine that R doesn't contain any built-in or packaged function to compute Gini coefficients, so we'll create one of our own.

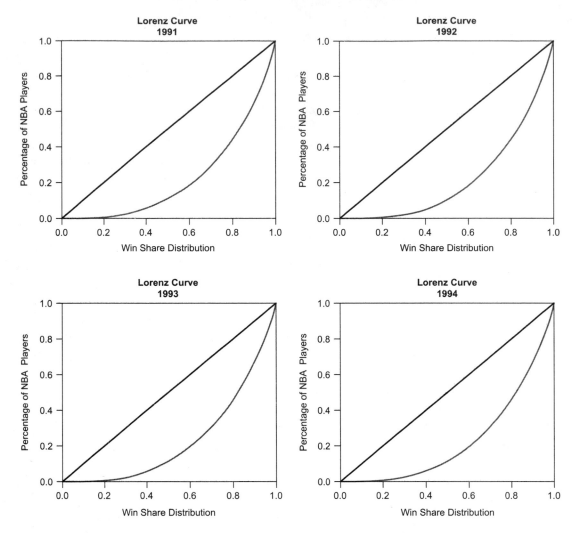

Figure 13.4   League-wide Lorenz curves for win share distributions between 1991 and 1994 created from a `for` **loop and base R**

13.7   *User-defined functions*

R is essentially a *functional* programming language, which means almost everything in R is derived from a built-in or packaged function. In this chapter alone, we've already called nearly 40 unique functions. Every function contains the following components:

- *Function name*—The actual name of the function. Function names are usually unique but not necessarily so given the ongoing proliferation of new packages and functions. Very simply, the function name for the `pivot_wider()` function is `pivot_wider`.

- *Arguments*—One or more arguments, or inputs, that functions require to run. When we call the `pivot_wider()` function, for instance, we then pass two arguments inside a pair of open and closed parentheses separated by a comma; those arguments tell R which variable from which data set to break out into new columns and from which other variable we should populate those new columns.
- *Function body*—More or less contains a collection of statements that define what the function is supposed to do. Unlike the function name and the function arguments, the function body is invisible to us; we know what a function is supposed to do from experience or from reading about it.
- *Return value*—The output we expect when a function runs. When, for instance, we call the `mean()` function against a continuous variable, we expect R to return a numeric value that represents the average, or mean.

When we say that R is a functional programming language, that's also because we can write our own functions, which are frequently referred to as user-defined functions. They contain the same components as built-in or packaged functions and even take on the same syntax.

Let's write a function that converts r, or the correlation coefficient between a pair of continuous variables, to r^2, which, if we were to regress one continuous variable against the other, represents the proportion of variance that can be explained in the target variable by the predictor variable.

Our function name, on the left side of the assignment operator, is called `r_to_rsquared()`. Function names should be more intuitive than creative. Our function requires just one argument, or input, and that is `r`. The function body and the return value are situated inside a pair of opening and closing curly brackets. Our `r_to_rsquared()` function converts r to r^2 by squaring it and then returning the result. Our first user-defined function follows:

```
r_to_rsquared <- function(r) {
   rsquared <- r^2
   return(rsquared)
 }
```

Then, we call the function and pass a value, `.42`, for r. Our function returns r^2, or 0.1764.

```
r_to_rsquared(.42)
## [1] 0.1764
```

Let's now write a second user-defined function, which converts r^2 to r:

- Our new function is called `rsquared_to_r()`.
- It requires one argument, a value for r^2, to run.
- It then converts r^2 to r by computing the square root and returning the result.

Our second user-defined function "looks" just like our first one:

```
rsquared_to_r <- function(rsquared) {
  r <- sqrt(rsquared)
  return(r)
}
```

We then call the function and pass 0.1764 as an argument to get 0.42 returned:

```
rsquared_to_r(.1764)
## [1] 0.42
```

Next, we'll create a function that estimates the Gini coefficient from a Lorenz curve:

- Our function takes on the name `gini.est()`.
- It requires exactly three arguments to be passed:
  - `a`, which represents the estimated cumulative population percentage when the cumulative win share distribution equals 40%.
  - `b`, which represents the estimated cumulative population percentage when the cumulative win share distribution equals 60%.
  - `c`, which represents the estimated cumulative population percentage when the cumulative win share distribution equals 80%. In other words, given three x-axis coordinates—40%, 60%, and 80%—we're estimating the corresponding y-axis coordinates through which a Lorenz curve passes. We already know y when x equals 0% or 100%.
- The function body computes the estimated Gini coefficient, shortened to equal gini, and returns the result. The estimated Gini coefficient is computed first by splitting the area *underneath* the Lorenz curve into mutually exclusive triangles, estimating the area for each, and adding the estimates together; that sum is then multiplied by 2, and that product is then subtracted by 1. With respect to the 1991 through 1994 NBA seasons, we should get Gini coefficients equal to or slightly greater than 0.50.

The area underneath each Lorenz curve is divided into four triangles, where the estimated area equals the width (the distance between two points along the x-axis) times the height (the distance between two points along the y-axis, where estimates for `a`, `b`, and `c` must be supplied) times 0.5:

```
gini.est <- function(a, b, c) {
  gini <- 1 - 2 * ((0.4 - 0.0) * (a + 0) * 0.5 +
                   (0.6 - 0.4) * (b + a) * 0.5 +
                   (0.8 - 0.6) * (c + b) * 0.5 +
                   (1.0 - 0.8) * (1 + c) * 0.5)
  return(gini)
}
```

Let's now run the `gini.est()` function but pass only two of the required three parameters:

```
gini.est(.05, .18)
## Error in gini.est(0.05, 0.18): argument "c" is missing, with no default
```

R throws an error because we supplied a and b, but not c.

Let's do it right this time. Based on the Lorenz curve we created for the 1991 NBA season, we're estimating that 40% of the win shares were accrued by 5% of the players in our data set who played that year, that 60% of the win shares were accrued by 18% of the players, and that 80% of the win shares were accrued by 44% of the players:

```
gini.est(.05, .18, .44)
## [1] 0.522
```

Our function returns an estimated Gini coefficient equal to 0.522; the actual Gini coefficient in 1991 was 0.56. So while our function isn't perfect, it nevertheless returned a reasonable enough estimate

Let's now run the `gini.est()` function for the 1992, 1993, and 1994 NBA seasons:

```
gini.est(.05, .19, .44)
## [1] 0.518
gini.est(.06, .20, .44)
## [1] 0.508
gini.est(.06, .20, .44)
## [1] 0.508
```

We're consistently lowballing our estimates—the Gini coefficient equaled, of course, 0.56 in 1992 and 0.54 in 1993 and 1994. Had we further decomposed the area underneath the curve and then performed additional geometric calculations, our function might have then proved more accurate. But more to the point, we've demonstrated how a user-defined function can be created in R. Let's now see how real Gini coefficients relate to winning and losing.

13.8   *Win share inequality and championships*

Our purpose here is to measure win share inequality grouped by championship-winning teams versus all other teams, perform a t-test to determine whether the variance in mean Gini coefficients between the groups is statistically significant, and then perform a pair of effect size tests around the same. In other words, we'll perform a mix of "old" and "new" tests in the process. However, there are a series of data wrangling operations that must be performed first.

13.8.1 *Wrangling data*

Our next chunk of code reshapes ws_gini2, our working data set before we demonstrated `for` loops and user-defined functions, so that individual win shares (WS) at every year (Year) and team (Tm) combination become their own columns:

- The variable rank doesn't figure into our analysis; it was created only to help us subset the data we originally imported. Therefore, we call the `dplyr select()` function to subset ws_gini2 on every variable but rank.

- Then, we pass the ws_gini2 data set to the `dplyr group_by()`, `mutate()`, and `row_number()` functions to create a new variable called id, which is merely a column of consecutive numbers with separate and independent sequences for every Year and Tm combination.

- We then call the `tidyr pivot_wider()` function to transpose the ws_gini2 data set from a long format to a wide format where the variable id is broken out into columns, and the values from the variable WS are then used to populate the cells in these new columns.

The result is a new tibble called ws_gini3. A call to the base R `head()` function returns the first six observations so that you get an idea of what was just created. This is just the first step toward prepping our data to join with another data set:

```
ws_gini2 %>%
  select(-c(rank)) -> ws_gini2

ws_gini2 %>%
  group_by(Tm, Year) %>%
  mutate(id = row_number(WS)) %>%
  pivot_wider(names_from = id, values_from = WS) -> ws_gini3
head(ws_gini3)
## # A tibble: 6 × 16
## # Groups:   Tm, Year [6]
##   Year  Tm      `1`   `2`   `3`   `4`   `5`   `6`
##   <fct> <fct> <dbl> <dbl> <dbl> <dbl> <dbl> <dbl>
## 1 1991  ATL     0     0     0     0     1.1   1.8
## 2 1991  BOS     0     0     0     0     0.3   1.2
## 3 1991  CHH     0     0.1   0.3   0.6   1.8   1.8
## 4 1991  CHI     0.5   0.9   1.5   1.7   2     2.3
## 5 1991  CLE     0     0     0.2   0.6   1     1.3
## 6 1991  DAL     0.1   0.4   0.6   0.6   0.6   0.7
##     `7`   `8`   `9`  `10`  `11`  `12`  `13`  `14`
##   <dbl> <dbl> <dbl> <dbl> <dbl> <dbl> <dbl> <dbl>
## 1 1.9   2.5   4     4.4   5.4   5.6   6.3   11.4
## 2 3.5   4.7   5.9   6.6   7.5   7.9   8.3   10
## 3 2     2     2.1   2.7   3     3     4.1   4.8
## 4 4.1   4.2   5.7  10.3  11.2  20.3  NA    NA
## 5 1.5   1.6   2     2.4   3.1   3.4   9     9.8
## 6 0.7   1     1.6   1.7   4.3   5.3   5.5   7.6
```

The numbered columns don't tie back at all to the variable rank; as a matter of fact, win shares are now sorted in ascending order from left to right. This is fine because the sort, or order, no longer matters.

We then call the names() function from base R to rename all of the ws_gini3 column names. That, of course, includes the variables Year and Tm, which will be renamed to season_end and team, respectively, to sync up with our chapter 12 data. The head() function, of course, returns the first six observations:

```
names(ws_gini3) = c("season_end", "team", "ws1", "ws2", "ws3", "ws4",
                    "ws5", "ws6", "ws7", "ws8", "ws9", "ws10", "ws11",
                    "ws12", "ws13", "ws14")
```

```
head(ws_gini3)
## # A tibble: 6 × 16
## # Groups:   team, season_end [6]
##    season_end team    ws1   ws2   ws3   ws4   ws5   ws6
##    <fct>      <fct> <dbl> <dbl> <dbl> <dbl> <dbl> <dbl>
## 1 1991        ATL     0     0     0     0     1.1   1.8
## 2 1991        BOS     0     0     0     0     0.3   1.2
## 3 1991        CHH     0     0.1   0.3   0.6   1.8   1.8
## 4 1991        CHI     0.5   0.9   1.5   1.7   2     2.3
## 5 1991        CLE     0     0     0.2   0.6   1     1.3
## 6 1991        DAL     0.1   0.4   0.6   0.6   0.6   0.7
##    ws7   ws8   ws9  ws10  ws11  ws12  ws13  ws14
##  <dbl> <dbl> <dbl> <dbl> <dbl> <dbl> <dbl> <dbl>
## 1 1.9   2.5   4     4.4   5.4   5.6   6.3  11.4
## 2 3.5   4.7   5.9   6.6   7.5   7.9   8.3  10
## 3 2     2     2.1   2.7   3     3     4.1   4.8
## 4 4.1   4.2   5.7  10.3  11.2  20.3  NA    NA
## 5 1.5   1.6   2     2.4   3.1   3.4   9     9.8
## 6 0.7   1     1.6   1.7   4.3   5.3   5.5   7.6
```

Next, we call the mutate() function to create a new variable called gini_index, which equals the computed Gini coefficient, rounded to two digits right of the decimal point, for every team and season_end combination in the ws_gini3 data set. The Gini coefficient is computed by again calling the ineq() function from the ineq package, which takes the variables ws1 through ws14 as arguments. By setting the na.rm argument to TRUE, we're instructing the ineq() function to skip Not Available (NA) values in our data; if we had instead set it to FALSE, the ineq() function would return NA for every team and season_end combination with fewer than 14 win shares.

The result is a new tibble called ws_gini4. The head() function prints the first six records:

```
ws_gini3 %>%
  mutate(gini_index = round(ineq(c(ws1, ws2, ws3, ws4, ws5, ws6, ws7,
                                   ws8, ws9, ws10, ws11, ws12, ws13,
                                   ws14, na.rm = TRUE)),
                            digits = 2)) -> ws_gini4
```

```
head(ws_gini4)
```

```
## # A tibble: 6 × 17
## # Groups:   team, season_end [6]
##   season_end team    ws1   ws2   ws3   ws4   ws5   ws6
##   <fct>      <fct> <dbl> <dbl> <dbl> <dbl> <dbl> <dbl>
## 1 1991       ATL     0     0     0     0     1.1   1.8
## 2 1991       BOS     0     0     0     0     0.3   1.2
## 3 1991       CHH     0     0.1   0.3   0.6   1.8   1.8
## 4 1991       CHI     0.5   0.9   1.5   1.7   2     2.3
## 5 1991       CLE     0     0     0.2   0.6   1     1.3
## 6 1991       DAL     0.1   0.4   0.6   0.6   0.6   0.7
##   ws7   ws8   ws9  ws10  ws11  ws12  ws13  ws14 gini_index
## <dbl> <dbl> <dbl> <dbl> <dbl> <dbl> <dbl> <dbl>      <dbl>
## 1 1.9   2.5   4     4.4   5.4   5.6   6.3  11.4       0.54
## 2 3.5   4.7   5.9   6.6   7.5   7.9   8.3  10         0.52
## 3 2     2     2.1   2.7   3     3     4.1   4.8       0.39
## 4 4.1   4.2   5.7  10.3  11.2  20.3  NA    NA         0.53
## 5 1.5   1.6   2     2.4   3.1   3.4   9     9.8       0.56
## 6 0.7   1     1.6   1.7   4.3   5.3   5.5   7.6       0.53
```

We then make a second call to the read_csv() function to import the records.csv file stored in our default working directory; this is the same .csv file we imported in chapter 12. We'll again call it records:

```
records <- read_csv("records.csv")
```

The records data set includes regular season wins and losses, regular season winning percentage, and a binary variable equal to 0 or 1, where 0 indicates a team didn't win a championship and 1 indicates otherwise. The data set contains these records for every NBA season between 1991 and 2018. Because the data set we downloaded from Kaggle goes through 2017, we then call the dplyr filter() function to subset the records data set where the variable season_end, now numeric, is less than 2018:

```
records %>%
  filter(season_end < 2018) -> records
```

Then, we convert the variables season_end, team, and champ (this is the binary variable referenced previously) to factor variables by calling the base R as.factor() function three times. As a reminder, variables should be factors if and when they can take on just a finite set of values:

```
records$season_end <- as.factor(records$season_end)
records$team <- as.factor(records$team)
records$champ <- as.factor(records$champ)
```

We're about to join ws_gini4 and records on the like variables season_end and team. However, the variable team in ws_gini4 is populated with every team's three-letter abbreviation (e.g, ATL), whereas the variable team in records is populated with full team names (e.g., Atlanta Hawks). Two calls to the base R levels() function allow us to cross-check the two:

```
levels(ws_gini4$team)
[1]  "ATL" "BOS" "BRK" "CHA" "CHH" "CHI" "CHO" "CLE" "DAL" "DEN"
[11] "DET" "GSW" "HOU" "IND" "LAC" "LAL" "MEM" "MIA" "MIL" "MIN"
[21] "NJN" "NOH" "NOK" "NOP" "NYK" "OKC" "ORL" "PHI" "PHO" "POR"
[31] "SAC" "SAS" "SEA" "TOR" "UTA" "VAN" "WAS" "WSB"
```

```
levels(records$team)
##  [1] "Atlanta Hawks"                        "Boston Celtics"
##  [3] "Brooklyn Nets"                        "Charlotte Bobcats"
##  [5] "Charlotte Hornets"                    "Chicago Bulls"
##  [7] "Cleveland Cavaliers"                  "Dallas Mavericks"
##  [9] "Denver Nuggets"                       "Detroit Pistons"
## [11] "Golden State Warriors"                "Houston Rockets"
## [13] "Indiana Pacers"                       "Los Angeles Clippers"
## [15] "Los Angeles Lakers"                   "Memphis Grizzlies"
## [17] "Miami Heat"                           "Milwaukee Bucks"
## [19] "Minnesota Timberwolves"               "New Jersey Nets"
## [21] "New Orleans Hornets"                  "New Orleans Pelicans"
## [23] "New Orleans/Oklahoma City Hornets"    "New York Knicks"
## [25] "Oklahoma City Thunder"                "Orlando Magic"
## [27] "Philadelphia 76ers"                   "Phoenix Suns"
## [29] "Portland Trail Blazers"               "Sacramento Kings"
## [31] "San Antonio Spurs"                    "Seattle SuperSonics"
## [33] "Toronto Raptors"                      "Utah Jazz"
## [35] "Vancouver Grizzlies"                  "Washington Bullets"
## [37] "Washington Wizards"
```

We then call the recode() function from the car package to rename every ws_gini4 instance of ATL to Atlanta Hawks, every instance of BOS to Boston Celtics, and so on, to align the variable team with the same variable in the records data set:

```
ws_gini4$team <- recode(ws_gini4$team, "'ATL' = 'Atlanta Hawks';
                        'BOS' = 'Boston Celtics';
                        'BRK' = 'Brooklyn Nets';
                        'CHA' = 'Charlotte Bobcats';
                        'CHH' = 'Charlotte Hornets';
                        'CHI' = 'Chicago Bulls';
                        'CHO' = 'Charlotte Hornets';
                        'CLE' = 'Cleveland Cavaliers';
                        'DAL' = 'Dallas Mavericks';
                        'DEN' = 'Denver Nuggets';
                        'DET' = 'Detroit Pistons';
                        'GSW' = 'Golden State Warriors';
                        'HOU' = 'Houston Rockets';
                        'IND' = 'Indiana Pacers';
                        'LAC' = 'Los Angeles Clippers';
                        'LAL' = 'Los Angeles Lakers';
                        'MEM' = 'Memphis Grizzlies';
                        'MIA' = 'Miami Heat';
                        'MIL' = 'Milwaukee Bucks';
                        'MIN' = 'Minnesota Timberwolves';
                        'NJN' = 'New Jersey Nets';
                        'NOH' = 'New Orleans Hornets';
                        'NOK' = 'New Orleans/Oklahoma City Hornets';
```

```
                              'NOP' = 'New Orleans Pelicans';
                              'NYK' = 'New York Knicks';
                              'OKC' = 'Oklahoma City Thunder';
                              'ORL' = 'Orlando Magic';
                              'PHI' = 'Philadelphia 76ers';
                              'PHO' = 'Phoenix Suns';
                              'POR' = 'Portland Trail Blazers';
                              'SAC' = 'Sacramento Kings';
                              'SAS' = 'San Antonio Spurs';
                              'SEA' = 'Seattle SuperSonics';
                              'TOR' = 'Toronto Raptors';
                              'UTA' = 'Utah Jazz';
                              'VAN' = 'Vancouver Grizzlies';
                              'WAS' = 'Washington Wizards';
                              'WSB' = 'Washington Bullets'")
```

Now that the variable `team` is aligned between ws_gini4 and records, we can combine the two objects into a single data set, ws_gini_records, by calling the `left_join()` function from the `dplyr` package:

```
left_join(ws_gini4, records,
          by = c("season_end", "team")) -> ws_gini_records
```

Then, we make a call to the `dplyr` `glimpse()` function to return a transposed view of the ws_gini_records data set:

```
glimpse(ws_gini_records)
## Rows: 786
## Columns: 21
## Groups: team, season_end [786]
## $ season_end <fct> 1991, 1991, 1991, 1991, 1991, 1991, 1991, 19…
## $ team       <fct> Atlanta Hawks, Boston Celtics, Charlotte Hor…
## $ ws1        <dbl> 0.0, 0.0, 0.0, 0.5, 0.0, 0.1, 0.1, 0.1, 0.1,…
## $ ws2        <dbl> 0.0, 0.0, 0.1, 0.9, 0.0, 0.4, 0.3, 0.1, 0.2,…
## $ ws3        <dbl> 0.0, 0.0, 0.3, 1.5, 0.2, 0.6, 0.3, 0.5, 0.2,…
## $ ws4        <dbl> 0.0, 0.0, 0.6, 1.7, 0.6, 0.6, 0.3, 0.5, 0.3,…
## $ ws5        <dbl> 1.1, 0.3, 1.8, 2.0, 1.0, 0.6, 0.5, 0.5, 1.0,…
## $ ws6        <dbl> 1.8, 1.2, 1.8, 2.3, 1.3, 0.7, 0.6, 1.3, 1.3,…
## $ ws7        <dbl> 1.9, 3.5, 2.0, 4.1, 1.5, 0.7, 0.7, 3.4, 1.7,…
## $ ws8        <dbl> 2.5, 4.7, 2.0, 4.2, 1.6, 1.0, 0.9, 3.5, 1.9,…
## $ ws9        <dbl> 4.0, 5.9, 2.1, 5.7, 2.0, 1.6, 1.0, 3.8, 2.1,…
## $ ws10       <dbl> 4.4, 6.6, 2.7, 10.3, 2.4, 1.7, 1.3, 4.8, 2.5…
## $ ws11       <dbl> 5.4, 7.5, 3.0, 11.2, 3.1, 4.3, 1.7, 5.5, 5.3…
## $ ws12       <dbl> 5.6, 7.9, 3.0, 20.3, 3.4, 5.3, 2.2, 8.0, 7.1…
## $ ws13       <dbl> 6.3, 8.3, 4.1, NA, 9.0, 5.5, 3.9, 8.7, 9.9,…
## $ ws14       <dbl> 11.4, 10.0, 4.8, NA, 9.8, 7.6, 6.3, 9.9, 12.…
## $ gini_index <dbl> 0.54, 0.52, 0.39, 0.53, 0.56, 0.53, 0.53, 0.…
## $ wins       <dbl> 43, 56, 26, 61, 33, 28, 20, 50, 44, 52, 41, …
## $ losses     <dbl> 39, 26, 56, 21, 49, 54, 62, 32, 38, 30, 41, …
## $ pct        <dbl> 0.52, 0.68, 0.32, 0.74, 0.40, 0.34, 0.24, 0.…
## $ champ      <fct> 0, 0, 0, 1, 0, 0, 0, 0, 0, 0, 0, 0, 0, 0, 0,…
```

The ws_gini_records data set contains 786 rows and 21 columns—786 rows because that's the row count from ws_gini4 and records, and 21 columns because that's the sum of variables between ws_gini4 and records minus the variables season_end and team. Yet we only need a subset of these variables. We therefore call the dplyr select() function to reduce the ws_gini_records data set to the variables season_end, team, gini_index, wins, losses, pct, and champ. The variables gini_index through champ occupy the last five positions in ws_gini_records:

```
ws_gini_records %>%
  select(season_end, team, gini_index:champ) -> ws_gini_records
```

Next, we'll measure the Gini coefficient for win share distribution grouped by the variable champ and then perform our first t-test.

13.8.2 T-test

Now that we have a single data set that contains the win shares Gini coefficient for every team and season_end combination between 1991 and 2017, as well as records for those same team and season_end combinations, we can begin our test and analysis efforts. It's never enough to merely compute a pair of group means, record the results, and highlight any variance. The difference in means may or may not be meaningful; we therefore perform a statistical test to determine if the variance is likely due to chance or if it's more significant than that.

We start with a chunk of dplyr code by which the ws_gini_records data set is passed to the group_by() and summarize() functions. The summarize() function computes the gini_index mean, rounded to two digits right of the decimal point, for each level, or factor, in the binary variable champ. Our results are cast into a tibble called ws_gini_summary2:

```
ws_gini_records %>%
  group_by(champ) %>%
  summarize(mean = round(mean(gini_index), digits = 2)) -> ws_gini_summary2
print(ws_gini_summary2)
## # A tibble: 2 × 2
##   champ  mean
##   <fct> <dbl>
## 1 0      0.49
## 2 1      0.51
```

Championship-winning teams in our data set—one per season between 1991 and 2017, or 27 in total—had an average Gini coefficient for win share distribution equal to 0.51, while teams that didn't win a league championship had an average Gini coefficient equal to 0.49. In other words, championship-winning teams between 1991 and 2017 had more unequal win share distributions than other teams.

We'll conduct a t-test to determine whether this amounts to a statistically significant variance. Once more, a t-test is a statistical test that compares the means from two data series. It considers the difference in means and the group variances in conjunction with the record counts to determine if the variance is due to chance and therefore essentially equal to zero or, alternatively, if the variance is meaningful and therefore different from zero. If the former, we'll fail to reject the null hypothesis and, in the case of the latter, we'll reject the null hypothesis and instead accept the alternative hypothesis. Our null hypothesis here is that Gini coefficients have no effect on who wins or doesn't win NBA championships. We'll fail to reject the null hypothesis if we get a high p-value, greater than our predefined 5% threshold, from our t-test; otherwise, we'll reject the null hypothesis, accept the alternative hypothesis, and conclude that higher Gini coefficients—that is, more unequal player productivity—contribute to NBA championships.

With that in mind, we establish two new data sets, ws_giniX, which is ws_gini_records filtered on the variable `champ` equaling `0`, and ws_giniY, which is ws_gini_records filtered on the variable `champ` instead equaling `1`. The t-test is performed against the ws_gini_records variable `gini_index`:

```
ws_gini_records %>%
  filter(champ == 0) -> ws_giniX
ws_gini_records %>%
  filter(champ == 1) -> ws_giniY

t.test(ws_giniX$gini_index, ws_giniY$gini_index)
##
##   Welch Two Sample t-test
##
## data:  ws_giniX$gini_index and ws_giniY$gini_index
## t = -2.5402, df = 31.156, p-value = 0.01628
## alternative hypothesis: true difference in means is not equal to 0
## 95 percent confidence interval:
##   -0.039949859 -0.004371617
## sample estimates:
## mean of x mean of y
## 0.4911726 0.5133333
```

The p-value of our t-test is equal to 0.02, and because it's below our predefined and generally accepted 0.05 threshold for significance, we thus reject the null hypothesis that the means are statistically equal, which means the variance is statistically significant. In other words, the fact that championship-winning teams have more *unequal* win share distributions than all other teams, at least between 1991 and 2017, is meaningful. Quite frankly, this flies in the face of conventional thought; it's always been assumed that the most "balanced" and "well-rounded" teams are also the most successful teams.

These results are best visualized with a pair of boxplots (see figure 13.5). But first, we call the base R `rbind()` function to join the ws_giniX and ws_giniY data sets by rows, thereby creating a new object called ws_giniXY in the process. Object ws_giniXY is then our data source. Our x-axis variable is the binary variable `champ`, and our y-axis variable is `gini_index`. The `scale_x_discrete()` function adds the x-axis labels `League Champions` and `All Other Teams` in lieu of `1` and `0`, respectively, from the variable `champ`.

The `ggplot()` function automatically draws horizontal lines to represent the medians; the `stat_summary()` function adds light dots to represent the means.

Following is our data wrangling and data visualization code:

```
ws_giniXY <- rbind(ws_giniX, ws_giniY)
ggplot(ws_giniXY, aes(x = champ, y = gini_index)) +
  geom_boxplot() +
  labs(title =
       "Comparison of Gini Coefficients based on Season-End Disposition",
       x = "",
       y = "Gini Coefficients", subtitle = "1991-2017") +
  geom_boxplot(color = "darkorange4", fill = "darkorange1") +
  stat_summary(fun = mean, geom = "point", shape = 20, size = 8,
               color = "white", fill = "white") +
  theme(plot.title = element_text(face = "bold")) +
  scale_x_discrete(breaks = c("1", "0"),
                   labels = c("League Champions", "All Other Teams"))
```

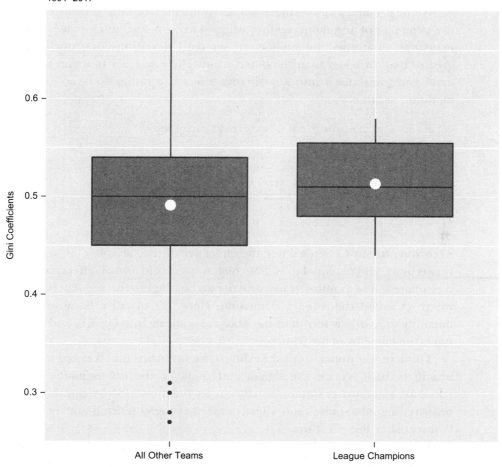

Comparison of Gini Coefficients based on Season−End Disposition
1991−2017

Figure 13.5   Paired boxplots that visualize the means, medians, and Gini coefficient distributions between championship-winning teams and all other teams

There isn't anything particularly remarkable about displaying the mean of one population versus the mean of a second population; however, our boxplots show the difference in population medians as well as the difference in distributions, where one is clearly less dispersed than the other.

While t-tests tell us if the variance in two means is equal to zero or nonzero, and thus whether or not we should reject a null hypothesis, effect size tests tell us how large or not so large the standardized difference is between two distributions. We'll pivot toward effect size testing next. Some of these tests haven't been introduced until now.

13.8.3 *Effect size testing*

The most popular, or most common, effect size test is Cohen's d, which computes the difference between two means and divides it by the average standard deviation between the same two populations. We've performed Cohen's d tests in prior chapters where we've also run t-tests.

We next make a call to the `cohen.d()` function from the `effsize` package, passing the same pair of arguments we first assigned to our t-test, and we get in return a d estimate that quantifies the number of standard deviations that one mean is either greater than or lesser than the other mean. The `cohen.d()` function takes that d estimate and translates it into a qualitative effect size rating equal to negligible, small, medium, or large:

```
cohen.d(ws_giniX$gini_index, ws_giniY$gini_index)
##
## Cohen's d
##
## d estimate: -0.3165796 (small)
## 95 percent confidence interval:
##        lower        upper
## -0.70133815  0.06817886
```

According to our Cohen's d test, the effect size of the variable gini_index in ws_giniX versus in ws_giniY is equal to –0.32, which translates to a small effect size. The Cohen's d estimate will be positive or negative depending on how we sequenced the arguments when we called the `cohen.d()` function. Here, it's negative because the gini_index mean in ws_giniX is less than the gini_index mean in ws_giniY, and Cohen's d subtracts the latter from the former.

Think of the numerator as the difference in means that is equal to the effect size, which, in turn, equals the signal, and think of the denominator as the average (pooled) standard deviation, which equals the noise. So in one sense, Cohen's d returns a signal-to-noise ratio where the farther the coefficient, or d estimate, is from 0, the greater the effect size.

Let's next run a Cohen's d test from the `effectsize` package as well as two other effect size tests from the same package, Hedges' g and Glass's delta, and compare and contrast the results. But first, here's some additional background on effect size testing:

- Once more, Cohen's d returns an effect size by computing the difference in two means and then dividing that by a pooled standard deviation between the two populations. Cohen's d therefore doesn't consider record counts, which is why we've previously stated that Cohen's d is a proper statistical test to *complement* a t-test and is thus not a suitable *replacement* for the same. After all, results are more likely due to chance when we have, let's say, just 50 records to evaluate, versus 5,000 records; a Cohen's d effect size test wouldn't recognize that.

- Another reason it's worth mentioning that Cohen's d ignores population sizes, or record counts, is that Cohen's d may supply an inflated estimate of the standardized difference between two means to its denominator when the population sizes are small or if the two population sizes are different. To address this, Hedges' g was introduced as an adjustment to Cohen's d. Hedges' g incorporates a correction factor to the denominator that accounts for the potential bias in small record counts, thereby providing a more accurate estimate of the effect size. It's an appropriate alternative when there are fewer than 20 records. Otherwise, Hedges' g works just like Cohen's d; for example, if Hedges' g also returned an effect size equal to –0.32, we would evaluate that estimate as a small effect.

- Glass's delta divides the difference in means by the standard deviation of the second group passed to the `glass_delta()` function instead of a pooled, or average, standard deviation between both groups. This means we should expect different results if the two standard deviations are different. We still get an effect size equal to some number between –1 and +1, which would be evaluated similarly to Cohen's d or Hedges' g.

- It might go without saying, but neither Hedges' g nor Glass's delta should be run in lieu of a t-test; like Cohen's d, both are only fitting complements to a t-test.

That all being said, we next make calls to the `cohens_d()`, `hedges_g()`, and `glass_delta()` functions in succession:

```
cohens_d(ws_giniX$gini_index, ws_giniY$gini_index)
## Cohen's d |         95% CI
## -----------------------
## -0.32     | [-0.70, 0.07]
##
## - Estimated using pooled SD.
hedges_g(ws_giniX$gini_index, ws_giniY$gini_index)
## Hedges' g |         95% CI
## -----------------------
## -0.32     | [-0.70, 0.07]
##
## - Estimated using pooled SD.
glass_delta(ws_giniX$gini_index, ws_giniY$gini_index)
## Glass' delta |         95% CI
## ---------------------------
## -0.51        | [-0.93, -0.09]
```

Our first, and maybe most obvious, takeaway is that the Cohen's d test returns the same results as our first Cohen's d test—as it should.

Our second takeaway is that the Hedges' g results match the Cohen's d results. This isn't surprising because the Hedges' g method for effect size is computed similarly to Cohen's d, where the difference in population means is divided by the average, or pooled, standard deviation—except that Hedges' g adds a "correction" by factoring counts in the denominator. As such, Hedges' g is usually recommended over Cohen's d when the population sizes are less than 20. When both are greater than 20 (as shown here), Hedges' g usually returns the same results as Cohen's d.

Our third, perhaps most significant, takeaway is that the Glass's delta method of effect size returns very different results from our Cohen's d and Hedges' g tests. Based on the Glass's delta effect size estimate alone, we would instead conclude that the difference in the variable `gini_index` between ws_giniX and ws_giniY is medium, rather than small, and therefore more significant than either the Cohen's d and Hedges' g tests otherwise suggest.

We're told to accept the Glass's delta estimate over Cohen's d and Hedges' g when the standard deviations between the two data series are significantly different. The base R `sd()` function returns the standard deviations; here, we front the `sd()` function with the `round()` function so that the returned standard deviations include two digits right of the decimal point rather than the default seven:

```
round(sd(ws_giniX$gini_index), digits = 2)
## [1] 0.07
round(sd(ws_giniY$gini_index), digits = 2)
## [1] 0.04
```

The standard deviation is equal to the square root of the variance, so we could also compute the standard deviations by calling the base R `sqrt()` and `var()` functions:

```
round(sqrt(var(ws_giniX$gini_index)), digits = 2)
## [1] 0.07
round(sqrt(var(ws_giniY$gini_index)), digits = 2)
## [1] 0.04
```

We then make a call to the `var.test()` function from base R to run what's called an F-test. An F-test computes the F statistic, or the ratio of two variances, and returns a p-value. The p-value should be evaluated just the same as a p-value from other statistical tests:

```
var.test(ws_giniX$gini_index, ws_giniY$gini_index)
##
##   F test to compare two variances
##
## data:  ws_giniX$gini_index and ws_giniY$gini_index
## F = 2.6659, num df = 758, denom df = 26, p-value = 0.003528
## alternative hypothesis: true ratio of variances is not equal to 1
## 95 percent confidence interval:
```

```
##  1.410118 4.349496
## sample estimates:
## ratio of variances
##            2.665942
```

Because the p-value essentially equals zero, we should reject the null hypothesis and conclude that the variances, and therefore the standard deviations, are statistically different. So we should therefore accept the Glass's delta effect size results over the Cohen's d and Hedges' g results and conclude that the effect size is medium instead of small.

Or should we? Whereas Cohen's d and Hedges' g average, or pool, the standard deviations from both data series, Glass's delta takes just the standard deviation from the *second* argument as a denominator. Let's then rerun our effect size tests, this time reversing the sequence of the arguments:

```
cohens_d(ws_giniY$gini_index, ws_giniX$gini_index)
## Cohen's d |        95% CI
## -----------------------
## 0.32      | [-0.07, 0.70]
##
## - Estimated using pooled SD.
hedges_g(ws_giniY$gini_index, ws_giniX$gini_index)
## Hedges' g |        95% CI
## -----------------------
## 0.32      | [-0.07, 0.70]
##
## - Estimated using pooled SD.
glass_delta(ws_giniY$gini_index, ws_giniX$gini_index)
## Glass' delta |       95% CI
## --------------------------
## 0.31         | [0.07, 0.56]
```

This time around, we essentially get the same results across all three effect size tests. Therefore, we can confidently settle on the idea that the effect size in the variable `gini_index` between the ws_giniX and ws_giniY data sets is small, which, of course, is more significant than negligible, but also less so than medium.

In the next section, we'll repeat these same tests and compare the Gini coefficient on win shares between winning and losing teams.

13.9 Win share inequality and wins and losses

There's no need for further data wrangling, so we'll jump right in with another t-test. Here, we'll be testing to determine whether or not Gini coefficients on win shares matter in regular season winning percentages.

13.9.1 T-test

We begin by passing the ws_gini_records data set to the `dplyr group_by()` and `summarize()` functions whereby `summarize()` computes the average Gini coefficient, rounded to two digits right of the decimal point, and `group_by()` separates the results by winning percentage. Because we've included a logical operator inside the argument to the `group_by()` function, our results, when passed to a tibble called ws_gini_summary3, will therefore be split between TRUE and FALSE:

```
ws_gini_records %>%
  group_by(pct >= 0.50) %>%
  summarize(mean = round(mean(gini_index), digits = 2)) -> ws_gini_summary3
print(ws_gini_summary3)
## # A tibble: 2 × 2
##   `pct >= 0.5`  mean
##   <lgl>        <dbl>
## 1 FALSE         0.48
## 2 TRUE          0.5
```

Winning teams, on average, have higher Gini coefficients, and therefore more unequal win share distributions, than teams with losing records, at least between the 1991 and 2017 seasons. The difference is relatively small, but given the record counts, probably statistically significant. We'll run a t-test to find out for sure.

We therefore establish two more data sets: ws_giniA, which is ws_gini_records subset where the variable `pct` is equal to or greater than 0.50, and ws_giniB, which is ws_gini_records subset where the variable `pct` is less than 0.50. Our t-test compares the `gini_index` means between ws_giniA, subset on teams between 1991 and 2017 that won at least half their regular season games, and ws_giniB, subset on teams that won fewer than half of their regular season games:

```
ws_gini_records %>%
  filter(pct >= 0.50) -> ws_giniA
ws_gini_records %>%
  filter(pct < 0.50) -> ws_giniB

t.test(ws_giniA$gini_index, ws_giniB$gini_index)
##
##  Welch Two Sample t-test
##
## data:  ws_giniA$gini_index and ws_giniB$gini_index
## t = 3.5935, df = 641.1, p-value = 0.0003513
## alternative hypothesis: true difference in means is not equal to 0
## 95 percent confidence interval:
##   0.008383264 0.028584666
## sample estimates:
## mean of x mean of y
##   0.500000  0.481516
```

The p-value essentially equals 0, so once again, we should reject the null hypothesis and conclude that the variance in Gini coefficients is therefore statistically significant.

We then produce a pair of `ggplot2` boxplots as a way of visualizing our results (see figure 13.6):

```
ws_giniAB <- rbind(ws_giniA, ws_giniB)
mutate(ws_giniAB, win_pct = ifelse(pct >= 0.50, "y", "n")) -> ws_giniAB
ggplot(ws_giniAB, aes(x = win_pct, y = gini_index)) +
  geom_boxplot() +
  labs(title =
        "Comparison of Gini Coefficients based on Winning Percentage",
       subtitle = "1991-2017",
       x = "",
       y = "Gini Coefficients") +
  geom_boxplot(color = "darkorange4", fill = "darkorange1") +
  stat_summary(fun = mean, geom = "point", shape = 20, size`= 8,
               color = "white", fill = "white") +
  theme(plot.title = element_text(face = "bold")) +
  scale_x_discrete(breaks = c("y", "n"),
                   labels = c("Winning Teams", "Losing Teams"))
```

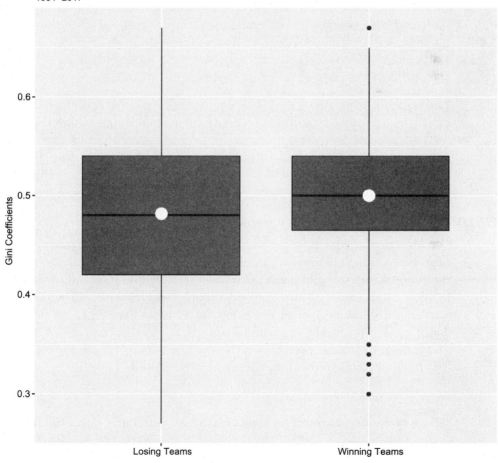

Figure 13.6   Paired boxplots that visualize the means, medians, and Gini coefficient distributions between winning and losing teams

We'll run a series of effect size tests next.

13.9.2   *Effect size testing*

In our next chunk of code, we call the `cohens_d()`, `hedges_g()`, and `glass_delta()` functions from the `effectsize` package:

```
cohens_d(ws_giniA$gini_index, ws_giniB$gini_index)
## Cohen's d |       95% CI
## ----------------------
## 0.27      | [0.12, 0.41]
##
## - Estimated using pooled SD.
hedges_g(ws_giniA$gini_index, ws_giniB$gini_index)
## Hedges' g |       95% CI
## ----------------------
## 0.27      | [0.12, 0.41]
##
## - Estimated using pooled SD.
glass_delta(ws_giniA$gini_index, ws_giniB$gini_index)
## Glass' delta |      95% CI
## -------------------------
## 0.24         | [0.11, 0.37]
```

The Cohen's d and Hedges' g estimates match one another, but the Glass's delta estimate is marginally different. In any event, these results suggest that the effect size in this case is small.

Finally, we'll create bands of winning percentages, as we did in chapter 12, and then plot the Gini coefficient for each band. Our point is to determine how regular season winning percentages might trend as inequality in player productivity increases.

13.10 *Gini coefficient bands versus winning percentage*

Our first action is to pass the ws_gini_records data set to the `dplyr` `mutate()` and `case_when()` functions to create a categorical variable called `ws_gini_band` derived from the numeric variable `gini_index`. When the variable `gini_index`, for instance, is equal to or greater than `0.50`, the derived variable `ws_gini_band` will equal `>0.50`; when `gini_index` is greater than or equal to `0.45` and less than `0.50`, the derived variable `ws_gini_band` then equals `>0.45`, and so on.

We then call the `as.factor()` function to convert `ws_gini_band` to a factor variable. The `head()` function returns the first three observations.

```
ws_gini_records %>%
  mutate(ws_gini_band =
            case_when(gini_index >= .50 ~ ">0.50",
                      gini_index >= .45 & gini_index < .50 ~ ">0.45",
                      gini_index >= .40 & gini_index < .45 ~ ">0.40",
                      gini_index >= .35 & gini_index < .40 ~ ">0.35",
                      gini_index >= .30 & gini_index < .35 ~ ">0.30",
                      gini_index >= .25 & gini_index < .30 ~ ">0.25",
```

```
                gini_index < .25 ~ "<0.25")) -> ws_gini_records

ws_gini_records$ws_gini_band <- as.factor(ws_gini_records$ws_gini_band)
head(ws_gini_records, n = 3)
## # A tibble: 3 x 8
## # Groups:   team, season_end [3]
##   season_end team              gini_index  wins losses   pct
##   <fct>      <fct>                  <dbl> <dbl>  <dbl> <dbl>
## 1 1991       Atlanta Hawks           0.54    43     39  0.52
## 2 1991       Boston Celtics          0.52    56     26  0.68
## 3 1991       Charlotte Hornets       0.39    26     56  0.32
##   champ ws_gini_band
##   <fct> <fct>
## 1 0     >0.50
## 2 0     >0.50
## 3 0     >0.35
```

Then, we pass ws_gini_records to the dplyr group_by() and summarize() functions,
where the summarize() function computes the mean of the variable pct, rounded two
digits to the right of the decimal point, and the group_by() function separates the
results by each level, or factor, in the variable ws_gini_band. The results are cast to a
tibble called gini_summary4:

```
ws_gini_records %>%
  group_by(ws_gini_band) %>%
  summarize(mean_pct = round(mean(pct), digits = 2)) -> ws_gini_summary4
print(ws_gini_summary4)
## # A tibble: 6 x 2
##   ws_gini_band mean_pct
##   <fct>           <dbl>
## 1 >0.25            0.22
## 2 >0.30            0.46
## 3 >0.35            0.43
## 4 >0.40            0.47
## 5 >0.45            0.52
## 6 >0.50            0.59
```

Note that no results are returned where the derived variable ws_gini_band equals <0.25.

Here's our ggplot2 bar chart that takes gini_summary4 as a data source and plots
the variable ws_gini_band along the x-axis and the variable mean_pct along the y-axis
(see figure 13.7):

```
ggplot(ws_gini_summary4, aes(x = ws_gini_band, y = mean_pct)) +
  geom_bar(stat = "identity", width = .6, fill = "steelblue1") +
  labs(title = "Gini Coefficients and Winning Percentages",
       subtitle = "1991-2017",
       x = "Gini Coefficient Bands",
       y = "Average Regular Season Winning Percentage") +
  ylim(0, 0.7) +
  geom_text(aes(x = ws_gini_band, y = mean_pct,
                label = mean_pct, vjust = -0.3, fontface = "bold")) +
  theme(plot.title = element_text(face = "bold"))
```

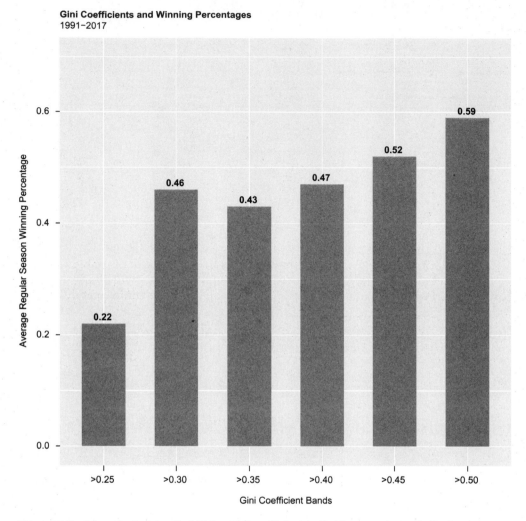

Figure 13.7   A bar chart shows that higher Gini coefficients—that is, more unequal win share distributions—are mostly aligned with higher regular season winning percentages.

Our bar chart shows that NBA teams between 1991 and 2017 mainly had incremental to significant increases in regular season winning percentages with each successive bump in Gini coefficient bands—the bands representing the inequality in player productivity. We have one anomaly, where the Gini coefficient is greater than 0.35 and less than 0.40, due to relatively low record counts.

So we've demonstrated that the most successful NBA teams, at least between 1991 and 2017, weren't the most "balanced" and "well-rounded" teams. Just the opposite, in fact. Put differently, we twice rejected our null hypothesis that Gini coefficients in win shares have no effect on outcomes, first with respect to league championships and then again with respect to regular season winning percentages. In other words, we've again challenged and contradicted the conventional wisdom. In chapter 14, we'll challenge the idea that defense wins championships.

In the meantime, hopefully we kept our promise that, despite working with Gini coefficients and Lorenz curves one more (and final) time, there was enough new statistical, data visualization, and programming material to keep your interest throughout. For instance, we learned that there are effect size tests, other than Cohen's d, to complement t-tests; we demonstrated how to run those and even discussed under what circumstances which of these tests might best fit. We ran our first F-test and reviewed how and when you should pull such a test out of your toolkit of statistical tests. We also demonstrated how to create a `for` loop to avoid writing repeatable chunks of code and then how to write your own function if R doesn't already have what you need. While not statistical, per se, you need to be comfortable with `for` loops and user-defined functions if you want to take your R skills to the highest levels.

Summary

- Statistical dispersion in general and Gini coefficients in particular are important concepts to understand in that they have many critical applications. Is there an association between city-level income inequality and school performance that should figure into funding and resource allocations? Is high income inequality correlated with exposure to contagious diseases, and, if so, should Gini coefficients drive prevention strategies? From a billing perspective, are there some medical procedures that have higher Gini coefficients than others, and if that's the case, are additional regulations in order? Should Gini coefficients in securities returns trigger calculations of risk and reward and influence investment decisions?

- In addition, we demonstrated `for` loops as just one way R lets us perform repeatable tasks without the repetition, thereby mitigating monotony from a development perspective and maintenance from a support perspective. There's most definitely a huge return on investment here for any serious R programmer.

- We also demonstrated how to create a user-defined function. Even though it seems R has more than one function for almost any operation, we nevertheless have the ability in R to write our own functions if the need arises.

- While effect size tests should only complement t-tests (or other like tests where we would reject or fail to reject a null hypothesis, such as a chi-square test for independence) and never replace them, their meaning and their results may actually resonate better with the laymen in your audience.

- Of the effect size tests demonstrated in this chapter (disregarding the Cramer's V tests from chapter 9), Cohen's d is the most common and the most robust of the three. In most instances, Hedges' g and Cohen's d will return similar results; however, you might want to run a Hedges' g test when you're working with just a few records. A Glass's delta test only makes sense if you want to control which of two standard deviations should be your effect size denominator, rather than it being an average of two standard deviations pooled from two groups.

- League-wide Gini coefficients around win share distributions are most recently down from where they were in the early 1990s.
- Nevertheless, unequal win share distributions are mostly associated with championship-winning teams and teams that win more regular season games than they lose. Conversely, win share distributions that are less unequal (they aren't really equal) are mostly associated with losing teams. These results are supported by our t-tests especially and our effect size tests. That these results are similar to our results from chapter 12 suggest that salaries and productivity are well aligned.

14

Intermediate and advanced modeling

This chapter covers

- Fitting and evaluating analysis of variance models and logistic regressions
- Computing probabilities, odds ratios, and log odds
- Computing and plotting sensitivity and specificity
- Running correlation tests
- Creating new and improved boxplots

The idea that "defense wins championships" might have come from legendary college football coach Paul "Bear" Bryant, who led the Alabama Crimson Tide to six national titles in the 1960s and 1970s. The same idea then extended into basketball, especially the NBA. Despite the fact that NBA teams spend roughly half their time and effort playing offense and the other half playing defense, the view that defense matters more than offense took hold and remains part of the sport's conventional wisdom.

Our purpose here is to repeatedly test the idea that defense, *much* more than offense, influences regular season wins and playoff appearances in the NBA. We'll compute correlation coefficients; run correlation tests; demonstrate how to fit and evaluate an analysis of variance (ANOVA) model, which is a type of statistical model used to analyze the differences between three or more group means and determine the significance of these differences; and show how to fit and evaluate a logistic regression, which is the most popular method of solving classification problems—all while comparing and contrasting the effects of defense versus offense.

We have several packages to load, including quite a few we haven't used yet. We'll start there.

14.1 Loading packages

As usual, we'll use a combination of built-in and packaged functions to accomplish our goals; no doubt, you're familiar with the `tidyverse` and `patchwork` packages by now, but here are the other packages we'll need throughout this chapter:

- Graphical displays of model outputs—diagnostic plots from our ANOVAs and a pair of receiver operating characteristic (ROC) curves from our logistic regressions—will be created from base R functionality. The remaining plots will be created from the `ggplot2` package, which is part of `tidyverse`. Additionally, we'll extend `ggplot2` by calling the `ggpaired()` function from the `ggpubr` package to create paired boxplots that are very different from our previous boxplots. You might recall that we previously loaded the `ggpubr` package in chapter 7, from which we called the `stat_compare_means()` function to automatically add p-values to paired `ggplot2` boxplots.

- We'll fit our logistic regressions from the base R `glm()` function. We'll then make calls to functions from the `pscl`, `SciViews`, `questionr`, `caret`, and `pROC` packages to return model results and provide other insights.

Rather than incrementally loading these packages by making eight successive calls to the base R `library()` function, we'll instead create a vector called packages and then pass it to the base R `lapply()` function (you may recall that we first called the `lapply()` function back in chapter 3):

```
packages <- c("tidyverse", "patchwork", "ggpubr", "pscl", "SciViews",
              "questionr", "caret", "pROC")

lapply(packages, library, character.only = TRUE)
```

We'll import and wrangle our data next, starting with the salaries data set we first introduced back in chapter 10. Remember that the salaries data set contains much more than the sum of player salaries for every NBA team between the 2000 and 2017 seasons; it also includes regular season wins and end-of-season disposition for the same.

14.2 Importing and wrangling data

The salaries data set is a .csv file saved in our default working directory; the file contains the following:

- Real and inflation-adjusted team payrolls for every NBA team between the 2000 and 2017 seasons. The real payrolls were obtained from a Boston Celtics fan site and the inflation-adjusted payrolls were computed using a tool from www.usinflationcalculator.com.

- Regular season win totals and postseason results for every team between these same seasons. These were scraped from www.basketball-reference.com.

We make a call to the read_csv() function from the readr package to import the salaries data set:

```
salaries <- read_csv("salaries.csv")
```

The salaries data set contains more data than we need and, at the same time, not enough data; furthermore, it isn't even formatted in a way that best suits our needs. Thus, we need to run a series of data wrangling operations—subsetting data, reshaping data sets, creating derived variables, and joining salaries with other data sets— before we can run any statistical tests and fit any models.

14.2.1 Subsetting and reshaping our data

We begin by making a pair of calls to the select() function from the dplyr package to subset salaries into two new data sets named first_salaries and second_salaries:

- The first_salaries data set contains the variable Team, as well as the variables w2017 through w2008. Team is a character string that includes the full name of every NBA team, and w2017 through w2008 are numeric variables that include their regular season win totals.

- The second_salaries data set contains the variable Team plus the variables pc2017 through pc2008. For now, pc2017 through pc2008 are numeric variables, but their cells are actually populated with one of just three season-ending, or postseason, result factors:

```
salaries %>%
  select(Team, w2017:w2008) -> first_salaries

salaries %>%
  select(Team, pc2017:pc2008) -> second_salaries
```

Next, we make a pair of calls to the tidyr pivot_longer() function to transpose the first_salaries and second_salaries data sets from wide to long formats.

In the first chunk of the following code, we pass first_salaries to the pivot_longer() function, where the variables w2017 through w2008 are converted to factors within a new variable called year, and their former values roll up under another a new variable called wins. The results are cast to a tibble called first_stats.

In the second code chunk, the second_salaries data set is passed to the pivot_longer() function, where new variables called season and playoffs take the place of pc2017 through pc2008. These results are then cast to yet another tibble called second_stats:

```
first_salaries %>%
  pivot_longer(col = c(w2017:w2008),
               names_to = "year",
               values_to = "wins") -> first_stats

second_salaries %>%
  pivot_longer(col = c(pc2017:pc2008),
               names_to = "season",
               values_to = "playoffs") -> second_stats
```

The base R dim() function returns the row and column counts for first_stats; it contains 300 rows, or one row for every unique team and year combination, and three columns. The head() and tail() functions, also from base R, return the first three and last three observations, respectively, from first_stats. By default, R returns six records, but you can tell R to return any number of records you want. Here, we're instructing R to just return three records each time:

```
dim(first_stats)
## [1] 300   3

head(first_stats, n = 3)
## # A tibble: 3 × 3
##    Team           year  wins
##    <chr>          <chr> <int>
## 1 Atlanta Hawks w2017    43
## 2 Atlanta Hawks w2016    48
## 3 Atlanta Hawks w2015    60

tail(first_stats, n = 3)
## # A tibble: 3 × 3
##    Team                year  wins
##    <chr>               <chr> <int>
## 1 Washington Wizards w2010    26
## 2 Washington Wizards w2009    19
## 3 Washington Wizards w2008    43
```

We then run these same three commands a second time, but we swap out the first_stats tibble in favor of second_stats in the process:

```
dim(second_stats)
## [1] 300   3

head(second_stats, n = 3)
## # A tibble: 3 × 3
##    Team           season  playoffs
##    <chr>          <chr>    <int>
## 1 Atlanta Hawks X2017pc     10
## 2 Atlanta Hawks X2016pc     10
## 3 Atlanta Hawks X2015pc     10
```

```
tail(second_stats, n = 3)
## # A tibble: 3 x 3
##   Team                season  playoffs
##   <chr>               <chr>      <int>
## 1 Washington Wizards  X2010pc        0
## 2 Washington Wizards  X2009pc        0
## 3 Washington Wizards  X2008pc       10
```

As a result, we now have two working data sets that are longer than their predecessors; each record in each object now contains a unique team and season combination complemented by regular season wins (in the case of first_stats) or season-ending results (in the case of second_stats). These are objects from which we can create derived variables, join with other data sets, and then ultimately drop into statistical tests and statistical models.

14.2.2 Extracting a substring to create a new variable

In our next upcoming code chunk, we call the dplyr mutate() function in tandem with the str_sub() function from the stringr package, which is part of the tidyverse, to convert all the elements in the variable year to a more readable and practical format where, for instance, w2017 becomes simply 2017. If for no other reason, our plots will make that much more sense if they include just the year rather than the year preceded by a single-byte character that once indicated regular season wins but has since been repurposed.

The mutate() function is called to create a new variable called season derived from the variable year, which is a character string. Then, we call the str_sub() function so that our new variable is a character vector but also a substring of year. The str_sub() function takes three arguments: the first is the name of the character string that requires manipulation; the second and third arguments are the start and end positions, going from right to left, that require extraction. We're extracting the first through the fourth characters, so -4 and -1 are therefore our next two arguments. Then we call the select() function to subset the first_stats data set on every variable but year.

Finally, we call the base R as.factor() function to convert our new variable from a character string to a factor variable. The head() function returns the first three records in the new and improved first_stats data set:

```
first_stats %>%
  mutate(season = str_sub(year, -4, -1)) -> first_stats

first_stats %>%
  select(-year) -> first_stats

first_stats$season <- as.factor(first_stats$season)

head(first_stats, n = 3)
## # A tibble: 3 x 3
```

```
##    Team              wins season
##    <chr>            <int> <fct>
## 1 Atlanta Hawks       43 2017
## 2 Atlanta Hawks       48 2016
## 3 Atlanta Hawks       60 2015
```

After all that, we merely replaced the variable `year`, which was a character string (e.g., `w2017`, `w2016`, etc.), with the variable `season`, which is a factor variable (e.g., `2017`, `2016`, etc.).

14.2.3 *Joining data*

With respect to second_stats, we again make a call to the `dplyr` `select()` function to reduce it to only contain the variable `playoffs`:

```
second_stats %>%
  select(playoffs) -> second_stats
```

Now we can join first_stats and second_stats and make a new data set by calling the `cbind()` function from base R. Whereas first_stats has a 300 × 3 dimension and second_stats now has a 300 × 1 dimension, our new data set, stats, contains 300 rows and four columns. We then call the `head()` function so that R returns the first three records:

```
stats <- cbind(first_stats, second_stats)
head(stats, n = 3)
##             Team wins season playoffs
## 1 Atlanta Hawks   43   2017       10
## 2 Atlanta Hawks   48   2016       10
## 3 Atlanta Hawks   60   2015       10
```

Now we have a single data set that contains regular season wins and season-end results for every unique team and season combination.

14.2.4 *Importing and wrangling additional data sets*

We have 10 additional .csv files to import. Each .csv file contains a season's worth of team-level statistics such as wins and losses, points scored per game, and the average difference between points scored and points allowed. The data was scraped and copied from the NBA's official website and pasted into Microsoft Excel; the files were then saved with .csv extensions and subsequently stored in our default working directory. We therefore call the `read_csv()` function 10 times to import these 10 files:

```
nba2017 <- read_csv("nba2017.csv")
nba2016 <- read_csv("nba2016.csv")
nba2015 <- read_csv("nba2015.csv")
nba2014 <- read_csv("nba2014.csv")
nba2013 <- read_csv("nba2013.csv")
nba2012 <- read_csv("nba2012.csv")
nba2011 <- read_csv("nba2011.csv")
```

```
nba2010 <- read_csv("nba2010.csv")
nba2009 <- read_csv("nba2009.csv")
nba2008 <- read_csv("nba2008.csv")
```

Each of these files contains 30 rows, or one row per team, and 27 columns of data. We then call the base R `rbind()` function to merge these 10 data sets into one data set called nba:

```
nba <- rbind(nba2017, nba2016, nba2015, nba2014, nba2013, nba2012,
             nba2011, nba2010, nba2009, nba2008)
```

A call to the `dim()` function then returns the row and column counts. This confirms that (1) while we previously had 30 records for each of the 10 data sets, we now have one data set that contains 300 rows (30 records × 10 data sets); and (2) we still have 27 columns, or variables:

```
dim(nba)
## [1] 300   27
```

Then we call the `mutate()` function to create a new nba variable called season. The `rep()` and `c()` functions populate our new variable, starting at the top, with 30 instances of 2017, then 30 instances of 2016, 30 instances of 2015, and so on, through 2008. A subsequent call to the `as.factor()` function converts season to a factor variable.

As stated in previous chapters, it's always a good practice to validate the integrity of infrequent operations *before* calling other data wrangling functions. First, we call the `head()` and `tail()` functions to print the first three and last three values in the variable season; we should get three instances of 2017 and then three instances of 2008. Then, we call the base R `summary()` function where season, rather than the entire nba data set, is passed as an argument. Because season is a factor variable, R will return the row counts for each level. We should, of course, get 10 counts of 30 rows:

```
nba %>%
  mutate(season = rep(c(2017:2008), each = 30)) -> nba
nba$season <- as.factor(nba$season)

head(nba$season, n = 3)
## [1] 2017 2017 2017
## Levels: 2008 2009 2010 2011 2012 2013 2014 2015 2016 2017

tail(nba$season, n = 3)
## [1] 2008 2008 2008
## Levels: 2008 2009 2010 2011 2012 2013 2014 2015 2016 2017

summary(nba$season)
## 2008 2009 2010 2011 2012 2013 2014 2015 2016 2017
##   30   30   30   30   30   30   30   30   30   30
```

Everything checks out, which means we can move forward with further data wrangling operations.

We again call the `mutate()` function to create a derived variable called `O_PTS`, which represents the average number of points *allowed* per game. Our data set contains a variable called `PTS`, which represents the average number of points *scored* per game, and another variable called `PTS_DIFF`, which is the difference between points scored and points allowed. So `O_PTS` equals the difference between `PTS` and `PTS_DIFF`:

```
nba %>%
  mutate(O_PTS = PTS - PTS_DIFF) -> nba
```

Then we call the `select()` function to subset nba on the variables `Team`, `PTS`, `PTS_DIFF`, `season`, and `O_PTS`:

```
nba %>%
  select(Team, PTS, PTS_DIFF, season, O_PTS) -> nba
```

A call the `dplyr` `glimpse()` function returns the reduced dimension of the nba data set as well as a transposed view of the data:

```
glimpse(nba)
## Rows: 300
## Columns: 5
## $ Team     <chr> "Golden State Warriors", "San Antonio Spurs", "Houst…
## $ PTS      <dbl> 115.9, 105.3, 115.3, 108.0, 110.3, 108.7, 106.9, 100…
## $ PTS_DIFF <dbl> 11.6, 7.2, 5.8, 2.6, 3.2, 4.3, 4.2, 3.9, 1.8, 0.8, -…
## $ season   <fct> 2017, 2017, 2017, 2017, 2017, 2017, 2017, 2017, 2017…
## $ O_PTS    <dbl> 104.3, 98.1, 109.5, 105.4, 107.1, 104.4, 102.7, 96.8…
```

Because the remaining columns in nba aren't necessarily arranged in the most logical order, we'll next demonstrate just one way to reorder columns in R. We've previously called the `select()` function from the `dplyr` package to subset a data set; here, by passing every remaining column in the nba data set, the `select()` function rearranges the columns in the order by which they're passed. Another call to the `glimpse()` function returns the results:

```
nba %>%
  select(Team, season, PTS, O_PTS, PTS_DIFF) -> nba

glimpse(nba)
## Rows: 300
## Columns: 5
## $ Team     <chr> "Golden State Warriors", "San Antonio Spurs", "Houst…
## $ season   <fct> 2017, 2017, 2017, 2017, 2017, 2017, 2017, 2017, 2017…
## $ PTS      <dbl> 115.9, 105.3, 115.3, 108.0, 110.3, 108.7, 106.9, 100…
## $ O_PTS    <dbl> 104.3, 98.1, 109.5, 105.4, 107.1, 104.4, 102.7, 96.8…
## $ PTS_DIFF <dbl> 11.6, 7.2, 5.8, 2.6, 3.2, 4.3, 4.2, 3.9, 1.8, 0.8, -…
```

The `glimpse()` function always returns, from top to bottom, the complete list of variables that otherwise run from left to right.

14.2.5 *Joining data (one more time)*

Going back to the stats data set, we call the `as.factor()` function to convert the variable `playoffs`, where every record can take on just one of three values, to a factor variable. The variable `playoffs` equals 0 when teams failed to qualify for postseason play; `playoffs` equals 10 when teams qualified for postseason play but were then eliminated; and `playoffs` equals 11 when teams won the NBA championship:

```
stats$playoffs <- as.factor(stats$playoffs)
```

Then, we call the `dplyr left_join()` function to join the nba and stats data sets by the two variables, `Team` and `season`, which they have in common:

```
nba_stats <- left_join(stats, nba, by = c("Team", "season"))
```

As a result, nba_stats contains seven columns, or every unique column between the nba and stats data sets.

Although a left join was used here, any of the join operations, described in the following list, would have worked with nba and stats and produced the same results:

- A left join, or left outer join (as used in the preceding code), merges every row in one data set with only matching rows from another data set.
- A right join, or right outer join, does the same, but the data sets are switched.
- An outer join, or full outer join, keeps every row from both data sets.
- A natural join, or inner join, keeps only matching rows from both data sets.

We'll demonstrate this by successively calling the `dplyr right_join()`, `inner_join()`, and `full_join` functions and then calling the `head()` function four times to return the top three records from each operation:

```
nba_stats_right <- right_join(stats, nba, by = c("Team", "season"))
nba_stats_full <- inner_join(stats, nba, by = c("Team", "season"))
nba_stats_inner <- full_join(stats, nba, by = c("Team", "season"))

head(nba_stats, n = 3)
##               Team wins season playoffs   PTS O_PTS PTS_DIFF
## 1 Atlanta Hawks   43   2017       10 103.2 104.1     -0.9
## 2 Atlanta Hawks   48   2016       10 102.8  99.2      3.6
## 3 Atlanta Hawks   60   2015       10 102.5  97.1      5.4
head(nba_stats_right, n = 3)
##               Team wins season playoffs   PTS O_PTS PTS_DIFF
## 1 Atlanta Hawks   43   2017       10 103.2 104.1     -0.9
## 2 Atlanta Hawks   48   2016       10 102.8  99.2      3.6
## 3 Atlanta Hawks   60   2015       10 102.5  97.1      5.4
head(nba_stats_full, n = 3)
##               Team wins season playoffs   PTS O_PTS PTS_DIFF
```

```
## 1 Atlanta Hawks    43    2017       10 103.2 104.1      -0.9
## 2 Atlanta Hawks    48    2016       10 102.8  99.2       3.6
## 3 Atlanta Hawks    60    2015       10 102.5  97.1       5.4
head(nba_stats_inner, n = 3)
##               Team wins season playoffs   PTS O_PTS PTS_DIFF
## 1 Atlanta Hawks    43    2017       10 103.2 104.1      -0.9
## 2 Atlanta Hawks    48    2016       10 102.8  99.2       3.6
## 3 Atlanta Hawks    60    2015       10 102.5  97.1       5.4
```

As you can see, the results are exactly the same, regardless of what join operation was called.

14.2.6 *Creating standardized variables*

Finally, we make three successive calls to the `dplyr` `group_by()` and `mutate()` functions to standardize three of the four numeric variables in the nba_stats data set. Once more, standardization is the process of converting variables to the same scale; when these same variables also span several years—and in our case, 10 NBA seasons, where periodic rule changes and style of play transformations make it difficult, even unsound, to compare year-over-year results—standardization just makes sense. Furthermore, by standardizing key measures, we get context that we can't get from the raw figures. From a more practical perspective, standardization corrects the 2012 regular season win totals because teams didn't play an 82-game regular season schedule that year due to a player strike.

Variables are standardized by computing their z-scores, which equal the number of standard deviations a data point is above or below a population mean. Let's use the variable `wins` as an example. By calling the `mutate()` function, we're creating a new variable called z_wins, which is the z-score for regular season wins. A z-score is computed by subtracting the mean for wins from actual wins and dividing that difference by the standard deviation. By first calling the `group_by()` function, we're instructing R to compute the z-scores annually. Subsequent calls to the `round()` function from base R reduce our z-scores to just two digits right of the decimal point.

```
nba_stats %>%
  group_by(season) %>%
  mutate(z_wins = (wins - mean(wins)) / sd(wins)) -> nba_stats
  nba_stats$z_wins <- round(nba_stats$z_wins, digits = 2)

nba_stats %>%
  group_by(season) %>%
  mutate(z_pts = (PTS - mean(PTS)) / sd(PTS)) -> nba_stats
  nba_stats$z_pts <- round(nba_stats$z_pts, digits = 2)

nba_stats %>%
  group_by(season) %>%
  mutate(z_o_pts = (O_PTS - mean(O_PTS)) / sd(O_PTS)) -> nba_stats
  nba_stats$z_o_pts <- round(nba_stats$z_o_pts, digits = 2)
```

The `head()` function returns the first three records:

```
head(nba_stats, n = 3)
## # A tibble: 3 × 10
## # Groups:   season [3]
##   Team            wins season playoffs   PTS O_PTS PTS_DIFF
##   <chr>          <dbl> <fct>  <fct>     <dbl> <dbl>    <dbl>
## 1 Atlanta Hawks     43 2017   10        103.  104.      -0.9
## 2 Atlanta Hawks     48 2016   10        103.   99.2      3.6
## 3 Atlanta Hawks     60 2015   10        102.   97.1      5.4
## z_wins z_pts z_o_pts
##  <dbl> <dbl>   <dbl>
## 1 0.18 -0.58   -0.37
## 2 0.5   0.04   -0.93
## 3 1.41  0.58   -0.97
```

Let's now take a look at the 2017 Atlanta Hawks for a representative example. Their 43 regular season wins were 0.18 standard deviations above the mean in 2017, which makes sense considering every team played an 82-game regular season schedule that year. Their 103.2 points scored per game were 0.58 standard deviations below the 2017 mean, so the Hawks finished the 2016–17 season with a winning record while scoring fewer points per game than the league average. But the Hawks were a much better defensive team; they allowed 104.1 points per game, which was 0.37 standard deviations below the 2017 mean. This means the 2017 Hawks allowed almost one more point per game than they scored.

Next, we'll create a `ggplot2` bar chart and a `ggplot2` histogram to provide some initial insights into our data.

14.3 Exploring data

To create a bar chart, we first need to summarize our data. We therefore call the `group_by()` and `summarize()` functions from the `dplyr` package to compute the mean for the numeric variable `PTS` for each of the 10 NBA seasons in the nba_stats data set. Our intent is to display the average points scored per game for every NBA season in our data set and to discover any trends during the same. The results are rounded to two digits right of the decimal point and then cast to a tibble called first_tibble:

```
nba_stats %>%
  group_by(season) %>%
  summarize(pts_avg = round(mean(PTS), digits = 2)) -> first_tibble
print(first_tibble)
## # A tibble: 10 × 2
##    season pts_avg
##    <fct>    <dbl>
## 1  2008      99.9
## 2  2009      99.9
## 3  2010     100.
```

```
##  4 2011     99.6
##  5 2012     96.3
##  6 2013     98.1
##  7 2014    101.
##  8 2015    100.
##  9 2016    103.
## 10 2017    106.
```

Our `ggplot2` bar chart takes first_tibble as a data source and plots the variable `season` along the x-axis and the variable `pts_avg` along the y-axis (see figure 14.1).

The `geom_bar()` function instructs R to create a bar chart. By default, R will compute and visualize row counts for each value of x; we override that and, in the process, tell R to tie each value of x to our y-axis variable by adding the `stat = "identity"` argument. Otherwise, the bars are half the default width and colored and filled with different shades of steel blue.

The `geom_text()` function affixes the y values atop the bars. Because of this add, we then need to call the `ylim()` function to extend the length of the y-axis:

```
ggplot(first_tibble, aes(x = season, y = pts_avg)) +
  geom_bar(stat = "identity", width = .5,
           color = "steelblue4", fill = "steelblue1") +
  labs(title = "Average Points per Game per Team by Season",
       subtitle = "2008-17",
       x = "Season",
       y = "Average Points per Game") +
  geom_text(aes(label = (pts_avg), vjust = -0.3, fontface = "bold")) +
  ylim(0, 110) +
  theme(plot.title = element_text(face = "bold"))
```

On one hand, we don't see a tremendous amount of year-over-year variation in points scored per game—which, of course, must also equal points allowed per game. On the other hand, however, we see a low of 96.26 in 2012 and a high of 105.59 in 2017, and that difference is significant.

Next, we plot a histogram to visualize the distribution of the variable PTS across the entire nba_stats data set (see figure 14.2). Therefore, nba_stats is our data source, and PTS is our x-axis variable.

Our histogram will contain 15 bins. The number of bins should scale with the record count in your data. One rule of thumb suggests the number of bins should approximately equal the square root of the record count, with a not-to-exceed equal to 20. We have 300 observations in the nba_stats data set; the square root of 300 equals 17.3, so 15 bins by this rule seems appropriate enough.

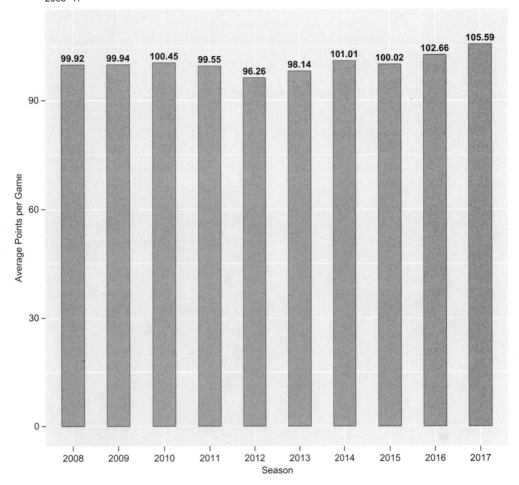

Average Points per Game per Team by Season
2008-17

Figure 14.1 **The average points scored per game and per team for every NBA season between 2008 and 2017**

A pair of calls to the geom_line() function tells R to draw two vertical lines, a dashed line that represents the population mean and a solid line—ggplot2 lines default to solid—that represents the population median:

```
ggplot(nba_stats, aes(x = PTS)) +
  geom_histogram(fill = "steelblue1", color = "steelblue4", bins = 15) +
    geom_vline(aes(xintercept = mean(PTS)),
            color = "black", linetype = "longdash", size = .8) +
    geom_vline(aes(xintercept = median(PTS)),
            color = "black", size = .8) +
```

```
labs(title = "Distribution of Points Scored per Game per Team",
     subtitle = "2008-17",
     caption = "dashed line represents the mean
       solid line represents the median",
     x = "Average Points Scored per Game",
     y = "Frequency") +
theme(plot.title = element_text(face = "bold"))
```

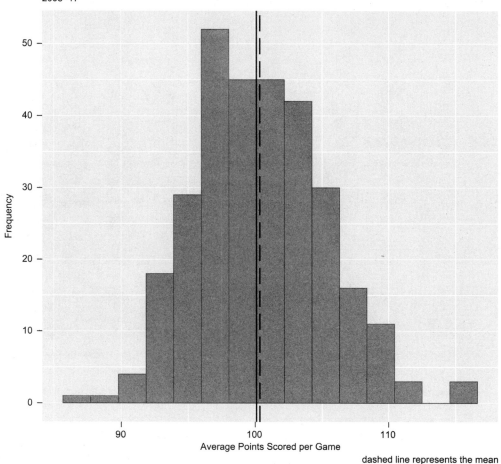

Distribution of Points Scored per Game per Team
2008–17

dashed line represents the mean
solid line represents the median

Figure 14.2   The distribution of points per game for every NBA team between 2008 and 2017

It appears that the variable PTS takes on a normal, or Gaussian, distribution. In other words, the distribution is symmetric about the mean, where the most frequent occurrences in the data are near the mean and the most infrequent occurrences are farthest from the mean.

But visual inspection isn't always reliable. Therefore, we next call the `shapiro.test()` function from base R to run a Shapiro-Wilk test, which is probably the most common normality test. In the case of a Shapiro-Wilk test, we're looking for a p-value above 0.05 to assume normality:

```
shapiro.test(nba_stats$PTS)
##
##   Shapiro-Wilk normality test
##
## data:  nba_stats$PTS
## W = 0.99016, p-value = 0.04124
```

Because the p-value is less than the 0.05 significance cutoff, we should assume the distribution of the variable PTS from the nba_stats data set isn't (quite) normal, despite appearances to the contrary. This is something to keep in mind as we conduct our tests, which we'll turn to next.

14.4 Correlations

We begin by computing and comparing the correlation coefficients between z_wins and z_o_pts versus z_wins and z_pts. So we're first computing the correlation coefficient between the standardized versions of regular season wins and points allowed and then computing the same between the standardized versions of wins and points scored. If points allowed matters more in terms of regular season wins than does points scored, or if defense matters more than offense, z_o_pts should have a stronger correlation with z_wins than z_pts has with z_wins. Then, we'll run a pair of correlation tests with the same combination of variables—and make similar assumptions based on a comparison of the p-values.

14.4.1 Computing and plotting correlation coefficients

Computing correlation coefficients in R is easy enough; we simply call the `cor()` function from base R and pass two numeric variables:

```
cor(nba_stats$z_wins, nba_stats$z_o_pts)
## [1] -0.5844698

cor(nba_stats$z_wins, nba_stats$z_pts)
## [1] 0.5282497
```

So points allowed does have a stronger correlation with wins (–0.58) than does points scored (0.53), but the difference in the two correlation coefficients is negligible. They are, in fact, almost equally distant from being perfectly neutral, which doesn't at all suggest that defense matters materially more than offense, at least as far as regular season wins between 2008 and 2017 are concerned.

Correlation coefficients are well visualized with correlation plots, often called scatterplots. These are constructed in ggplot2 by passing the data source and two numeric variables as arguments to the ggplot() function and then calling the geom_point() function (see figure 14.3).

The geom_smooth() function adds a linear regression line and, by default, 95% confidence intervals above and below the line—which we're overriding by adding the argument se = FALSE to geom_smooth(). The xlim() function ensures that the x-axes of both plots match one another. The first of our two correlation plots, p1, visualizes the correlation between points allowed and wins, while our second correlation plot, p2, visualizes the correlation between points scored and wins:

```
p1 <- ggplot(nba_stats, aes(x = z_o_pts, y = z_wins)) +
  geom_point() +
  labs(title = " Points Allowed vs. Wins (2008-17)",
       subtitle = "correlation coefficient = -0.58",
       x = "Points Allowed (standardized)", y = "Wins (standardized)") +
  geom_smooth(method = lm, se = FALSE) +
  xlim(-3.3, 3.3) +
  theme(plot.title = element_text(face = "bold"))

p2 <- ggplot(nba_stats, aes(x = z_pts, y = z_wins)) +
  geom_point() +
  labs(title = "Points Scored vs. Wins (2008-17)",
       subtitle = "correlation coefficient = 0.53",
       x = "Points Scored (standardized)", y = "Wins (standardized)") +
  geom_smooth(method = lm, se = FALSE) +
  xlim(-3.3, 3.3) +
  theme(plot.title = element_text(face = "bold"))
```

We then call the plot_layout() function from the patchwork package to bundle p1 and p2 into a single object where the two plots are placed side by side for easy purposes of comparison (see figure 14.3):

```
p1 + p2 + plot_layout(ncol = 2)
```

These two plots are basically mirror images of each other.

Let's plot the net correlation coefficient between O_PTS and wins and PTS and wins by season. We'll first need to create another summarization of the nba_stats data set. Therefore, we make another call to the dplyr group_by() and summarize() functions which, together, compute the absolute difference—note the calls to the base R abs() function—between the PTS and wins correlation coefficient and the O_PTS and wins correlation coefficient for each NBA season in the nba_stats data set. Because we're subsetting these results by season, it's perfectly appropriate to use the raw data rather than their standardized equivalents (e.g., wins rather than z_wins).

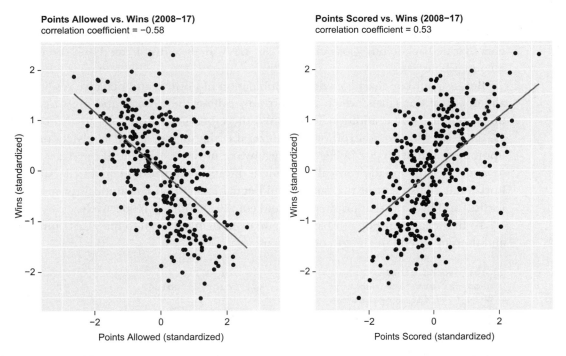

Figure 14.3   The correlation between points allowed and wins is visualized on the left; the correlation between points scored and wins is visualized on the right.

The results are rounded to two digits right of the decimal point and then cast to a tibble called second_tibble:

```
nba_stats %>%
  group_by(season) %>%
  summarize(cor_dif = round(cor(PTS, wins) - abs(cor(O_PTS, z_wins)),
                            digits = 2)) -> second_tibble
print(second_tibble)
## # A tibble: 10 × 2
##     season cor_dif
##     <fct>    <dbl>
##  1 2008     -0.03
##  2 2009     -0.36
##  3 2010     -0.16
##  4 2011     -0.35
##  5 2012      0.08
##  6 2013      0.08
##  7 2014     -0.06
##  8 2015      0.23
##  9 2016      0.01
## 10 2017     -0.01
```

We then visualize these results with a second `ggplot2` bar chart (see figure 14.4). Once again, we call the `geom_text()` function to add labels just beyond the "height" of the bars that tie back to our y-axis variable, `cor_dif`, which we just created and threw into second_tibble.

Because our bar chart contains a combination of positive and negative results, the alignment of our labels, which we control by calling the `vjust()` and `hjust()` functions, requires some additional logic. We therefore make two calls to the base R `ifelse()` function to control, or customize, the alignment of our labels contingent upon the variable `cor_dif` being a nonnegative or negative number. If `cor_dif` is equal to or greater than `0`, the vertical adjustment of our labels should equal `-0.5`, and the horizontal adjustment of the same should equal `0.5`; if that condition isn't met, the vertical and horizontal adjustments should equal `1.3` and `0.5`, respectively.

To fit the labels inside our bar chart, we need to make a call to the `ylim()` function and thereby extend the length of the y-axis:

```
ggplot(second_tibble, aes(x = season, y = cor_dif)) +
  geom_bar(stat = "identity", width = .7, color = "gold4",
           fill = "gold1") +
  labs(title = "Annual Differences in Absolute Correlations",
       subtitle = "2008-17",
       caption = "when negative, points allowed mattered more;
           when positive, points scored mattered more",
       x = "Season",
       y = "Absolute Correlation Difference") +
  geom_text(aes(label = cor_dif, y = cor_dif, fontface = "bold",
                vjust = ifelse(cor_dif >= 0, -0.5, 1.3),
                hjust = ifelse(cor_dif >= 0, 0.5, 0.5))) +
  ylim(-.4, .4) +
  theme(plot.title = element_text(face = "bold"))
```

Each bar represents the absolute difference in the correlation coefficients between PTS and wins and between O_PTS and wins. Take the 2010 season as an example—the correlation coefficient between PTS and wins minus the correlation coefficient between O_PTS and wins equals -0.16. In other words, in 2010, O_PTS had a stronger correlation with wins than did PTS, which suggests that defense then mattered more than offense. In fact, points allowed had stronger correlations with regular season wins every year between 2008 and 2011, but then points scored had stronger correlations with wins than points allowed in four of the next six NBA seasons.

Our bar chart gives us a year-over-year view of what might be the relative significance between points scored versus points allowed with respect to regular season wins; this is a perspective we don't get merely by computing the correlation coefficients across the entire data series. Our results suggest that, more recently, offense has actually mattered more than defense. But the differences are usually negligible either way; at the very least, between 2012 and 2017, we haven't seen differences in correlation coefficients like those in 2009 and 2011.

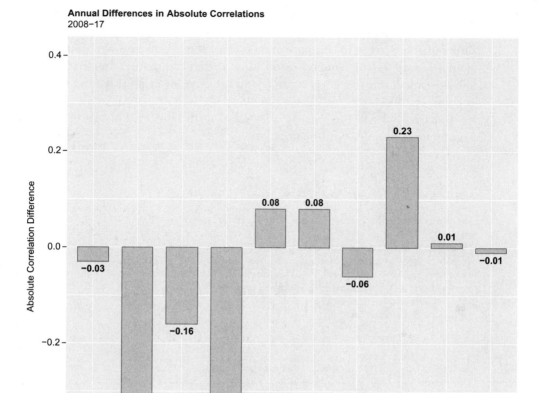

Figure 14.4   **Annual differences in correlation coefficients between points scored and wins versus points allowed and wins**

14.4.2 *Running correlation tests*

Even when a correlation coefficient equals some number other than 0, it may or may not be significantly different from 0, at least in any statistical sense, which is why a correlation test adds value. A correlation test, like other statistical tests, returns a p-value that, based on a predefined 5% significance level, we can either reject or fail to reject a null hypothesis of no correlation. Our null hypothesis is that there is no meaningful relationship or correlation; we'll reject this hypothesis if the returned p-value is less than or equal to 0.05 or fail to reject it if otherwise.

We therefore call the base R cor.test() function twice to run a pair of correlation tests, the first between z_wins and z_o_pts and the second between z_wins and z_pts. Our purpose here is to compare and contrast the results between points allowed and points scored versus regular season wins. If defense matters more than offense, we should expect our first correlation test to return a lower p-value than our second correlation test.

But first, we call the options() function from base R and pass the scipen = 999 argument to disable scientific notation:

```
options(scipen = 999)

cor.test(nba_stats$z_wins, nba_stats$z_o_pts)
##
##  Pearson's product-moment correlation
##
## data:  nba_stats$z_wins and nba_stats$z_o_pts
## t = -12.434, df = 298, p-value < 0.00000000000000022
## alternative hypothesis: true correlation is not equal to 0
## 95 percent confidence interval:
##  -0.6543987 -0.5046282
## sample estimates:
##        cor
## -0.5844698

cor.test(nba_stats$z_wins, nba_stats$z_pts)
##
##  Pearson's product-moment correlation
##
## data:  nba_stats$z_wins and nba_stats$z_pts
## t = 10.74, df = 298, p-value < 0.00000000000000022
## alternative hypothesis: true correlation is not equal to 0
## 95 percent confidence interval:
##  0.4414140 0.6052828
## sample estimates:
##        cor
## 0.5282497
```

Both correlations are statistically significant due to the fact that the p-value for both tests is less than the 0.05 significance threshold; in fact, the p-values are exactly the same between the two correlation tests, thereby suggesting no material difference between points allowed and points scored versus regular season wins.

Based on these results—and these results alone, for we have additional tests to perform—we can't conclude that points allowed are more significant than points scored or that defense matters more than offense when it comes to regular season wins. Next, we'll fit a pair of one-way ANOVA models.

14.5 *Analysis of variance models*

Whereas a t-test is a statistical test that determines whether or not the means from *two* data series are significantly different, analysis of variance (ANOVA) is a method that determines if the means from *three or more* data series are statistically different from each other. We'll wrangle our data some first, visualize the same, and then fit and evaluate a pair of ANOVA models. Otherwise, we'll continue evaluating regular season wins and points scored versus points allowed.

14.5.1 *Data wrangling and data visualization*

ANOVAs require a categorical predictor variable and a quantitative target variable. We have a quantitative dependent variable in z_wins, but we don't yet have any categorical predictor variables. In the following chunk of code, we call the dplyr mutate() and case_when() functions to create a new categorical variable, o_pts_cat, derived from the variable z_o_points. When z_o_pts is less than −1, o_pts_cat equals A; when z_o_pts is greater than or equal to −1 and less than 0, o_pts_cat equals B; when z_o_pts is equal to or greater than 0 and less than or equal to 1, o_pts_cat equals C; and when z_o_pts is greater than 1, o_pts_cat equals D. Our new variable is then converted to a factor by calling the base R as.factor() function:

```
nba_stats %>%
  mutate(o_pts_cat = case_when(z_o_pts < -1 ~ "A",
                               z_o_pts >= -1 & z_o_pts < 0 ~ "B",
                               z_o_pts >= 0 & z_o_pts <= 1 ~ "C",
                               z_o_pts > 1 ~ "D")) -> nba_stats
nba_stats$o_pts_cat <- as.factor(nba_stats$o_pts_cat)
```

Then, we call the mutate() and case_when() functions again to create a like variable derived from z_pts. This variable, too, is then converted to a factor by again calling the as.factor() function:

```
nba_stats %>%
  mutate(pts_cat = case_when(z_pts < -1 ~ "A",
                             z_pts >= -1 & z_pts < 0 ~ "B",
                             z_pts >= 0 & z_pts <= 1 ~ "C",
                             z_pts > 1 ~ "D")) -> nba_stats
nba_stats$pts_cat <- as.factor(nba_stats$pts_cat)
```

We then make a pair of calls to the base R summary() function to return the record counts for each factor level, or category, in the variables o_pts_cat and pts_cat. For numeric variables, the summary() function returns a series of basic, or descriptive, statistics, but for factor variables such as the two we just created, summary() instead returns the record counts:

```
summary(nba_stats$o_pts_cat)
##   A   B   C   D
##  43 103 105  49
summary(nba_stats$pts_cat)
##   A   B   C   D
##  49 109  97  45
```

Most significantly, there are no Not Availables (NAs, or missing data), so we've success-fully assigned a o_pts_cat and pts_cat category to every record in the nba_stats data set. Otherwise, these variables equal B or C for more than two-thirds of the 300 obser-vations in our data set, which means more than two-thirds of the NBA teams between the 2008 and 2017 seasons were within ± one standard deviation from the league mean in points allowed and points scored.

Let's plot how well, or not so well, o_pts_cat and pts_cat are associated with the variable z_wins through two series of boxplots. But first, here's a quick refresher on boxplots, which are sometimes referred to as box and whisker plots:

- The box represents the Interquartile Range (IQR), or every data point between the 25th and 75th percentiles; the IQR therefore contains the middle 50% of the data.
- The whiskers, or the lines extending from the top and bottom of the box, repre-sent the upper and lower quartiles.
- Any data points beyond the whiskers are considered outliers; this data is approximately three standard deviations or more from the population median.
- The horizontal line in each box represents the population median; R automati-cally draws this line for us.

Our first series of boxplots, p3, points to the nba_stats data set. These box plots are a bit different from those we have previously created; here's what you need to know before we introduce the code:

- Inside the aes() function, we're passing o_pts_cat as our x-axis variable and z_wins as our y-axis variable, so we're visualizing the distribution of standardized regular season wins by each factor level in o_pts_cat.
- Additionally, we're passing o_pts_cat to equal the fill, which means our box-plots will take on the default ggplot2 palette rather than a designated or uni-form fill. Recall that fill defines the color by which a geom is filled, whereas the color argument defines the boundary color.
- We've added two optional arguments to the geom_boxplot() function:
  - When notch equals TRUE (the default is FALSE), we're instructing R to draw notched, rather than standard, boxplots. From a visual perspective, the notch "squeezes" the box around the median; from a statistical perspective, the notch is a display of the confidence interval around the median. The value added is that notches are used to compare groups; if and when the notches of two or more boxes do *not* overlap, we have strong evidence that the medians are significantly different. And while we're more interested in group means than medians, the two measures are in fact very close to each other, regardless of the o_pts_cat factor level.
  - The second argument inside the boxplot() function, alpha, adjusts the opac-ity of the boxes; in fact, the alpha argument can be passed to adjust the opac-ity of any geom. Values must range from 0 to 1, where lower values equal more opacity.

- By calling the `stat_summary()` function, we're adding a solid white dot to each box that represents the mean.
- We're adding a legend and positioning it at the bottom of each plot. Legends can be placed almost anywhere, including inside the plot itself.
- Finally, a call to the `scale_fill_discrete()` function allows us to customize the legend name and legend labels. By default, our legend would otherwise be named `o_pts_cat`, and the labels would equal the `o_pts_cat` factor levels—neither of which would be very intuitive.

The code chunk just described follows:

```
p3 <- ggplot(nba_stats, aes(x = o_pts_cat, y = z_wins, fill = o_pts_cat)) +
  geom_boxplot(notch = TRUE, alpha = 0.5) +
  labs(title = "Points Allowed vs. Wins",
       subtitle = "2008-17",
       x = "Standardized Points Allowed Category",
       y = "Standardized Regular Season Wins") +
  stat_summary(fun = mean, geom = "point",
               shape = 20, size = 8, color = "white", fill = "white") +
  theme(legend.position = "bottom") +
  scale_fill_discrete(name = "Points\nAllowed\nZ-Score",
                      labels = c("< -1", "-1 to 0", "0 to 1","> 1")) +
  theme(plot.title = element_text(face = "bold"))
```

Our second series of boxplots, p4, is similar to p3, except that we've swapped out `o_pts_cat` in favor of `pts_cat` as our x-axis variable and fill. So here, we're plotting the distribution of standardized regular season wins against each factor level in `pts_cat`:

```
p4 <- ggplot(nba_stats, aes(x = pts_cat, y = z_wins, fill = pts_cat)) +
  geom_boxplot(notch = TRUE, alpha = 0.5) +
  labs(title = "Points Scored vs. Wins",
       subtitle = "2008-17",
       x = "Standardized Points Scored Category",
       y = "Standardized Regular Season Wins") +
  stat_summary(fun = mean, geom = "point",
               shape = 20, size = 8, color = "white", fill = "white") +
  theme(legend.position = "bottom") +
  scale_fill_discrete(name = "Points\nScored\nZ-Score",
                      labels = c("< -1", "-1 to 0", "0 to 1", "> 1")) +
  theme(plot.title = element_text(face = "bold"))
```

Our two plots have been held in memory. We then bundle p3 and p4 together by calling the `plot_layout()` function from the `patchwork` package and print our boxplots as one graphical object (see figure 14.5):

```
p3 + p4 + plot_layout(ncol = 2)
```

Clearly, teams that were more successful on defense or offense between the 2008 and 2017 NBA seasons were generally more successful in the regular season. Furthermore,

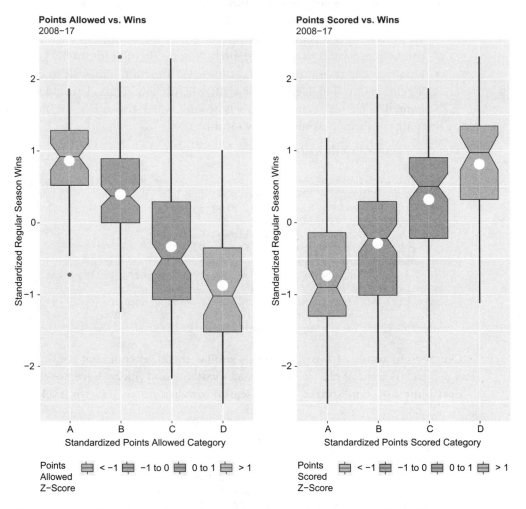

Figure 14.5 On the left, four standardized points allowed categories are plotted against standardized regular season wins; on the right, four standardized points scored categories are plotted against standardized regular season wins.

it appears that we don't have overlapping notches in either plot, thereby suggesting the potential for variances that are statistically significant.

14.5.2 *One-way ANOVAs*

Let's now conduct a pair of one-way ANOVAs—"one-way" because we're analyzing how just *one* predictor variable, o_pts_cat and then pts_cat, affects a target variable, z_wins. Our purpose is to determine whether there is a statistically significant difference between the factor levels in o_pts_cat and pts_cat *and* then to establish if one group of factor levels has a greater effect on z_wins than the other group of factor levels.

We fit a one-way ANOVA similarly to fitting a simple linear regression, except that we call the base R `aov()` function rather than the `lm()` function. We then pass the target and predictor variables, separated by a tilde, and a pointer to our data source, nba_stats, as arguments:

```
fit1 <- aov(z_wins ~ o_pts_cat, data = nba_stats)
```

Then, we call the `summary()` function to return the results:

```
summary(fit1)
##              Df Sum Sq Mean Sq F value              Pr(>F)
## o_pts_cat     3  96.56   32.19   49.32 <0.0000000000000002 ***
## Residuals   296 193.16    0.65
## ---
## Signif. codes:  0 '***' 0.001 '**' 0.01 '*' 0.05 '.' 0.1 ' ' 1
```

The p-value is essentially equal to 0, which means there is a statistically significant difference in the mean for z_wins that ties back to the four factor levels in the variable o_pts_cat.

Let's now examine a pair of diagnostic plots by calling the base R `plot()` function (see figure 14.6). Diagnostic plots are used to assess model integrity. By default, R returns up to four diagnostic plots, but we're interested in checking for equal variances across groups and normality in the residuals, so just two of the four diagnostic plots, Residuals vs. Fitted and Normal QQ, are sufficient. As such, we pass the which argument to the base R `plot()` function to print just two plots (in one column) rather than four:

```
plot(fit1, which = c(2, 1))
```

The Residuals vs. Fitted plot displays the relationship between residuals and fitted values, that is, the relationship between each team's standardized regular season wins and the z_wins mean for their respective o_pts_cat factor level. Teams that had more regular season wins than their group or category mean have positive residuals; teams that had fewer regular season wins than their group or category mean have negative residuals. For fit1 to perfectly satisfy the one-way ANOVA assumption for equal variances across groups, the residuals should be equally dispersed for each level of fitted values. However, we can clearly see that the residuals are less dispersed at the highest fitted values versus the other levels, so the equal variances across groups assumption has likely been violated, albeit not significantly so.

The Normal QQ plot does not, per se, display the distribution of the residuals, but it does provide a visual clue as to whether or not the residuals are normally distributed. If the residuals were normally distributed, the Normal QQ points would overlay the diagonal line; if not, we would instead see serious deviations from the diagonal line, most likely at one or both of the tails. In our case, the points deviate slightly at both tails, but on the whole, they overlay the diagonal line very well. In conclusion,

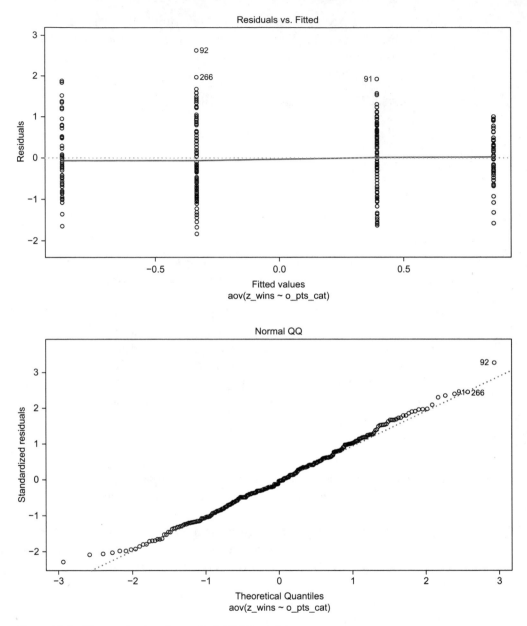

Figure 14.6　Diagnostic plots for our first ANOVA model

while fit1 might be a model of less-than-perfect integrity, it does *not* qualify as a "bad" model that requires corrective action and a do-over.

Let's now fit a second ANOVA by which we swap out predictor variables: fit2 therefore tests the effect of the categorical variable pts_cat on the numeric variable z_wins.

We call the `aov()` function to run our ANOVA and then the `summary()` function to return the results:

```
fit2 <- aov(z_wins ~ pts_cat, data = nba_stats)
summary(fit2)
##              Df Sum Sq Mean Sq F value            Pr(>F)
## pts_cat       3  75.04  25.014   34.49 <0.0000000000000002 ***
## Residuals   296 214.68   0.725
## ---
## Signif. codes:  0 '***' 0.001 '**' 0.01 '*' 0.05 '.' 0.1 ' ' 1
```

Once again, the p-value essentially equals 0, which means there is also a statistically significant difference in the mean for `z_wins` that can be attributed to the four factor levels in `pts_cat`.

Let's print the fit2 diagnostics and compare to our first ANOVA by again calling the `plot()` function (see figure 14.7):

```
plot(fit2, which = c(2, 1))
```

First, with respect to the Residuals vs. Fitted plot, the fit2 residuals appear to be more equally dispersed for each level of fitted values than they were for fit1, thereby suggesting equal variances across groups. Second, with respect to the Normal QQ plot, the points appear to overlay the diagonal line more than the fit1 residuals, thereby suggesting a more normal distribution.

Finally, we pass fit1 and fit2 to the base R `AIC()` function so as to compute the Akaike Information Criterion (AIC) for both ANOVAs. AIC weighs the variation explained against the number of predictors and returns a score. For a single model, AIC means nothing, but for the purposes of model selection—especially fit1 versus fit2, where we have equal p-values—AIC is a popular best-fit measure where the lower AIC score the better:

```
AIC(fit1, fit2)
##      df      AIC
## fit1  5 729.2831
## fit2  5 760.9676
```

It would appear, at least based on these two AIC scores, that fit1 better explains variations in `z_wins` than does fit2; in other words, defense explains variances in regular season wins better than offense. This may certainly be true, but the advantage is negligible at best and therefore hardly overwhelming.

Thus, based on correlation tests and ANOVA models, we can confidently conclude that defense has, at best, a small advantage over offense in terms of affecting regular season wins. Next, we'll run a pair of logistic regressions to determine if defense or offense better predicts which teams qualify, or don't qualify, for postseason play.

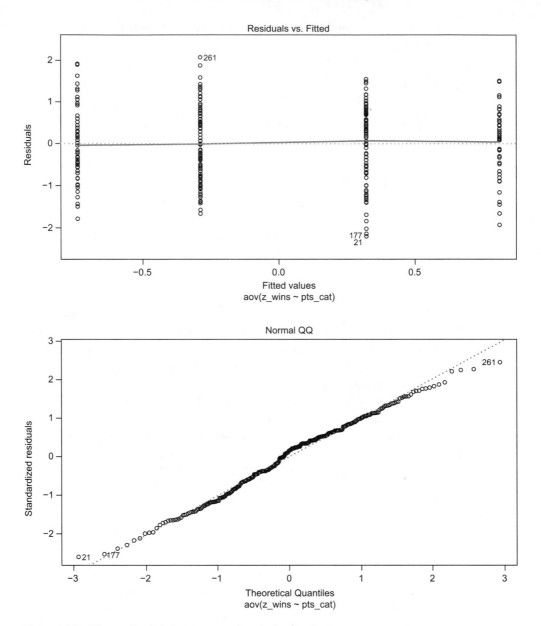

Figure 14.7 Diagnostic plots for our second analysis of variance

14.6 *Logistic regressions*

Back in chapter 5, we fit a pair of linear regressions to identify which hustle statistics might have a statistically significant influence on wins and by how much; put differently, we regressed a continuous variable against other continuous variables. Logistic regression, on the other hand, is a method by which we regress a binary target variable against one or more (usually) continuous predictor variables. Our purpose here is to run a pair of simple logistic regressions—simple because each model will contain just one predictor variable, either z_o_pts or z_pts, rather than multiple predictors—to compare and contrast the offensive and defensive influence on postseason qualification.

Before we get into the nuts and bolts of logistic regression—which, be warned, is more complex than linear regression—let's wrangle the nba_stats data set by creating a derived target variable and then split nba_stats into two mutually exclusive subsets for training and predicting.

14.6.1 Data wrangling

First, we pass nba_stats to the dplyr mutate() function and base R ifelse() function to create a new variable called playoffs2. If the variable playoffs—which is a factor variable with levels 0, 10, and 11—equals 0, then playoffs2 should also equal 0; if playoffs equals anything other than 0, then playoffs2 should instead equal 1.

The base R head() and tail() functions return the first 10 and last 10 observations in nba_stats, respectively, but with a slight twist. Rather than return every column in nba_stats, we instead instruct R to only return those variables in positions 1, 3, 4, and 13. Note that we must include the position numbers in order for this code to run; if we were to instead apply the variable names, R would throw an error:

```
nba_stats %>%
  mutate(playoffs2 = ifelse(playoffs == 0, 0, 1)) -> nba_stats
head(nba_stats[,c(1, 3, 4, 13)], 10)
## # A tibble: 10 × 4
## # Groups:   season [10]
##     Team          season playoffs playoffs2
##     <chr>         <fct>  <fct>        <dbl>
##  1 Atlanta Hawks 2017   10               1
##  2 Atlanta Hawks 2016   10               1
##  3 Atlanta Hawks 2015   10               1
##  4 Atlanta Hawks 2014   10               1
##  5 Atlanta Hawks 2013   10               1
##  6 Atlanta Hawks 2012   10               1
##  7 Atlanta Hawks 2011   10               1
##  8 Atlanta Hawks 2010   10               1
##  9 Atlanta Hawks 2009   10               1
## 10 Atlanta Hawks 2008   10               1

tail(nba_stats[,c(1, 3, 4, 13)], 10)
## # A tibble: 10 × 4
## # Groups:   season [10]
##     Team               season playoffs playoffs2
##     <chr>              <fct>  <fct>        <dbl>
##  1 Washington Wizards 2017   10               1
##  2 Washington Wizards 2016   0                0
##  3 Washington Wizards 2015   10               1
##  4 Washington Wizards 2014   10               1
##  5 Washington Wizards 2013   0                0
##  6 Washington Wizards 2012   0                0
##  7 Washington Wizards 2011   0                0
##  8 Washington Wizards 2010   0                0
```

```
##  9 Washington Wizards 2009   0                    0
## 10 Washington Wizards 2008   10                   1
```

Then, we pass nba_stats to the dplyr `filter()` and `row_number()` functions to divert approximately one out of every four records into a subset called test. Next, by calling the dplyr `anti_join()` function, we throw every nba_stats record *not* in test into another subset called train:

```
nba_stats %>%
  filter(row_number() %% 4 == 1) -> test
train <- anti_join(nba_stats, test)
```

We'll train our logistic regressions on train and then predict on test. This is the exact same approach we took back in chapter 5 with respect to our multiple linear regressions; in fact, this is the same code we first used in that chapter to split our data into train and test.

Successive calls to the base R `dim()` function return the row and column counts for train and test:

```
dim(train)
## [1] 220   13
dim(test)
## [1] 80 13
```

We see that train contains 220 of the 300 records from nba_stats, or about 73% of the total record count, and that test contains the remaining 80 records.

14.6.2 *Model development*

First, let's consider a few critical details about logistic regression:

- The response, or target, variable must be binary where the factor levels usually equal 0 or 1, or 0 for No and 1 for Yes. In fact, we just created a binary target variable called `playoffs2` where 0 means a team failed to qualify for postseason play and 1 means a team did qualify for postseason play.
- Logistic regression is a method by which we predict the probability of a target variable equaling 1. For example, we could run a logistic regression to predict the probability of a high school senior getting accepted into Harvard, the probability of rain tomorrow, or the probability of an NBA team making the playoffs.
- Our logistic regressions will model the probability of qualifying for postseason play given the standardized scores between points allowed and then points scored. For instance, the probability of qualifying for postseason play given the value of the predictor variable `z_o_pts` can be written as Pr(playoffs2 = Yes|z_o_pts), or p(playoffs2) for short.
- The probability will always equal some number between 0 and 1. We'll then predict playoffs2 = Yes for any team where p(playoffs2) is equal to or greater than 0.50.

- This is why we can't run a linear regression to solve a classification problem; a linear model is actually capable of predicting probabilities less than 0 and greater than 1 when the predictor variable equals a relatively extreme value. To avoid mathematically impossible results, logistic regression uses a method known as *maximum likelihood estimation* to predict probabilities that will always fall between 0 and 1.

- The maximum likelihood estimation predicts probabilities from the following equation: $\log[p(X) / (1 - p(X))] = B_0 + B_1 X_1$. The left-hand side of this equation is called the log odds, or logit; the right-hand side therefore is how we compute the log odds, where X_1 equals the predictor variable and B_1 equals the predictor variable's coefficient. We'll talk much more on this when we get around to evaluating the results of our first model.

Let's now fit the first of our two regressions.

FITTING OUR FIRST OF TWO MODELS

To fit a logistic regression, we call the base R `glm()` function, short for generalized linear models, which represents a class of models that includes logistic regression. The syntax for a logistic regression is otherwise similar to a linear model and the base R `lm()` function, except that we need to pass the `family = "binomial"` argument to tell R to run a logistic regression versus some other generalized linear model. Note that we're fitting the model against train and not nba_stats.

We regress the target binary variable `playoffs2` against the continuous predictor variable `z_o_pts`. Then, we call the base R `summary()` function and pass the model name, fit3, to return the results:

```
fit3 <- glm(playoffs2 ~ z_o_pts, family = "binomial", data = train)
summary(fit3)
##
## Call:
## glm(formula = playoffs2 ~ z_o_pts, family = "binomial", data = train)
##
## Deviance Residuals:
##      Min        1Q    Median        3Q       Max
## -2.17428  -0.77250  -0.01473   0.76694   2.13669
##
## Coefficients:
##              Estimate Std. Error z value      Pr(>|z|)
## (Intercept)    0.1998     0.1727   1.157         0.247
## z_o_pts       -1.7210     0.2317  -7.428 0.00000000000011 ***
## ---
## Signif. codes:  0 '***' 0.001 '**' 0.01 '*' 0.05 '.' 0.1 ' ' 1
##
## (Dispersion parameter for binomial family taken to be 1)
##
##     Null deviance: 304.98  on 219  degrees of freedom
## Residual deviance: 210.91  on 218  degrees of freedom
## AIC: 214.91
##
## Number of Fisher Scoring iterations: 5
```

Let's alternately review a subset of these results and fetch some additional metrics. First, the p-value for z_o_pts essentially equals 0, which means it has a statistically significant effect on playoffs2; that is, points allowed definitely have an effect on whether or not an NBA team qualifies for the postseason.

Second, whereas a linear regression returns R^2 and Adjusted R^2 statistics that measure the amount of collective variance explained by the model's predictors, a logistic regression has no such equivalent. However, the pR2() function from the pscl package returns what's called a McFadden's pseudo-R^2 measure for generalized linear models. It otherwise measures the goodness of fit in logistic regression models. It quantifies the proportion of variance explained by the model by comparing the log-likelihood of the fitted model with that of a null model by returning some value between 0 and 1, where the higher the number, the more predictive power. A pseudo-R^2 as "low" as 0.4 or even 0.2 is generally considered to indicate a good fit. In the following code, we pass the model name, fit3, to the pR2() function to get McFadden's pseudo-R^2:

```
pR2(fit3)["McFadden"]
## fitting null model for pseudo-r2
##  McFadden
## 0.3084425
```

Because McFadden's pseudo-R^2 equals 0.31, we can therefore conclude that z_o_pts is a good fit for the data.

Third, the caret package includes a function called varImp(), which quantitatively measures the importance or relevance of model predictors. The metric means nothing by itself, but when compared to other predictors in the same model or another predictor in a competing simple regression, it allows us to compare and contrast their influence on the same target variable. All we then need to do is pass fit3 to the varImp() function. We'll return to these results after running our second logistic regression:

```
varImp(fit3)
##          Overall
## z_o_pts 7.428127
```

Fourth, the fit3 AIC equals 214.91; the summary() function returns this measure for generalized linear models, whereas for linear regressions and ANOVAs, we need to run the AIC() function to get the AIC. Once again, the AIC doesn't mean anything until we're comparing competing models, so we'll keep the AIC in our back pocket for the time being.

Fifth, we now need to continue our conversation about the predictor variable's coefficient; in fit3, the z_o_pts coefficient equals -1.72. First and foremost, it's important to understand how a probability is converted to log odds and vice versa:

- Probability is the likelihood of some event occurring. For example, there might be a 70% probability of our flight from New York to London departing on time.
- Odds, or more accurately the odds of success, equals the probability of success divided by the probability of failure. So the odds of our flight departing on time equals the odds ratio, or 0.70 divided by 0.30, which equals 2.33.

- The log odds is merely the natural logarithm of the odds ratio. One way of computing the natural logarithm in R is by calling the `ln()` function from the SciViews package and passing the odds ratio:

```
ln(2.33)
## [1] 0.8458683
```

More importantly for our purposes, here's how to convert a log odds to an odds ratio and an odds ratio to a probability that we can all understand:

- The odds ratio equals e^{log} odds, where e is a mathematical constant equal to 2.72, and, in our example, the log odds equals 0.85. R makes this easy for us—we simply call the base R `exp()` function and pass the log odds to convert the log odds to the odds ratio:

```
exp(0.85)
## [1] 2.339647
```

- The probability equals the odds ratio, or 2.34 in our example, divided by the sum of 1 and 2.34, or 3.34:

```
2.34 / 3.34
## [1] 0.7005988
```

After all that, we're back to a 70% probability of our New York to London flight departing on time.

Now, with respect to our logistic regression model, we can convert the `z_o_pts` coefficient from log odds to a probability and then evaluate the average change in our dependent variable, `playoffs2`, when the `z_o_pts` coefficient increases or decreases by one unit.

Rather than convert the log odds to an odd ratio and then convert the odds ratio to a probability, we'll merely pass the log odds to the base R `plogis()` function to compute the probability directly from the log odds:

```
plogis(-1.72)
## [1] 0.1518712
```

So a one-unit increase or decrease in `z_o_pts` will correspond to a roughly 15% change in the probability of qualifying for the playoffs.

Now that we've fit our logistic regression on the train data set, we can use it to make predictions against the test data set. We therefore pass our model and our data to the base R `predict()` function. By adding `type = "response"` as a third argument to the `predict()` function, we're instructing R to return the predicted probabilities in the form Pr(playoffs2 = Yes|z_o_pts).

```
predicted_fit3 <- predict(fit3, test, type = "response")
```

If we were to then call the `print()` function, R would return a matrix of probabilities, all equaling some number between 0 and 1, for all 80 records in test. Instead, we'll pass test to the `dplyr` `select()` function to create a subset called actuals that just includes the variable `playoffs2`. However, we first make a call to the `dplyr` `ungroup()` function to decouple the variables `playoffs2` and `season`; otherwise, actuals would unnecessarily include both variables:

```
test %>%
  ungroup(season) %>%
  select(playoffs2) -> actuals
```

Then, we pass actuals to the `dplyr` `rename()` function; `rename()` takes the variable on the right side of the assignment operator and renames it to whatever is on the left side:

```
actuals %>%
  rename(actual_values = playoffs2) -> actuals
```

Switching gears somewhat, we then create a new object called predictions, which equals predicted_fit3 that's been converted from a matrix to a data frame by making a call to the base R `as.data.frame()` function:

```
predictions <- as.data.frame(predicted_fit3)
```

We then pass predictions to the `rename()` function; as a matrix and then as a data frame, the one variable in predicted_fit3 is actually `predicted_fit3`. By calling the `rename()` function, we change that to instead equal `predicted_values`:

```
predictions %>%
  rename(predicted_values = predicted_fit3) -> predictions
```

Next, we pass predictions to the `dplyr` `mutate()` and base R `ifelse()` functions to create a derived variable based on conditional logic. When the variable `predicted_values` is equal to or greater than `0.50`, `predicted_values2` should equal 1; otherwise, it should equal 0:

```
predictions %>%
  mutate(predicted_values2 =
         ifelse(predicted_values >= 0.50, 1, 0)) -> predictions
```

Now we have a pair of single-variable objects that both tie back to test—actuals contains a binary variable called `actual_values`, which indicates whether an NBA team qualified for postseason play, and predictions contains a binary variable called `predicted_values`, which indicates whether predicted_fit3 predicted those same teams to make the playoffs.

We then pass both those variables to the base R `table()` function to create what's called a confusion matrix. The `print()` function returns the results. The passed variables must absolutely be binary in order for this to run:

```
confusion_matrix <- table(actuals$actual_values,
    predictions$predicted_values2)
print(confusion_matrix)
##    0  1
## 0 19 11
## 1 10 40
```

Our confusion matrix is both like and unlike the contingency table we created back in chapter 9, as explained here:

- A confusion matrix is a table that summarizes the performance of a classification model by displaying the counts of true positives (TP), true negatives (TN), false positives (FP), and false negatives (FN). The confusion matrix is the source from which we can then derive critical predicted_fit3 performance measures.
- A true positive refers to a case in which the model correctly predicted a positive outcome. Where a positive outcome is the equivalent of an NBA team qualifying for the postseason, we have 40 such instances.
- A true negative refers to a case in which the model correctly predicted a negative outcome. Where a negative outcome is the equivalent of an NBA team not qualifying for postseason play, we have 19 such instances.
- A false positive refers to a case where the model incorrectly predicted a positive outcome. We have 11 such instances.
- A false negative refers to a case where the model incorrectly predicted a negative outcome. We have 10 such instances.
- Sensitivity, otherwise known as the true positive rate, is a measure of the proportion of true positives correctly identified by a classification model out of all positive instances.
  - Sensitivity = TP / (TP + FN)
- Specificity, also known as the true negative rate, is a measure of the proportion of true negatives correctly identified by a classification model out of all negative instances.
  - Specificity = TN / (TN + FP)
- The relative importance of sensitivity versus specificity usually depends on the context. Consider tests for a rare but highly aggressive form of cancer. False negatives can possibly lead to severe consequences because they could delay or even prevent treatments, resulting in fatal outcomes. Maximizing true positives and minimizing false negatives are much more important than minimizing false positives. Another example to consider is law and order, particularly in democracies, where it's so important to minimize wrongful convictions, or false positives. In other cases, such as whether NBA teams are successful in qualifying for postseason play, sensitivity and specificity might be of equal importance.
- Misclassification error, sometimes called the classification error or just the error rate, is a measure of misclassified instances in a classification model. It therefore represents the percentage of incorrect predictions.
  - Misclassification error = (FP + FN) / n

- Model accuracy is the inverse of the error rate; it therefore represents the percentage of correct predictions.
  - Model accuracy = (TP + TN) / n or 1 − (FP + FN) / n

It's easy enough in R to compute the sensitivity and specificity rates; we simply pass our binary variables, `actual_values` and `predicted_values2`, to the `sensitivity()` and `specificity()` functions from the `caret` package. To get correct results, you must pass the variables in the same sequence in which they were previously passed to the `table()` function:

```
sensitivity(actuals$actual_values, predictions$predicted_values2)
## [1] 0.8
specificity(actuals$actual_values, predictions$predicted_values2)
## [1] 0.6333333
```

Because the sensitivity rate is higher than the specificity rate, we can therefore conclude that our first logistic regression, predicted_fit3, is better at identifying true positives than true negatives.

Then, we use arithmetic operations to calculate the error rate and to derive model accuracy. Once more, the misclassification error, or simply the error rate, is equal to the sum of false positives and false negatives divided by the record count:

```
print(misclassification_error <- (11 + 10) / 80)
## [1] 0.2625
```

Model accuracy is simply the inverse of the error rate:

```
print(accuracy <- 1 - misclassification_error)
[## 1] 0.7375
```

An accuracy rate this high indicates that predicted_fit3 has fairly strong predictive power.

Finally, we'll combine the `roc()` function from the pROC package and the `plot()` function from base R to compute what's called the area under the curve (AUC) and then draw the ROC curve, which was discussed earlier in this chapter. The AUC quantifies the predictive power of a classification model by equally considering the sensitivity and specificity rates. When the AUC equals a maximum of 1, a model perfectly distinguishes both positive and negative instances; when equal to 0.5, the model performs no better than random chance. Thus, the higher the AUC, the better. A ROC curve visualizes the same by plotting the specificity rate along the x-axis and the sensitivity rate along the y-axis.

Whereas the error rate measures the proportion of misclassified instances from the total record count, and therefore focuses on individual predictions, the AUC measures the overall discriminatory power of a classified model from how well it distinguishes positive versus negative instances. Though the measures are thus different, they usually align very well with one another.

In the following code, we pass `actual_values` and `predicted_values2`—in that order—to the `roc()` function and `print()` function to get the AUC:

```
roc_curve <- roc(actuals$actual_values, predictions$predicted_values2)
print(roc_curve)
## Call:
## roc.default(response = actuals$actual_values,
##     predictor = predictions$predicted_values2)
##
## Data: predictions$predicted_values2 in 30 controls
##    (actuals$actual_values 0) < 50 cases (actuals$actual_values 1).
## Area under the curve: 0.73
```

An AUC equal to 0.73 is an indication of a fairly strong model.

We then get an ROC curve by making a call to the `plot()` function (see figure 14.8). Base R plots are more functional than they are elegant, yet we can color-code the curve and customize the title and axis labels:

```
plot(roc_curve,
     col = "red",
     main = "ROC Curve: AUC = 0.73",
     xlab = "Specificity: TN / (TN + FP)",
     ylab = "Sensitivity: TP / (TP + FN)")
```

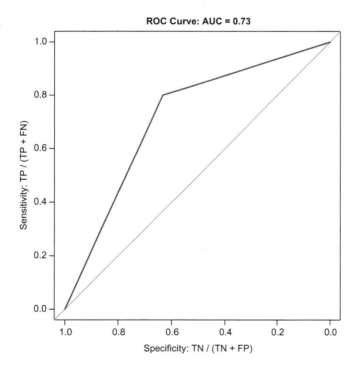

Figure 14.8 ROC curve for our first of two logistic regressions that plot true negatives along the x-axis and true positives along the y-axis

Let's fit a second regression and then compare and contrast our two models.

FITTING OUR SECOND OF TWO MODELS

Our second and last model, fit4, regresses `playoffs2` against `z_pts`. We plot a second ROC curve at the end (see figure 14.9):

```
fit4 <- glm(playoffs2 ~ z_pts, family = "binomial", data = train)
summary(fit4)
##
## Call:
## glm(formula = playoffs2 ~ z_pts, family = "binomial", data = train)
##
## Deviance Residuals:
##     Min      1Q    Median      3Q      Max
## -1.8007  -1.0788  -0.0708   1.1246   1.5395
##
## Coefficients:
##               Estimate Std. Error z value  Pr(>|z|)
## (Intercept)   -0.02059    0.14104  -0.146     0.884
## z_pts          0.63463    0.15263   4.158 0.0000321 ***
## ---

## Signif. codes:  0 '***' 0.001 '**' 0.01 '*' 0.05 '.' 0.1 ' ' 1
##
## (Dispersion parameter for binomial family taken to be 1)
##
##     Null deviance: 304.98  on 219  degrees of freedom
## Residual deviance: 285.32  on 218  degrees of freedom
## AIC: 289.32
##
## Number of Fisher Scoring iterations: 4

plogis(0.63)
## [1] 0.6524895

pR2(fit4)["McFadden"]
## fitting null model for pseudo-r2
##   McFadden
## 0.06446806

varImp(fit4)
##        Overall
## z_pts 4.157984

predicted_fit4 <-predict(fit4, test, type = "response")

predictions <- as.data.frame(predicted_fit4)

predictions %>%
  rename(predicted_values = predicted_fit4) -> predictions

predictions %>%
  mutate(predicted_values2 =
           ifelse(predicted_values >= 0.50, 1, 0)) -> predictions

confusion_matrix <- table(actuals$actual_values,
```

```
                                  predictions$predicted_values2)
print(confusion_matrix)
##    0  1
## 0 27  3
## 1 22 28

sensitivity(actuals$actual_values, predictions$predicted_values2)
## [1] 0.56
specificity(actuals$actual_values, predictions$predicted_values2)
## [1] 0.9

print(misclassification_error <- (3 + 22) / 80)
## [1] 0.3125

print(accuracy <- 1 - misclassification_error)
## [1] 0.6875

roc_curve <- roc(actuals$actual_values, predictions$predicted_values2)
print(roc_curve)
## Call:
## roc.default(response = actuals$actual_values,
##       predictor = predictions$predicted_values2)
##
## Data: predictions$predicted_values2 in 30 controls
##     (actuals$actual_values 0) < 50 cases (actuals$actual_values 1).
## Area under the curve: 0.73

plot(roc_curve,
     col = "blue",
     main = " ROC Curve: AUC = 0.73",
     xlab = "Specificity: TN / (TN + FP)",
     ylab = "Sensitivity: TP / (TP + FN)")
```

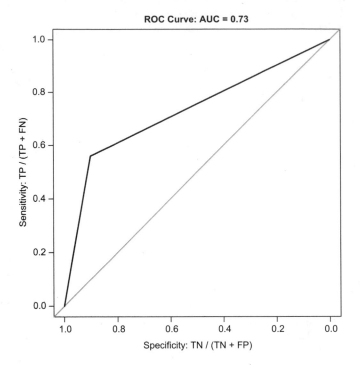

Figure 14.9   ROC curve for our second of two logistic regressions that plot true negatives along the x-axis and true positives along the y-axis. Whereas our first model returned a higher sensitivity rate than specificity rate, our second model returned just the opposite. However, the respective AUCs are essentially equal.

Let's review the results and evaluate the same against fit3 and predicted_fit3 (see table 14.1).

Table 14.1   Side-by-side results from our logistic regression models

Metric	fit3	fit4	Notes
Predictor p-value	0.00000000000011	0.0000321	Both z_o_pts and z_pts have statistically significant influences on playoffs2. z_o_pts has a lower p-value than z_pts, however.
pseudo-R^2	0.31	0.06	z_o_pts is the better of the two predictors.
AIC	214.91	289.32	AIC evaluates models on a combination of fit and complexity, where the lower the AIC, the better. Because both models are simple regressions, the AIC scores otherwise suggest that fit3 is a better fit for the data.
Variable importance	7.43	4.16	z_o_pts is the more important contributor to differences in the target variable playoffs2.

Table 14.1 Side-by-side results from our logistic regression models *(continued)*

Metric	predicted_fit3	predicted_fit4	Notes
Sensitivity	0.80	0.56	predicted_fit3 is the stronger of the two models with respect to true positive rates.
Specificity	0.63	0.90	predicted_fit4 is the stronger of the two models with respect to true negative rates.
Error rate	0.26	0.31	predicted_fit3 has the lower error rate.
Model accuracy	0.74	0.69	predicted_fit3 therefore has the higher model accuracy rate.
AUC	0.73	0.73	predicted_fit4 has a slightly higher AUC.

All things considered, based on our logistic regressions alone, we have to conclude that points allowed has a larger effect on whether NBA teams, at least between the 2007 and 2018 seasons, qualify for postseason play.

But as in our correlation tests and ANOVA models, any advantage z_o_pts might have over z_pts is negligible at best. In fact, the best overall conclusion is that points allowed and points scored have roughly equal influences on regular season wins and whether teams qualify for postseason play. In other words, defense doesn't matter *much* more than offense.

That being said, why do so many people—players, coaches, and general managers included—still cling to the idea that defense clearly and unmistakably matters more than offense? We might actually have an answer for that next.

14.7 Paired data before and after

The answer might tie back to the regular season and postseason differences in points scored and especially points allowed for most NBA championship-winning teams. Let's explore this possibility.

We begin by passing the nba_stats data set to the dplyr filter() function to subset nba_stats on the 10 records where the factor variable playoffs equals 11. The factor level equals 11 for league champions only. Then, nba_stats is passed to the dplyr select() function to subset it on the variables Team, season, PTS, and O_PTS. Finally, we make a call to the dplyr arrange() function to sort nba_stats on the variable season. The results are cast to a 10 × 3 tibble called df1:

```
nba_stats %>%
  filter(playoffs == 11) %>%
  select(Team, season, PTS, O_PTS) %>%
  arrange(season) -> df1
```

Then, we make another call to the select() function to subset df1 on every variable except Team:

```
df1 %>%
  select(-Team) -> df1
```

We now have a tidy object that contains the regular season points scored and points allowed averages for the 10 NBA champions from nba_stats. Next, we call the base R data.frame() function to create a postseason equivalent of df1.

Our new object, df2, contains three vectors: a factor variable called season, which equals 2008 through 2017; a numeric variable called PTS, which equals points scored per game; and a numeric variable called O_PTS, which equals points allowed per game (postseason results were grabbed from www.basketball-reference.com):

```
df2 <- data.frame(season = as.factor(c(2008:2017)),
                  PTS = c(94.0, 102.4, 101.1, 98.2, 97.3, 97.1,
                          106.3, 103.3, 104.8, 119.3),
                  O_PTS = c(88.8, 95.2, 97.3, 92.4, 90.2, 90.7,
                            97.0, 95.5, 96.2, 105.8))
```

We then pass df1 and df2 to the rbind() function, which concatenates data objects by rows. In the process, we create a 20 × 4 tibble called df3:

```
df3 <- rbind(df1, df2)
```

Lastly, we append a new variable to df3 called Season (once more, R is a case-sensitive programming language, so Season is different than season), where the first 10 records equal Regular Season and the last 10 records equal Playoffs. We then call the print() function to return df3 in its entirety:

```
df3$Season <- rep(c("Regular Season", "Playoffs"), each = 10)
print(df3)
## # A tibble: 20 × 4
## # Groups:   season [10]
##    season   PTS O_PTS Season
##    <fct>  <dbl> <dbl> <chr>
##  1 2008   100.   90.2 Regular Season
##  2 2009   107.   99.2 Regular Season
##  3 2010   102.   97   Regular Season
##  4 2011   100.   96   Regular Season
##  5 2012    98.5  92.5 Regular Season
##  6 2013   103.   95   Regular Season
##  7 2014   105.   97.7 Regular Season
##  8 2015   110    99.9 Regular Season
##  9 2016   104.   98.3 Regular Season
## 10 2017   116.  104.  Regular Season
## 11 2008    94    88.8 Playoffs
## 12 2009   102.   95.2 Playoffs
## 13 2010   101.   97.3 Playoffs
## 14 2011    98.2  92.4 Playoffs
## 15 2012    97.3  90.2 Playoffs
## 16 2013    97.1  90.7 Playoffs
## 17 2014   106.   97   Playoffs
## 18 2015   103.   95.5 Playoffs
## 19 2016   105.   96.2 Playoffs
## 20 2017   119.  106.  Playoffs
```

We then pass df3, and specifically the variables `Season` and `O_PTS`, to the `ggpaired()` function from the `ggpubr` package to plot regular season and postseason points allowed. The `ggpaired()` function creates a pair of before and after boxplots that displays the regular season and postseason points allowed distributions *and* draws connecting lines between the same teams so that we can compare each team's performance (see figure 14.10).

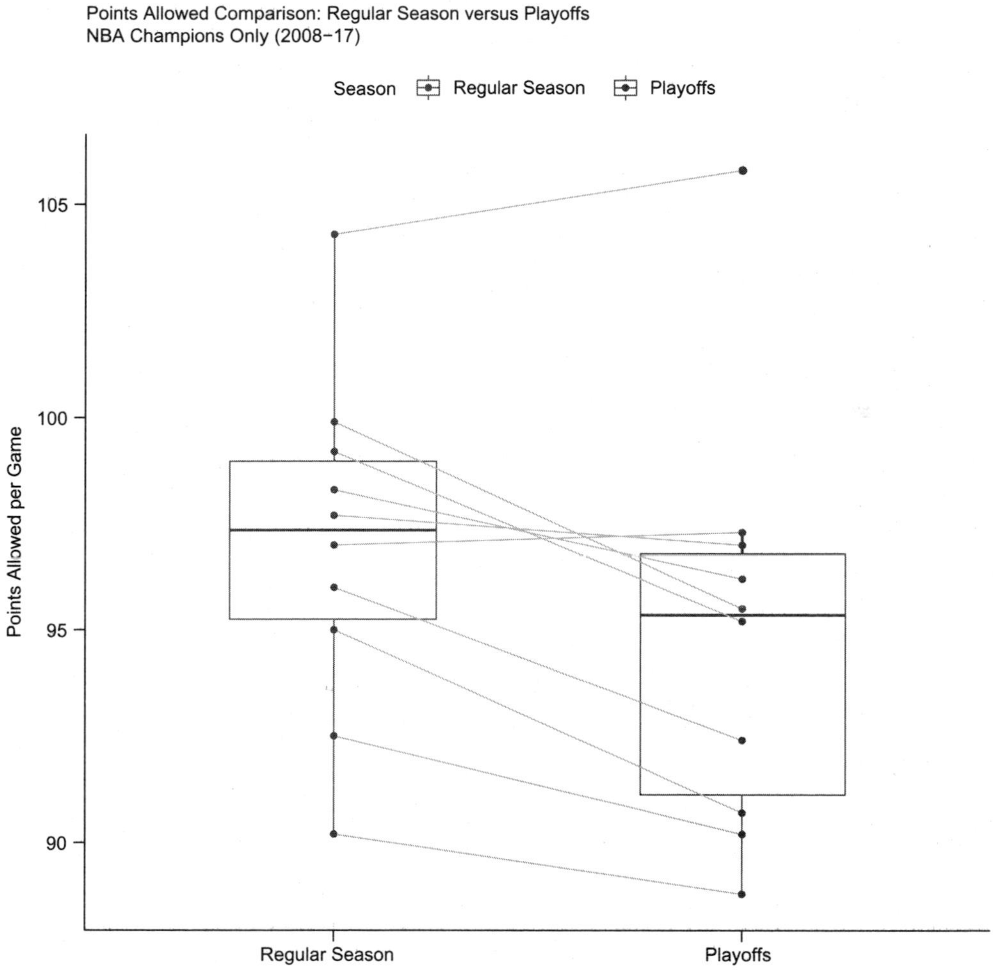

Figure 14.10   Paired boxplots displaying the per-game points allowed between the regular season and postseason for all NBA championship-winning teams between the 2008 and 2017 seasons. Most teams allowed fewer points per game in the postseason than they did during the regular season.

We can also customize the color and width of the connecting lines and choose a color scheme for the boxes and whiskers from several `ggplot2` palettes (`aaas`, short for the American Association for the Advancement of Science, is one of many scientific journal color palettes):

```
ggpaired(df3, x = "Season", y = "O_PTS",
        color = "Season", line.color = "gray", line.size = 0.4,
        palette = "aaas",
        main = "Points Allowed Comparison: Regular Season versus Playoffs
            NBA Champions Only (2008-17)",
        xlab = "",
        ylab = "Points Allowed per Game")
```

Here's the key takeaway: 8 of the 10 NBA champions between the 2008 and 2017 seasons allowed fewer points in the postseason than they did during the regular season.

But most of these same teams also *scored* fewer points per game in the playoffs then they did in the regular season (see figure 14.11); this therefore suggests their opponents also played better defense in the postseason:

```
ggpaired(df3, x = "Season", y = "PTS",
        color = "Season", line.color = "gray", line.size = 0.4,
        palette = "aaas",
        main = "Points Scored Comparison: Regular Season versus Playoffs
            NBA Champions Only (2008-17)",
        xlab = "",
        ylab = "Points Scored per Game")
```

The fact that fewer points are scored in most postseason games than in most regular season games may very well be responsible for creating the *impression* that defense, much more so than offense, wins championships. But at the end of the day, defense doesn't win championships; based on our series of test results, defense at best is marginally more of a differentiator than offense, and that's hardly the equivalent of today's conventional wisdom. We're drawing this conclusion based on the consistency of our analysis between computing correlation coefficients, running correlation tests, fitting ANOVA models, and then fitting a pair of logistic regressions.

In the next chapter, we'll explore the 80-20 rule and demonstrate how to create charts, really Pareto charts, that contain two y-axes.

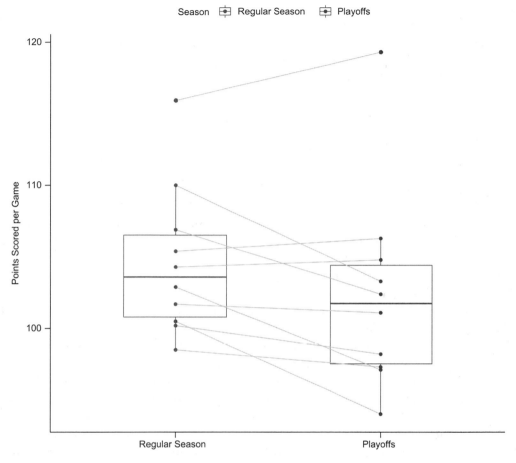

Points Scored Comparison: Regular Season versus Playoffs
NBA Champions Only (2008–17)

Figure 14.11 Paired boxplots displaying the per-game points scored between the regular season and postseason for all NBA championship-winning teams between the 2008 and 2017 seasons. Most teams also scored fewer points per game during the postseason than they did during the regular season.

Summary

- We applied three statistical techniques—correlation tests, ANOVAs, and logistic regressions—alternately testing the effects of points allowed and points scored on regular season wins and postseason qualification against a 10-season NBA data set. All of our tests returned statistically significant results, and all strongly suggest that defense might be *slightly* more important than offense, which is hardly equivalent to the conventional wisdom that defense matters much more than offense.

- Points allowed and points scored per game are almost equally *correlated* with regular season wins. Furthermore, correlation tests between the two paired with wins returned like results where the p-values were well below the predefined 5% threshold for significance.

- Points allowed and points scored have similar effects on regular season wins, based on our one-way ANOVAs where, again, our models returned equal p-values well below the threshold for significance.

- Based on our logistic regressions, points allowed and points scored per regular season game are, by and large, equally effective predictors (or at least roughly so) for who will qualify, or not qualify, for postseason play when we net out the results of our two models. One predictive model had a lower error rate and therefore a higher model accuracy rate, but the other had a higher AUC.

- Once more, all of our tests produced statistically significant results, but there's no evidence that defense clearly and unmistakably matters more than offense.

- Otherwise, it's absolutely necessary to standardize variables when they're on different scales; at other times, it's a best practice to standardize the same variables when the data spans several years. Converting raw data to z-scores is probably the most common standardization method, but we'll introduce other standardization techniques in chapter 19.

- It's critical to understand which statistical test to run under which conditions. In prior chapters, we've run t-tests and chi-square tests; however, ANOVAs should be your method of choice when comparing three or more data series when there is a quantitative target variable and categorical predictor variables. Linear regressions should be fit when working with a continuous target variable; logistic regressions should be fit instead when working with a binary target variable.

- Logistic regression is probably the most common of classification models. To understand and apply the results correctly, it's absolutely critical to know the differences between probabilities, odds ratios, and log odds, and to understand how to convert values from one to the other. It's equally critical to know how to create and interpret a confusion matrix and how to derive key measures from it to accurately assess model fit.

The Lindy effect

15

This chapter covers

- Examining the 80-20 rule
- Visualizing the 80-20 rule with Pareto charts
- Creating violin plots
- Creating paired histograms

The Lindy effect, or Lindy's Law, suggests that nonperishable items, such as a book in print or a business, have life expectancies equal to their current age. For instance, if *The Great Gatsby* has been in print for 100 years, we can expect it to remain in print for another 100 years. Basically, the longer something has been in existence, the longer it's likely to continue existing. The concept is named after a *former* delicatessen in New York City named Lindy's that nonetheless remained open for nearly a century. The Lindy effect doesn't apply to human beings, fruit, or other perishable items; after all, we can't expect a man aged 75 years to live another 75 years or a banana to stay ripe indefinitely.

From a statistical perspective, the Lindy effect follows a right-skewed, or positive-skewed, probability distribution; that is, the distribution of a numeric variable over a continuous interval peaks when x is close to 0 and then tapers as x increases. Our first visualization (see figure 15.1) demonstrates this effect; it's a ggplot2 density plot that displays the distribution of NBA franchises by years present, from 1946, when the NBA was founded, through 2020 (where the number of franchises equals unique team names between cities, states, and nicknames). Put simply, it shows that most NBA franchises existed, or have existed, for just a few years, whereas fewer franchises have been, or were, in existence for many years.

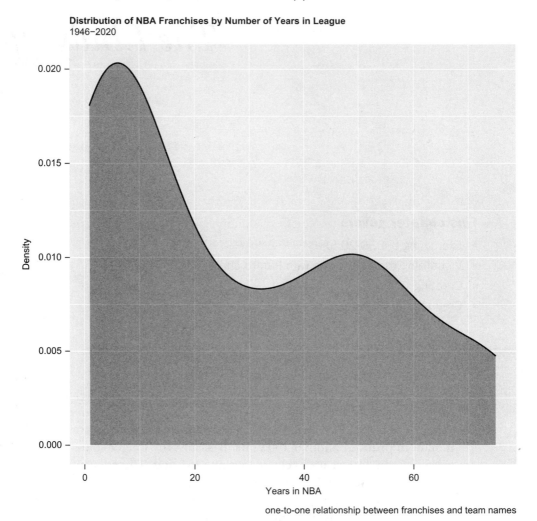

Figure 15.1   **The distribution of NBA franchises visualized by number of years in the league; when the Lindy effect applies, we'll see a right-skewed, or positive-skewed, distribution. Thus, the Lindy effect corresponds to a Pareto probability distribution that is closely aligned with the 80-20 rule.**

The distribution is clearly right-skewed; there are more values clustered around the left tail of the distribution than anywhere else, while the right tail of the distribution is significantly longer. This sort of distribution corresponds well with a Pareto probability distribution. Named after the Italian civil engineer, economist, and sociologist Vilfredo Pareto, the Pareto distribution is a power law and, therefore, nonlinear probability distribution that, at least in spirit if not the letter, suggests that 80% of all outcomes are due to just 20% of causes. For instance, 80% of a company's sales are generated from 20% of its clients, or 80% of all R code is powered by just 20% of the libraries. The inverse is also true: you might wear only 20% of your wardrobe 80% of the time, or maybe you watch just 20% of your television channels 80% of the time. We all know this as the 80-20 rule.

Our purpose here is to test the 80-20 rule with respect to games played and games won across all NBA franchises between 1946 and 2020. Might it be true that 20% of all NBA franchises—which continuously come and go—account for 80% of the games played and won? In the process, we'll demonstrate two ways in which to create a Pareto chart, which is a combination bar and line chart that displays unit and incremental frequencies across primary and secondary y axes, respectively. We'll start, as usual, by loading our required packages.

15.1 Loading packages

Once again, we'll use a combination of familiar and not-so-familiar packages:

- Our data will be wrangled with a mix of `dplyr` and `tidyr` functions, and some of our visualizations will be created in `ggplot2`, so we start by loading the `tidyverse` package.
- Some of our visualizations will be bundled into a single graphical object for printing and presentation purposes, so we then load the `patchwork` package.
- We'll again make a call to the `recode()` function from the `car` package to rename elements in a vector.
- Through the `ggpubr` package, we'll introduce two new visualization types: a violin plot and a paired histogram.
- The `ggQC` and `gcc` packages are new. Our first of two Pareto charts will be created with a combination of `ggplot2` and `ggQC` functions; our second Pareto chart will be created with the `gcc` package.

We therefore call the `library()` function six times to sequentially load these six packages:

```
library(tidyverse)
library(patchwork)
library(car)
library(ggpubr)
library(ggQC)
library(qcc)
```

We'll import our data set next.

15.2 Importing and viewing data

Our data set is a Microsoft Excel spreadsheet saved in our default working directory with a .csv extension; it contains the number of games played and won for every NBA franchise between the 1946 and 2020 seasons, scraped from www.nba.com and www.basketball-reference.com. We make a call to the `readr` `read_csv()` function to import our data:

```
df1 <- read_csv("nba_lindy.csv")
```

Then, we call the `glimpse()` function from the `dplyr` package to return a transposed view of our data set:

```
glimpse(df1)
## Rows: 89
## Columns: 8
## $ franchise       <chr> "Atlanta Hawks", "Atlanta Hawks", "St. Louis …
## $ parent_child    <chr> "parent", "child", "child", "child", "child",…
## $ active_inactive <chr> "active", "active", "inactive", "inactive", "…
## $ start           <dbl> 1949, 1968, 1955, 1951, 1949, 1946, 1976, 201…
## $ end             <dbl> 2020, 2020, 1967, 1954, 1950, 2020, 2020, 202…
## $ years           <dbl> 72, 53, 13, 4, 2, 75, 45, 9, 35, 1, 31, 21, 1…
## $ games           <dbl> 5693, 4273, 1008, 280, 132, 5869, 3622, 718, …
## $ wins            <dbl> 2808, 2109, 555, 90, 54, 3462, 1533, 325, 118…
```

Our data set, df1, contains 89 rows, or 1 row per NBA franchise, and just eight columns. Bear in mind that while the NBA now comprises 30 teams or franchises, the NBA usually had only eight teams between 1946 and 1965, had no more than 20 teams until 1977, and didn't have 30 teams until the 2004 season. Here's a variable-by-variable breakdown:

- `franchise`—The full name of every franchise in NBA history dating back to 1946. Let's walk through a pair of examples. The Atlanta Hawks are one of 30 active NBA teams (franchises). Their roots go back to 1949, when they alternated their home games between three small towns in Illinois and Iowa and were then known as the Tri-Cities Blackhawks. In 1951, they relocated to Milwaukee and became the Milwaukee Hawks; in 1955, they relocated again, this time to St. Louis, and thus became the St. Louis Hawks. Finally, in 1968, they relocated to Atlanta. Consequently, there are five "Hawks" records in df1—one for each unique team, or child, plus one roll-up, or parent, record that aggregates the sums of all the child records. Or take a team (franchise) such as the Boston Celtics. They've always played in Boston and have always been known as the Celtics, so df1 contains just one record for the Boston Celtics franchise. This is now a character string, but in a moment, we'll be converting it to a factor variable.
- `parent_child`—Now a character string that will soon be converted to a factor variable. This variable equals `parent`, `parent_only`, or `child`. With respect to the lone Boston Celtics record in df1, `parent_child` equals `parent_only` because there are no child records. With respect to the five "Hawks" records, `parent_child` equals parent for the one roll-up record and child for the remaining four records.
- `active_inactive`—Also a character variable that will be converted to a factor; this variable equals `active` for all parent and child records if the team (franchise) is currently in the NBA; if not, it equals `inactive`.

- start—Equals the first season for any franchise or franchise name where, for instance, 1949 equals the 1948–49 season. This is now an integer and will remain an integer.

- end—Equals the final season for any franchise or franchise name; this is also an integer.

- years—Equals the number of years, or seasons, in existence; this is another integer.

- games—An integer that equals the total number of games played.

- wins—An integer that equals the total number of games won.

Let's now convert the variables franchise, parent_child, and active_inactive to factors by calling the base R as.factor() function three times. Once more, variables are best being factors if and when they can only take on a finite set of values:

```
df1$franchise <- as.factor(df1$franchise)
df1$parent_child <- as.factor(df1$parent_child)
df1$active_inactive <- as.factor(df1$active_inactive)
```

We then call the base R summary() function, which returns descriptive statistics on our df1 numeric variables and record counts by level on our factor variables:

```
summary(df1)
##                   franchise      parent_child active_inactive
##   Atlanta Hawks         : 2   child      :42   active  :46
##   Baltimore Bullets     : 2   parent     :16   inactive:43
##   Brooklyn Nets         : 2   parent_only:31
##   Charlotte Hornets     : 2
##   Detroit Pistons       : 2
##   Golden State Warriors : 2
##   (Other)               :77
##       start          end           years          games
##   Min.   :1946   Min.   :1946   Min.   : 1.00   Min.   :  60
##   1st Qu.:1949   1st Qu.:1962   1st Qu.: 5.00   1st Qu.: 328
##   Median :1967   Median :2020   Median :19.00   Median :1522
##   Mean   :1968   Mean   :1995   Mean   :26.94   Mean   :2140
##   3rd Qu.:1978   3rd Qu.:2020   3rd Qu.:50.00   3rd Qu.:4025
##   Max.   :2015   Max.   :2020   Max.   :75.00   Max.   :5869
##
##       wins
##   Min.   :  11
##   1st Qu.: 147
##   Median : 704
##   Mean   :1062
##   3rd Qu.:1938
##   Max.   :3462
```

Here's a synopsis of what the summary() function just told us about our data set:

- There are 31 franchises, including the Boston Celtics, with no child records. These are teams that never relocated or changed names, but they aren't necessarily active.

- There are 16 additional franchises (so 47 in all) that either started play in some other city from where they are now located or at least changed their name one or more times since their first year in the league.
- There are 30 active franchises, which is derived by subtracting the 46 active franchise count by the 16 records where the `parent_child` variable equals `parent`.
- At least one team played only one year, and at least one team has been around for 75 years.
- At least one team played only 60 games before they folded, and one team has played in 5,869 games.
- At least one team won just 11 games, while at least one other team has won 3,462 games.
- With respect to the variables `years`, `games`, and `wins`, the mean is consistently greater than the median; this, of course, corresponds well with right-skewed, or positive-skewed, distributions.

Now that we have some good, but mostly tabular, insights into our data, we'll next visualize much of the same by creating two violin plots and paired histograms. You'll see that violin plots share many of the same properties as boxplots; however, violin plots also display the density of a numeric variable at different values along the y-axis. Paired histograms, sometimes referred to as overlaid histograms (you'll see why in just a moment), provide a type of visualization by which two distributions are compared side by side rather than in separate plots, which, of course, makes it that much easier to compare and contrast the distributions of two numeric variables at once. One of the aims of this book is to introduce visualizations outside the mainstream, discuss best cases for their use, and demonstrate how to create them. This chapter in particular includes a few such plots.

15.3 *Visualizing data*

Our next order of business is to call the `filter()` function from the `dplyr` package to subset df1 where the variable `parent_child` doesn't equal parent; once more, the `!=` operator in R means not equal to. In other words, we're subsetting df1—and creating a new object called f2—where the variable `parent_child` equals `parent_only` or `child`. So we've effectively eliminated the df1 roll-up records while creating df2:

```
df1 %>%
  filter(parent_child != "parent") -> df2
```

Then, we call the `dim()` function from base R, which returns the dimension of df2, or the row and column counts:

```
dim(df2)
## [1]  73   8
```

We still have the original eight variables, of course, but df2 contains just 73 records whereas df1 contains 89.

15.3.1 *Creating and evaluating violin plots*

Now let's create our pair of violin plots. A violin plot is a hybrid between a boxplot and a density plot that visualizes the distribution of a numeric data series. Our first plot visualizes the distribution of the variable games, and the second visualizes the distribution of the variable wins:

- Both plots are created by calling the ggviolin() function from the ggpubr package, which is just one of many ggplot2 extensions. If there's a challenge with ggpubr and other ggplot2 extensions, it's with the syntax; they tend to use a random mix of ggplot2, base R, and other miscellaneous commands. But if you can work through the idiosyncrasies of the code, the reward will be worth the effort.
- The object we just created, df2, is the data source for both plots. This means we're visualizing the distributions of games and wins for every unique franchise or team name and disregarding those records where in df1 the variable parent_child equals parent.
- Violin plots require just a y-axis variable; y equals games in our first plot and wins in our second plot.
- Our violin plots each contain an embedded boxplot; that way, we can still make out the Interquartile Range (IQR), mean and median, lower and upper quartiles, and any outliers. As with our previous boxplots in prior chapters, R automatically denotes the median with a horizontal line somewhere within the IQR; after the ggviolin() function, we add the stat_summary() function, as we've done so many times before, to add a solid dot that represents the mean.
- The ggplot2 theme() function applies a bold font to both titles.

The chunks of code for both plots, p2 and p3, are shown here:

```
p2 <- ggviolin(df2, y = "games",
               color = "darkslategray1", fill = "salmon1",
               add = "boxplot", add.params = list(fill = "white"),
               main = "Distribution of Games Played:\nAll NBA Franchises",
               font.main = "bold",
               subtitle = "1946-2020",
               xlab = "",
               ylab = "Games Played") +
  stat_summary(fun = mean, geom = "point", shape = 20, size = 8,
               color = "darkslategray1", fill = "darkslategray1") +
  theme(axis.text.x = element_blank())

p3 <- ggviolin(df2, y = "wins",
               color = "darkslategray1", fill = "salmon1",
               add = "boxplot", add.params = list(fill = "white"),
               main = "Distribution of Games Won:\nAll NBA Franchises",
               font.main = "bold",
               subtitle = "1946-2020",
               xlab = "",
               ylab = "Games Won") +
```

```
stat_summary(fun = mean, geom = "point", shape = 20, size = 8,
            color = "darkslategray1", fill = "darkslategray1") +
theme(axis.text.x = element_blank())
```

Rather than instantly printing our violin plots, we'll instead hold them in memory while we proceed with creating our `ggpubr` paired histograms. But first, we need to do a bit of data wrangling.

15.3.2 *Creating paired histograms*

We pass the df2 data set via the pipe operator to the `pivot_longer()` function from the `tidyr` package. The `pivot_longer()` function takes the df2 variables `games` and `wins`, converts them to levels within a new variable called `games`, and throws their values to another new variable called `counts`. The end result is a tibble called df3. Then we call the `as.factor()` function to convert the variable `games` from a character string to a factor; the `counts` variable is an integer.

Next, we call the `recode()` function from the `car` package to rename the `games` and `wins` elements within the `games` variable to `Played` and `Won`, respectively. The `recode()` function is typically called to modify values in a variable, but as we're demonstrating here, it can also be called when there's a need to rename variables. Thus, it's a suitable substitute for the `rename()` function.

The base R `head()` function returns the first 10 records in df3, but subset on the variables `franchise`, `games`, and `counts`. You must include the variable positions rather than the variable names for this last line of code to run:

```
df2 %>%
  pivot_longer(cols = c("games", "wins"),
               names_to = "games",
               values_to = "counts") -> df3

df3$games <- as.factor(df3$games)

df3$games <- recode(df3$games, "games" = "Played",
                     "wins" = "Won")
head(df3[,c(1, 7, 8)], 10)
## # A tibble: 10 × 3
##    franchise              games  counts
##    <fct>                  <fct>  <int>
##  1 Atlanta Hawks          Played  4273
##  2 Atlanta Hawks          Won     2109
##  3 St. Louis Hawks        Played  1008
##  4 St. Louis Hawks        Won      555
##  5 Milwaukee Hawks        Played   280
##  6 Milwaukee Hawks        Won       90
##  7 Tri-Cities Blackhawks  Played   132
##  8 Tri-Cities Blackhawks  Won       54
##  9 Boston Celtics         Played  5869
## 10 Boston Celtics         Won     3462
```

Now we can create our paired histograms by calling the gghistogram() function from the ggpubr package. By calling the gghistogram() function, we're creating two histograms within the same graphical object. We're able to overlay two plots in the same visualization because gghistogram() automatically prints both histograms in opaque hues, thereby making it possible to view both distributions even when and where they overlap one another:

- The tibble we just created, df3, is our data source.
- Whereas boxplots only require a y-axis variable, histograms just require an x-axis variable; here, our x-axis variable is counts. Because counts ties back to the factor variable games, with levels equal to games and wins, one of our histograms therefore visualizes the distribution of games, or games played, and our other histogram visualizes the distribution of wins.
- As with ggplot2 boxplots, we control the number of bins. Both of our boxplots contain 15 bins, which is close enough to the square root of the df3 record count.
- The add argument inserts vertical dashed lines that represent the mean for each distribution.
- By setting the rug argument equal to TRUE, R adds a rug plot in the margin along the x-axis. A rug plot is a one-dimensional display of a data distribution in the form of marks, which often complements a two-dimensional display of the same data series. Rug plots are only practical when your data set contains a relatively modest number of records.

The code chunk for our paired histograms, p4, follows:

```
p4 <- gghistogram(df3, x = "counts", bins = 15,
    add = "mean", rug = TRUE,
    main = "Distributions of Games Played and Won",
    font.main = "bold",
    subtitle = "1946-2020",
    xlab = "Games Played / Games Won",
    ylab = "Frequency",
    legend.title = "", font.legend = "bold",
    legend = "top",
    color = "games", fill = "games")
```

15.3.3 *Printing our plots*

We temporarily hold p4 in memory and then bundle it with p2 and p3 into a single object by calling the plot_layout() function from the patchwork package (see figure 15.2). Plots p2 and p3 are printed side by side on the top row, and plot p4, which assumes a width equal to p2 plus p3, is displayed on the bottom row (take note of the minus operator in our code):

```
p2 + p3 - p4 + plot_layout(ncol = 1)
```

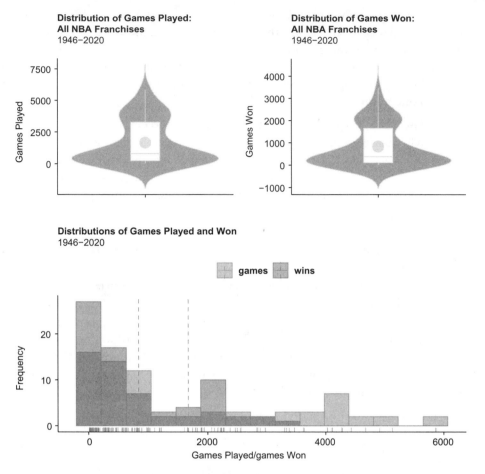

Figure 15.2   Violin plots on the top display the distributions of games played and games won, respectively, by all current and past NBA franchises between 1946 and 2020. On the bottom, paired histograms visualize the same data series.

While violin plots are less common, or less popular, than boxplots, and therefore might not resonate as well across a random sample of end users, there is at least one reason why you should favor violin plots: they display the full distribution of a data series, whereas boxplots merely show the summary statistics. (Of course, we've chosen to provide the best of both worlds by adding embedded boxplots to our violin plots.) You might want to select one or the other depending upon the sophistication level of your audience.

Violin plots also display the shape of a data series by using a probability density function (PDF) just like a density plot. In fact, if it were possible to slice our violin plots vertically down the middle and then rotate the left halves 90 degrees, they would look very much like the density plot we created earlier (refer to figure 15.1). The width of the PDF represents how frequently corresponding values can be observed in the data, where wider regions indicate higher frequencies and tapered regions indicate lower frequencies.

The data is right-skewed. We know this because the widest regions in both of our violin plots are where y equals some number not far from 0. We also know this because both means, represented by the solid dots inside our embedded boxplots, are greater than the medians, represented by the horizontal lines inside the same. That the data is right-skewed is perhaps made more obvious by our paired histograms. Plotting two histograms within the same visualization is a good technique to know when you want or need to compare and contrast two distributions down to the factor level.

However, our violin plots and paired histograms don't tell us if the 80-20 rule is in effect; in other words, we don't yet know if 20% of current and past NBA franchises account for 80% of games played or won. The data is definitely nonlinear, but *how* nonlinear we haven't yet figured out. That's why we need Pareto charts.

15.4 Pareto charts

Let's talk about Pareto charts for a moment before we demonstrate how to create and interpret them. A Pareto chart is both a bar chart and a line chart with primary and secondary y-axes. The bar length usually represents frequency, but it can also represent time, money, or some other cost function. The bars are usually arranged vertically and must be in descending order. Whereas the bars represent unit frequencies, the line represents cumulative frequency measured in percentages; the points along the line therefore correspond to the bars.

A Pareto chart is essentially a quality control tool that provides a visual cue into causes and effects that are, more often than not, on the order of 80-20 or at least nonlinear. For instance, a Pareto chart might show that 80% of application failures are caused by just 20% of the known bugs. To an application development manager prioritizing their team's workload, that's more than just an interesting tidbit of information—it's an actionable insight. Here are some more examples to consider:

- A customer service manager is analyzing complaints. A Pareto chart might show that 80% of in-store complaints tie back to associate behavior and poor lighting, which when combined account for just 20% of all complaint types. This suggests that complaint volume can be reduced by as much as 80% merely by addressing these two areas.
- A call center supervisor is reviewing average speed to answer data that reveals daily breaches to self-imposed service levels. A Pareto analysis subsequently shows that 80% of the inbound calls with unacceptable average speeds to answer occur within just 20% of the 30-minute time intervals. The supervisor then knows when or where to staff up.
- The principal of a car dealership is presented with a Pareto chart which shows that 80% of the vehicles are sold by just 20% of the salespeople. Now the manager knows which employees merit rewards and which employees may require additional sales training.

■ An e-commerce director sees that 80% of their customer's browsing time is spent on just 20% of the website pages; this tells the director where to stick most of the ads and how to charge for them.

A Pareto chart might not always display 80-20 proportions, and that's okay. It's the *spirit* of the 80-20 rule that truly matters, which simply suggests that most outcomes have a small number of causes. That means many problems can be resolved, or at least mitigated, with lower effort levels.

We'll now create a pair of Pareto charts that display relatively innocuous relationships between NBA franchises and games played and then games won. Our Pareto charts will be created from different R packages so you can choose the packages and the methods that work best for you.

15.4.1 *ggplot2 and ggQC packages*

Our first of two Pareto charts is built from a combination of `ggplot2` and a package called `ggQC`, which can be used to create a number of quality control charts. We start by creating a data source for both Pareto charts. We call the `dplyr` `filter()` function to subset df1 where the variable `parent_child` doesn't equal `child`, which also means we're subsetting df1 where the same variable equals `parent` or `parent_only`:

```
df1 %>%
  filter(parent_child != "child") -> df4
```

Then, we run the `dim()` function from base R to get the row count from the data set we just created, df4:

```
dim(df4)
## [1] 47   8
```

Our data set contains 47 rows. The following chunk of `dplyr` code tallies the record counts by the variable `active_inactive`:

```
df4 %>%
  group_by(active_inactive) %>%
  tally()
## # A tibble: 2 × 2
##   active_inactive      n
##   <fct>            <int>
## 1 active              30
## 2 inactive            17
```

These results make perfect sense—the NBA now comprises 30 teams or franchises, so the fact that df4 contains 30 active franchises and 17 inactive franchises is the result we should have expected.

Our first Pareto chart (see figure 15.3) plots the number of games played for each of the 47 past and present NBA franchises (the bars) and the cumulative percentage of total games played (the line).

Because we're creating a `ggplot2` visualization, we initialize our plot with the `ggplot()` function using df4, where the variable `games` is grouped by the variable `franchise`, as a data source. If we were to instead create our `ggplot2` Pareto chart without first piping `dplyr code` to the `ggplot()` function, our x-axis labels would not be properly sequenced.

Our x-axis variable is `franchise`, and our primary y-axis variable is `games`. The `stat_pareto()` function from the `ggQC` package automatically draws a line that maps to a secondary y-axis. The x-axis labels are angled at 90 degrees for fit:

```
df4 %>%
  group_by(franchise) %>%
  summarize(games) %>%
ggplot(aes(x = franchise, y = games)) +
        theme(axis.text.x = element_text(angle = 90,
                                         hjust = 1, vjust = 0.5)) +
        stat_pareto() +
  ggtitle("Pareto Chart: Games Played (1946-2020)") +
  xlab("") +
  ylab("Games Played") +
  theme(plot.title = element_text(face = "bold"))
```

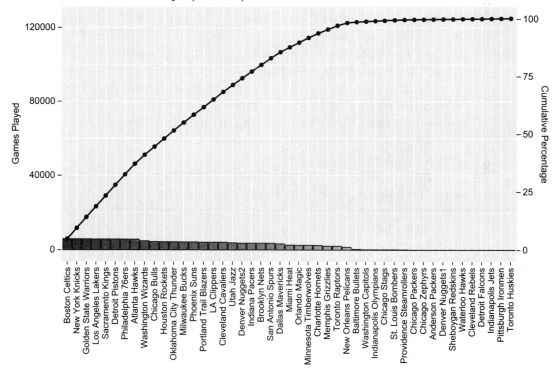

Figure 15.3 A Pareto chart built in `ggplot2` and `ggQC` that displays the nonlinear relationship between NBA franchises and games played

A few points bear mentioning:

- Our primary y-axis (on the left) represents all games played by all NBA franchises; if our 47 bars were stacked on top of each other instead of representing different ticks along the x-axis, the one bar would reach the exact same height as the line.

- Had we binned the 47 NBA franchises into, let's say, 8 or 10 groups, we would, of course, have fewer, but much taller, bars. While this operation surely would have improved the aesthetics by eliminating much of the white space, it also would have camouflaged the results. Think of the Pareto chart for our fictional call center supervisor—binning the 30-minute increments into one-hour increments might conceal the results and, more significantly, make it that much more challenging to implement a corrective action plan.

- The 80-20 rule isn't in effect—20% of the active and inactive franchises participated in less than 50% of all NBA games between the 1946 and 2020 seasons, and 80% of the games played tie back to about 45% of all NBA franchises, past or present. But while the 80-20 rule isn't in effect, the relationship between NBA franchises and games played is nevertheless nonlinear.

- Our Pareto chart—or any Pareto chart, for that matter—resembles a plot of diminishing returns. The law of diminishing returns says that, for instance, throwing additional headcount into a project that's behind schedule will yield incrementally less benefit to the point where no value is gained from supplementary new hires. For another example, consider a multiple linear regression: we can throw more and more independent variables into a model, thereby increasing R^2, but meanwhile, the adjusted R^2 incrementally drops with each subsequent variable that adds zero predictive value. The active NBA franchises account for more than 98% of all NBA games played between 1946 and 2020; thus, we didn't necessarily need the other 17 franchises to get a comprehensive-enough read on the total games count.

- Pareto charts are mirror images of Lorenz curves (see chapters 12 and 13). One shows nonlinearity, and the other displays inequality, but at the end of the day, the two are more or less synonymous. Both nonlinearity and inequality represent departures from uniformity or linearity. Nonlinearity pertains to the deviation from a straight, proportional, or linear relationship, while inequality refers to the deviation from equal distribution or treatment.

Now, let's move on to our second Pareto chart.

15.4.2 *qcc package*

Our second and final Pareto chart uses the `pareto.chart()` function from the `qcc` package, which is yet another package that enables the build of quality control charts. This time, our purpose is to visualize the relationship between past and present NBA franchises with games won. What's nice about the `pareto.chart()` function is that it not only draws a Pareto chart but also returns a tabular view of the data. Otherwise, take note of the following operations to trim our plot (see figure 15.4):

- We've added an x-axis label and defaulted both y-axis labels.
- We've modified the color scheme for the bars, at least when viewed online, so that they resemble a heat index.
- The `pareto.chart()` function takes a data set and a numeric variable as an argument; unlike `ggplot()`, it doesn't allow us to set an x-axis variable. Consequently, the `pareto.chart()` function inserts a letter and number scheme for the x-axis labels that tie back to the tabular results. We then chose to remove those with the `xaxt` argument:

```
pareto.chart(df4$wins,
  main = "Pareto Chart: Games Won (1946-2020)",
  xlab = "NBA Franchises",
  col = heat.colors(length(df4$wins)),
  xaxt = "n")
```

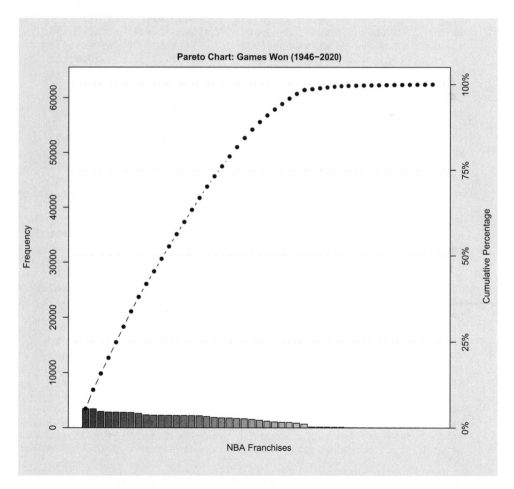

Figure 15.4 A Pareto chart built with the `gcc` package that displays a similar nonlinear relationship with respect to games won, followed by a tabular view of the data, both of which are simultaneously produced with the same code base

```
##
## Pareto chart analysis for df4$wins
    Frequency     Cum.Freq.       Percentage    Cum.Percent.
## B  3462.00000000  3462.00000000     5.54612156      5.54612156
## N  3429.00000000  6891.00000000     5.49325558     11.03937714
## W  2950.00000000  9841.00000000     4.72589792     15.76527506
## T  2840.00000000 12681.00000000     4.54967800     20.31495306
## J  2826.00000000 15507.00000000     4.52725001     24.84220307
## A  2808.00000000 18315.00000000     4.49841402     29.34061709
## I  2774.00000000 21089.00000000     4.44394604     33.78456313
## Z  2624.00000000 23713.00000000     4.20364615     37.98820929
## U  2349.00000000 26062.00000000     3.76309634     41.75130563
## K  2286.00000000 28348.00000000     3.66217039     45.41347602
## X  2271.00000000 30619.00000000     3.63814040     49.05161642
## E  2258.00000000 32877.00000000     3.61731441     52.66893083
## Q  2231.00000000 35108.00000000     3.57406043     56.24299125
## A1 2227.00000000 37335.00000000     3.56765243     59.81064368
## Y  2211.00000000 39546.00000000     3.54202044     63.35266412
## D1 2187.00000000 41733.00000000     3.50357246     66.85623658
## C1 2060.00000000 43793.00000000     3.30011855     70.15635513
## F  1889.00000000 45682.00000000     3.02617667     73.18253180
## L  1823.00000000 47505.00000000     2.92044472     76.10297651
## H  1796.00000000 49301.00000000     2.87719073     78.98016725
## M  1706.00000000 51007.00000000     2.73301080     81.71317805
## G  1657.00000000 52664.00000000     2.65451283     84.36769088
## C  1533.00000000 54197.00000000     2.45586492     86.82355580
## P  1378.00000000 55575.00000000     2.20755503     89.03111083
## V  1212.00000000 56787.00000000     1.94162315     90.97273397
## D  1083.00000000 57870.00000000     1.73496524     92.70769921
## R  1003.00000000 58873.00000000     1.60680529     94.31450450
## B1  982.00000000 59855.00000000     1.57316331     95.88766781
## O   864.00000000 60719.00000000     1.38412739     97.27179520
## S   704.00000000 61423.00000000     1.12780750     98.39960270
## H1  158.00000000 61581.00000000     0.25311589     98.65271859
## T1  157.00000000 61738.00000000     0.25151389     98.90423248
## I1  147.00000000 61885.00000000     0.23549390     99.13972638
## N1  132.00000000 62017.00000000     0.21146391     99.35119029
## R1  122.00000000 62139.00000000     0.19544391     99.54663420
## P1   46.00000000 62185.00000000     0.07369197     99.62032617
## G1   37.00000000 62222.00000000     0.05927397     99.67960014
## J1   30.00000000 62252.00000000     0.04805998     99.72766012
## E1   25.00000000 62277.00000000     0.04004998     99.76771010
## Q1   22.00000000 62299.00000000     0.03524398     99.80295409
## S1   22.00000000 62321.00000000     0.03524398     99.83819807
## L1   20.00000000 62341.00000000     0.03203999     99.87023806
## U1   19.00000000 62360.00000000     0.03043799     99.90067604
## F1   18.00000000 62378.00000000     0.02883599     99.92951203
## M1   18.00000000 62396.00000000     0.02883599     99.95834802
## O1   15.00000000 62411.00000000     0.02402999     99.98237801
## K1   11.00000000 62422.00000000     0.01762199    100.00000000
```

While the aesthetics are obviously different from our first Pareto chart, the results aren't so different—between the 1946 and 2020 NBA seasons, 20% of the active and inactive franchises won approximately 45% of all the games played, and 80% of the games won tie back to roughly 42% of all past and present franchises. Again, no 80-20 rule is in effect, but there is more nonlinearity nonetheless.

In the next chapter, we'll consider the possibility that randomness might actually be present when others see causality.

Summary

- It's impossible to understand most cause-and-effect relationships without first understanding the 80-20 rule.
- The 80-20 rule is really a euphemism for nonlinearity; after all, 80% of outcomes don't always map to 20% of root causes. That much of the world is nevertheless nonlinear to *some* extent, and therefore untidy, must be understood and accepted to then trigger the right sort of analysis.
- Pareto charts are a best solution for visualizing causes and effects and enabling "best-bang-for-the-buck" corrective actions.
- R provides a plethora of options for Pareto chart creation, including built-in functions and `ggplot2` without extensions. We demonstrated just two of the best options.
- In the process, we also demonstrated that the relationships between NBA franchises and games played and won are both nonlinear.
- We introduced new visualization techniques: violin plots as yet another alternative for graphically displaying the distribution of continuous data, and then paired histograms within the same plot.

16

Randomness versus causality

Way back in the 18th century, a French scholar and polymath by the name of Pierre-Simon Laplace developed a formula to compute probabilities starting from low observation counts. Assume there have been n independent trials that can only result in success or failure; we might then compute the probability (p) of success (s) on the next trial (n) by applying the following formula: $p = s / n$. However, let's say there have been just five independent trials and five successes. The probability of success on the sixth trial would therefore equal 100%; alternatively, if there had instead been five failures, the probability of success would equal 0%. The traditional or customary way of computing probabilities doesn't make an allowance for a different outcome where and when the observation count is low and the opportunity for variance is relatively minimal, and therefore not terribly meaningful.

Enter Laplace. Ironically, Laplace developed what then became the rule of succession, not by observing some rare phenomena, but by estimating the probability of the sun rising. If p equals the probability of success, s equals the number of prior successes, and n equals the number of completed trials, then Laplace's rule of succession estimates that $p = (s + 1) / (n + 2)$. So if there have been five successes on five independent trials, the probability of success on the sixth trial will not equal 100%, but rather 86%. If the five previous trials all resulted in failures, Laplace's rule of succession estimates a 14% chance that the sixth trial will actually be a success.

A series of independent trials most often leads to some mix of successes and failures. But the most popular use case for Laplace's rule of succession is estimating the probability of success following a string of prior successes, regardless of the prior independent trial count.

This is why we're here. Our purpose is to learn about the Laplace probability curve and then explore whether or not free throw percentage follows such a curve, at least in spirit, given a prior string of successes. Our questions will include the following:

- Does free throw percentage increase with each subsequent success, or does free throw percentage not follow any pattern whatsoever?
- Is it possible to estimate the success of a free throw attempt from prior attempts, or do makes and misses resemble a series of coin flips?
- Is there order and causality when we analyze a series of free throw makes and misses, or is there just randomness?
- Is there such a thing as a "hot hand," or is the hot hand merely a cognitive illusion?

We'll load our packages, import our data, run a series of data wrangling operations, further discuss the rule of succession and the hot hand, and then conduct our analysis. Our analysis will be divided into two parts: we'll examine free throw shooting from three of the league leaders in attempts, and then we'll evaluate the same from every player in a single data series. Be prepared for a serious plot twist.

16.1 Loading packages

Other than `tidyverse` (we'll wrangle data with `dplyr` functions and create visualizations with `ggplot2` functions), we just need to load a relatively obscure package called `runner`, which contains functions for scoping and sizing streaks. We therefore make a pair of calls to the `library()` function to load the `tidyverse` and `runner` packages:

```
library(tidyverse)
library(runner)
```

Next, we'll import—or reimport—the same data set we used earlier in chapter 8.

16.2 *Importing and wrangling data*

We then make a call to the read_csv() function to import a .csv file downloaded from www.bigdataball.com and subsequently saved in our default working directory. Our data set—the same data we first imported in chapter 8 when we explored the optimal stopping rule—contains details on almost every play from the 2019–20 NBA regular season and postseason. In the process, we establish an object called ft.

We already know that our data is 543,149 rows long and 44 columns wide; thus, if you're working on a personal computer and not a server, loading the play-by-play data set will likely take several seconds:

```
ft <- read_csv("pbp.csv")
```

Our data is wider and longer than what we need. Therefore, we next make a call to the select() function from the dplyr package to subset our data on just a few variables:

```
ft %>%
  select(date, event_type, player, points, result, type) -> ft
```

We've reduced ft to the following variables:

- date—The date, in yyyy-mm-dd format, on which each play occurred. This is now a character string that will soon be converted to a date class.
- event_type—The type of play (e.g., jump ball, foul, turnover). Back in chapter 8, we converted event_type from a character string to a factor variable and then eventually subset the data where event_type equaled shot (which represents a made field goal) or miss (which represents a missed field goal attempt).
- player—The name of the player, in "firstname lastname" format, responsible for the event type, or play. This is now a character string that will remain a character string.
- points—The number of points scored as a direct result of any play. This equals a minimum of 0 and a maximum of 3 where and when a play can directly lead to points; when a play can't possibly result in any points—a rebound, an ejection, or a timeout, for instance—points equals NA. This is now and will remain an integer.
- result—Equals made or missed following a field goal or free throw attempt; otherwise, equals NA. This is now a character string that will be converted to a factor variable.
- type—Similar to event_type, but slightly more descriptive. For example, where the variable event_type equals rebound, the variable type might equal rebound offensive; or where event_type equals miss, the type might equal Floating Jump Shot. This is now a character string that will be converted to a factor variable.

Then, we call the filter() function, also from dplyr, to reduce the length of our data:

```
ft %>%
  filter(event_type == "free throw", type != "Free Throw Technical") -> ft
```

We've subset ft where the variable `event_type` equals `free throw` and the variable `type` doesn't equal `Free Throw Technical`. Some explanation is in order.

Back in chapter 8, we subset the play-by-play data on all field goal attempts, which required us to apply the `filter()` function where `event_type` was equal to `shot` or `miss`—because `shot` represents successful field goal attempts and `miss` represents unsuccessful field goal attempts. Conversely, every free throw attempt—make or miss—is accounted for where `event_type` equals `free throw`; we then have to couple `event_type` with the variable `result`, which equals `made` or `missed`, to know whether any attempted free throw was or wasn't successful.

If you're not familiar with basketball, you might be wondering what the heck a free throw is. Many defensive fouls result in an offensive player being allowed to shoot one or usually two free throws—sometimes, even three free throws are shot, depending on the circumstances. A free throw is an uninhibited, or undefended, shot attempted from behind a line 15 feet from the basket. The game clock is paused, and every player on the court must stand to the side or behind the shooter and remain still until the final free throw has been attempted. Successful free throws, frequently referred to as foul shots, are always worth one point. A good shooter or scorer might make 45% of his field goal attempts, but 80% or more of his free throws.

We're excluding technical free throws, which comprise just a small fraction of all attempted free throws, because doing so simplifies our efforts to scope and size streaks of successful attempts. To provide some context here, Giannis Antetokounmpo, a power forward for the Milwaukee Bucks nicknamed the Greek Freak, attempted 629 free throws during the 2019–20 regular season, second in the league, and then an additional 81 free throws during the subsequent playoffs. Only 3 of these 710 total attempts were technical free throws, that is, free throws resulting from a technical foul being called on the opposing team. You'll hear more on Antetokounmpo shortly.

Contrast free throws, then, with field goal attempts, which can vary from a contested jump shot 25 feet from the basket to an open layup. This is why we've selected free throws, and not field goals, to compare to a Laplace probability curve and to determine whether or not there is such a thing as a hot hand. Free throws are attempted in a mostly controlled environment, whereas field goals are frequently attempted in the midst of chaotic situations.

That said, we next call the base R `as.Date()` function to convert the ft variable `date` from a character string to a date class. The `as.Date()` function is especially straightforward when the format equals %Y-%m-%d, as it does here, or %Y/%m/%d. Then, we call the `class()` function, also from base R, to return and confirm the converted class:

```
ft$date <- as.Date(ft$date, "%Y-%m-%d")
class(ft$date)
## [1] "Date"
```

Next, we make three calls to the base R `as.factor()` function to convert three of the four remaining ft character strings to factors:

```
ft$event_type <- as.factor(ft$event_type)
ft$result <- as.factor(ft$result)
ft$type <- as.factor(ft$type)
```

Finally, we call the `dplyr` `glimpse()` function, which returns a transposed, yet truncated, view of our data. Additionally, `glimpse()` returns the ft row and column counts as well as the class for each of the surviving variables. So in a single snapshot, we get a fair view into the output of our data wrangling operations:

```
glimpse(ft)
## Rows: 51,722
## Columns: 6
## $ date       <date> 2019-10-22, 2019-10-22, 2019-10-22, 2019-10-22,…
## $ event_type <fct> free throw, free throw, free throw, free throw, …
## $ player     <chr> "Kyle Lowry", "Kyle Lowry", "Pascal Siakam", "Pa…
## $ points     <dbl> 1, 0, 1, 1, 1, 1, 1, 1, 1, 2, 0, 1, 1, 0, 1, 1, …
## $ result     <fct> made, missed, made, made, made, made, made, made…
## $ type       <fct> Free Throw 1 of 2, Free Throw 2 of 2, Free Throw…
```

Next, we'll elaborate on Laplace's rule of succession.

16.3   *Rule of succession and the hot hand*

If free throw percentage at least roughly follows a Laplace probability curve when successes (s) equal trials (n), then it *might* be reasonable to conclude there is such a thing as a hot hand. This broadly suggests that success inevitably leads to further success, meaning, from a statistical perspective, that a power law evolves from a string of early successes instead of an immediate regression to the mean. To be clear, a power law describes a mathematical relationship by which one variable is proportional to a power of another variable; results aren't linear but rather exponential. In contrast, regression to the mean is a phenomenon by which extreme outcomes are succeeded by more moderate outcomes or equally extreme outcomes in the opposite direction that average each other out.

On the other hand, we must accept the fact that much of the world is indiscriminate and therefore not tidy or predictable, and avoid the trap of confusing randomness for order and causality. Take a series of coin flips, which we can simulate in R by calling the built-in `sample()` function. The `sample()` function takes the following four arguments:

- `x`—A vector that contains the elements from which to choose. Because we're flipping a two-sided coin, we assign a pair of integers to represent heads (0) and tails (1). These integers are then passed as arguments to the base R `c()` function to form the vector.

- `size`—Equal to the number of desired coin flips. Because we can just as easily demonstrate the `sample()` function with 10 flips as with 10,000, we set `size` equal to `10`.

- prob—A second vector that contains the probabilities of a single coin flip coming up heads or tails. Because we're simulating flips of a fair coin and not a weighted coin, prob must therefore contain 0.5 and 0.5 as elements.
- replace—Equals TRUE when sampling with replacement or FALSE otherwise. Coin flips are meant to be independent trials where each flip has an equal probability of resulting in heads or tails regardless of previous flips. This is why we must sample with replacement. (By the way, independent trials that can result in just one of two outcomes are often referred to as Bernoulli, or binomial, trials.)

The sample() function returns a series of 10 values, each of which will equal 0 or 1. Results, of course, will differ every time you call the sample() function; what's displayed here is what was returned when sample() was called for the first time:

```
sample(x = c(0, 1), size = 10, prob = c(0.5, 0.5), replace = TRUE)
## [1] 0 1 1 1 1 1 1 0 1 0
```

Our first simulated coin flip resulted in heads, the next six flips resulted in tails, and two of the final three flips resulted in heads. There are no problems with our code nor any defects with the sample() function—we fairly simulated 10 coin flips where there was an equal probability of getting heads versus tails.

Probabilities do not equate to guaranteed outcomes, especially over small samples. If we were to simulate 10,000 coin flips, it's unlikely we would get tails on 70% of those flips; however, it's equally unlikely we would get heads exactly 5,000 times and tails 5,000 times.

If we were to run our code again, we could get the same results, and therefore our two series of coin flips would resemble a power law in effect. We could instead get seven heads and three tails, or at least five heads and five tails, and thus our two series of coin flips would reveal a regression to the mean.

That our simulated coin turned up tails on six consecutive flips doesn't, of course, mean it got hot. Each flip of the coin represents an independent trial where outcomes have no connection to past or future events. But what about an NBA player shooting free throws? Is each free throw also an independent trial, or because a string of attempted free throws are actually dependent events, do six consecutive made shots therefore constitute a hot hand?

Put differently, is the hot hand a cognitive illusion, like the infamous Monty Hall problem? Or is it a real phenomenon?

The Monty Hall problem

Monty Hall was the original host of the television game show *Let's Make a Deal*. Contestants were often presented with three prizes hidden behind three closed doors and asked to select one of the three. Behind one of the doors is a car; behind the other two doors are farm animals. You, as the contestant, select door number 1.

(continued)

Monty Hall, who knows what's behind each door, then opens door number 3, behind which is a billy goat. He then asks if you want to stick with door number 1 or switch to door number 2. You might conclude that it doesn't matter—with two remaining doors the odds must be even. However, you actually double your chances of winning the car by switching to door number 2. That's because there is a 33.3% probability that the car is behind door number 1 and a 66.7% probability that the car is behind one of the other two doors. And because Monty Hall has already opened door number 3, there is twice the probability that the car is behind door number 2 versus door number 1. Contestants who switched doors won a car about two-thirds of the time.

If the hot hand is a real phenomenon, then free throw percentage would approximately follow a Laplace probability curve where the number of trials (shots) and successes (made free throws) are the same. Let's now demonstrate exactly what a Laplace probability curve looks like with 20 successes over 20 trials.

We first create a pair of vectors, `prior_successes` and `independent_trials`, that both contain integers 1 through 20 as elements. The base R `seq()` function generates a sequence of numbers from one passed argument to the other passed argument; by default, R increments the sequence by one. Then, we create a data frame, df, by passing our two vectors to the base R `data.frame()` function:

```
prior_successes <-seq(1, 20)
independent_trials <- seq(1, 20)

df <- data.frame(prior_successes, independent_trials)
print(df)
##     prior_successes independent_trials
## 1                 1                  1
## 2                 2                  2
## 3                 3                  3
## 4                 4                  4
## 5                 5                  5
## 6                 6                  6
## 7                 7                  7
## 8                 8                  8
## 9                 9                  9
## 10               10                 10
## 11               11                 11
## 12               12                 12
## 13               13                 13
## 14               14                 14
## 15               15                 15
## 16               16                 16
## 17               17                 17
## 18               18                 18
## 19               19                 19
## 20               20                 20
```

Next, we pass df via the pipe operator to the `dplyr` `mutate()` function to create a new variable. Our new variable, `laplace`, equals Laplace's rule of succession formula, which is then multiplied by 100 to convert decimals to percentages:

```
df %>%
  mutate(laplace = (prior_successes + 1) /
           (independent_trials + 2) * 100) -> df
print(df)
##    prior_successes independent_trials  laplace
## 1                1                  1 66.66667
## 2                2                  2 75.00000
## 3                3                  3 80.00000
## 4                4                  4 83.33333
## 5                5                  5 85.71429
## 6                6                  6 87.50000
## 7                7                  7 88.88889
## 8                8                  8 90.00000
## 9                9                  9 90.90909
## 10              10                 10 91.66667
## 11              11                 11 92.30769
## 12              12                 12 92.85714
## 13              13                 13 93.33333
## 14              14                 14 93.75000
## 15              15                 15 94.11765
## 16              16                 16 94.44444
## 17              17                 17 94.73684
## 18              18                 18 95.00000
## 19              19                 19 95.23810
## 20              20                 20 95.45455
```

Of course, it's always more effective to visualize results than it is to read rows of numbers, which you can do in figure 16.1:

- We, therefore, pass our simulated data to the `ggplot()` function from the `ggplot2` package.
- Our x-axis variable is `independent_trials`, and our y-axis variable is `laplace`.
- Our visualization will be a line chart with points layered on top of the line; thus, we call a pair of geoms to draw our plot, `geom_line()` and `geom_point()`. Our line is 1.5 times the default width, and our points are three times the default size.
- The `scale_x_continuous()` function in tandem with the `seq()` function allows us to manipulate the x-axis tick marks and therefore override the `ggplot2` default. Our x-axis will contain 20 tick marks incremented by one instead of four tick marks incremented by five.

The precise y-axis values are mostly meaningless to us. We're merely interested in the arc of the probability curve as the number of trials and successes increases:

```
p1 <- ggplot(df, aes(x = independent_trials, y = laplace, group = 1)) +
      geom_line(aes(y = laplace), color = "purple", size = 1.5) +
      geom_point(size = 3, color = "purple") +
```

```
    labs(title = "Laplace's Rule of Succession",
         subtitle = "success leads to more success",
         x = "Independent Trials",
         y = "Probability of Success") +
    scale_x_continuous(breaks = seq(0, 20)) +
    theme(plot.title = element_text(face = "bold"))
print(p1)
```

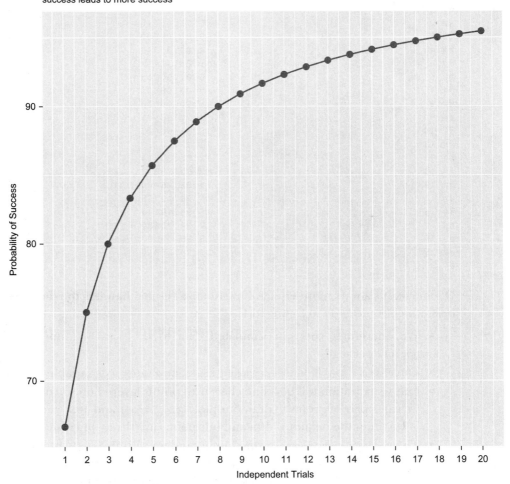

Figure 16.1   A Laplace probability curve when the number of successes equals a relatively small number of independent trials

The probability of success increases at a decreasing rate as the number of independent trials (and successes) increases, but it will never reach 100%. Laplace's rule of succession accounts for some probability of a different outcome, irrespective of how many successful trials were previously run.

Let's begin our analysis by examining player-specific free throw percentages, broken down by consecutive attempts and makes. We'll then compare the results to our Laplace probability curve.

16.4   *Player-level analysis*

We've hand-picked three players for our analysis. All three were among the 2019–20 regular season leaders in attempted free throws; however, their respective percentages of made attempts vary significantly. Therefore, lots of observations to support our analysis are spread across three players who have unequal free throw shooting skills.

16.4.1   *Player 1 of 3: Giannis Antetokounmpo*

We'll start with Giannis Antetokounmpo, who plays the power forward position for the Milwaukee Bucks. Antetokounmpo attempted 707 free throws during the 2019–20 regular season and postseason, not including technical free throws, and was successful on 442, or 62.5%, of those attempts, according to www.basketball-reference.com. Antetokounmpo is one of the NBA's best players and scorers, but free throw shooting isn't one of his strengths.

Our first operation is a call to the `filter()` function to subset the ft data set where the variable `player` equals `Giannis Antetokounmpo`. The end result is a new data set called giannis.

We can confirm the integrity of our data—or at least corroborate it with the statistics we lifted from www.basketball-reference.com—by running a pair of base R functions. The `dim()` function returns the giannis row and column counts; giannis contains 707 records, which match the number of free throws he attempted during the regular season and postseason. The `sum()` function adds the integers contained in the variable points, where `0` equals a missed free throw and `1` equals a made free throw; the sum equals 442, which, sure enough, equals the number of successful free throws:

```
ft %>%
  filter(player == "Giannis Antetokounmpo") -> giannis

dim(giannis)
## [1] 707    6
sum(giannis$points)
## [1] 442
```

Then we pipe the giannis data set to the `dplyr` `group_by()` and `mutate()` functions. From `mutate()`, we get a new variable called `streak`, and `group_by()` splits the results by the variable date.

Our new variable is derived by calling the `streak_run()` function from the `runner` package. The `lag()` function from `dplyr-streak_run()` computes a running series of consecutive elements and tells `streak_run()` to ingest the variable points from the *previous* record before crunching the data. (The `dplyr` package also contains a `lead()` function, which is the opposite of `lag()`; also, it's possible to look back or forward by two or more records.)

We're splitting these results by the variable date because if there is such a phenomenon as a hot hand, it most definitely exists within single games only and therefore
doesn't carry over from one game to the next. This approach also keeps the record
counts to a minimum and therefore qualifies as a best fit for Laplace's rule of succession.

Our results are cast to a tibble called giannis_final. The base R `head()` function
returns the first 10 observations:

```
giannis %>%
  group_by(date) %>%
  mutate(streak = streak_run(lag(points))) -> giannis_final

head(giannis_final, n = 10)
## # A tibble: 10 × 7
## # Groups:    date [1]
##     date       event_type player                     points result
##     <date>     <fct>      <chr>                       <dbl> <fct>
##  1 2019-10-24 free throw Giannis Antetokounmpo            0 missed
##  2 2019-10-24 free throw Giannis Antetokounmpo            1 made
##  3 2019-10-24 free throw Giannis Antetokounmpo            0 missed
##  4 2019-10-24 free throw Giannis Antetokounmpo            0 missed
##  5 2019-10-24 free throw Giannis Antetokounmpo            0 missed
##  6 2019-10-24 free throw Giannis Antetokounmpo            1 made
##  7 2019-10-24 free throw Giannis Antetokounmpo            1 made
##  8 2019-10-24 free throw Giannis Antetokounmpo            1 made
##  9 2019-10-24 free throw Giannis Antetokounmpo            1 made
## 10 2019-10-24 free throw Giannis Antetokounmpo            1 made
##     type              streak
##     <fct>             <int>
##  1 Free Throw 1 of 2      0
##  2 Free Throw 2 of 2      1
##  3 Free Throw 1 of 2      1
##  4 Free Throw 2 of 2      1
##  5 Free Throw 1 of 2      2
##  6 Free Throw 2 of 2      3
##  7 Free Throw 1 of 1      1
##  8 Free Throw 1 of 2      2
##  9 Free Throw 2 of 2      3
## 10 Free Throw 1 of 2      4
```

Let's walk through the data—at least the first few records—to further explain how the
`streak_run()` function does its thing:

- The variable `streak` will always equal `0` when the date flips; and it will always
  equal `1` following the first free throw attempt of a game, regardless of whether
  that attempt was a make or a miss.
- Antetokounmpo missed his first free throw attempt on 10/24/19 and then
  made his second attempt. Therefore, `streak` equals `1` for his third attempted
  free throw. Because Antetokounmpo missed that attempt, `streak` also equals `1`
  for his fourth free throw attempt.
- Eventually, Antetokounmpo makes five consecutive free throws; thus, the variable `streak` increments by one for each successive attempt.

We then pass giannis_final to the `dplyr` `group_by()` and `slice()` functions to effectively delete the first record for every unique date. Streaks are automatically stopped when each game ends; therefore, we're only interested in the second free throw attempt onward for every unique date or game:

```
giannis_final %>%
  group_by(date) %>%
  slice(-1) -> giannis_final
```

A call to the `dim()` function returns the new giannis_final dimension:

```
dim(giannis_final)
## [1] 635    7
```

As a result of removing the first record for each unique date or game (once more, we're segmenting the records by date because streaks don't carry over from one game to the next, so the first free throw attempt in every game is superfluous), giannis_final now contains 635 records, or 72 fewer records than it did before. This makes sense because Antetokounmpo played in 72 regular season and postseason games in 2019–20. (Note that the 2019–20 NBA season was cut short due to COVID-19.)

We're not quite finished with reducing the giannis_final record count because at this point, we're tracking streaks for makes *and* misses, yet we only care about successful and unsuccessful free throw attempts immediately following a made free throw. So in our next chunk of code, we pass giannis_final to the `filter()` function to subset our data where the one-record lag in the variable `points` equals 1.

Then, we call the `dplyr` `group_by()` and `summarize()` functions to tally makes and misses by the variable `streak`. Our results are cast to a tibble called giannis_tbl1:

```
giannis_final %>%
  filter(lag(points) == 1) %>%
  group_by(streak) %>%
  summarize(makes = sum(points == 1),
            misses = sum(points == 0)) -> giannis_tbl1
print(giannis_tbl1)
## # A tibble: 12 x 3
##    streak makes misses
##     <int> <int>  <int>
##  1      1    74     46
##  2      2    63     30
##  3      3    41     16
##  4      4    27      8
##  5      5    14      7
##  6      6     6      4
##  7      7     3      1
##  8      8     3      0
##  9      9     2      0
## 10     10     1      1
## 11     11     1      0
## 12     12     1      0
```

Finally, we make another call to `mutate()` to create a new variable, `pct`, which is equal to the number of makes divided by the total number of free throw attempts. The variable `pct` therefore represents Giannis Antetokounmpo's free throw percentage for each integer contained in the variable `streak`:

```
giannis_tbl1 %>%
  mutate(pct = makes / (makes + misses) * 100) -> giannis_tbl2
print(giannis_tbl2)
## # A tibble: 12 x 4
##    streak makes misses   pct
##     <int> <int>  <int> <dbl>
## 1       1    74     46  61.7
## 2       2    63     30  67.7
## 3       3    41     16  71.9
## 4       4    27      8  77.1
## 5       5    14      7  66.7
## 6       6     6      4  60
## 7       7     3      1  75
## 8       8     3      0 100
## 9       9     2      0 100
## 10     10     1      1  50
## 11     11     1      0 100
## 12     12     1      0 100
```

These results are then visualized with a `ggplot2` line chart with points layered on top of the line for every x-axis tick mark (see figure 16.2):

```
p2 <- ggplot(giannis_tbl2, aes(x = streak, y = pct, group = 1)) +
  geom_line(aes(y = pct), color = "steelblue", size = 1.5) +
  geom_point(size = 3, color = "steelblue") +
  labs(title = "Giannis Antetokounmpo",
       subtitle = "Free Throw Percentage Following Consecutive Makes",
       x = "Consecutive Makes (Streak)",
       y = "Free Throw Shooting Percentage",
       caption = "2019-20 regular season and postseason\n
                Antetokounmpo shot 62.5% from the line during
       the regular season and postseason combined") +
  scale_x_continuous(breaks = seq(0, 12, 1)) +
  theme(plot.title = element_text(face = "bold"))
print(p2)
```

Our plot doesn't at all resemble a Laplace probability curve, and therefore we can't conclude a hot hand was in effect. Yes, Antetokounmpo shot successfully higher percentages from the foul line when he had streaks of one to four made free throws, but his free throw percentage then regressed to approximately 67% when he had a streak of five successful attempts and again to 60% when he had six consecutive makes. And, yes, Antetokounmpo usually shot 100% from the foul line when his streak of successful free throw attempts reached and then exceeded eight makes, but the record count is so low at those numbers as to render the results statistically meaningless.

Giannis Antetokounmpo
Free Throw Percentage Following Consecutive Makes

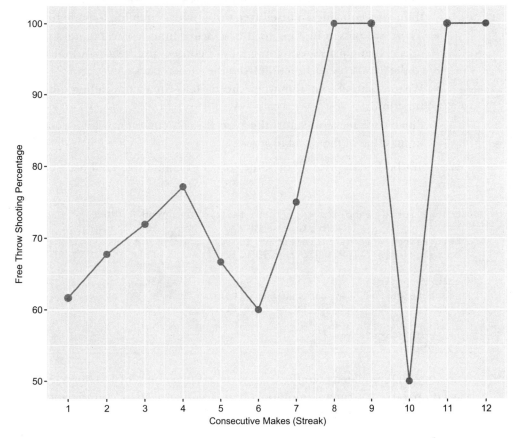

2019–20 regular season and postseason

Antetokounmpo shot 62.5% from the line during
the regular season and postseason combined

Figure 16.2   Giannis Antetokounmpo's free throw percentages following consecutive makes during the 2019–20 season

More significantly, however, those last results ignore the fact that even a flipped coin at even odds can come up heads or tails many times in a row. Our simulated coin flips previously returned tails six consecutive times on just 10 flips. Let's see what sort of streak we might get on 700 flips, which is approximately equal to the number of free throws Antetokounmpo attempted in 2019–20.

We make another call to the `sample()` function (once more, results will differ every time `sample()` is called):

- Because we're now simulating 700 coin flips rather than just 10, we change the size argument of the `sample()` function to `700`.

- Our results are saved in a data frame called coin_flips and specifically a column called heads_tails, where 0 again equals heads and 1 equals tails. We can also think of 0 equaling a missed free throw and 1 equaling a made free throw.
- Then, we pass coin_flips to the mutate() function to create a variable called streak that equals an ongoing tally of consecutive heads and tails, thanks again to the streak_run() function from the runner package.
- We then subset coin_flips where heads_tails equals 1 by calling the dplyr filter() function.
- Finally, we make a call to the base R max() function, which returns the maximum value of the variable streak.

We won't bother to print all or some subset of coin_flips; we'll just share the results here:

```
coin_flips <- sample(x = c(0, 1), size = 700, prob = c(0.5, 0.5),
                     replace = TRUE)
coin_flips <- as.data.frame(coin_flips)
colnames(coin_flips) <- c("heads_tails")

coin_flips %>%
  mutate(streak = streak_run(heads_tails)) %>%
  filter(heads_tails == 1) -> coin_flips

max(coin_flips$streak)
## [1] 11
```

So after 700 simulated coin flips, we got tails a maximum of 11 consecutive times. This is comparable to Antetokounmpo's best streak, especially considering we simulated fair, and not weighted, coin flips for which the odds are 50/50.

16.4.2 *Player 2 of 3: Julius Randle*

Our next player is Julius Randle, a power forward and center for the New York Knicks. Randle attempted 350 free throws, not including a pair of technical free throws, during the 2019–20 regular season (the Knicks didn't qualify for postseason play); he made 257, or 73.4%, of these attempts. Once more, these statistics were lifted from www.basketball-reference.com.

We begin by calling the filter() function and subsetting the ft data set where the variable player equals Julius Randle. Subsequent calls to the dim() and sum() functions confirm that our data corresponds perfectly with like statistics from the Basketball Reference website—dim() returns the record count, which is equal to the number of attempted free throws, and sum() returns the number of made free throws by adding the integers from the variable points, where 0 equals a missed free throw and 1 equals a made free throw:

```
ft %>%
  filter(player == "Julius Randle") -> randle

dim(randle)
## [1] 350    6
sum(randle$points)
## [1] 257
```

Then, we create a variable called streak, not unlike our previous variable by the same name, grouped by the variable date. Our results are cast to a new object called randle_final.

We get the first 10 observations in randle_final returned to us by making a call to the head() function:

```
randle %>%
  group_by(date) %>%
  mutate(streak = streak_run(lag(points))) -> randle_final

head(randle_final, n = 10)
## # A tibble: 10 × 7
## # Groups:   date [2]
##    date       event_type  player       points result
##    <date>     <fct>       <chr>         <dbl> <fct>
##  1 2019-10-23 free throw  Julius Randle     1 made
##  2 2019-10-23 free throw  Julius Randle     0 missed
##  3 2019-10-23 free throw  Julius Randle     1 made
##  4 2019-10-23 free throw  Julius Randle     1 made
##  5 2019-10-23 free throw  Julius Randle     0 missed
##  6 2019-10-23 free throw  Julius Randle     1 made
##  7 2019-10-25 free throw  Julius Randle     0 missed
##  8 2019-10-25 free throw  Julius Randle     0 missed
##  9 2019-10-25 free throw  Julius Randle     1 made
## 10 2019-10-25 free throw  Julius Randle     1 made
##    type               streak
##    <fct>               <int>
##  1 Free Throw 1 of 1       0
##  2 Free Throw 1 of 2       1
##  3 Free Throw 2 of 2       1
##  4 Free Throw 1 of 1       1
##  5 Free Throw 1 of 2       2
##  6 Free Throw 2 of 2       1
##  7 Free Throw 1 of 2       0
##  8 Free Throw 2 of 2       1
##  9 Free Throw 1 of 2       2
## 10 Free Throw 2 of 2       1
```

We then pass randle_final via the pipe operator to the group_by() and slice() functions to delete the first randle_final record for each unique date or game:

```
randle_final %>%
  group_by(date) %>%
  slice(-1) -> randle_final
```

This reduces the length of randle_final to 289 records:

```
dim(randle_final)
## [1] 289    7
```

Another call to the `filter()` function further reduces randle_final, this time by subsetting it where a one-record lag in the variable points equals 1. These results are then passed to the `group_by()` and `summarize()` functions to tally makes and misses for each integer in the variable streak. Our summary results are cast to a tibble called randle_tbl1:

```
randle_final %>%
  filter(lag(points) == 1) %>%
  group_by(streak) %>%
  summarize(makes = sum(points == 1),
            misses = sum(points == 0)) -> randle_tbl1
print(randle_tbl1)
## # A tibble: 8 × 3
##    streak makes misses
##     <int> <int>  <int>
## 1      1    39     10
## 2      2    35     24
## 3      3    18     10
## 4      4    10      5
## 5      5     5      3
## 6      6     2      1
## 7      7     2      0
## 8      8     1      0
```

This is then passed to `mutate()` to create a new variable equal to Randle's free throw percentage for each length of consecutive makes:

```
randle_tbl1 %>%
  mutate(pct = makes / (makes + misses) * 100) -> randle_tbl2
```

```
print(randle_tbl2)
## # A tibble: 8 × 4
##    streak makes misses    pct
##     <int> <int>  <int>  <dbl>
## 1      1    39     10   79.6
## 2      2    35     24   59.3
## 3      3    18     10   64.3
## 4      4    10      5   66.7
## 5      5     5      3   62.5
## 6      6     2      1   66.7
## 7      7     2      0  100
## 8      8     1      0  100
```

Finally, we visualize Julius Randle's free throw percentages by drawing a `ggplot2` line chart sourced from the randle_tbl2 tibble we just created (see figure 16.3):

```
p3 <- ggplot(randle_tbl2, aes(x = streak, y = pct, group = 1)) +
  geom_line(aes(y = pct), color = "steelblue", size = 1.5) +
  geom_point(size = 3, color = "steelblue") +
```

```
labs(title = "Julius Randle",
     subtitle = "Free Throw Percentage Following Consecutive Makes",
     x = "Consecutive Makes (Streak)",
     y = "Free Throw Shooting Percentage",
     caption = "2019-20 regular season and postseason\n
                Randle shot 73.4% from the line during
     the regular season") +
  scale_x_continuous(breaks = seq(0, 8, 1)) +
  theme(plot.title = element_text(face = "bold"))
print(p3)
```

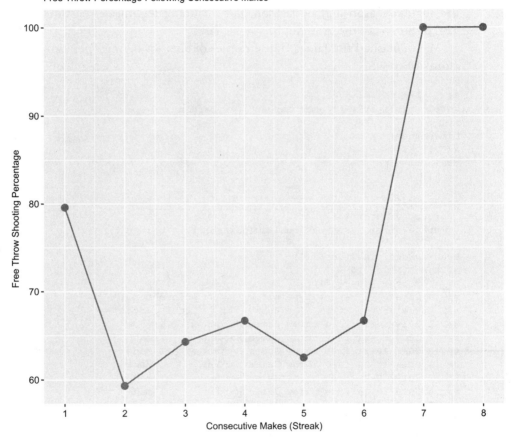

Figure 16.3   Julius Randle's free throw percentages following consecutive makes during the 2019–20 season

Randle shot almost 80% from the line following one successful free throw attempt, but then less than 70% when he previously made anywhere between two and six consecutive free throws. Once more, there is no resemblance to a Laplace probability curve, so we again fail to see any evidence of a hot hand.

16.4.3 *Player 3 of 3: James Harden*

Our third and final player is James Harden, a guard who was playing for the Houston Rockets back in the 2019–20 season (he has since played for three other teams). Year over year, Harden is one of the NBA's top scorers, in large part because he draws a lot of shooting fouls and thus attempts a lot of free throws. In 2019–20, Harden attempted almost 200 more foul shots than any other player. According to his www.basketball-reference.com stat line, Harden attempted 873 free throws between the regular season and postseason, not including technical free throws, and made 754, or 86.4%, of those attempts.

We've mashed the James Harden series of data wrangling operations into a single chunk of code:

```
ft %>%
  filter(player == "James Harden") -> harden

dim(harden)
## [1] 873    6
sum(harden$points)
## [1] 754

harden %>%
  group_by(date) %>%
  mutate(streak = streak_run(lag(points))) -> harden_final

head(harden_final, n = 10)
## # A tibble: 10 × 7
## # Groups:   date [1]
##    date       event_type player       points result
##    <date>     <fct>      <chr>         <dbl> <fct>
## 1 2019-10-24 free throw James Harden      1 made
## 2 2019-10-24 free throw James Harden      1 made
## 3 2019-10-24 free throw James Harden      1 made
## 4 2019-10-24 free throw James Harden      1 made
## 5 2019-10-24 free throw James Harden      1 made
## 6 2019-10-24 free throw James Harden      1 made
## 7 2019-10-24 free throw James Harden      1 made
## 8 2019-10-24 free throw James Harden      1 made
## 9 2019-10-24 free throw James Harden      1 made
## 10 2019-10-24 free throw James Harden     1 made
##    type              streak
##    <fct>             <int>
## 1 Free Throw 1 of 2       0
## 2 Free Throw 2 of 2       1
## 3 Free Throw 1 of 3       2
## 4 Free Throw 2 of 3       3
## 5 Free Throw 3 of 3       4
## 6 Free Throw 1 of 3       5
## 7 Free Throw 2 of 3       6
```

```
##  8 Free Throw 3 of 3        7
##  9 Free Throw 1 of 2        8
## 10 Free Throw 2 of 2        9

harden_final %>%
  group_by(date) %>%
  slice(-1) -> harden_final

dim(harden_final)
## [1] 793    7

harden_final %>%
  filter(lag(points) == 1) %>%
  group_by(streak) %>%
  summarize(makes = sum(points == 1),
            misses = sum(points == 0)) -> harden_tbl1
print(harden_tbl1)
## # A tibble: 23 × 3
##     streak makes misses
##      <int> <int>  <int>
##  1       1    70     13
##  2       2   104     17
##  3       3    86     12
##  4       4    66     14
##  5       5    46      8
##  6       6    35      7
##  7       7    27      4
##  8       8    19      4
##  9       9    16      1
## 10      10    13      2
## # … with 13 more rows

harden_tbl1 %>%
  mutate(pct = makes / (makes + misses) * 100) -> harden_tbl2
print(harden_tbl2)
## # A tibble: 23 × 4
##     streak makes misses   pct
##      <int> <int>  <int> <dbl>
##  1       1    70     13  84.3
##  2       2   104     17  86.0
##  3       3    86     12  87.8
##  4       4    66     14  82.5
##  5       5    46      8  85.2
##  6       6    35      7  83.3
##  7       7    27      4  87.1
##  8       8    19      4  82.6
##  9       9    16      1  94.1
## 10      10    13      2  86.7
## # … with 13 more rows
```

Harden's free throw percentages for every integer in the variable `streak` are represented in tabular format in the preceding chunk through the tibble harden_tbl2 and, in the following chunk, in graphical format through another `ggplot2` line chart in figure 16.4:

```
p4 <- ggplot(harden_tbl2, aes(x = streak, y = pct, group = 1)) +
  geom_line(aes(y = pct), color = "steelblue", size = 1.5) +
  geom_point(size = 3, color = "steelblue") +
  labs(title = "James Harden",
       subtitle = "Free Throw Percentage Following Consecutive Makes",
       x = "Consecutive Makes (Streak)",
       y = "Free Throw Shooting Percentage",
       caption = "2019-20 regular season and postseason\n
                  Harden shot 86.4% from the line during
       the regular season and postseason combined") +
  scale_x_continuous(breaks = seq(0, 23, 1)) +
  theme(plot.title = element_text(face = "bold"))
print(p4)
```

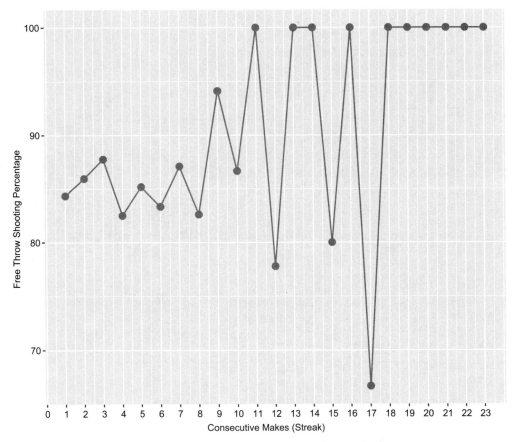

James Harden
Free Throw Percentage Following Consecutive Makes

2019–20 regular season and postseason

Harden shot 86.4% from the line during
the regular season and postseason combined

Figure 16.4   James Harden's free throw percentages following consecutive makes during the 2019–20 season

Once more, we see nothing but randomness—no Laplace probability curve, no power law, no hot hand. Next up, however, is the plot twist we candidly dropped in the beginning.

16.5 League-wide analysis

We end by plotting and analyzing the entire NBA in a single data series. Our data wrangling operations are again mashed into a single code chunk; there's nothing new here except that, when necessary, we're grouping data operations by date *and* player:

```
ft %>%
  group_by(date, player) %>%
  mutate(streak = streak_run(lag(points))) -> ft_final

head(ft_final, n = 10)
## # A tibble: 10 x 7
## # Groups:   date, player [4]
##     <date>      <fct>        <chr>          <dbl> <fct>
##  1 2019-10-22 free throw Kyle Lowry          1 made
##  2 2019-10-22 free throw Kyle Lowry          0 missed
##  3 2019-10-22 free throw Pascal Siakam       1 made
##  4 2019-10-22 free throw Pascal Siakam       1 made
##  5 2019-10-22 free throw Pascal Siakam       1 made
##  6 2019-10-22 free throw Pascal Siakam       1 made
##  7 2019-10-22 free throw Fred VanVleet       1 made
##  8 2019-10-22 free throw Kyle Lowry          1 made
##  9 2019-10-22 free throw Kyle Lowry          1 made
## 10 2019-10-22 free throw Josh Hart           2 made
##     <fct>              <int>
##  1 Free Throw 1 of 2      0
##  2 Free Throw 2 of 2      1
##  3 Free Throw 1 of 2      0
##  4 Free Throw 2 of 2      1
##  5 Free Throw 1 of 2      2
##  6 Free Throw 2 of 2      3
##  7 Free Throw 1 of 1      0
##  8 Free Throw 1 of 2      1
##  9 Free Throw 2 of 2      1
## 10 Free Throw 1 of 2      0

ft_final %>%
  group_by(date, player) %>%
  slice(-1) -> ft_final

ft_final %>%
  filter(lag(points) == 1) %>%
  group_by(streak) %>%
  summarize(makes = sum(points == 1),
            misses = sum(points == 0)) -> ft_tbl1
print(ft_tbl1)
## # A tibble: 23 x 3
##    streak makes misses
##     <int> <int>  <int>
##  1      1  3209    980
```

```
##  2       2  5285  1386
##  3       3  3257   774
##  4       4  1796   399
##  5       5  1110   225
##  6       6   645   130
##  7       7   404    68
##  8       8   245    42
##  9       9   151    21
## 10      10    90    13
## # … with 13 more rows
```

```
ft_tbl1 %>%
  mutate(pct = makes / (makes + misses) * 100) -> ft_tbl2
print(ft_tbl2)
## # A tibble: 23 × 4
##     streak makes misses   pct
##      <int> <int>  <int> <dbl>
##  1       1  3209    980  76.6
##  2       2  5285   1386  79.2
##  3       3  3257    774  80.8
##  4       4  1796    399  81.8
##  5       5  1110    225  83.1
##  6       6   645    130  83.2
##  7       7   404     68  85.6
##  8       8   245     42  85.4
##  9       9   151     21  87.8
## 10      10    90     13  87.4
## # … with 13 more rows
```

This leads to our final visualization, yet another ggplot2 line chart that displays league-wide free throw percentages for every possible streak of consecutive makes from the foul line (see figure 16.5). Note that Antetokounmpo, Randle, and Harden's figures are included in these results; in fact, any player who attempted at least one free throw during the 2019–20 regular season or postseason is factored into these results.

However, we've added a very cool feature to this last plot—we've inserted p1 in the upper-left corner so that we can readily compare (imperfect) league-wide results to a (perfect) Laplace probability curve. We make this happen by calling the ggplot2 annotation_custom() function. The first argument passed to annotation_custom() is the ggplotGrob() function, which generates a ggplot2 grid graphical object from a preexisting plot. The remaining four arguments establish the x and y coordinates for the inset:

```
p5 <- ggplot(ft_tbl2, aes(x = streak, y = pct, group = 1)) +
  geom_line(aes(y = pct), color = "steelblue", size = 1.5) +
  geom_point(size = 3, color = "steelblue") +
  labs(title = "Entire NBA",
       subtitle = "Free Throw Percentage Following Consecutive Makes",
       x = "Consecutive Makes (Streak)",
       y = "Free Throw Shooting Percentage",
       caption = "2019-20 regular season and postseason") +
  scale_x_continuous(breaks = seq(0, 23, 1)) +
```

```
    theme(plot.title = element_text(face = "bold")) +
    annotation_custom(ggplotGrob(p1), xmin = 1, xmax = 11,
                      ymin = 89, ymax = 101)
print(p5)
```

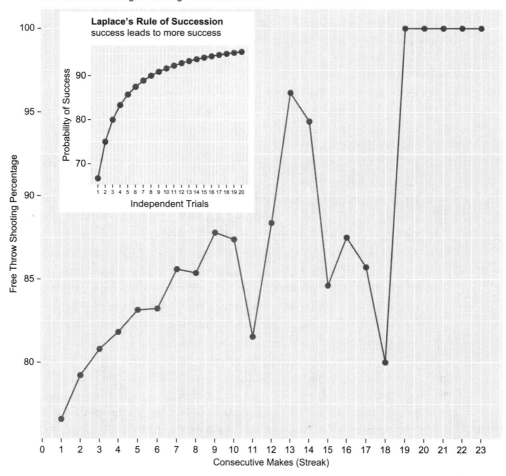

Entire NBA
Free Throw Percentage Following Consecutive Makes

2019–20 regular season and postseason

Figure 16.5   League-wide free throw percentages following consecutive makes during the 2019–20 season. Unlike our results at the player level, these results approximate a Laplace probability curve.

We actually get a visualization that approximates a Laplace probability curve now that we're plotting thousands of data points instead of just a few hundred. It's hardly perfect, of course, but we do see incrementally higher free throw percentages as the number of consecutive makes increases; we even see a series of increases at a decreasing rate, at least until the number of consecutive made free throws equals 9. We then see regressions when consecutive makes equal 11, then 15, and again when it equals 18;

however, by and large, we see higher free throw percentages when the number of prior made free throws increases. We therefore see what appears to be a hot hand when we examine the NBA as a whole instead of a few select players. This time, it makes sense, however, to separate the Laplace probability curve from the hot hand. After all, while the NBA-wide results approximate a Laplace probability curve, a hot hand applies only to the individual player level over finite periods of time.

In the next chapter, we'll investigate whether a wisdom in crowds exists by comparing opening and closing odds released by Las Vegas sportsbooks to final scores.

Summary

- Even in an era of big data, small data is everywhere. Laplace's rule of succession is the best alternative to the conventional probability formula when working with few observations and/or when the number of independent trials and successes are the same.

- It can't be emphasized enough how critical it is to recognize (and accept) randomness when others might see (or want) order. We demonstrated how simulated coin flips might (or will) contain streaks of heads or tails and that real-life events, like free throw shooting, actually resemble random and independent flips of a coin instead of an orderly and predicable process.

- So, no, free throw percentage, at least at the player level, doesn't consistently increase with each subsequent success; makes and misses do resemble coin flips more than they approximate a Laplace probability curve; there is randomness that others mistake for order and causality; and there is no hot hand in the NBA, at least based on free throw shooting during the 2019–20 regular season and postseason.

- The `runner` package was introduced as a "relatively obscure package," which is true. Over the course of 2022, it's been downloaded about 2,000 times on average per month. Conversely, `ggplot2` has been downloaded about 3 million times per month over the 2022 calendar year. But the `runner` package is nevertheless a great example of how versatile and extensible the R programming language is—regardless of what you want to do in R, there's an excellent chance someone else has already completed the exact same task *and* published a package to help you with the heavy lifting.

- One point around the hot hand must absolutely be made, especially in consideration of the inconsistent results that were presented here: the player-specific results are much more meaningful than the league-wide results. That's because the hot hand applies to individuals acting within discrete periods of time, and not toward many individuals operating in different spaces at different times. Thus, based on the balance of evidence, our best conclusion is that free throw shooting resembles coin flips more than it does a hot hand phenomenon.

- In the meantime, we demonstrated how to simulate coin flips with just a single line of R code. And it doesn't have to necessarily be a fair coin. If you want to simulate an event with, let's say, 70/30 odds rather than 50/50, that can be done merely by changing the `probs` argument to the `sample()` function.

- Finally, we showed how to inset a `ggplot2` object into another `ggplot2` object. This is a great data visualization technique to apply when you want to compare a new plot to an "older" plot.

Collective intelligence

This chapter covers

- Automated exploratory data analysis
- Conducting baseline EDA tasks with the `tableone` package
- Performing advanced EDA operations with the `DataExplorer` and `SmartEDA` packages
- Applying new functional and aesthetic techniques to `ggplot2` bar charts

Our first purpose here is to establish who might be smarter—the small number of Las Vegas oddsmakers with advanced data science degrees who establish *opening* odds using very sophisticated algorithms where millions of dollars are at stake for the casinos they work for, or the thousands of gamblers, professionals and amateurs with skin in the game, who then wager their hard-earned money and, in the process, influence the *closing* odds.

For instance, on October 17, 2018, the Memphis Grizzlies played at the Indiana Pacers. The opening total from Las Vegas oddsmakers—that is, the estimated number of points to be scored by the Grizzlies and Pacers combined—was 209. Wagers were then placed on what is otherwise known as the over/under until the betting line closed. Money wagered on the over comes from gamblers who think the Grizzlies and Pacers will score more than 209 points; money wagered on the under comes from gamblers who think the two teams will combine for fewer than 209 points. It doesn't matter who wins, who loses, or what the final margin is; all that matters is whether or not the combined point total is greater than or less than 209.

The opening total is meant to encourage even money on the over and the under. When that's *not* the case, the opening total subsequently moves up or down—up to encourage more bets on the under and down to encourage additional bets on the over. With respect to the Grizzlies-Pacers game, the over/under closed at 204.5 (this is also known as the closing total), which, of course, means most of the betting money was on the under as opposed to the over.

The opening point spread—often called the opening spread, or just the spread— was Indiana –7, or Memphis +7. In other words, the same Las Vegas oddsmakers estimated that Indiana would win by seven points (or that Memphis would lose by seven points). Money therefore wagered on the Pacers comes from gamblers who think the Pacers will win *and* win by more than seven points; money wagered instead on the Grizzlies comes from gamblers who think the Grizzlies will lose by fewer than seven points *or* maybe win outright.

Like the over/under, the opening spread is supposed to encourage equal amounts of money to be wagered on both teams—Indiana to cover or Memphis to cover. And like the over/under, the spread then moves based on actual bets. With regard to the Grizzlies-Pacers game, the spread closed at Indiana –7.5, which means most of the betting money (probably not much more than half) was on the Pacers to win and to win by more than seven points.

The Pacers defeated the Grizzlies 111–83, which means that the closing total and the closing spread were nearer the final results than the opening total and the opening spread. At least with respect to this one game, the gamblers knew more than the oddsmakers. We'll examine every NBA game from the 2018–19 regular season to see if this was the rule or just one exception to the rule.

Our second purpose is to introduce ways that R makes exploratory data analysis (EDA) quick and easy; we'll present and review three automated EDA packages and discuss their advantages and disadvantages versus more methodical EDA approaches. We'll begin by loading our packages.

17.1 Loading packages

We'll wrangle our data with a combination of `dplyr` and `tidyr` functions and visualize our results with `ggplot2` bar charts and facet plots. Otherwise, we'll sequentially explore our data through three automated EDA packages—`tableone`, `DataExplorer`, and `SmartEDA`—as shown here:

```
library(tidyverse)
library(tableone)
library(DataExplorer)
library(SmartEDA)
```

We'll next import our one data set.

17.2   *Importing data*

We import our data by making a call to the `read_csv()` function from the `readr` package and pass a file called 2018-2019 NBA_Box_Score_Team-Stats.csv that was downloaded from www.bigdataball.com and subsequently stored in our default working directory. Our data set, at least for now, is called oddsdf1:

```
oddsdf1 <- read_csv("018-2019_NBA_Box_Score_Team-Stats.csv")
```

Then, we pass oddsdf1 to the base R `dim()` function to return the row and column counts:

```
dim(oddsdf1)
## [1] 2624   57
```

Our data set contains 2,624 records and 57 variables, which is both more and less than what we need for our analysis. In other words, it contains rows and columns that won't factor into our analysis, but it doesn't (yet) contain other variables that we'll instead have to derive ourselves. Thus, we'll run several data wrangling operations to transform our raw data into an object that's much more useful to us.

17.3   *Wrangling data*

We start by reducing the length of our data. The oddsdf1 data set contains records for the 2018–19 NBA regular season (which we want) and the 2019 playoffs (which we don't want). So we make a call to the `filter()` function from the `dplyr` package to subset oddsdf1 on those observations where the variable DATASET doesn't equal NBA 2019 Playoffs (the `!=` operator means not equal to):

```
oddsdf1 %>%
  filter(DATASET != "NBA 2019 Playoffs") -> oddsdf1
```

Then, we reduce the width of our data. Although much of the data in oddsdf1 is interesting, it's hardly necessary for our purposes, so we call the `dplyr` `select()` function to subset oddsdf1 on just the few variables we absolutely require:

```
oddsdf1 %>%
  select(GAME_ID, DATE, TEAM, VENUE, PTS, OPENING_SPREAD, OPENING_TOTAL,
         CLOSING_SPREAD, CLOSING_TOTAL) -> oddsdf1
```

Our surviving variables include the following:

- GAME_ID—A unique and sequential identifier for each game that increments by one chronologically using date and start time.
- DATE—The date of each game in mm/dd/yy format. This is now a character string.

- TEAM—The abbreviated team name (e.g., Philadelphia rather than Philadelphia 76ers, or Boston instead of Boston Celtics); the two teams based in Los Angeles, the LA Clippers and the LA Lakers, are the exceptions. This is now a character string.
- VENUE—Equals R for road teams and H for home teams. This is now a character string.
- PTS—Equals the total points scored for each participating team. This is now numeric and will remain numeric.
- OPENING_SPREAD—Equals the predicted point spread before any wagers have been placed. When the spread is, for instance, 4.5, the underdog must win outright or lose by 4 or fewer points to cover; when the spread is –4.5, the favorite must win by 5 or more points to cover. This is now numeric and will remain numeric.
- OPENING_TOTAL—Equals the predicted total points scored by the participating teams; also known as the over/under. Gamblers bet the over or under based on the actual number of combined points they expect to be scored. This is now numeric and will remain numeric.
- CLOSING_SPREAD—Equals the predicted point spread after all wagers have been placed and the betting line has closed. This is now numeric and will remain numeric.
- CLOSING_TOTAL—Equals the predicted number of combined points after all wagers have been placed and the betting line has closed. This is now numeric and will remain numeric.

You might have figured out that oddsdf1 actually contains two records for each game. The top record pertains to the road team, and the bottom record pertains to the home team. Here are the specifics:

- The variables GAME_ID and DATE are the same for each pair of records. The first game of the 2018–19 regular season matched the Philadelphia 76ers at the Boston Celtics. Therefore, GAME_ID equals 21800001, and DATE equals 10/16/18 for the first two oddsdf1 records.
- The variables TEAM, VENUE, and PTS are unique to the road and home teams. The final score is therefore reflected in the two values under PTS.
- The variables OPENING_SPREAD and CLOSING_SPREAD are exact opposites of each other. For instance, if OPENING_SPREAD or CLOSING_SPREAD equals 4.5 for the road team, it equals -4.5 for the home team.
- The variables OPENING_TOTAL and CLOSING_TOTAL are the same for each pair of records.

However, this isn't the structure we want or need; our analysis requires that our data set contains one record, not two, for each game. So our next order of business is to break oddsdf1 into two equal halves and then join the two halves by rows.

To make this happen, we first call the `filter()` function again, this time to subset oddsdf1 where the variable VENUE equals R; our new object is called roadodds:

```
oddsdf1 %>%
  filter(VENUE == "R") -> roadodds
```

Then, we pass roadodds via the pipe operator to the `rename()` function to rename every variable. The `rename()` function requires the *new* variable names to be left of the assignment operator and the *old* variable names to be on the right. For instance, we're renaming PTS to ptsR:

```
roadodds %>%
  rename(ID = GAME_ID, date = DATE, teamR = TEAM, venueR = VENUE,
         ptsR = PTS, openspreadR = OPENING_SPREAD,
         opentotal = OPENING_TOTAL, closespreadR = CLOSING_SPREAD,
         closetotal = CLOSING_TOTAL) -> roadodds
```

Next, the remaining oddsdf1 records, where the variable VENUE equals H, are thrown into a new object called homeodds:

```
oddsdf1 %>%
  filter(VENUE == "H") -> homeodds
```

We then subset homeodds so that it just includes the variables TEAM, VENUE, PTS, OPENING_SPREAD, and CLOSING_SPREAD. The variables GAME_ID, DATE, OPENING_TOTAL, and CLOSING_TOTAL, which are the same between each pair of oddsdf1 records, are contained in roadodds and are therefore not needed in homeodds as well:

```
homeodds %>%
  select(TEAM, VENUE, PTS, OPENING_SPREAD, CLOSING_SPREAD) -> homeodds
```

The surviving homeodds variables are then renamed to distinguish them from their road team equivalents:

```
homeodds %>%
  rename(teamH = TEAM, venueH = VENUE, ptsH = PTS,
         openspreadH = OPENING_SPREAD,
         closespreadH = CLOSING_SPREAD) -> homeodds
```

Finally, we create a new object called oddsdf2 by calling the base R `cbind()` function, which joins roadodds and homeodds by rows into a single data set:

```
oddsdf2 <- cbind(roadodds, homeodds)
```

We then call the `dim()` function—oddsdf2 contains 1,230 rows and 14 columns. An NBA regular season schedule, where all 30 teams play 82 games, equals 1,230 games, so this checks out:

```
dim(oddsdf2)
## [1] 1230   14
```

Then, we call the base R `as.factor()` function to convert four of the five oddsdf2 character strings (all but the variable `date`) to factor variables:

```
oddsdf2$teamR <- as.factor(oddsdf2$teamR)
oddsdf2$teamH <- as.factor(oddsdf2$teamH)
oddsdf2$venueR <- as.factor(oddsdf2$venueR)
oddsdf2$venueH <- as.factor(oddsdf2$venueH)
```

We convert `date` from a character string to a date class by calling the `as.Date()` function from base R. The second argument to the `as.Date()` function is an instruction to R to keep the current mm/dd/yy format—for now:

```
oddsdf2$date <- as.Date(oddsdf2$date, "%m/%d/%Y")
```

Next, we create a new variable by passing oddsdf2 to the `dplyr` `mutate()` function; our new variable, called `month`, is derived from the variable `date`. For instance, where `date` equals `10/27/18`, `month` equals `October`; likewise, where `date` equals `2/9/19`, `month` equals `February`:

```
oddsdf2 %>%
  mutate(month = format(date, "%B")) -> oddsdf2
```

The 2018–19 NBA regular season started on October 16 and ended on April 10. Therefore, October was the first month in the 2018–19 regular season schedule, November the second month, December the third month, and so on. That being said, we pass oddsdf2 to the `dplyr` `mutate()` and `case_when()` functions—`mutate()` creates another new variable and `case_when()` assigns conditional values to the cells. When the variable `month` equals `October`, our new variable, `month2`, should equal `1`; when `month` equals `November`, `month2` should instead equal `2`; and so forth.

Our new variable is then converted to a factor by calling the `as.factor()` function from base R:

```
oddsdf2 %>%
  mutate(month2 = case_when(month == "October" ~ 1,
                            month == "November" ~ 2,
                            month == "December" ~ 3,
                            month == "January" ~ 4,
                            month == "February" ~ 5,
                            month == "March" ~ 6,
                            month == "April" ~ 7)) -> oddsdf2

oddsdf2$month2 <- as.factor(oddsdf2$month2)
```

We then call the `select()` function to drop the variables `ID`, `date`, and `month` from oddsdf2 (notice the minus signs in front of the variable names):

```
oddsdf2 %>%
  select(-ID, -date, -month) -> oddsdf2
```

Now, let's start to explore our data, immediately starting with the `tableone` package. This package was designed to return summary data on both continuous and categorical variables mixed within one table.

17.4 *Automated exploratory data analysis*

Exploratory data analysis (EDA) is a combination of computing basic statistics and creating visual content to get an initial read on a data set and to establish a scope for further analysis. There are several R packages that allow us to automate EDA tasks, or at least to create more content with fewer lines of code versus a manual and more methodical EDA approach (see chapter 2, for instance).

We're going to demonstrate three of these packages. The first of these is called `tableone`.

17.4.1 *Baseline EDA with tableone*

The `tableone` package was inspired by a typical *Table 1* found in many research publications, which usually includes several lines of summary statistics; as such, `tableone`, as you might have guessed, returns results in tabular format only and, therefore, doesn't produce any visual representations of the data.

Maybe the most simple and straightforward EDA task is to summarize an entire data set. With `tableone`, we can do that by passing a data set, in this case oddsdf2, to the `CreateTableOne()` function. We subsequently get a stack of summary statistics returned when we then call the base R `print()` function (due to space considerations, some output isn't included):

```
tableOne <- CreateTableOne(data = oddsdf2)
print(tableOne)
##
##                          Overall
##   n                       1230
##   teamR (%)
##      Atlanta              41 (  3.3)
##      Boston               41 (  3.3)
##      Brooklyn             41 (  3.3)

##      Toronto              41 (  3.3)
##      Utah                 41 (  3.3)
##      Washington           41 (  3.3)
##   venueR = R (%)          1230 (100.0)
##   ptsR (mean (SD))      109.85 (12.48)
##   openspreadR (mean (SD))   2.49 (6.45)
##   opentotal (mean (SD))   221.64 (8.62)
##   closespreadR (mean (SD))   2.62 (6.59)
##   closetotal (mean (SD))  221.69 (8.79)
##   teamH (%)
##      Atlanta              41 (  3.3)
##      Boston               41 (  3.3)
##      Brooklyn             41 (  3.3)
```

```
##     Toronto                   41 (   3.3)
##     Utah                      41 (   3.3)
##     Washington                41 (   3.3)
##   venueH = H (%)            1230 (100.0)
##   ptsH (mean (SD))         112.57 (12.68)
##   openspreadH (mean (SD))   -2.49 (6.45)
##   closespreadH (mean (SD))  -2.62 (6.59)
##   month2 (%)
##     1                        110 (   8.9)
##     2                        219 (  17.8)
##     3                        219 (  17.8)
##     4                        221 (  18.0)
##     5                        158 (  12.8)
##     6                        224 (  18.2)
##     7                         79 (   6.4)
```

So here's what we can glean just by running a single `tableone` function:

- The oddsdf2 data set contains 1,230 records.

- All 30 teams played 41 road games and 41 home games during the 2018–19 regular season.

- Each team was therefore the road team in 3.3% of all 2018–19 regular season games and the home team in an additional 3.3% of all games.

- Road teams averaged 109.85 points per game that year while home teams averaged 112.57 points per game.

- The dispersion in points scored, represented by the standard deviation (SD) in the variables `ptsR` and `ptsH`, is about the same between road and home teams. This means that in roughly two-thirds of the 2018–19 regular season games, the road team scored approximately 110 plus or minus 13 points and the home team scored approximately 113 plus or minus 13 points.

- The opening spread and especially the closing spread accurately represent the average margin in points scored per game between road and home teams.

- On average, the closing spread is slightly greater than the opening spread; home teams are favored more frequently than road teams.

- On average, there was almost no movement between the opening and closing totals; but that is probably not an accurate reflection of game-over-game variation.

- Finally, we get a breakdown of the regular season game count by month. Take away the partial months of October and April and the month of February, which, of course, has just 28 days and is further shortened because of the all-star break, and the regular season schedule appears to be equally spaced.

The `summary()` function returns even more detail. Summary statistics on continuous variables, including the mean, median, minimum, and maximum values, and the first and third quartiles, are always returned first, followed by observation counts for the oddsdf2 categorical variables.

But first, we disable scientific notation by passing the `scipen = 999` argument to the base R `options()` function (again, some results aren't included due to space considerations):

```
options(scipen = 999)
summary(tableOne)
##
##       ### Summary of continuous variables ###
##
## strata: Overall
##                 n miss p.miss mean sd median p25 p75 min max skew kurt
## ptsR         1230    0      0  110 12    110 101 118  68 168  0.1  0.2
## openspreadR  1230    0      0    2  6      3  -2   8 -16  18 -0.2 -0.6
## opentotal    1230    0      0  222  9    222 216 228 196 243 -0.2 -0.4
## closespreadR 1230    0      0    3  7      4  -2   8 -17  18 -0.2 -0.7
## closetotal   1230    0      0  222  9    222 216 228 194 244 -0.1 -0.3
## ptsH         1230    0      0  113 13    112 104 121  77 161  0.2  0.1
## openspreadH  1230    0      0   -2  6     -3  -8   2 -18  16  0.2 -0.6
## closespreadH 1230    0      0   -3  7     -4  -8   2 -18  17  0.2 -0.7
##
## =======================================================================
##
##       ### Summary of categorical variables ###
##
## strata: Overall
##    var     n miss p.miss      level freq percent cum.percent
##   teamR 1230    0    0.0    Atlanta   41     3.3         3.3
##                               Boston   41     3.3         6.7
##                             Brooklyn   41     3.3        10.0
##
##                              Toronto   41     3.3        93.3
##                                 Utah   41     3.3        96.7
##                           Washington   41     3.3       100.0
##
##  venueR 1230    0    0.0          R 1230   100.0       100.0
##
##   teamH 1230    0    0.0    Atlanta   41     3.3         3.3
##                               Boston   41     3.3         6.7
##                             Brooklyn   41     3.3        10.0
##
##                              Toronto   41     3.3        93.3
##                                 Utah   41     3.3        96.7
##                           Washington   41     3.3       100.0
##
##  venueH 1230    0    0.0          H 1230   100.0       100.0
##
##  month2 1230    0    0.0          1  110     8.9         8.9
##                                   2  219    17.8        26.7
##                                   3  219    17.8        44.6
##                                   4  221    18.0        62.5
##                                   5  158    12.8        75.4
##                                   6  224    18.2        93.6
##                                   7   79     6.4       100.0
##
```

The summary() function doesn't return anything new and interesting with respect to the oddsdf2 categorical variables, but it does provide some additional insights on our continuous variables. For instance, we get the skewness (skew) and kurtosis (kurt) for each of those variables. Skewness represents the degree of distortion from a normal, or Gaussian, distribution; it therefore measures asymmetry in a data's distribution. When negative, the distribution is negatively skewed or left-skewed; when positive, the distribution is positively skewed or right-skewed; and when equal to 0, the distribution is actually symmetrical. Skewness, then, could complement or even replace a Shapiro-Wilk test, where any results greater than 2 or less than –2 would qualify as non-normal distributions.

Kurtosis, on the other hand, is a measure of how long, or not so long, the tails are in a distribution. When equal to or close to 0, the distribution is normal; when negative, the distribution has thin tails; and when positive, the distribution has fat tails.

Next, we'll plot some of these same distributions as part of a broader exercise to further explore our data through another automated EDA package called DataExplorer.

17.4.2 Over/under EDA with DataExplorer

Our scope for further EDA, at least for the time being, will be around the opening and closing totals, or the over/under; we'll save the opening and closing point spreads for a subsequent EDA exercise with yet another package. That being said, we'll create a new data set, oddsdf3, by subsetting oddsdf2, add five new oddsdf3 variables, and then introduce the capabilities of the DataExplorer package to learn more about our data.

WRANGLING DATA

We create oddsdf3 by passing oddsdf2 to the dplyr select() function and subsetting oddsdf2 on 9 of its 13 variables:

```
oddsdf2 %>%
  select(teamR, venueR, ptsR, opentotal, closetotal, teamH, venueH,
         ptsH, month2) -> oddsdf3
```

Then, we go about creating our new variables. The first of these, ptsT, is the total points scored per game between the road and home teams; therefore, we pass oddsdf3 to the dplyr mutate() function and sum the variables ptsR and ptsH to equal ptsT:

```
oddsdf3 %>%
  mutate(ptsT = ptsR + ptsH) -> oddsdf3
```

Our second variable, diff_ptsT_opentotal, is the absolute difference between the variables ptsT and opentotal. The abs() function is a base R function that keeps positive numbers positive and converts negative numbers to positive:

```
oddsdf3 %>%
  mutate(diff_ptsT_opentotal = abs(ptsT - opentotal)) -> oddsdf3
```

Our third variable, `diff_ptsT_closetotal`, is the absolute difference between the variables `ptsT` and `closetotal`:

```
oddsdf3 %>%
  mutate(diff_ptsT_closetotal = abs(ptsT - closetotal)) -> oddsdf3
```

Our fourth variable requires that we combine the `mutate()` function with the `case_when()` function. When `closetotal` is greater than `opentotal`, our new variable, `totalmove`, should equal `up`; when `closetotal` is less than `opentotal`, `totalmove` should equal `down`; and when `closetotal` equals `opentotal`, `totalmove` should equal `same`. Then, we call the `as.factor()` function to convert `totalmove` to a factor variable; after all, it can assume just one of three potential values:

```
oddsdf3 %>%
  mutate(totalmove = case_when(closetotal > opentotal ~ "up",
                               closetotal < opentotal ~ "down",
                               closetotal == opentotal ~ "same")) -> oddsdf3

oddsdf3$totalmove <- as.factor(oddsdf3$totalmove)
```

Our fifth variable, `versusPTS`, also requires `mutate()` in combination with `case_when()`. When `diff_ptsT_opentotal` is greater than `diff_ptsT_closetotal`, or when the absolute difference between total points scored and the opening total is greater than the absolute difference between total points scored and the closing total, `versusPTS` should equal `closetotal`. When the opposite condition is true, `versusPTS` should instead equal `opentotal`. And when there's no difference between `diff_ptsT_opentotal` and `diff_ptsT_closetotal`, the new variable `versusPTS` should equal `same`. Then, we convert `versusPTS` to a factor variable by once more calling the `as.factor()` function:

```
oddsdf3 %>%
  mutate(versusPTS =
          case_when(diff_ptsT_opentotal >
                       diff_ptsT_closetotal ~ "closetotal",
                    diff_ptsT_closetotal >
                       diff_ptsT_opentotal ~ "opentotal",
                    diff_ptsT_opentotal ==
                       diff_ptsT_closetotal ~ "same")) -> oddsdf3

oddsdf3$versusPTS <- factor(oddsdf3$versusPTS)
```

As a result of all this wrangling, the oddsdf3 variables aren't necessarily sequenced left to right in any logical order. One way of rearranging the variable order in R is to simply call the `select()` function. Rather than instructing `select()` to subset our data, we'll pass *every* oddsdf3 variable—actually, their current position numbers—to the `select()` function and, by doing so, R will then rearrange the variables in the order by which the variables are passed as arguments.

A call to the `head()` function from base R returns the top six records:

```
oddsdf3 %>%
  select(9, 1, 2, 3, 6, 7, 8, 10, 4, 5, 11, 12, 13, 14) -> oddsdf3
head(oddsdf3)
##    month2              teamR venueR ptsR        teamH
## 1       1    Philadelphia      R   87        Boston
## 2       1   Oklahoma City      R  100  Golden State
## 3       1       Milwaukee      R  113      Charlotte
## 4       1        Brooklyn      R  100        Detroit
## 5       1         Memphis      R   83        Indiana
## 6       1           Miami      R  101        Orlando
##   venueH ptsH ptsT opentotal closetotal diff_ptsT_opentotal
## 1      H  105  192     208.5      211.5                16.5
## 2      H  108  208     223.5      220.5                15.5
## 3      H  112  225     217.0      222.0                 8.0
## 4      H  103  203     212.0      213.0                 9.0
## 5      H  111  194     209.0      204.5                15.0
## 6      H  104  205     210.5      208.0                 5.5
##   diff_ptsT_closetotal totalmove   versusPTS
## 1                 19.5        up   opentotal
## 2                 12.5      down  closetotal
## 3                  3.0        up  closetotal
## 4                 10.0        up   opentotal
## 5                 10.5      down  closetotal
## 6                  3.0      down  closetotal
```

We now have a data set by which we can readily compare and contrast opening and closing totals against total points scored.

CREATING THE DATA PROFILING REPORT

Let's now introduce the DataExplorer package. We previously suggested that the most encompassing EDA activity—summarizing an entire data set—might also be the most basic. By passing the oddsdf3 data set to the DataExplorer create_report() function, we actually get a comprehensive data profiling report in the form of an interactive HTML file (see figure 17.1). The create_report() function automatically runs many of the DataExplorer EDA functions and then stacks the results, not in the RStudio Console, but rather in a standalone report that can be saved and shared:

```
create_report(oddsdf3)
```

If *cool* is synonymous with effortless style, then the DataExplorer package is most definitely a head turner. While we absolutely created more with less—that is, more content, most of it visual, with less code and therefore requiring less time and effort than a manual alternative—some of the content (most of which we're about to share) doesn't actually add any value—and that's the trade-off. Are you under the gun to put something in front of your boss, even if it's a mix of relevant and not-so-relevant content? Or would you—and your boss—be better served by a more surgical approach?

Consider the EDA from chapter 2. That necessitated a lot of brainpower and a lot of code, but every plot communicated a relevant message. There wasn't a bit of noise. The message here is that manual and automated EDA approaches both have their

Data Profiling Report

- Basic Statistics
  - Raw Counts
  - Percentages
- Data Structure
- Missing Data Profile
- Univariate Distribution
  - Histogram
  - Bar Chart (with frequency)
  - QQ Plot
- Correlation Analysis
- Principal Component Analysis

Basic Statistics

Raw Counts

Name	Value
Rows	1,230
Columns	13
Discrete columns	6
Continuous columns	7
All missing columns	0
Missing observations	0
Complete Rows	1,230
Total observations	15,990
Memory allocation	106.6 Kb

Figure 17.1 A screen capture of a data profiling report that was created by passing a data set as the only argument to a simple function from the `DataExplorer` package

pros and cons; depending on the project and mitigating factors, you'll have to decide what works best for you.

Let's now explore the content we get from the data profiling report.

BASIC STATISTICS

The data profiling report first displays a graphical representation of some basic statistics: how our data set is split between categorical and continuous variables and how much missing data we might have. We can produce this visualization by passing odd-sdf3 to the `plot_intro()` function (see figure 17.2):

```
plot_intro(oddsdf3)
```

Note that only `create_report()` publishes results in a standalone report; when you run individual commands such as `plot_intro()` that are otherwise packed into the `create_report()` function, the results are instead displayed in RStudio.

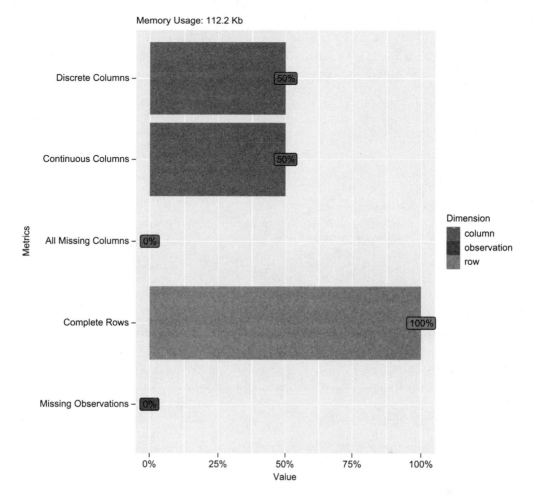

Figure 17.2   A graphical display of basic statistics on a data set from the `DataExplorer` package

We also can get the same in tabular format by passing oddsdf3 to the `introduce()` function:

```
introduce(oddsdf3)
##   rows columns discrete_columns continuous_columns all_missing_columns
## 1 1230      14                7                  7                   0
##   total_missing_values complete_rows total_observations memory_usage
## 1                    0          1230              17220       114856
```

Half of the 14 oddsdf3 variables are continuous, and the other half are categorical (or discrete). In addition, we have no missing data.

DATA STRUCTURE

There are two ways of getting a graphical representation of a data set's structure—basically, a visual alternative to the `dplyr glimpse()` function. One way is to call the `plot_str()` function (see figure 17.3):

```
plot_str(oddsdf3)
```

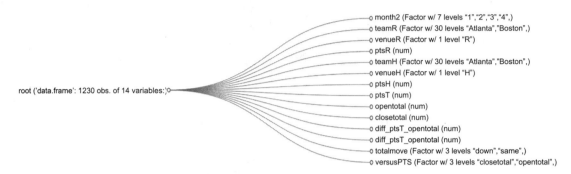

Figure 17.3   A visual representation of a data set's structure. The base R `str()` function and `dplyr glimpse()` function both return similar information, but not in a graphical format.

The second way is to again call `plot_str()`, but to then add the `type = "r"` argument, which tells R to plot the data structure in the form of a radial network (see figure 17.4):

```
plot_str(oddsdf3, type = "r")
```

Either way, we see that `month2`, for instance, is a factor variable with seven levels and that `closetotal` is one of the seven oddsdf3 continuous (or numeric) variables.

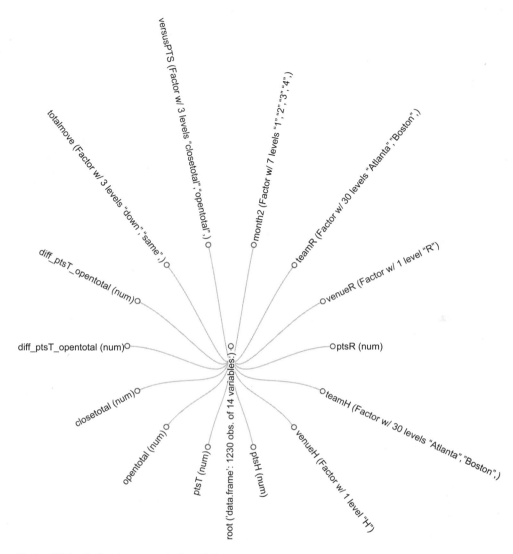

Figure 17.4 A visual representation of the same data structure, but in the form of a radial network. This and the previous view are made possible by the `DataExplorer` package.

MISSING DATA PROFILE

By previously running the `plot_intro()` and `introduce()` functions, we already know that oddsdf3 doesn't contain any missing data. But if the opposite were true, neither of those functions would tell us anything specific about Not Availables (NAs) or incomplete observations in our data set. But the `plot_missing()` function returns a visualization that displays the missing values profile by variable (see figure 17.5):

```
plot_missing(oddsdf3)
```

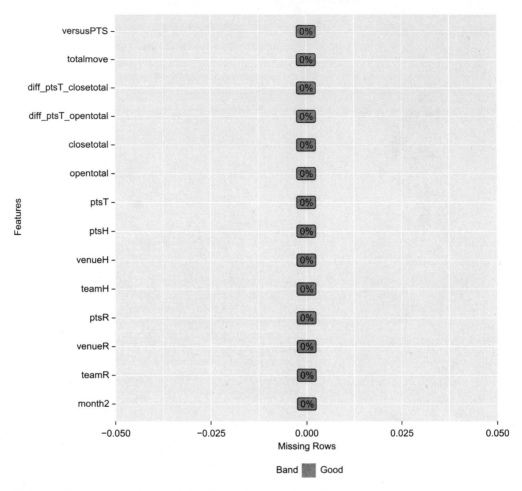

Figure 17.5   A `DataExplorer` **plot that provides a missing values profile**

UNIVARIATE DISTRIBUTION

There are three methods of plotting the distribution of continuous data with `Data-Explorer`. When we run the `create_report()` function, `DataExplorer` automatically detects which variables are continuous and then returns histograms and quantile-quantile (QQ) plots for each. In addition, we have the option of telling `DataExplorer` to print density plots in lieu of or in addition to histograms or QQ plots.

The `plot_histogram()` function returns a matrix of histograms that displays frequency distributions for each of our continuous variables (see figure 17.6). By default, `DataExplorer` usually returns plots in alphabetical order by variable name:

```
plot_histogram(oddsdf3)
```

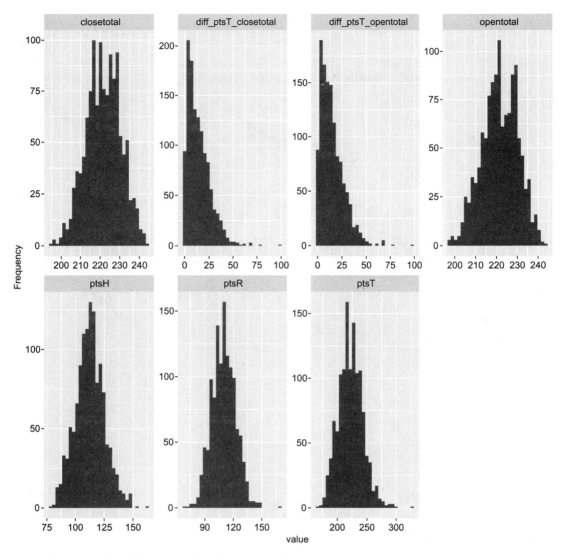

Figure 17.6   A matrix of histograms from the `DataExplorer` package

Some of our continuous variables appear to be normally distributed, or at least close enough, but the variables `diff_ptsT_closetotal` and `diff_ptsT_opentotal` are clearly right-skewed.

The `plot_qq()` function returns a matrix of QQ plots (see figure 17.7). When data is normally distributed, or at least close enough to assuming a Gaussian distribution, the points will fall on top of or very near the diagonal line in a QQ plot; otherwise, we'll instead observe points at one or both tails that deviate, sometimes significantly so, from a QQ plot diagonal line (e.g., see `diff_ptsT_closetotal` and `diff_ptsT_opentotal`):

```
plot_qq(oddsdf3)
```

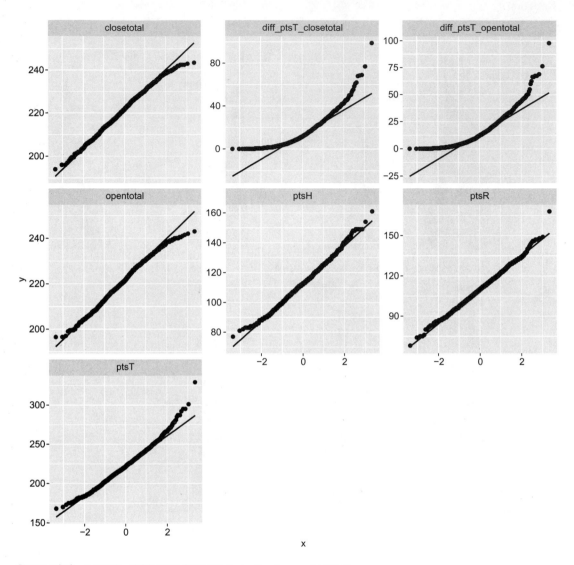

Figure 17.7   A matrix of QQ plots from the `DataExplorer` package

Finally, the `plot_density()` function returns a series of density plots (see figure 17.8).

```
plot_density(oddsdf3)
```

The data profiling report, by default, calls the `plot_histogram()`, `plot_qq()`, and `plot_density()` functions, and therefore returns three series of like visualizations on the same variables, so we get three views into frequency distributions when often just one will suffice. That being said, many statistical tests, such as linear regression, for instance (see chapter 5), assume normality in numeric data, so understanding frequency distributions first is absolutely critical.

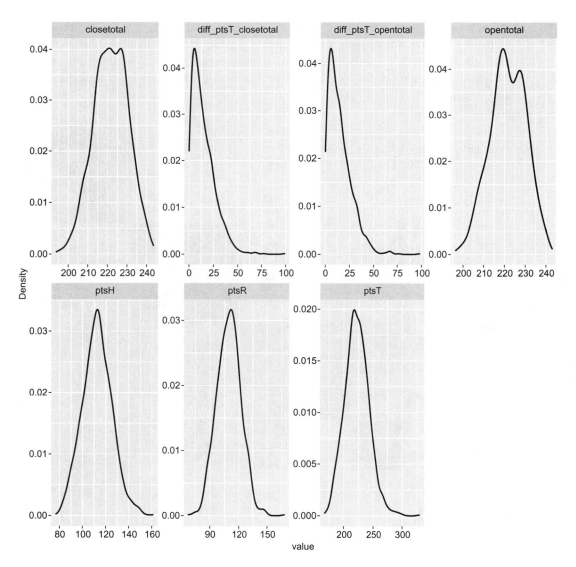

Figure 17.8   A matrix of density plots from the `DataExplorer` package

CORRELATION ANALYSIS

When we make a call to the `DataExplorer` `plot_correlation()` function, we get a correlation matrix, or heat map, returned with the computed correlation coefficients added as data labels (see figure 17.9). By default, the `create_report()` function adds a correlation heat map to the data profiling report that includes continuous *and* categorical variables. By adding `type = "c"` as a second argument, we're manually limiting the results to the oddsdf3 continuous variables only:

```
plot_correlation(oddsdf3, type = "c")
```

What's especially nice about the `plot_correlation()` function is that `DataExplorer` automatically ignores any missing values and then generates the heat map anyway. Note that the correlation coefficients between `closetotal` and `ptsR`, `ptsH`, and `ptsT` are (slightly) higher than the correlation coefficients between `opentotal` and these same three variables.

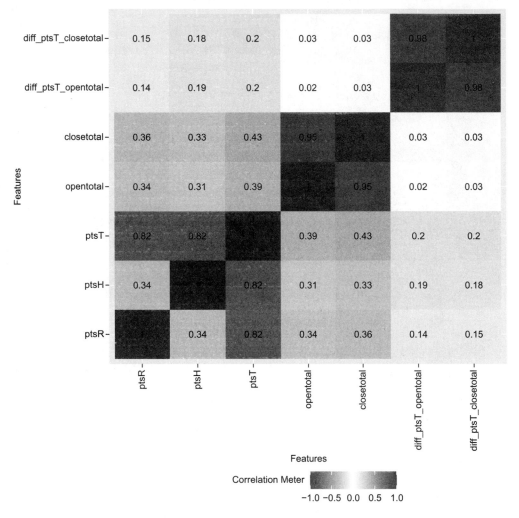

Figure 17.9   A correlation matrix, or heat map, from the `DataExplorer` package; by default, correlation heat maps include all variables, continuous or categorical. Here, we've limited the results to include the oddsdf3 continuous variables only.

CATEGORICAL VARIABLE ANALYSIS

Finally, let's pivot and tell `DataExplorer` to provide some visual insights into the oddsdf3 categorical variables. The data profiling report that is generated by calling the `create_report()` function automatically contains bar charts for every categorical variable as a means of visualizing frequencies, or counts. We can replicate that automation by passing the oddsdf3 data set to the `plot_bar()` function (see figure 17.10):

```
plot_bar(oddsdf3)p
```

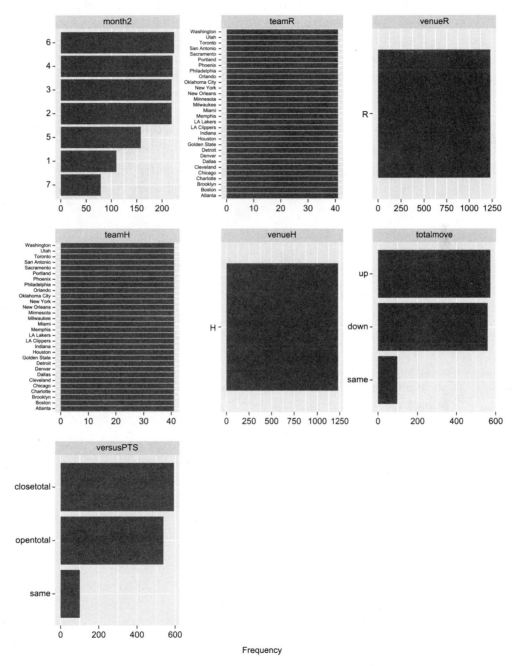

Figure 17.10 `DataExplorer` **bar charts for every oddsdf3 categorical variable**

But as you can see, some of these plots are absolutely meaningless and, of course, would never be generated if it weren't for automation. There are a couple of interesting takeaways, however, after sifting through the noise:

- The opening total was greater than the closing total almost as frequently as the closing total was greater than the opening total. Otherwise, they were the same about 100 times out of 1,230 games in our data set.
- More significantly for our purposes, the margin between the closing total (the over/under when the betting line closed) and total points scored was usually less than the margin between the opening total (the over/under when the betting line opened) and total points scored. This suggests that the closing total (influenced by gamblers) more frequently performed better than the opening total (generated by oddsmakers and their algorithms).

It's also possible to create a series of bar charts grouped by a discrete variable. In the line of code that follows, we create six stacked bar charts by the variable month2 (see figure 17.11):

```
plot_bar(oddsdf3, by = "month2")
```

A close examination of the totalmove and versusPTS stacked bar charts suggests month-over-month performance variances between or across the factor levels of those two variables.

Aside from the principal components analysis, which we purposely kept out of scope, we otherwise demonstrated almost every DataExplorer function; in the process, we gained some insights into our data and established a scope for further analysis. We'll get to that additional analysis soon enough, but in the meantime, we're going to explore opening and closing point spreads with the help of yet another automated EDA package.

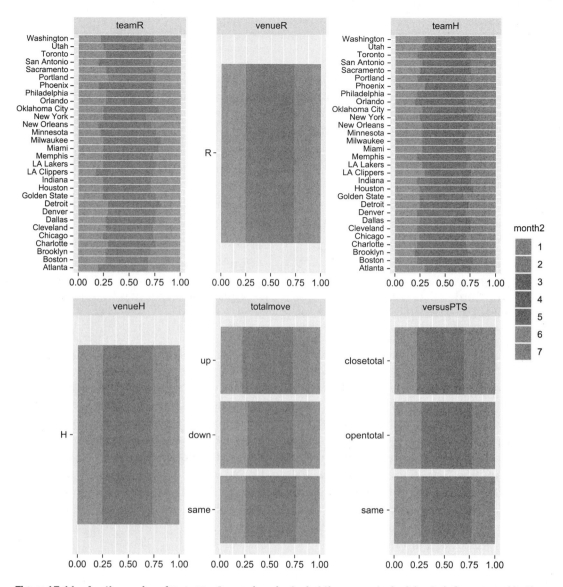

Figure 17.11   Another series of `DataExplorer` bar charts, but these are stacked due to being grouped by the `oddsdf3` variable `month2`

17.4.3   *Point spread EDA with SmartEDA*

Our new scope will be around the opening and closing point spreads and how they compare to final scores. We'll first create a new data set subset from oddsdf2, add some derived variables, and then explore the data with a package called `SmartEDA`.

WRANGLING DATA

By making a call to the `dplyr select()` function, we subset the oddsdf2 data set and pass the results to a new data set called oddsdf4:

```
oddsdf2 %>%
  select(teamR, venueR, ptsR, openspreadR, closespreadR, teamH,
         venueH, ptsH, openspreadH, closespreadH, month2) -> oddsdf4
```

Then, we go about creating our new variables and appending each of them to odd-sdf4. The first of these, called `margin`, is a continuous variable that equals the difference between `ptsR` and `ptsH`, or the difference between the number of points scored between the road and home teams:

```
oddsdf4 %>%
  mutate(margin = ptsR - ptsH) -> oddsdf4
```

Our second new variable, `diff_margin_openspreadH`, equals the absolute difference between the variables `margin` and `openspreadH`:

```
oddsdf4 %>%
  mutate(diff_margin_openspreadH = abs(margin - openspreadH)) -> oddsdf4
```

Our third variable, `diff_margin_closespreadH`, equals the absolute difference between the variables `margin` and `closespreadH`:

```
oddsdf4 %>%
  mutate(diff_margin_closespreadH = abs(margin - closespreadH)) -> oddsdf4
```

Our fourth and final variable, `spreadmove`, again requires that we call the `mutate()` function in tandem with the `case_when()` function. When the absolute value of `closespreadH` is greater than the absolute value of `openspreadH`, `spreadmove` should then equal `up`; from the perspective of home teams, then, when the absolute value of the closing spread is greater than the absolute value of the opening spread (it went, e.g., from 6 to 7 or –6 to –7), `spreadmove` should equal `up`. When the opposite condition is true, `spreadmove` should instead equal `down`. And, when there is no difference in the absolute values of opening and closing spreads, then `spreadmove` should equal `same`. Because `spreadmove` should be a categorical variable, we then call the `as.factor()` function to make it just that:

```
oddsdf4 %>%
  mutate(spreadmove = case_when(abs(closespreadH) >
                                abs(openspreadH) ~ "up",
                                abs(closespreadH) <
                                abs(openspreadH) ~ "down",
                                abs(closespreadH) ==
                                abs(openspreadH) ~ "same")) -> oddsdf4

oddsdf4$spreadmove <- factor(oddsdf4$spreadmove)
```

We then call the `select()` function to rearrange the oddsdf4 variables in a more logical order. A subsequent call to the `head()` function returns the top six oddsdf4 records:

```
oddsdf4 %>%
  select(11, 1, 2, 3, 6, 7, 8, 4, 5, 9, 10, 12, 13, 14, 15) -> oddsdf4

head(oddsdf4)
##   month2        teamR venueR ptsR       teamH venueH ptsH openspreadR
## 1      1 Philadelphia      R   87       Boston      H  105         5.0
## 2      1 Oklahoma City     R  100 Golden State      H  108        11.5
## 3      1     Milwaukee     R  113    Charlotte      H  112        -1.5
## 4      1      Brooklyn     R  100      Detroit      H  103         4.5
## 5      1       Memphis     R   83      Indiana      H  111         7.0
## 6      1         Miami     R  101      Orlando      H  104        -2.0
##   closespreadR openspreadH closespreadH margin diff_margin_openspreadH
## 1          4.5        -5.0         -4.5    -18                    13.0
## 2         12.0       -11.5        -12.0     -8                     3.5
## 3         -3.0         1.5          3.0      1                     0.5
## 4          6.0        -4.5         -6.0     -3                     1.5
## 5          7.5        -7.0         -7.5    -28                    21.0
## 6         -2.5         2.0          2.5     -3                     5.0
##   diff_margin_closespreadH spreadmove
## 1                     13.5       down
## 2                      4.0         up
## 3                      2.0         up
## 4                      3.0         up
## 5                     20.5         up
## 6                      5.5         up
```

CREATING THE EDA REPORT

The SmartEDA package is a cross of sorts between tableone and DataExplorer because it returns results in both tabular and graphical formats. But all things considered, SmartEDA bears more of a resemblance to DataExplorer; one reason is that, as we did with DataExplorer, we can also create an interactive HTML report that automatically aggregates other SmartEDA EDA functions into one function.

However, you'll readily notice that the SmartEDA functions aren't as intuitive or as simple as their DataExplorer equivalents. In addition, many of these same functions, when run manually, work best when you first break up your data set or just ask SmartEDA to output a random sample; we didn't have to do either with the DataExplorer package, or even the tableone package, for that matter.

In any event, we get a SmartEDA HTML report by passing two mandatory arguments, the oddsdf4 data set and the output file name, to the ExpReport() function (see figure 17.12). This will take several seconds to run:

```
ExpReport(oddsdf4, op_file = "oddsdf4.html")
```

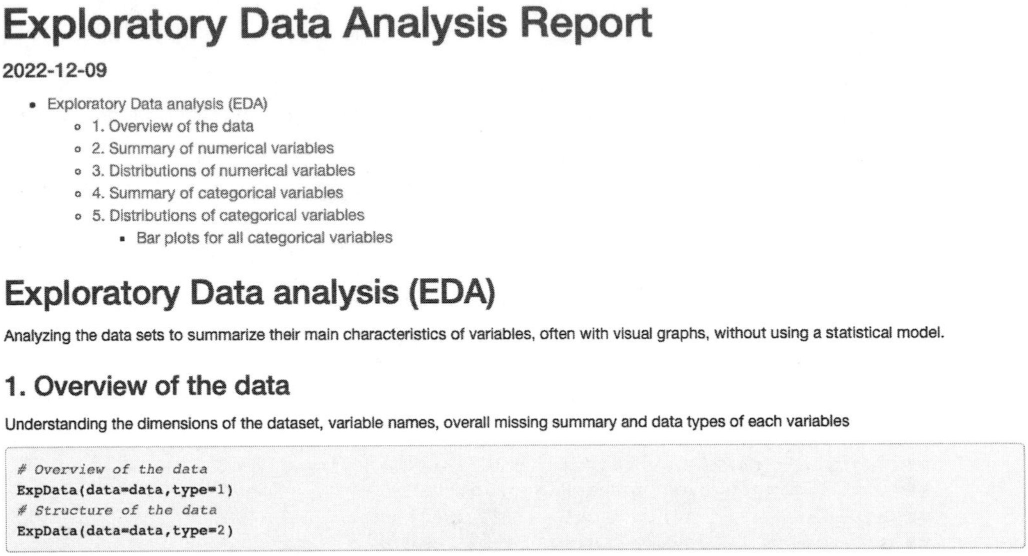

Exploratory Data Analysis Report

2022-12-09

- Exploratory Data analysis (EDA)
  - 1. Overview of the data
  - 2. Summary of numerical variables
  - 3. Distributions of numerical variables
  - 4. Summary of categorical variables
  - 5. Distributions of categorical variables
    - Bar plots for all categorical variables

Exploratory Data analysis (EDA)

Analyzing the data sets to summarize their main characteristics of variables, often with visual graphs, without using a statistical model.

1. Overview of the data

Understanding the dimensions of the dataset, variable names, overall missing summary and data types of each variables

```
# Overview of the data
ExpData(data=data,type=1)
# Structure of the data
ExpData(data=data,type=2)
```

Figure 17.12 The top of an interactive HTML EDA report from the `SmartEDA` package

OVERVIEW OF THE DATA

`SmartEDA` aggregates the following functions and bundles the outputs in the standalone HTML file we just created. Otherwise, when we pass oddsdf4 and the `type = 1` argument to the `ExpData()` function, `SmartEDA` returns a high-level overview of our data in the form of a table. We get the dimension, the number of variables for each class, and information around missing cases published in RStudio:

```
ExpData(oddsdf4, type = 1)
##                                          Descriptions     Value
## 1                                 Sample size (nrow)      1230
## 2                            No. of variables (ncol)        15
## 3                  No. of numeric/interger variables         9
## 4                            No. of factor variables         6
## 5                              No. of text variables         0
## 6                           No. of logical variables         0
## 7                        No. of identifier variables         0
## 8                              No. of date variables         0
## 9           No. of zero variance variables (uniform)         2
## 10             %. of variables having complete cases 100% (15)
## 11   %. of variables having >0% and <50% missing cases    0% (0)
## 12 %. of variables having >=50% and <90% missing cases    0% (0)
## 13           %. of variables having >=90% missing cases    0% (0)
```

When we instead pass the `type = 2` argument to the `ExpData()` function, `SmartEDA` returns the structure of our data, namely, the oddsdf4 variable names, their type, the row counts, and more information around missing data (of which there is none, of course):

```
ExpData(oddsdf4, type = 2)
##      Index            Variable_Name Variable_Type Sample_n Missing_Count
## 1        1                   month2        factor     1230             0
## 2        2                    teamR        factor     1230             0
## 3        3                   venueR        factor     1230             0
## 4        4                     ptsR       numeric     1230             0
## 5        5                    teamH        factor     1230             0
## 6        6                   venueH        factor     1230             0
## 7        7                     ptsH       numeric     1230             0
## 8        8              openspreadR       numeric     1230             0
## 9        9             closespreadR       numeric     1230             0
## 10      10              openspreadH       numeric     1230             0
## 11      11             closespreadH       numeric     1230             0
## 12      12                   margin       numeric     1230             0
## 13      13  diff_margin_openspreadH       numeric     1230             0
## 14      14 diff_margin_closespreadH       numeric     1230             0
## 15      15               spreadmove        factor     1230             0
##      Per_of_Missing No_of_distinct_values
## 1                 0                     7
## 2                 0                    30
## 3                 0                     1
## 4                 0                    74
## 5                 0                    30
## 6                 0                     1
## 7                 0                    71
## 8                 0                    63
## 9                 0                    63
## 10                0                    63
## 11                0                    63
## 12                0                    81
## 13                0                    82
## 14                0                    79
## 15                0                     3
```

SUMMARY OF CONTINUOUS VARIABLES

We get a summary of the oddsdf4 continuous variables by calling the ExpNumStat() function. By adding the Outlier = TRUE argument, we're instructing SmartEDA to return the lower hinge, upper hinge, and number of outliers in our data, among other measures that we get by default. The lower hinge (LB.25%) is the median of the lower half of the data up to and including the median; the upper hinge (UB.75%) is the median of the upper half of the data up to and including the median; we otherwise know these as the lower and upper quartiles. In addition, by adding round = 2 as a second argument, we're telling SmartEDA to return all the results with just two digits right of the decimal point.

There's a lot more to unpack here, but let's take a look at the nNeg, nZero, and nPos measures—these amount to, respectively, the number of records where each variable equals either a negative number, zero, or a positive number. The variables openspreadH and closespreadH equal negative numbers for almost two-thirds of the 1,230 oddsdf4 records, which means that the home team opened and/or closed as the favorite in almost 66% of the games during the 2018–19 NBA regular season. Now take a look at these same measures with respect to the derived variable margin, which is equal to ptsR minus ptsH: margin is negative just 729 times, corresponding to about 59% of the records. This aligns very well with what we learned back in chapter 9—that home teams win about 58% to 59% of all regular season games:

```
ExpNumStat(oddsdf4, Outlier = TRUE, round = 2)
##                              Vname  Group    TN  nNeg  nZero  nPos  NegInf  PosInf
## 6                     closespreadH    All  1230   804      1   425       0       0
## 4                     closespreadR    All  1230   425      1   804       0       0
## 9  diff_margin_closespreadH         All  1230     0     22  1208       0       0
## 8   diff_margin_openspreadH         All  1230     0     20  1210       0       0
## 7                           margin    All  1230   729      0   501       0       0
## 5                      openspreadH    All  1230   790     30   410       0       0
## 3                      openspreadR    All  1230   410     30   790       0       0
## 2                             ptsH    All  1230     0      0  1230       0       0
## 1                             ptsR    All  1230     0      0  1230       0       0
##      NA_Value  Per_of_Missing       sum     min    max     mean  median     SD
## 6            0              0   -3222.5   -18.5   17.0    -2.62    -3.5   6.59
## 4            0              0    3222.5   -17.0   18.5     2.62     3.5   6.59
## 9            0              0   12201.5     0.0   55.0     9.92     8.0   8.12
## 8            0              0   12365.0     0.0   53.5    10.05     8.0   8.22
## 7            0              0   -3351.0   -50.0   56.0    -2.72    -4.0  14.41
## 5            0              0   -3066.0   -18.5   16.0    -2.49    -3.0   6.45
## 3            0              0    3066.0   -16.0   18.5     2.49     3.0   6.45
## 2            0              0  138462.0    77.0  161.0   112.57   112.0  12.68
## 1            0              0  135111.0    68.0  168.0   109.85   110.0  12.48
##       CV   IQR  Skewness  Kurtosis  LB.25%  UB.75%  nOutliers
## 6  -2.52  10.0      0.20     -0.74  -22.50   17.50          0
## 4   2.52  10.0     -0.20     -0.74  -17.50   22.50          0
## 9   0.82   9.5      1.35      2.26  -10.25   27.75         49
## 8   0.82  10.0      1.37      2.32  -11.00   29.00         40
## 7  -5.29  19.0      0.06      0.23  -40.50   35.50         11
## 5  -2.59   9.5      0.18     -0.63  -21.75   16.25          0
## 3   2.59   9.5     -0.18     -0.63  -16.25   21.75          0
## 2   0.11  17.0      0.17      0.10   78.50  146.50         12
## 1   0.11  17.0      0.14      0.24   75.50  143.50         13
```

DISTRIBUTIONS OF CONTINUOUS VARIABLES

Most of the remaining SmartEDA content is visual. A call to the ExpOutQQ() function returns QQ plots of all continuous variables (see figure 17.13):

```
ExpOutQQ(oddsdf4, Page = c(2, 2), sample = 4)
```

It's fascinating to discover that the DataExplorer package, and now the SmartEDA package as well, feature QQ plots first and foremost to graphically represent the distribution of continuous data; after all, while QQ plots are regularly returned when running regression diagnostics, they are rarely featured in EDA. Here, we're instructing SmartEDA to return a random sample of four plots and to arrange them in a 2 × 2 matrix. Once more, when the plotted data falls on top of the diagonal line in a QQ plot, that data is normally distributed; if not, the data is skewed one way or another.

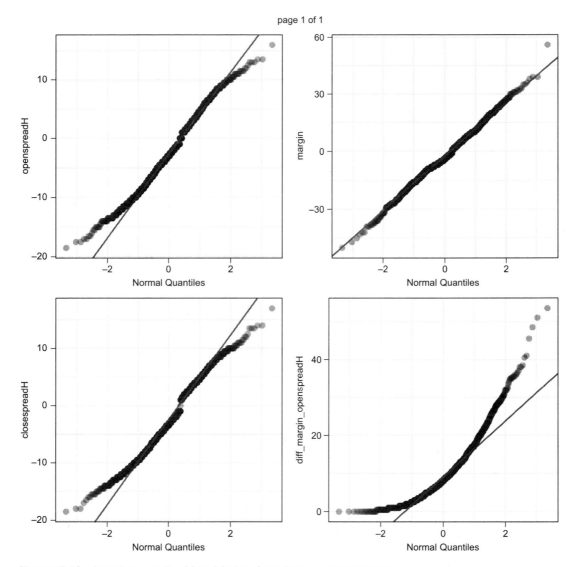

Figure 17.13   A random sample of four QQ plots from the `SmartEDA` package

Then, we call the `ExpNumViz()` function to get a random sample of four density plots, also arranged in a 2×2 matrix (see figure 17.14):

```
ExpNumViz(oddsdf4, Page = c(2,2), sample = 4)
```

It so happens that `SmartEDA` returned QQ plots and density plots for the variables `openspreadH` and `diff_margin_closespreadH`; `openspreadH` is normally distributed, whereas `diff_margin_closespreadH` isn't. Notice the probability distributions from their respective density plots, and compare those to their corresponding QQ plots. In addition, what's nice about these density plots is that `SmartEDA` prints the skewness and

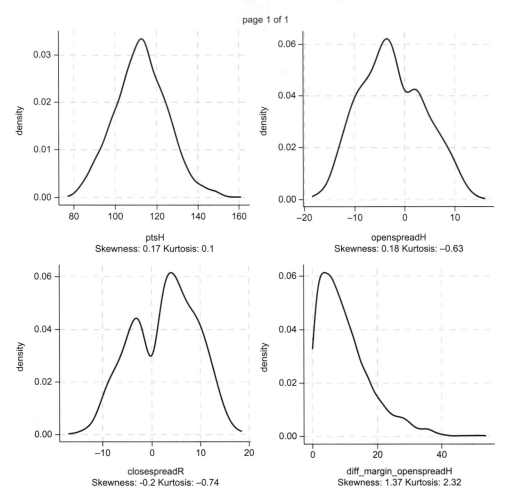

Figure 17.14   A random sample of four density plots from the `SmartEDA` package

kurtosis numbers. When the data is normally distributed, as it is for the variable `openspreadH`, skewness and kurtosis will both equal some number close to 0; alternatively, when the data is otherwise skewed, as it is for the variable `diff_margin_closespreadH`, skewness and kurtosis will instead equal numbers, positively or negatively, further from 0. In fact, skewness and kurtosis are positive or negative depending on how the data is skewed; when positively skewed, the measures are positive, and when negatively skewed, both measures are negative.

Finally, another call to `ExpNumVix()`, this time with `scatter = TRUE` passed as an additional argument, returns a random sample of four scatterplots arranged in a 2 × 2 matrix (see figure 17.15):

```
ExpNumViz(oddsdf4, Page = c(2,2), scatter = TRUE, sample = 4)p
```

Unfortunately, it's not possible to create a correlation matrix with SmartEDA; therefore, the only way to visualize the relationship between pairs of continuous variables is to create a series of scatterplots. The output file we previously created by calling the ExpReport() function actually contained 36 scatterplots.

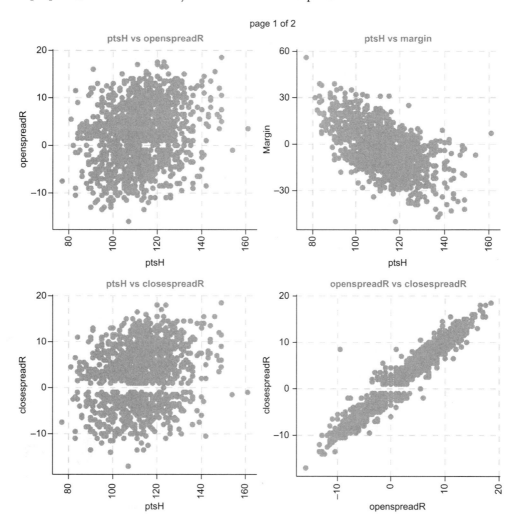

Figure 17.15   A random sample of four scatterplots from the SmartEDA package

CATEGORICAL VARIABLE ANALYSIS

That's it for our continuous data. As for our categorical variables, we first make a call to the ExpTable() function, which returns basic statistics for month2 and spreadmove in a tabular format. What's really nice is that ExpTable() breaks down our categorical data by factor level and provides the roll-ups for each. It's interesting to discover that the opening point spread increased almost 52% of the time and decreased just 32% of the time (it otherwise closed where it opened nearly 16% of the time):

```
ExpCTable(oddsdf4)
##       Variable Valid Frequency Percent CumPercent
## 1       month2     1       110    8.94       8.94
## 2       month2     2       219   17.80      26.74
## 3       month2     3       219   17.80      44.54
## 4       month2     4       221   17.97      62.51
## 5       month2     5       158   12.85      75.36
## 6       month2     6       224   18.21      93.57
## 7       month2     7        79    6.42      99.99
## 8       month2 TOTAL      1230      NA         NA
## 9    spreadmove  down       397   32.28      32.28
## 10   spreadmove  same       194   15.77      48.05
## 11   spreadmove    up       639   51.95     100.00
## 12   spreadmove TOTAL      1230      NA         NA
```

Finally, we twice subset our data on each categorical variable and then call the `ExpCatViz()` function. We get a pair of bar charts that graphically represent the data previously returned by calling the `ExpTable()` function (see figure 17.16):

```
select(oddsdf4, month2) -> temp1
ExpCatViz(temp1, Page = c(1, 1))

select(oddsdf4, spreadmove) -> temp2
ExpCatViz(temp2, Page = c(1, 1))
```

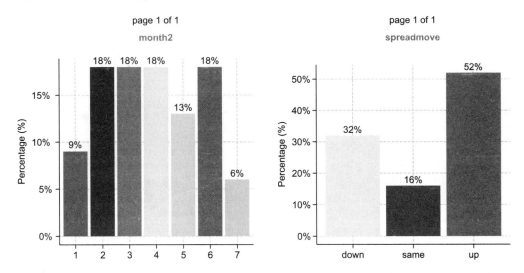

Figure 17.16   On the left, the bar chart displays the `month2` frequencies by factor level, and on the right, the bar chart displays the `spreadmove` frequencies by factor level.

Remember, the purpose of EDA is to get an initial read on a data set—it's not the be-all and end-all. That's up next, where we bring everything together.

17.5   Results

Regardless of how we subsequently slice and dice the data, the closing total outperformed the opening total, and the closing point spread outperformed the opening point spread—at least as far as the 2018–19 regular season is concerned. That is, closing totals and closing point spreads were more often nearer to game results than were opening totals and opening point spreads. This suggests that the masses—at least those who follow the NBA and are disposed to risk their earnings—add value above and beyond the expert predictions from the Las Vegas oddsmakers. We'll share the over/under results first.

17.5.1 Over/under

Our EDA exercise with the `DataExplorer` package returned some interesting insights and provided a good foundation from which to move forward. One of the bar charts showed that the variable `versusPTS` equals `closetotal` more frequently than it equals `opentotal`, though without providing the counts. Put differently, there appeared to be more games during the 2018–19 NBA regular season where the difference between the closing over/under and total points scored was less than the opening over/under and total points scored.

PLOTTING OPENING TOTAL AND CLOSING TOTAL PERFORMANCE VERSUS COMBINED POINTS

In the chunk of code that follows, we first pass the oddsdf3 data set to the `dplyr` `summarize()` function—SUM1 equals the number of instances where `diff_ptsT_opentotal` is greater than `diff_ptsT_closetotal`, SUM2 equals the number of instances where the opposite condition is true, and SUM3 equals the number of instances where `diff_ptsT_opentotal` and `diff_ptsT_closetotal` are the same.

These results are then passed to the `tidyr` `pivot_longer()` function, which increases the row count at the expense of the column count. Two new variables are created in the process, `sum` and `total`; SUM1, SUM2, and SUM3 are then converted to factors within `sum`, and their values are placed in the cells within `total`. All of this gets us an object we can then throw into a plot and analyze. The end result is a tibble called tblA:

```
oddsdf3 %>%
  summarize(SUM1 = sum(diff_ptsT_opentotal > diff_ptsT_closetotal),
            SUM2 = sum(diff_ptsT_closetotal > diff_ptsT_opentotal),
            SUM3 = sum(diff_ptsT_opentotal == diff_ptsT_closetotal)) %>%
  pivot_longer(cols = c("SUM1", "SUM2", "SUM3"),
               names_to = "sum",
               values_to = "total") -> tblA
```

Then we call the `ggplot2` `ggplot()` and `geom_bar()` functions to visualize tblA with a bar chart (see figure 17.17):

- Our x-axis variable is `sum`, and our y-axis variable is `total`. By adding the `fill` argument, we're telling R to color-code the bars by the variable `sum` rather than printing them in grayscale.
- By passing the `stat = "identity"` argument to the `geom_bar()` function, we're instructing R to map the height of the bars to the y-axis variable previously supplied to the `ggplot` aesthetic.

- Affixing labels that tie back to the y-axis variable is always a nice enhancement to any bar chart; here, the `geom_text()` function places the y-axis totals atop the bars and prints them in a bold font. If we preferred to affix the labels somewhere inside the bars, we would merely modify the `vjust` argument (short for vertical adjustment) to a positive number.
- Adding labels atop the bars usually requires, for aesthetic purposes, that we then extend the length of the y-axis by calling the `ylim()` function and specifying the starting and ending points.
- By calling the `scale_x_discrete()` function, we replace SUM1, SUM2, and SUM3 with more descriptive labels, which then preclude the need to take up space with a legend.

All of this comes together in the following chunk of code:

```
p1 <- ggplot(tblA, aes(x = sum, y = total, fill = sum)) +
  geom_bar(stat = "identity") +
  geom_text(aes(label = total), vjust = -0.2, fontface = "bold") +
  labs(title =
          "Opening Total and Closing Total Performance vs. Combined Points",
          subtitle = "Closing Total performed ~10% better than Opening Total",
          caption = "2018-19 Regular Season",
          x = "",
          y = "Counts") +
  ylim(0, 625) +
  theme(plot.title = element_text(face = "bold")) +
  scale_x_discrete(labels = c("SUM1" = "closetotal\nBEAT\nopentotal",
                              "SUM2" = "opentotal\nBEAT\nclosetotal",
                              "SUM3" = "closetotal\nEQUALED\nopentotal")) +
  theme(legend.position = "none")
print(p1)
```

As it turns out, the closing total outperformed the opening total by approximately 10%.

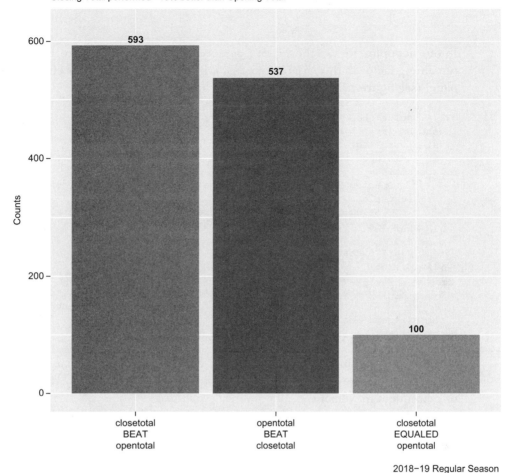

Opening Total and Closing Total Performance versus Combined Points
Closing Total performed ~10% better than Opening Total

2018–19 Regular Season

Figure 17.17   A bar chart shows that the closing total outperformed the opening total versus total points scored by approximately 10%.

BY MOVEMENT

The next chunk of code is a replication of the `dplyr` and `tidyr` code that produced tblA—except that we're inserting the `dplyr` `group_by()` function to group the results by each factor in the variable `totalmove` and then adding the `filter()` function to exclude the 100 instances where `diff_ptsT_opentotal` equals `diff_ptsT_closetotal`. Our results are then cast to a tibble called tblB:

```
oddsdf3 %>%
  group_by(totalmove) %>%
  summarize(SUM1 = sum(diff_ptsT_closetotal > diff_ptsT_opentotal),
            SUM2 = sum(diff_ptsT_opentotal > diff_ptsT_closetotal),
            SUM3 = sum(diff_ptsT_opentotal == diff_ptsT_closetotal)) %>%
```

```
        pivot_longer(cols = c("SUM1", "SUM2", "SUM3"),
                    names_to = "sum",
                    values_to = "total") %>%
filter(total > 100) -> tblB
```

In our next plot, we call the `ggplot2 facet_wrap()` function to create a panel for each remaining factor in the variable `totalmove`. R then creates a like bar chart within each panel (see figure 17.18):

```
p2 <- ggplot(tblB, aes(x = sum, y = total, fill = sum))+
  geom_bar(stat = "identity") +
  facet_wrap(~totalmove) +
  geom_text(aes(label = total), vjust = -0.2, fontface = "bold") +
  labs(title =
           "Opening Total and Closing Total Performance by O/U Movement",
       subtitle =
          "Closing Total performed ~10% better than Opening Total",
       caption = "2018-19 Regular Season",
       x = "",
       y = "Counts") +
  ylim(0, 325) +
  theme(plot.title = element_text(face = "bold")) +
  scale_x_discrete(labels = c("SUM1" = "opentotal\nBEAT\nclosetotal",
                              "SUM2" = "closetotal\nBEAT\nopentotal")) +
  theme(legend.position = "none")
print(p2)
```

Whether the opening total then went up or down before closing is largely immaterial. It turns out that the closing total outperformed the opening total by 10%, irrespective of subsequent movement.

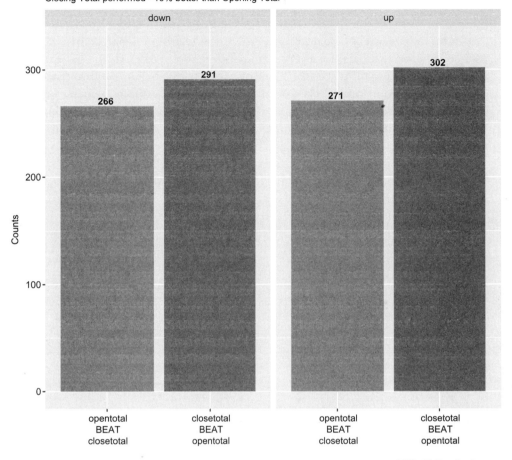

Figure 17.18   A facet plot that breaks down opening and closing totals versus points scored by factors in the variable `totalmove`. **It turns out that the closing total outperformed the opening total by about 10%, irrespective of whether the opening total then went up or down.**

BY MONTH

Next, we pass oddsdf3 to the `group_by()` and `summarize()` functions to tally the number of instances where `diff_ptsT_opentotal` is less than `diff_ptsT_closetotal` and where `diff_ptsT_closetotal` is less than `diff_ptsT_opentotal` by each factor in the variable month2. These results are then passed to the `pivot_longer()` function so that we get SUM1 and SUM2 results for every month. Our final results are reflected in a tibble called tblC:

```
oddsdf3 %>%
  group_by(month2) %>%
  summarize(SUM1 = sum(diff_ptsT_opentotal < diff_ptsT_closetotal),
            SUM2 = sum(diff_ptsT_closetotal < diff_ptsT_opentotal)) %>%
```

```
    pivot_longer(cols = c("SUM1", "SUM2"),
                 names_to = "sum",
                 values_to = "total") -> tblC
```

Our next `ggplot2` visualization is therefore a grouped bar chart where we get two results, or two bars, for every month (see figure 17.19). The `geom_bar()` position = "dodge" argument places each pair of bars side by side and adjoins them.

To prevent our labels from then straddling each pair of bars, we must add the `position_dodge()` function to the `geom_text()` function. By specifying the width to equal 0.9, the labels are centered atop the bars; even a minor adjustment from 0.9 to 1 would instead affix the labels left of center.

By calling the `scale_x_discrete()` function, we're able to map each `month2` factor to actual months, so that `1` equals October, `2` equals November, and so forth. And because our x-axis labels tie back to the variable `month2` and not the variable `sum`, a legend, placed beneath the plot, is therefore in order:

```
p3 <-ggplot(tblC, aes(x = month2, y = total,
                      fill = factor(sum, levels = c("SUM1", "SUM2")))) +
  geom_bar(position = "dodge", stat = "identity") +
  geom_text(aes(label = total), position = position_dodge(width = 0.9),
            vjust = -0.2, fontface = "bold") +
  labs(title =
         "Month-over-Month Opening Total and Closing Total Performance",
       subtitle = "Closing Total beat Opening Total in 4 of 7 Months",
       caption = "2018-19 Regular Season",
       x = "Month",
       y = "Counts") +
  ylim(0, 120) +
  scale_fill_discrete(name = "",
                      labels = c("Opening Total", "Closing Total")) +
  scale_x_discrete(labels = c("1" = "October", "2" = "November",
                              "3" = "December", "4" = "January",
                              "5" = "February", "6" = "March",
                              "7" = "April")) +
  theme(legend.position = "bottom") +
  theme(plot.title = element_text(face = "bold"))
print(p3)
```

The closing total outperformed the opening total in four months out of seven. However, the most fascinating, and maybe most significant, results are from October and November 2018. In these first two months of the regular season, with relatively few observations to work from, the closing total substantially outperformed the opening total.

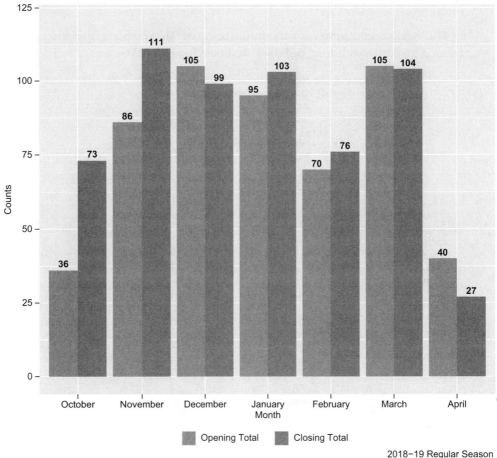

Figure 17.19   Opening total versus closing total performance by month. The 2018–19 NBA regular season started in October and ended the following April.

PLOTTING OPENING TOTAL AND CLOSING TOTAL VARIANCES VERSUS COMBINED POINTS

Now we're interested in the average variances between the opening and closing totals and the combined point totals between opposing teams. We pass oddsdf3 to the summarize() function, which computes the means for diff_ptsT_opentotal and diff_ptsT_closetotal. The initial results are then passed to the pivot_longer() function to convert AVG1 and AVG2 to factors within a new variable called avg and to place their values within another new variable called value. The final results are cast to a tibble called tblD:

```
oddsdf3 %>%
    summarize(AVG1 = mean(diff_ptsT_opentotal),
              AVG2 = mean(diff_ptsT_closetotal)) %>%
```

```
pivot_longer(cols = c("AVG1", "AVG2"),
        names_to = "avg",
        values_to = "value") -> tblD
```

Our next visualization is a very simple bar chart that displays opening total and closing total variances with total points scored (see figure 17.20).

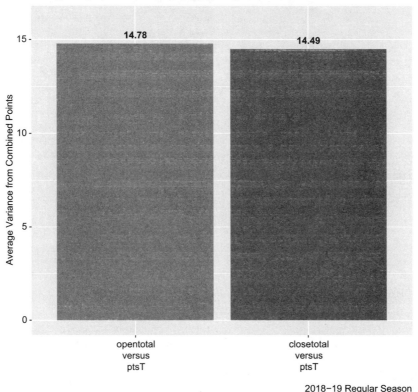

Figure 17.20   The average variances between opening and closing totals and combined points scored by opposing teams

Rather than calling the `geom_bar()` function and passing the `stat = "identity"` argument, we merely call the `geom_col()` function instead. By inserting the base R `round()` function inside the `geom_text()` function, our labels are guaranteed to include only two digits right of the decimal point:

```
p4 <- ggplot(tblD, aes(x = avg, y = value, fill = avg)) +
  geom_col() +
  geom_text(aes(label = round(value, 2)), vjust = -0.2,
            fontface = "bold") +
  labs(title =
```

```
                "Variances: Opening and Closing Totals vs. Combined Points",
              subtitle = "Closing Total performed ~2% better than Opening Total",
              caption = "2018-19 Regular Season",
              x = "",
              y = "Average Variance from Combined Points") +
      ylim(0, 16) +
      theme(plot.title = element_text(face = "bold")) +
      scale_x_discrete(labels = c("AVG1" = "opentotal\nversus\nptsT",
                                  "AVG2" = "closetotal\nversus\nptsT")) +
      theme(legend.position = "none")
print(p4)
```

The variances are obviously very similar, but the closing total did, in fact, outperform the opening total by about 2%.

BY MOVEMENT

We then break down these same results by whether the opening total went up or down before closing; therefore, we insert the `group_by()` function into a copy of our `dplyr` and `tidyr` code to group the results by each factor in the variable `totalmove`. Then, we call the `filter()` function to limit the final results to where `totalmove` doesn't equal `same`. We subsequently get a tibble called tblE:

```
oddsdf3 %>%
  group_by(totalmove) %>%
  summarize(AVG1 = mean(diff_ptsT_opentotal),
            AVG2 = mean(diff_ptsT_closetotal)) %>%
  pivot_longer(cols = c("AVG1", "AVG2"),
               names_to = "avg",
               values_to = "value") %>%
filter(totalmove != "same") -> tblE
```

Our next visualization is a facet plot (see figure 17.21) that contains one panel for each of the remaining factors in the tblE variable `totalmove`. Once more, we've replaced the `geom_bar()` function with `geom_col()`. In addition, we've modified the aesthetic parameter `vjust` from `-0.2` to `1.5`, which affixes our labels *below* the top of the bars. As a result, it then becomes unnecessary to call the `ylim()` function to extend the length of the y-axis:

```
p5 <- ggplot(tblE, aes(x = avg, y = value, fill = avg)) +
  geom_col() +
  facet_wrap(~totalmove) +
  geom_text(aes(label = round(value, 2)), vjust = 1.5,
            fontface = "bold") +
  labs(title =
         "Opening Total and Closing Total Performance by O/U Movement",
       subtitle =
         "Closing Total performed ~2% better than Opening Total",
       caption = "2018-19 Regular Season",
       x = "",
       y = "Average Variance from Combined Points") +
  theme(plot.title = element_text(face = "bold")) +
```

```
    scale_x_discrete(labels = c("AVG1" = "opentotal",
                                "AVG2" = "closetotal")) +
    theme(legend.position = "none")
print(p5)
```

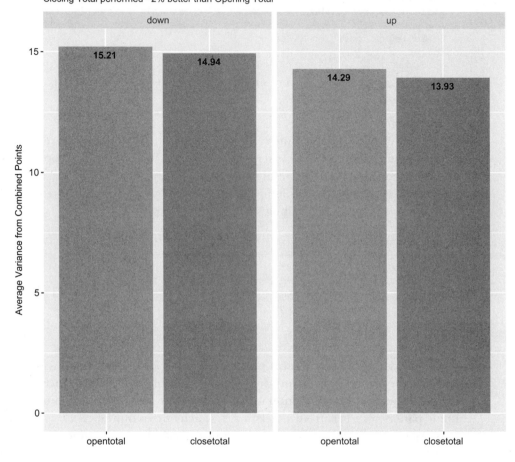

Figure 17.21   The average variances between opening and closing totals and combined points scored by opposing teams separated by each remaining factor in the variable `totalmove`

The variances are again very similar regardless of which direction the opening total went before closing. Nevertheless, the closing total outperformed the opening total by 2% irrespective of whether the opening total went up or down.

BY MONTH

Finally, we'll plot these variances by month. We therefore pass the oddsdf3 data set to the `group_by()` and `summarize()` functions to compute the `diff_ptsT_opentotal` and diff_ptsT_closetotal means by each factor in the variable month2. By subsequently calling the pivot_longer() function, we transform AVG1 and AVG2 from variables to factors within a new variable called avg and place their values within yet another new variable called value. Our results are cast to a tibble called tblF:

```
oddsdf3 %>%
  group_by(month2) %>%
  summarize(AVG1 = mean(diff_ptsT_opentotal),
            AVG2 = mean(diff_ptsT_closetotal)) %>%
  pivot_longer(cols = c("AVG1", "AVG2"),
               names_to = "avg",
               values_to = "value") -> tblF
```

We've made some aesthetic changes from our previous month-over-month plot (see figure 17.22). Rather than pass the position = "dodge" argument to the geom_bar() function, this time, we pass position_dodge() and specify a width of 0.5, which effectively obscures half the width of one series of bars by the other series. As a result, we then round the labels to the nearest whole number; otherwise, the labels would often blend together and be indecipherable. To center these same labels atop the bars, we also add the position_dodge() function to the geom_text() function; however, this time we specify the width to also equal 0.5 rather than 0.9 as before:

```
p6 <-ggplot(tblF, aes(x = month2, y = value,
                      fill = factor(avg, levels = c("AVG1", "AVG2")))) +
  geom_bar(position = position_dodge(width = 0.5), stat = "identity") +
  geom_text(aes(label = round(value, 0)),
            position = position_dodge(width = 0.5), vjust = -0.2,
            fontface = "bold") +
  labs(title =
         "Month-over-Month Opening Total and Closing Total Performance",
       subtitle =
         "Closing Total beat or equaled Opening Total in 7 of 7 Months",
       caption = "2018-19 Regular Season",
       x = "Month",
       y = "Average Variance from Combined Points") +
  ylim(0,18) +
  scale_fill_discrete(name = "", labels = c("Opening Total",
                                            "Closing Total")) +
  scale_x_discrete(labels = c("1" = "October", "2" = "November",
                              "3" = "December", "4" = "January",
                              "5" = "February", "6" = "March",
                              "7" = "April")) +
  theme(legend.position = "bottom") +
  theme(plot.title = element_text(face = "bold"))
print(p6)
```

The closing total beat or at least equaled the opening total in all seven months of the 2018–19 NBA regular season—if we go by the rounded variances. If we instead go by the visual representation of the same results, the closing total bested the opening total in five out of seven months. The most significant variances favoring the closing total

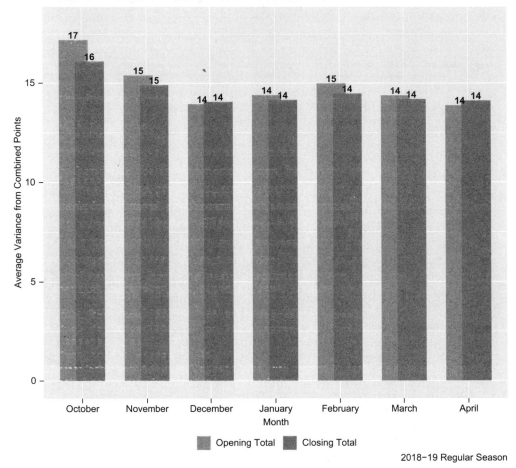

Figure 17.22   The month-over-month average variances between opening and closing totals and combined points scored. The labels affixed atop the bars have been rounded to the nearest whole number.

were in October and November 2018 when, again, relatively few games had been played, and thus there were just a handful of observations to work from.

We'll now pivot and report on the performance differences between the opening and closing point spreads.

17.5.2   *Point spreads*

To minimize the presentation of duplicate lines of code (notwithstanding variable swaps), we'll display our results by printing tibbles and eschewing any further visualizations. We'll begin by tallying the number of times the closing spread was closer to the final margin than was the opening spread, the number of times the opening spread was closer to the final margin, and the number of times the closing and opening spreads were the same. The following chunk of code matches the dplyr and tidyr code that previously produced tblA; here, we're casting the results to a tibble called tblG:

```
oddsdf4 %>%
  summarize(SUM1 = sum(diff_margin_openspreadH >
                         diff_margin_closespreadH),
            SUM2 = sum(diff_margin_closespreadH >
                         diff_margin_openspreadH),
            SUM3 = sum(diff_margin_openspreadH ==
                         diff_margin_closespreadH)) %>%
  pivot_longer(cols = c("SUM1", "SUM2", "SUM3"),
               names_to = "sum",
               values_to = "total") -> tblG
print(tblG)
## # A tibble: 3 x 2
##    sum   total
##    <chr> <int>
## 1 SUM1    553
## 2 SUM2    493
## 3 SUM3    184
```

The closing total outperformed the opening total by approximately 11% (equal to the inverse of SUM2 divided by SUM1).

Next, we break down these same results by whether the opening spread then moved up or down; our final results don't include instances where the variable spreadmove equals same or where the variable sum equals SUM3. The following lines of code that ultimately produce a tibble called tblH are similar to the code that produced tblB:

```
oddsdf4 %>%
  group_by(spreadmove) %>%
  summarize(SUM1 = sum(diff_margin_closespreadH >
                         diff_margin_openspreadH),
            SUM2 = sum(diff_margin_openspreadH >
                         diff_margin_closespreadH),
            SUM3 = sum(diff_margin_openspreadH ==
                         diff_margin_closespreadH)) %>%
  pivot_longer(cols = c("SUM1", "SUM2", "SUM3"),
               names_to = "sum",
               values_to = "total") %>%
  filter(spreadmove != "same", sum != "SUM3") -> tblH
print(tblH)
## # A tibble: 4 x 3
##    spreadmove sum   total
##    <fct>      <chr> <int>
## 1 down        SUM1    185
## 2 down        SUM2    212
## 3 up          SUM1    303
## 4 up          SUM2    331
```

The closing spread outperformed the opening spread regardless of whether the opening spread subsequently moved up or down before closing, but the results vary by the spreadmove factor level. When the opening spread went down, the closing spread outperformed the opening spread by about 13%; when the opening spread went up, the closing spread outperformed the opening spread by about 8%.

Then, we compute how the opening and closing spreads performed against the final margins by each factor in the variable month2. The following chunk of code, which produces a tibble called tblI, matches the tblC code very well:

```
oddsdf4 %>%
  group_by(month2) %>%
  summarize(SUM1 = sum(diff_margin_openspreadH <
                       diff_margin_closespreadH),
            SUM2 = sum(diff_margin_closespreadH <
                       diff_margin_openspreadH)) %>%
  pivot_longer(cols = c("SUM1", "SUM2"),
               names_to = "sum",
               values_to = "total") -> tblI
print(tblI)
## # A tibble: 14 × 3
##    month2 sum   total
##    <fct>  <chr> <int>
##  1 1      SUM1     52
##  2 1      SUM2     43
##  3 2      SUM1     85
##  4 2      SUM2     90
##  5 3      SUM1     75
##  6 3      SUM2    110
##  7 4      SUM1     95
##  8 4      SUM2     94
##  9 5      SUM1     70
## 10 5      SUM2     71
## 11 6      SUM1     87
## 12 6      SUM2    108
## 13 7      SUM1     29
## 14 7      SUM2     37
```

The closing spread outperformed the opening spread in five out of seven months—two of the first three months of the 2018–19 NBA regular season plus, curiously, the last three months.

Next, we compute the average variance between the opening and closing spreads versus the final margin and cast the results to a tibble called tblJ (see the tblD code for comparison purposes):

```
oddsdf4 %>%
  summarize(AVG1 = mean(diff_margin_openspreadH),
            AVG2 = mean(diff_margin_closespreadH)) %>%
  pivot_longer(cols = c("AVG1", "AVG2"),
               names_to = "avg",
               values_to = "value") -> tblJ
print(tblJ)
```

```
## # A tibble: 2 × 2
##    avg    value
##    <chr>  <dbl>
## 1  AVG1   10.1
## 2  AVG2    9.92
```

The closing spread outperformed the opening spread by approximately 2%.

We then compute these same variances by whether the opening spread moved up or down. Our results, pushed to a tibble called tblK, don't include instances where the variable spreadmove equals same (see the code for tblE for a comparison):

```
oddsdf4 %>%
  group_by(spreadmove) %>%
  summarize(AVG1 = mean(diff_margin_openspreadH),
            AVG2 = mean(diff_margin_closespreadH)) %>%
  pivot_longer(cols = c("AVG1", "AVG2"),
               names_to = "avg",
               values_to = "value") %>%
  filter(spreadmove != "same") -> tblK
print(tblK)
## # A tibble: 4 × 3
##    spreadmove avg   value
##    <fct>      <chr> <dbl>
## 1  down       AVG1  10.8
## 2  down       AVG2  10.6
## 3  up         AVG1   9.79
## 4  up         AVG2   9.68
```

The closing spread outperformed the opening spread more or less equally irrespective of whether the opening spread then moved up or down before closing.

Finally, we compute the month-over-month opening and closing performances against the final margins (see the tblF code for a comparison):

```
oddsdf4 %>%
  group_by(month2) %>%
  summarize(AVG1 = mean(diff_margin_openspreadH),
            AVG2 = mean(diff_margin_closespreadH)) %>%
  pivot_longer(cols = c("AVG1", "AVG2"),
               names_to = "avg",
               values_to = "value") -> tblL
print(tblL)
## # A tibble: 14 × 3
##    month2 avg   value
##    <fct>  <chr> <dbl>
## 1  1      AVG1   9.92
## 2  1      AVG2   9.98
## 3  2      AVG1  10.4
## 4  2      AVG2  10.3
## 5  3      AVG1  10.4
## 6  3      AVG2  10.1
## 7  4      AVG1   9.79
## 8  4      AVG2   9.75
```

```
##  9 5      AVG1    9.46
## 10 5      AVG2    9.33
## 11 6      AVG1   10.2
## 12 6      AVG2    9.96
## 13 7      AVG1    9.80
## 14 7      AVG2    9.66
```

The closing spread outperformed the opening spread in every month of the 2018–19 NBA regular season, except (curiously) in the first month.

While some of these variances—not just between the opening and closing spreads, but also between the opening and closing totals—might appear small, they are hardly immaterial. In the gambling world, small variances usually have large financial ramifications, for the casinos and wagerers alike. In the final analysis, if only based on 2018–19 regular season data, the closing total and the closing spread, influenced by gamblers, were more often than not nearer end-of-game results than the opening total and the opening spread established by Las Vegas oddsmakers. Furthermore, the "value add" from gamblers was more prevalent early in the 2018–19 season, when there wasn't much historical data to work with, than later on. The relative lack of training data therefore appeared to affect the oddsmakers more than it affected the collective intelligence of the wagerers.

In the next chapter, we'll examine how the salary cap, which the NBA implemented between the 1983–84 and 1984–85 seasons, *might* have affected intra-season and inter-season parity. We'll introduce several statistical measures of dispersion to quantify parity before and after 1985 to determine whether the salary cap actually improved parity as the league said it would.

Summary

- The upside to automated EDA is that you can produce more with less, that is, more content with fewer lines of code. This also allows you to focus on running statistical tests, developing predictive models, creating unsupervised algorithms, and so on.

- The downside to automated EDA is that you probably won't get optimal content returned; that is, you'll likely get results that don't matter and won't get other results that would and should matter.

- Manual, or methodical, EDA approaches compel you to think about your data and, along the way, provide a tremendous learning opportunity. Automated EDA is akin to a global positioning system—you'll get to a predetermined destination, but you might not know how you got there.

- When it comes to automated or manual, it doesn't necessarily have to be either/or; some mix of automated and manual EDA could conceivably be a great solution for many projects. In addition, you can pick and choose which `tableone`, `DataExplorer`, and/or `SmartEDA` functions you might want to run manually to complement base R and `tidyverse` functions.

- One more point about automated EDA and specifically the three packages that were demonstrated: though `tableone`, `DataExplorer`, and `SmartEDA` are no doubt three of the mostly popular automated EDA packages, that doesn't necessarily mean they've been adequately vetted. The manual functions from `SmartEDA` are quirky at best and buggy at worst. `DataExplorer` outputs a relatively polished and thorough combination of tabular and graphical results that can be saved in a standalone file and then shared; it's therefore the best of these three automated EDA packages.

- Our results consistently demonstrated that closing totals and closing spreads are nearer to final results than opening totals and opening spreads. Gamblers add value, especially early in the season when there are relatively few games or results from which to establish opening odds.

- Wisdom therefore exists in crowds; the idea that a mass of people operating independently and with skin in the game are smarter than a much smaller number of experts may very well be true.

Statistical
dispersion methods 18

This chapter covers

- Measures of statistical dispersion
- Variance method
- Standard deviation method
- Range method
- Mean absolute deviation method
- Median absolute deviation method
- Computing churn
- Creating pyramid plots

Our primary purpose here is to introduce several methods of statistical dispersion. Otherwise known as statistical variability or spread, statistical dispersion is a measure of how much a vector of continuous data is spread out or scattered around a middle value. It's often not enough to just know the mean or median; knowing the methods by which to compute statistical dispersion is essential for gaining a true understanding of numeric data, with practical implications around assessing risk and measuring consistency and volatility frequently on the line.

Here's the context for us: between the 1983–84 and 1984–85 seasons, the NBA introduced a salary cap. This meant that teams could only spend so much money every year on player salaries, with some allowable exceptions. (The salary cap remains in effect, with annual adjustments for inflation, increases in roster sizes, and other factors.) According to the NBA powers that be, the purported justification for a salary cap—or to put it more bluntly, the reason for restricting the amount of money players could make—was to create parity, where teams would have roughly equivalent talent that would lead to less predictable outcomes. The league convinced the players—and their union—that parity was good for the financial health and long-term sustainability of the league; the players (and everyone else, including fans) would benefit by a financially and otherwise secure NBA supported by a salary cap–driven condition of everlasting parity.

Just to be clear, we're now talking about *intra*-season parity, where the dispersion in regular season wins across the league, post–salary cap, should be less than what it was pre–salary cap.

Did the NBA really have an intra-season parity problem prior to the 1984–85 season? If so, did the salary cap effectively solve that problem? Our plan is to answer these questions by incrementally demonstrating several statistical measures of dispersion, computing the same across a vector of regular season wins grouped by season, and plotting the results before and after the salary cap.

However, there's also *inter*-season parity, where the year-over-year churn of the NBA's best teams should be greater after the salary cap than it was before.

Did the salary cap increase the annual turnover at the top of the league from the pre–salary cap years, or did it not? Our secondary purpose is to therefore evaluate what effect, if any, the salary cap had on inter-season parity; we'll demonstrate one way of computing churn and plot the same year-over-year before and after the salary cap. When all is said and done, we want to validate the salary cap's effects on intra-season and inter-season parity or sow doubt regarding those effects. Spoiler alert: we'll sow doubt.

We'll begin by loading the one package we need to go above and beyond base R and accomplish these goals.

18.1 Loading a package

We'll wrangle our data with `dplyr` and `tidyr` functions and visualize our intra-season and inter-season results with `ggplot2` functions. Our first and only call to the `library()` function loads the `tidyverse` universe of packages; otherwise, base R functions will suit us just fine:

```
library(tidyverse)
```

We'll import our two data sets next.

18.2 Importing data

The first of our two data sets contains annual salary cap figures in real dollars scraped from www.basketball-reference.com and the same in 2021 dollars, adjusted for inflation using a tool from www.usinflationcalculator.com. Whereas we previously imported a similar file that spanned the 2000 through 2017 NBA seasons, this file—salary_cap2.csv, which equals an object called cap—covers the 1985 through 2021 seasons.

The second of our two data sets—team_records.csv (downloaded from Kaggle), which equals an object called records—contains annual won-loss records for every NBA team between the 1961 and 2018 regular seasons.

We import both data sets and save them in our default working directory by calling the readr read_csv() function twice:

```
cap <- read_csv("salary_cap2.csv")

records <- read_csv("team_records.csv")
```

More on these two data sets is coming up next.

18.3 *Exploring and wrangling data*

We previously visualized NBA salary cap data, real and adjusted, with a time-series chart; here, we'll visualize the same with what's called a pyramid chart. A pyramid chart, sometimes called a triangle chart, is a terrific option when displaying hierarchical data, either right side up or upside down.

Our choice of visualizations means we'll first have to wrangle the cap data set. A pyramid chart somewhat resembles a stacked bar chart—which displays numeric values across two or more categorical variables—that's been rotated 90 degrees; the pyramid, or triangle, effect is created by originating each "half" of every bar at 0 and drawing them in opposite directions. This means we have to convert real or adjusted dollars to negative numbers, so we'll convert real dollars to negatives simply by multiplying every cell by –1.

A call to the base R head() function then returns the first six observations in cap:

```
cap$real <- cap$real * -1

head(cap)
##    season        real    adjusted
## 1 2020-21 -109140000 109140000
## 2 2019-20 -109140000 114267422
## 3 2018-19 -101869000 107970613
## 4 2017-18  -99093000 106931428
## 5 2016-17  -94143000 101015531
## 6 2015-16  -70000000  76710179
```

Then, we pass cap to the tidyr pivot_longer() function; the former columns real and adjusted become factors within a new column called type, and their values fall within another new column called cap. These changes are reflected in a tibble called new_cap. Another call to the head() function reveals the aftereffect of this operation:

```
cap %>%
  pivot_longer(cols = c("real", "adjusted"),
               names_to = "type",
```

```
                    values_to = "cap") -> new_cap

head(new_cap)
## # A tibble: 6 × 3
##   season  type            cap
##   <chr>   <chr>         <dbl>
## 1 2020-21 real     -109140000
## 2 2020-21 adjusted  109140000
## 3 2019-20 real     -109140000
## 4 2019-20 adjusted  114267422
## 5 2018-19 real     -101869000
## 6 2018-19 adjusted  107970613
```

Next, we define the breaks and labels for our pyramid chart. The breaks are defined by calling the base R `seq()` function and passing three arguments that represent the y-axis minimum and maximum values and how the ticks should be incremented. The labels are defined by calling the base R `paste0()` function, which rescales the ticks and concatenates the values with an uppercase `M`; as a result, a figure such as 120000000 is converted to 120M:

```
breaks <- seq(-120000000, 120000000, 10000000)
labels <- paste0(as.character(c(seq(120, 0, -10), seq(10, 120, 10))), "M")
```

Now, here are the nuts and bolts of our forthcoming `ggplot2` pyramid chart (see figure 18.1):

- We initialize the plot by calling the `ggplot()` function; new_cap is our data source, the variable season is our x-axis variable, and the variable cap is our y-axis variable. The `fill` argument establishes a color scheme for the chart around the two factors within the variable `type`; the `scale_fill_discrete()` function tells R to create a legend pointing to the same. By default, legends are deployed to the right of a `ggplot2` chart, but they can be moved almost anywhere you prefer; here, we've made the decision to position the legend at the bottom of the plot.
- The `geom_col()` function is a way to tell R to then draw a bar chart (remember, a pyramid chart, at least in some ways, resembles a bar chart). The `geom_col()` function equals the `geom_bar()` function when the `stat = "identity"` argument is passed to the latter. Otherwise, we want R to draw the bars at 60% of the default width.
- The `scale_y_continuous()` function inserts the breaks and labels we established up front.
- The `coord_flip()` function rotates our chart, including the x- and y-axes, 90 degrees, thereby producing an upside-down pyramid chart (upside down because the x-axis is stacked in reverse chronological order from top to bottom).

Following is the `ggplot2` code chunk for our pyramid chart:

```
p1 <- ggplot(new_cap, aes(x = season, y = cap, fill = type)) +
  geom_col(width = .6) +
  scale_y_continuous(breaks = breaks,
                     labels = labels) +
  coord_flip() +
  labs(title = "NBA Salary Cap History: 1984-85 to 2020-21",
       x = "Season",
       y = "Real or Adjusted Cap",
       caption = "salary cap was introduced prior to the 1984-85 season") +
  scale_fill_discrete(name = "",
                      labels = c("Adjusted Dollars", "Real Dollars")) +
  theme(plot.title = element_text(face = "bold")) +
  theme(axis.text.x = element_text(angle = 45, hjust = 1)) +
  theme(legend.position = "bottom")
print(p1)
```

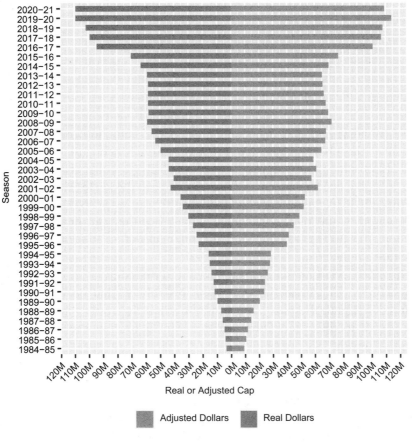

Figure 18.1   A pyramid chart that displays the year-over-year increases in the NBA salary cap, in both real and inflation-adjusted dollars, between 1984–85 and 2020–21

Once more, a pyramid chart is ideal when you want or need to visualize an order or hierarchy. For instance, you might choose to create a pyramid chart to display sales by country, with units on the left and (rescaled) dollars on the right; to display population counts by gender and age group; or to represent credit card delinquency rates between units and balances for every due stage.

Let's now pivot away from the cap data set and toward the records data set. We reduce the dimension of records two ways: first by calling the dplyr select() function, which subsets records on just the few variables we absolutely need, and second, by calling the dplyr filter() function, which reduces records to only include observations that meet a given criteria:

```
records %>%
  select(Season, Lg, Team, W, L) -> records

records %>%
  filter(Lg == "NBA" & Season > "1969-70" & Season < "1998-99") -> records
```

Then, we call the dplyr glimpse() function to return the records dimension as well as a truncated and transposed view of the data:

```
glimpse(records)
## Rows: 650
## Columns: 5
## $ Season <chr> "1997-98", "1996-97", "1995-96", "1994-95", "1993-94", "…
## $ Lg     <chr> "NBA", "NBA", "NBA", "NBA", "NBA", "NBA", "NBA", "NBA", …
## $ Team   <chr> "Boston Celtics", "Boston Celtics", "Boston Celtics", "B…
## $ W      <dbl> 36, 15, 33, 35, 32, 48, 51, 56, 52, 42, 57, 59, 67, 63, …
## $ L      <dbl> 46, 67, 49, 47, 50, 34, 31, 26, 30, 40, 25, 23, 15, 19, …
```

Here's what the records data now looks like:

- Season—This now equals a minimum of 1970-71 and a maximum of 1997-98. We therefore have 14 seasons of data pre–salary cap and another 14 seasons of data post–salary cap, which is enough to compare and contrast results before and since the salary cap introduction prior to the 1984–85 season.

- Lg—This now equals NBA for all remaining observations, but originally equaled NBA or ABA. The ABA, or American Basketball Association, was a rival professional league that folded way back in 1976. Because our salary cap analysis applies to the NBA only, we filtered out all ABA observations.

- Team—This equals full NBA team names (e.g., Detroit Pistons, Houston Rockets). An asterisk indicates the team qualified for postseason play.

- W—This equals the number of regular season wins over an 82-game schedule.

- L—This equals the number of regular season losses. Wins (W) plus losses (L) equals 82 for every remaining record.

Now that we have a good read on our data, let's move on to our analysis. We'll begin with intra-season parity and demonstrate how we can quantify the same, before and after the salary cap, through different measures of statistical dispersion.

18.4   *Measures of statistical dispersion and intra-season parity*

Measures of statistical dispersion quantify the spread, or distribution, of numeric data around a central value; in other words, measures of dispersion describe the variability of data. As variability increases, dispersion increases as well. If the salary cap actually improved intra-season parity, we should therefore see higher dispersion figures before the 1984-85 season than afterward.

If you're a low-risk investor contemplating the purchase of one stock over another, it would probably be wise to calculate the dispersion of both stock prices over time and then invest in the stock with the lower dispersion value. As another example, you may be a human resources manager who wants to understand the dispersion in compensation across the same industry when adjusting salary bands. You might also be preparing for a trip and want to compute the dispersion of temperatures in your destination before deciding what and how much to pack. In each of these scenarios, simply computing the mean or median would be insufficient at best and misleading at worst.

To understand intra-season parity in the NBA–before there was a salary cap and after–we need to compute the annual dispersion in regular season wins and plot those values over time, which is exactly what we're about to do.

Our intent is to introduce five common statistical measures of dispersion, compute results for each year, or season, in the records data set, plot the results in ggplot2 line charts, and insert regression lines into our visualizations to determine how intra-season parity trended before and after the salary cap. You'll learn more about dispersion and how to compute these measures in R; in the meantime, we'll determine if the NBA did, in fact, have an intra-season parity problem when it established a salary cap in 1984, and if so, if the salary cap then had a positive effect.

Before we begin by introducing the variance method, note that each of the following methods has its own advantages and disadvantages. It's worth your while to consider multiple measures of statistical dispersion to get a comprehensive understanding of a data's spread.

18.4.1   *Variance method*

Variance measures the average squared deviation of every data point from the group mean; thus, variance considers the differences between individual data points and a single mean. It's computed by summing the squared differences between each data point from the mean and then dividing each difference by the record count. In R, we simply make a call to the base R var() function. The variance method thus considers *all* data points, but it can be somewhat sensitive to any outliers in the data.

In the following chunk of code, we pass the records data set to the group_by() and summarize() functions from the dplyr package to compute the league-wide variance in regular season wins per season. The annual variance in regular season wins is represented by a variable called v_wins in a tibble called var_records. The head() and tail() functions return the first three and last three observations in var_records:

```
records %>%
  group_by(Season) %>%
  summarize(v_wins = var(W)) -> var_records

head(var_records, n = 3)
## # A tibble: 3 × 2
##    Season  v_wins
##    <chr>    <dbl>
## 1 1970-71    143.
## 2 1971-72    235.
## 3 1972-73    264.

tail(var_records, n = 3)
## # A tibble: 3 × 2
##    Season  v_wins
##    <chr>    <dbl>
## 1 1995-96    197.
## 2 1996-97    245.
## 3 1997-98    241.
```

These results are then plotted in a `ggplot2` line chart (see figure 18.2):

- The tibble we just created, var_records, is our data source. One variable, `Season`, is the x-axis variable, and the other variable, `v_wins`, is the y-axis variable.

- The `geom_line()` function draws a line one-half the default `ggplot2` width. The `geom_point()` function overlays the line with data points that are five times the default size.

- The `ylim()` function draws the y-axis from and to the values that are passed as arguments.

- The `geom_smooth()` function, called twice, draws regression lines from the 1970–71 season through 1983–84 and from the 1984–85 season through 1997–98.

- The `annotate()` function, also called twice, adds light, but separate, color blocks to readily distinguish the pre–salary cap era versus the post–salary cap era. Thus, the colored blocks correspond with the lengths of our regression lines.

- The second call to the `theme()` function orients the x-axis ticks at an angle equal to 45 degrees.

Our subsequent line charts will be created with this same basic syntax:

```
p2 <- ggplot(var_records, aes(x = Season, y = v_wins, group = 1)) +
  geom_line(aes(y = v_wins), color = "black", size = .5) +
  geom_point(size = 5, color = "dodgerblue") +
  labs(title = "Year-over-Year Variance in Regular Season Wins",
       subtitle = "1970-98",
       x = "Season",
       y = "Variance",
       caption = "salary cap was introduced prior to the 1984-85 season") +
  ylim(0, 300) +
  theme(plot.title = element_text(face = "bold")) +
  theme(axis.text.x = element_text(angle = 45, hjust = 1)) +
  geom_smooth(method = lm, color = "red", se = FALSE,
```

```
                data = var_records[as.character(var_records$Season) <
                                   "1984-85",]) +
      geom_smooth(method = lm, color = "red", se = FALSE,
                data = var_records[as.character(var_records$Season) >
                                   "1983-84",]) +
      annotate("rect", xmin = "1970-71", xmax = "1983-84",
               ymin = 0, ymax = 300, alpha = 0.1, fill = "orange") +
      annotate("rect", xmin = "1984-85", xmax = "1997-98",
               ymin = 0, ymax = 300, alpha = 0.1, fill = "green")
print(p2)
```

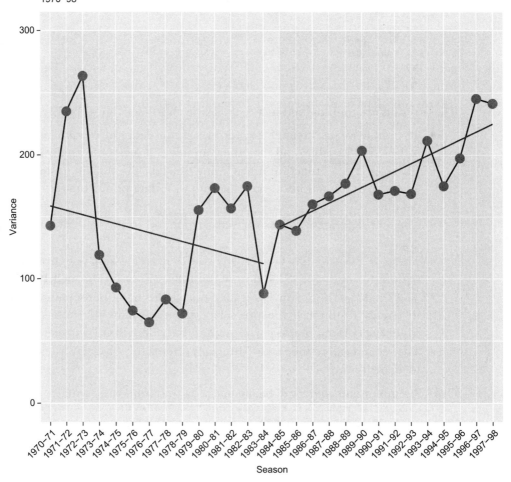

Figure 18.2   Year-over-year dispersion in regular season wins based on the variance method

Based on the variance method, intra-season parity actually trended *downward* between the 1970–71 and 1983–84 seasons and then trended *upward* during the salary cap era.

In the league's defense, the NBA might have trimmed their historical perspective by only considering the 1979–80 through 1982–83 seasons, where the dispersion in regular season wins was higher than it was in seven of the previous nine years. Even so, based on this analysis at least, the salary cap clearly failed to have a positive effect on intra-season parity.

18.4.2 Standard deviation method

Another downside of the variance method is that it often (including in this case) produces dispersion values that are difficult to understand. In contrast, an upside of the standard deviation method is that it's simply the square root of the variance; in R, the standard deviation is computed by prefacing the `var()` function with the base R `sqrt()` function or calling the base R `sd()` function.

In the following chunk of code, we again pass records to the `group_by()` and `summarize()` functions to compute the year-over-year standard deviation in regular season wins. The results are cast to a tibble called sd_records. Once more, the `head()` and `tail()` functions return the top three and bottom three observations:

```
records %>%
  group_by(Season) %>%
  summarize(sd_wins = sd(W)) -> sd_records

head(sd_records, n = 3)
## # A tibble: 3 × 2
##    Season  sd_wins
##    <chr>     <dbl>
## 1 1970-71    12.0
## 2 1971-72    15.3
## 3 1972-73    16.2

tail(sd_records, n = 3)
## # A tibble: 3 × 2
##    Season  sd_wins
##    <chr>     <dbl>
## 1 1995-96    14.0
## 2 1996-97    15.7
## 3 1997-98    15.5
```

Then, we pass sd_records to the `ggplot()` function and create a second line chart with the same look and feel as our first line chart (see figure 18.3):

```
p3 <- ggplot(sd_records, aes(x = Season, y = sd_wins, group = 1)) +
  geom_line(aes(y = sd_wins), color = "black", size = .5) +
  geom_point(size = 5, color = "dodgerblue") +
  labs(title = "Year-over-Year Standard Deviation in Regular Season Wins",
       subtitle = "1970-98",
       x = "Season",
       y = "Standard Deviation",
       caption = "salary cap was introduced prior to the 1984-85 season") +
```

```
ylim(0, 20) +
theme(plot.title = element_text(face = "bold")) +
theme(axis.text.x = element_text(angle = 45, hjust = 1)) +
geom_smooth(method = lm, color = "red", se = FALSE,
            data = sd_records[as.character(sd_records$Season) <
                              "1984-85",]) +
geom_smooth(method = lm, color = "red", se = FALSE,
            data = sd_records[as.character(sd_records$Season) >
                              "1983-84",]) +
annotate("rect", xmin = "1970-71", xmax = "1983-84",
         ymin = 0, ymax = 20, alpha = 0.1, fill = "orange") +
annotate("rect", xmin = "1984-85", xmax = "1997-98",
         ymin = 0, ymax = 20, alpha = 0.1, fill = "green")
print(p3)
```

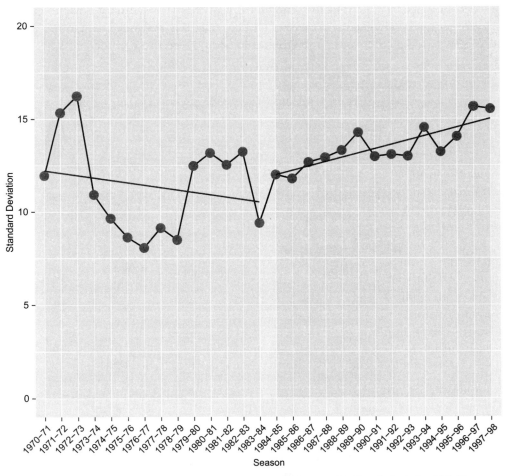

Year–over–Year Standard Deviation in Regular Season Wins
1970–98

salary cap was introduced prior to the 1984–85 season

Figure 18.3   Year-over-year dispersion in regular season wins based on the standard deviation method

Because the standard deviation is derived from the variance, it's no surprise that these results match our previous results—except for the fact that the standard deviation method returns dispersion measures we can all readily relate to. If the variable `wins` assumed a normal, or Gaussian, distribution—and it does—we could then deduce that roughly two-thirds of all NBA teams won somewhere between 33 and 49 regular season games during the 1976–77 season (equal to plus or minus 8 wins, the approximate standard deviation in wins in 1976–77, from a mean of 41). We could also deduce that, in 1996–97, two-thirds of the teams won somewhere between 25 and 57 regular season games. This shows significantly more dispersion and therefore less parity.

18.4.3 *Range method*

The range method is undoubtedly the simplest and most straightforward dispersion statistic; however, because it only considers the most extreme values, rather than every data point like the variance and standard deviation methods, it's especially sensitive to outliers and inconsiderate of the total distribution. It equals the difference between the highest and lowest values in a data set. In R, we get those values by calling the base R `max()` and `min()` functions and then the range by subtracting the latter from the former. The `group_by()` and `summarize()` functions otherwise instruct R to compute the range by each factor in the variable `Season` and to push the results to a variable called r_wins and a tibble called r_records. The `head()` and `tail()` functions give us a pair of small glimpses into the results:

```
records %>%
  group_by(Season) %>%
  summarize(r_wins = max(W) - min(W)) -> r_records

head(r_records, n = 3)
## # A tibble: 3 × 2
##    Season   r_wins
##    <chr>     <int>
## 1 1970-71      51
## 2 1971-72      51
## 3 1972-73      59

tail(r_records, n = 3)
## # A tibble: 3 × 2
##    Season   r_wins
##    <chr>     <int>
## 1 1995-96      57
## 2 1996-97      55
## 3 1997-98      51
```

Another `ggplot2` line chart visualizes the same (see figure 18.4):

```
p4 <- ggplot(r_records, aes(x = Season, y = r_wins, group = 1)) +
  geom_line(aes(y = r_wins), color = "black", size = .5) +
  geom_point(size = 5, color = "dodgerblue") +
  labs(title = "Year-over-Year Range in Regular Season Wins",
       subtitle = "1970-98",
       x = "Season",
       y = "Range",
```

```
        caption = "salary cap was introduced prior to the 1984-85 season") +
ylim(0, 60) +
theme(plot.title = element_text(face = "bold")) +
theme(axis.text.x = element_text(angle = 45, hjust = 1)) +
geom_smooth(method = lm, color = "red", se = FALSE,
            data = r_records[as.character(r_records$Season) <
                             "1984-85",]) +
geom_smooth(method = lm, color = "red", se = FALSE,
            data = r_records[as.character(r_records$Season) >
                             "1983-84",]) +
annotate("rect", xmin = "1970-71", xmax = "1983-84",
   ymin = 0, ymax = 60, alpha = 0.1, fill = "orange") +
annotate("rect", xmin = "1984-85", xmax = "1997-98",
   ymin = 0, ymax = 60, alpha = 0.1, fill = "green")
print(p4)
```

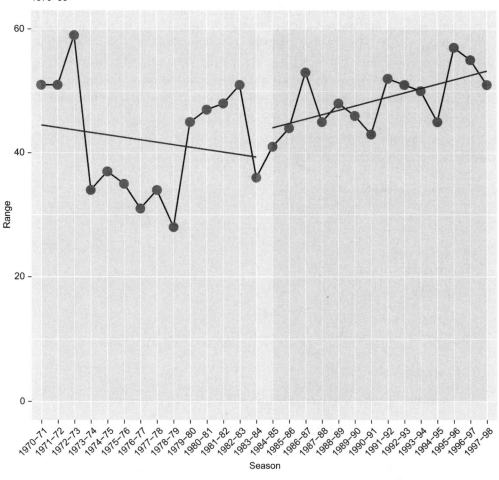

Figure 18.4   Year-over-year dispersion in regular season wins based on the range method

Even by the range method, the NBA's intra-season parity "problem" incrementally improved over the 14 seasons immediately preceding the salary cap (though it did increase during each subsequent season from 1978–79 through 1982–83). By this measure as well, the salary cap had no positive effect on furthering intra-season parity; in fact, in every season from 1984–85 through 1997–98, the dispersion in regular season wins exceeded that from 1983–84, the final NBA season of the pre–salary cap era.

18.4.4 *Mean absolute deviation method*

If the range method is the simplest and most straightforward dispersion statistic to be demonstrated here, then the mean and median deviation methods (see also section 18.4.5) are just as surely the most complex (but only in a relative sense, not in any absolute sense). Both methods are less sensitive to outliers than the alternatives.

We need two steps to compute the year-over-year dispersion in regular season wins based on the mean deviation method. First, we pass the records data set to the dplyr group_by() and mutate() functions; from mutate(), we create a new variable called mad_wins, which equals the absolute value of the difference between wins and the mean of wins, and from group_by(), we compute mad_wins for each season in records. The results are cast to a tibble called mad_records. The head() and tail() functions return the first three and last three mad_records observations:

```
records %>%
  group_by(Season) %>%
  mutate(mad_wins = abs(W - mean(W))) -> mad_records

head(mad_records, n = 3)
## # A tibble: 3 × 6
## # Groups:    Season [3]
##    Season  Lg    Team              W     L mad_wins
##    <chr>   <chr> <chr>         <int> <int>    <dbl>
## 1 1997-98 NBA   Boston Celtics    36    46        5
## 2 1996-97 NBA   Boston Celtics    15    67       26
## 3 1995-96 NBA   Boston Celtics    33    49        8

tail(mad_records, n = 3)
## # A tibble: 3 × 6
## # Groups:    Season [3]
##    Season  Lg    Team                 W     L mad_wins
##    <chr>   <chr> <chr>            <int> <int>    <dbl>
## 1 1997-98 NBA   Vancouver Grizzlies   19    63       22
## 2 1996-97 NBA   Vancouver Grizzlies   14    68       27
## 3 1995-96 NBA   Vancouver Grizzlies   15    67       26
```

Then, we pass mad_records, not records, to the group_by() and summarize() functions. Here, we're taking the sum of the variable mad_wins and dividing it by the sum of observations where the variable wins is greater than 0. Of course, because every NBA team has more than 0 regular season wins, the divisor is therefore equal to the total observation count. And that's the point—the condition is such that we get *n* in a way that works with `group_by()` and `summarize()`.

The first and last three observations of a new tibble called mad_records2 are printed by successive calls to the `head()` and `tail()` functions:

```
mad_records %>%
  group_by(Season) %>%
  summarize(mad_wins2 = sum(mad_wins) / sum(W > 0)) -> mad_records2

head(mad_records2, n = 3)
## # A tibble: 3 × 2
##    Season  mad_wins2
##    <chr>      <dbl>
## 1 1970-71      8.71
## 2 1971-72     13.2
## 3 1972-73     13.3

tail(mad_records2, n = 3)
## # A tibble: 3 × 2
##    Season  mad_wins2
##    <chr>      <dbl>
## 1 1995-96     11.1
## 2 1996-97     13.2
## 3 1997-98     12.6
```

We then display our results with another `ggplot2` line chart (see figure 18.5):

```
p5 <- ggplot(mad_records2, aes(x = Season, y = mad_wins2, group = 1)) +
  geom_line(aes(y = mad_wins2), color = "black", size = .5) +
  geom_point(size = 5, color = "dodgerblue") +
  labs(title =
          "Year-over-Year Mean Absolute Deviation in Regular Season Wins",
       subtitle = "1970-98",
       x = "Season",
       y = "Mean Absolute Deviation",
       caption = "salary cap was introduced prior to the 1984-85 season") +
  ylim(0, 14) +
  theme(plot.title = element_text(face = "bold")) +
  theme(axis.text.x = element_text(angle = 45, hjust = 1)) +
  geom_smooth(method = lm, color = "red", se = FALSE,
              data = mad_records2[as.character(mad_records2$Season) <
                                   "1984-85",]) +
  geom_smooth(method = lm, color = "red", se = FALSE,
              data = mad_records2[as.character(mad_records2$Season) > "1983-
                ➡ 84",]) +
  annotate("rect", xmin = "1970-71", xmax = "1983-84",
           ymin = 0, ymax = 14, alpha = 0.1, fill = "orange") +
  annotate("rect", xmin = "1984-85", xmax = "1997-98",
           ymin = 0, ymax = 14, alpha = 0.1, fill = "green")
print(p5)
```

Year-over-Year Mean Absolute Deviation in Regular Season Wins
1970–98

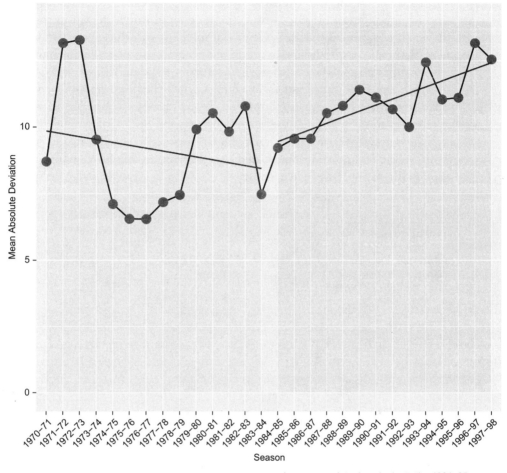

salary cap was introduced prior to the 1984–85 season

Figure 18.5   Year-over-year dispersion in regular season wins based on the mean absolute deviation method

Although we used a different measure and method, we got the same results. It doesn't appear that the NBA had an intra-season parity problem in the years leading up to the salary cap introduction, or, if it did, by this and other measures, the problem was more or less taking care of itself. More significantly, perhaps, the salary cap did nothing to improve intra-season parity, based on this method and other methods, at least during the first 14 seasons of the salary cap era.

18.4.5 *Median absolute deviation method*

It turns out that the year-over-year differences in mean and median regular season wins are immaterial. In other words, the median absolute deviation method—where the mean is swapped out in favor of the median—produces results almost just like those that came from the mean absolute deviation method. This is hardly surprising considering we're working with normally distributed data.

From the following chunks of code, we get the following—(1) a tibble called mdad_records, which equals records plus a new variable called `mdad_wins` that, in turn, equals the annual absolute difference between wins and median wins; (2) another tibble called mdad_records2, which contains the median absolute deviation method results in the form of a variable called `mdad_wins`; and (3) a fifth `ggplot2` line chart that displays the results (see figure 18.6):

```
records %>%
  group_by(Season) %>%
  mutate(mdad_wins = abs(W - median(W))) -> mdad_records

head(mdad_records, n = 3)
## # A tibble: 3 × 6
## # Groups:    Season [3]
##    Season  Lg    Team                W      L mdad_wins
##    <chr>   <chr> <chr>           <int> <int>     <dbl>
## 1 1997-98  NBA   Boston Celtics     36    46         7
## 2 1996-97  NBA   Boston Celtics     15    67        25
## 3 1995-96  NBA   Boston Celtics     33    49         8

tail(mdad_records, n = 3)
## # A tibble: 3 × 6
## # Groups:    Season [3]
##    Season  Lg    Team                  W     L mdad_wins
##    <chr>   <chr> <chr>             <int> <int>     <dbl>
## 1 1997-98  NBA   Vancouver Grizzlies   19    63        24
## 2 1996-97  NBA   Vancouver Grizzlies   14    68        26
## 3 1995-96  NBA   Vancouver Grizzlies   15    67        26

mdad_records %>%
  group_by(Season) %>%
  summarize(mdad_wins2 = sum(mdad_wins) / sum(W > 0)) -> mdad_records2

head(mdad_records2, n = 3)
## # A tibble: 3 × 2
##    Season  mdad_wins2
##    <chr>        <dbl>
## 1 1970-71       8.65
## 2 1971-72      13
## 3 1972-73      13.2

tail(mdad_records2, n = 3)
```

```
## # A tibble: 3 x 2
##   Season  mdad_wins2
##   <chr>        <dbl>
## 1 1995-96       11.1
## 2 1996-97       13.1
## 3 1997-98       12.4

p6 <- ggplot(mdad_records2, aes(x = Season, y = mdad_wins2, group = 1)) +
  geom_line(aes(y = mdad_wins2), color = "black", size = .5) +
  geom_point(size = 5, color = "dodgerblue") +
  labs(title =
         "Year-over-Year Median Absolute Deviation in Regular Season Wins",
       subtitle = "1970-98",
       x = "Season",
       y = "Median Absolute Deviation",
       caption = "salary cap was introduced prior to the 1984-85 season") +
  ylim(0, 14) +
  theme(plot.title = element_text(face = "bold")) +
  theme(axis.text.x = element_text(angle = 45, hjust = 1)) +
  geom_smooth(method = lm, color = "red", se = FALSE,
              data = mdad_records2[as.character(mdad_records2$Season) <
                                     "1984-85",]) +
  geom_smooth(method = lm, color = "red", se = FALSE,
              data = mdad_records2[as.character(mdad_records2$Season) >
                                     "1983-84",]) +
  annotate("rect", xmin = "1970-71", xmax = "1983-84",
    ymin = 0, ymax = 14, alpha = 0.1, fill = "orange") +
  annotate("rect", xmin = "1984-85", xmax = "1997-98",
    ymin = 0, ymax = 14, alpha = 0.1, fill = "green")
print(p6)
```

It's impossible to know—nearly 40 years later—how the NBA might have concluded it had an *intra*-season parity problem. We do know this, however—whatever intra-season parity problem the NBA did have during the seasons leading up to the salary cap, the problem (if it can be called that) was dissipating on its own volition, at least based on the measures of statistical dispersion demonstrated herein. Furthermore, based on these same measures, the salary cap had absolutely zero effect on reducing the league-wide dispersion in regular season wins; on the contrary, dispersion actually trended upward over the first 14 seasons in the salary cap era.

In the next section, we'll compute the annual churn within the league's top eight teams—that is, the number of teams in the top eight that weren't in the top eight at the end of the previous season—as a way of testing for *inter*-season parity.

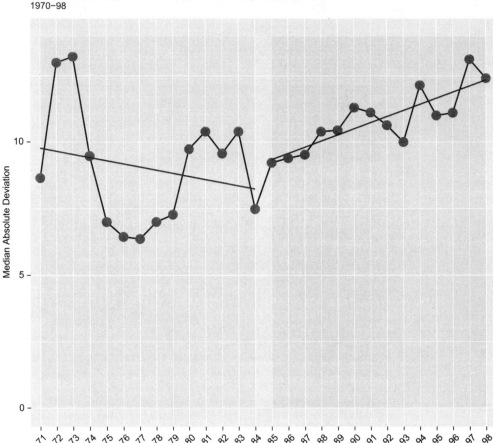

Figure 18.6   **Year-over-year dispersion in regular season wins based on the median absolute deviation method**

18.5   *Churn and inter-season parity*

So there wasn't necessarily an intra-season parity problem by the time the NBA capped player salaries just before the start of the 1984–85 season, and even if there was, the salary cap didn't come close to solving anything. But what about *inter*-season parity?

Our purpose here is to explore the year-over-year churn of the NBA's top teams, pre– and post–salary cap, to determine whether the cap on player salaries might have triggered higher year-over-year turnover rates at the very top of the league. We'll rank regular season wins per season, divide the NBA into two groups based on rank, compute the annual churn, and plot the same in a final ggplot2 line chart.

18.5.1 *Data wrangling*

We have some further data wrangling operations to run before we can analyze and visualize any results. Our first order of business is to create an exact copy of the records data set, which we'll call churn:

```
records -> churn
```

You might recall that cells within the records variable Team include an asterisk at the end if the team qualified for postseason play. We need to remove the asterisks because going forward, we don't want R to think Boston Celtics* is any different from Boston Celtics.

We therefore make a call to the base R gsub() function, which changes out every pattern match from a string and replaces it with whatever we want or need. The gsub() function takes the following three arguments: (1) the string to be matched, (2) the replacement string, and (3) the string vector.

In the following code, the first argument instructs R to remove any and all special characters, asterisks included; the second argument is blank because we don't want or need a replacement string; and the third argument is the object and string we want to change:

```
churn$Team <- gsub('[^[:alnum:] ]', '', churn$Team)
```

We then pass the churn data set to the group_by() and mutate() functions to create a new variable called rank derived from the original variable W. Per every season in churn, the team with the most regular season wins should receive a rank of 1, the next best team should receive a rank of 2, and so forth. The best teams should therefore receive lower-digit ranks, and the worst teams should get higher-digit ranks—hence the minus sign in front of the variable W in our code. In addition, teams with equal regular season win totals from the same season should receive the same ranks, so we use the ties.method argument to assign tied elements to the average and same rank:

```
churn %>%
  group_by(Season) %>%
  mutate(rank = rank(-W, ties.method = "average")) -> churn
```

Next, we call the mutate() function again, this time in combination with the ifesle() function, to create another derived variable, called topTeam. If the variable rank is greater than 8, then topTeam should equal 0; if not, then topTeam should instead equal 1. Put differently, we're segmenting the top eight teams from the rest of the NBA:

```
churn %>%
  mutate(topTeam = ifelse(rank > 8, 0, 1)) -> churn
```

Then, we pass churn to the `arrange()` function to sort the data first by the variable `Team` and then, in descending order, the variable `Season`. We make yet another call to `mutate()` to create one more derived variable, `topTeam2`, which equals `topTeam` from the *succeeding* record. For instance, if `topTeam` equals 1 for the 1996–97 Atlanta Hawks, then `topTeam2` should equal 1 for the 1997–98 Atlanta Hawks. The `dplyr` `lead()` function instructs R to fill `topTeam2` by copying the `topTeam` value from the next record, which is why the argument n equals 1; alternatively, if we instead wanted R to fill `topTeam2` with the *preceding* `topTeam` values, we would call the `dplyr` `lag()` function rather than `lead()`. This operation is grouped by the variable `Team` because, for instance, we don't want the Atlanta Hawks extracting results from the Baltimore Bullets:

```
churn %>%
  arrange(Team, desc(Season)) %>%
  group_by(Team) %>%
  mutate(topTeam2 = lead(topTeam, n = 1)) -> churn
```

```
head(churn, n = 30)
## # A tibble: 30 × 8
## # Groups:   Team [2]
##    Season  Lg    Team             W     L  rank topTeam topTeam2
##    <chr>   <chr> <chr>        <int> <int> <dbl>   <dbl>    <dbl>
## 1  1997-98 NBA   Atlanta Hawks   50    32  10        0        1
## 2  1996-97 NBA   Atlanta Hawks   56    26   7.5      1        0
## 3  1995-96 NBA   Atlanta Hawks   46    36  11.5      0        0
## 4  1994-95 NBA   Atlanta Hawks   42    40  14        0        1
## 5  1993-94 NBA   Atlanta Hawks   57    25   3.5      1        0
## 6  1992-93 NBA   Atlanta Hawks   43    39  12.5      0        0
## 7  1991-92 NBA   Atlanta Hawks   38    44  17.5      0        0
## 8  1990-91 NBA   Atlanta Hawks   43    39  13        0        0
## 9  1989-90 NBA   Atlanta Hawks   41    41  17        0        1
## 10 1988-89 NBA   Atlanta Hawks   52    30   5.5      1        1
```

As a result, churn contains Not Available (NA) for the variable `topTeam2` where the variable `Season` equals 1970–71. We don't want NAs in our data, so we next call the `na.omit()` function from base R to remove every observation in churn that contains an NA:

```
na.omit(churn) -> churn
```

We're now ready to compute churn and visualize the year-over-year results.

18.5.2 *Computing and visualizing churn*

Churn is an especially critical metric for companies that offer subscription-based services (e.g., mobile carriers, cable providers, software as a service suppliers) where customers can opt out without penalty. Companies therefore develop churn models—usually decision trees (see chapter 5) or logistic regressions (see chapter 14)—to identify high-risk customers, pinpoint the factors (e.g., age, gender, usage, contract length) that make them high risk, and devise meticulous retention strategies. Other companies develop similar models to reduce workforce churn.

So number one, churn is almost always a bad thing, financially and otherwise. Number two, it's usually computed by dividing the number of lost customers (but this could also be lost employees) by the customer count at the start of some previously defined time period (usually monthly, quarterly, or annually) and then multiplying the quotient by 100. This makes perfect sense when circumstances are fairly fluid.

Let's now consider the NBA and the purported motive behind the salary cap. Churn at the top of the NBA—that is, inter-season churn that we'll measure by one-year turnovers in the league's best eight teams—isn't just a good thing, but maybe a necessary thing to ensure the long-term viability of the league. In addition, because our situation is fixed, rather than measuring churn by plugging numbers into the normal formula, we'll instead compute churn by merely bean-counting the number of teams in the top eight that weren't among the top eight at the end of the previous season.

We start by passing the churn data set to the `group_by()` and `count()` functions to tally the number of records for each season in our data where the value in `topTeam` exceeded the value in `topTeam2`. In other words, we're counting the number of records where the variable `topTeam` equals 1 and the variable `topTeam2` equals 0. Our results are cast to a tibble called churn_tbl. Then, we call the `head()` function to return the first six churn_tbl records:

```
churn %>%
  group_by(Season) %>%
  count(topTeam > topTeam2) -> churn_tbl

head(churn_tbl)
## # A tibble: 6 × 3
## # Groups:   Season [3]
##   Season `topTeam > topTeam2`     n
##   <chr>  <lgl>                <int>
## 1 1971-72 FALSE                  14
## 2 1971-72 TRUE                    1
## 3 1972-73 FALSE                  14
## 4 1972-73 TRUE                    2
## 5 1973-74 FALSE                  15
## 6 1973-74 TRUE                    1
```

Because we instructed R to perform a logical operation, we get the annual counts where the condition equals both TRUE and FALSE. We don't want or need any records where the logical condition equals FALSE; the first two lines of code in the next chunk extract the even-numbered rows in churn_tbl.

The first line of code creates a dummy indicator that breaks down every row as even or odd. The `seq_len()` function is a base R function that creates a sequence starting at 1 and, in this case, ending at 54, which equals the churn_tbl row count; the `%%` operator is the modulo operator that returns either a 1 or 0 when the churn_tbl row numbers are divided by 2. The second line of code then extracts the even-numbered rows, or where row_odd equals 0.

Then, we call the `select()` function to subset churn_tbl on the variables `Season` and n only; the `print()` function prints every churn_tbl record:

```
row_odd <- seq_len(nrow(churn_tbl)) %% 2
churn_tbl[row_odd == 0, ] -> churn_tbl
churn_tbl %>%
  select(Season, n) -> churn_tbl
print(churn_tbl)
## # A tibble: 27 × 2
## # Groups:   Season [27]
##    Season       n
##    <chr>    <int>
##  1 1971-72      1
##  2 1972-73      2
##  3 1973-74      1
##  4 1974-75      4
##  5 1975-76      3
##  6 1976-77      3
##  7 1977-78      3
##  8 1978-79      3
##  9 1979-80      3
## 10 1980-81      2
## # … with 17 more rows
```

Next, we visualize the results with another `ggplot2` line chart that displays the year-over-year churn before and after the salary cap (see figure 18.7):

```
p7 <- ggplot(churn_tbl, aes(x = Season, y = n, group = 1)) +
  geom_line(aes(y = n), color = "black", size = .5) +
  geom_point(size = 5, color = "orange") +
  labs(title = "Year-over-Year Churn in the NBA's Top 8",
       subtitle = "1971-98",
       x = "Season",
       y = "Number of New Top 8 Teams from Prior Season",
       caption = "salary cap was introduced prior to the 1984-85 season") +
  ylim(0, 6) +
  theme(plot.title = element_text(face = "bold")) +
  theme(axis.text.x = element_text(angle = 45, hjust = 1)) +
  geom_smooth(method = lm, color = "red", se = FALSE,
              data = churn_tbl[as.character(churn_tbl$Season) <
                                 "1984-85",]) +
  geom_smooth(method = lm, color = "red", se = FALSE,
              data = churn_tbl[as.character(churn_tbl$Season) >
                                 "1983-84",]) +
  annotate("rect", xmin = "1971-72", xmax = "1983-84",
    ymin = 0, ymax = 6, alpha = 0.1, fill = "blue") +
  annotate("rect", xmin = "1984-85", xmax = "1997-98",
    ymin = 0, ymax = 6, alpha = 0.1, fill = "green")
print(p7)
```

Year–over–Year Churn in the NBA's Top 8
1971–98

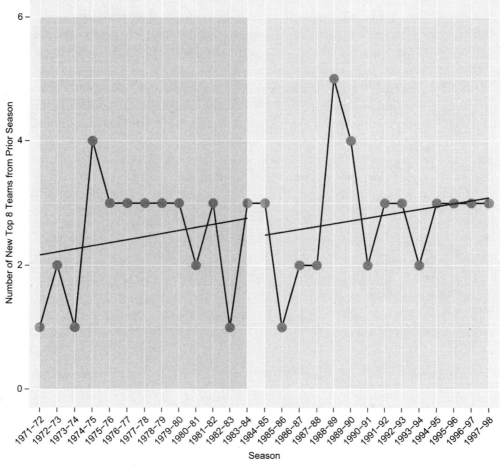

salary cap was introduced prior to the 1984–85 season

Figure 18.7   The annual number of NBA teams among the top eight in regular season wins that weren't among the top eight in the prior season. Once more, our plot is segmented by colored blocks to represent pre– and post–salary cap.

Clearly, the salary cap had no effect on inter-season parity either, at least based on the method we've chosen to measure it. Our purpose here was to test whether the NBA's salary cap achieved its *declared* purpose of introducing parity—intra-season parity by multiple measures of dispersion and inter-season parity by measuring churn. While the salary cap surely yielded other benefits (no doubt it has kept overall expenses in check, which improves margins), bringing about parity hasn't been one of them.

In the next chapter, we'll introduce data standardization techniques and apply the same to get a different historical perspective on the NBA's leading points scorers.

Summary

- There are many measures of statistical dispersion; we just demonstrated what might be the five most popular or most common measures.

- There are built-in functions to compute some of these measures, such as variance and standard deviation; where R doesn't have a function, it's hardly a problem to write arithmetic code.

- Of the five measures of statistical dispersion that were demonstrated—variance, standard deviation, range, mean absolute deviation, and median absolute deviation—the standard deviation method probably strikes the best balance between thoroughness, ease, and identification.

- However, as previously stated, it's often beneficial to apply multiple methods to get a better understanding of your data.

- Based on our analyses, the salary cap essentially had zero effect on intra-season or inter-season parity.

Data standardization

19

This chapter covers

- Methods of data standardization
- Z-score method
- Standard deviation method
- Centering method
- Range method
- Coloring data frames and highlighting observations
- Comparing data sets

It's not often that an NBA player scores 50 or more points in a game. In fact, during the 2021–22 regular season (1,230 games), it happened only 12 times. The top five scorers in NBA history—Lebron James (still playing), Kareem Abdul-Jabbar, Karl Malone, Kobe Bryant, and Michael Jordan—scored at least 50 points in a regular season game 73 times over a grand total of 93 seasons between them.

But during the 1961–62 season, Wilt Chamberlain, then playing for the Philadelphia Warriors, *averaged* 50 points per game; he then averaged almost 45 points per game the very next year. No player has since come close to matching these figures. Sixty years later, we remain amazed at Chamberlain's scoring prowess. However, many of us of have ignored the fact that rule changes and style of play transformations have frequently changed the pace of play. During the 1961–62 season, teams attempted roughly 110 shots, or field goals, per game and about 25 free throws per game; when Neil Johnston led the NBA in scoring during the 1952–53 season, averaging "just" 22.3 points per game, teams then attempted only 70 shots and 20 free throws per game. Nowadays, teams take about 85 shots every game and attempt about 20 free throws. More shot attempts equals more scoring; fewer shot attempts equals less scoring.

You've probably figured out, then, that the difference between Chamberlain's scoring average in 1961–62 and Johnston's scoring average in 1952–53 might actually be less significant than the raw data might otherwise suggest. We sometimes standardize data—that is, we convert a variable from its raw format to a simple and uniform scale—to control for epochal changes, seasonal effects, and other external factors. Take gasoline prices, for instance; it's neither fair nor accurate to outright compare today's cost for a gallon of gas to, let's say, the 1980 cost for the same without adjusting for inflation. As another example, consider a collections agent; it wouldn't be fair to evaluate an agent's performance in, let's say, November or December, when many customers are unwilling or unable to cure their debt, versus March or April, when many delinquent customers are in receipt of their tax returns and so have disposable income.

Our purpose here is to demonstrate different standardization techniques on an NBA data set containing annual scoring leaders and then visualize the results against the raw data. By converting points per game from its raw format to its standardized equivalents, we eliminate the influence of rule changes, style of play transformations, and other external factors that, over the course of many generations, affect basic statistics. Depending on the method, our presumption is that we're likely to see results that are very different from what has been reported over many decades.

Let's go back to our collections agent and briefly discuss why standardization is so important to understand and appreciate. The raw performance numbers during the holidays compared to March and April from the same year might put the agent on corrective action. But the standardized performance numbers might otherwise show that the agent's collections effectiveness is entirely consistent with seasonal ebbs and flows. Standardizing data might not only provide a fresh perspective but also enable best actions.

We'll start by loading the only package we'll need.

19.1   Loading a package

We'll load data with `readr`, wrangle and fetch data with `dplyr` functions only, and visualize the same exclusively with `ggplot2` functions; therefore, the `tidyverse` universe of packages will suffice:

```
library(tidyverse)
```

Otherwise, the remainder of our heavy lifting will be through a series of simple arithmetic operations to standardize our data. Next, we'll import our data set and briefly explore its contents.

19.2 *Importing and viewing data*

Our data set is a .csv file downloaded from Kaggle that contains scraped data from www.basketball-reference.com; it specifically contains player statistics, including games played and total points scored, for every NBA season between 1949–50 and 2016–17. Soon enough, we'll trim the data so that the 1998–99 is the maximum season—thereby leaving us with 50 seasons of data, still quite sufficient for our purposes. It has since been saved in our default working directory as season_stats.csv.

We make a call to the readr read_csv() function to import season_stats.csv and in the process create a data set called dat1:

```
dat1 <- read_csv("seasons_stats.csv")
```

Then, we call the base R dim() function to return the dat1 dimension:

```
dim(dat1)
## [1] 24624    53
```

Our data set contains 24,624 rows and 53 columns.

Going forward, we only need six of the 53 dat1 variables; therefore, we next call the select() function from the dplyr package to subset dat1 on these six variables. In addition, due to space considerations more than anything else, we'll confine our analysis to the first 50 seasons where we have data. We then call the dplyr filter() function to subset dat1 where the variable Year, now numeric, is less than or equal to 1999:

```
dat1 %>%
  select(Year, Player, Pos, Tm, G, PTS) -> dat1

dat1 %>%
  filter(Year <= 1999) -> dat1
```

The glimpse() function, also from dplyr, prints a transposed and truncated snapshot of dat1. We also get the new row and column counts after previously calling select() and filter():

```
glimpse(dat1)
## Rows: 14,420
## Columns: 6
## $ Year   <dbl> 1950, 1950, 1950, 1950, 1950, 1950, 1950, 1950, 195…
## $ Player <chr> "Curly Armstrong", "Cliff Barker", "Leo Barnhorst",…
## $ Pos    <chr> "G-F", "SG", "SF", "F", "F", "F", "G", "G-F", "F-C"…
## $ Tm     <chr> "FTW", "INO", "CHS", "TOT", "DNN", "NYK", "INO", "T…
## $ G      <dbl> 63, 49, 67, 15, 13, 2, 60, 3, 65, 36, 29, 57, 60, 5…
## $ PTS    <dbl> 458, 279, 438, 63, 59, 4, 895, 10, 661, 382, 279, 2…
```

Here's a breakdown of our six surviving variables:

- Year—Equivalent to season where, for instance, the year 1975 is equivalent to the 1974–75 season; has a minimum value of 1950 (1949–50 season) and a maximum value of 1999 (1998–99 season). This is now an integer, but it will be converted to a factor variable.

- Player—A player's full name, in firstname lastname format. An asterisk beside a player's name indicates he is a Hall of Famer. This is now and will remain a character string.

- Pos—A player's position or positions where, for example, G equals Guard, F equals Forward, and G-F equals Guard-Forward. This is now an integer, but it will be converted to a factor.

- Tm—A player's team in abbreviated format so that, for example, BOS equals the Boston Celtics. This is yet another character string, but it will be converted to a factor.

- G—The number of regular season games played by any player for any year. This is now an integer and will remain an integer.

- PTS—The total points scored in regular season games by any player for any year. This is another integer that will remain an integer.

Our data requires further wrangling before we can create standardized variables and analyze the results.

19.3   *Wrangling data*

Our first order of business is fairly mundane by now—convert the variables Year, Pos, and Tm from character strings to factors by calling the as.factor() function from base R three times:

```
dat1$Year <- as.factor(dat1$Year)
dat1$Pos <- as.factor(dat1$Pos)
dat1$Tm <- as.factor(dat1$Tm)
```

Our second order of business, however, isn't so straightforward. Our data set contains duplicate records brought about by midseason trades and other transactions that caused some players to play for two or more teams in the same NBA season. These records must be treated somehow to not compromise the integrity of our standardization equations.

19.3.1   *Treating duplicate records*

The most significant challenge with our data set is that it contains one record for each unique year, player, and team combination. So someone who played for, let's say, two teams during the 1949–50 season actually takes up three records in dat1—one for each of the two teams he played for plus one additional record that aggregates his statistics, where the variable Tm equals TOT (presumably short for TOTAL).

That being said, we next call the distinct() function from the dplyr package to subset dat1 on every unique, or distinct, Year/Player/Pos combination; the results are then cast into a new data set called test1. Then, we call the dim() function to return the record count; test1 contains 12,239 records, or 2,181 fewer observations than dat1:

```
dat1 %>%
  distinct(Year, Player, Pos) -> test1
dim(test1)
## [1] 12239     3
```

Put somewhat differently, that means dat1 contains 2,181 records (not unique players) where the variable Tm equals TOT or duplicate Year/Player/Pos combinations that otherwise roll up to a record where the variable Tm equals TOT.

We then write a short chunk of dplyr code to pull the record count from dat1 where the variable Tm equals TOT. We pass dat1 to the filter() function via the pipe operator and then pass the results to the tally() function, which returns the number of dat1 observations where Tm equals TOT:

```
dat1 %>%
  filter(Tm == "TOT") %>%
  tally()
##      n
## 1 1172
```

So we have 1,172 players in dat1 who switched teams *during* an NBA season at least once.

Let's take a look at just one example. Ed Bartels was a 6-5 forward who played collegiately at North Carolina State. In 1950, he appeared in 13 games for the Denver Nuggets, scoring 59 points, plus 2 games for the New York Knicks, scoring 4 points. His total 1950 productivity was therefore 15 games played and 63 points scored.

We make another call to the filter() function to subset dat1 where the variable Year equals 1950 and the variable Player equals Ed Bartels; our results are cast into a new data set called test2. The base R print() function returns the results:

```
dat1 %>%
  filter(Year == 1950, Player == "Ed Bartels") -> test2
print(test2)
##   Year     Player Pos  Tm  G PTS
## 1 1950 Ed Bartels   F TOT 15  63
## 2 1950 Ed Bartels   F DNN 13  59
## 3 1950 Ed Bartels   F NYK  2   4
```

We don't want our data to contain more than one record per unique Year/Player/Pos combination. So we'll delete every dat1 observation where Tm equals TOT and then aggregate the variables games (G) and points (PTS) for every surviving record. This might seem counterintuitive; however, this sequence of steps is easier from an execution standpoint than the alternative of retaining the observations where Tm equals TOT and then deleting the two or more observations "beneath" them.

Therefore, we make another call to the `filter()` function to subset dat1 where Tm equals anything other than TOT (note the use of the `!=` operator). The `dim()` function returns the row and column counts:

```
dat1 %>%
  filter(Tm != "TOT") -> dat1
dim(dat1)
## [1] 13248      6
```

Our data set now contains 13,248 records, which equals the 14,420 original record count minus the 1,172 players who changed teams midseason.

Then, we pass dat1 to the dplyr `group_by()` and `summarize()` functions to sum games and points for every Year/Player/Pos combination. For most of the dat1 records, this operation will have zero effect; however, where we have duplicate Year/Player/Pos combinations, the `group_by()` and `summarize()` functions essentially consolidate the statistics from two or more records into just one record. These results are cast into a tibble called dat2. Afterward, we call the `dim()` function to get the dat2 dimension:

```
dat1 %>%
  group_by(Year, Player, Pos) %>%
  summarize(G = sum(G), PTS = sum(PTS)) -> dat2
dim(dat2)
## [1] 12136      5
```

Note that we've lost the variable Tm; dat1 contains six columns, whereas dat2 has only five. We instructed R to summarize two of the six dat1 variables grouped by three of the remaining four variables; therefore, we didn't provide R with any instructions with respect to Tm. This is okay because going forward, we don't need Tm to drive any further data wrangling operations or to support any of our analysis.

Now let's run a couple more tests. First, we call the `filter()` function again to subset dat2 on the variable Year equaling 1950 and the variable Player equaling Ed Bartels. Our results are cast into a new data set called test3 and then printed:

```
dat2 %>%
  filter(Year == 1950, Player == "Ed Bartels") -> test3
print(test3)
## # A tibble: 1 × 5
## # Groups:   Year, Player [1]
##    Year Player      Pos       G   PTS
##   <fct> <chr>      <fct> <int> <int>
## 1 1950  Ed Bartels  F        15    63
```

This dat2 record resembles the dat1 equivalent where the variable Tm in dat1 was equal to TOT; dat2, of course, doesn't contain a variable called Tm, but more importantly, the variables G and PTS match up perfectly.

Second, let's confirm that the records for a player who never switched teams mid-season, such as George Mikan, who played center for the Lakers when the team was based in Minneapolis, weren't affected (more on Mikan in a bit). In the process, we'll demonstrate a pair of operations we haven't yet introduced.

Take a look at the last line in the following code chunk—colorDF is a package that adds color to a returned data frame or tibble, and the highlight() function draws attention to one or more records that satisfy a given condition when viewed online. We didn't previously load the colorDF package by making a call to the library() function; instead, we're simultaneously loading the colorDF package and calling the highlight() function from the same by separating the two with a pair of colons. The highlight() function takes a data frame–like object as one argument (test4, created with the preceding dplyr code) and a condition as a second argument (where the variable Year from test4 equals 1962).

NOTE   colorDF must first be installed before performing this operation. It's still a good practice to load your packages up front, but this is a valuable technique to know when calling functions that cross packages (highlight() isn't one of them). R will get confused if you fail to combine the package and function names in the same line of code.

```
dat2 %>%
  group_by(Year) %>%
  filter(Player == 'George Mikan*') -> test4
colorDF::highlight(test4, test4$Year == 1950)
## # Tibble (class tbl_df) 6 x 6:
## # Groups: Year [6]
## |Year |Player        |Pos |Tm  |G   |PTS
## 1|1950 |George Mikan* |C   |MNL |  68| 1865
## 2|1951 |George Mikan* |C   |MNL |  68| 1932
## 3|1952 |George Mikan* |C   |MNL |  64| 1523
## 4|1953 |George Mikan* |C   |MNL |  70| 1442
## 5|1954 |George Mikan* |C   |MNL |  72| 1306
## 6|1956 |George Mikan* |C   |MNL |  37|  390
```

Then, we pass dat2 instead of dat1 to a similar code chunk, thereby allowing us to compare the outputs:

```
dat2 %>%
  group_by(Year) %>%
  filter(Player == 'George Mikan*') -> test5
colorDF::highlight(test5, test5$Year == 1950)
## # Tibble (class tbl_df) 5 x 6:
## # Groups: Year [6]
## |Year  |Player        |Pos |G   |PTS
## 1|1950 |George Mikan* |C   |  68| 1865
## 2|1951 |George Mikan* |C   |  68| 1932
## 3|1952 |George Mikan* |C   |  64| 1523
## 4|1953 |George Mikan* |C   |  70| 1442
## 5|1954 |George Mikan* |C   |  72| 1306
## 6|1956 |George Mikan* |C   |  37|  390
```

Aside from the fact that test4 includes a variable called Tm and test5 doesn't—after all, test4 is derived from dat1, whereas test5 is derived instead from dat2—the outputs are similar. The compraredf() function from the arsenal package takes two data sets as arguments, compares the two, and returns a summary of findings. This is especially helpful when you need to compare two objects with dimensions much larger than test4 or test5:

```
arsenal::comparedf(test4, test5)
## Compare Object
##
## Function Call:
## arsenal::comparedf(x = test4, y = test5)
##
## Shared: 5 non-by variables and 6 observations.
## Not shared: 1 variables and 0 observations.
##
## Differences found in 0/5 variables compared.
## 0 variables compared have non-identical attributes.
```

Our third and final order of data wrangling business—at least for the time being—is to create one new variable and then remove superfluous data (rows and columns) from our working data set. We'll do that next.

19.3.2 *Final trimmings*

Moving forward, because our analysis will be directed at points scored per game, not total points scored, we call the dplyr mutate() function to create a new variable called PPG, which equals the quotient of the dividend PTS and the divisor G. The format() function from base R restricts PPG to include just one digit right of the decimal point. While we usually round or format our results to include up to two digits right of the decimal point, the NBA has historically recorded points per game and other metrics to include just one digit after the decimal point. The head() function returns the first six records:

```
dat2 %>%
  mutate(PPG = format(PTS/G, digits = 1, nsmall = 1)) -> dat2
head(dat2)
## # A tibble: 6 × 6
## # Groups:   Year, Player [6]
##   Year  Player       Pos       G   PTS PPG
##   <fct> <chr>        <fct> <int> <int> <chr>
## 1 1950  Al Cervi*    PG       56   573 10.2
## 2 1950  Al Guokas    F-G      57   214 3.8
## 3 1950  Al Miksis    C         8    27 3.4
## 4 1950  Alex Groza   C        64  1496 23.4
## 5 1950  Alex Hannum* PF       64   482 7.5
## 6 1950  Andrew Levane F-G     60   332 5.5
```

Our data set contains records for many marginal players; as previously mentioned, these are players at the end of the bench and quite possibly in the NBA on part-time contracts. By and large, they should therefore be removed from our data set to exclude them from our analysis. A quick and easy way of doing so is to again call the `filter()` function and reduce dat2 to include only players who averaged at least two points per game or who appeared in at least one-quarter of the games. It's hardly a stretch to label any player as marginal if he's failed to average at least one basket per game (a basket is the equivalent of a made shot and is worth at least two points) or play in more than 20 games during an 80-game or 82-game regular season schedule:

```
dat2 %>%
  filter(PPG >= 2 & G >= 20) -> dat2
dim(dat2)
## [1] 6390    6
```

These criteria significantly reduce the length of our data—dat2 previously contained 12,136 records and now contains just 6,390 observations.

At this point, we no longer need the variables `Pos`, `G`, and `PTS`; therefore, we next call the `select()` function from the `dplyr` package to subset dat2 on the variables `Year`, `Player`, and `PPG`:

```
dat2 %>%
  select(Year, Player, PPG) -> dat2
```

Finally, we convert our derived variable `PPG` from a character string to numeric by calling the base R `as.numeric()` function:

```
dat2$PPG <- as.numeric(dat2$PPG)
```

In the next section, we'll create a `ggplot2` bar chart that visualizes the year-over-year points per game averages for the NBA's leading scorers, demonstrate different methods of standardizing a numeric vector, and create like bar charts on the standardized data so that we can compare and contrast results across methods and against the raw data.

19.4   Standardizing data

No doubt, most of us have used data to challenge prior assumptions that stuck for years when data wasn't accessible or analysts weren't available to mine it. Standardization dares us to take different perspectives when data has, in fact, been stored, mined, and packaged for public consumption for a long while.

We start by making one enhancement to the dat2 data set by making a new variable called `Year_Player`, which is simply a concatenation of the existing variables `Year` and `Player`, made possible by the built-in `paste0()` function. The `paste0()` function takes `Year` as one argument, inserts a space, and then takes `Player` as a second argument. As a result, where `Year` might equal `1999` and `Player` might equal `Will Perdue`, our new variable `Year_Player` equals `1999 Will Perdue`. The base R `head()` and `tail()` functions return the first three and last three observations:

```
dat2$Year_Player <- paste0(as.character(dat2$Year)," ",
                           as.character(dat2$Player))
```

```
head(dat2, n = 3)
## # A tibble: 3 × 4
## # Groups:   Year, Player [3]
##   Year  Player          PPG Year_Player
##   <fct> <chr>         <dbl> <chr>
## 1 1950  Al Guokas       3.8 1950 Al Guokas
## 2 1950  Alex Groza     23.4 1950 Alex Groza
## 3 1950  Alex Hannum*    7.5 1950 Alex Hannum*
```

```
tail(dat2, n = 3)
## # A tibble: 3 × 4
## # Groups:   Year, Player [3]
##   Year  Player          PPG Year_Player
##   <fct> <chr>         <dbl> <chr>
## 1 1999  Walt Williams   9.3 1999 Walt Williams
## 2 1999  Walter McCarty  5.7 1999 Walter McCarty
## 3 1999  Will Perdue     2.4 1999 Will Perdue
```

Our intent is to use `Year_Player`, instead of `Year` *or* `Player`, as the x-axis variable in our forthcoming `ggplot2` bar charts—just so that we can display and fit both of these variables and not have to choose between one or the other. This will improve both the readability and aesthetics of our visual content.

Then, we pass dat2 to the `dplyr` `group_by()` and `slice()` functions—the `slice()` function extracts the one observation for every year in dat2 where the variable `PPG`, points per game, is the maximum. Our intent, after all, is to display just the annual points per game leaders; therefore, we need a data source which exactly satisfies that requirement. The results are then cast to a tibble called dat3:

```
dat2 %>%
  group_by(Year) %>%
  slice(which.max(PPG)) -> dat3
```

Next, we create our first `ggplot2` bar chart, where dat3 is the data source, `Year_Player` is our x-axis variable, and `PPG` is our y-axis variable (see figure 19.1). We are therefore visualizing the year-over-year NBA scoring leaders between the 1949–50 and 1998–99 seasons and their respective points per game average; it's our raw data baseline by which subsequent results will be compared and contrasted:

```
p1 <- ggplot(dat3, aes(x = Year_Player, y = PPG)) +
  geom_bar(stat = "identity", color = "dodgerblue", fill = "dodgerblue") +
  geom_text(aes(label = PPG),
            position = position_dodge(width = 0.8), vjust = -0.3,
            fontface = "bold", size = 2) +
  labs(title = "Leading Scorer (PPG) by Year",
       subtitle = "1950 to 1999",
       caption = "* Hall of Fame member",
       x = "Year and Leading Scorer",
```

```
                  y = "Points per Game") +
      theme(plot.title = element_text(face = "bold")) +
      theme(axis.text.x = element_text(angle = 90))
  print(p1)
```

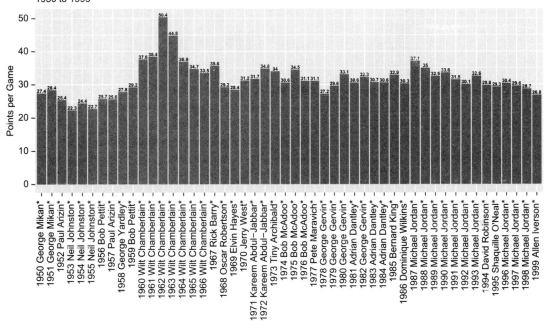

Figure 19.1   Year-over-year NBA scoring leaders and their average points scored per game, between the 1949–50 and 1998–99 seasons

Wilt Chamberlain's 50.4 points per game in 1961–62 and 44.8 average in 1962–63 clearly stand out. Next, we'll demonstrate various standardization techniques and compare the results to the year-over-year raw numbers we just displayed. If our original presumption is correct, one or more of the following methods should return very different results.

19.4.1 Z-score method

The z-score method is probably the most common or most popular way of standardizing data. It represents the number of standard deviations a raw number is above or below a population mean. The z-score is computed by subtracting the population mean from the raw number and then dividing the difference by the standard deviation.

In the next chunk of code, we pass dat2 to the group_by() and mutate() functions to compute z-scores for every dat2 record, where populations are segmented by the variable Year. For instance, George Mikan's 1950 PPG z-score is computed from a different mean and standard deviation than Wilt Chamberlain's 1962 z-score. The results are thrown into a tibble called dat4a. The `head()` and `tail()` functions return the first three and last three records, respectively:

```
dat2 %>%
  group_by(Year) %>%
  mutate(z_ppg = round((PPG - mean(PPG)) / sd(PPG), digits = 1)) -> dat4a
```

```
head(dat4a, n = 3)
## # A tibble: 3 × 5
## # Groups:   Year [1]
##   Year  Player         PPG Year_Player       z_ppg
##   <fct> <chr>        <dbl> <chr>             <dbl>
## 1 1950  Al Guokas      3.8 1950 Al Guokas     -0.8
## 2 1950  Alex Groza    23.4 1950 Alex Groza     5.6
## 3 1950  Alex Hannum*   7.5 1950 Alex Hannum*   0.4
```

```
tail(dat4a, n = 3)
## # A tibble: 3 × 5
## # Groups:   Year [1]
##   Year  Player           PPG Year_Player        z_ppg
##   <fct> <chr>          <dbl> <chr>              <dbl>
## 1 1999  Walt Williams    9.3 1999 Walt Williams   0.5
## 2 1999  Walter McCarty   5.7 1999 Walter McCarty -0.2
## 3 1999  Will Perdue      2.4 1999 Will Perdue    -0.9
```

In 1950, an average of 3.8 points scored per game was 0.8 standard deviations below the 1950 mean, while 23.4 points per game was 5.6 standard deviations above the 1950 mean.

There is a quick and easy way—actually, two quick and easy ways—of validating the integrity of the variable we just created, z_ppg. A vector of z-scores should have a mean equal to 0 and a variance equal to 1; we then call the base R `mean()` and `var()` functions to check for these:

```
mean(dat4a$z_ppg)
## [1] 0.0002503912
```

```
var(dat4a$z_ppg)
## [1] 0.9933541
```

When rounded, the z_ppg mean does, in fact, equal 0, and the z_ppg variance, a measure of dispersion that equals the standard deviation squared, equals 1. We should not have expected the mean to *exactly* equal 0 or for the variance to *exactly* equal 1 for the simple reason that we created z_ppg by each factor in the variable Year and not holistically.

Then, we pass dat4a to the `group_by()` and `slice()` functions, which cast the maximum z_ppg for each factor in the variable Year to a tibble called dat4b:

```
dat4a %>%
  group_by(Year) %>%
  slice(which.max(z_ppg)) -> dat4b
```

What's nice about the `slice()` function versus `summarize()` is that `slice()` pulls every variable for every applicable record; had we called the `summarize()` function instead, dat4b would instead contain only the variables `z_ppg` and `Year`. It's dat4b that we then throw into a second `ggplot2` bar chart, where `Year_Player` is again our x-axis variable and `z_ppg`, rather than `PPG`, is our y-axis variable (see figure 19.2):

```
p2 <- ggplot(dat4b, aes(x = Year_Player, y = z_ppg)) +
  geom_bar(stat = "identity", color = "darkorange", fill = "darkorange") +
  geom_text(aes(label = z_ppg),
            position = position_dodge(width = 0.8), vjust = -0.3,
            fontface = "bold", size = 2) +
  labs(title = "Leading Scorer (Z-Score) by Year",
       subtitle = "1950 to 1999",
       caption = "* Hall of Fame member",
       x = "Year and Leading Scorer",
       y = "Z-Score (standard deviations from mean)") +
  theme(plot.title = element_text(face = "bold")) +
  theme(axis.text.x = element_text(angle = 90))
print(p2)
```

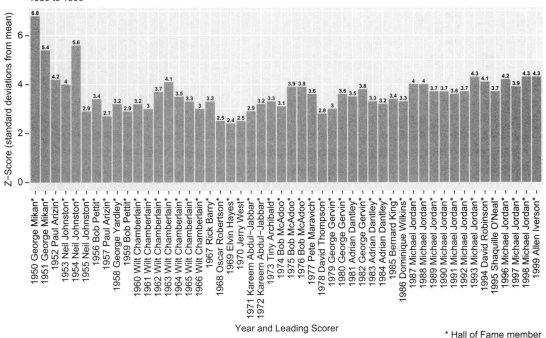

Figure 19.2   Year-over-year NBA scoring leaders and their average points scored per game, by z-score, between the 1949–50 and 1998–99 seasons

These results shed a totally different perspective on historical points per game averages. Wilt Chamberlain's 50.4 points per game average during the 1961–62 season was "only" 4.1 standard deviations above the mean for that year. Meanwhile, George Mikan's 1950 points per game average of 27.4 points was almost 7 standard deviations above the mean.

19.4.2 *Standard deviation method*

Another method of standardizing data is the standard deviation method. Whereas the z-score method subtracts the population mean from the raw data and then divides the difference by the standard deviation, the standard deviation method excludes the mean and simply divides the raw data by the standard deviation.

We pass dat2 to the `dplyr group_by()` and `mutate()` functions to compute the standard deviation method by each factor in the variable Year and persist the results in a new variable called sd_ppg. We get a new tibble called dat5a, which, of course, equals dat2 plus the variable sd_ppg. We get a peek at the first three and last three records in dat5a by calling the `head()` and `tail()` functions:

```
dat2 %>%
  group_by(Year) %>%
  mutate(sd_ppg = round((PPG / sd(PPG)), digits = 1)) -> dat5a

head(dat5a, n = 3)
## # A tibble: 3 × 5
## # Groups:   Year [1]
##   Year  Player          PPG Year_Player         sd_ppg
##   <fct> <chr>         <dbl> <chr>                <dbl>
## 1 1950  Al Guokas       3.8 1950 Al Guokas         1.2
## 2 1950  Alex Groza     23.4 1950 Alex Groza        7.5
## 3 1950  Alex Hannum*    7.5 1950 Alex Hannum*      2.4

tail(dat5a, n = 3)
## # A tibble: 3 × 5
## # Groups:   Year [1]
##   Year  Player          PPG Year_Player         sd_ppg
##   <fct> <chr>         <dbl> <chr>                <dbl>
## 1 1999  Walt Williams   9.3 1999 Walt Williams       2
## 2 1999  Walter McCarty  5.7 1999 Walter McCarty    1.2
## 3 1999  Will Perdue     2.4 1999 Will Perdue       0.5
```

The variance for sd_ppg, like the variance for z_ppg, equals 1:

```
var(dat5a$sd_ppg)
## [1] 1.018061
```

Then, we pass the tibble we just created, dat5a, to the `dplyr group_by()` and `slice()` functions. Together, these two functions effectively reduce dat5a to include just the one record per year where the variable sd_ppg is the maximum. These results are cast into yet another tibble called dat5b:

```
dat5a %>%
  group_by(Year) %>%
  slice(which.max(sd_ppg)) -> dat5b
```

Our results are then visualized with a `ggplot2` bar chart where dat5b is our data source, `Year_Player` is again our x-axis variable, and sd_ppg is our y-axis variable (see figure 19.3):

```
p3 <- ggplot(dat5b, aes(x = Year_Player, y = sd_ppg)) +
  geom_bar(stat = "identity", color = "salmon3", fill = "salmon3") +
  geom_text(aes(label = sd_ppg),
            position = position_dodge(width = 0.8), vjust = -0.3,
            fontface = "bold", size = 2) +
  labs(title = "Leading Scorer (Standard Deviation Method) by Year",
       subtitle = "1950 to 1999", caption = "* Hall of Fame member",
       x = "Year and Leading Scorer",
       y = "PPG / Standard Deviation") +
  theme(plot.title = element_text(face = "bold")) +
  theme(axis.text.x = element_text(angle = 90))
print(p3)
```

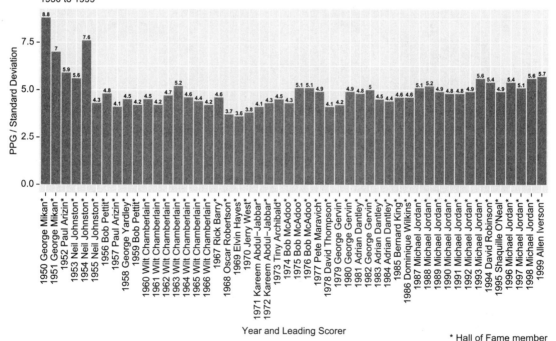

Figure 19.3 Year-over-year NBA scoring leaders and their average points scored per game, based on the standard deviation method, between the 1949–50 and 1998–99 seasons

These results look very similar to our previous results, suggesting that the annual mean in points scored per game, which factors into the z-score method but not the standard deviation method, is essentially neutral, or immaterial. When these results are otherwise compared with the raw data, George Mikan's 1950 season again stands out. Neal Johnston's 1954 season stands out too, and Allen Iverson's 1998–99 season with the Philadelphia 76ers is the most significant outlier in the last 45-plus NBA seasons.

19.4.3 *Centering method*

The centering method simply subtracts some constant—such as the minimum or maximum, but usually the mean—from the raw data. We'll subtract the annual mean, but if our prior assumption about the points per game mean is correct—that it's neutral—our results should therefore resemble the raw data.

First, we pass dat2 to the `group_by()` and `summarize()` functions to compute the annual points per game mean. The results are then cast into a tibble called dat6a. We get the first three and last three dat6a records returned by calling the `head()` and `tail()` functions:

```
dat2 %>%
  group_by(Year) %>%
  summarize(mean = round(mean(PPG), digits = 1)) -> dat6a

head(dat6a, n = 3)
## # A tibble: 3 × 2
##    Year   mean
##    <fct>  <dbl>
## 1 1950    6.1
## 2 1951    6.6
## 3 1952    7.1

tail(dat6a, n = 3)
## # A tibble: 3 × 2
##    Year   mean
##    <fct>  <dbl>
## 1 1997    7.2
## 2 1998    6.7
## 3 1999    6.8
```

Second, we call the `left_join()` function from the `dplyr` package to merge, or join, dat3 and dat6a by the variable `Year`, which is the one variable these two tibbles have in common. Whereas dat3 has a 68 × 4 dimension and dat6a has a 68 × 2 dimension, dat6b has a 68 × 5 dimension. The `head()` and `tail()` functions return the top three and bottom three dat6b observations:

```
left_join(dat3, dat6a, by = "Year") -> dat6b

head(dat6b, n = 3)
## # A tibble: 3 × 5
## # Groups:    Year [3]
##    Year  Player          PPG Year_Player          mean
##    <fct> <chr>         <dbl> <chr>               <dbl>
## 1 1950  George Mikan*  27.4 1950 George Mikan*   6.1
## 2 1951  George Mikan*  28.4 1951 George Mikan*   6.6
## 3 1952  Paul Arizin*   25.4 1952 Paul Arizin*    7.1
```

```
tail(dat6b, n = 3)
## # A tibble: 3 × 5
## # Groups:   Year [3]
##   Year  Player          PPG Year_Player          mean
##   <fct> <chr>          <dbl> <chr>               <dbl>
## 1 1997  Michael Jordan* 29.6 1997 Michael Jordan*  7.2
## 2 1998  Michael Jordan* 28.7 1998 Michael Jordan*  6.7
## 3 1999  Allen Iverson*  26.8 1999 Allen Iverson*   6.8
```

Now we have the per-year maximum PPG and the per-year population mean in a single object.

Third, we pass dat6b to the `mutate()` function to create a new dat6b variable called c_ppg, which equals PPG minus the mean. Now you know why we just performed a left join—we needed these two variables in the same object to derive c_ppg. To continue providing visibility into all these steps, we again call the `head()` and `tail()` functions to return six records between them:

```
dat6b %>%
  mutate(c_ppg = PPG - mean) -> dat6b

head(dat6b, n = 3)
## # A tibble: 3 × 6
## # Groups:   Year [3]
##   Year  Player          PPG Year_Player          mean c_ppg
##   <fct> <chr>          <dbl> <chr>               <dbl> <dbl>
## 1 1950  George Mikan*   27.4 1950 George Mikan*    6.1  21.3
## 2 1951  George Mikan*   28.4 1951 George Mikan*    6.6  21.8
## 3 1952  Paul Arizin*    25.4 1952 Paul Arizin*     7.1  18.3

tail(dat6b, n = 3)
## # A tibble: 3 × 6
## # Groups:   Year [3]
##   Year  Player          PPG Year_Player          mean c_ppg
##   <fct> <chr>          <dbl> <chr>               <dbl> <dbl>
## 1 1997  Michael Jordan* 29.6 1997 Michael Jordan*  7.2  22.4
## 2 1998  Michael Jordan* 28.7 1998 Michael Jordan*  6.7  22
## 3 1999  Allen Iverson*  26.8 1999 Allen Iverson*   6.8  20
```

Fourth, we create yet another `ggplot2` bar chart as a way of visualizing outcomes (see figure 19.4); dat6b is our data source, `Year_Player` runs along the x-axis, and c_ppg runs along the y-axis:

```
p4 <- ggplot(dat6b, aes(x = Year_Player, y = c_ppg)) +
  geom_bar(stat = "identity", color = "aquamarine4",
           fill = "aquamarine4") +
  geom_text(aes(label = c_ppg),
            position = position_dodge(width = 0.8), vjust = -0.3,
            fontface = "bold", size = 2) +
  labs(title = "Leading Scorer (Centering Method) by Year",
       subtitle = "1950 to 2017",
       caption = "* Hall of Fame member",
       x = "Year and Leading Scorer",
```

```
            y = "PPG - Annual Mean") +
    theme(plot.title = element_text(face = "bold")) +
    theme(axis.text.x = element_text(angle = 90))
  print(p4)
```

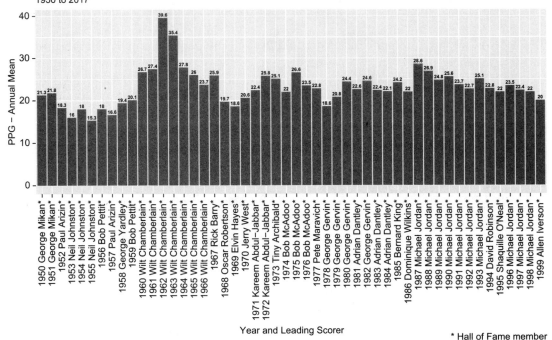

Figure 19.4   Year-over-year NBA scoring leaders and their average points scored per game, based on the centering method, between the 1949–50 and 1998–99 seasons

It's no surprise that these results are a near copy of the raw numbers. Yes, the totals affixed to the top of the bars are less, of course, than the raw numbers, but that's because we subtracted the annual population mean in points scored per game from the variable PPG. More significantly, though, the year-over-year comparisons match perfectly with the raw data.

19.4.4   Range method

In this fourth and final method, we divide the raw numbers by the annual range, which is equal to the maximum points per game average minus the minimum points per game average for each factor in Year.

Thus, we pass dat2 to the group_by() and mutate() functions, thereby creating a new variable called r_ppg, which is equal to PPG divided by the maximum PPG minus the minimum PPG. We then get the first three and last three records in dat7a, the tibble we just created, by calling the head() and tail() functions:

```
dat2 %>%
  group_by(Year) %>%
  mutate(r_ppg = round((PPG) / (max(PPG) - min(PPG)), digits = 1)) -> dat7a

head(dat7a, n = 3)
## # A tibble: 3 × 5
## # Groups:   Year [1]
##   Year  Player          PPG Year_Player       r_ppg
##   <fct> <chr>         <dbl> <chr>             <dbl>
## 1 1950  Al Guokas       3.8 1950 Al Guokas     0.2
## 2 1950  Alex Groza     23.4 1950 Alex Groza    0.9
## 3 1950  Alex Hannum*    7.5 1950 Alex Hannum*  0.3

tail(dat7a, n = 3)
## # A tibble: 3 × 5
## # Groups:   Year [1]
##   Year  Player          PPG Year_Player          r_ppg
##   <fct> <chr>         <dbl> <chr>                <dbl>
## 1 1999  Walt Williams   9.3 1999 Walt Williams    0.4
## 2 1999  Walter McCarty  5.7 1999 Walter McCarty   0.2
## 3 1999  Will Perdue     2.4 1999 Will Perdue      0.1
```

Next, we cut a tibble called dat7b, which includes only those records, one for each Year factor, where our derived variable r_ppg is the maximum. It turns out that r_ppg equals 1.1 for every dat7b record. Rather than create a (rather unremarkable) bar chart, we'll instead show the first 10 and last 10 results:

```
dat7b %>%
  group_by(Year) %>%
  slice(which.max(r_ppg)) -> dat7b

head(dat7b, n = 10)
## # A tibble: 10 × 5
## # Groups:   Year [10]
##    Year  Player           PPG Year_Player           r_ppg
##    <fct> <chr>          <dbl> <chr>                 <dbl>
## 1  1950  George Mikan*   27.4 1950 George Mikan*     1.1
## 2  1951  George Mikan*   28.4 1951 George Mikan*     1.1
## 3  1952  Paul Arizin*    25.4 1952 Paul Arizin*      1.1
## 4  1953  Neil Johnston*  22.3 1953 Neil Johnston*    1.1
## 5  1954  Neil Johnston*  24.4 1954 Neil Johnston*    1.1
## 6  1955  Neil Johnston*  22.7 1955 Neil Johnston*    1.1
## 7  1956  Bob Pettit*     25.7 1956 Bob Pettit*       1.1
## 8  1957  Bob Pettit*     24.7 1957 Bob Pettit*       1.1
## 9  1958  George Yardley* 27.8 1958 George Yardley*   1.1
## 10 1959  Bob Pettit*     29.2 1959 Bob Pettit*       1.1

tail(dat7b, n = 10)
## # A tibble: 10 × 5
## # Groups:   Year [10]
##    Year  Player            PPG Year_Player            r_ppg
##    <fct> <chr>           <dbl> <chr>                  <dbl>
## 1  1990  Michael Jordan*  33.6 1990 Michael Jordan*    1.1
## 2  1991  Michael Jordan*  31.5 1991 Michael Jordan*    1.1
```

```
## 3 1992  Michael Jordan*     30.1 1992 Michael Jordan*     1.1
## 4 1993  Michael Jordan*     32.6 1993 Michael Jordan*     1.1
## 5 1994  David Robinson*     29.8 1994 David Robinson*     1.1
## 6 1995  Shaquille O'Neal*   29.3 1995 Shaquille O'Neal*   1.1
## 7 1996  Michael Jordan*     30.4 1996 Michael Jordan*     1.1
## 8 1997  Michael Jordan*     29.6 1997 Michael Jordan*     1.1
## 9 1998  Michael Jordan*     28.7 1998 Michael Jordan*     1.1
## 10 1999 Allen Iverson*      26.8 1999 Allen Iverson*      1.1
```

While we have demonstrated four methods of standardizing a single variable, sometimes it's necessary to standardize two or more variables where the raw numbers are on vastly different scales. That's because we don't want one variable, such as transaction amounts, which can range between hundreds or even thousands of dollars, to weigh more heavily in a customer segmentation or other similar analysis versus another variable, such as transaction counts, which usually ranges between single and double digits. The range method makes more sense when standardizing two or more variables, as opposed to a single variable, such as PPG, that spans decades.

Returning to our analysis, we demonstrated that standardization has the potential to present data in radically different ways from what we otherwise might be used to, and therefore challenges us to rethink prior conventions. Almost everyone still talks about Wilt Chamberlain, but barely anyone pays any attention to George Mikan's exploits. Based on what we've presented here, that should definitely change.

Our next and last chapter is a summarization of the first 19 chapters.

Summary

- Standardization is a critical statistical concept to know and apply when you have a single continuous variable, such as average points scored per game, that spans a long time horizon. The raw data therefore has different "meanings" over time because of changing external factors. Think inflation and why we convert older dollars to current dollars.

- When you have two or more continuous variables where the raw data is on very different scales, to prevent one of those variables from having undue influence, it's important to convert the variables to like scales—using like methods—and then cast the standardized versions of your data into your analysis.

- We demonstrated four data standardization methods because there's no one-size-fits-all data standardization solution. Which of these methods might be the best for your use case mostly depends on your data and whether you're standardizing just a single variable or multiple variables. It's good practice to test different methods and not settle on a single, predefined method.

- We also showed how you can add color to data frame–like objects and even highlight records that meet a logical criteria. These are good techniques to know that might aid your real-time analysis efforts or when you intend to inject (albeit crude) R outputs directly into a PowerPoint presentation, RMarkdown file, or other document type.

- We introduced and demonstrated some different data wrangling techniques—extracting observations that meet a specific criterion with `slice()`, selecting only unique, or distinct, records from a data set with `distinct()`, comparing two objects and getting a report on the differences with `comparedf()`, and concatenating strings with `paste0()`.

- We also demonstrated how best to call functions that cross between packages. Rather than separately loading those packages and calling their functions, it's actually best to load the packages and call the applicable function within the same line of code. There might actually be more of a need to apply this technique going forward as the number of R functions and packages increases every year.

Finishing up

Our purpose in these last few pages is to survey the results from chapters 2 through 19 and review the techniques we used along the way. Rather than go chapter by chapter and therefore repeat our journey in the same sequence, we'll instead consolidate our findings into nine "learning areas" that are further broken down by packages, applied techniques, and chapter references. For instance, between chapters 5 and 14, we developed four types of models—linear regression, regression tree, analysis of variance (ANOVA), and logistic regression—using a mix of base R and packaged functions; accordingly, modeling is one of our nine learning areas. Once we get to section 20.4, we'll review which models were applied where and for what ends.

The following learning areas are listed in the order in which they will be presented:

- Cluster analysis (20.1)
- Significance testing (20.2)
- Effect size testing (20.3)
- Modeling (20.4)
- Operations research (20.5)
- Probability (20.6)
- Statistical dispersion (20.7)
- Standardization (20.8)
- Summary statistics and visualization (20.9)

In addition, we've created a series of Sankey diagrams (see chapter 3), one for each learning area, that plot the relationships between learning areas, packages and base R functions, techniques, and chapter numbers. These final visualizations are therefore visual snapshots of the same confluences.

20.1 Cluster analysis

Cluster analysis is a type of unsupervised learning method and multivariate analysis technique that classifies objects (e.g., automobiles, neighborhoods, almost anything, really) into one of multiple groups, or clusters, based on their similarity. A department store chain might segment its customers based on demographic data and prior purchases with the intent of then mapping made-to-order marketing strategies with clusters. No doubt, the most common or most popular clustering algorithms are hierarchical clustering and K-means clustering. We featured these two clustering techniques in chapters 3 and 11, respectively.

We began this journey by making the case that tanking is a perfectly logical (albeit repugnant) strategy for down-and-out NBA teams who plan to rebuild their rosters through the amateur draft. That's because the league rewards its worst teams with the first few picks, and about the only possible way of selecting a future superstar—the sort of player who can reverse a team's fortunes—is to pick at or near the very top of the draft. We concluded our case by developing a hierarchical clustering using a series of base R functions.

More to the point, we created a distance matrix based on mean career win shares grouped by first-round pick number from the 2000 to 2009 NBA drafts. A hierarchical clustering begins by treating every object, or observation, as its own cluster. It then iterates by merging two similar clusters at a time until all the clusters—30 in our case, or 1 cluster per first-round selection—are merged into one. The end result is a dendrogram, or upside-down tree, that displays the original clusters along the x-axis and results from the distance matrix along the y-axis.

What's especially nice about creating dendrograms in R is that we have the option of drawing a *K* number of transparent boxes on top of the plot to further differentiate clusters. We set *K* equal to 2 to see if R would then draw one transparent box around draft picks 1 through 5 and another box around picks 6 through 30, and therefore return similar results from our previous analyses. Sure enough, that's exactly what R did for us.

In chapter 10 and again in chapter 11, we explored the relationship between team payrolls and regular season wins, postseason appearances, and championships—concluding that, minus a couple of exceptions, team payrolls are otherwise leading indicators of team trajectories. We finished our analysis with a K-means clustering.

A K-means clustering differs from a hierarchical clustering in at least two ways—(1) we must tell R up front how many clusters to create, and (2) we get a *K* number of clusters based on two or more continuous variables that, for plotting purposes, are automatically standardized or rescaled for us. We plotted adjusted payrolls and regular season wins between the 2000 and 2017 seasons.

We first demonstrated a pair of methods to compute optimal cluster counts (versus randomly generating K), using functions from the `factoextra` package. The within-cluster sum of squares method, sometimes called the elbow method because it suggests an optimal cluster count at the (unprecise) location where the ensuing scree plot bends, returned six clusters; the silhouette method returned two clusters.

We decided to split the difference and instruct R to segment the results into four clusters. A K-means clustering crunches numbers through (possibly) several iterative steps until the total sum of squares between the data and their respective centroid, or the center position of a cluster, is minimized, without, of course, violating the predetermined requirement for K. Maybe the most fascinating part of our results is that R relegated the New York Knicks, which had a payroll more than three standard deviations *above* the league mean and a regular season win count more than one standard deviation *below* the mean, to its own cluster. Meanwhile, the San Antonio Spurs, winners of more regular season games between 2000 and 2017 than any other team on a below-average payroll, were clustered with 10 other teams. Results were returned from base R functionality and then visualized through the `factoextra` package.

Unsupervised learning methods in general and cluster analysis in particular return results that are more subjective than, let's say, a linear regression or a t-test. We further demonstrated in chapter 11 that results can and will vary significantly when we apply different values to K; thus, the idiosyncrasies of cluster analysis, especially K-means, escalate as we increase K. A pair of customers who seemingly share similar profiles and therefore deserve to be on the receiving end of like marketing campaigns when K equals 2 can and do get partitioned into different clusters when K then equals 3 or more. Nevertheless, cluster analysis is an essential technique for exploring data and evaluating groups, as well as a critical enabler for applying different treatments that usually get better returns than all-in-one strategies.

The first of our Sankey diagrams—indeed, all of the Sankey diagrams that follow—should be read from left to right (see figure 20.1). The left-most node is the applicable learning area; the next node, or series of nodes, represents the packages and/or built-in functions that were called; the next set of nodes represents the applied techniques; and the right-most set of nodes are the chapter references. So hierarchical clustering was developed with base R functions only, whereas our K-means clustering was developed with a combination of base R and `factoextra` functions. Hierarchical clustering was demonstrated in chapter 3 and K-means clustering was demonstrated in chapter 11. (By the way, the width of the connectors, or links, between node groupings doesn't mean anything.)

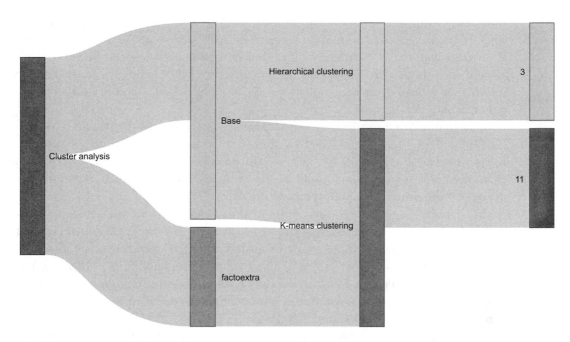

Figure 20.1 Hierarchical clustering was demonstrated in chapter 3 as the final piece of evidence supporting tanking; K-means clustering was demonstrated in chapter 11 as a way of segmenting like teams based on a combination of their respective payrolls and regular season wins. Our hierarchical clustering was developed and visualized exclusively with base R functions; conversely, our K-means clustering was mostly developed with built-in functions, but visualized through the `factoextra` package.

20.2 Significance testing

Any significance test—whether a t-test, a chi-square test for independence, a correlation test, or an F-test—should revolve around a null hypothesis (H_0) and its opposite, an alternative hypothesis (H_1). We always start with a null hypothesis; that is, we assume going in that any variances are due to chance. We then run a significance test that tells us either to reject the null hypothesis or to fail to reject it. By rejecting the null hypothesis, we're therefore accepting the alternative hypothesis.

Let's say we have two like groups of delinquent customers getting different collections treatments. A significance test tells us if performance differences are due to chance or if they should instead be attributed to dissimilarities in treatments. We fail to reject the null hypothesis if the former, or we reject the null hypothesis if the latter. If the results are significant, it would then make sense to apply the winning treatment to all customers.

The p-value from a significance test tells us whether to reject a null hypothesis. We consistently applied a predefined 5% threshold, which is most common—when the returned p-value was greater than 5%, we failed to reject our null hypothesis, and when it was instead less than 5%, we rejected that null hypothesis and accepted the alternative hypothesis. Significance thresholds are sometimes set as low as 1% and sometimes as high as 10%. This means a significance test essentially returns a binary result; that is, based on the applied significance threshold, observed variances are either immaterial or consequential.

Bear in mind that results from significance testing, especially t-tests and chi-square tests for independence, are based on the variances as well as the size of the data. If you're ever asked to design a test and control (sometimes referred to as a champion/challenger), you should divide your test and control populations and determine the duration of your test accordingly.

In chapter 7, we explored the possibility that home-court advantage, so prevalent in the NBA, could be due, at least in part, to biased officiating. Of course, officials don't influence which shots are made or missed or which team recovers a loose ball, but they are responsible for calling—or not calling—personal fouls, which are typically discretionary. Personal foul calls usually result in free throw attempts—and more points—for the opposing team. But in a broader sense, they can disrupt substitution patterns and therefore affect the flow of a game.

Visiting teams are whistled for more personal foul calls than home teams, and as a result, home teams attempt more free throws than visiting teams, at least based on data from the 2018–19 and 2019–20 seasons. Raw numbers, however, don't tell us if these variances are merely due to chance or if there's some meaning behind them. This is where significance testing comes in.

A t-test is an appropriate significance, or hypothesis, test when we want to compare means from two groups—and only two groups—and we have continuous data to work with. Our null, or going-in, hypothesis is that the group means are essentially equal; we therefore require a very low p-value to reject a null hypothesis that the means are statistically equal and instead accept the alternative hypothesis that something other than chance is at the root cause of any variances. We ran eight t-tests in chapter 7; while the raw numbers were consistently slanted in favor of home teams—or even *designated* home teams when games were played at a neutral site—our tests returned statistically significant results where we had large record counts and insignificant results otherwise. Significant tests, including t-tests, are usually run from base R functions, but in chapter 7, we also ran t-tests from the ggpubr package, which then allowed us to automatically insert the results into ggplot2 boxplots.

Then, in chapters 12 and 13, we discovered that championship-winning teams between 1991 and 2018 have more unequal salary distributions and more unequal win share distributions than other teams; by the same token, winning teams—not just winning teams that then won a league title, but teams with regular season winning percentages above .500—have more unequal salary distributions and more unequal win share distributions than losing teams. We ran additional t-tests to determine if the variances in the Gini coefficient means between groups was or was not statistically significant; every t-test returned a p-value below the .05 threshold for significance. In layman terms, the salary distributions and win share distributions are key differentiators when it comes to winning, and winning championships.

A correlation test is another significance test run with continuous data. We ran our first correlation test in chapter 10 to determine whether team payrolls and regular season wins, at least between the 2000 and 2017 seasons, have a statistically significant association, or relationship. Our null hypothesis is that they don't, but our correlation test returned a p-value below .05, so we rejected the null hypothesis and instead concluded that there is, in fact, a meaningful relationship between payrolls and wins.

We ran two more correlation tests in chapter 14—the first between wins and points allowed and the second between wins and points scored. Our variables were first rescaled to mitigate the effects of time. You might recall that our purpose in chapter 14 was to measure the relative influences of defense and offense on winning. If defense truly matters more than offense, as conventional thinking has suggested for many years, then our two correlation tests should return very different results. They didn't, however—our two tests returned statistically significant and identical results, thereby suggesting that defense and offense have equal effects on winning. Correlation tests are run from the base R functionality.

Switching gears a bit, we ran a different sort of significance test, a chi-square test for independence, in chapter 9, where we explored wins and losses between home and visiting teams based on different permutations of prior days of rest. A chi-square test rather than a t-test (or certainly a correlation test) was the more appropriate significance test because we were working with categorical data in chapter 9 instead of continuous data.

Nevertheless, we start with a null hypothesis and then reject, or fail to reject, that null hypothesis based on the test's p-value. We ultimately rejected the null hypothesis and therefore concluded that permutations of days of rest matter in wins and losses. Our chi-square test for independence was run from base R, and we then visualized the results two ways, once from the `gtools` package and again from the `vcd` package.

Finally, we ran an F-test from base R in chapter 13 to help us decide which results to accept from three competing effect size tests (see section 20.3). As with t-tests and chi-square tests, our starting point is a null hypothesis, and the finish line is a p-value less than or equal to .05. Our second Sankey diagram (see figure 20.2) visually summarizes the significance testing learning area.

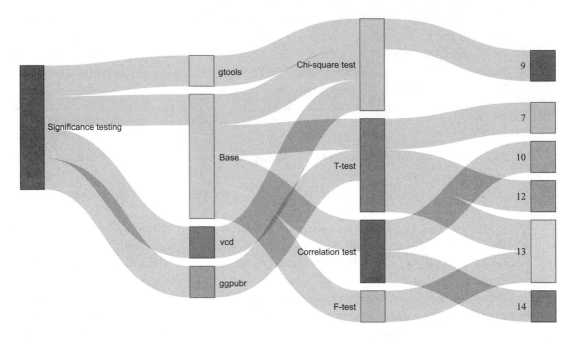

Figure 20.2   Significance tests start with a null hypothesis that is subsequently rejected or not rejected based on a p-value with a 5% threshold. Which significance test to run is conditioned on the data (usually, but not always, continuous versus categorical). Significance tests are usually run from base R functions, and the results are typically visualized through packaged functions.

20.3   *Effect size testing*

Whereas a statistical test of significance returns a p-value that tells us, usually at a 5% threshold, whether or not the variance between observed and expected results are statistically significant, effect size tests tell us how large or not so large that same variance happens to be. Consider the following about effect size testing:

- Effect size tests should complement, or supplement, statistical tests of significance and not take their place. We don't reject or fail to reject a null hypothesis based on effect size testing.

- Like other statistical tests, choosing the right effect size test depends on the data. Cohen's d, Hedges' g, and Glass's delta effect size tests are run against continuous data, so they complement t-tests. A Cramer's V effect size test, on the other hand, is run against categorical data, so it complements chi-square tests for independence.

- Cohen's d is the most popular effect size test for continuous data. We ran Cohen's d tests in chapters 7, 12, and 13, and we ran Hedges' g and Glass's delta tests in chapter 13 only.

- Our Cohen's d tests were run from the `effsize` package in chapters 7, 12, and 13 and again from the `effectsize` package in chapter 13 only. Our Hedges' g and Glass's delta tests were therefore run from the `effectsize` package only.

- Cramer's V is the go-to effect size test for categorical data. We twice ran Cramer's V effect size tests in chapter 9, once from the `questionr` package and again from the `rcompanion` package.

- Results between statistical tests of significance and effect size tests might not always line up. For instance, a t-test that returns a p-value well below the 5% threshold won't necessarily translate into a large effect size; conversely, a t-test or other significance test that returns a p-value above 5% might, in fact, equate to a large effect size. Once more, significance tests consider record counts, whereas effect size tests do not.

- In general, when the quantitative result equals 0.2 or less, the effect size is considered small; when the result is at or around 0.5, the effect size is considered to be medium; and when the result is equal to or above 0.8, the effect size is considered to be large.

Our next Sankey diagram (see figure 20.3) visualizes these very same associations.

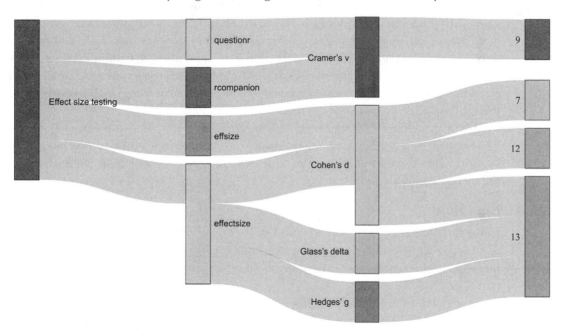

Figure 20.3 Effect size tests should complement or supplement, and not replace, significance testing. Cohen's d, Hedges' g, and Glass's delta are effect size tests that were run to complement t-tests, where the data is continuous; Cramer's V is an effect size test that was run to complement a chi-square test for independence, where the data is categorical rather than continuous. A Cohen's d test, the most popular effect size test for continuous data, was run from the `effsize` package in chapters 7, 12, and 13 and from the `effectsize` package in chapter 13; Hedges' g and Glass's delta tests were run from the `effectsize` package in chapter 13 only. Cramer's V was run twice in chapter 9, once from the `questionr` package and once from the `rcompanion` package.

In chapter 7, we explored the possibility that game officials are biased toward home teams by quantifying personal foul calls and free throw attempts between road and home teams and then testing and measuring the variances. Regardless of the preceding t-test results, our Cohens' d tests—where group means and standard deviations are crunched and record counts are ignored—returned negligible effect sizes. We tested the 2018–19 regular season and postseason and the 2019–20 regular season, pre- and post-COVID.

In chapter 12, we explored the relationship between salary inequality and winning, using a data set that spanned 28 NBA seasons. We discovered that teams with higher regular season winning percentages have more unequal salary distributions than teams with lower winning percentages; we also discovered that championship-winning teams have more unequal salary distributions than the rest of the league. We then ran a pair of Cohen's d effect size tests to measure the salary distribution differences—in both cases, Cohen's d returned medium effect sizes.

In chapter 13, we analyzed win share distributions across teams (as a substitute for salary inequality) versus winning. We subsequently learned that teams with more unequal win share distributions are the same teams that win more regular season games and also win championships. We used chapter 13 as an opportunity to further demonstrate effect size testing by introducing another package, which then allowed us to run Hedges' g and Glass's delta effect size tests in addition to Cohen's d tests. These other tests returned the same results as our final Cohen's d tests, despite small differences in how the effect sizes are computed. The effect sizes were small irrespective of the method and regardless of the test.

As for our Cramer's V tests from chapter 9, where we set out to measure the effect size between rest and winning versus losing, our results indicated that rest has a small to moderate effect on game results, at least based on regular season games between the 2012–13 and 2017–18 seasons.

20.4   *Modeling*

In the 2016–17 regular season, the NBA started measuring hustle statistics—plays such as blocked shots, deflections, and loose balls recovered. We set out in chapter 5 to investigate which of these hustle statistics, if any, matter in the grand scheme of wins and losses.

Our starting point was a multiple linear regression, where regular season wins (a continuous variable) were regressed against the NBA's hustle statistics (other continuous variables), prefaced by an exhaustive data exploration and data wrangling effort that included the following:

- Identifying outliers by drawing boxplots for each variable and, where outliers were present, eliminating them by increasing their value to equal the so-called minimum or decreasing their value to equal the maximum—because outliers could disproportionately bias model results. The process of "capping" values is called winsorization.
- Checking for normal distributions by drawing density plots and running Shapiro-Wilk tests and, where applicable, removing variables with non-normal

distributions as candidate predictors—because linear regression assumes, even requires, that variables take on a Gaussian distribution. We assume normality when a Shapiro-Wilk test returns a p-value above 0.05.

- Creating a matrix that displays the correlations between every pair of remaining variables and returns the correlation coefficients between the same—because we wanted to identify those variables that had the most promise as predictors.

Furthermore, we followed other best practices in the model development process, including the following:

- Splitting the data into mutually exclusive subsets for developing and predicting
- Checking for multicollinearity among the predictors
- Running diagnostics
- Fitting a second, or competing, model and comparing our two regressions for the best fit of the data

Our best multiple linear regression explains less than 20% of the variance in regular season wins (the total variance ties back to the R^2, or better yet, adjusted R^2 statistics); however, our intent wasn't to explain wins but rather to isolate those hustle statistics that actually influence wins and to quantify their collective effect. Points scored from screens, pass deflections on defense, and loose balls recovered have a statistically significant influence on the variance in regular season wins; that is, our best regression returned p-values less than .05 for these three variables.

Whereas linear regression draws a straight but diagonal line that minimizes the distances between it and the data, a regression tree—often referred to as a decision tree regression—draws a jagged line over the data through a series of if-else statements. We then fit a regression tree to see if a different type of model would return similar or dissimilar results.

In addition, whereas results from linear models are returned in tabular format (aside from the diagnostics), the results from tree-based models are returned in graphical format only. We get an upside-down tree by which the most significant predictors and splits are at the "top" of the tree, and the remaining predictors and splits are at the "bottom." It turned out that our regression tree isolated the same three variables—points from screens, deflections, and loose balls recovered—as having the most influence on regular season wins.

Linear regressions are developed from base R. We checked for multicollinearity by using the `car` package, and we called on functions from the `broom` package—part of the `tidyverse` universe of packages—to return a subset of our results. Our regression tree was developed from the `tree` package (though R offers other packaged alternatives) and visualized from base R.

We returned to modeling in chapter 14 as part of our effort to establish—or refute—the idea that defense matters more than offense, using a data set that spanned the 2007 through 2018 seasons. An analysis of variance (ANOVA) requires a continuous, or quantitative, dependent variable and a categorical predictor variable split between at least three data series. We separately tested a standardized conversion of regular season wins against standardized conversions of points allowed and then points scored; if defense is more important than offense, then our first model should better explain wins than our second model. However, the two models returned identical results. ANOVAs are fit using base R.

A logistic regression requires a binary dependent variable and one or more (usually) continuous predictor variables. We separately regressed a dependent variable that equals 0 for teams that failed to qualify for postseason play and equals 1 for teams that did make the postseason against the same predictors we threw into our ANOVAs. Again, if defense actually matters more than offense, our first logistic regression should better explain or predict whether or not teams qualify for postseason play. In fact, our first regression was stronger than our second model, but the differences were negligible. Overall, the fairest conclusion we could come to is that defense and offense have roughly equal influences on regular season wins and whether or not teams qualify for the postseason.

Logistic regressions are developed from base R; however, we then called a mix of packaged functions to get our results. Those details are reflected in the following Sankey diagram (see figure 20.4).

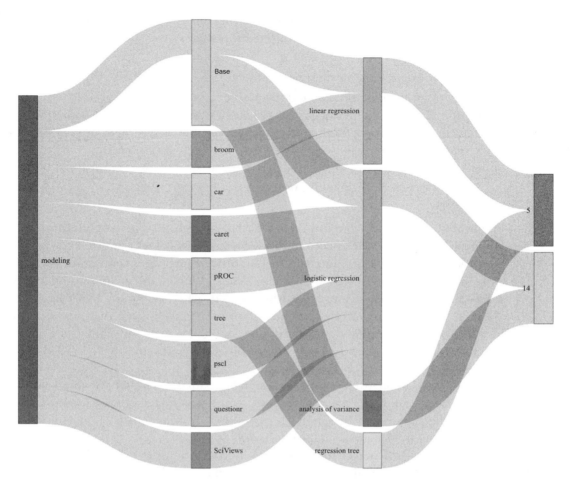

Figure 20.4   In chapter 5, we developed linear regression and regression tree models to isolate hustle statistics that might have a statistically significant effect on wins and losses. From both model types, we discovered that points scored from screens, pass deflections on defense, and loose balls recovered matter more than other like statistics and do, in fact, contribute to wins and losses. In chapter 14, we developed ANOVA and logistic regression models to establish if defense matters more than offense in terms of regular season wins from the former and postseason qualification from the latter. Our models returned statistically significant results, but it wasn't clear and unmistakable that defense matters more than offense.

20.5   *Operations research*

Unlike the previous learning areas, operations research contains a melting pot of techniques. Once more, we made a case for tanking in chapters 2 and 3 for teams that choose to rebuild via the amateur draft. Other teams, however, can and do choose instead to rebuild their rosters by acquiring veteran players via free agency. In chapter 4, we demonstrated how a fictional NBA team could optimize their free agent acquisitions and eliminate the guesswork by setting up a constrained optimization problem. Constrained optimization is an operations research technique by which some function is maximized or minimized while obeying one or more hard constraints. Our fictional team sought to maximize projected win shares across its free agent acquisitions within the following constraints:

- Exactly five free agents must be acquired.
- Each free agent must play a unique position.
- Annual salaries could not exceed $90,000,000; salaries could be distributed any which way between the five free agents, but their aggregated annual salaries must equal $90,000,000 or less.
- The average age of the five free agents at the time of signing must not exceed 30; there were no age limits per free agent, but the average must be equal to or less than 30.

The heavy lifting comes from the `lpSolve` package—the function to be maximized or minimized must be linear and continuous (win shares—check) and the constraints must also be linear and continuous (exact number of free agent acquisitions—check, exact number of acquisitions by position—check, maximum salary allocation per year—check, maximum average age when signed—check). From a short list of 24 available players, our constrained optimization problem returned the names of five free agents to acquire: one point guard, one shooting guard, one center, one power forward, and one small forward with annual salary demands that totaled $89,500,000 and an average age that equaled 28.4.

Any other solution would have been less than optimal or would have necessitated a breach of one or more of the hard constraints. Our constrained optimization problem can easily be repurposed by simply changing out the function to be maximized or minimized and by changing out the constraints.

By the time we reached chapter 8, we had effectively transitioned from "front office" analytics to "in-game" analytics. Here, we explored how well the optimal stopping rule applies when teams have 24 seconds by which to attempt a shot and avoid a turnover. There's a reason why optimal stopping is also known as the 37% rule—NBA teams should theoretically pass and dribble, not shoot, during the first 37% of their allotted time and then take the first shot that compares favorably to a previous shot opportunity. Likewise, if you're a hiring manager interviewing for an open role in your organization, you should automatically pass on the first 37% of the candidates and then hire the first applicant who compares favorably to the previous candidates. Optimal stopping is fixed on returning the highest probability of a best outcome, versus several alternatives, while preempting wasteful efforts—*when there are no second chances.*

Our analysis suggested that the *letter* of optimal stopping applied fairly well to the Milwaukee Bucks and Charlotte Hornets, but not necessarily to the Atlanta Hawks; further analysis also suggested that ongoing, or back-and-forth, regressions to the mean were more at play than the optimal stopping rule. However, the *spirit* of optimal stopping applied very well to the league as a whole; points scored and field goal percentage both dropped precipitously as the shot clock ticked down. Over the course of this analysis, we used a combination of functions from the tidyverse universe of packages as well as from the janitor package.

In chapter 9, before we explored the influence of rest on wins and losses, we had a very fundamental problem to resolve first: with respect to prior days of rest between opposing home and road teams, are we dealing with combinations or permutations? Ultimately, our intent was to tally and plot results by every conceivable grouping of prior days off, but because combinations and permutations aren't synonymous and are therefore computed differently, it was imperative that we first correctly established which was which.

To be brief, we're dealing with permutations because the order matters. (In fact, your combination lock should actually be called a permutation lock.) For any given game, the home team might be playing on two days of rest while the road team might be playing on just one day of rest, which, of course, isn't the same as the home team having one day off and the visiting team two days off. In fact, we're actually dealing with permutations with replacement instead of permutations without replacement because home and road teams could absolutely have the same number of prior days off, and they frequently do. From the gtools package, we computed the number of permutations we needed to account for and then provided instructions to R to print the actual permutations.

In chapter 15, we explored the parallels between the Lindy effect, right-skewed probability distributions, nonlinearity, and the 80-20 rule. Our specific interest was around measuring the distribution of games played and won across the NBA's franchises between 1946 and 2020—could it be that 20% of the league's franchises account for 80% of all the games that have been played and won?

You can't perform an 80-20 analysis without creating a Pareto chart. A Pareto chart is a combination bar chart and line chart with primary and secondary y-axes. The bar length can represent *unit* frequency, but it can also represent units of time, money, or some other cost function; they are usually arranged vertically, must absolutely be in descending order, and tie back to the primary y-axis. The line represents *cumulative* frequency measured in percentages, and it ties back to the secondary y-axis. The point is to visualize, let's say, how many problems can be solved with a much smaller number of fixes.

A Pareto chart is basically a quality control tool that provides a visual representation of causes and effects that are usually nonlinear and sometimes as extreme as 80-20. It should therefore come as no surprise that we used a pair of quality control packages to draw two Pareto charts. The first of these, from the ggQC package, displayed the number of games played per each NBA franchise, with ggplot2 aesthetics, whereas the second chart, from the qcc package, displayed the number of games won per franchise. The Pareto charts clearly showed nonlinearity in effect, but not on the order of 80-20.

Our next Sankey diagram (see figure 20.5) visualizes the operations research learning area.

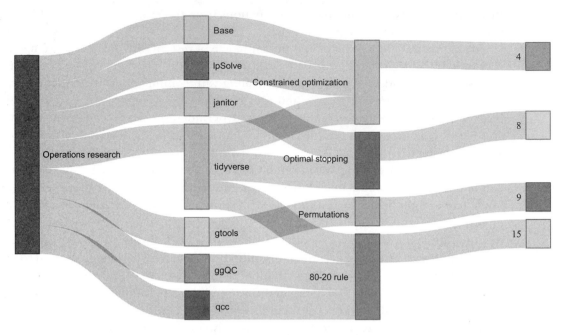

Figure 20.5   The operations research learning area contains a hodgepodge of techniques. In chapter 4, we demonstrated how an NBA team in the free agent market could get the biggest bang for its buck by setting up a constrained optimization problem; in chapter 8, we tested how well the optimal stopping rule, otherwise known as the 37% rule, works with a 24-second shot clock; in chapter 9, we examined permutations versus combinations (before computing permutations of prior days off between home and road teams); and in chapter 15, we demonstrated the 80-20 rule, often called the Pareto principle, and visualized how it applies to games played and won by all-time NBA franchises.

20.6   *Probability*

Let's look back to chapter 3 one more time to discuss expected value analysis—a technique in which contending outcomes are multiplied by their probabilities, and their products are then summed to get an expected value. We computed the expected value of a top-five draft pick as well as the expected value of any other first-round selection, anticipating that R would return very different results.

First-round selections from the 2000 to 2009 NBA drafts were assigned one of five statuses, or career outcomes, based on their subsequent win shares; for instance, a first-round pick was designated a superstar if he then earned more than 100 career win shares. We then computed the probabilities for each career outcome, split by whether or not the player was a top-five pick. The probability of getting a future superstar when selecting at or near the top of the draft equals 24%; when selecting anywhere else in the first round, the probability equals just 1%.

Then, we computed the median win shares for each outcome, again split by whether or not the player was a top-five selection. A future superstar picked in the top five then earned an average of 127 career win shares; future superstars picked below the top five averaged 111 career win shares.

The expected values were reached by multiplying probabilities by median win shares and then tallying the products. The expected value of a top-five pick equals 57.53 win shares, whereas the expected value of any other first-round pick equals just 21.21 win shares. This is the difference between getting a long-time starter versus just a marginal player—and further explains why getting to the top of the draft, by any means necessary, makes perfect sense. We called a combination of base R and `dplyr` functions to get these results, as the top-half of our next Sankey diagram shows (see figure 20.6).

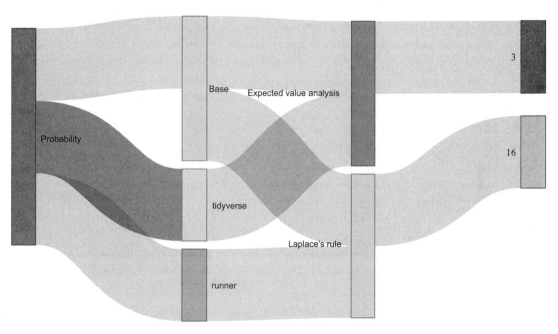

Figure 20.6 Our expected value analysis in chapter 3 clearly demonstrated that not all first-round NBA picks are created equal; teams should have very different expectations of their first-round selections depending on where they are drafting from. Then, in chapter 16, we set out to determine if free throw shooting resembles a Laplace probability curve, where success fuels additional success, or if it appears more random instead; we ultimately concluded the latter.

In chapter 16, we examined free throw shooting—specifically, streaks of successful free throw attempts—to determine if such shooting streaks best resemble a Laplace probability curve or flips of a coin. If the hot hand is a real phenomenon, a player's ongoing free throw percentage—his probability of success on the next attempt—should increase with each successive made shot. On the other hand, if a player's free throw percentage plotted by the length of consecutive makes fails to follow a Laplace probability curve, or at least thereabouts, then we should dismiss the hot hand phenomenon and instead conclude that free throw shooting is more random.

We first examined the free throw shooting of three players, all of whom finished the 2019–20 season among the lead leaders in free throw attempts: Giannis Antetokounmpo (roughly a 63% free throw shooter), Julius Randle (73%), and James Harden

(86%). Using the `runner` package, we tallied streaks of successful free throws and then computed the shooting percentage for each integer of consecutive makes. At the end of the day, free throw shooting appeared to be random. To prove this, we simulated 700 coin flips (Antetokounmpo attempted just over 700 free throws in 2019–20); our simulation returned streaks (tails) that very much resembled Antetokounmpo's free throw percentages.

But then, we plotted free throw percentages across the entire NBA—and got very different results. By grouping every player into a single series of computations, we got free throw percentages that, when plotted, looked much more like a Laplace probability curve than did our player-level analyses. Our key takeaway, however, was that the player-specific results were far more meaningful than the league-wide results because the hot hand, if it exists, applies to individual players performing within discrete periods of time, and not toward many players performing in different spaces at different times.

20.7 *Statistical dispersion*

We worked with Gini coefficients, using the `ineq` package, in chapters 12 and 13 (see sections 20.2 and 20.3), but it was really in chapter 18 where we most seriously considered measures of statistical dispersion. The NBA introduced a player salary cap just before the start of the 1984–85 season, ostensibly to create or at least improve parity across the league. We set about measuring pre–salary cap intra-season parity to determine if the NBA had a legitimate parity problem before 1984 that absolutely required corrective action and post–salary cap intra-season parity to establish whether the salary cap then improved the situation. The following methods were applied:

- *Variance method*—Equal to squaring the difference between each value in a data set and the mean of all values in the same data set and dividing it by the number of observations
- *Standard deviation method*—Equal to the square root of the variance
- *Range method*—Equal to the difference between the highest and lowest values in a data set
- *Mean absolute deviation method*—Equal to the aggregated and absolute difference between each data point from a data set and the mean from the same data divided by the number of records
- *Median absolute deviation method*—Equal to the aggregated and absolute difference between each data point from a data set and the median from the same data divided by the number of records

With respect to the variance and standard deviation methods, base R functions were called; with respect to the range, mean absolute deviation, and median absolute deviation methods, arithmetic operations, which also come out-of-the-box, were written. When considering thoroughness, ease, and identification, the standard deviation method strikes the best balance of all the methods that were tested. However, there is no one-size-fits-all measure of statistical dispersion; all methods should be applied to gain a best understanding of the data. Our next Sankey diagram (see figure 20.7) captures what methods were used and where.

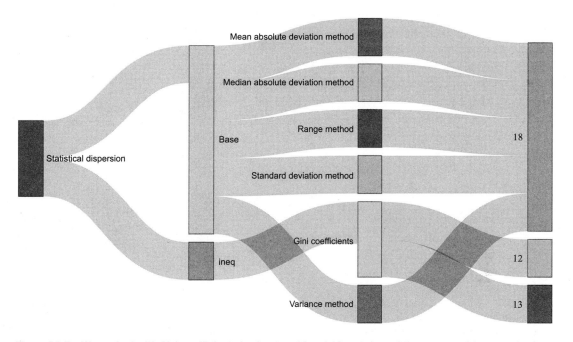

Figure 20.7   **We worked with Gini coefficients in chapters 12 and 13 and showed that teams with unequal salary and win share distributions, by that measure, were more successful than other teams. Five measures of statistical dispersion were then demonstrated in chapter 18 to quantify pre–salary cap and post–salary cap intra-season parity across the NBA. By all five measures of dispersion, intra-season parity actually improved between the 1970-71 and 1983–84 seasons and then worsened between the 1984–85 and 1997–98 seasons. Base R functions were used throughout.**

Our analysis failed to establish what the NBA might have been thinking when it claimed back in the day that it had a parity problem. We clearly demonstrated that, by the same five measures, the salary cap didn't produce its intended (or, at least, declaratory) effect.

20.8 *Standardization*

We worked with z-scores—a z-score tells us how far a raw value is above or below a population mean—in chapter 11 and again in chapter 14, but it was in chapter 19 where we most purposely worked with z-scores and other data standardization techniques (see figure 20.8).

Back in the 1961–62 season, the great Wilt Chamberlain averaged 50.4 points per game, and then in 1962–63, he averaged 44.8 points scored per game. (Chamberlain actually led the NBA in scoring for seven consecutive seasons, from 1960 through 1966.) No other player, before or since, has even averaged 40 points per game.

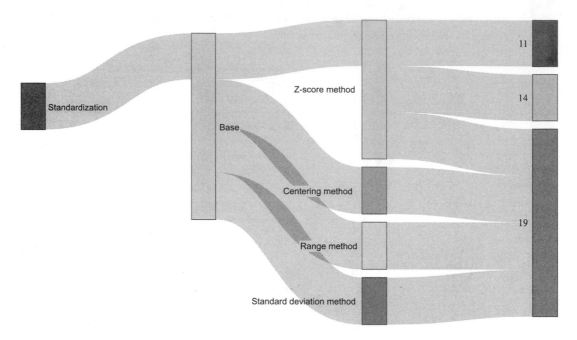

Figure 20.8   **While we worked with z-scores in chapters 11 and 14, it was in chapter 19 when we gave them, along with other standardization techniques, their full due. In chapter 19, we standardized historical points per game averages to mitigate the effects of rules changes and style of play transformations and, in the process, provided a fresh perspective on the past.**

Chamberlain was absolutely a one-of-a-kind player, yet our ongoing admiration for his scoring prowess nevertheless ignores the fact that rule changes and playing style transformations have affected the pace of play from the NBA's first season through today. Teams attempted fewer field goals and fewer free throws before and after Chamberlain's dominance in the 1960s; consequently, fewer points were scored in the 1940s and 1950s and then again from the 1970s onward.

We control for changes over time by standardizing the raw data; we therefore put a fresh perspective on historical points per game averages (or almost anything, really) by comparing annual scoring leaders against the league means of their time instead of across a span of several decades. Using base R functions, we tested the following four methods:

- *Z-score method*—Equal to the raw data minus the population mean and then dividing the difference by the standard deviation
- *Standard deviation method*—Equal to the raw data divided by the standard deviation
- *Centering method*—Equal to the raw data minus the mean
- *Range method*—Equal to the raw data divided by the difference between the maximum and minimum values

The z-score and standard deviation methods returned very different looks and results from the conventional perspective. According to both methods, George Mikan, in 1950, might very well have had the league's best scoring average between that year and 1999. Mikan's 1950 scoring average was 6.8 standard deviations above the league mean; by comparison, Chamberlain's 50.4 average more than a decade later was just 3.7 standard deviations above the league mean. The standard deviation method returned an even larger discrepancy between Mikan and Chamberlain. In other words, Mikan was a better scorer in his day than Chamberlain was in his.

20.9 Summary statistics and visualization

Our last learning area, summary statistics and visualization, is a sort of catch-all. That's because every previous chapter, to some extent, contains summary (or descriptive) statistics complemented by a mix of visualizations. To avoid any repetition from the prior learning areas, our scope is therefore relegated to the following:

- The automated (exploratory data analysis) EDA packages—`tableone`, `DataExplorer`, and `SmartEDA`—that were featured in chapter 17.
- The manual EDA exercises that were especially exhaustive or weren't necessarily complemented by the subsequent application of one or more statistical techniques. For instance, chapter 2 was almost wholly a demonstration of best EDA practices; chapter 5 showed how to best go about exploring a data set (and then wrangling it, as necessary) in preparation for fitting linear regressions; and though we introduced correlation tests in chapter 10, we otherwise relied solely on computing summary statistics and plotting the same.

All of this, of course, makes our scope somewhat subjective, but no less weighty than our other learning areas. Our next and final Sankey diagram (see figure 20.9) provides a visual snapshot of the discussion to come.

Our purpose in chapter 17 was to investigate opening totals versus closing totals and opening point spreads versus closing point spreads. Over the course of that investigation, we introduced and demonstrated a trio of automated EDA packages that subsequently provided the first indications that closing totals and closing point spreads, influenced by thousands of gamblers risking their own earnings, are usually more accurate than the opening totals and opening point spreads established by a much smaller number of oddsmakers and data scientists employed by Las Vegas casinos.

Here are the specifics:

- We called on the `tableone` package to baseline our data set and return results in tabular formats.
- We then pivoted to the `DataExplorer` package for insights into opening and closing totals (otherwise known as the opening and closing over/under), which returned a combination of results in tabular and visual formats.
- Finally, we demonstrated the `SmartEDA` package when we needed initial insights into opening and closing point spreads.

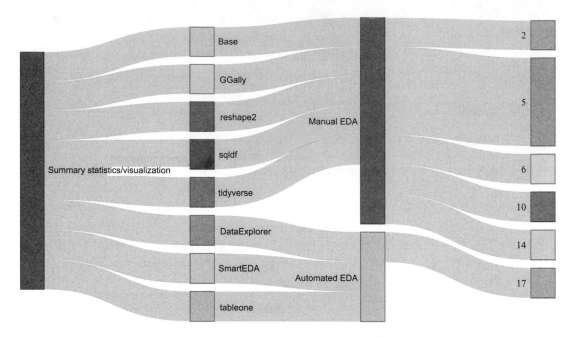

Figure 20.9　We computed summary, or descriptive, statistics in every chapter and then visualized the same by demonstrating a wide range of plotting techniques. However, the manual EDA exercises in chapters 2, 5, 6, 10, and 14, plus the automated EDA demonstrations in chapter 17, were more exhaustive than like efforts from other chapters.

What's especially nice about the `DataExplorer` and `SmartEDA` packages is that both aggregate several EDA commands—that we then demonstrated manually—into a single operation and then output the results to a standalone HTML file.

On the whole, however, if it were simply one or the other, we prefer manual EDA over automated EDA, due to content control and required brainpower. In chapter 2, we computed basic statistics and then created a mix of visualizations—one histogram, one correlation matrix, and several boxplots, bar charts, and facet plots—to best understand how our data was associated with career win shares.

In chapter 5, we drew boxplots, over scatterplots and histograms, to help us identify (and then remove) outliers in our data; density plots to help us determine if our variables were normally distributed; and a correlation matrix to isolate the best candidate predictors in preparation for linear models to come (also see section 20.4).

In chapter 6, we relied solely on basic data analysis and data visualization techniques to show that games aren't usually won in the fourth quarter, as conventional thinking has suggested for decades, but that they are actually won, more often than not, in the third quarter.

In chapter 10, we created correlation plots (and computed correlation coefficients) to show that team payrolls and regular season wins are positively correlated; dot plots binned by three season-ending classifications to show that teams with the highest payrolls win championships and generally qualify for postseason play, whereas teams with the lowest payrolls usually fail to make the playoffs; and lollipop charts, an alternative to bar charts, that show an even more definite association between payrolls and end-of-season disposition, especially since the 2006 season.

In chapter 14, we called on a number of EDA techniques that returned results, even before we ran our statistical tests, suggesting defense and offense more or less equally contribute to winning games and championships, rather than defense mattering more than offense.

Finally, this brings us back to chapter 1 and specifically how this book was intended to work. Our goal from the very beginning was to deliver a different—yet more effective and more interesting—way of learning statistics using the R programming language. While there are hundreds of websites and several books in print that, for instance, more than adequately demonstrate how to summarize data or create a ggplot2 bar chart or fit a linear regression, *none* explain how to tie together very different, seemingly unrelated, techniques and deliver actionable insights. There's no such thing as a data summarization project, a data visualization project, or a linear regression project, but *every* project in the real world requires you to logically and sequentially apply some combination of these and other techniques with foresight and prudence. Your data, for example, must first be summarized—and maybe transposed and wrangled as well—in a precise format to then use it as a source for a fixed plot or to run a suitable statistical test.

The most compelling way to deliver actionable insights is to visualize your results, if at all possible. Our visualizations were intended to be unassuming on one hand and always professional grade on the other. It's way more important to create plots that allow your readers to readily draw at minimum two or three critical conclusions than to dazzle them with aesthetics. We demonstrated how to create *lots* of visualizations, many of which—dendrograms, Sankey diagrams, pyramid plots, facet plots, Cleveland dot plots, and Lorenz curves, to name just a few—are outside the mainstream. Our intent wasn't to be different, per se, but to otherwise demonstrate that there's a proper time and space for these and other types of visualizations.

Finally, while it's unlikely you're in the business of analyzing basketball statistics, hopefully the use of NBA data sets made the learning more captivating than if we had instead imported packaged data sets or even used mocked-up data. Notwithstanding the common thread of NBA data sets, every technique we demonstrated is absolutely transferrable to your line of work—professional, academic, or otherwise. Even the concepts that we presented, from constrained optimization, for instance, to optimal stopping, to the 80-20 rule, have an infinite number of use cases in almost any vertical.

Now, make it happen!

*appendix
More ggplot2
visualizations*

This appendix includes correlation plots, dot plots, and lollipop charts covering the 2002 through 2017 NBA seasons—48 additional visualizations in all (which is why we're placing this content here and not in chapter 10). The code behind these visualizations is not included here because it's not materially different from the code that produced the correlation plots, dot plots, and lollipop charts covering the 2000 and 2001 seasons that are included in chapter 10. Otherwise, the plots are arranged by visualization type and then chronologically.

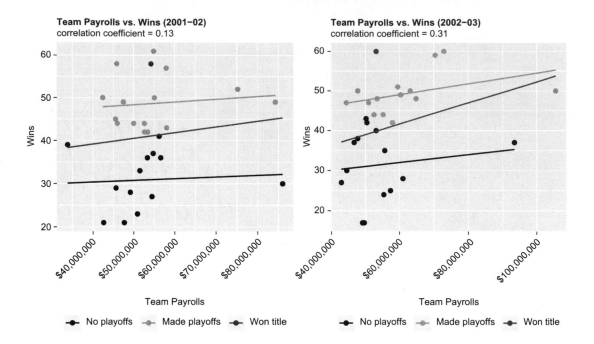

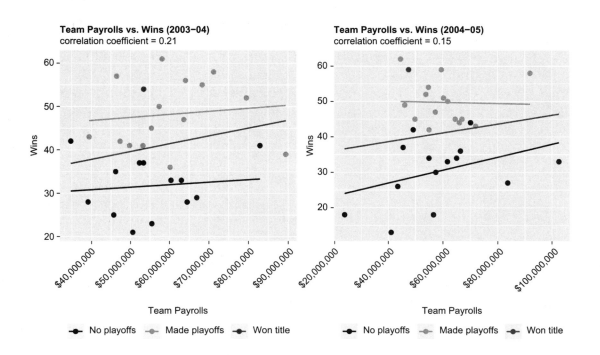

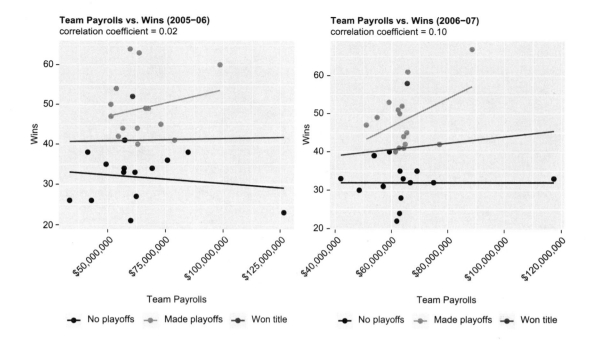

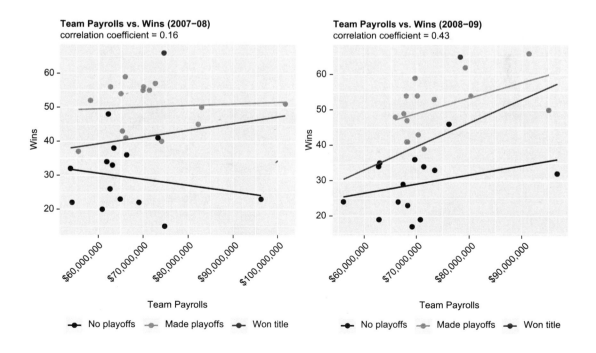

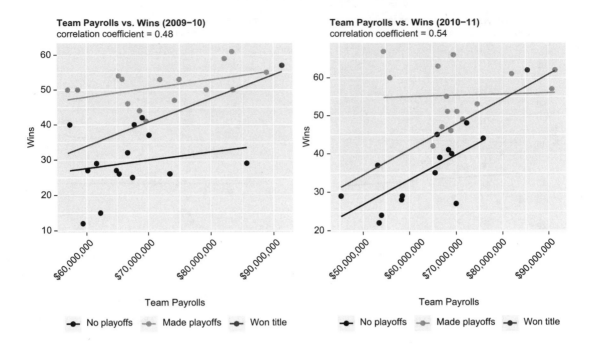

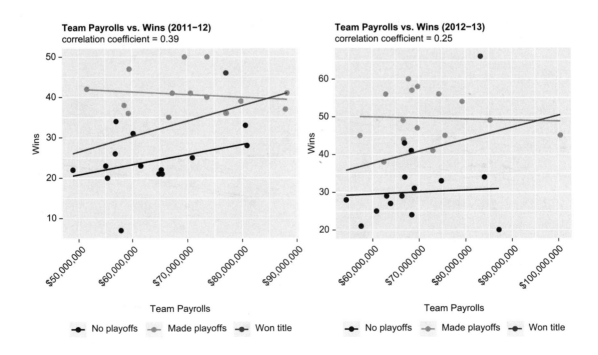

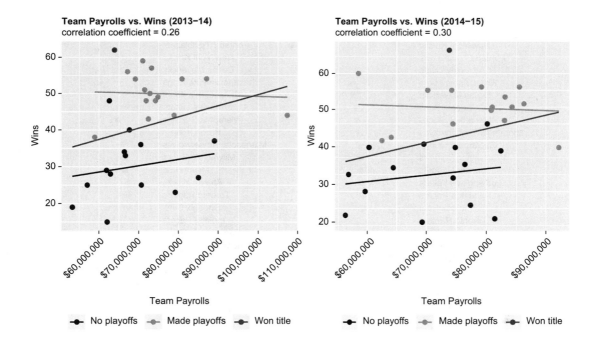

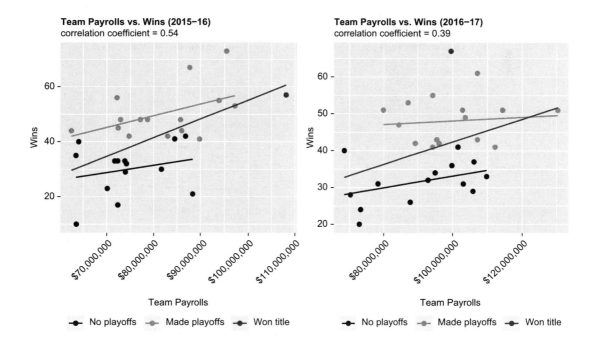

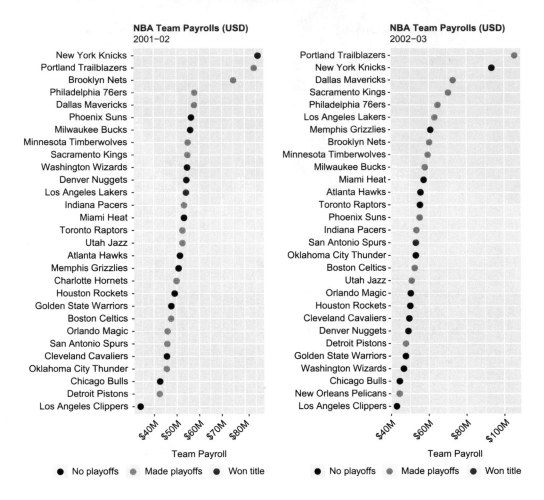

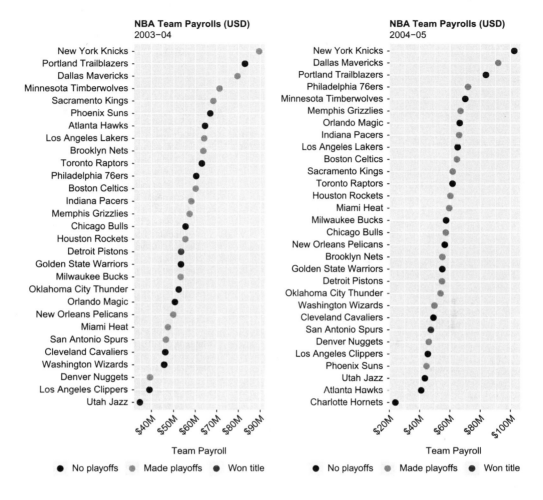

NBA Team Payrolls (USD)
2003–04

New York Knicks
Portland Trailblazers
Dallas Mavericks
Minnesota Timberwolves
Sacramento Kings
Phoenix Suns
Atlanta Hawks
Los Angeles Lakers
Brooklyn Nets
Toronto Raptors
Philadelphia 76ers
Boston Celtics
Indiana Pacers
Memphis Grizzlies
Chicago Bulls
Houston Rockets
Detroit Pistons
Golden State Warriors
Milwaukee Bucks
Oklahoma City Thunder
Orlando Magic
New Orleans Pelicans
Miami Heat
San Antonio Spurs
Cleveland Cavaliers
Washington Wizards
Denver Nuggets
Los Angeles Clippers
Utah Jazz

$40M $50M $60M $70M $80M $90M

Team Payroll

● No playoffs   ● Made playoffs   ● Won title

NBA Team Payrolls (USD)
2004–05

New York Knicks
Dallas Mavericks
Portland Trailblazers
Philadelphia 76ers
Minnesota Timberwolves
Memphis Grizzlies
Orlando Magic
Indiana Pacers
Los Angeles Lakers
Boston Celtics
Sacramento Kings
Toronto Raptors
Houston Rockets
Miami Heat
Milwaukee Bucks
Chicago Bulls
New Orleans Pelicans
Brooklyn Nets
Golden State Warriors
Detroit Pistons
Oklahoma City Thunder
Washington Wizards
Cleveland Cavaliers
San Antonio Spurs
Denver Nuggets
Los Angeles Clippers
Phoenix Suns
Utah Jazz
Atlanta Hawks
Charlotte Hornets

$20M $40M $60M $80M $100M

Team Payroll

● No playoffs   ● Made playoffs   ● Won title

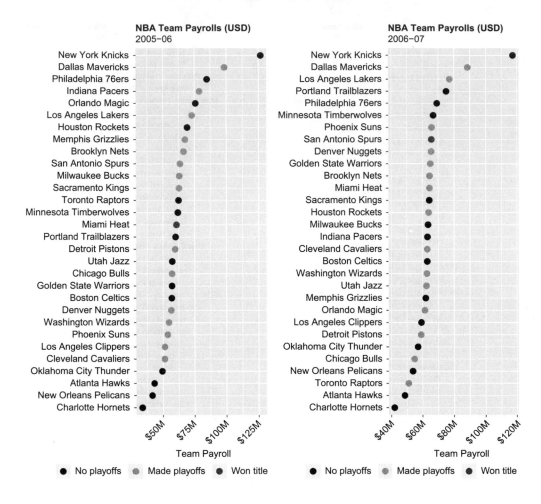

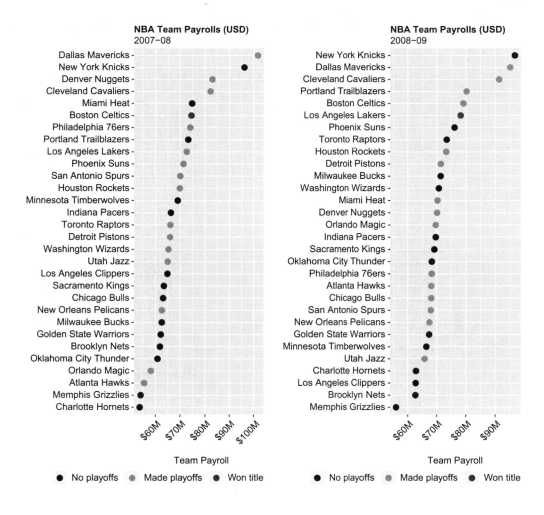

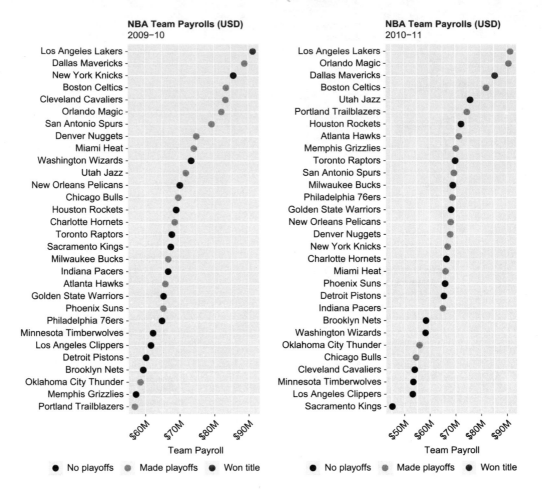

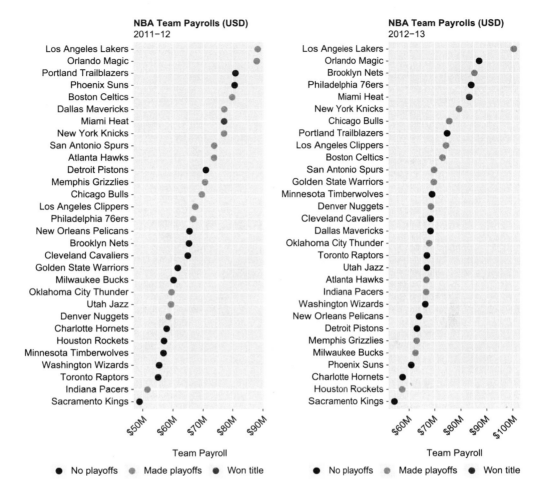

NBA Team Payrolls (USD)
2011–12

NBA Team Payrolls (USD)
2012–13

Team Payroll

● No playoffs   ● Made playoffs   ● Won title

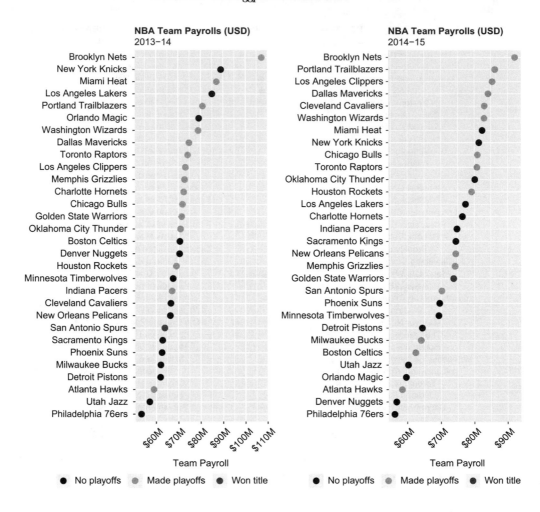

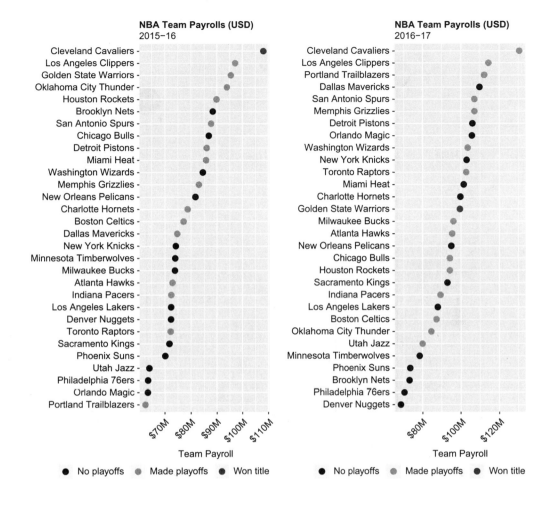

NBA Team Payrolls (USD)
2015–16

Cleveland Cavaliers
Los Angeles Clippers
Golden State Warriors
Oklahoma City Thunder
Houston Rockets
Brooklyn Nets
San Antonio Spurs
Chicago Bulls
Detroit Pistons
Miami Heat
Washington Wizards
Memphis Grizzlies
New Orleans Pelicans
Charlotte Hornets
Boston Celtics
Dallas Mavericks
New York Knicks
Minnesota Timberwolves
Milwaukee Bucks
Atlanta Hawks
Indiana Pacers
Los Angeles Lakers
Denver Nuggets
Toronto Raptors
Sacramento Kings
Phoenix Suns
Utah Jazz
Philadelphia 76ers
Orlando Magic
Portland Trailblazers

$70M $80M $90M $100M $110M

Team Payroll

● No playoffs   ● Made playoffs   ● Won title

NBA Team Payrolls (USD)
2016–17

Cleveland Cavaliers
Los Angeles Clippers
Portland Trailblazers
Dallas Mavericks
San Antonio Spurs
Memphis Grizzlies
Detroit Pistons
Orlando Magic
Washington Wizards
New York Knicks
Toronto Raptors
Miami Heat
Charlotte Hornets
Golden State Warriors
Milwaukee Bucks
Atlanta Hawks
New Orleans Pelicans
Chicago Bulls
Houston Rockets
Sacramento Kings
Indiana Pacers
Los Angeles Lakers
Boston Celtics
Oklahoma City Thunder
Utah Jazz
Minnesota Timberwolves
Phoenix Suns
Brooklyn Nets
Philadelphia 76ers
Denver Nuggets

$80M $100M $120M

Team Payroll

● No playoffs   ● Made playoffs   ● Won title

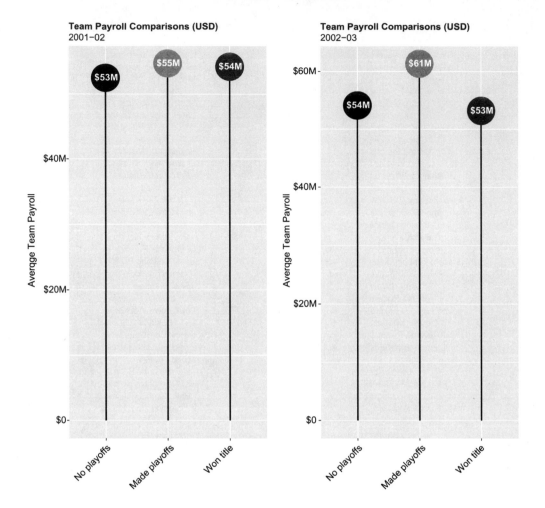

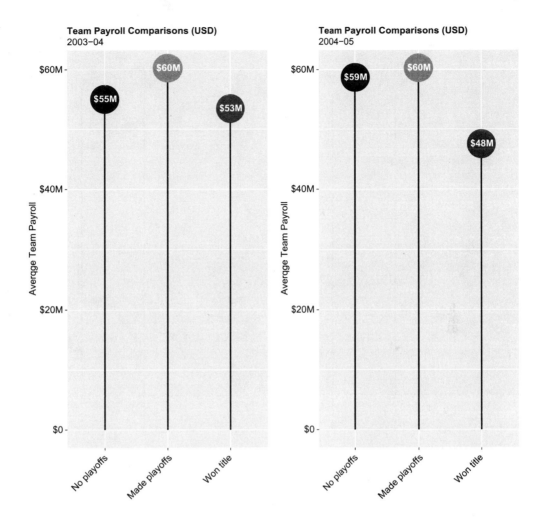

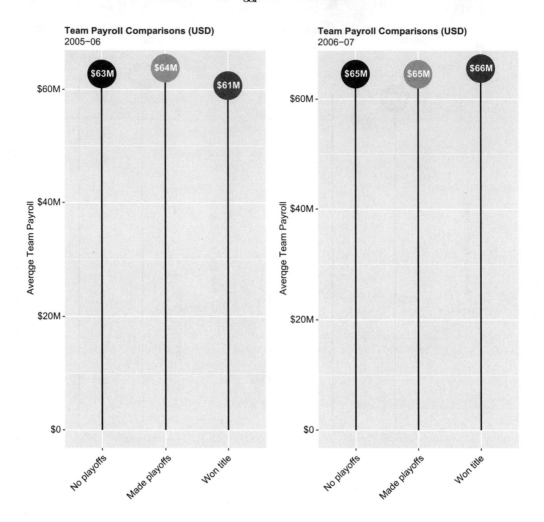

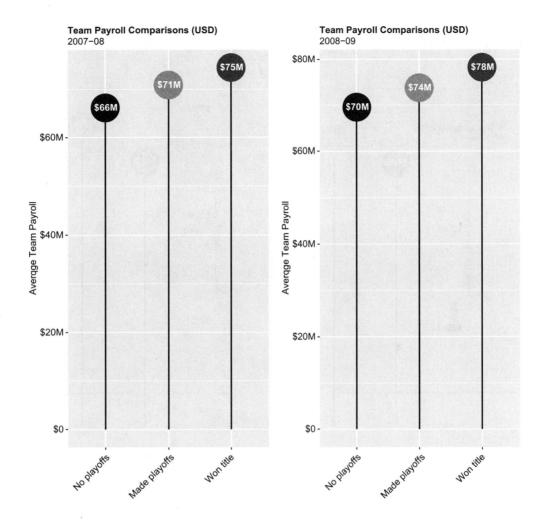

Team Payroll Comparisons (USD)
2007–08

Team Payroll Comparisons (USD)
2008–09

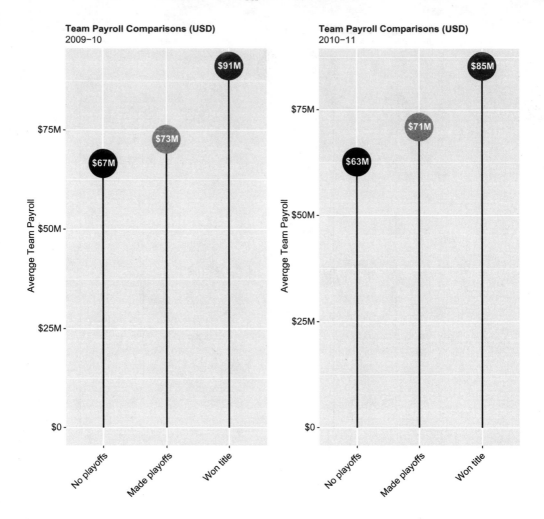

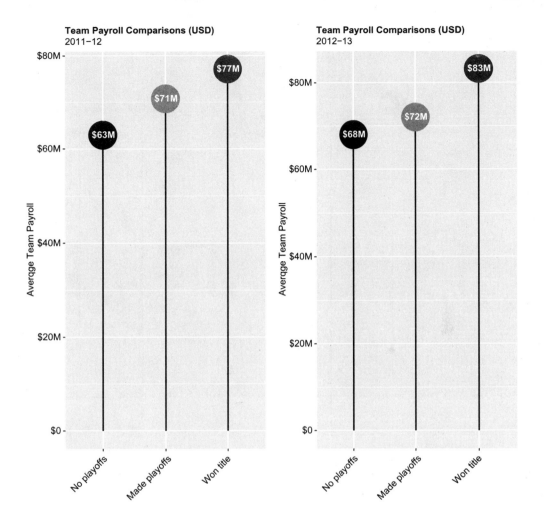

Team Payroll Comparisons (USD)
2011–12

Team Payroll Comparisons (USD)
2012–13

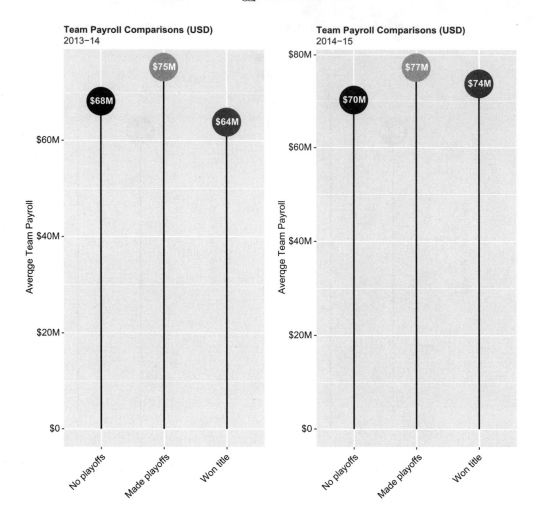

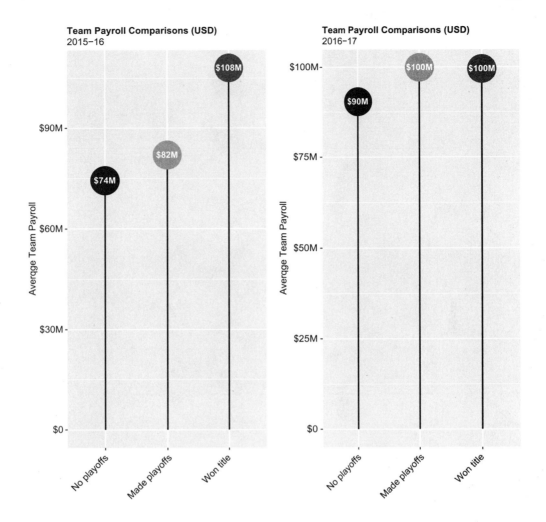

index

T

R in Action, Third Edition
by Robert I. Kabacoff

ISBN 9781617296055
656 pages, $59.99
March 2022

Practical Data Science with R, Second Edition
by Nina Zumel and John Mount
Foreword by Jeremy Howard and Rachel Thomas

ISBN 9781617295874
568 pages, $49.99
November 2019

Math for Programmers
by Paul Orland

ISBN 9781617295355
688 pages, $59.99
November 2020

The Quick Python Book, Third Edition
by Naomi Ceder
Foreword by Nicholas Tollervey

ISBN 9781617294037
472 pages, $39.99
May 2018

For ordering information go to www.manning.com

A new online reading experience

liveBook, our online reading platform, adds a new dimension to your Manning books, with features that make reading, learning, and sharing easier than ever. A liveBook version of your book is included FREE with every Manning book.

This next generation book platform is more than an online reader. It's packed with unique features to upgrade and enhance your learning experience.

- Add your own notes and bookmarks
- One-click code copy
- Learn from other readers in the discussion forum
- Audio recordings and interactive exercises
- Read all your purchased Manning content in any browser, anytime, anywhere

As an added bonus, you can search every Manning book and video in liveBook—even ones you don't yet own. Open any liveBook, and you'll be able to browse the content and read anything you like.*

Find out more at www.manning.com/livebook-program.

Open reading is limited to 10 minutes per book daily